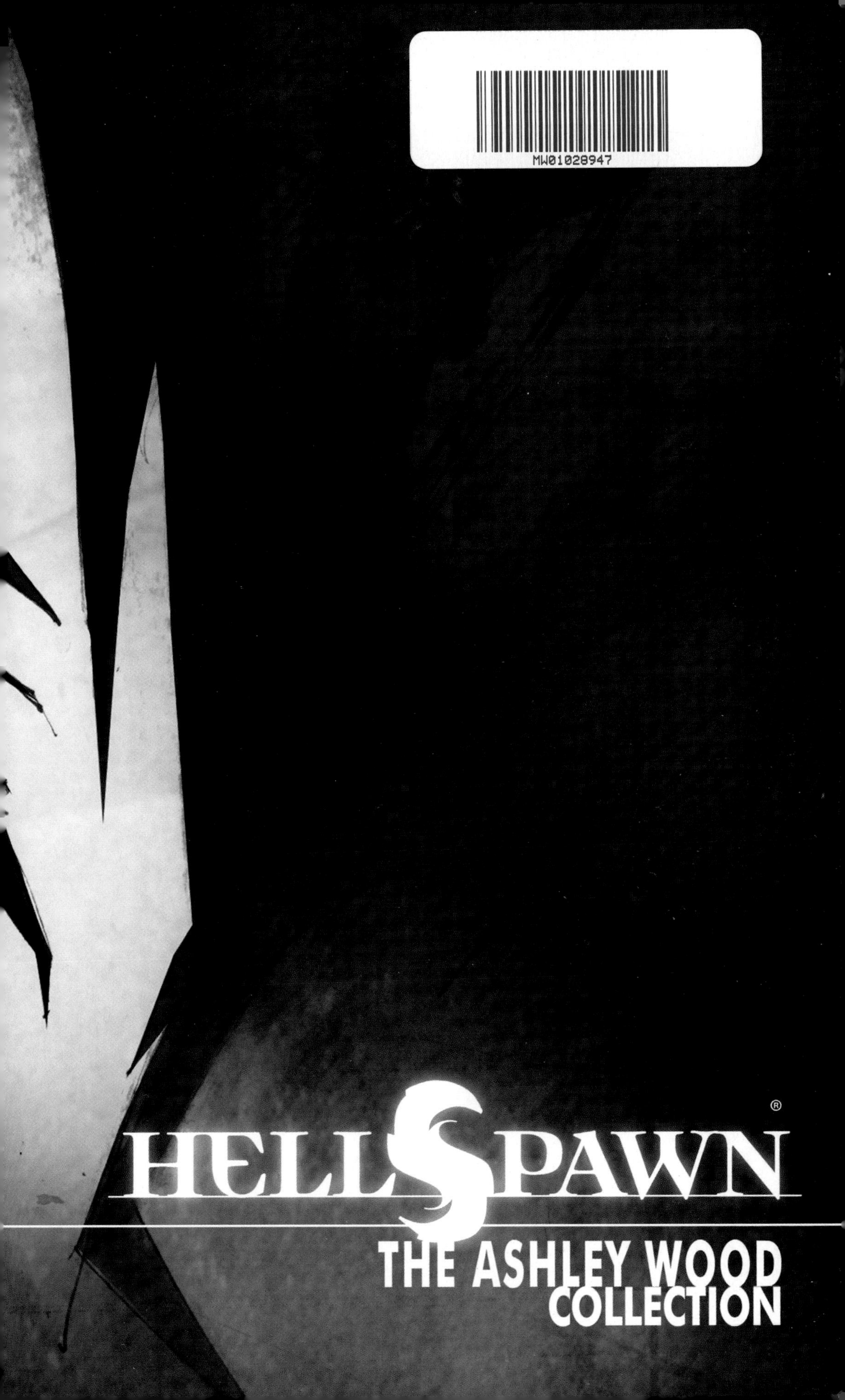

HELLSPAWN®
THE ASHLEY WOOD COLLECTION

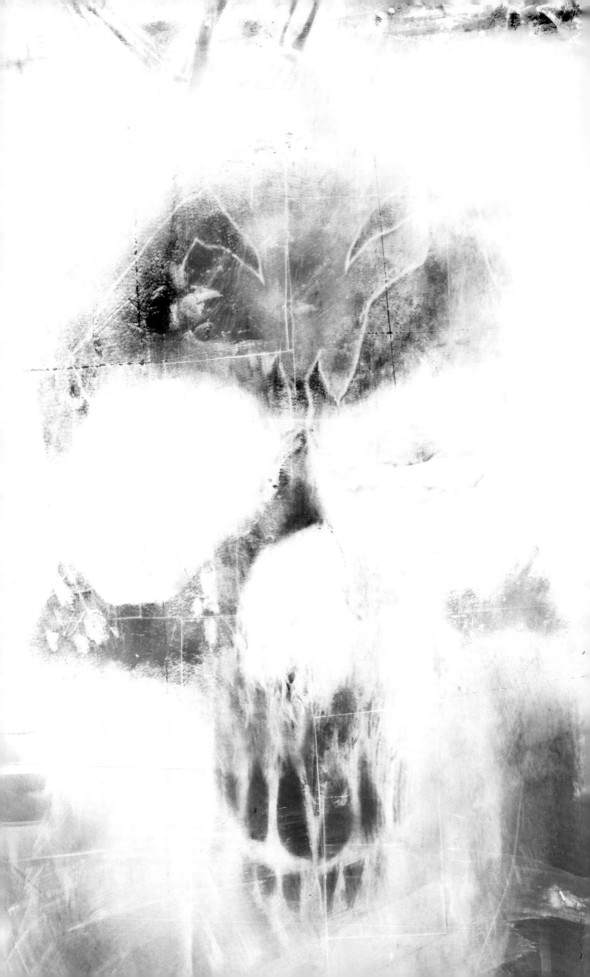

TODD McFARLANE AND
IMAGE COMICS PRESENT

HELLSPAWN

THE ASHLEY WOOD COLLECTION

STORY
BRIAN MICHAEL BENDIS
STEVE NILES

ART
ASHLEY WOOD

LETTERING
RICHARD STARKINGS
AND COMICRAFT'S
OSCAR GONGORA

COVER
ASHLEY WOOD

EDITOR IN CHIEF
BRIAN HABERLIN

PRESIDENT
MCFARLANE TOYS
LARRY MARDER

PRESIDENT OF
ENTERTAINMENT
TERRY FITZGERALD

EXECUTIVE DIRECTOR
OF SPAWN.COM
TYLER JEFFERS

MANAGER OF
INT'L. PUBLISHING
FOR TMP
SUZY THOMAS

PUBLISHER FOR
IMAGE COMICS
ERIK LARSEN

SPAWN CREATED BY
TODD McFARLANE

TODD McFARLANE
PRODUCTIONS
SPAWN.COM

HELLSPAWN: THE ASHLEY WOOD COLLECTION VOL.1 April 2006. Collects issues 1-10 of Hellspawn. First Printing. Published by IMAGE COMICS, 1942 University Ave.
Berkeley, CA 94704, $24.95 USA $28.00 CAN. Hellspawn, its logo and its symbol are registered trademarks © 2006 Todd McFarlane Productions, Inc. All other related characters
are TM and © 2006 Todd McFarlane Productions, Inc. All rights reserved. The characters, events and stories in this publication are entirely fictional. With exception of artwork used
for review purposes, none of the contents of this publication may be reprinted without the permission of Todd McFarlane Productions, Inc. PRINTED IN CANADA.

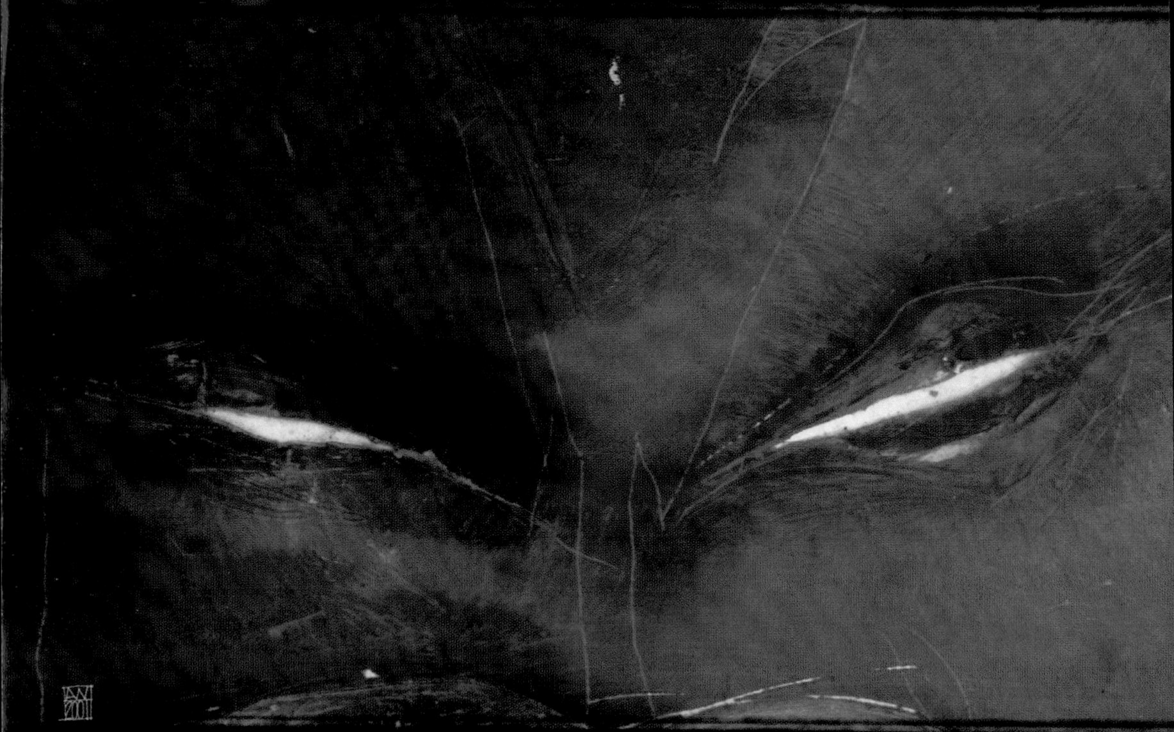

ISSUE ONE

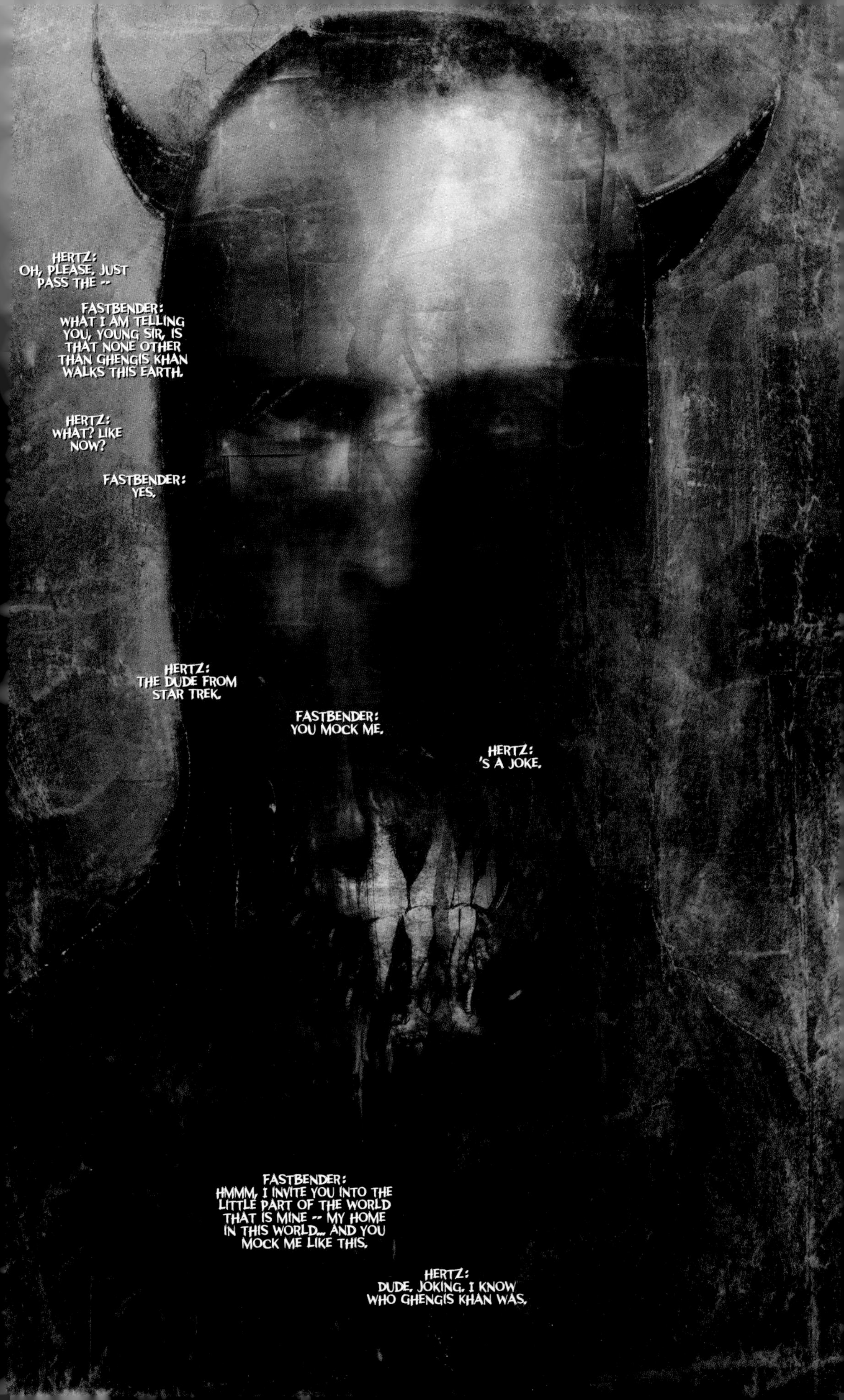
HERTZ: OH, PLEASE. JUST PASS THE --
FASTBENDER: WHAT I AM TELLING YOU, YOUNG SIR, IS THAT NONE OTHER THAN GHENGIS KHAN WALKS THIS EARTH.
HERTZ: WHAT? LIKE NOW?
FASTBENDER: YES.
HERTZ: THE DUDE FROM STAR TREK.
FASTBENDER: YOU MOCK ME.
HERTZ: 'S A JOKE.
FASTBENDER: HMMM. I INVITE YOU INTO THE LITTLE PART OF THE WORLD THAT IS MINE -- MY HOME IN THIS WORLD... AND YOU MOCK ME LIKE THIS.
HERTZ: DUDE. JOKING. I KNOW WHO GHENGIS KHAN WAS.

FASTBENDER:
WHO THEN?

HERTZ:
WHO?

FASTBENDER:
WHO WAS KHAN?

HERTZ:
WHO? HE WAS THAT--
DUDE, THAT GUY...

FASTBENDER:
HE, YOUNG MAN WHO HAS MUCH TO LEARN,
WAS THE FIRST MONGOLIAN LEADER WHO
ACHIEVED A DURABLE MONGOLIAN UNION. HE
ENDED THE PETTY TRIBAL SQUABBLING AND
ORGANIZED THE MONGOL NATION.

HERTZ:
OH YEAH -- SURE, I KNOW.

FASTBENDER:
AT THE TIME OF HIS SUPPOSED
DEATH IN 1227, HIS EMPIRE
WOULD REACH FROM PEKING
TO THE CASPIAN SEA.

HERTZ:
WOW, WELL THAT--
WAIT... SUPPOSED?

FASTBENDER:
THERE ARE THOSE, LIKE MYSELF, WHO
BELIEVE THAT THE GREAT AND MIGHTY
WARRIOR TRADED HIS VERY SOUL IN
RETURN FOR THE COUNTLESS VICTORIES
THAT UNITED HIS MEN AND COUNTRY.

HERTZ:
UH HUH.

FASTBENDER:
AND IN RETURN, THIS GREAT WARRIOR SOUL
HAS BEEN BORN AGAIN AND AGAIN AND AGAIN
IN THE FORM OF WHAT SOME ILL-INFORMED
LABEL AS THE SHADOW OF DEATH. BUT IN
REALITY HE IS NOTHING SHORT OF A WARRIOR
FROM HELL, A HELLSPAWN WARRIOR. THEY SAY
HE IS THE FACE OF DEATH AND THE FACE OF...

HERTZ:
'THEY' WHO?

FASTBENDER:
THEY!

HERTZ:
'THEY' WHO? I ALWAYS HEAR
ABOUT THIS 'THEY.' 'THEY' SAID
THIS AND 'THEY' SAID THIS...

FASTBENDER:
SIR...

HERTZ:
I'M JUST SAYING, I'D LIKE
TO MEET THIS 'THEY' ONE
DAY. PASS THE BOTTLE --

FASTBENDER:
SIR...

HERTZ:
HAVE YOU
MET 'THEM?'

FASTBENDER:
YOU MOCK ME STILL?

HERTZ:
OH COME ON. I'M JUST
PLAYIN' WITH YOU. JUST-

FASTBENDER:
I TELL YOU THAT THERE ARE
FORCES AT WORK IN THIS WORLD
THAT ARE BEYOND US. I TELL
YOU THAT I HAVE FIRST HAND
KNOWLEDGE OF THIS.

HERTZ:
YOU DO? FORCES?

FASTBENDER:
I TELL YOU THIS IN HOPES
THAT THE INFORMATION-

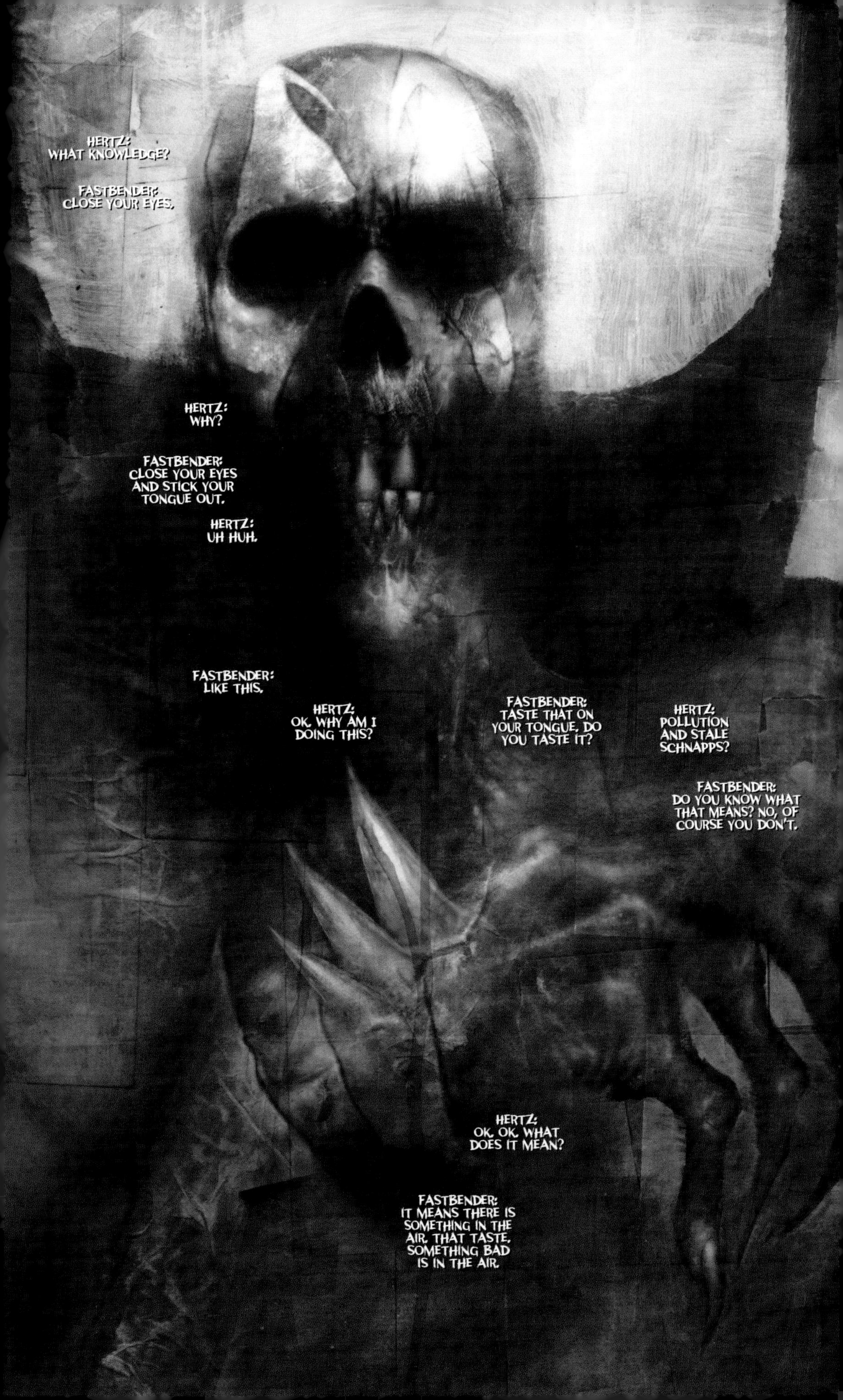
HERTZ: WHAT KNOWLEDGE?
FASTBENDER: CLOSE YOUR EYES.
HERTZ: WHY?
FASTBENDER: CLOSE YOUR EYES AND STICK YOUR TONGUE OUT.
HERTZ: UH HUH.
FASTBENDER: LIKE THIS.
HERTZ: OK. WHY AM I DOING THIS?
FASTBENDER: TASTE THAT ON YOUR TONGUE, DO YOU TASTE IT?
HERTZ: POLLUTION AND STALE SCHNAPPS?
FASTBENDER: DO YOU KNOW WHAT THAT MEANS? NO, OF COURSE YOU DON'T.
HERTZ: OK, OK, WHAT DOES IT MEAN?
FASTBENDER: IT MEANS THERE IS SOMETHING IN THE AIR, THAT TASTE. SOMETHING BAD IS IN THE AIR.

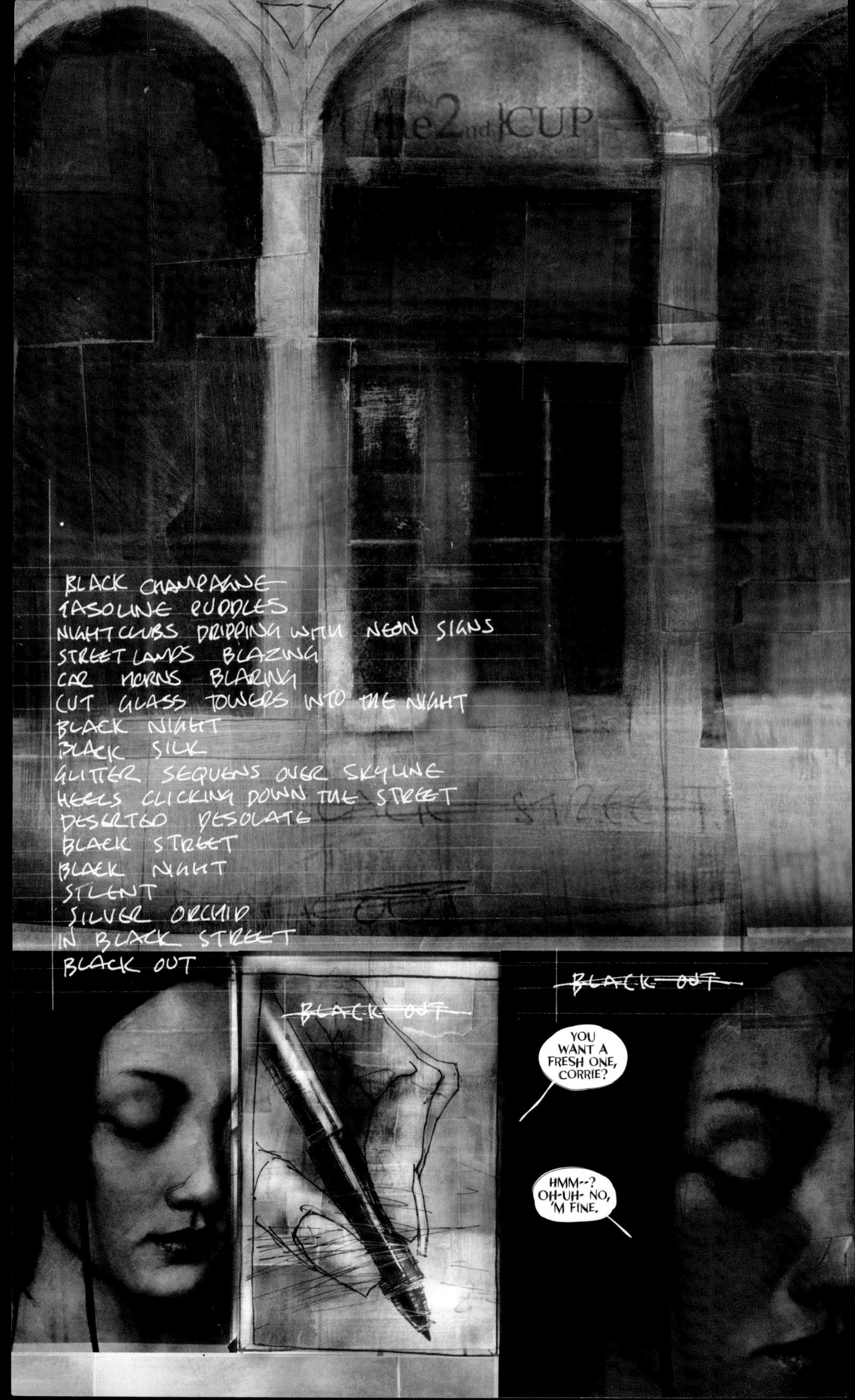
the 2nd CUP
BLACK CHAMPAGNE
GASOLINE PUDDLES
NIGHTCLUBS DRIPPING WITH NEON SIGNS
STREETLAMPS BLAZING
CAR HORNS BLARING
CUT GLASS TOWERS INTO THE NIGHT
BLACK NIGHT
BLACK SILK
GLITTER SEQUENS OVER SKYLINE
HEELS CLICKING DOWN THE STREET
DESERTED DESOLATE
BLACK STREET
BLACK NIGHT
SILENT
SILVER ORCHID
IN BLACK STREET
BLACK OUT
~~BLACK OUT~~
~~BLACK OUT~~
YOU WANT A FRESH ONE, CORRIE?
HMM--? OH-UH- NO, 'M FINE.

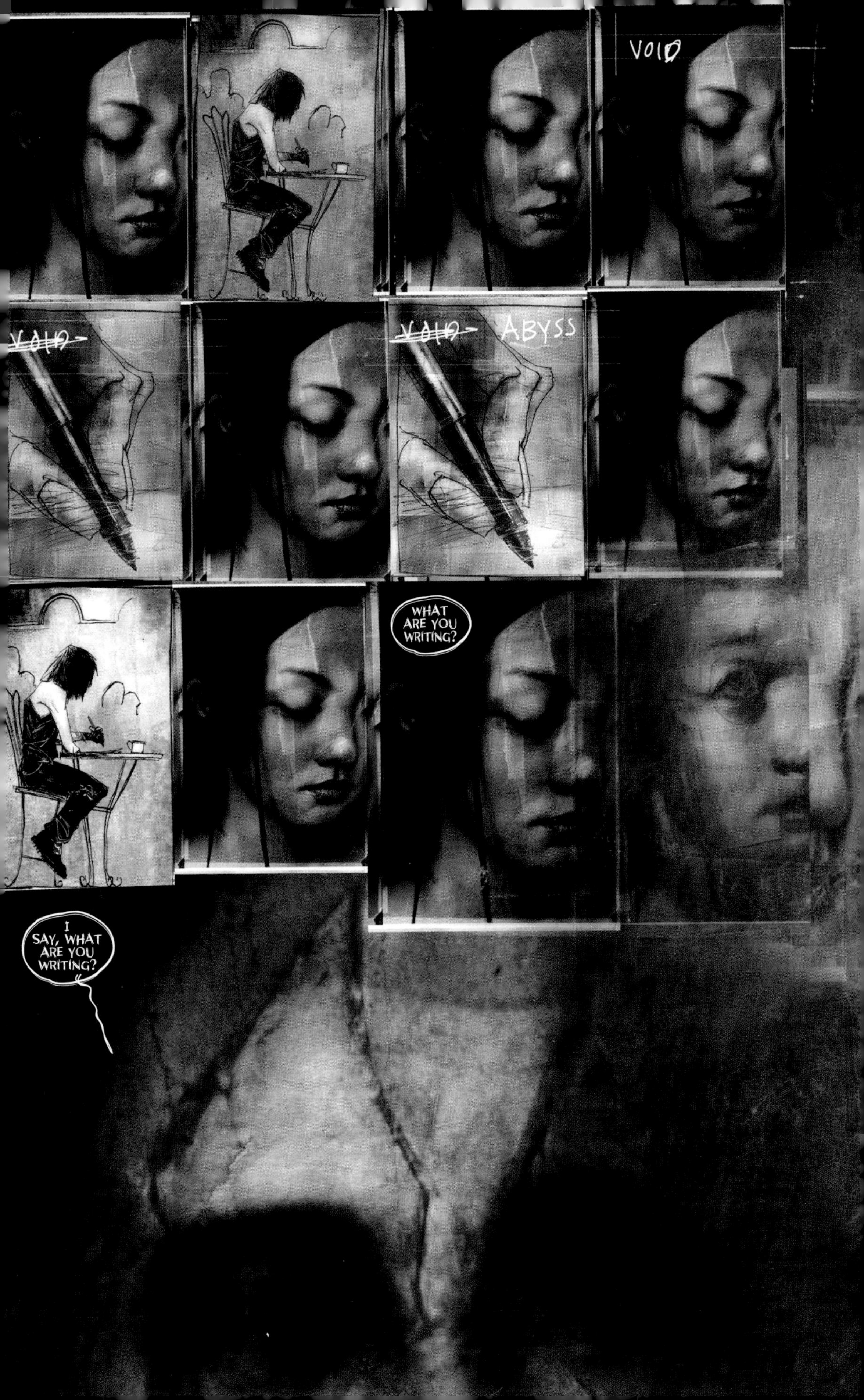
VOID
~~VOID~~
~~VOID~~ ABYSS
WHAT ARE YOU WRITING?
I SAY, WHAT ARE YOU WRITING?

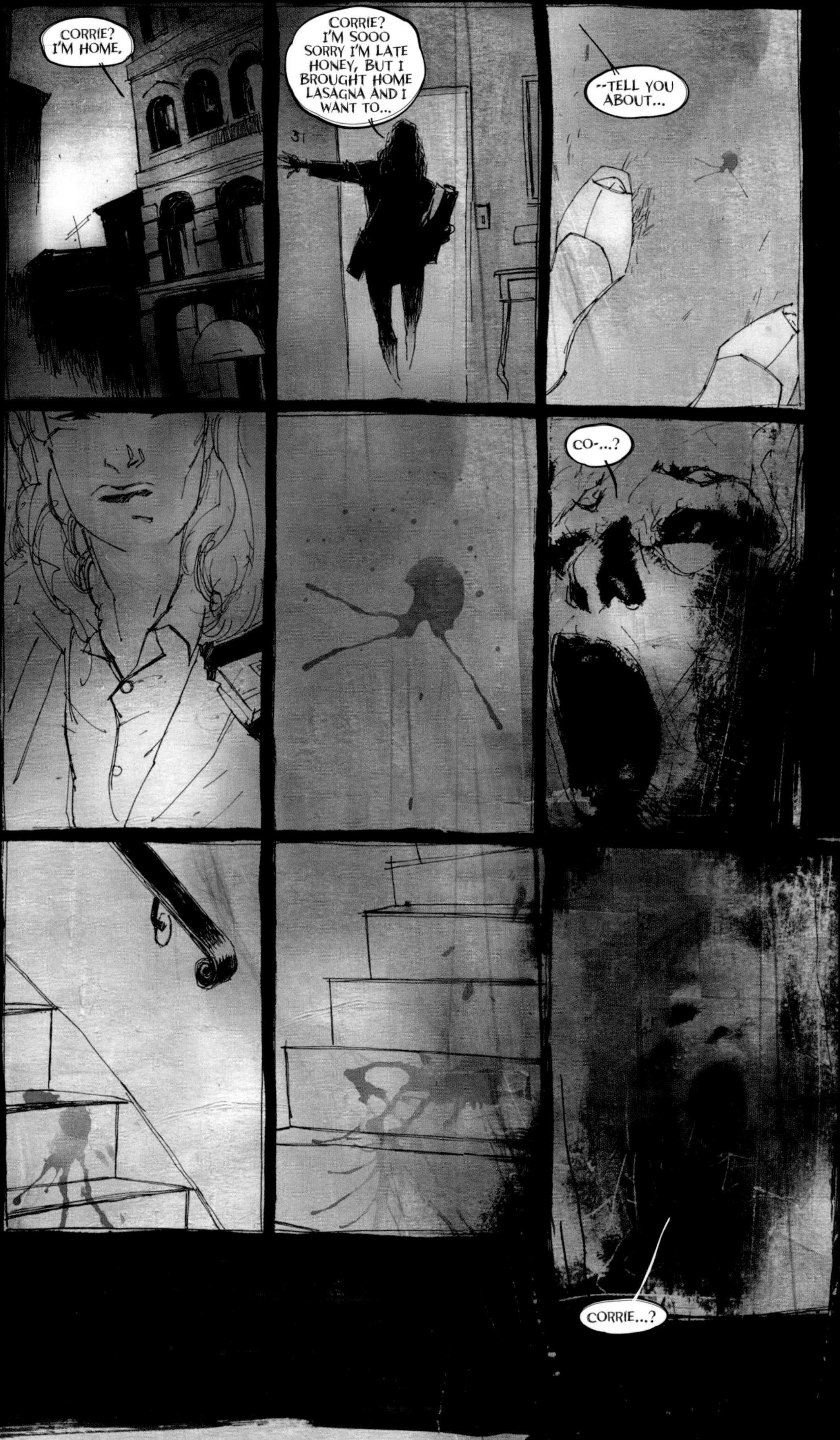
CORRIE? I'M HOME.
CORRIE? I'M SOOO SORRY I'M LATE HONEY, BUT I BROUGHT HOME LASAGNA AND I WANT TO...
--TELL YOU ABOUT...
CO-...?
CORRIE...?

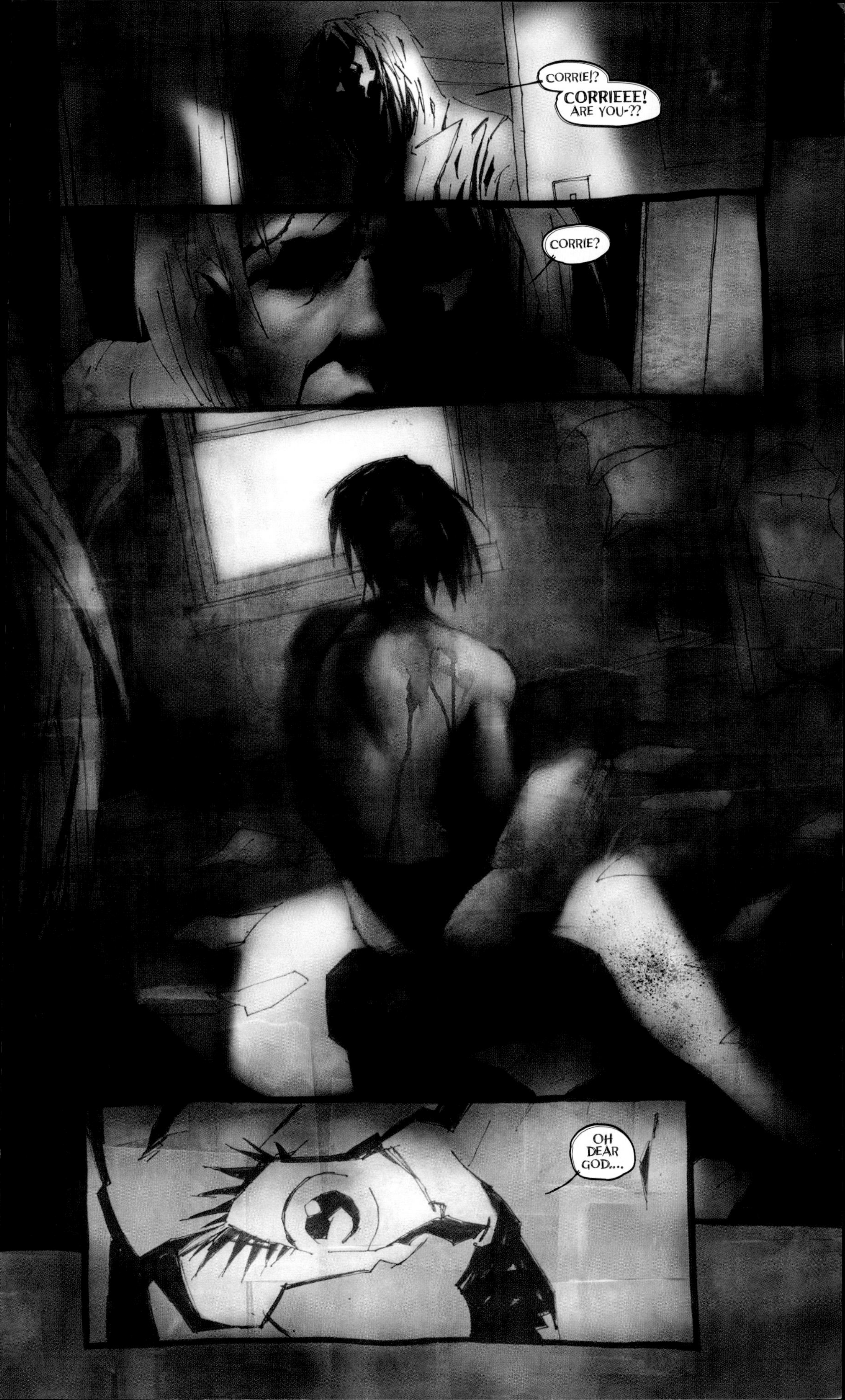
CORRIE!? CORRIEEE! ARE YOU-??
CORRIE?
OH DEAR GOD....

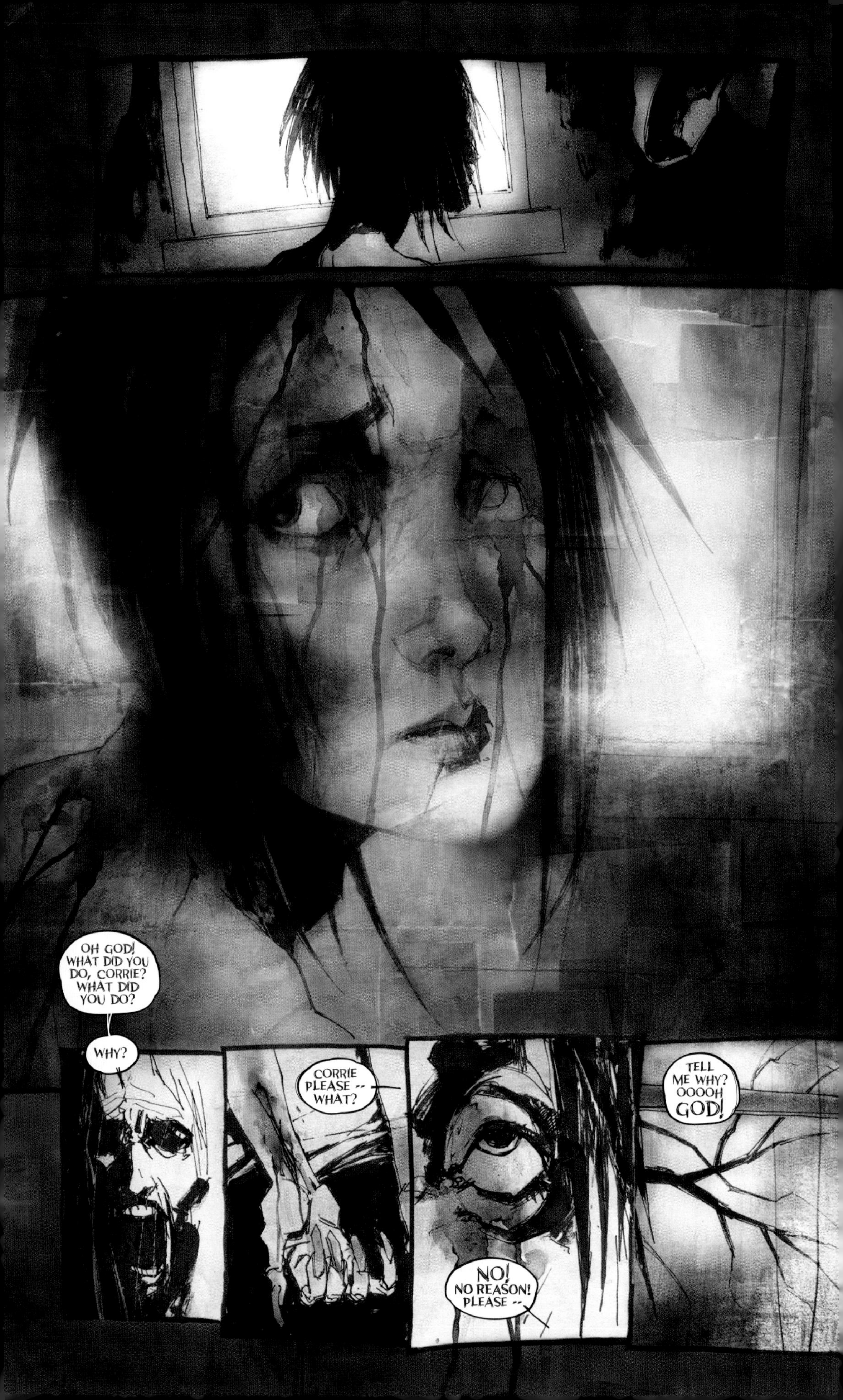
OH GOD! WHAT DID YOU DO, CORRIE? WHAT DID YOU DO?
WHY?
CORRIE PLEASE -- WHAT?
NO! NO REASON! PLEASE --
TELL ME WHY? OOOOH GOD!

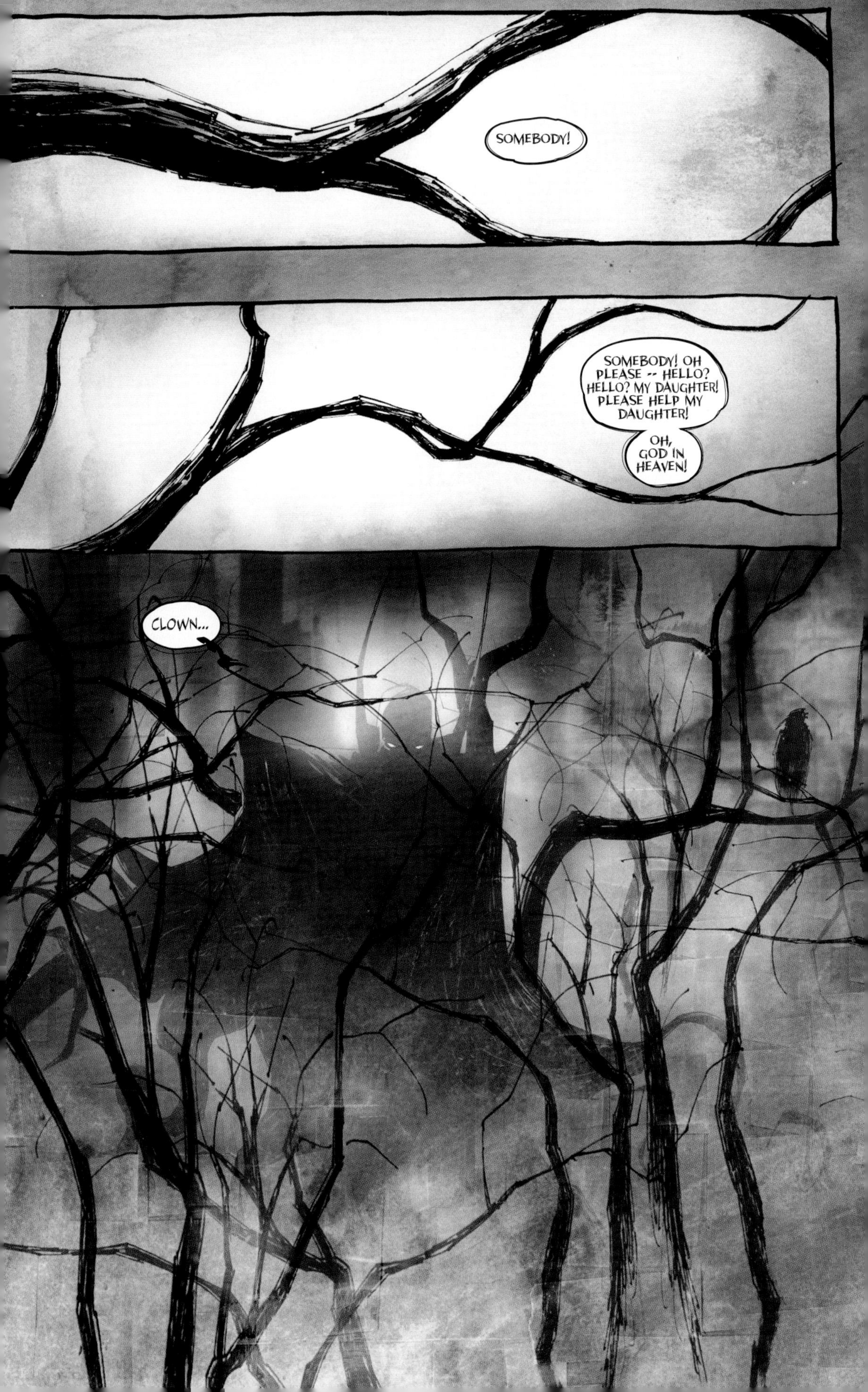
SOMEBODY!
SOMEBODY! OH PLEASE -- HELLO? HELLO? MY DAUGHTER! PLEASE HELP MY DAUGHTER!
OH, GOD IN HEAVEN!
CLOWN...

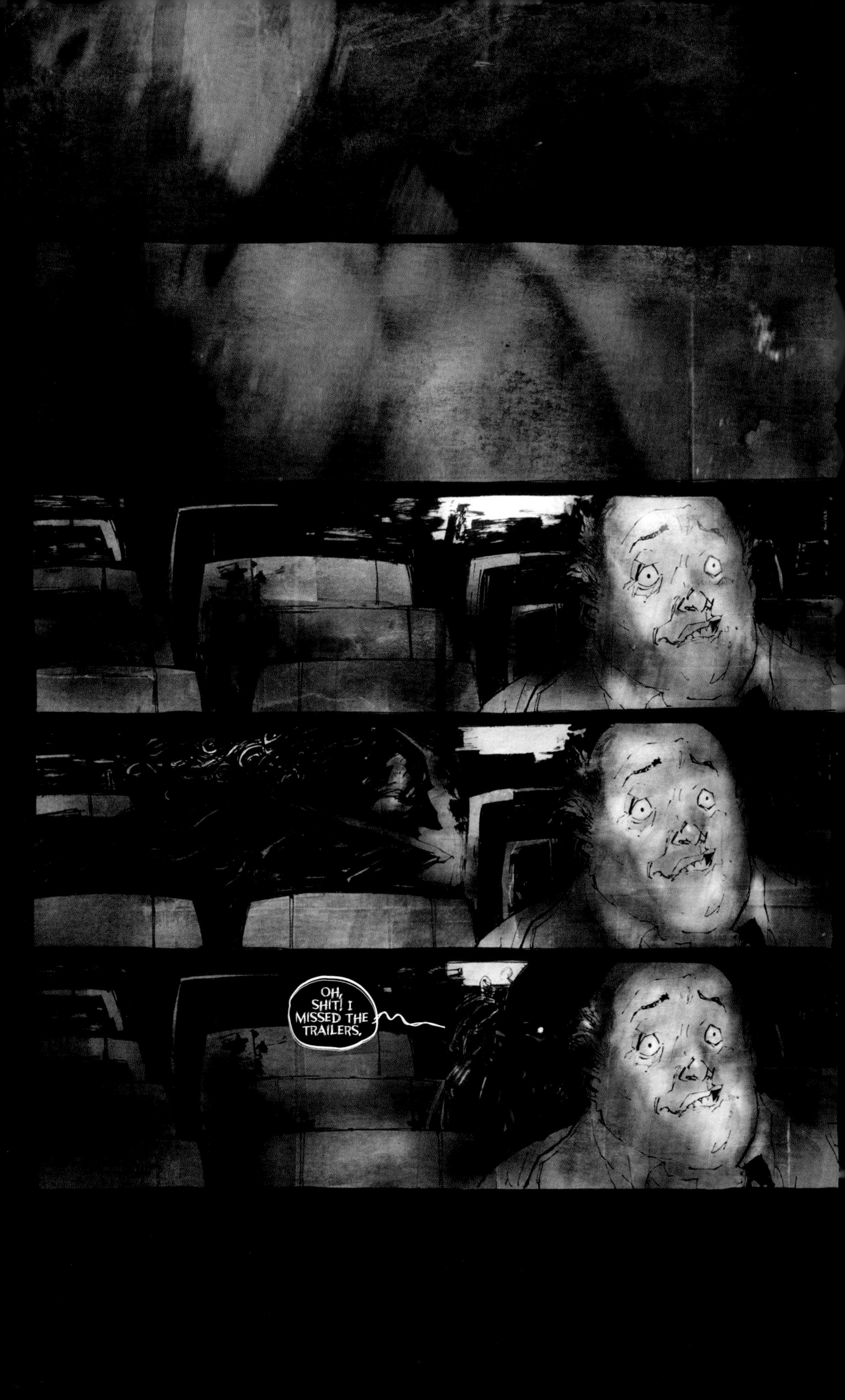
OH, SHIT! I MISSED THE TRAILERS.

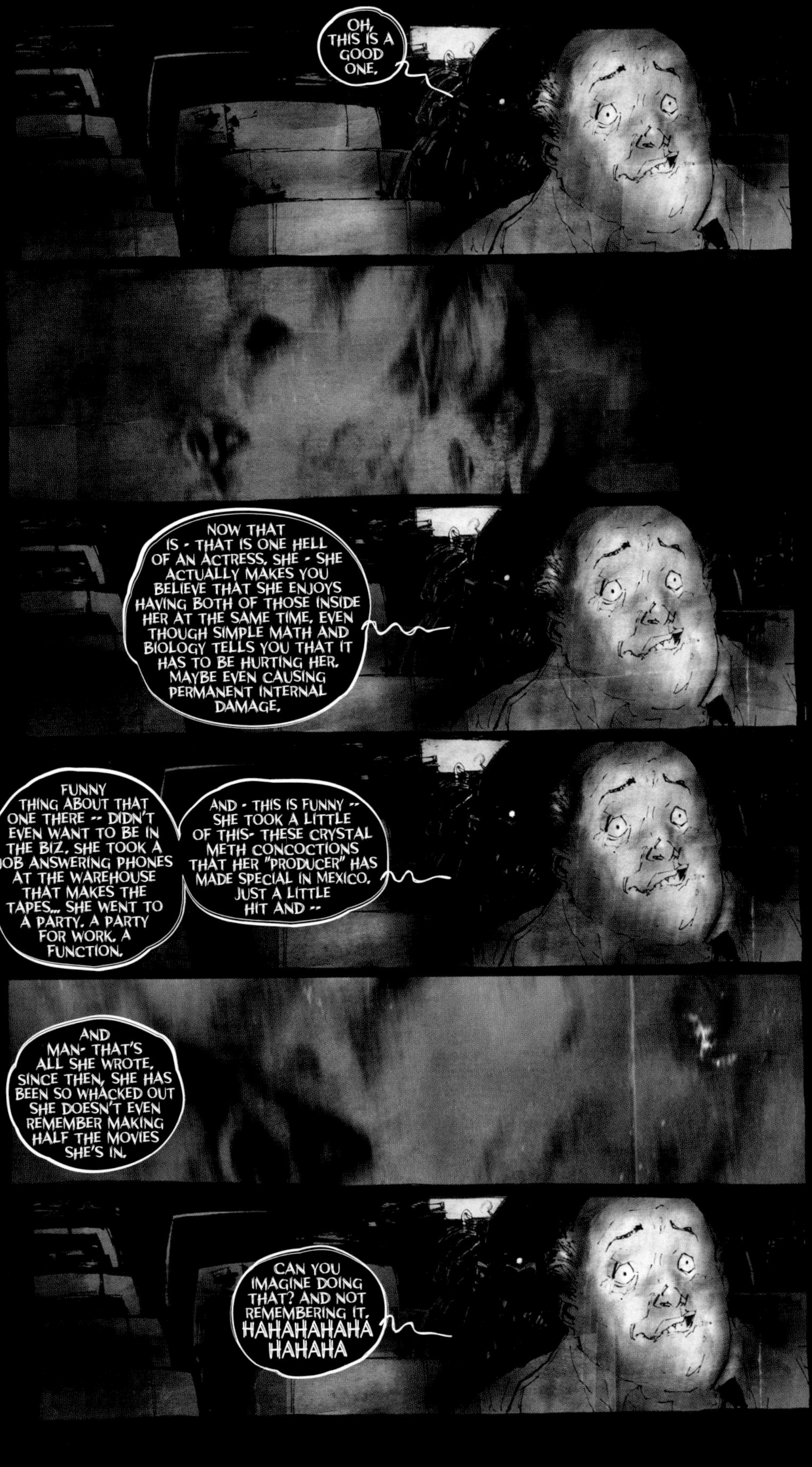
OH, THIS IS A GOOD ONE.
NOW THAT IS - THAT IS ONE HELL OF AN ACTRESS. SHE - SHE ACTUALLY MAKES YOU BELIEVE THAT SHE ENJOYS HAVING BOTH OF THOSE INSIDE HER AT THE SAME TIME, EVEN THOUGH SIMPLE MATH AND BIOLOGY TELLS YOU THAT IT HAS TO BE HURTING HER. MAYBE EVEN CAUSING PERMANENT INTERNAL DAMAGE.
FUNNY THING ABOUT THAT ONE THERE -- DIDN'T EVEN WANT TO BE IN THE BIZ. SHE TOOK A JOB ANSWERING PHONES AT THE WAREHOUSE THAT MAKES THE TAPES... SHE WENT TO A PARTY. A PARTY FOR WORK. A FUNCTION.
AND - THIS IS FUNNY -- SHE TOOK A LITTLE OF THIS- THESE CRYSTAL METH CONCOCTIONS THAT HER "PRODUCER" HAS MADE SPECIAL IN MEXICO. JUST A LITTLE HIT AND --
AND MAN- THAT'S ALL SHE WROTE. SINCE THEN, SHE HAS BEEN SO WHACKED OUT SHE DOESN'T EVEN REMEMBER MAKING HALF THE MOVIES SHE'S IN.
CAN YOU IMAGINE DOING THAT? AND NOT REMEMBERING IT. HAHAHAHAHA HAHAHA

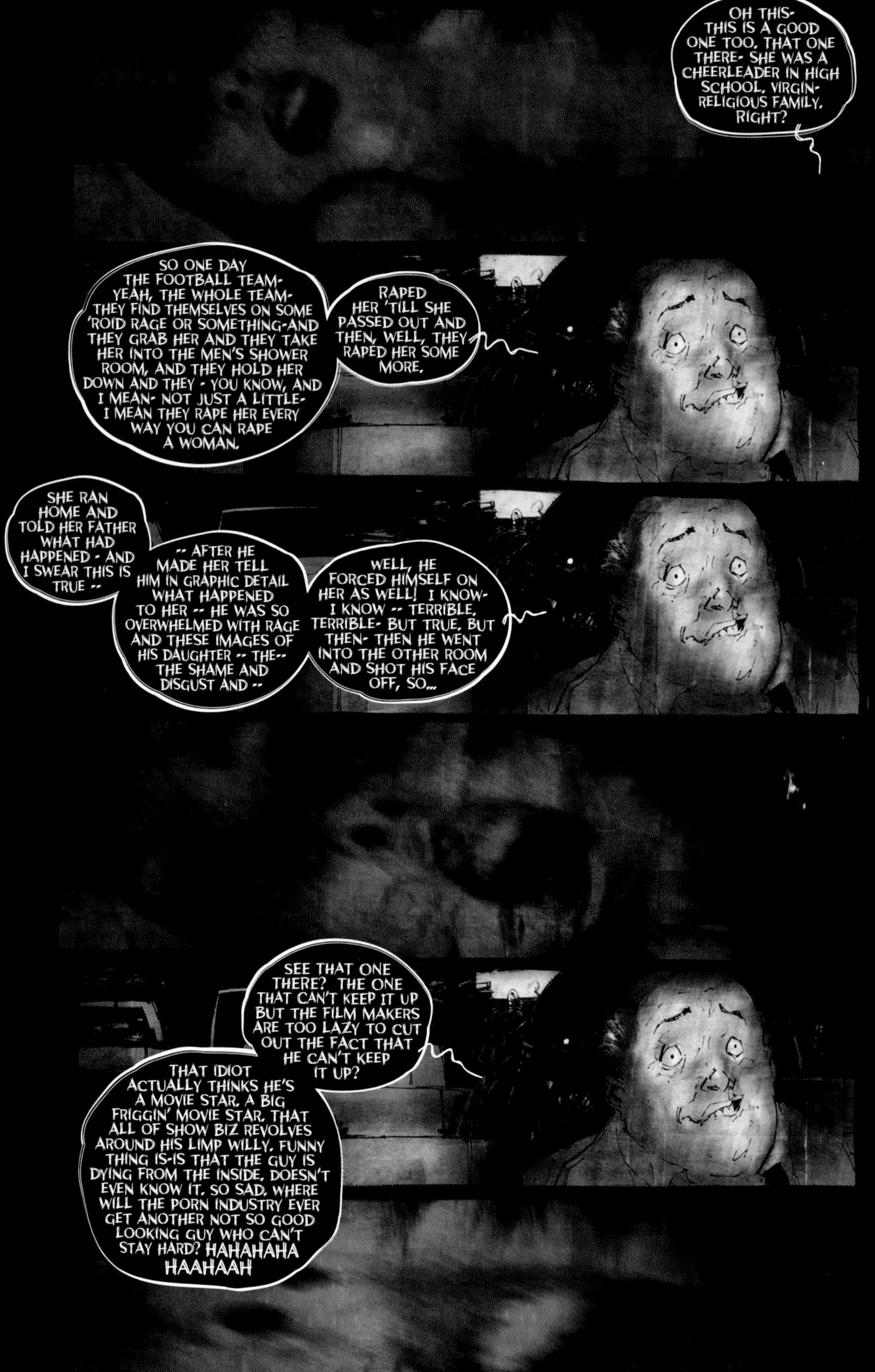
OH THIS- THIS IS A GOOD ONE TOO. THAT ONE THERE- SHE WAS A CHEERLEADER IN HIGH SCHOOL. VIRGIN- RELIGIOUS FAMILY. RIGHT?
SO ONE DAY THE FOOTBALL TEAM- YEAH, THE WHOLE TEAM- THEY FIND THEMSELVES ON SOME 'ROID RAGE OR SOMETHING-AND THEY GRAB HER AND THEY TAKE HER INTO THE MEN'S SHOWER ROOM, AND THEY HOLD HER DOWN AND THEY - YOU KNOW, AND I MEAN- NOT JUST A LITTLE- I MEAN THEY RAPE HER EVERY WAY YOU CAN RAPE A WOMAN.
RAPED HER 'TILL SHE PASSED OUT AND THEN, WELL, THEY RAPED HER SOME MORE.
SHE RAN HOME AND TOLD HER FATHER WHAT HAD HAPPENED - AND I SWEAR THIS IS TRUE --
-- AFTER HE MADE HER TELL HIM IN GRAPHIC DETAIL WHAT HAPPENED TO HER -- HE WAS SO OVERWHELMED WITH RAGE AND THESE IMAGES OF HIS DAUGHTER -- THE-- THE SHAME AND DISGUST AND --
WELL, HE FORCED HIMSELF ON HER AS WELL! I KNOW- I KNOW -- TERRIBLE, TERRIBLE- BUT TRUE. BUT THEN- THEN HE WENT INTO THE OTHER ROOM AND SHOT HIS FACE OFF, SO...
SEE THAT ONE THERE? THE ONE THAT CAN'T KEEP IT UP BUT THE FILM MAKERS ARE TOO LAZY TO CUT OUT THE FACT THAT HE CAN'T KEEP IT UP?
THAT IDIOT ACTUALLY THINKS HE'S A MOVIE STAR. A BIG FRIGGIN' MOVIE STAR. THAT ALL OF SHOW BIZ REVOLVES AROUND HIS LIMP WILLY. FUNNY THING IS-IS THAT THE GUY IS DYING FROM THE INSIDE. DOESN'T EVEN KNOW IT. SO SAD. WHERE WILL THE PORN INDUSTRY EVER GET ANOTHER NOT SO GOOD LOOKING GUY WHO CAN'T STAY HARD? HAHAHAHA HAAHAAH

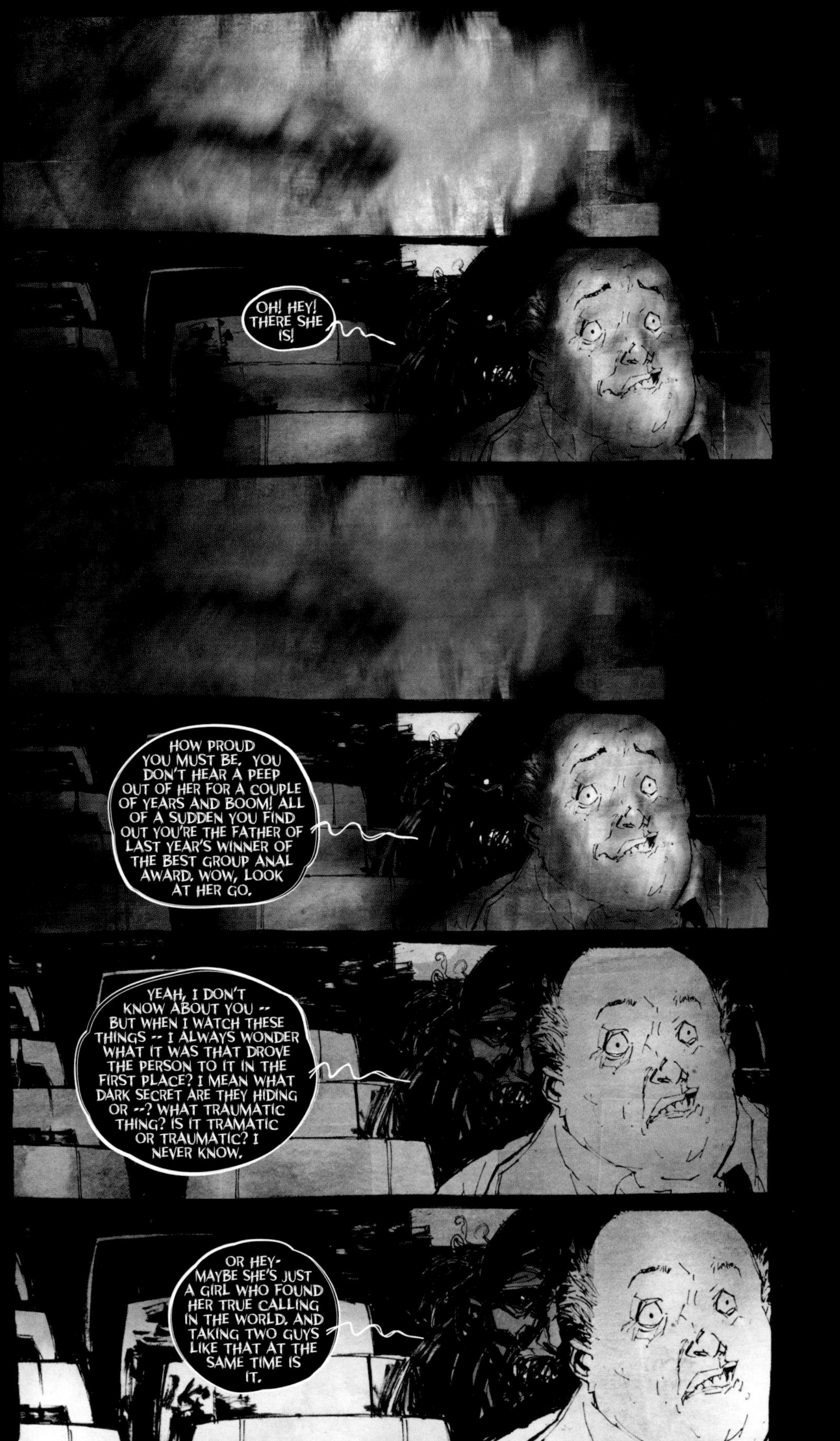
OH! HEY! THERE SHE IS!
HOW PROUD YOU MUST BE. YOU DON'T HEAR A PEEP OUT OF HER FOR A COUPLE OF YEARS AND BOOM! ALL OF A SUDDEN YOU FIND OUT YOU'RE THE FATHER OF LAST YEAR'S WINNER OF THE BEST GROUP ANAL AWARD. WOW, LOOK AT HER GO.
YEAH, I DON'T KNOW ABOUT YOU -- BUT WHEN I WATCH THESE THINGS -- I ALWAYS WONDER WHAT IT WAS THAT DROVE THE PERSON TO IT IN THE FIRST PLACE? I MEAN WHAT DARK SECRET ARE THEY HIDING OR --? WHAT TRAUMATIC THING? IS IT TRAMATIC OR TRAUMATIC? I NEVER KNOW.
OR HEY- MAYBE SHE'S JUST A GIRL WHO FOUND HER TRUE CALLING IN THE WORLD. AND TAKING TWO GUYS LIKE THAT AT THE SAME TIME IS IT.

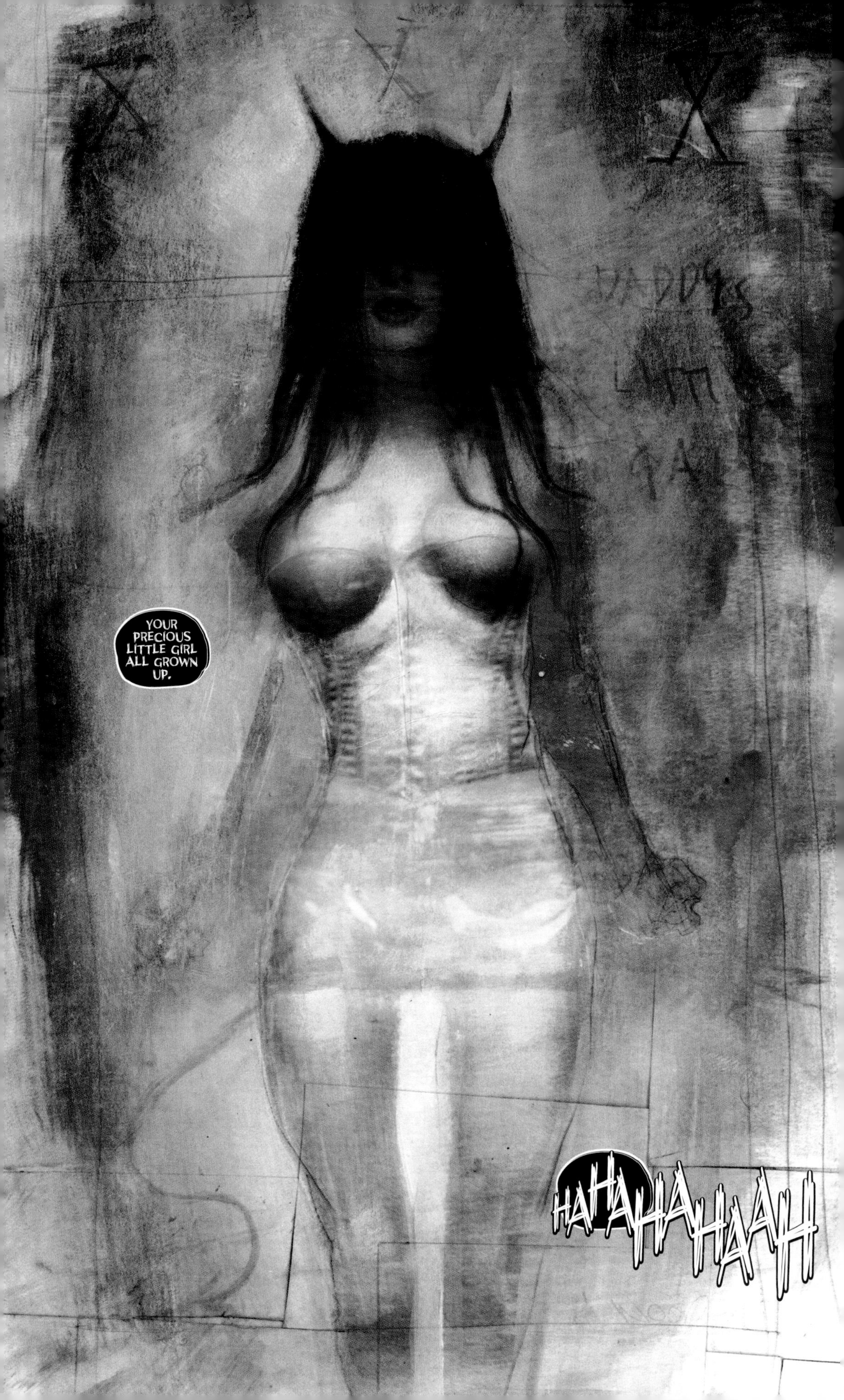
YOUR PRECIOUS LITTLE GIRL ALL GROWN UP.
HAHAHAHAHAAH

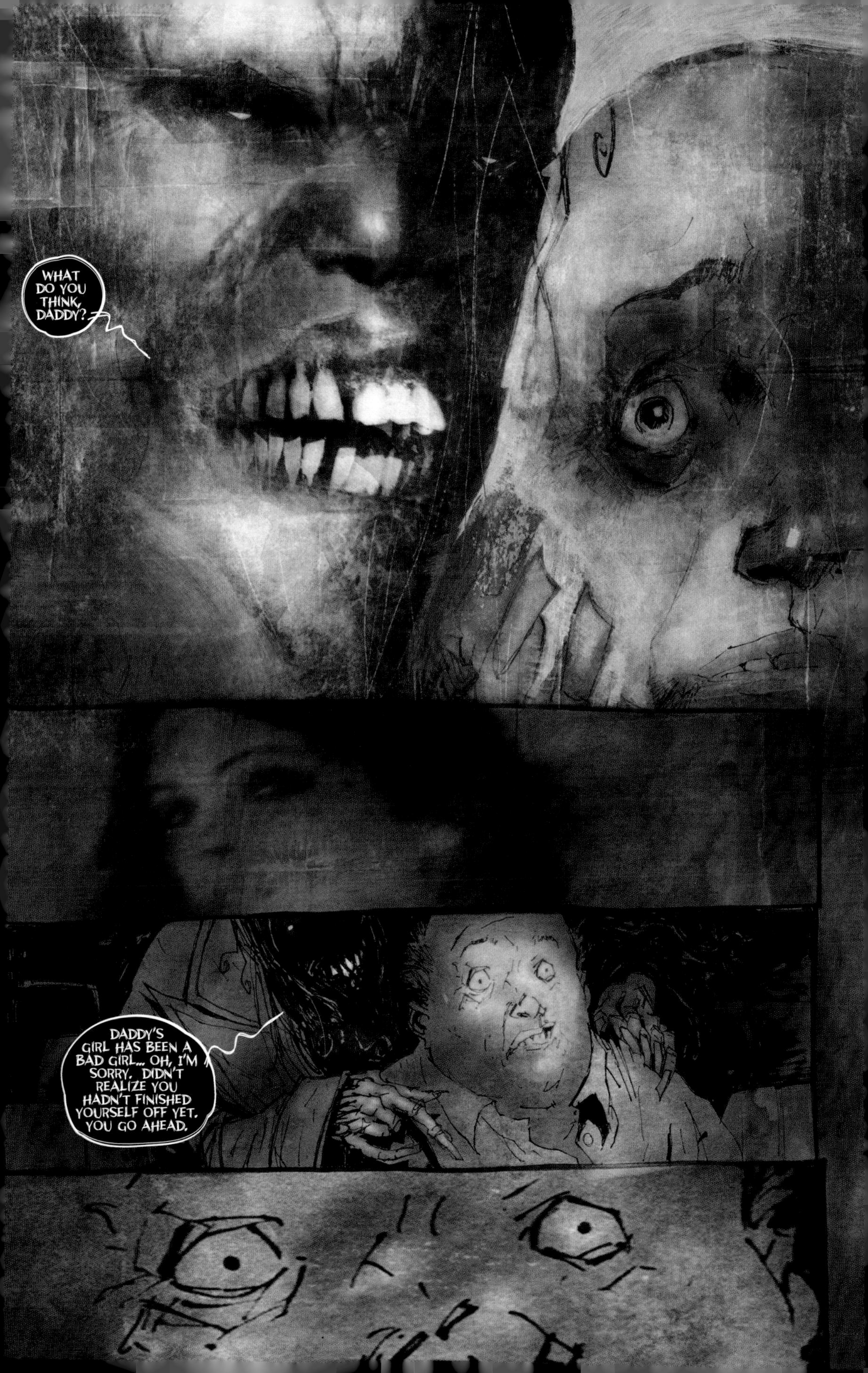
WHAT DO YOU THINK, DADDY?
DADDY'S GIRL HAS BEEN A BAD GIRL... OH, I'M SORRY. DIDN'T REALIZE YOU HADN'T FINISHED YOURSELF OFF YET. YOU GO AHEAD.

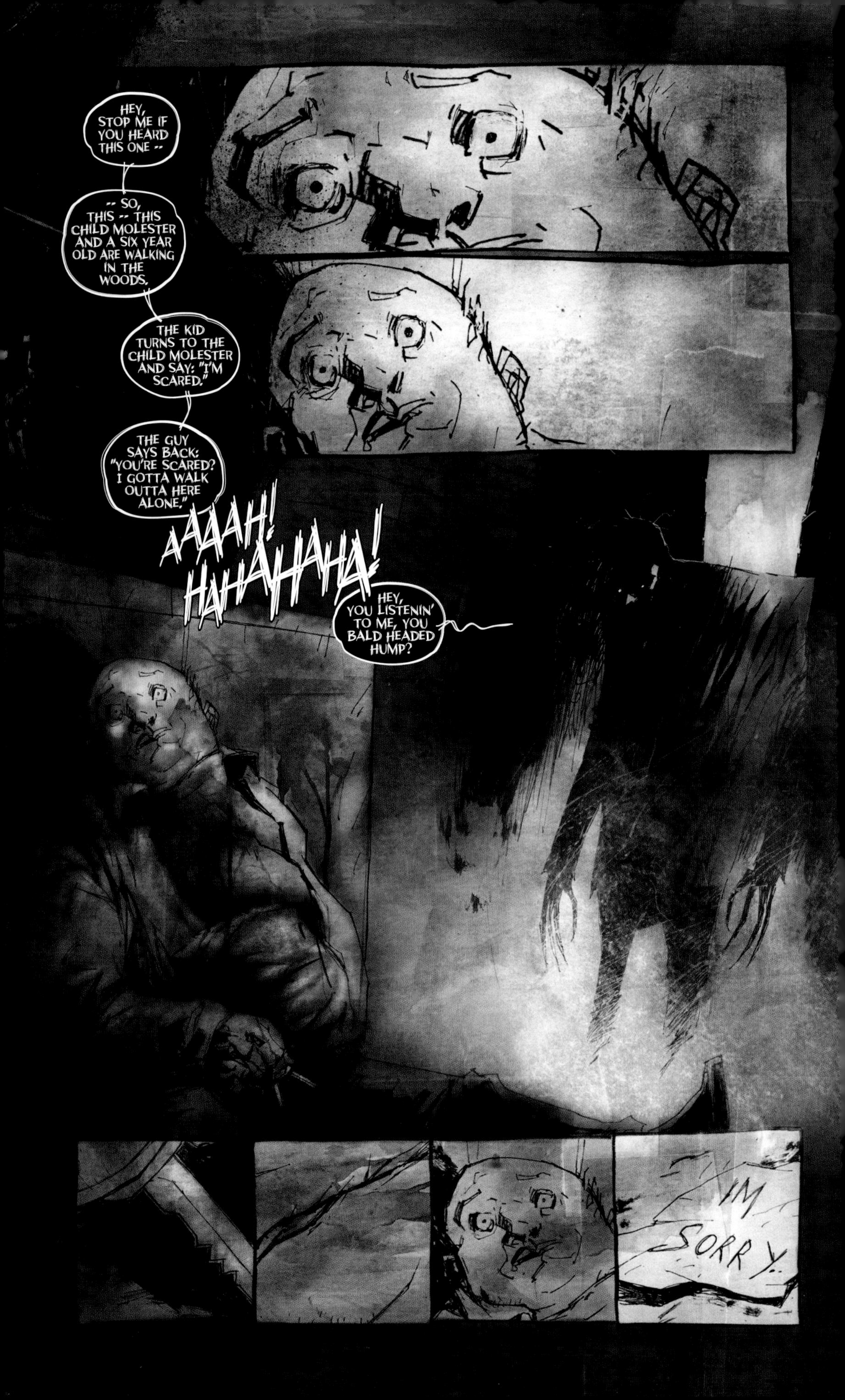
HEY, STOP ME IF YOU HEARD THIS ONE --
-- SO, THIS -- THIS CHILD MOLESTER AND A SIX YEAR OLD ARE WALKING IN THE WOODS.
THE KID TURNS TO THE CHILD MOLESTER AND SAY: "I'M SCARED."
THE GUY SAYS BACK: "YOU'RE SCARED? I GOTTA WALK OUTTA HERE ALONE."
AAAAH! HAHAHAHA!
HEY, YOU LISTENIN' TO ME, YOU BALD HEADED HUMP?
I'M SORRY.

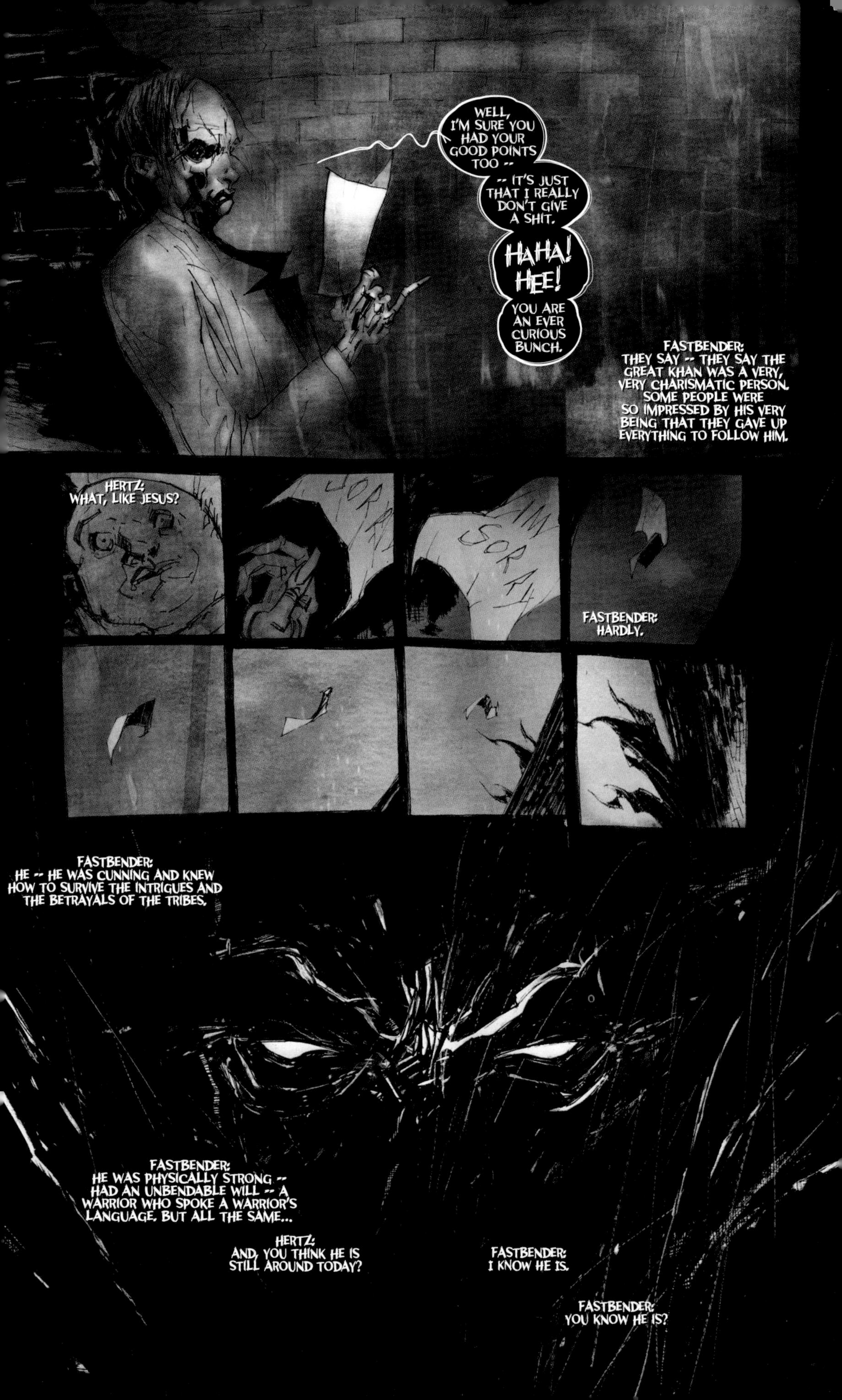

WELL, I'M SURE YOU HAD YOUR GOOD POINTS TOO --
-- IT'S JUST THAT I REALLY DON'T GIVE A SHIT.
HAHA! HEE!
YOU ARE AN EVER CURIOUS BUNCH.
FASTBENDER: THEY SAY -- THEY SAY THE GREAT KHAN WAS A VERY, VERY CHARISMATIC PERSON. SOME PEOPLE WERE SO IMPRESSED BY HIS VERY BEING THAT THEY GAVE UP EVERYTHING TO FOLLOW HIM.
HERTZ: WHAT, LIKE JESUS?
SORRY
AM SORRY
FASTBENDER: HARDLY.
FASTBENDER: HE -- HE WAS CUNNING AND KNEW HOW TO SURVIVE THE INTRIGUES AND THE BETRAYALS OF THE TRIBES.
FASTBENDER: HE WAS PHYSICALLY STRONG -- HAD AN UNBENDABLE WILL -- A WARRIOR WHO SPOKE A WARRIOR'S LANGUAGE. BUT ALL THE SAME...
HERTZ: AND, YOU THINK HE IS STILL AROUND TODAY?
FASTBENDER: I KNOW HE IS.
FASTBENDER: YOU KNOW HE IS?

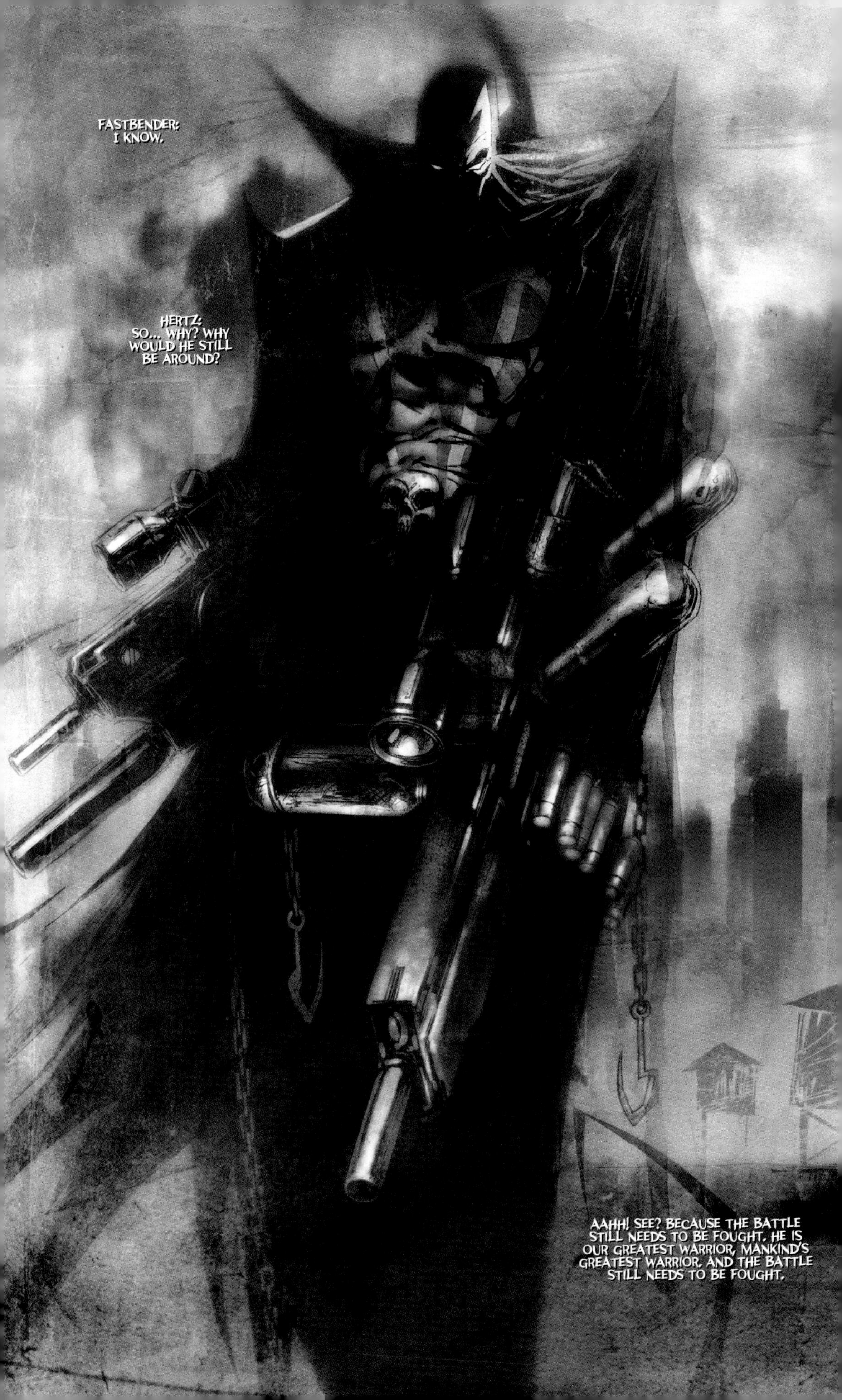
FASTBENDER: I KNOW.
HERTZ: SO... WHY? WHY WOULD HE STILL BE AROUND?
AAHH! SEE? BECAUSE THE BATTLE STILL NEEDS TO BE FOUGHT. HE IS OUR GREATEST WARRIOR, MANKIND'S GREATEST WARRIOR. AND THE BATTLE STILL NEEDS TO BE FOUGHT.

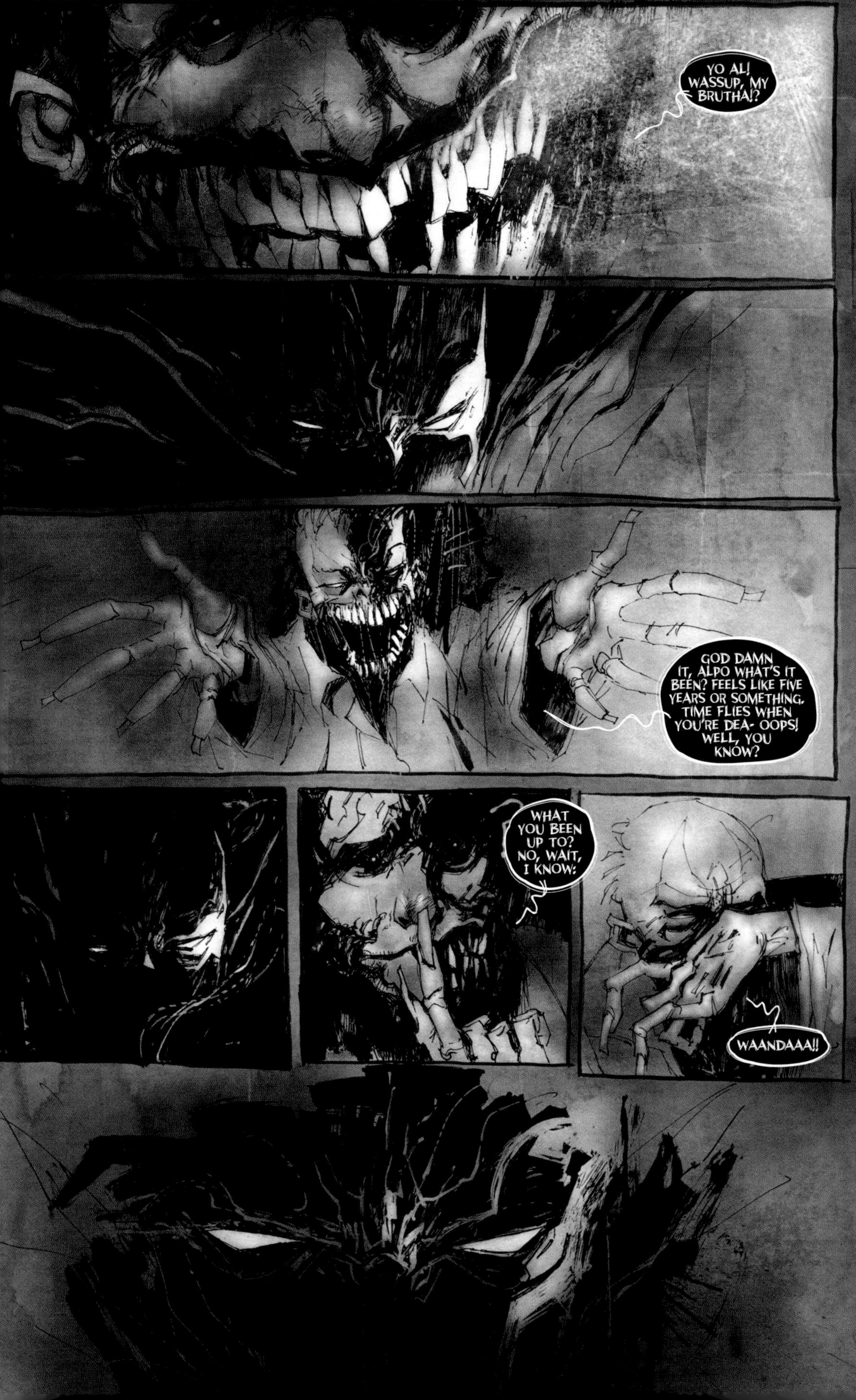
YO AL! WASSUP, MY BRUTHA!?
GOD DAMN IT, ALPO WHAT'S IT BEEN? FEELS LIKE FIVE YEARS OR SOMETHING. TIME FLIES WHEN YOU'RE DEA- OOPS! WELL, YOU KNOW?
WHAT YOU BEEN UP TO? NO, WAIT, I KNOW:
WAANDAAA!!

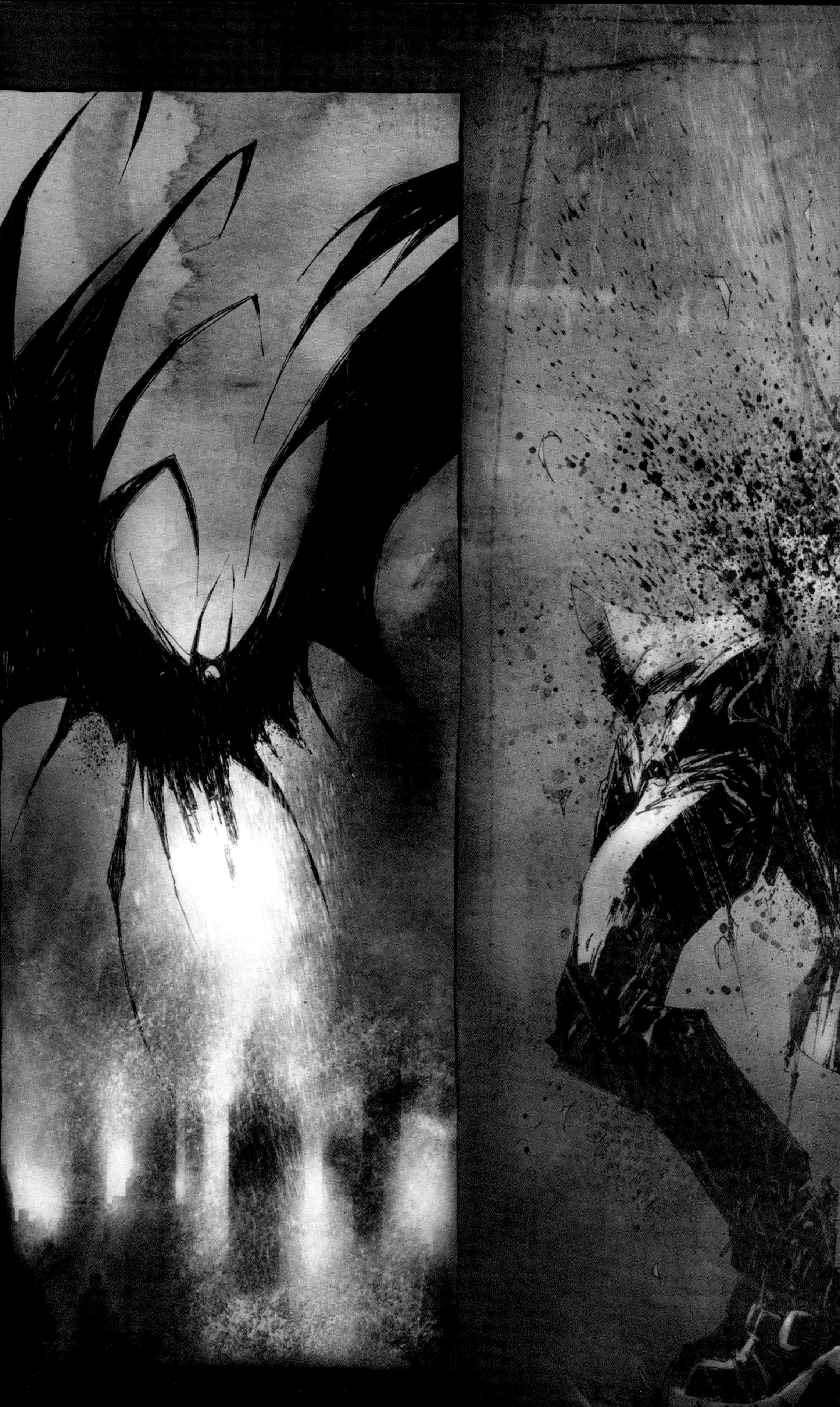

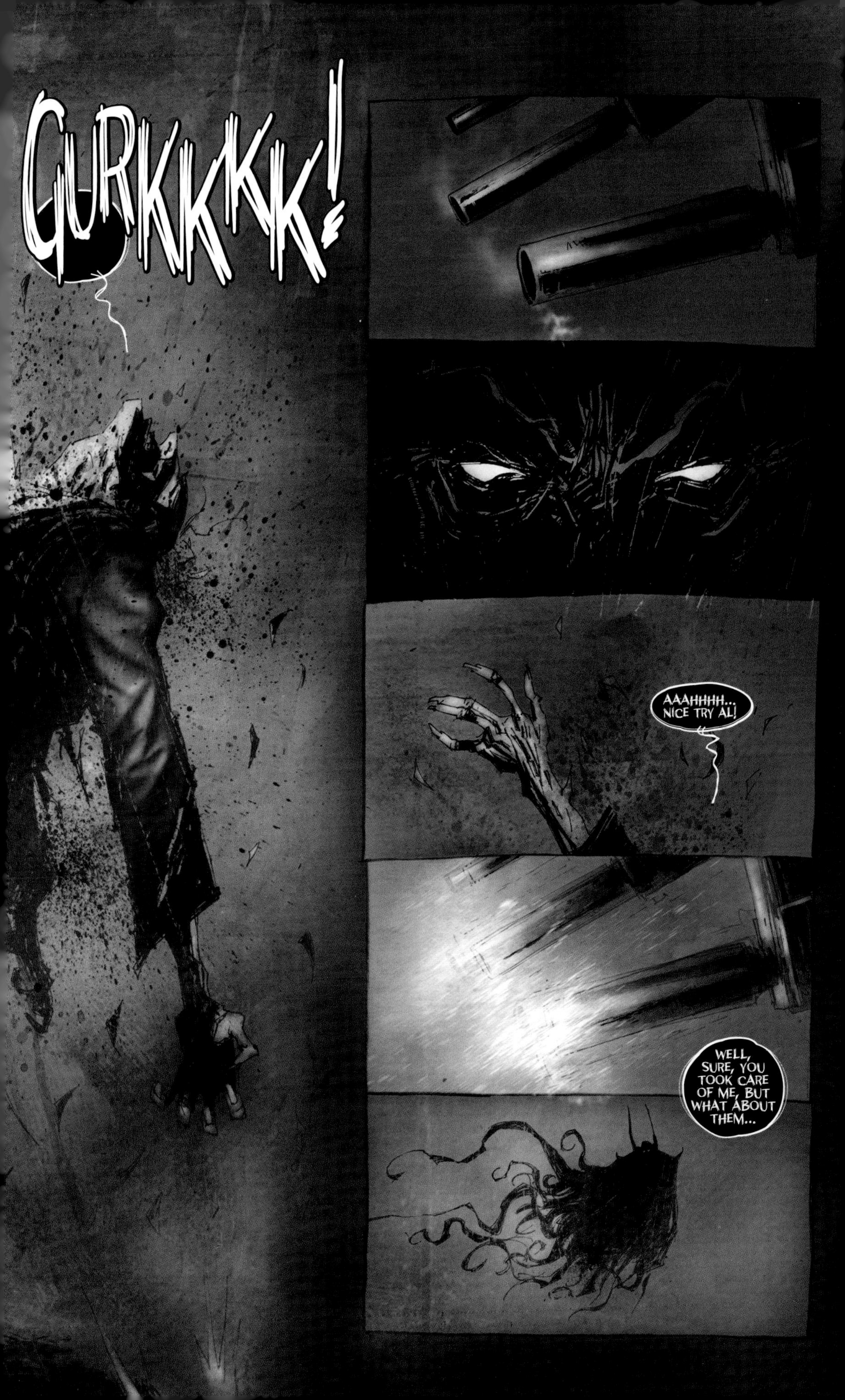
GURKKKK!
AAAHHHH... NICE TRY AL!
WELL, SURE, YOU TOOK CARE OF ME, BUT WHAT ABOUT THEM...

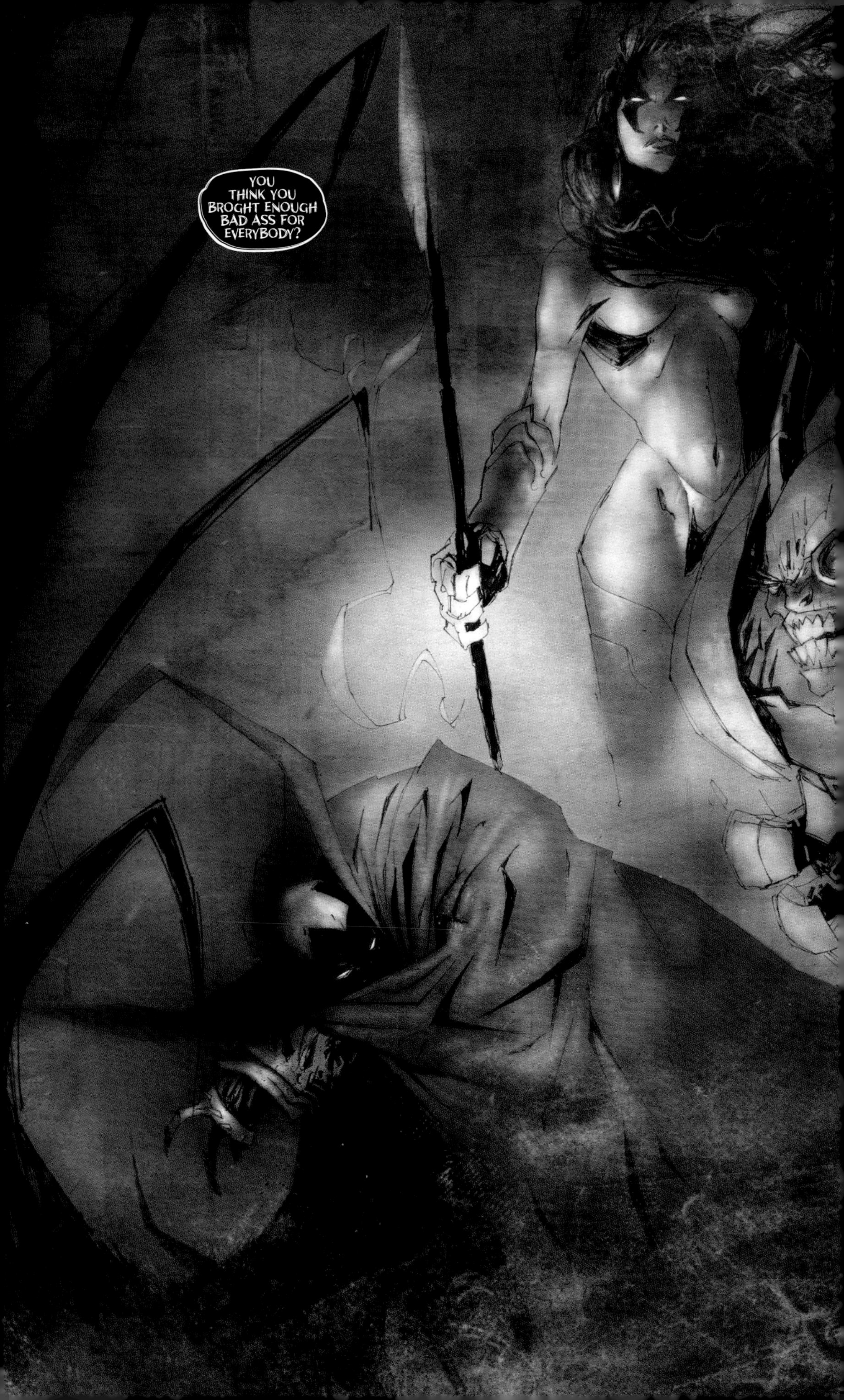
YOU THINK YOU BROGHT ENOUGH BAD ASS FOR EVERYBODY?

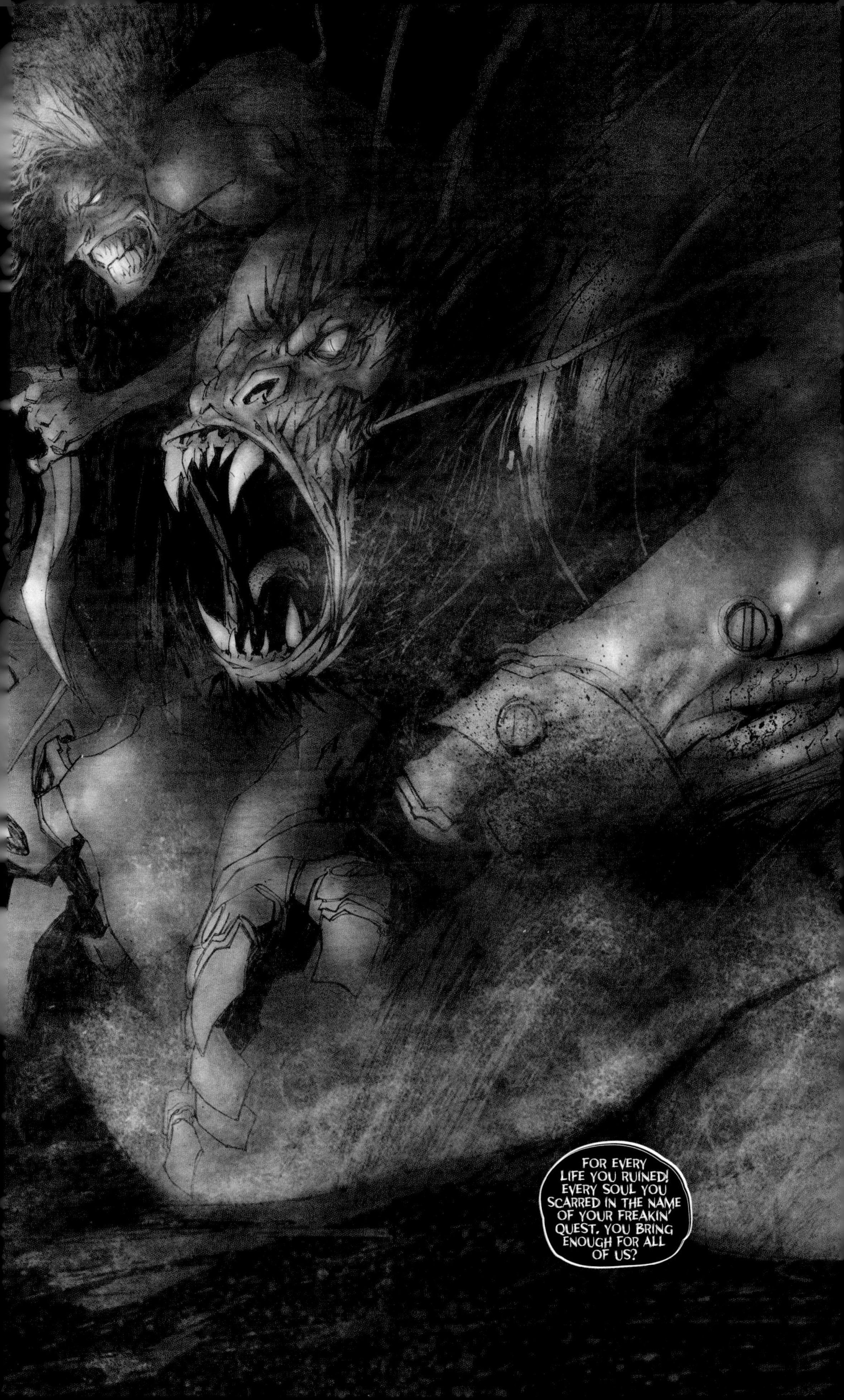
FOR EVERY LIFE YOU RUINED! EVERY SOUL YOU SCARRED IN THE NAME OF YOUR FREAKIN' QUEST. YOU BRING ENOUGH FOR ALL OF US?

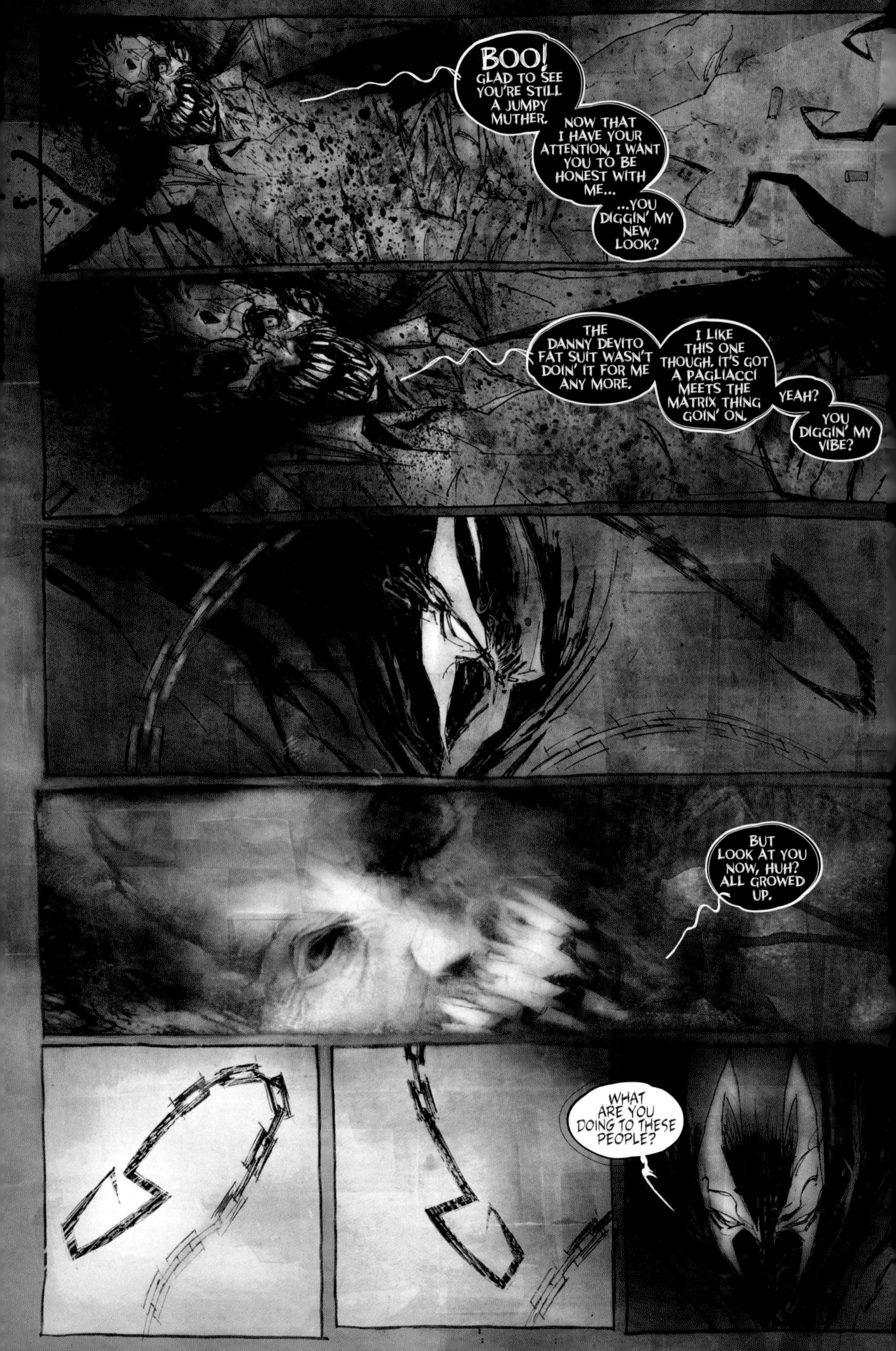
BOO! GLAD TO SEE YOU'RE STILL A JUMPY MUTHER.
NOW THAT I HAVE YOUR ATTENTION, I WANT YOU TO BE HONEST WITH ME...
...YOU DIGGIN' MY NEW LOOK?
THE DANNY DEVITO FAT SUIT WASN'T DOIN' IT FOR ME ANY MORE.
I LIKE THIS ONE THOUGH. IT'S GOT A PAGLIACCI MEETS THE MATRIX THING GOIN' ON.
YEAH?
YOU DIGGIN' MY VIBE?
BUT LOOK AT YOU NOW, HUH? ALL GROWED UP.
WHAT ARE YOU DOING TO THESE PEOPLE?

JUST SCREWIN' AROUND. WHY? YOU WANNA GO GET SOMETHIN' TO EAT? GET LAID OR-- ASACCK!

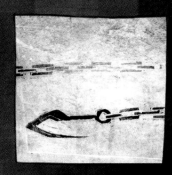

LISTEN UP, FREAK!

YOU TELL ME WHAT THIS IS ALL ABOUT? WHAT ARE YOU DOING HERE? WHAT ARE YOU DOING TO THESE PEOPLE?

TELL YOU WHAT AL -- YOU'RE SO SCARY SMART...

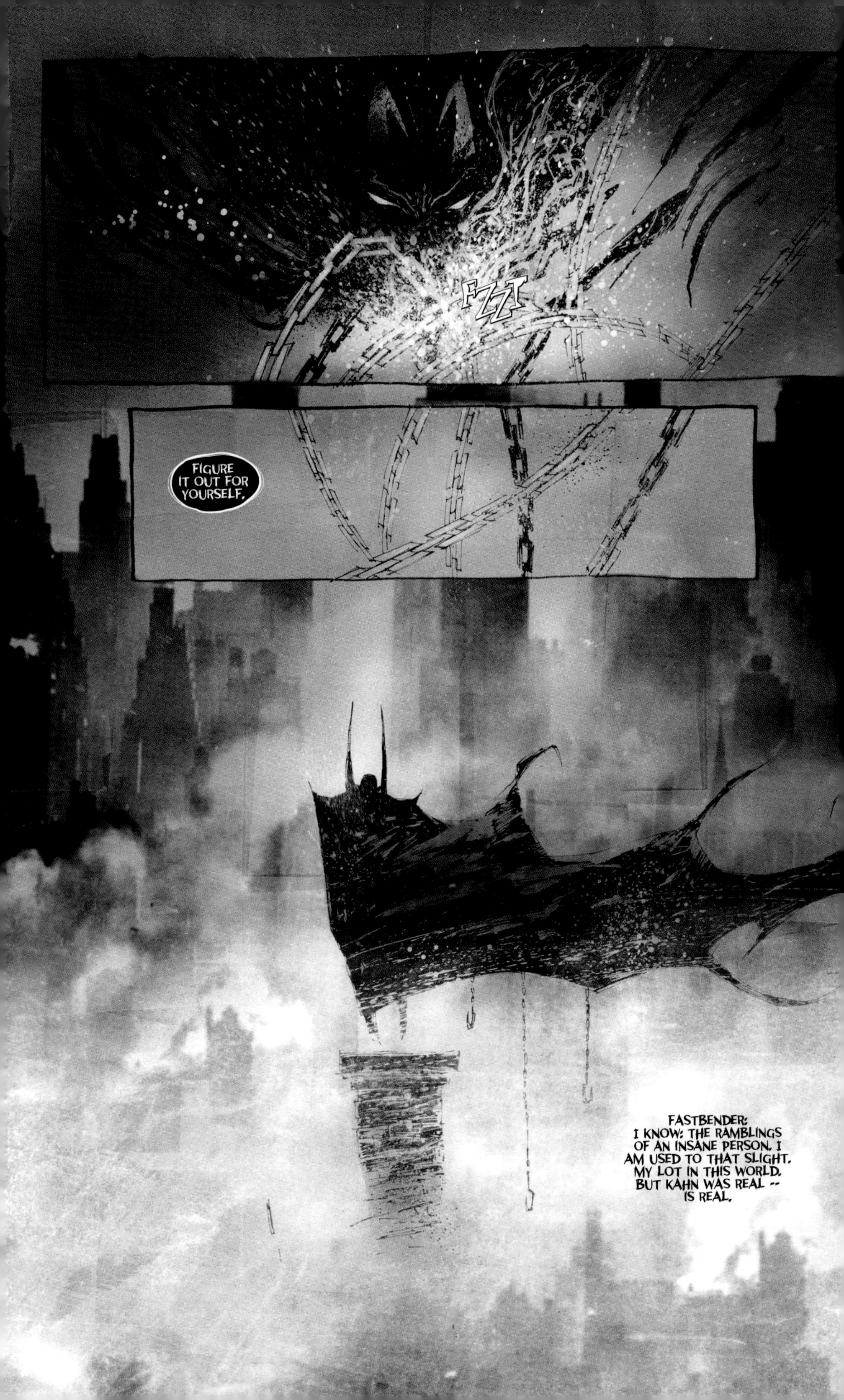
FZZT
FIGURE IT OUT FOR YOURSELF.
FASTBENDER: I KNOW: THE RAMBLINGS OF AN INSANE PERSON. I AM USED TO THAT SLIGHT. MY LOT IN THIS WORLD. BUT KAHN WAS REAL -- IS REAL.

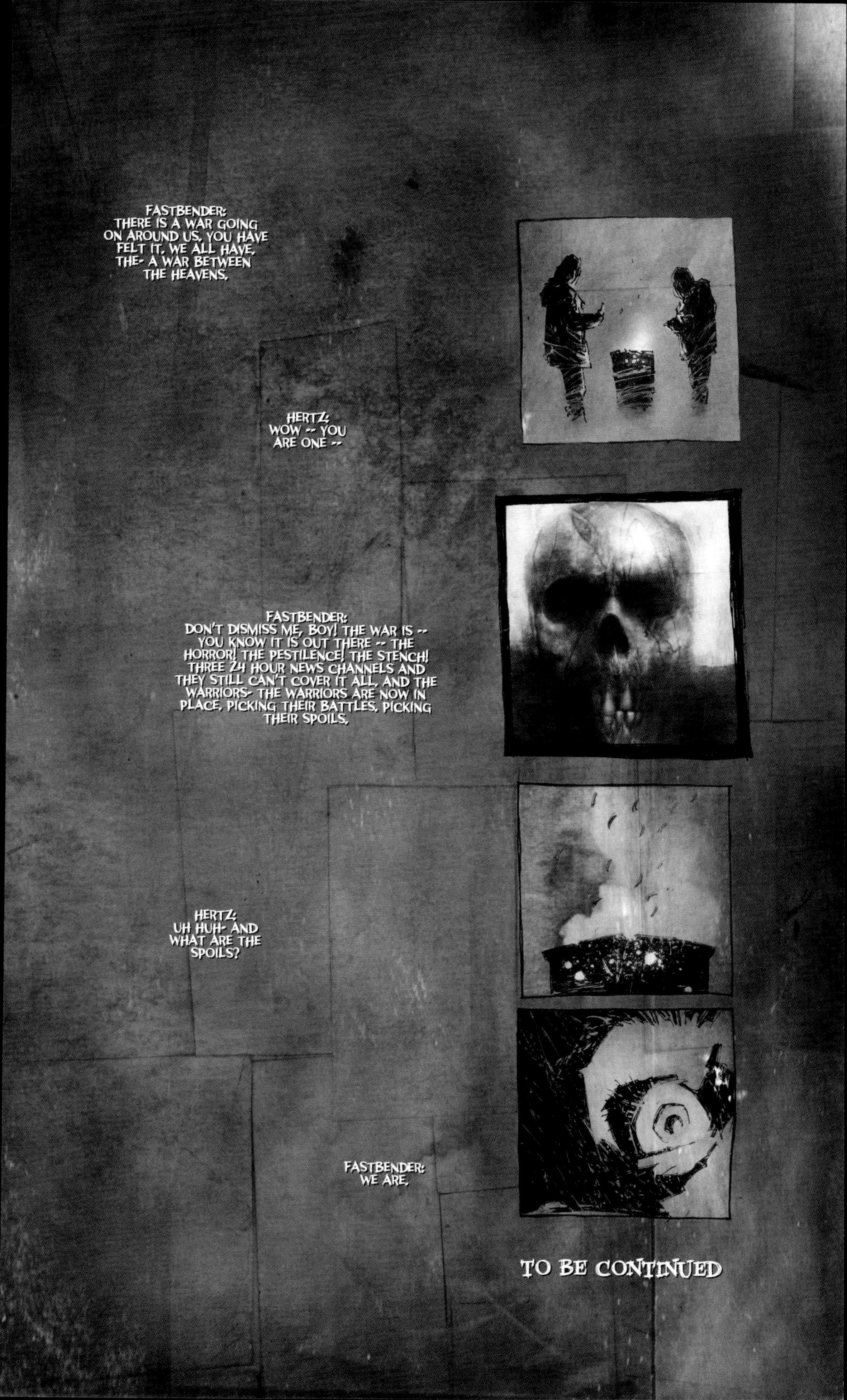
FASTBENDER: THERE IS A WAR GOING ON AROUND US. YOU HAVE FELT IT. WE ALL HAVE. THE- A WAR BETWEEN THE HEAVENS.
HERTZ: WOW -- YOU ARE ONE --
FASTBENDER: DON'T DISMISS ME, BOY! THE WAR IS -- YOU KNOW IT IS OUT THERE -- THE HORROR! THE PESTILENCE! THE STENCH! THREE 24 HOUR NEWS CHANNELS AND THEY STILL CAN'T COVER IT ALL. AND THE WARRIORS- THE WARRIORS ARE NOW IN PLACE, PICKING THEIR BATTLES, PICKING THEIR SPOILS.
HERTZ: UH HUH- AND WHAT ARE THE SPOILS?
FASTBENDER: WE ARE.
TO BE CONTINUED

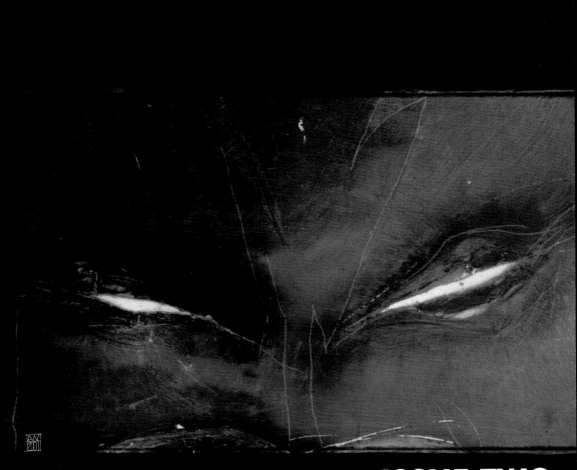

ISSUE TWO

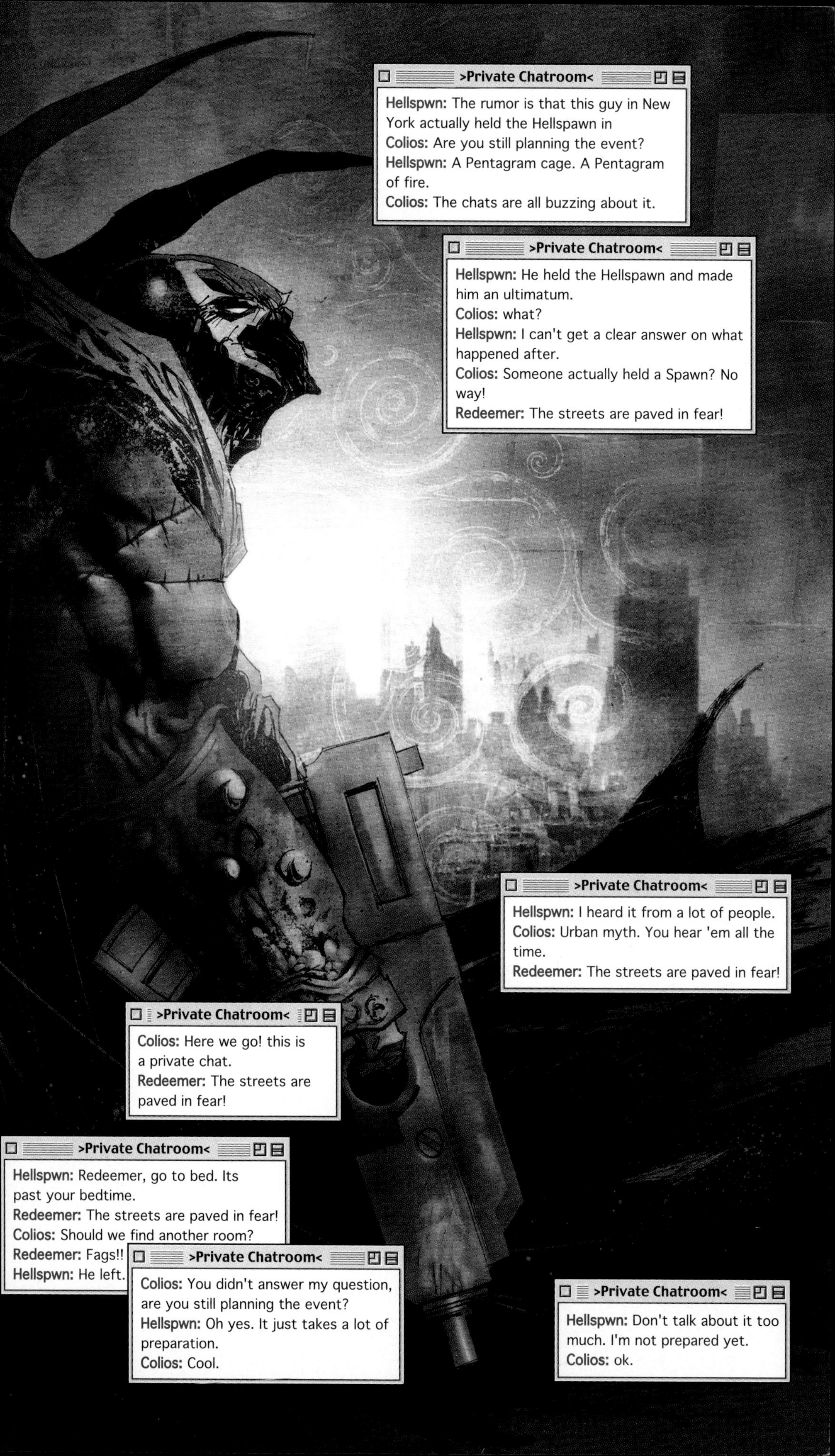
>Private Chatroom<
Hellspwn: The rumor is that this guy in New York actually held the Hellspawn in
Colios: Are you still planning the event?
Hellspwn: A Pentagram cage. A Pentagram of fire.
Colios: The chats are all buzzing about it.
>Private Chatroom<
Hellspwn: He held the Hellspawn and made him an ultimatum.
Colios: what?
Hellspwn: I can't get a clear answer on what happened after.
Colios: Someone actually held a Spawn? No way!
Redeemer: The streets are paved in fear!
>Private Chatroom<
Hellspwn: I heard it from a lot of people.
Colios: Urban myth. You hear 'em all the time.
Redeemer: The streets are paved in fear!
>Private Chatroom<
Colios: Here we go! this is a private chat.
Redeemer: The streets are paved in fear!
>Private Chatroom<
Hellspwn: Redeemer, go to bed. Its past your bedtime.
Redeemer: The streets are paved in fear!
Colios: Should we find another room?
Redeemer: Fags!!
Hellspwn: He left.
>Private Chatroom<
Colios: You didn't answer my question, are you still planning the event?
Hellspwn: Oh yes. It just takes a lot of preparation.
Colios: Cool.
>Private Chatroom<
Hellspwn: Don't talk about it too much. I'm not prepared yet.
Colios: ok.

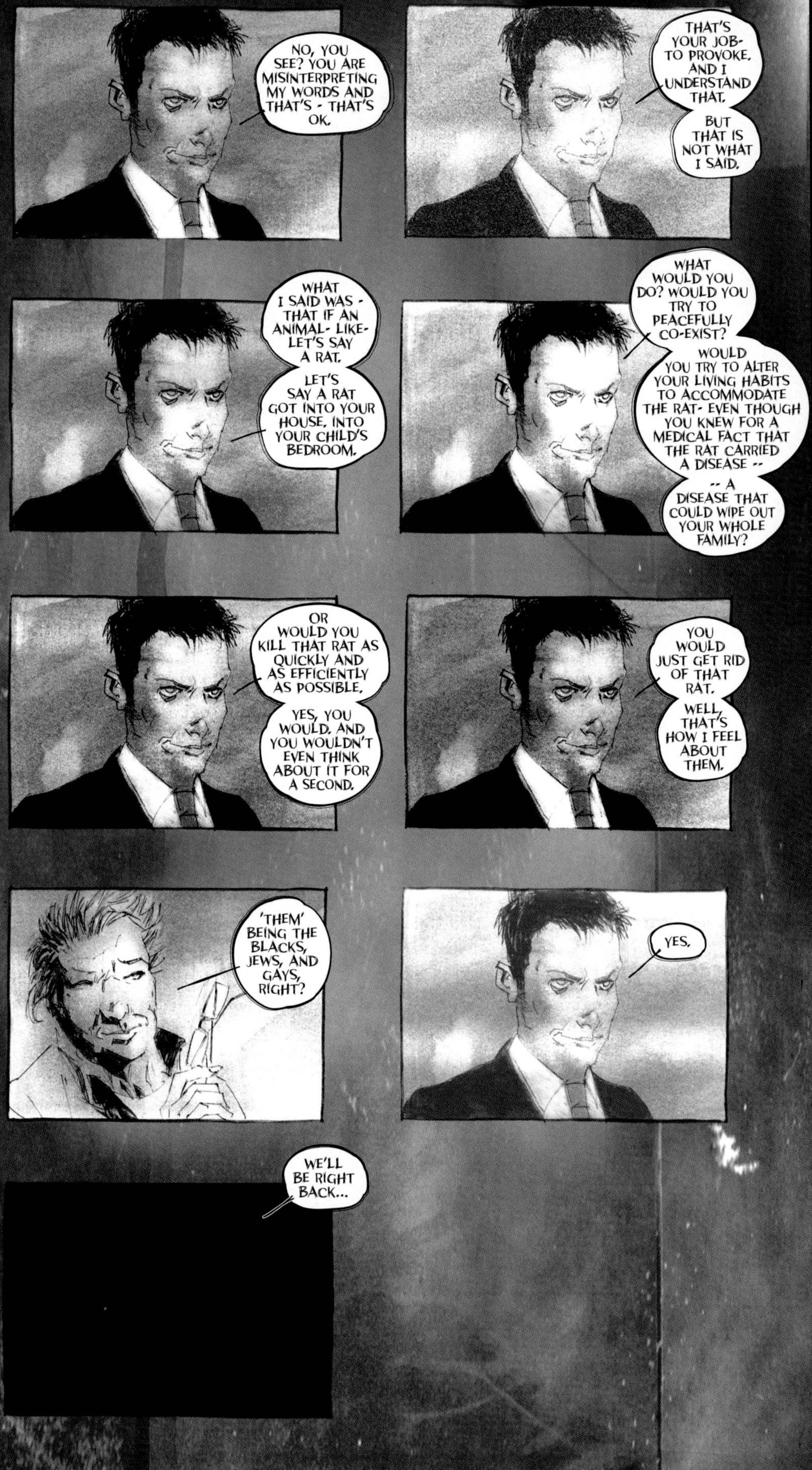

NO, YOU SEE? YOU ARE MISINTERPRETING MY WORDS AND THAT'S - THAT'S OK.
THAT'S YOUR JOB- TO PROVOKE. AND I UNDERSTAND THAT.
BUT THAT IS NOT WHAT I SAID.
WHAT I SAID WAS - THAT IF AN ANIMAL- LIKE- LET'S SAY A RAT.
LET'S SAY A RAT GOT INTO YOUR HOUSE. INTO YOUR CHILD'S BEDROOM.
WHAT WOULD YOU DO? WOULD YOU TRY TO PEACEFULLY CO-EXIST?
WOULD YOU TRY TO ALTER YOUR LIVING HABITS TO ACCOMMODATE THE RAT- EVEN THOUGH YOU KNEW FOR A MEDICAL FACT THAT THE RAT CARRIED A DISEASE --
-- A DISEASE THAT COULD WIPE OUT YOUR WHOLE FAMILY?
OR WOULD YOU KILL THAT RAT AS QUICKLY AND AS EFFICIENTLY AS POSSIBLE.
YES, YOU WOULD. AND YOU WOULDN'T EVEN THINK ABOUT IT FOR A SECOND.
YOU WOULD JUST GET RID OF THAT RAT.
WELL, THAT'S HOW I FEEL ABOUT THEM.
'THEM' BEING THE BLACKS, JEWS, AND GAYS, RIGHT?
YES.
WE'LL BE RIGHT BACK...

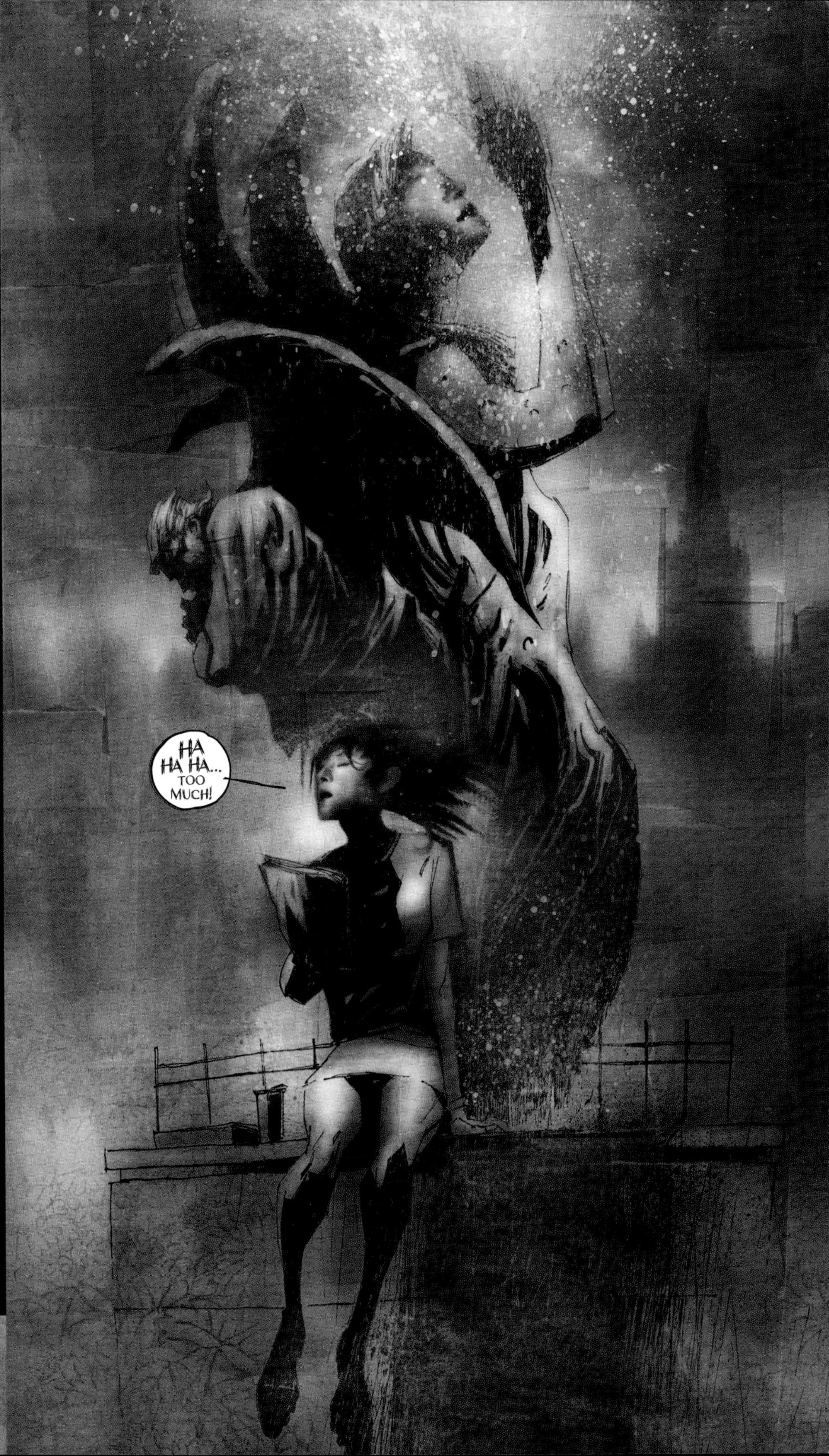
HA HA HA... TOO MUCH!

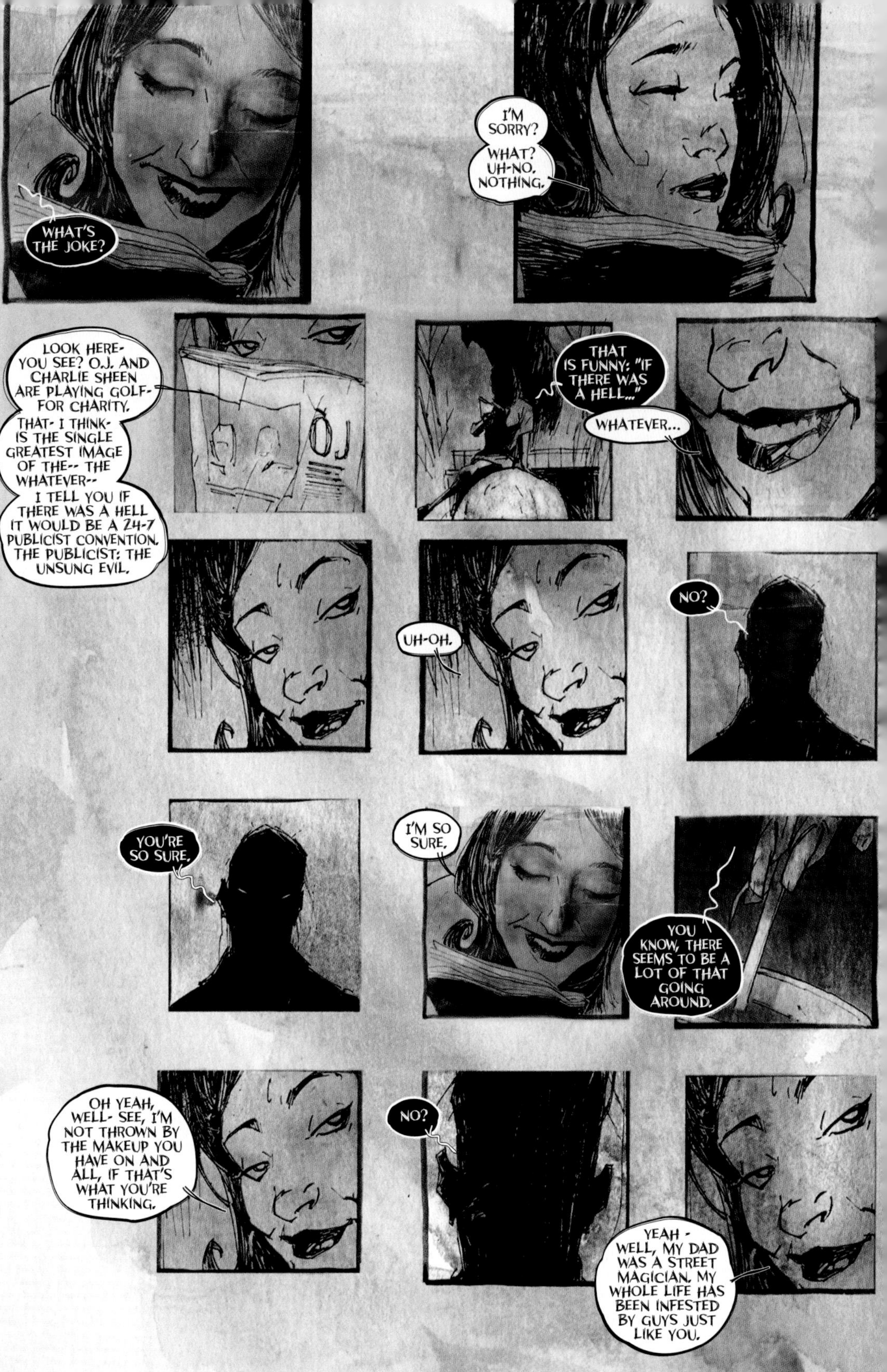
WHAT'S THE JOKE?
I'M SORRY?
WHAT? UH-NO. NOTHING.
LOOK HERE- YOU SEE? O.J. AND CHARLIE SHEEN ARE PLAYING GOLF- FOR CHARITY.
THAT- I THINK- IS THE SINGLE GREATEST IMAGE OF THE-- THE WHATEVER--
I TELL YOU IF THERE WAS A HELL IT WOULD BE A 24-7 PUBLICIST CONVENTION. THE PUBLICIST: THE UNSUNG EVIL.
THAT IS FUNNY: "IF THERE WAS A HELL..."
WHATEVER...
UH-OH.
NO?
YOU'RE SO SURE.
I'M SO SURE.
YOU KNOW, THERE SEEMS TO BE A LOT OF THAT GOING AROUND.
OH YEAH, WELL- SEE, I'M NOT THROWN BY THE MAKEUP YOU HAVE ON AND ALL, IF THAT'S WHAT YOU'RE THINKING.
NO?
YEAH - WELL, MY DAD WAS A STREET MAGICIAN. MY WHOLE LIFE HAS BEEN INFESTED BY GUYS JUST LIKE YOU.

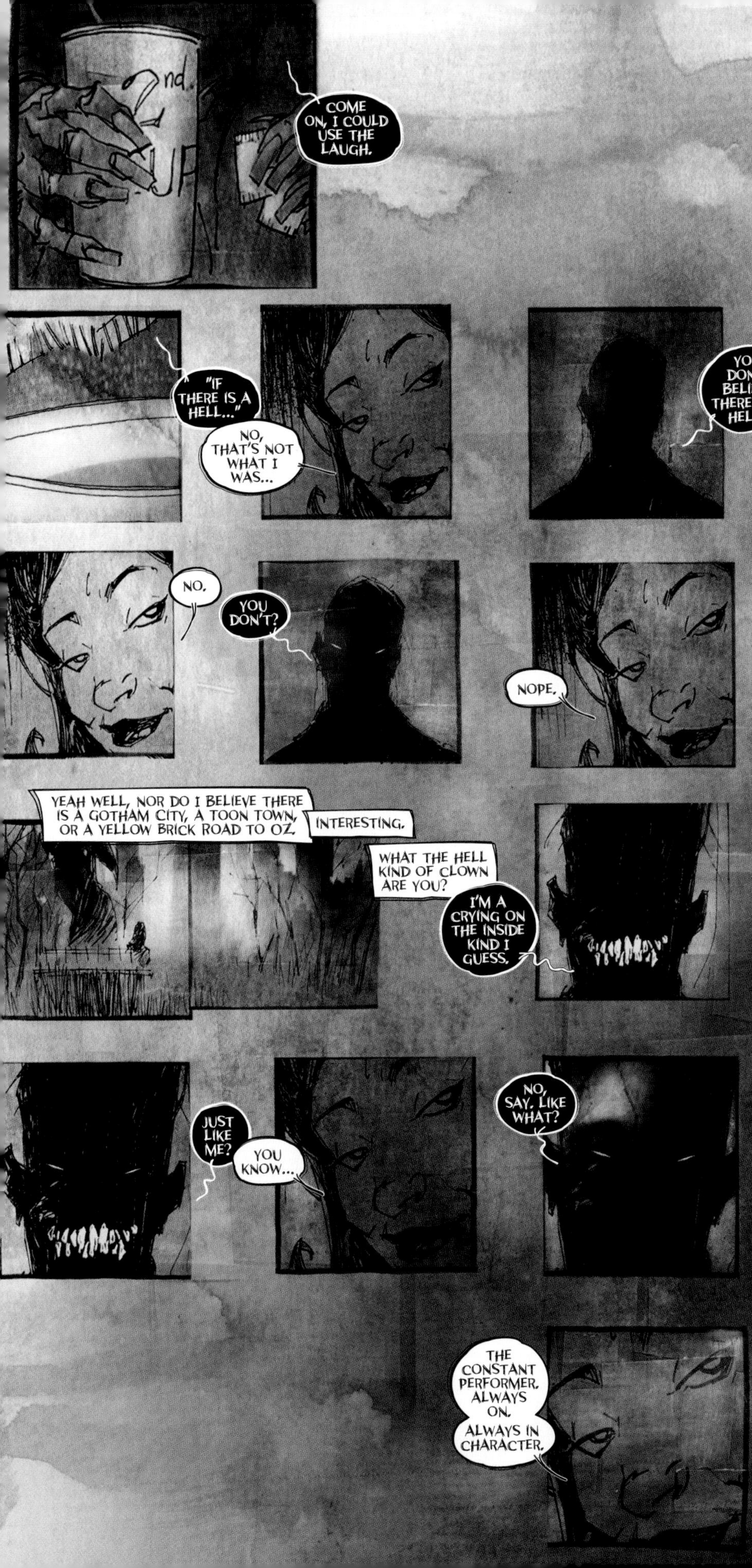
COME ON, I COULD USE THE LAUGH.
"IF THERE IS A HELL..."
NO, THAT'S NOT WHAT I WAS...
YOU DON'T BELIEVE THERE IS A HELL?
NO.
YOU DON'T?
NOPE.
YEAH WELL, NOR DO I BELIEVE THERE IS A GOTHAM CITY, A TOON TOWN, OR A YELLOW BRICK ROAD TO OZ.
INTERESTING.
WHAT THE HELL KIND OF CLOWN ARE YOU?
I'M A CRYING ON THE INSIDE KIND I GUESS.
JUST LIKE ME?
YOU KNOW...
NO, SAY, LIKE WHAT?
THE CONSTANT PERFORMER. ALWAYS ON.
ALWAYS IN CHARACTER.

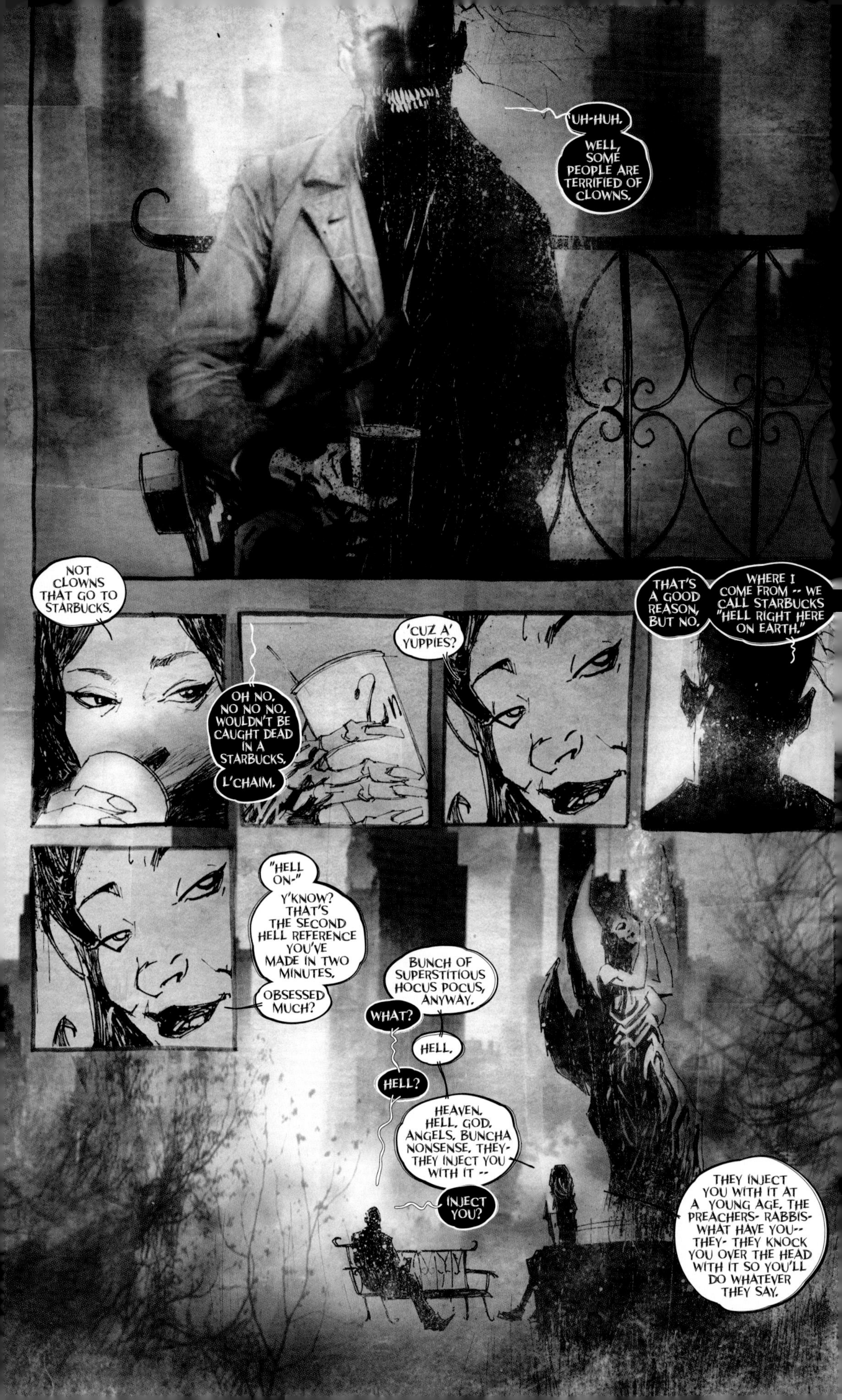
UH-HUH.
WELL, SOME PEOPLE ARE TERRIFIED OF CLOWNS.
NOT CLOWNS THAT GO TO STARBUCKS.
OH NO, NO NO NO. WOULDN'T BE CAUGHT DEAD IN A STARBUCKS.
L'CHAIM.
'CUZ A' YUPPIES?
THAT'S A GOOD REASON, BUT NO.
WHERE I COME FROM -- WE CALL STARBUCKS "HELL RIGHT HERE ON EARTH."
"HELL ON-"
Y'KNOW? THAT'S THE SECOND HELL REFERENCE YOU'VE MADE IN TWO MINUTES.
OBSESSED MUCH?
BUNCH OF SUPERSTITIOUS HOCUS POCUS, ANYWAY.
WHAT?
HELL.
HELL?
HEAVEN, HELL, GOD, ANGELS, BUNCHA NONSENSE. THEY- THEY INJECT YOU WITH IT --
INJECT YOU?
THEY INJECT YOU WITH IT AT A YOUNG AGE. THE PREACHERS- RABBIS- WHAT HAVE YOU-- THEY- THEY KNOCK YOU OVER THE HEAD WITH IT SO YOU'LL DO WHATEVER THEY SAY.

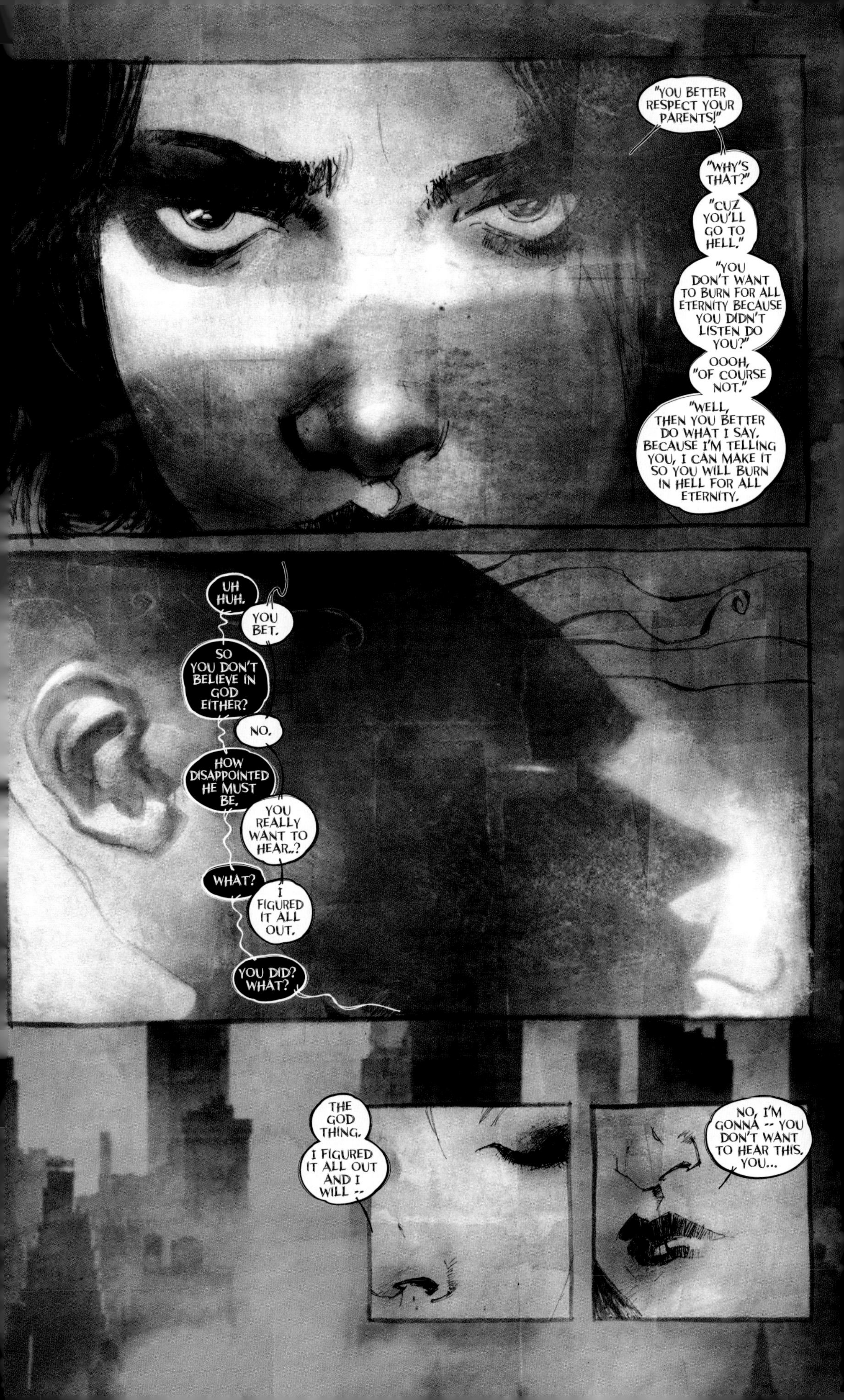
"YOU BETTER RESPECT YOUR PARENTS!"
"WHY'S THAT?"
"CUZ YOU'LL GO TO HELL."
"YOU DON'T WANT TO BURN FOR ALL ETERNITY BECAUSE YOU DIDN'T LISTEN DO YOU?"
OOOH, "OF COURSE NOT."
"WELL, THEN YOU BETTER DO WHAT I SAY. BECAUSE I'M TELLING YOU, I CAN MAKE IT SO YOU WILL BURN IN HELL FOR ALL ETERNITY.
UH HUH.
YOU BET.
SO YOU DON'T BELIEVE IN GOD EITHER?
NO.
HOW DISAPPOINTED HE MUST BE.
YOU REALLY WANT TO HEAR..?
WHAT?
I FIGURED IT ALL OUT.
YOU DID? WHAT?
THE GOD THING.
I FIGURED IT ALL OUT AND I WILL --
NO, I'M GONNA -- YOU DON'T WANT TO HEAR THIS. YOU...

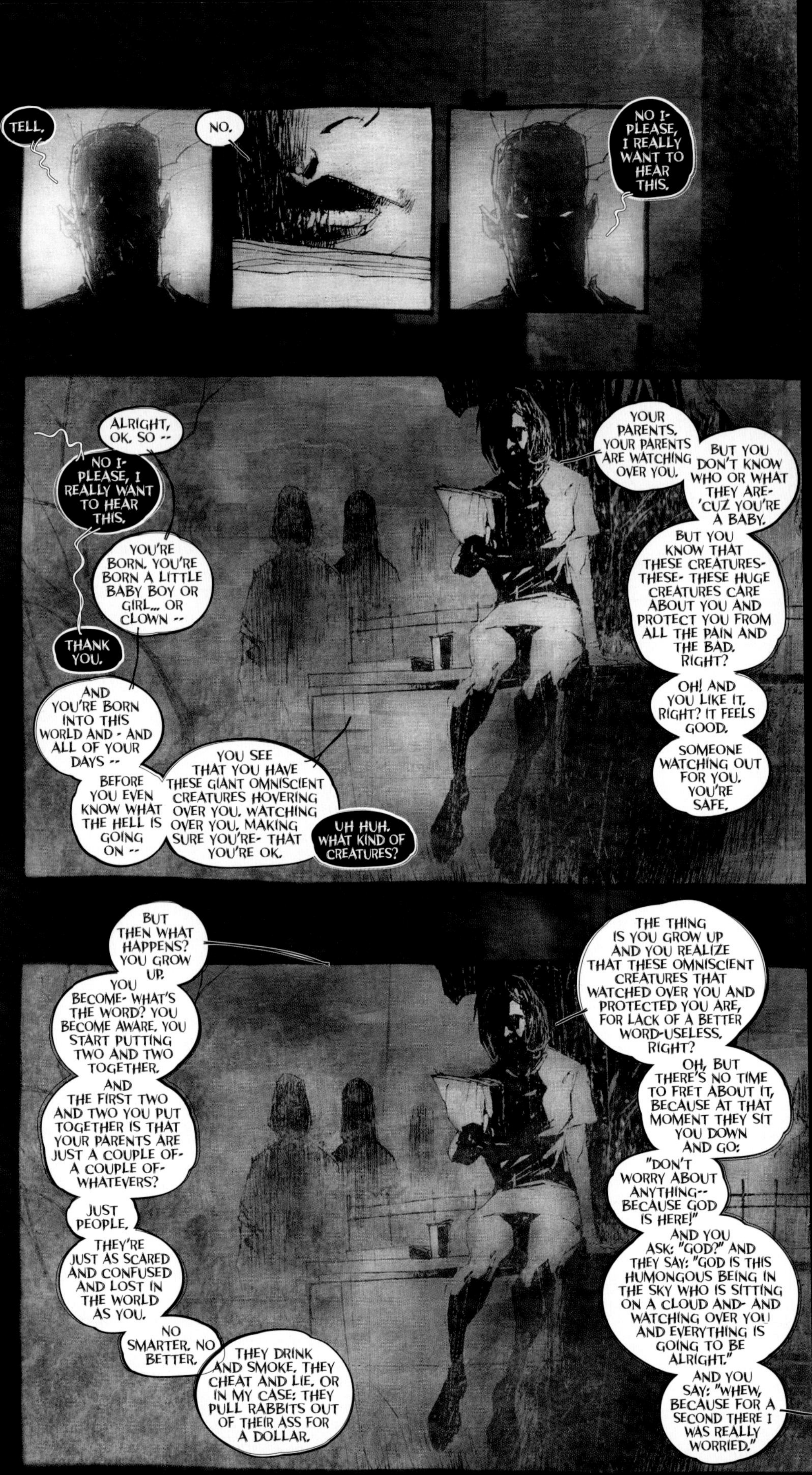
TELL.
NO.
NO I- PLEASE, I REALLY WANT TO HEAR THIS.
ALRIGHT, OK. SO --
NO I- PLEASE, I REALLY WANT TO HEAR THIS.
YOU'RE BORN. YOU'RE BORN A LITTLE BABY BOY OR GIRL... OR CLOWN --
THANK YOU.
AND YOU'RE BORN INTO THIS WORLD AND - AND ALL OF YOUR DAYS --
BEFORE YOU EVEN KNOW WHAT THE HELL IS GOING ON --
YOU SEE THAT YOU HAVE THESE GIANT OMNISCIENT CREATURES HOVERING OVER YOU. WATCHING OVER YOU. MAKING SURE YOU'RE- THAT YOU'RE OK.
UH HUH. WHAT KIND OF CREATURES?
YOUR PARENTS. YOUR PARENTS ARE WATCHING OVER YOU.
BUT YOU DON'T KNOW WHO OR WHAT THEY ARE- 'CUZ YOU'RE A BABY.
BUT YOU KNOW THAT THESE CREATURES- THESE- THESE HUGE CREATURES CARE ABOUT YOU AND PROTECT YOU FROM ALL THE PAIN AND THE BAD. RIGHT?
OH! AND YOU LIKE IT. RIGHT? IT FEELS GOOD.
SOMEONE WATCHING OUT FOR YOU. YOU'RE SAFE.
BUT THEN WHAT HAPPENS? YOU GROW UP.
YOU BECOME- WHAT'S THE WORD? YOU BECOME AWARE. YOU START PUTTING TWO AND TWO TOGETHER.
AND THE FIRST TWO AND TWO YOU PUT TOGETHER IS THAT YOUR PARENTS ARE JUST A COUPLE OF- A COUPLE OF- WHATEVERS?
JUST PEOPLE.
THEY'RE JUST AS SCARED AND CONFUSED AND LOST IN THE WORLD AS YOU.
NO SMARTER. NO BETTER.
THEY DRINK AND SMOKE. THEY CHEAT AND LIE. OR IN MY CASE: THEY PULL RABBITS OUT OF THEIR ASS FOR A DOLLAR.
THE THING IS YOU GROW UP AND YOU REALIZE THAT THESE OMNISCIENT CREATURES THAT WATCHED OVER YOU AND PROTECTED YOU ARE, FOR LACK OF A BETTER WORD-USELESS. RIGHT?
OH, BUT THERE'S NO TIME TO FRET ABOUT IT, BECAUSE AT THAT MOMENT THEY SIT YOU DOWN AND GO:
"DON'T WORRY ABOUT ANYTHING-- BECAUSE GOD IS HERE!"
AND YOU ASK: "GOD?" AND THEY SAY: "GOD IS THIS HUMONGOUS BEING IN THE SKY WHO IS SITTING ON A CLOUD AND- AND WATCHING OVER YOU AND EVERYTHING IS GOING TO BE ALRIGHT."
AND YOU SAY: "WHEW, BECAUSE FOR A SECOND THERE I WAS REALLY WORRIED."

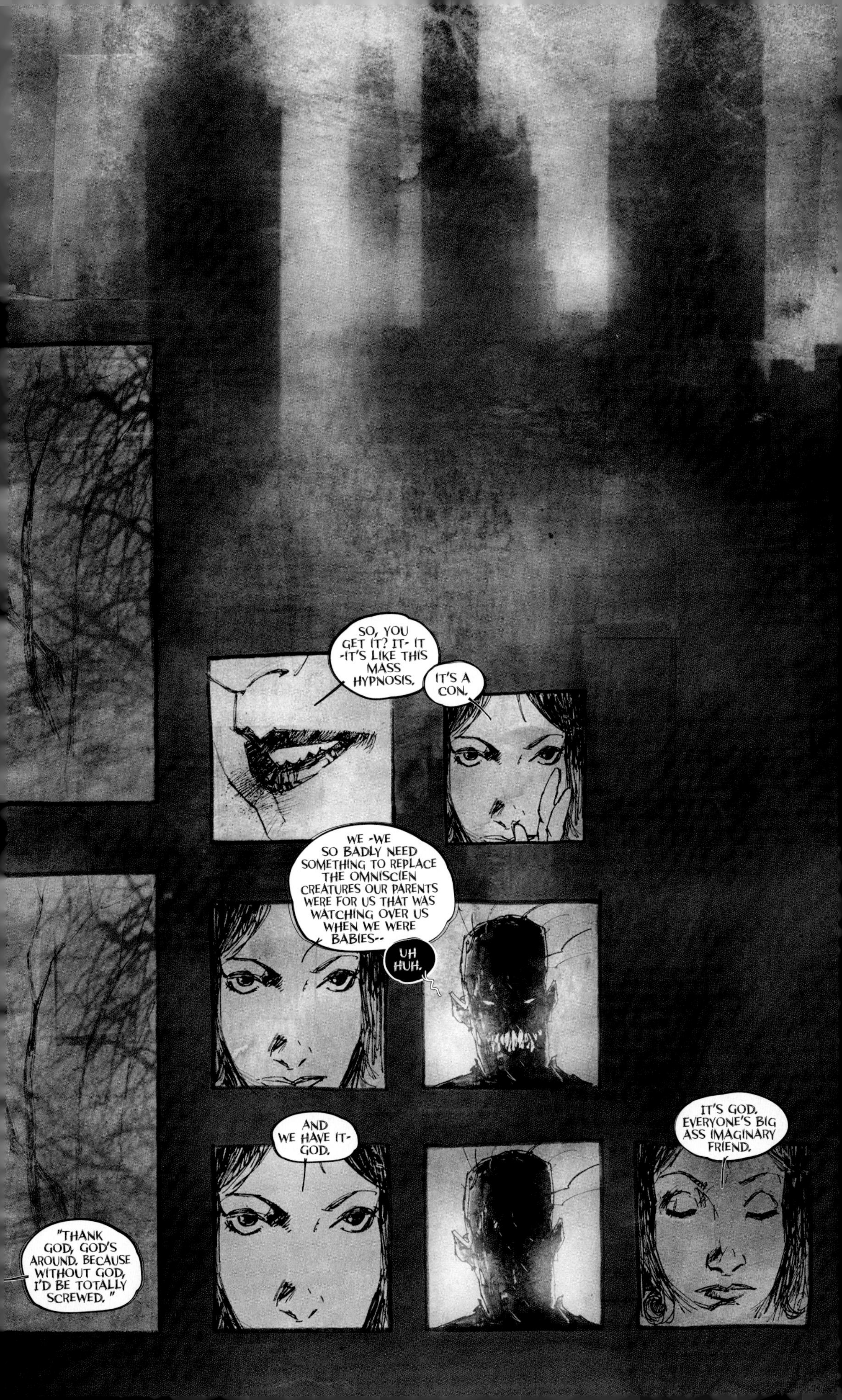

SO, YOU GET IT? IT- IT -IT'S LIKE THIS MASS HYPNOSIS.
IT'S A CON.
WE -WE SO BADLY NEED SOMETHING TO REPLACE THE OMNISCIEN CREATURES OUR PARENTS WERE FOR US THAT WAS WATCHING OVER US WHEN WE WERE BABIES--
UH HUH.
"THANK GOD, GOD'S AROUND. BECAUSE WITHOUT GOD, I'D BE TOTALLY SCREWED."
AND WE HAVE IT- GOD.
IT'S GOD. EVERYONE'S BIG ASS IMAGINARY FRIEND.

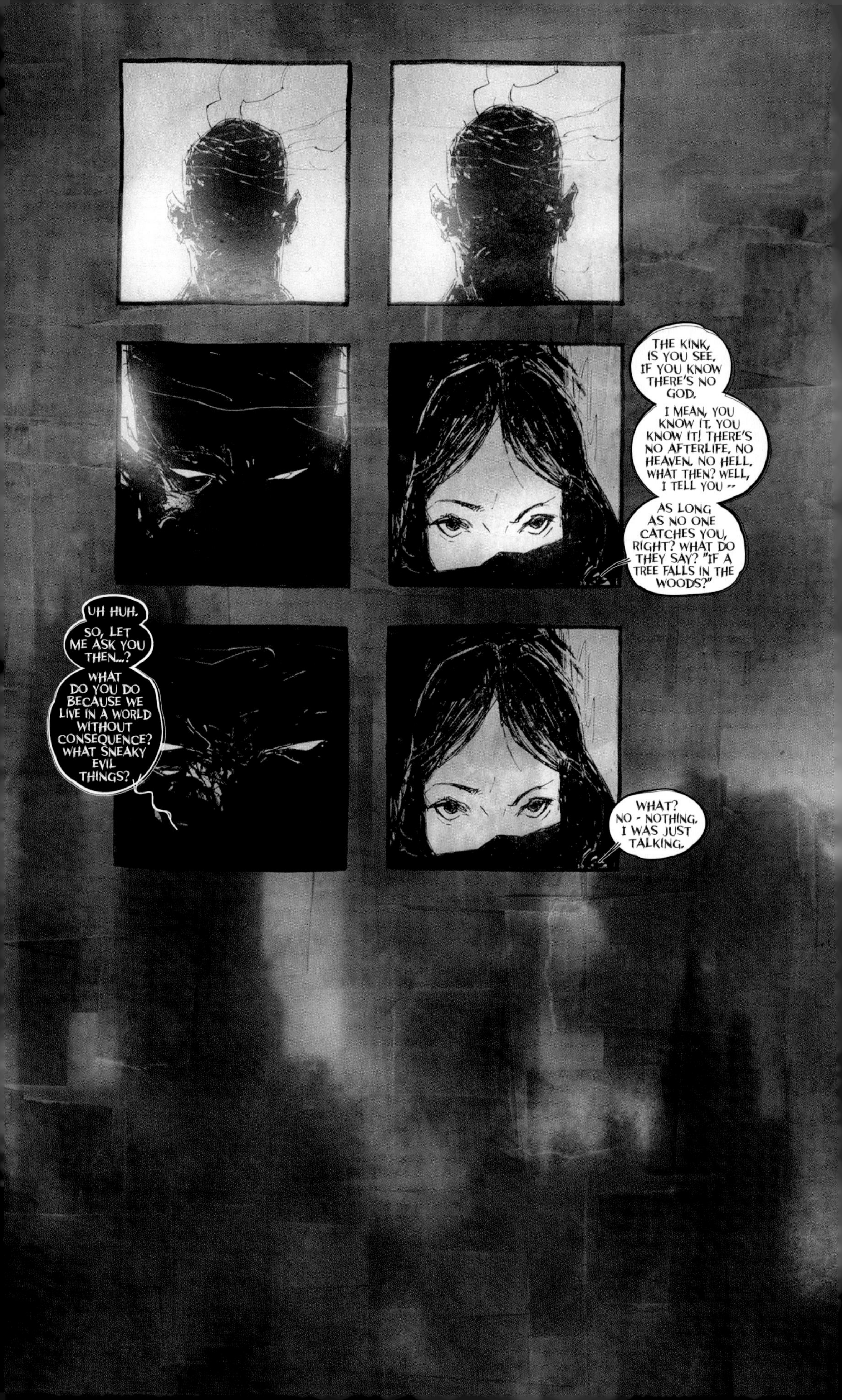
THE KINK, IS YOU SEE, IF YOU KNOW THERE'S NO GOD.
I MEAN, YOU KNOW IT. YOU KNOW IT! THERE'S NO AFTERLIFE, NO HEAVEN, NO HELL. WHAT THEN? WELL, I TELL YOU --
AS LONG AS NO ONE CATCHES YOU, RIGHT? WHAT DO THEY SAY? "IF A TREE FALLS IN THE WOODS?"
UH HUH.
SO, LET ME ASK YOU THEN...?
WHAT DO YOU DO BECAUSE WE LIVE IN A WORLD WITHOUT CONSEQUENCE? WHAT SNEAKY EVIL THINGS?
WHAT? NO - NOTHING. I WAS JUST TALKING.

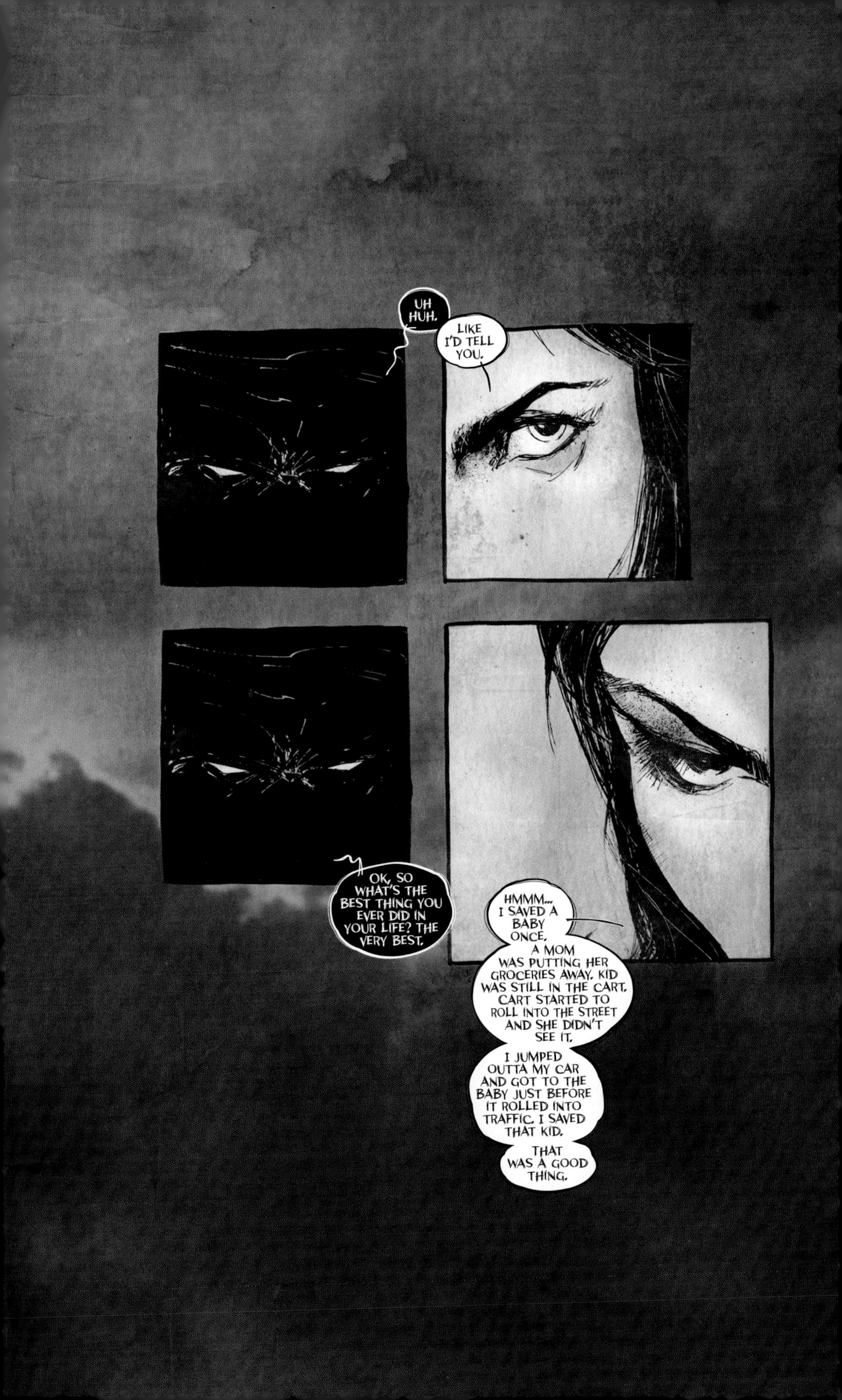

UH HUH.
LIKE I'D TELL YOU.
OK, SO WHAT'S THE BEST THING YOU EVER DID IN YOUR LIFE? THE VERY BEST.
HMMM... I SAVED A BABY ONCE.
A MOM WAS PUTTING HER GROCERIES AWAY. KID WAS STILL IN THE CART. CART STARTED TO ROLL INTO THE STREET AND SHE DIDN'T SEE IT.
I JUMPED OUTTA MY CAR AND GOT TO THE BABY JUST BEFORE IT ROLLED INTO TRAFFIC. I SAVED THAT KID.
THAT WAS A GOOD THING.

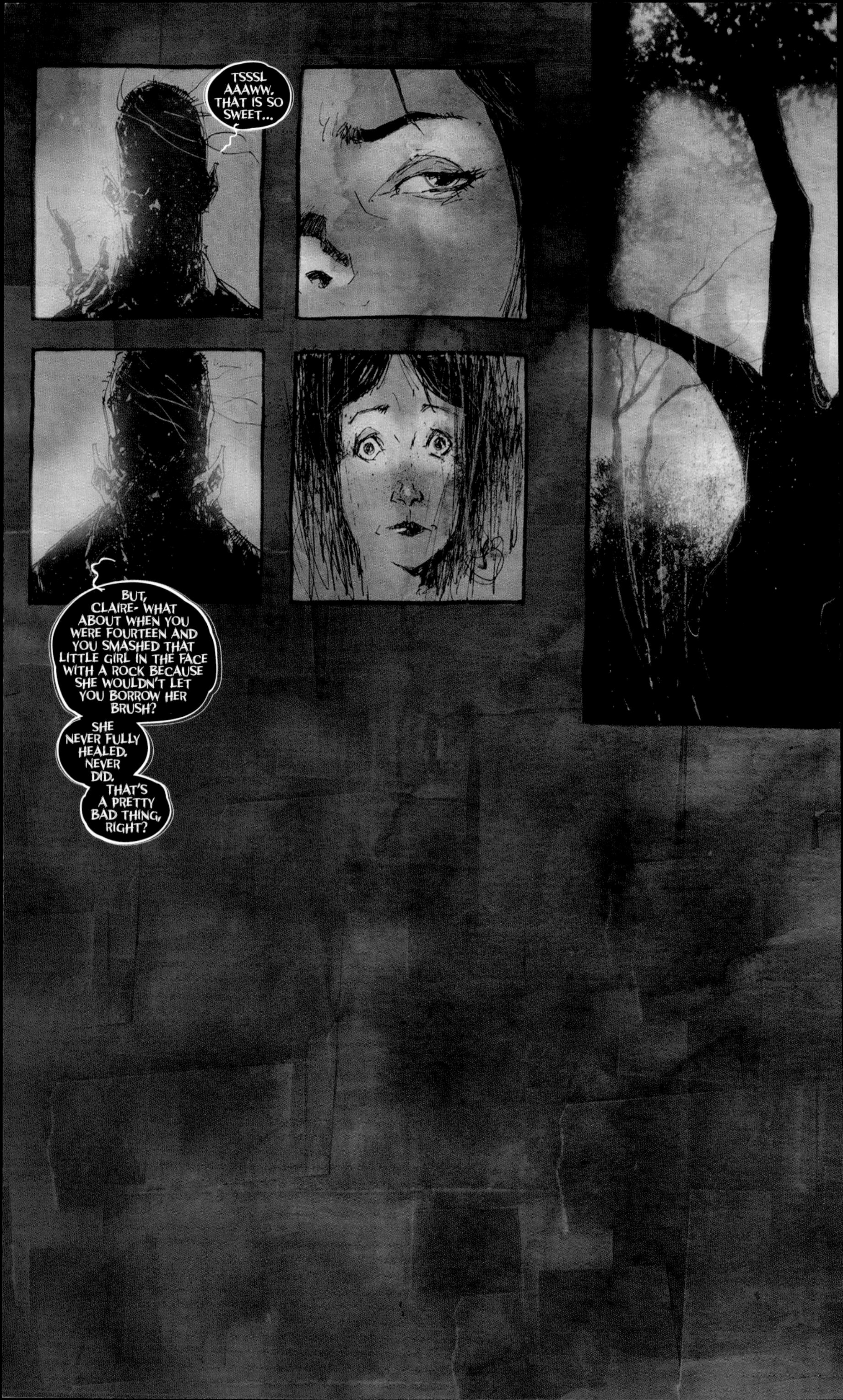
TSSSL AAAWW. THAT IS SO SWEET...
BUT, CLAIRE- WHAT ABOUT WHEN YOU WERE FOURTEEN AND YOU SMASHED THAT LITTLE GIRL IN THE FACE WITH A ROCK BECAUSE SHE WOULDN'T LET YOU BORROW HER BRUSH?
SHE NEVER FULLY HEALED. NEVER DID.
THAT'S A PRETTY BAD THING, RIGHT?

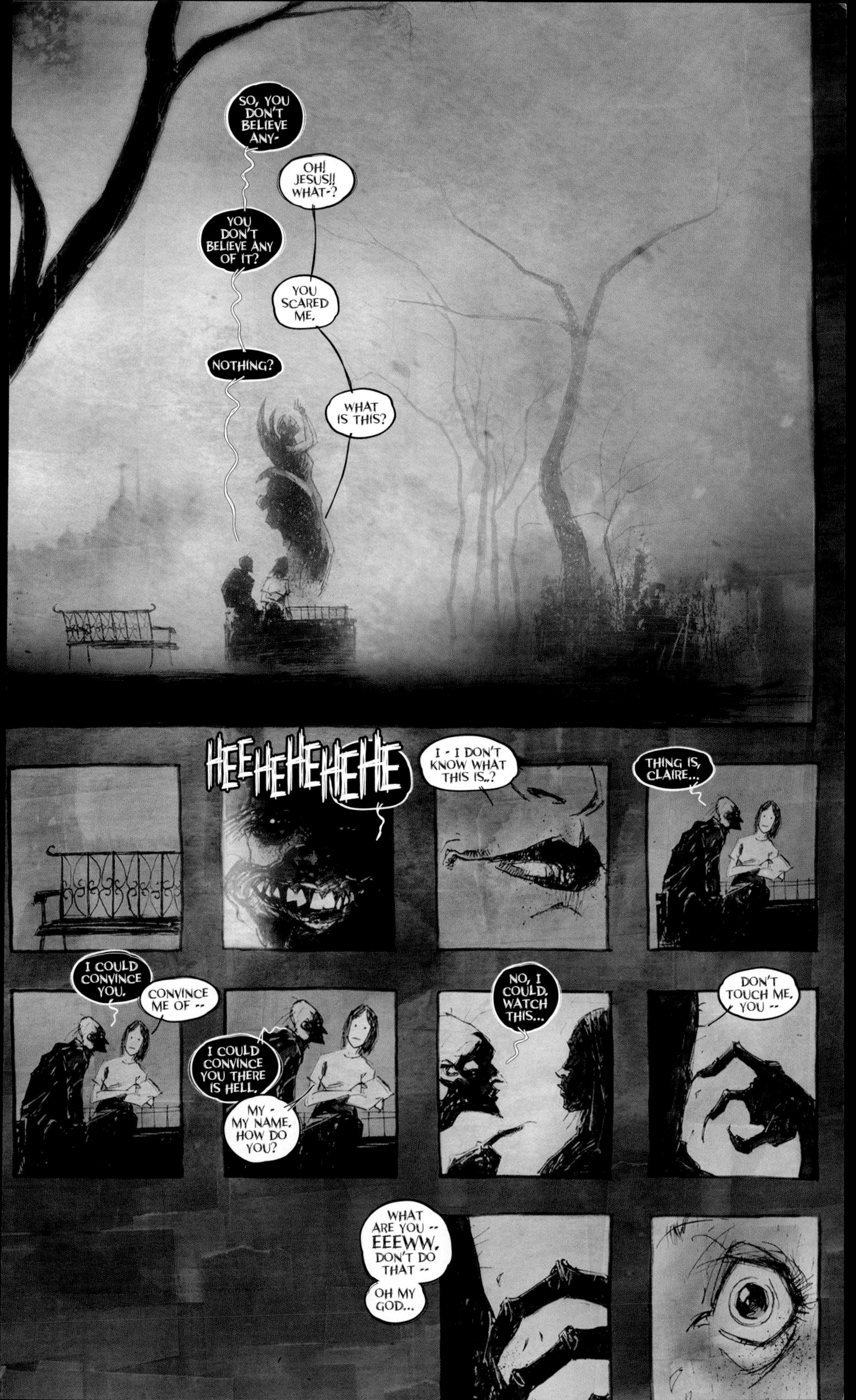
SO, YOU DON'T BELIEVE ANY-
OH! JESUS!! WHAT-?
YOU DON'T BELIEVE ANY OF IT?
YOU SCARED ME.
NOTHING?
WHAT IS THIS?
HEEHEHEHEHEHE
I - I DON'T KNOW WHAT THIS IS..?
THING IS, CLAIRE...
I COULD CONVINCE YOU.
CONVINCE ME OF --
I COULD CONVINCE YOU THERE IS HELL.
MY - MY NAME. HOW DO YOU?
NO, I COULD. WATCH THIS...
DON'T TOUCH ME, YOU --
WHAT ARE YOU -- EEEWW. DON'T DO THAT --
OH MY GOD...

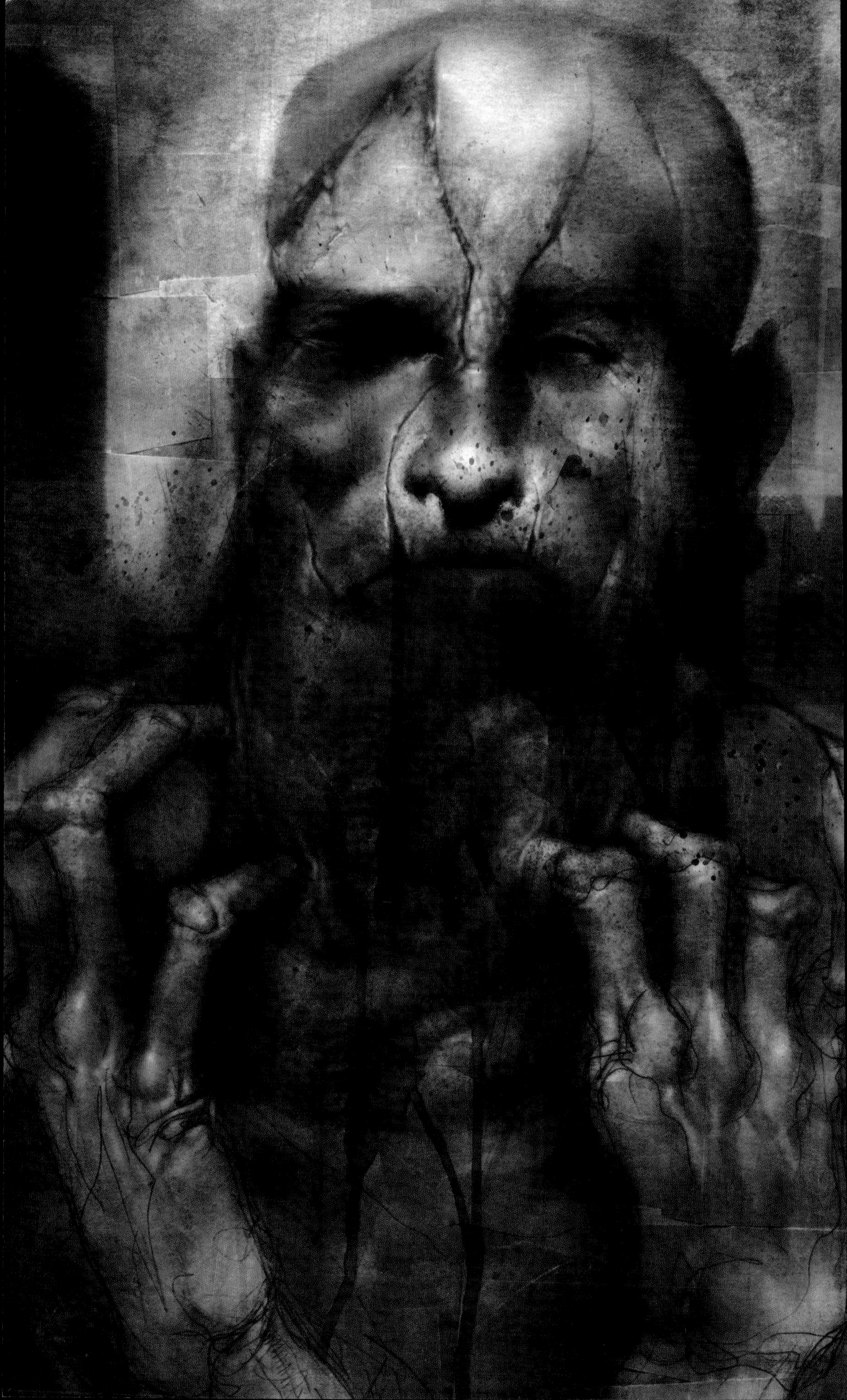

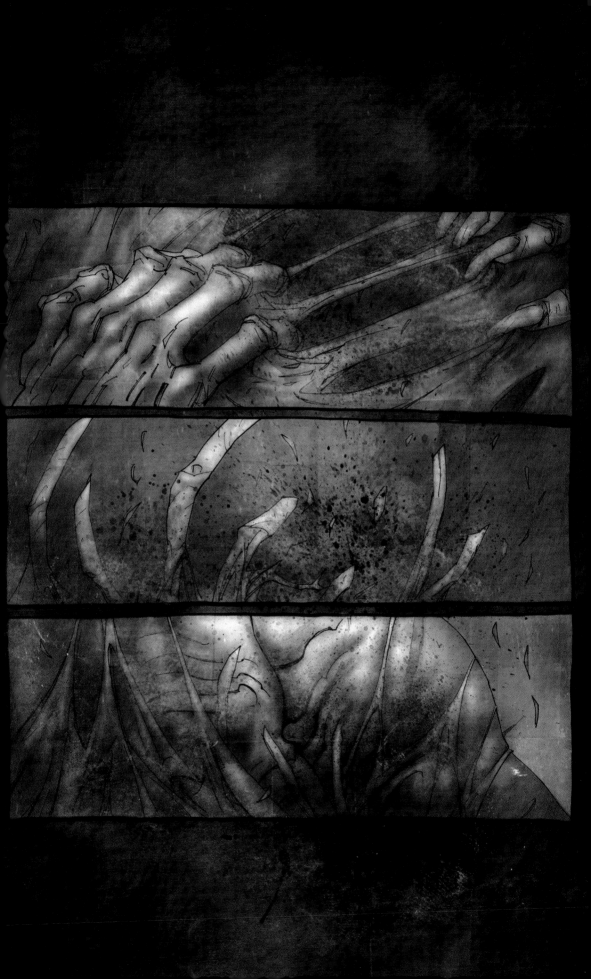

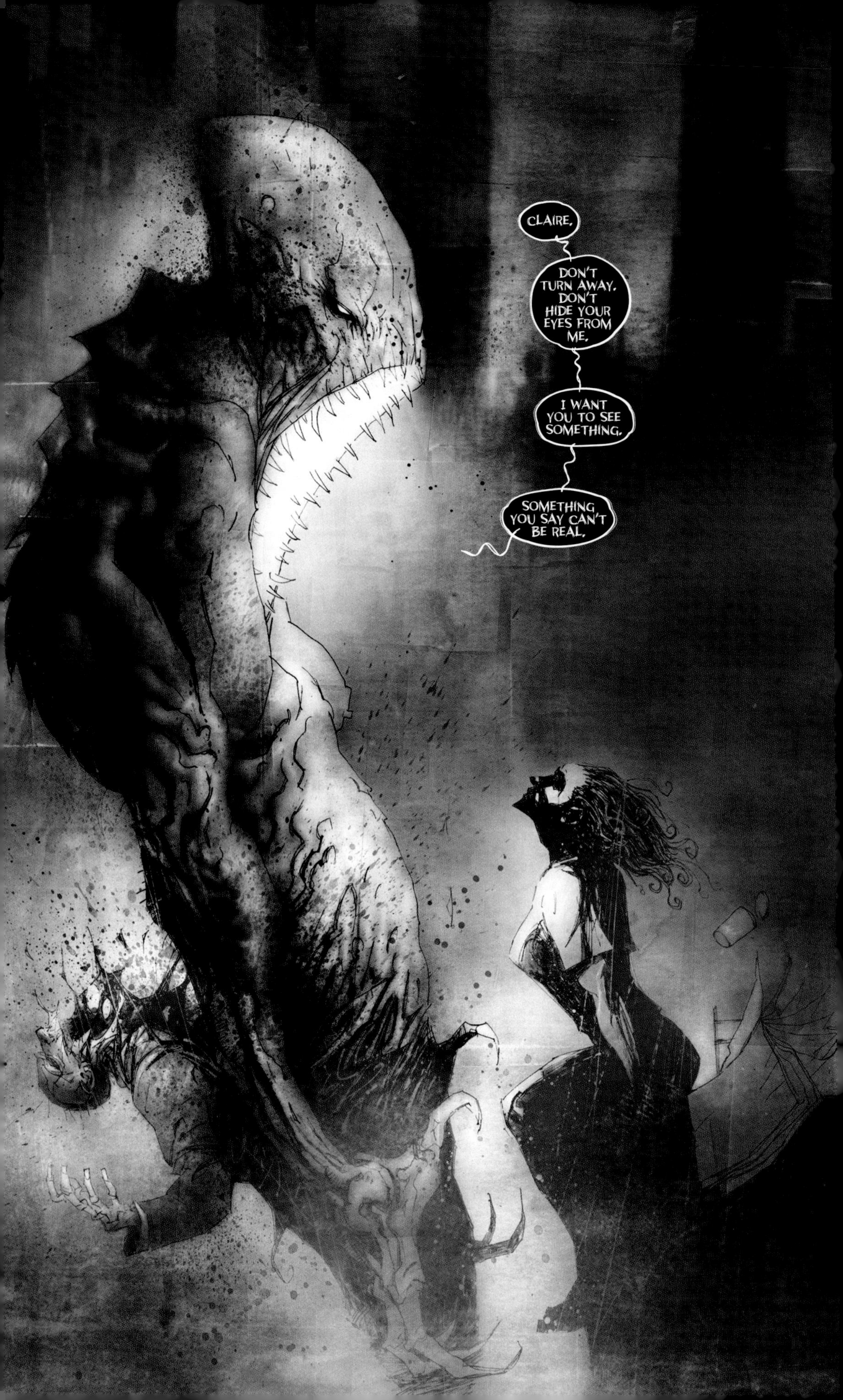
CLAIRE,
DON'T TURN AWAY. DON'T HIDE YOUR EYES FROM ME.
I WANT YOU TO SEE SOMETHING.
SOMETHING YOU SAY CAN'T BE REAL.

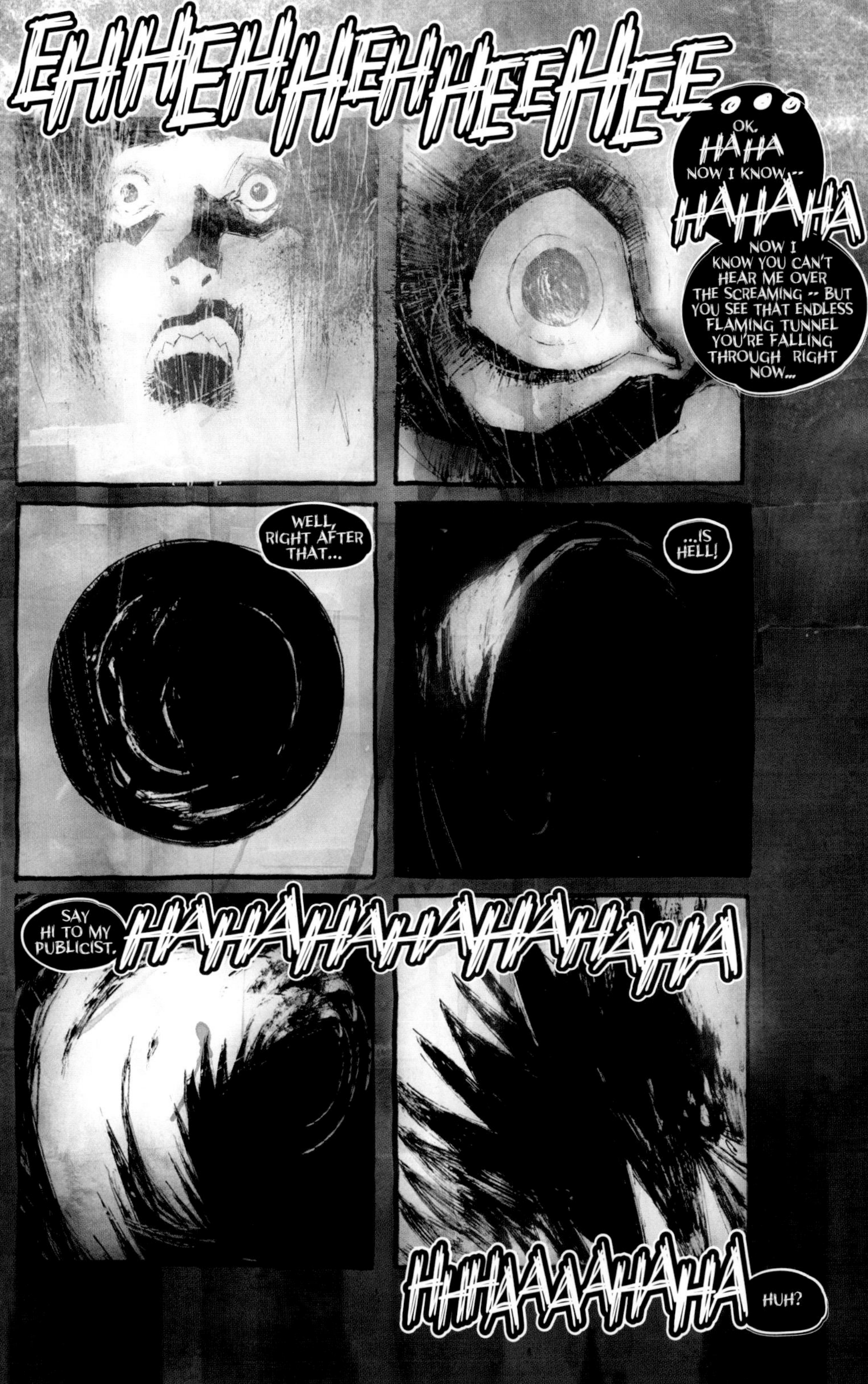
EHHEHHEHHEEHEE...
OK. HAHA NOW I KNOW... HAHAHA
NOW I KNOW YOU CAN'T HEAR ME OVER THE SCREAMING -- BUT YOU SEE THAT ENDLESS FLAMING TUNNEL YOU'RE FALLING THROUGH RIGHT NOW...
WELL, RIGHT AFTER THAT...
...IS HELL!
SAY HI TO MY PUBLICIST.
HAHAHAHAHAHAHAHAHA
HHHAAAAHAHA
HUH?

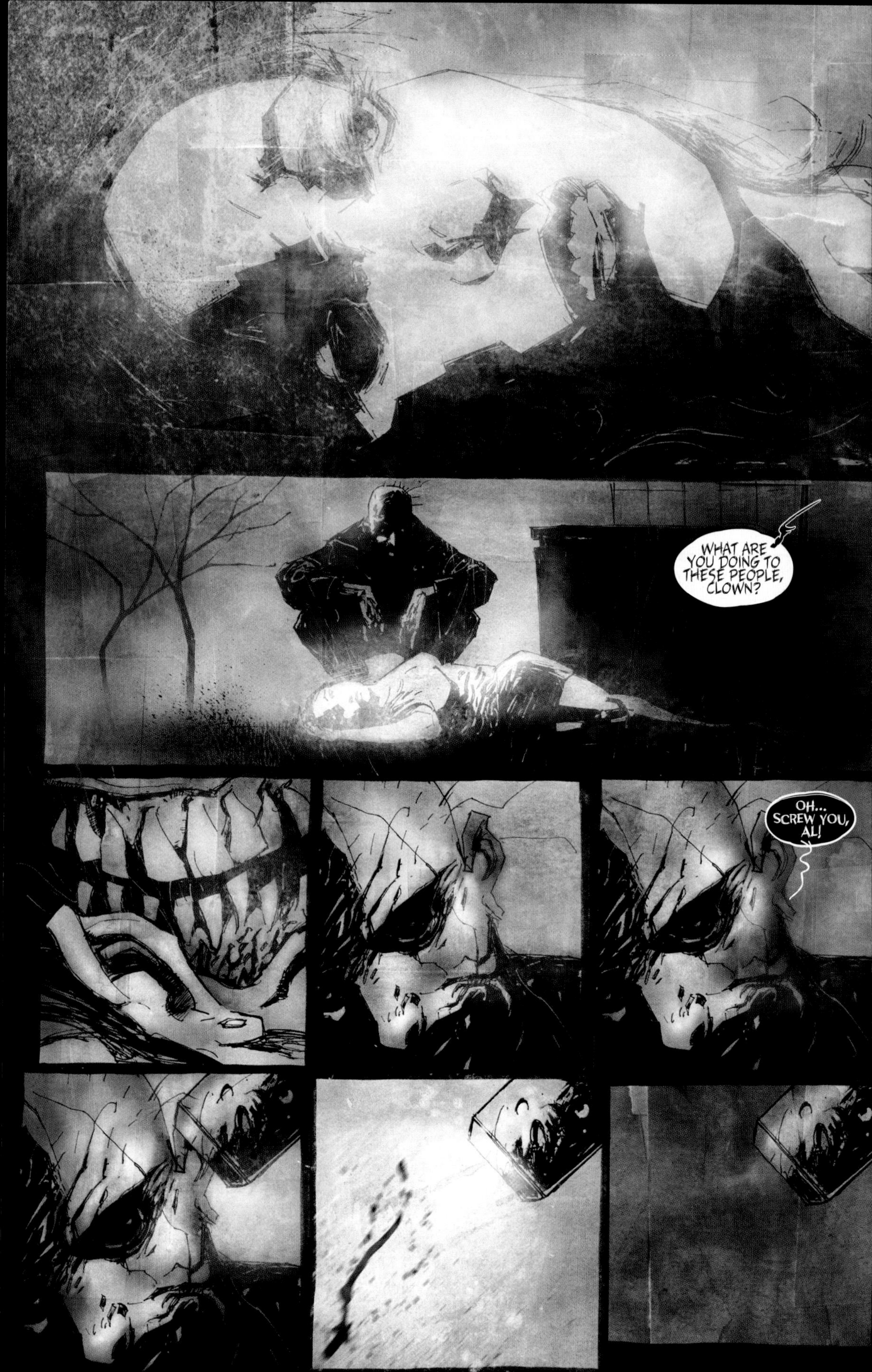
WHAT ARE YOU DOING TO THESE PEOPLE, CLOWN?
OH... SCREW YOU, AL!

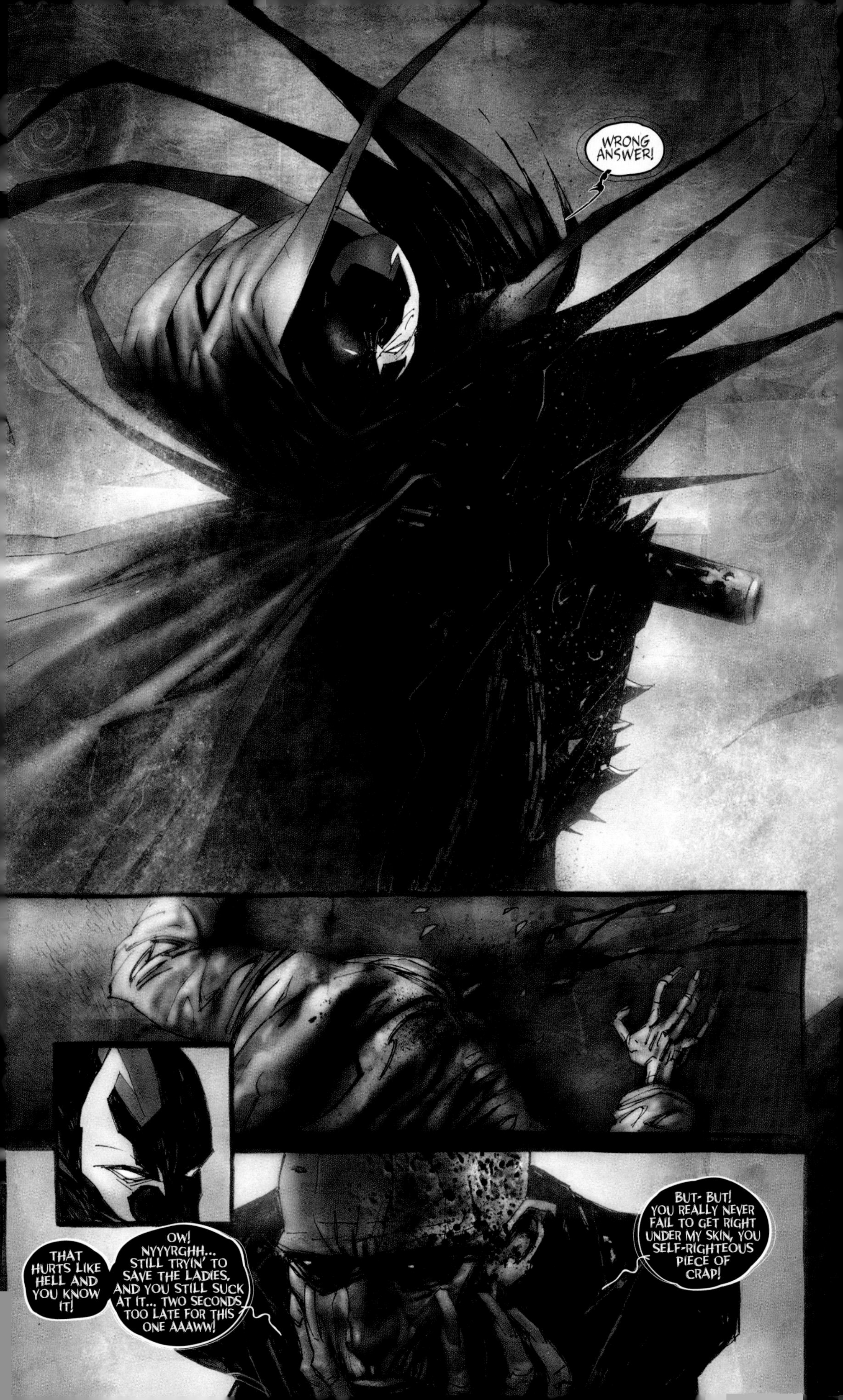
WRONG ANSWER!
THAT HURTS LIKE HELL AND YOU KNOW IT!
OW! NYYYRGHH... STILL TRYIN' TO SAVE THE LADIES, AND YOU STILL SUCK AT IT... TWO SECONDS TOO LATE FOR THIS ONE AAAWW!
BUT- BUT! YOU REALLY NEVER FAIL TO GET RIGHT UNDER MY SKIN, YOU SELF-RIGHTEOUS PIECE OF CRAP!

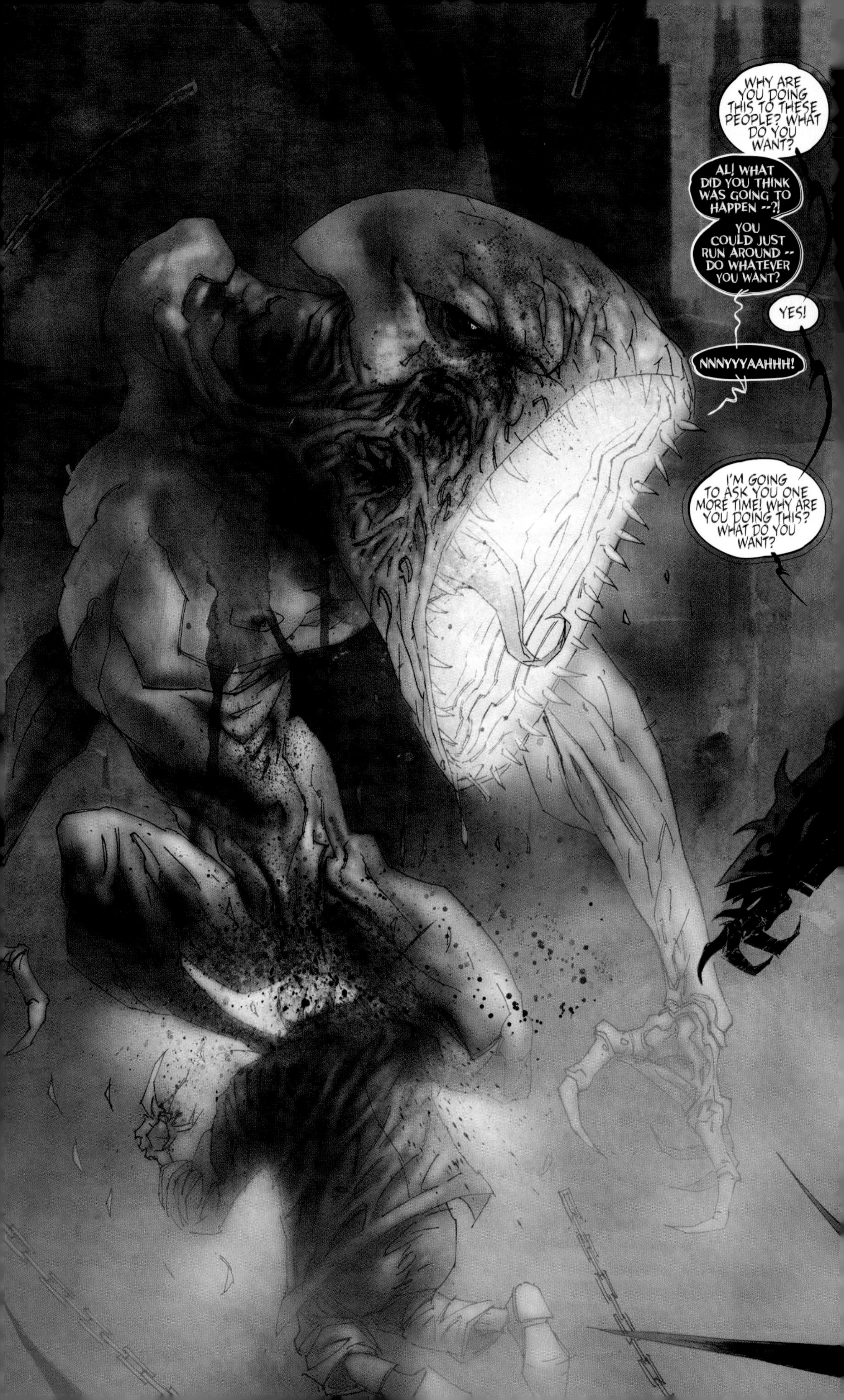
WHY ARE YOU DOING THIS TO THESE PEOPLE? WHAT DO YOU WANT?
AL! WHAT DID YOU THINK WAS GOING TO HAPPEN --?!
YOU COULD JUST RUN AROUND -- DO WHATEVER YOU WANT?
YES!
NNNYYYAAHHH!
I'M GOING TO ASK YOU ONE MORE TIME! WHY ARE YOU DOING THIS? WHAT DO YOU WANT?

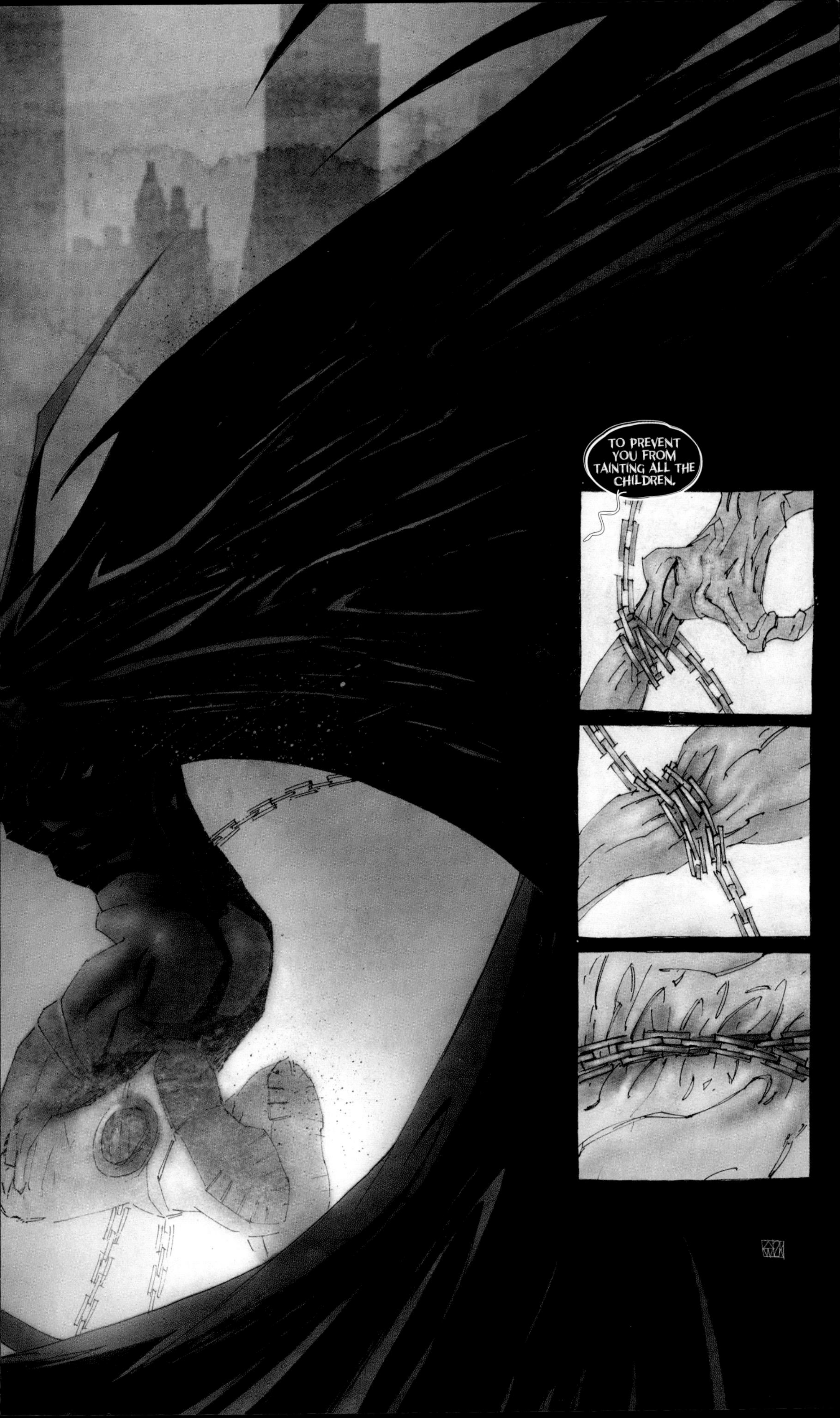
TO PREVENT YOU FROM TAINTING ALL THE CHILDREN.

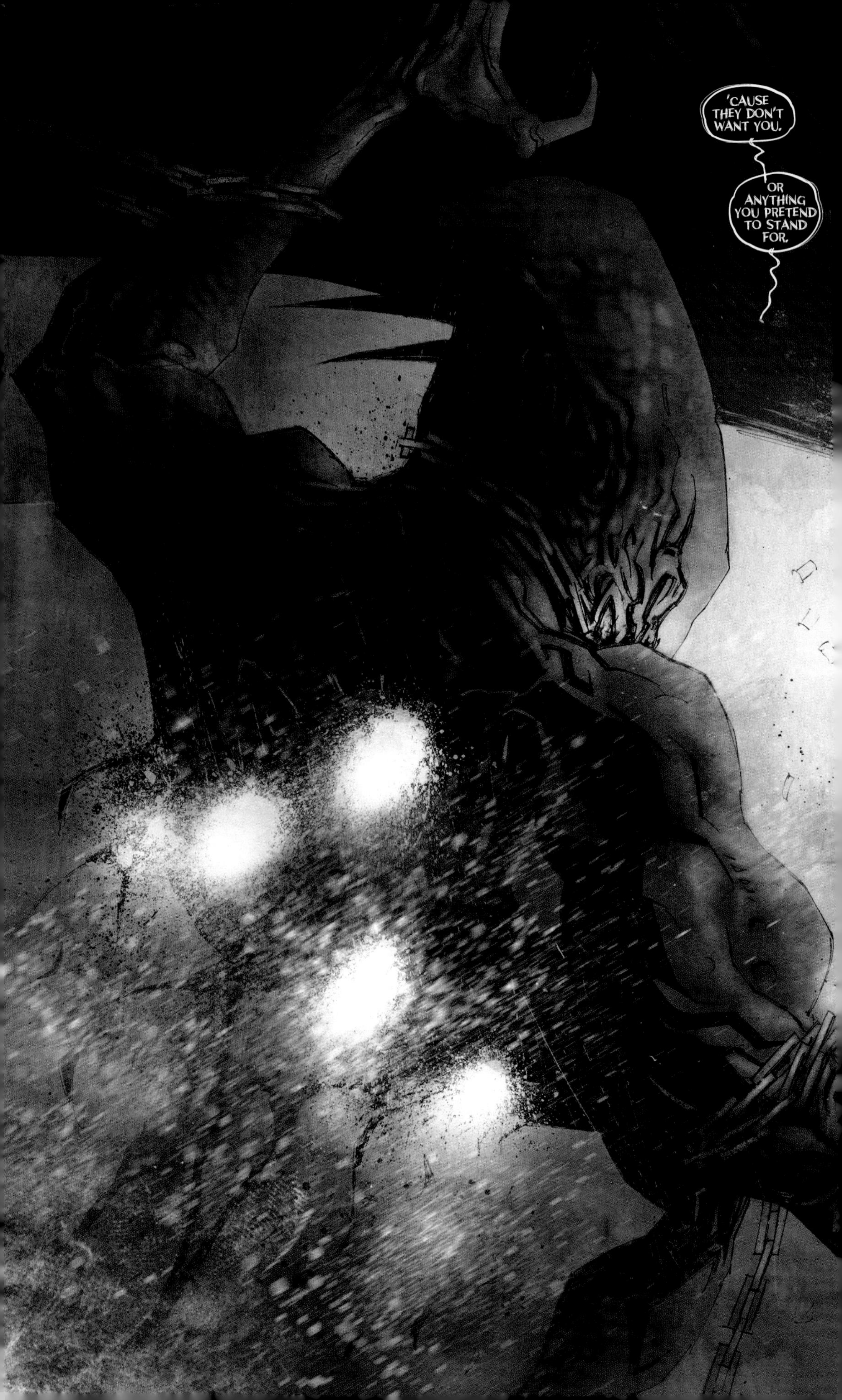
'CAUSE THEY DON'T WANT YOU.
OR ANYTHING YOU PRETEND TO STAND FOR.

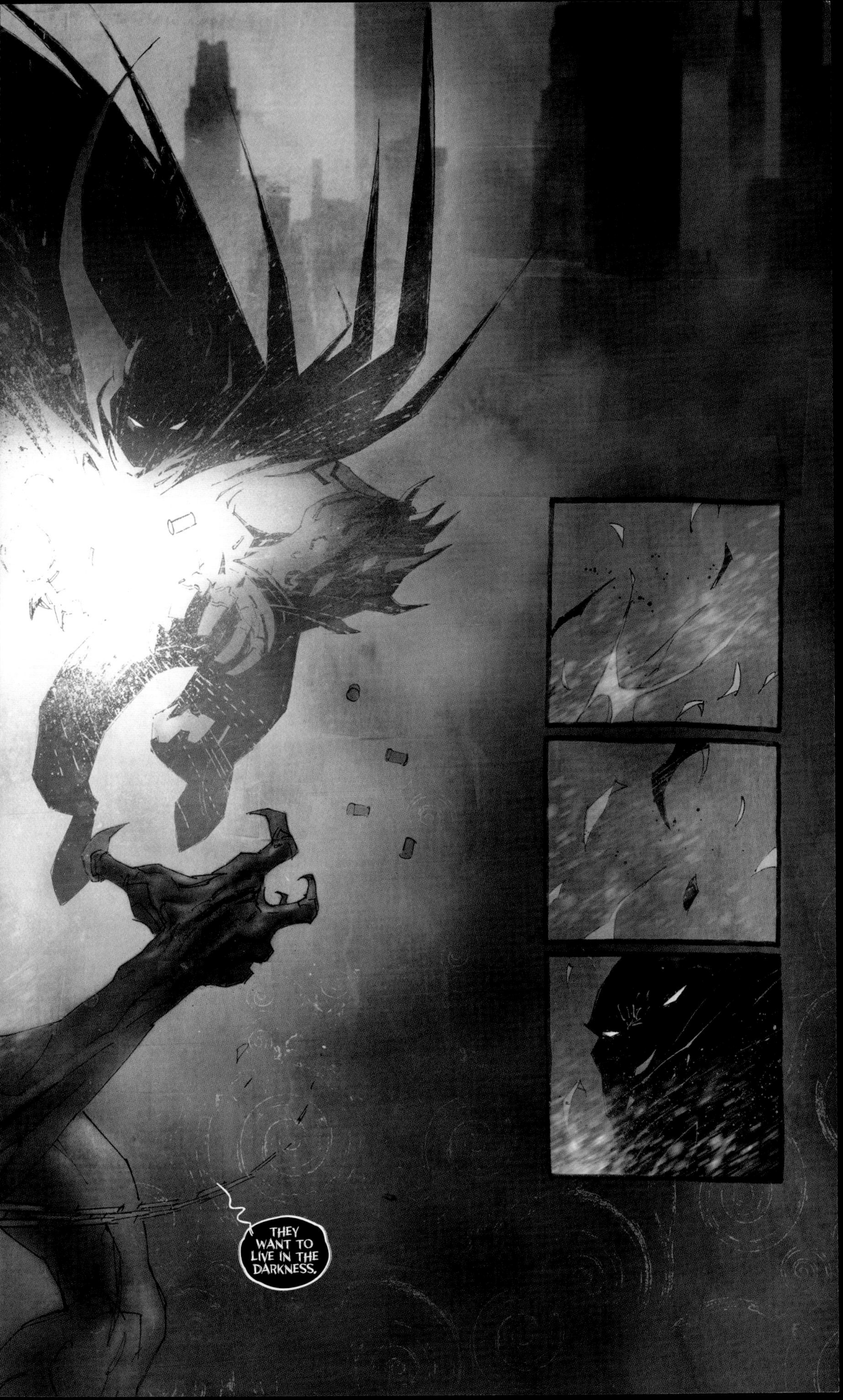
THEY WANT TO LIVE IN THE DARKNESS.

...WOMAN WAS FOUND DEAD TODAY IN CENTRAL PARK FROM AN APPARENT CARDIAC ARREST.

POLICE BELIEVE THAT HER PURSE AND CLOTHING WERE TAKEN AFTER HER DEMISE. AN INVESTIGATION IS STILL PENDING.

A 92-YEAR-OLD WOMAN WAS FOUND RAPED IN HER HOME.

THE POLICE REPORT THAT PROSTITUTES, TRANSIENTS, AND DRUG ADDICTS HAD MOVED INTO HER HOME AND HAD BEEN LIVING THERE FOR SOMETIME.

THAT REMINDS ME, MOTHER'S DAY IS RIGHT AROUND THE CORNER. WHAT ARE YOU GETTING YOUR MOTHER FOR MOTHER'S DAY, BRAD?

WHY IT'S A SURPRISE, CANDY.

HA HA HA HA HA

ON A LIGHTER NOTE, ALL HELL BROKE LOOSE ON A TAPING OF 'THE SUZIE BOOKER SHOW.'

CONTROVERSIAL RELIGIOUS LEADER, REVEREND GARY DANES WAS APPEARING ON A PANEL ABOUT RACE RELATIONS...

AS THIS EXCLUSIVE FOOTAGE SHOWS, COMMENTS MADE BY THE REVEREND STARTED A RIOT DURING TAPING.

SEVERAL PEOPLE WERE INJURED INCLUDING REVEREND DANES.

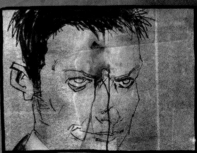

A SPOKESMAN FOR 'THE SUZIE BOOKER SHOW' STATED VIA PRESS RELEASE THAT THEY DO NOT CONDONE OR AGREE WITH REVEREND DANES! HORRIBLE REMARKS AND FIND THEM OFFENSIVE ON MANY LEVELS.

'THE SUZIE BOOKER SHOW' ANNOUNCED THAT THEY WILL RUN THE SHOW IN ITS ENTIRETY, UNEDITED IN A TWO HOUR SPECIAL. WE'LL BE RIGHT BACK.

TO BE CONTINUED

HELL**S**PAWN

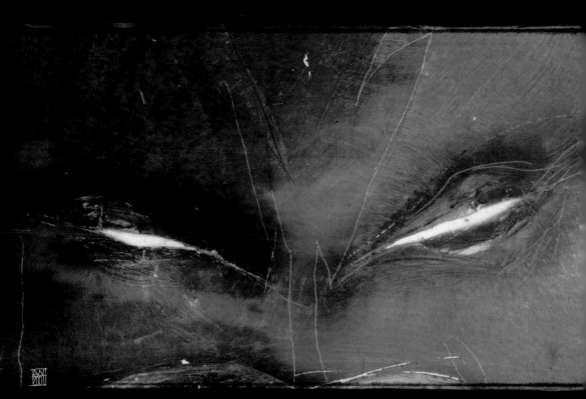

ISSUE THREE

FASTBENDER
WHY? SO YOU MAY MOCK
ME SOME MORE? NO.

HERTZ
NO? COME ON. YOU SAID SOMETHING --
SOMETHING ABOUT A WAR BETWEEN
HEAVEN AND HELL OR SOMETHING. I
WANT TO HEAR MORE ABOUT IT. I DO.

FASTBENDER
NO.

HERTZ
NO?

FASTBENDER
NO.

HERTZ
CAN I STILL
HAVE A SIP?

FASTBENDER
NO.

HERTZ
WAIT -- THERE'S A WAR GOING ON- ON
EARTH -- BETWEEN HEAVEN AND HELL,
AND YOU KNOW ALL ABOUT IT- AND YOU
AREN'T GOING TO TELL ANYONE ABOUT
IT? SEEMS KIND OF SELFISH TO --

FASTBENDER
YOU ARE JUST USING ME FOR
MY BOOZE. HUMORING ME. I
KNOW WHAT'S GOING ON.

HERTZ
NO. COME ON--

FASTBENDER
NO.

HERTZ
A WAR. YOU ARE
A FUNNY DUDE.

FASTBENDER
OH-- THERE'S A WAR
GOING ON MY FRIEND.

HERTZ
WELL, IF I HAD THIS KIND OF INFO
AT MY FINGERTIPS I WOULDN'T BE
SITTING HERE BEING ALL MR.
CRYPTIC. I WOULD BE SCREAMING
ABOUT IT FROM THE RAFTERS.

FASTBENDER
THAT IS READILY APPARENT.

HERTZ
I CERTAINLY HAVEN'T SEEN
ANY EVIDENCE OF THIS.

FASTBENDER
MY FRIEND -- YOU JUST
DON'T KNOW WHERE TO
LOOK. IT IS EVERY --

HERTZ
JUST SAYING YOU CAN'T HAVE IT BOTH WAYS. YOU CAN'T
BE WISE BEYOND YOUR YEARS AND MR. CRYPTIC. IT JUST --

FASTBENDER
THE EVENTS THAT ARE SHAPING THE WAR ARE BIGGER
THAN I. THEY ARE BIGGER THAN THE TWO OF US.

HERTZ
UH HUH.

FASTBENDER
THEY ARE BIGGER THAN ANYTHING I CAN SAY OR --

HERTZ
HOW BIG?

FASTBENDER
BIG.

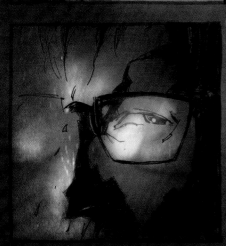

HERTZ
HOW BIG?

FASTBENDER
I TOLD YOU.

HERTZ
HOW BIG?

FASTBENDER
HOW BIG?

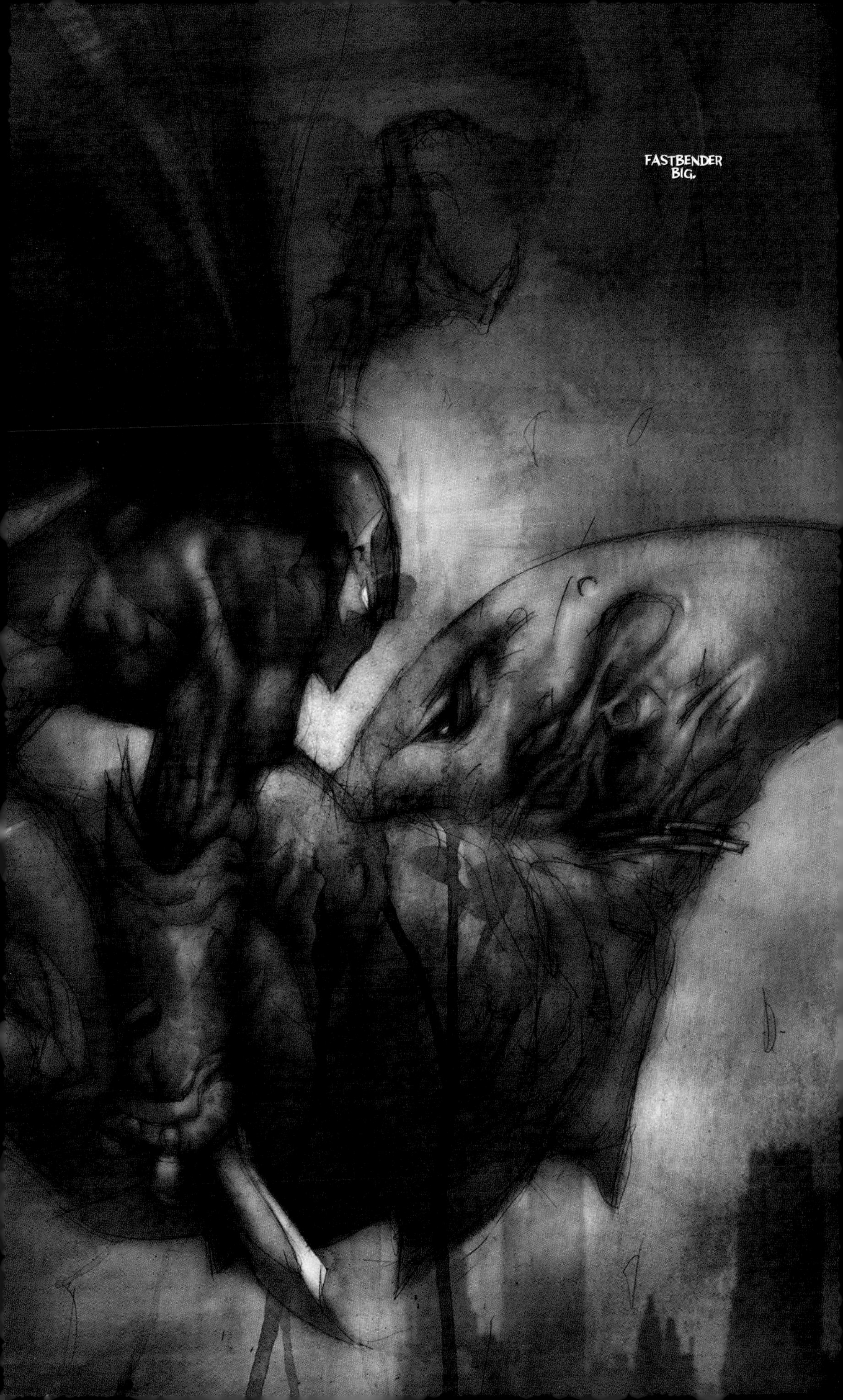
FASTBENDER
BIG.

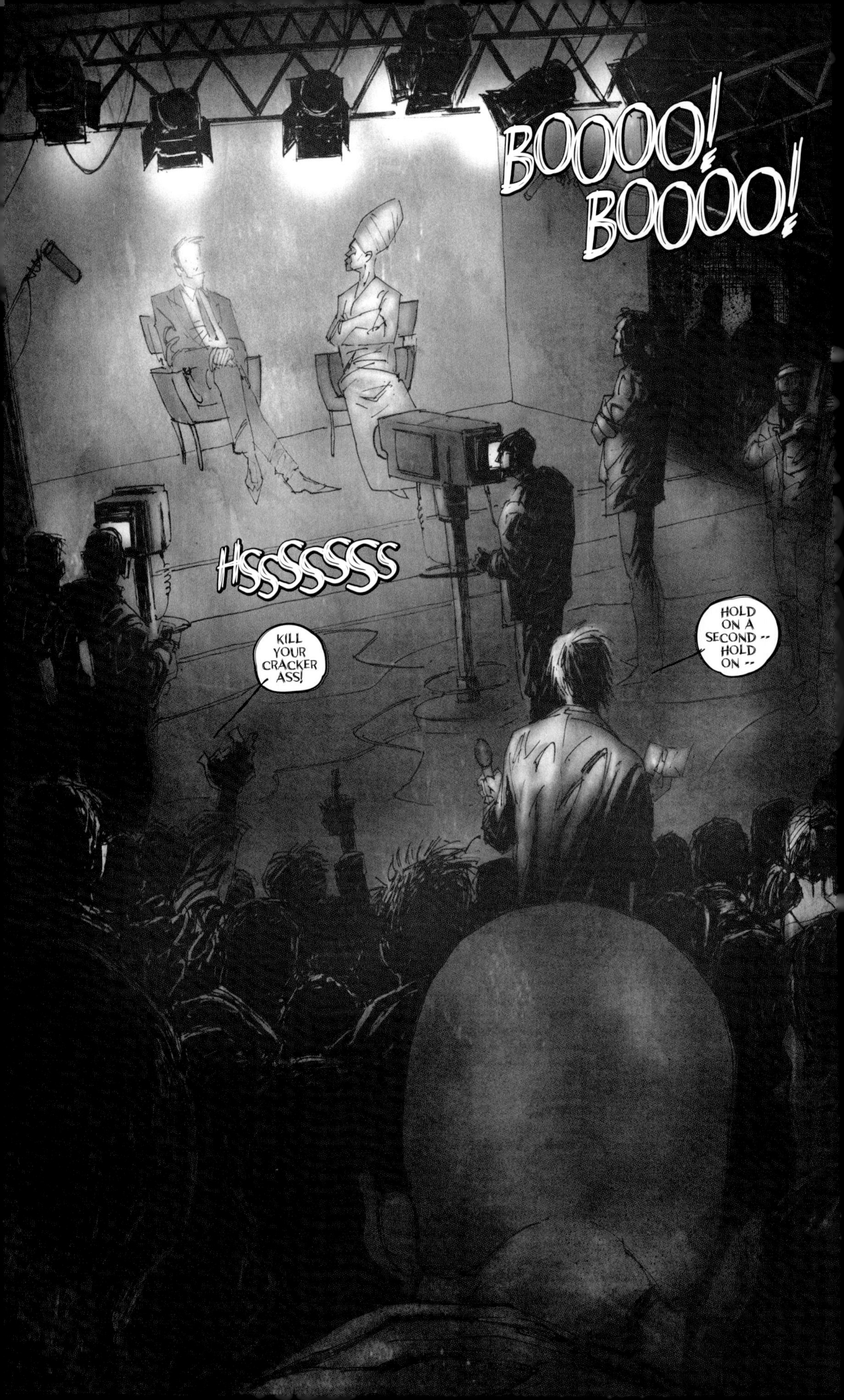
BOOOO! BOOOO!
HSSSSSSS
KILL YOUR CRACKER ASS!
HOLD ON A SECOND -- HOLD ON --

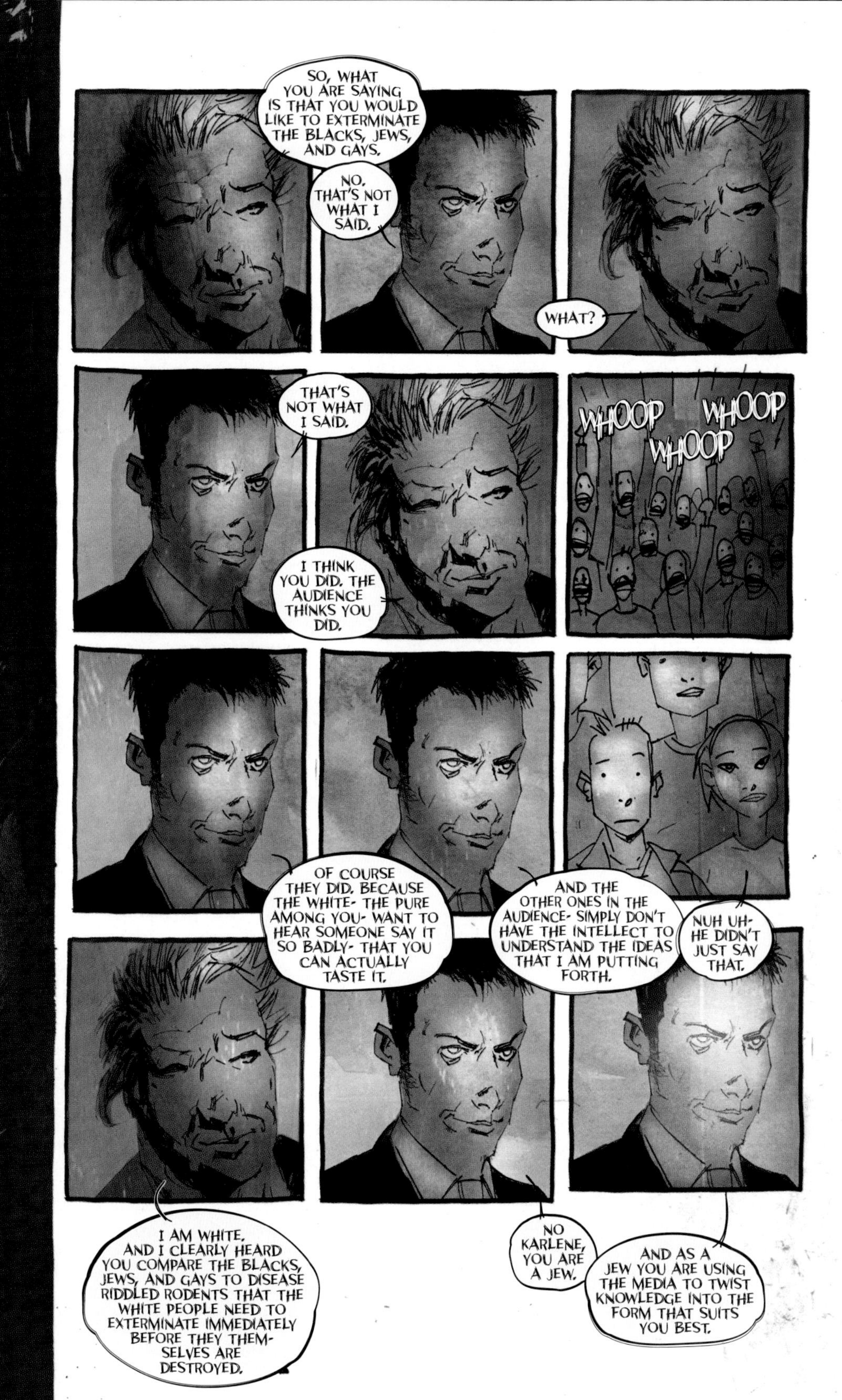
SO, WHAT YOU ARE SAYING IS THAT YOU WOULD LIKE TO EXTERMINATE THE BLACKS, JEWS, AND GAYS.
NO. THAT'S NOT WHAT I SAID.
WHAT?
THAT'S NOT WHAT I SAID.
I THINK YOU DID. THE AUDIENCE THINKS YOU DID.
WHOOP WHOOP WHOOP
OF COURSE THEY DID. BECAUSE THE WHITE- THE PURE AMONG YOU- WANT TO HEAR SOMEONE SAY IT SO BADLY- THAT YOU CAN ACTUALLY TASTE IT.
AND THE OTHER ONES IN THE AUDIENCE- SIMPLY DON'T HAVE THE INTELLECT TO UNDERSTAND THE IDEAS THAT I AM PUTTING FORTH.
NUH UH- HE DIDN'T JUST SAY THAT.
I AM WHITE. AND I CLEARLY HEARD YOU COMPARE THE BLACKS, JEWS, AND GAYS TO DISEASE RIDDLED RODENTS THAT THE WHITE PEOPLE NEED TO EXTERMINATE IMMEDIATELY BEFORE THEY THEM-SELVES ARE DESTROYED.
NO KARLENE, YOU ARE A JEW.
AND AS A JEW YOU ARE USING THE MEDIA TO TWIST KNOWLEDGE INTO THE FORM THAT SUITS YOU BEST.

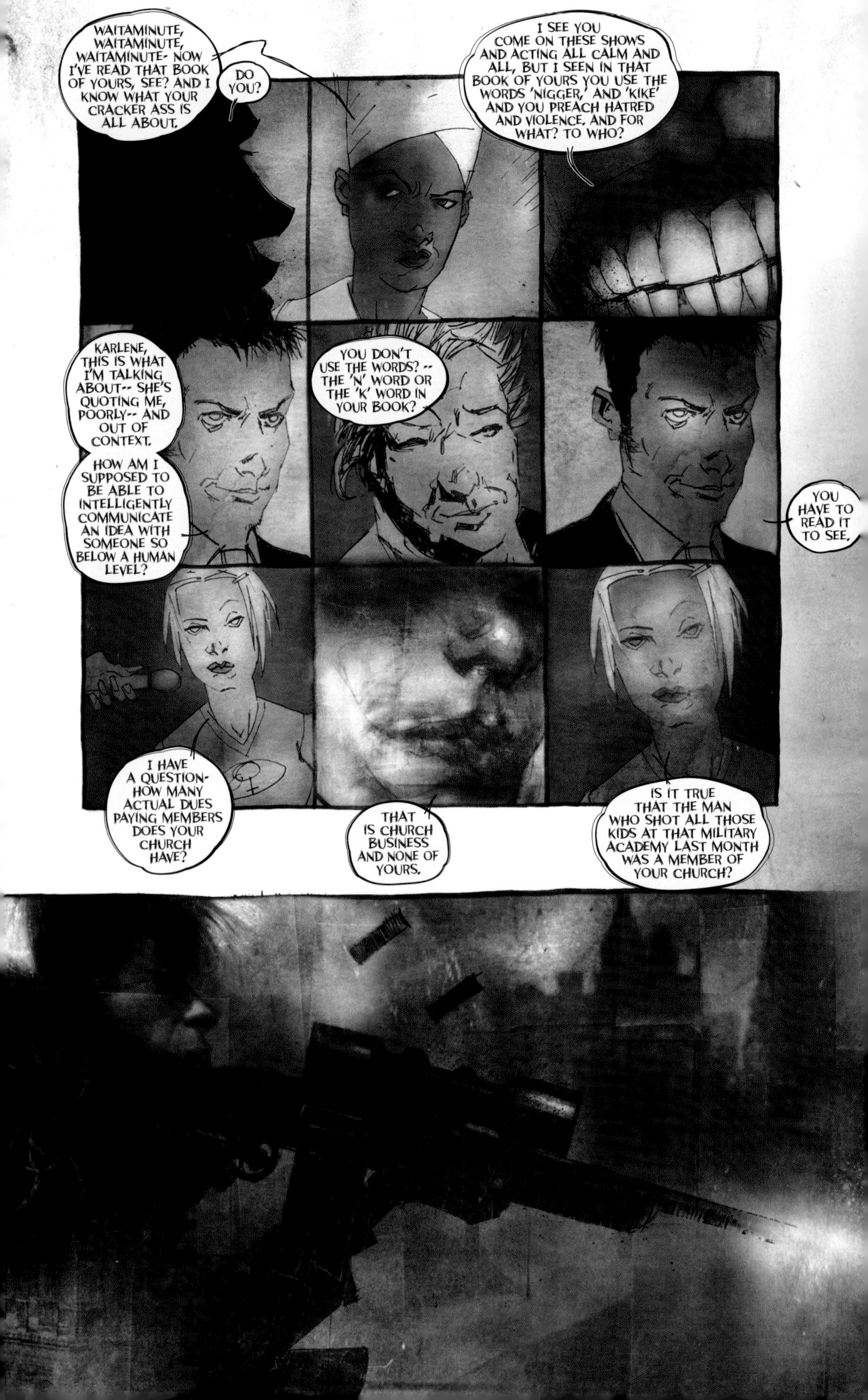
WAITAMINUTE, WAITAMINUTE, WAITAMINUTE- NOW I'VE READ THAT BOOK OF YOURS, SEE? AND I KNOW WHAT YOUR CRACKER ASS IS ALL ABOUT.
DO YOU?
I SEE YOU COME ON THESE SHOWS AND ACTING ALL CALM AND ALL, BUT I SEEN IN THAT BOOK OF YOURS YOU USE THE WORDS 'NIGGER,' AND 'KIKE' AND YOU PREACH HATRED AND VIOLENCE. AND FOR WHAT? TO WHO?
KARLENE, THIS IS WHAT I'M TALKING ABOUT-- SHE'S QUOTING ME, POORLY-- AND OUT OF CONTEXT.
HOW AM I SUPPOSED TO BE ABLE TO INTELLIGENTLY COMMUNICATE AN IDEA WITH SOMEONE SO BELOW A HUMAN LEVEL?
YOU DON'T USE THE WORDS? -- THE 'N' WORD OR THE 'K' WORD IN YOUR BOOK?
YOU HAVE TO READ IT TO SEE.
I HAVE A QUESTION- HOW MANY ACTUAL DUES PAYING MEMBERS DOES YOUR CHURCH HAVE?
THAT IS CHURCH BUSINESS AND NONE OF YOURS.
IS IT TRUE THAT THE MAN WHO SHOT ALL THOSE KIDS AT THAT MILITARY ACADEMY LAST MONTH WAS A MEMBER OF YOUR CHURCH?

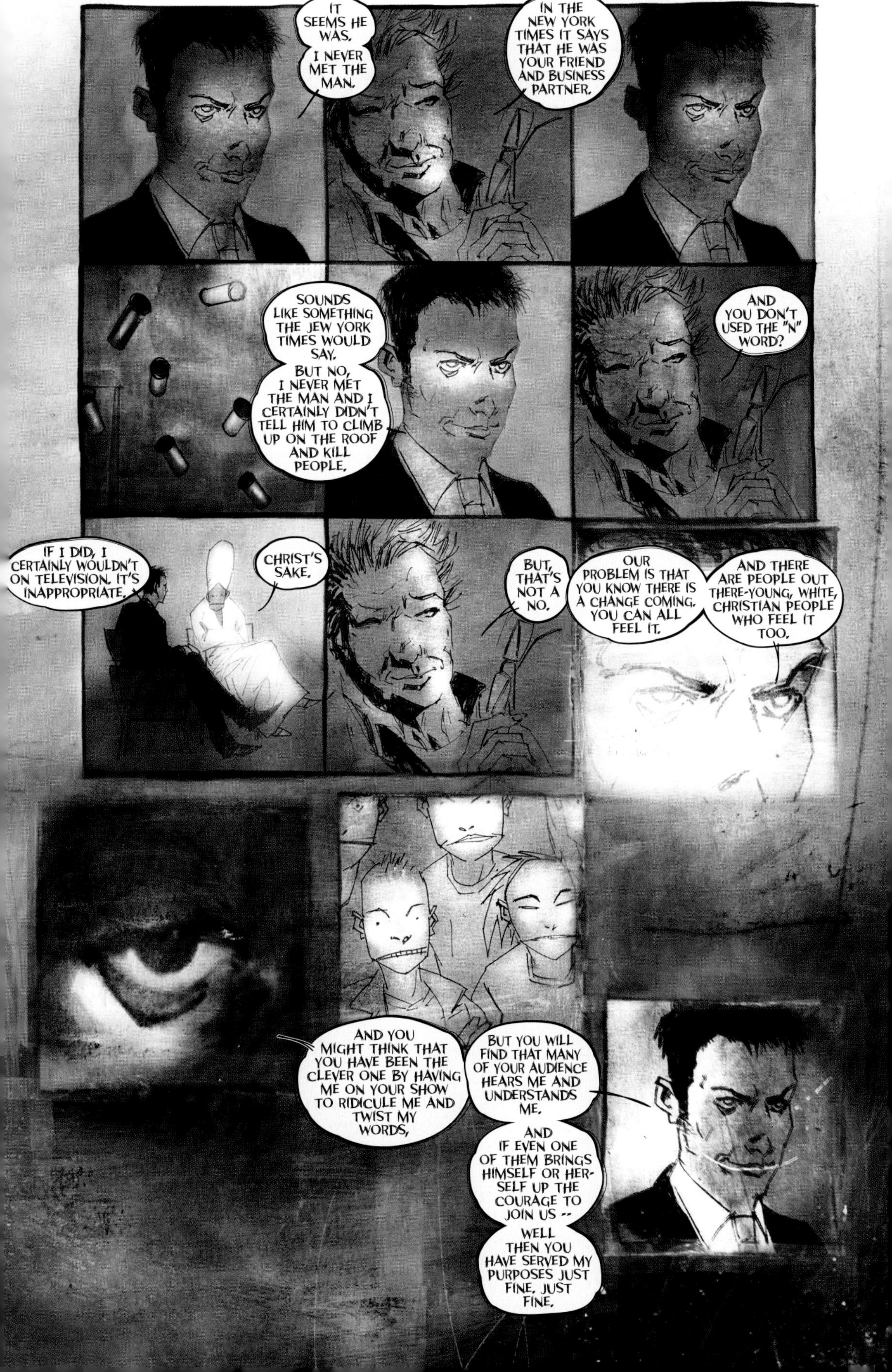
IT SEEMS HE WAS.
I NEVER MET THE MAN.
IN THE NEW YORK TIMES IT SAYS THAT HE WAS YOUR FRIEND AND BUSINESS PARTNER.
SOUNDS LIKE SOMETHING THE JEW YORK TIMES WOULD SAY.
BUT NO, I NEVER MET THE MAN AND I CERTAINLY DIDN'T TELL HIM TO CLIMB UP ON THE ROOF AND KILL PEOPLE.
AND YOU DON'T USED THE "N" WORD?
IF I DID, I CERTAINLY WOULDN'T ON TELEVISION. IT'S INAPPROPRIATE.
CHRIST'S SAKE.
BUT, THAT'S NOT A NO.
OUR PROBLEM IS THAT YOU KNOW THERE IS A CHANGE COMING. YOU CAN ALL FEEL IT.
AND THERE ARE PEOPLE OUT THERE-YOUNG, WHITE, CHRISTIAN PEOPLE WHO FEEL IT TOO.
AND YOU MIGHT THINK THAT YOU HAVE BEEN THE CLEVER ONE BY HAVING ME ON YOUR SHOW TO RIDICULE ME AND TWIST MY WORDS,
BUT YOU WILL FIND THAT MANY OF YOUR AUDIENCE HEARS ME AND UNDERSTANDS ME.
AND IF EVEN ONE OF THEM BRINGS HIMSELF OR HER-SELF UP THE COURAGE TO JOIN US --
WELL THEN YOU HAVE SERVED MY PURPOSES JUST FINE. JUST FINE.

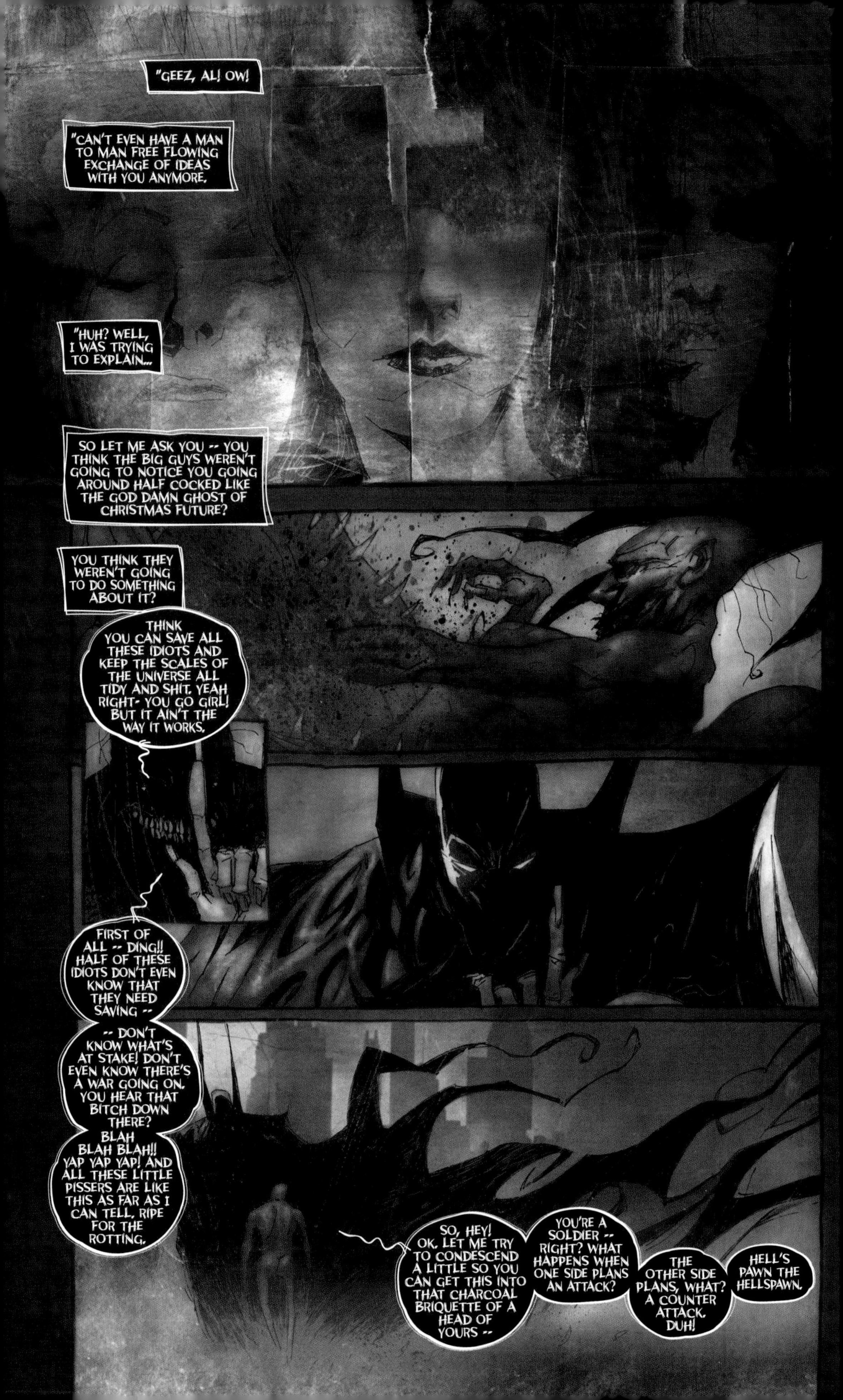
"GEEZ, AL! OW!
"CAN'T EVEN HAVE A MAN TO MAN FREE FLOWING EXCHANGE OF IDEAS WITH YOU ANYMORE.
"HUH? WELL, I WAS TRYING TO EXPLAIN...
SO LET ME ASK YOU -- YOU THINK THE BIG GUYS WEREN'T GOING TO NOTICE YOU GOING AROUND HALF COCKED LIKE THE GOD DAMN GHOST OF CHRISTMAS FUTURE?
YOU THINK THEY WEREN'T GOING TO DO SOMETHING ABOUT IT?
THINK YOU CAN SAVE ALL THESE IDIOTS AND KEEP THE SCALES OF THE UNIVERSE ALL TIDY AND SHIT. YEAH RIGHT- YOU GO GIRL! BUT IT AIN'T THE WAY IT WORKS.
FIRST OF ALL -- DING!! HALF OF THESE IDIOTS DON'T EVEN KNOW THAT THEY NEED SAVING --
-- DON'T KNOW WHAT'S AT STAKE! DON'T EVEN KNOW THERE'S A WAR GOING ON. YOU HEAR THAT BITCH DOWN THERE?
BLAH BLAH BLAH!! YAP YAP YAP! AND ALL THESE LITTLE PISSERS ARE LIKE THIS AS FAR AS I CAN TELL. RIPE FOR THE ROTTING.
SO, HEY! OK. LET ME TRY TO CONDESCEND A LITTLE SO YOU CAN GET THIS INTO THAT CHARCOAL BRIQUETTE OF A HEAD OF YOURS --
YOU'RE A SOLDIER -- RIGHT? WHAT HAPPENS WHEN ONE SIDE PLANS AN ATTACK?
THE OTHER SIDE PLANS, WHAT? A COUNTER ATTACK. DUH!
HELL'S PAWN THE HELLSPAWN.

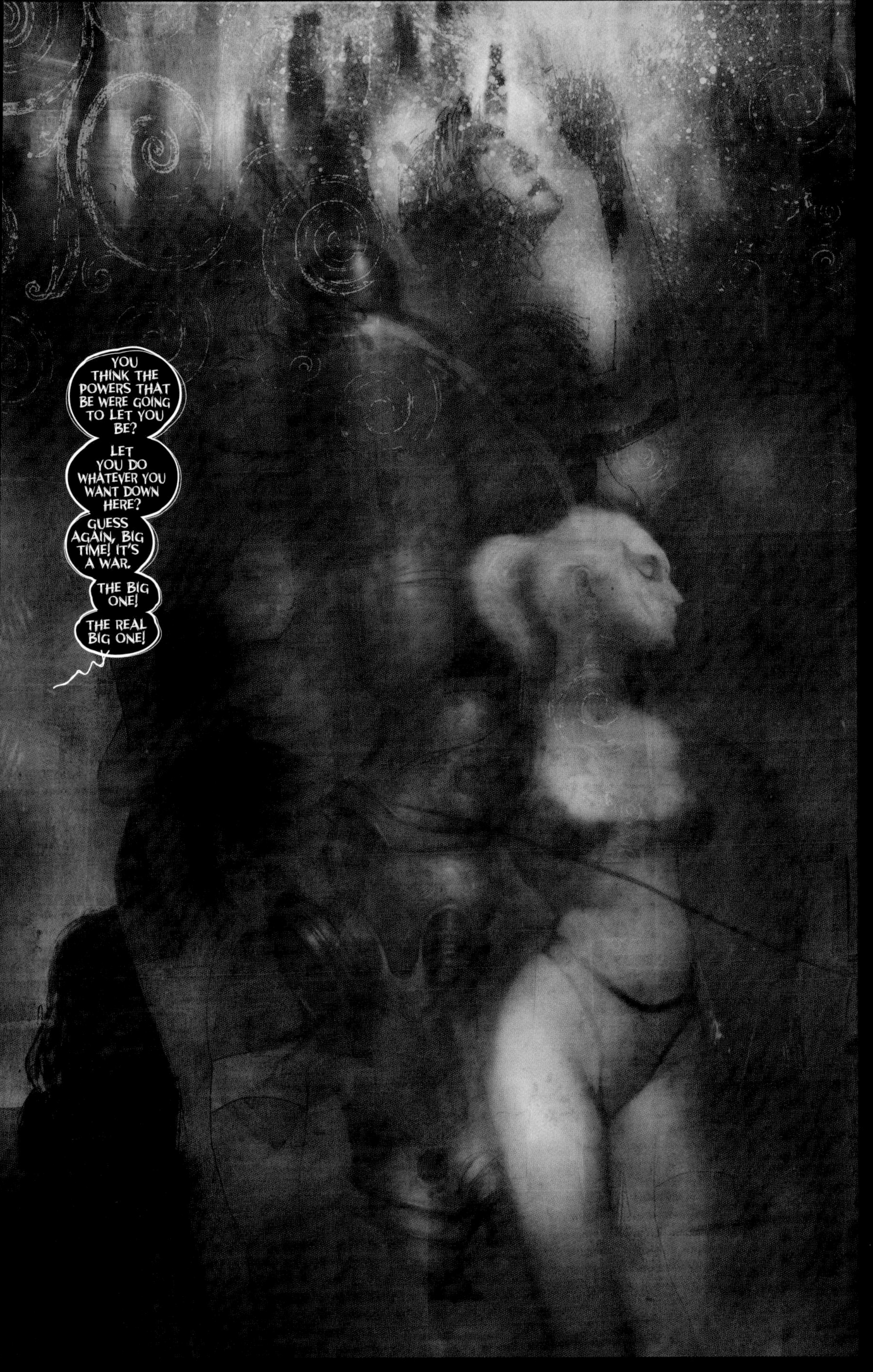
YOU THINK THE POWERS THAT BE WERE GOING TO LET YOU BE?
LET YOU DO WHATEVER YOU WANT DOWN HERE?
GUESS AGAIN, BIG TIME! IT'S A WAR.
THE BIG ONE!
THE REAL BIG ONE!

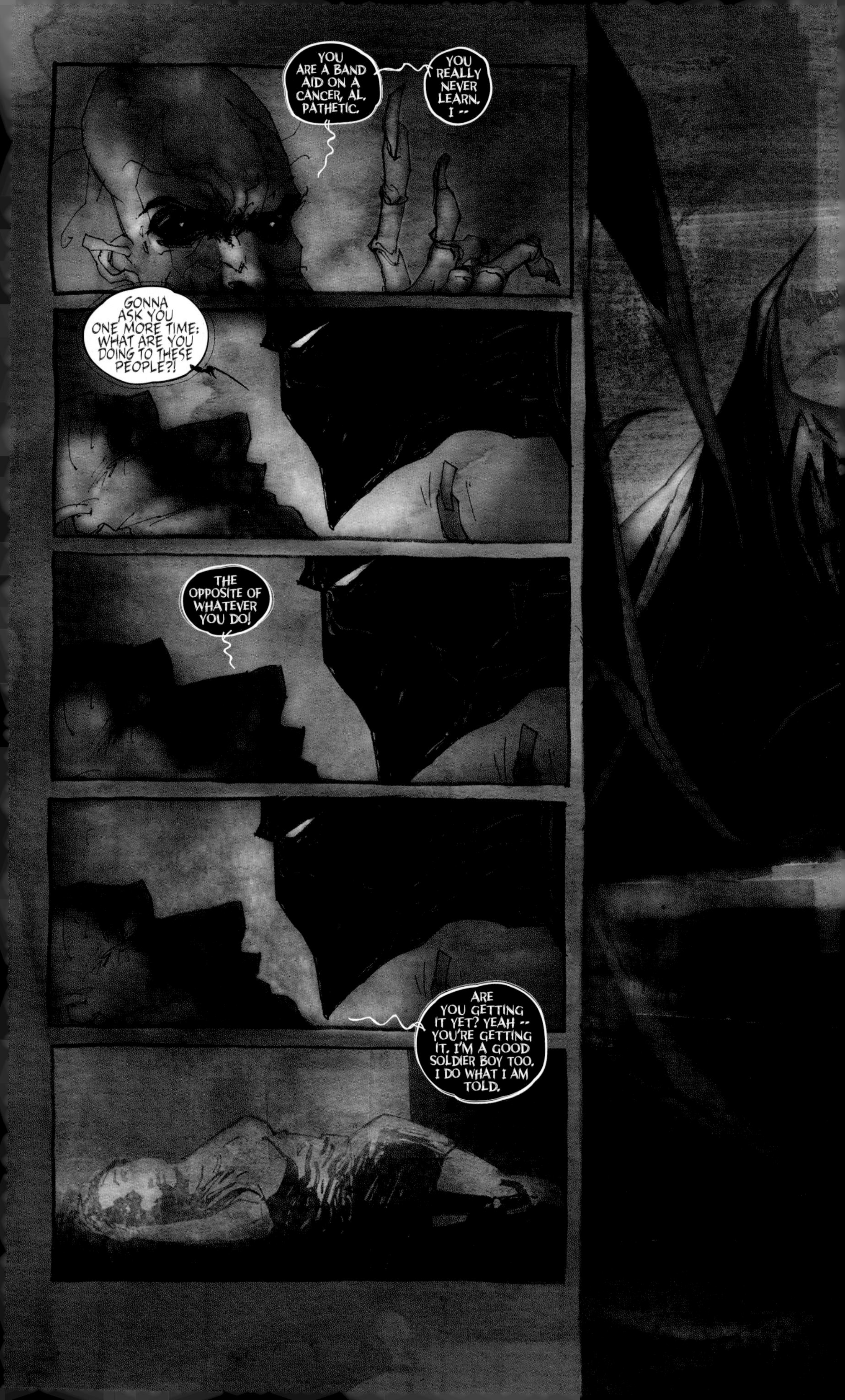
YOU ARE A BAND AID ON A CANCER, AL, PATHETIC.
YOU REALLY NEVER LEARN. I --
GONNA ASK YOU ONE MORE TIME: WHAT ARE YOU DOING TO THESE PEOPLE?!
THE OPPOSITE OF WHATEVER YOU DO!
ARE YOU GETTING IT YET? YEAH -- YOU'RE GETTING IT. I'M A GOOD SOLDIER BOY TOO. I DO WHAT I AM TOLD.

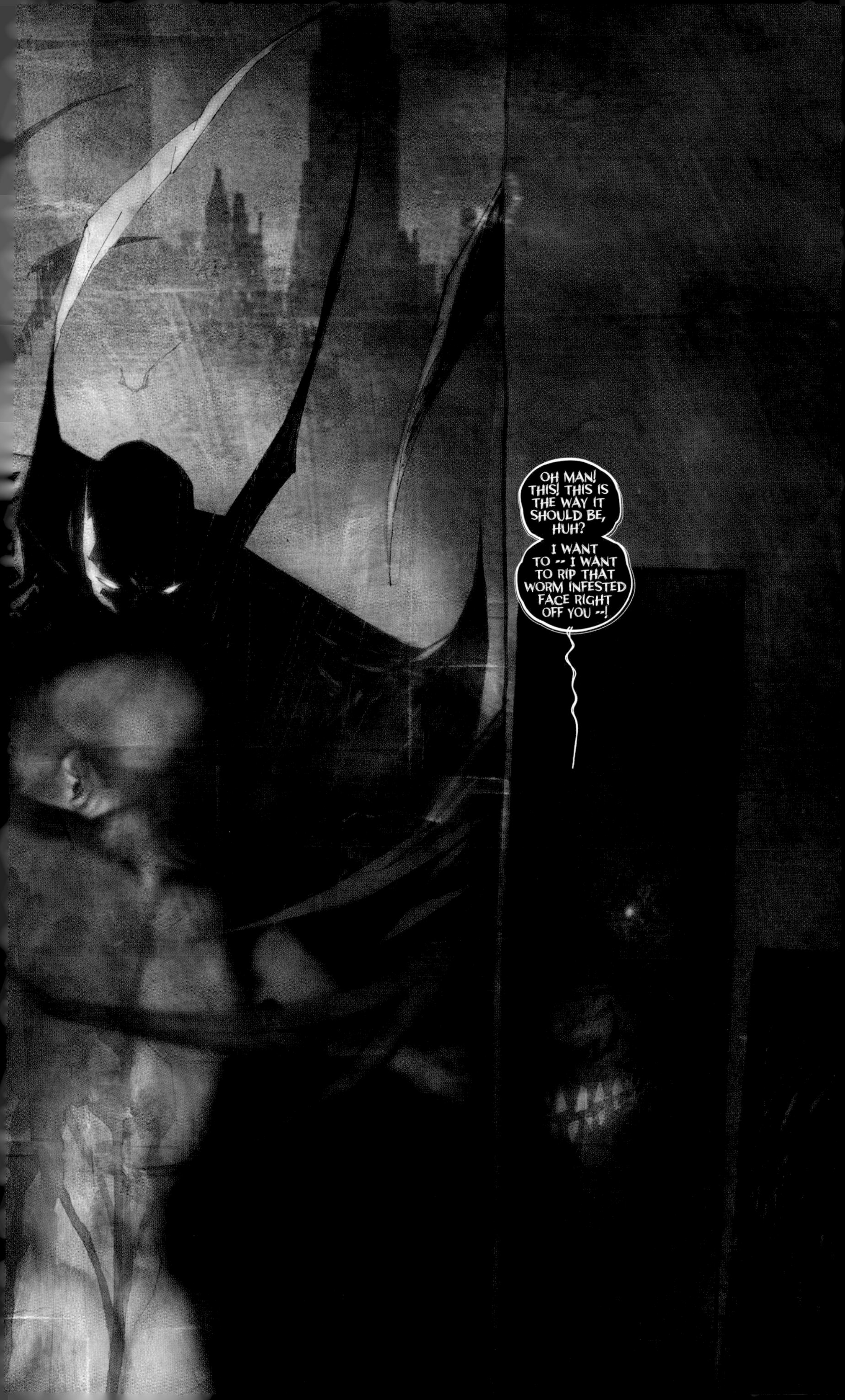
OH MAN! THIS! THIS IS THE WAY IT SHOULD BE, HUH?
I WANT TO -- I WANT TO RIP THAT WORM INFESTED FACE RIGHT OFF YOU --!

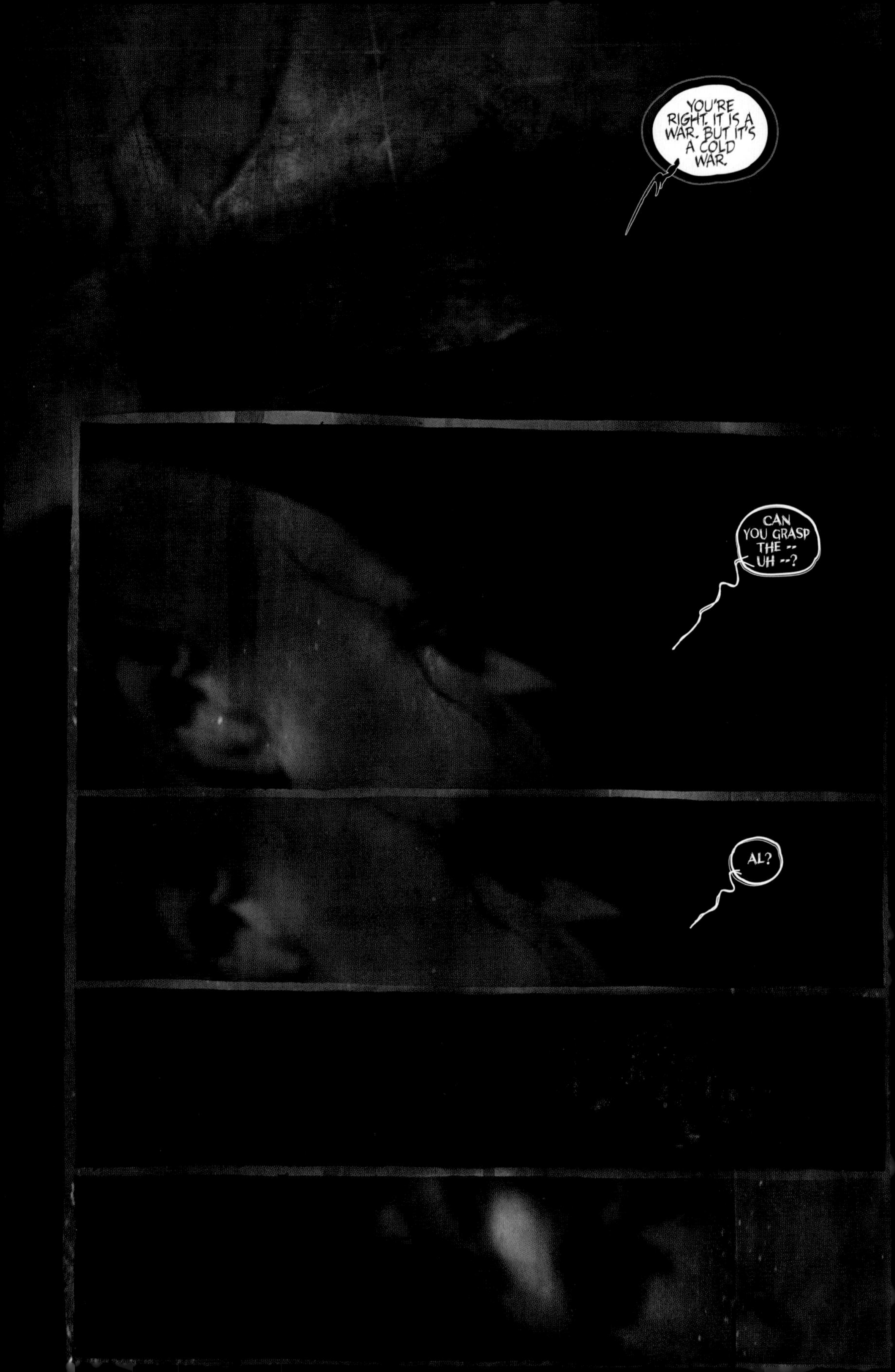
YOU'RE RIGHT. IT IS A WAR. BUT IT'S A COLD WAR.
CAN YOU GRASP THE -- UH --?
AL?

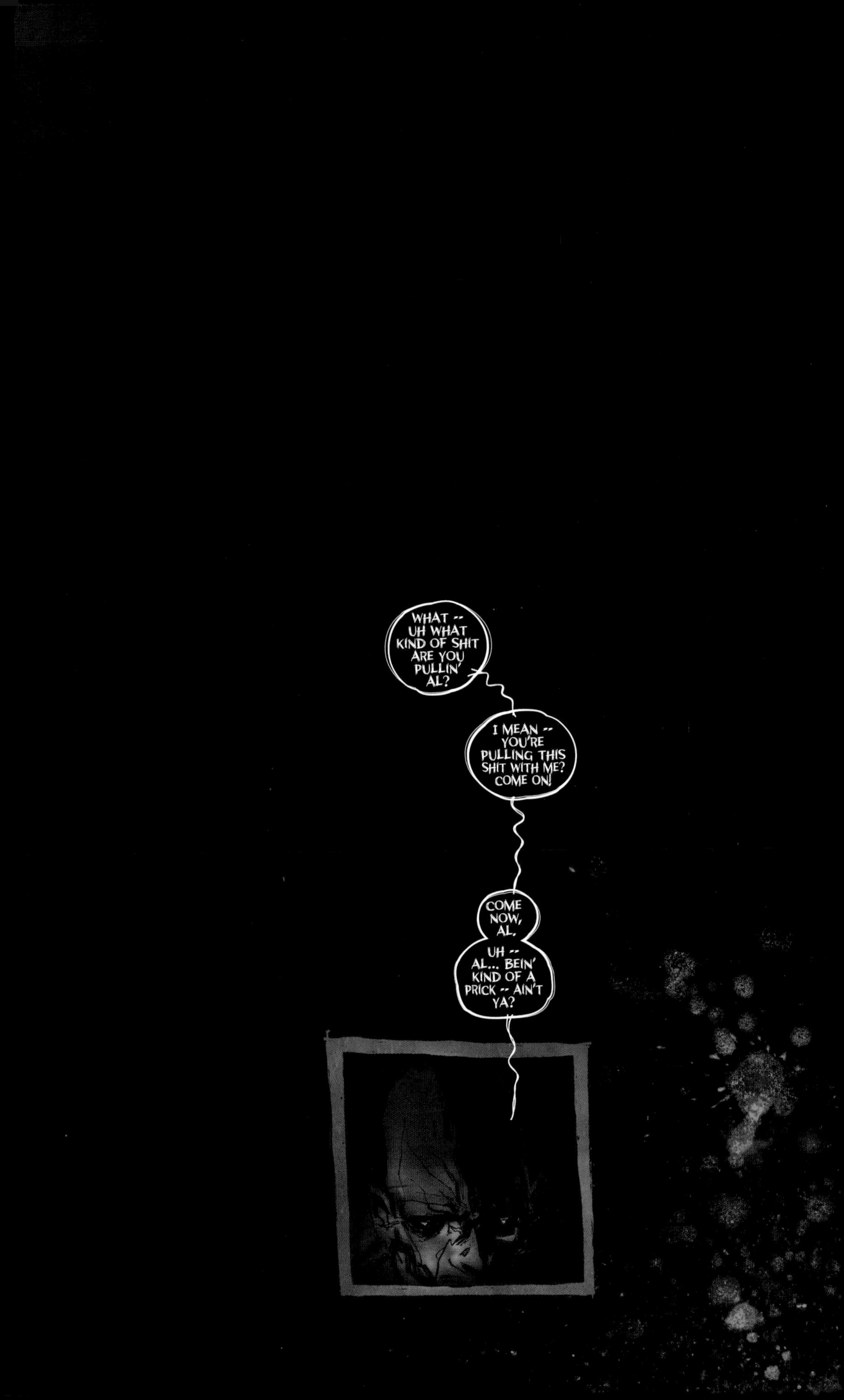
WHAT -- UH WHAT KIND OF SHIT ARE YOU PULLIN' AL?
I MEAN -- YOU'RE PULLING THIS SHIT WITH ME? COME ON!
COME NOW, AL.
UH -- AL... BEIN' KIND OF A PRICK -- AIN'T YA?

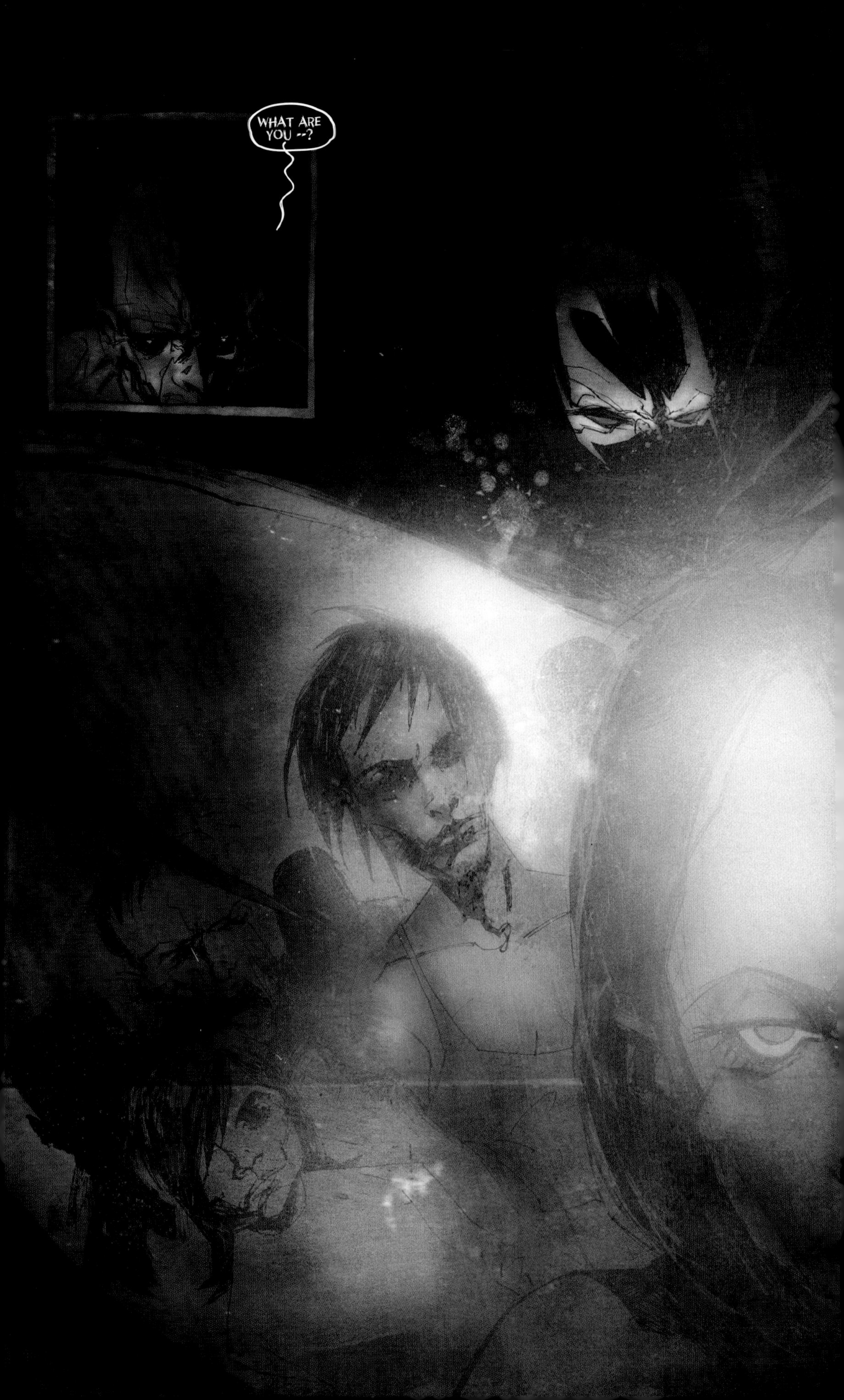
WHAT ARE YOU --?

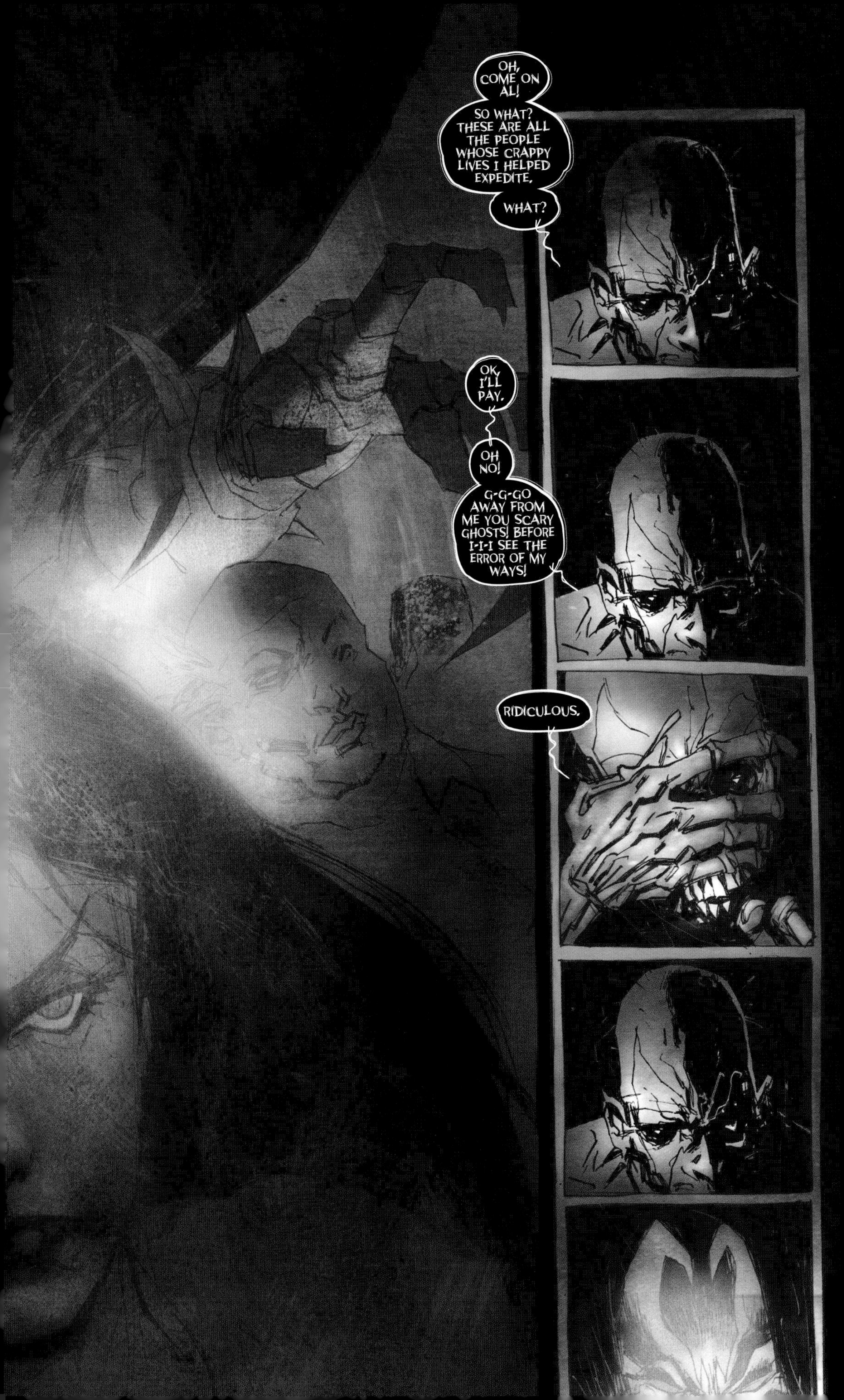
OH, COME ON AL!
SO WHAT? THESE ARE ALL THE PEOPLE WHOSE CRAPPY LIVES I HELPED EXPEDITE.
WHAT?
OK, I'LL PAY.
OH NO!
G-G-GO AWAY FROM ME YOU SCARY GHOSTS! BEFORE I-I-I SEE THE ERROR OF MY WAYS!
RIDICULOUS.

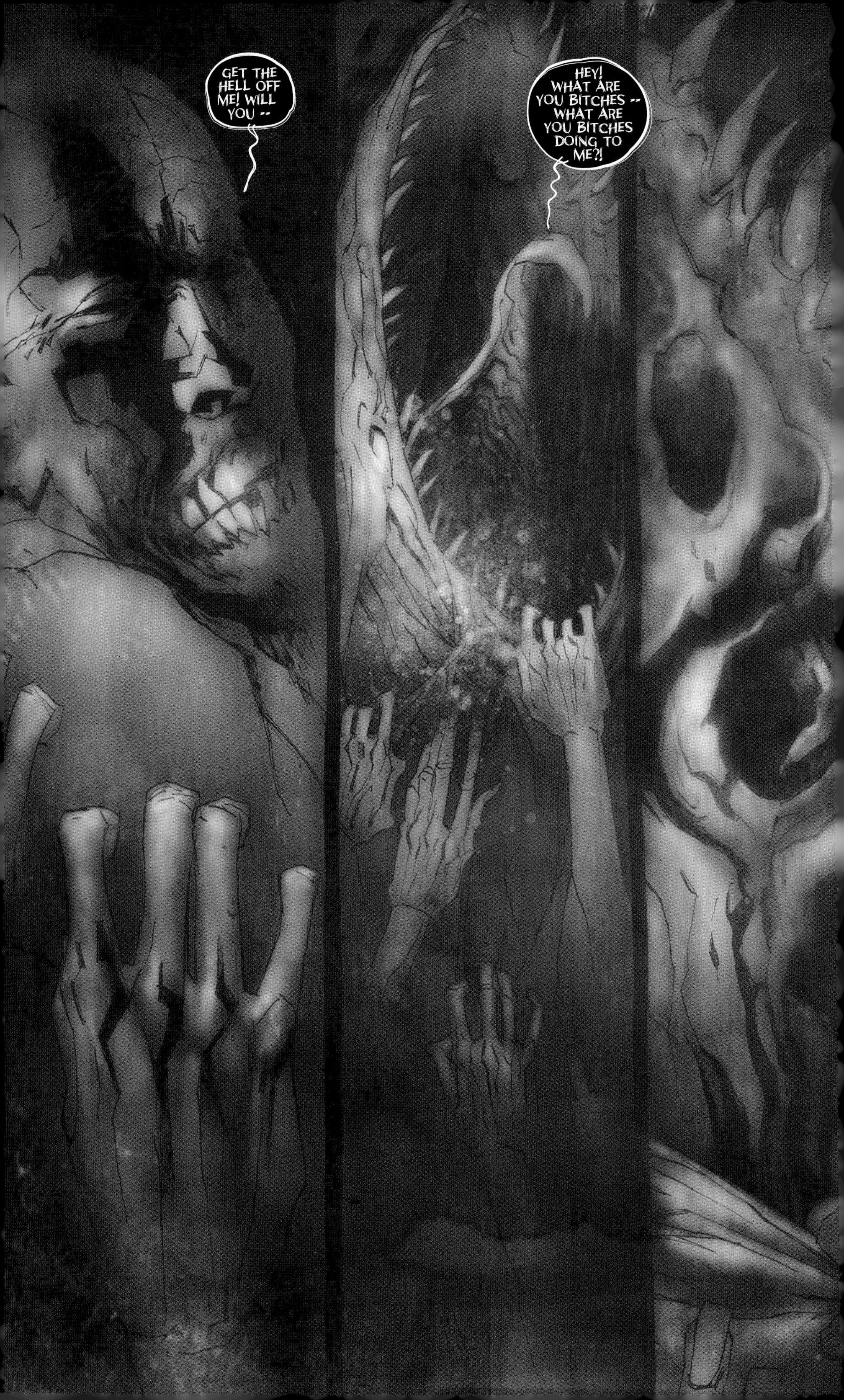
GET THE HELL OFF ME! WILL YOU --
HEY! WHAT ARE YOU BITCHES -- WHAT ARE YOU BITCHES DOING TO ME?!

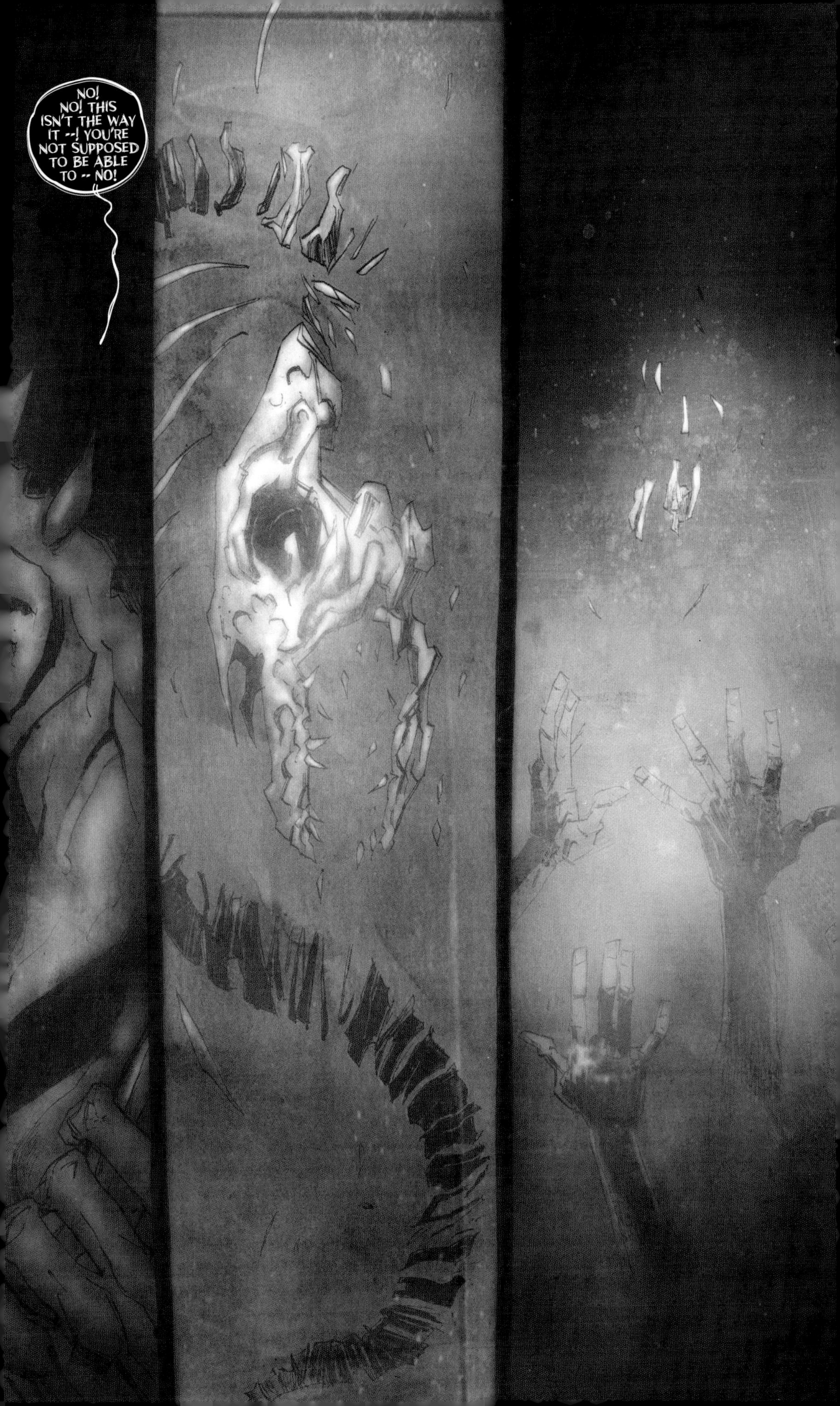
NO! NO! THIS ISN'T THE WAY IT --! YOU'RE NOT SUPPOSED TO BE ABLE TO -- NO!

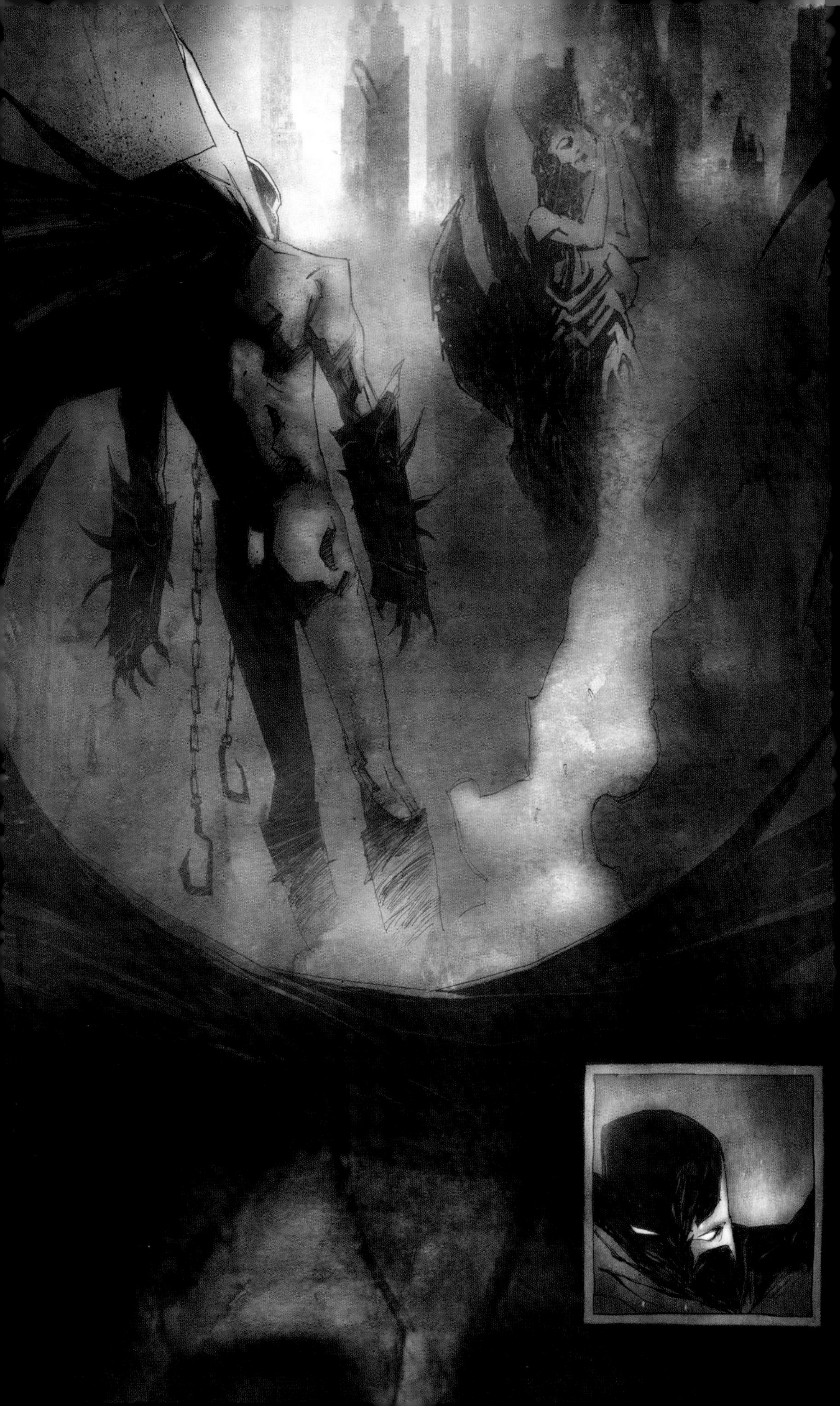

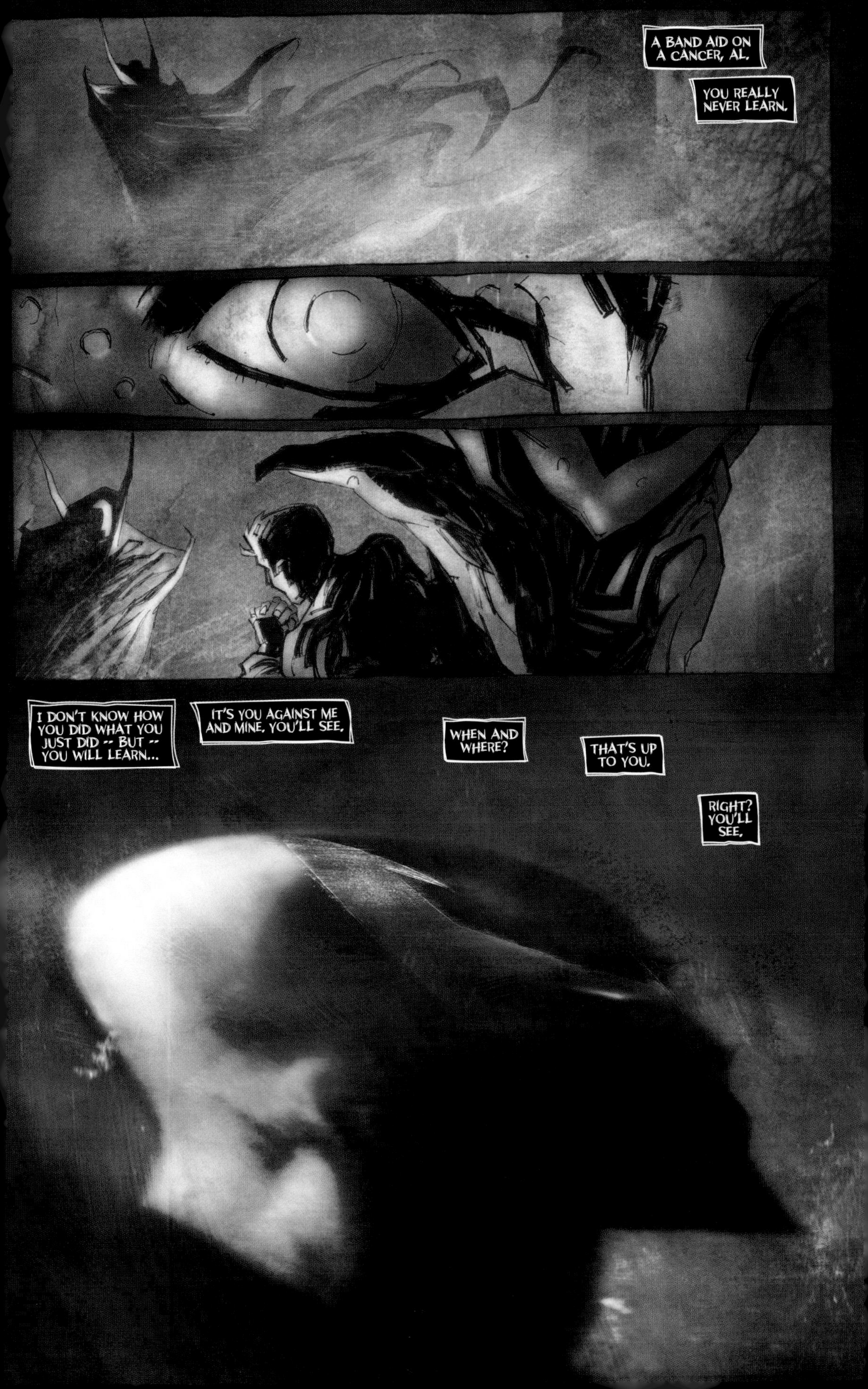
A BAND AID ON A CANCER, AL.
YOU REALLY NEVER LEARN.
I DON'T KNOW HOW YOU DID WHAT YOU JUST DID -- BUT -- YOU WILL LEARN...
IT'S YOU AGAINST ME AND MINE. YOU'LL SEE.
WHEN AND WHERE?
THAT'S UP TO YOU.
RIGHT? YOU'LL SEE.

WE'LL SEE...

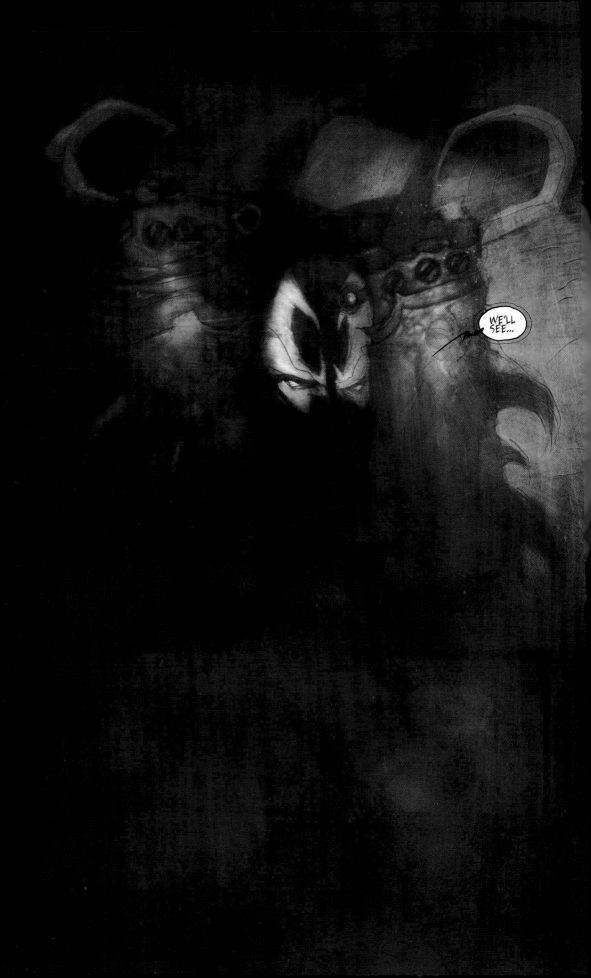

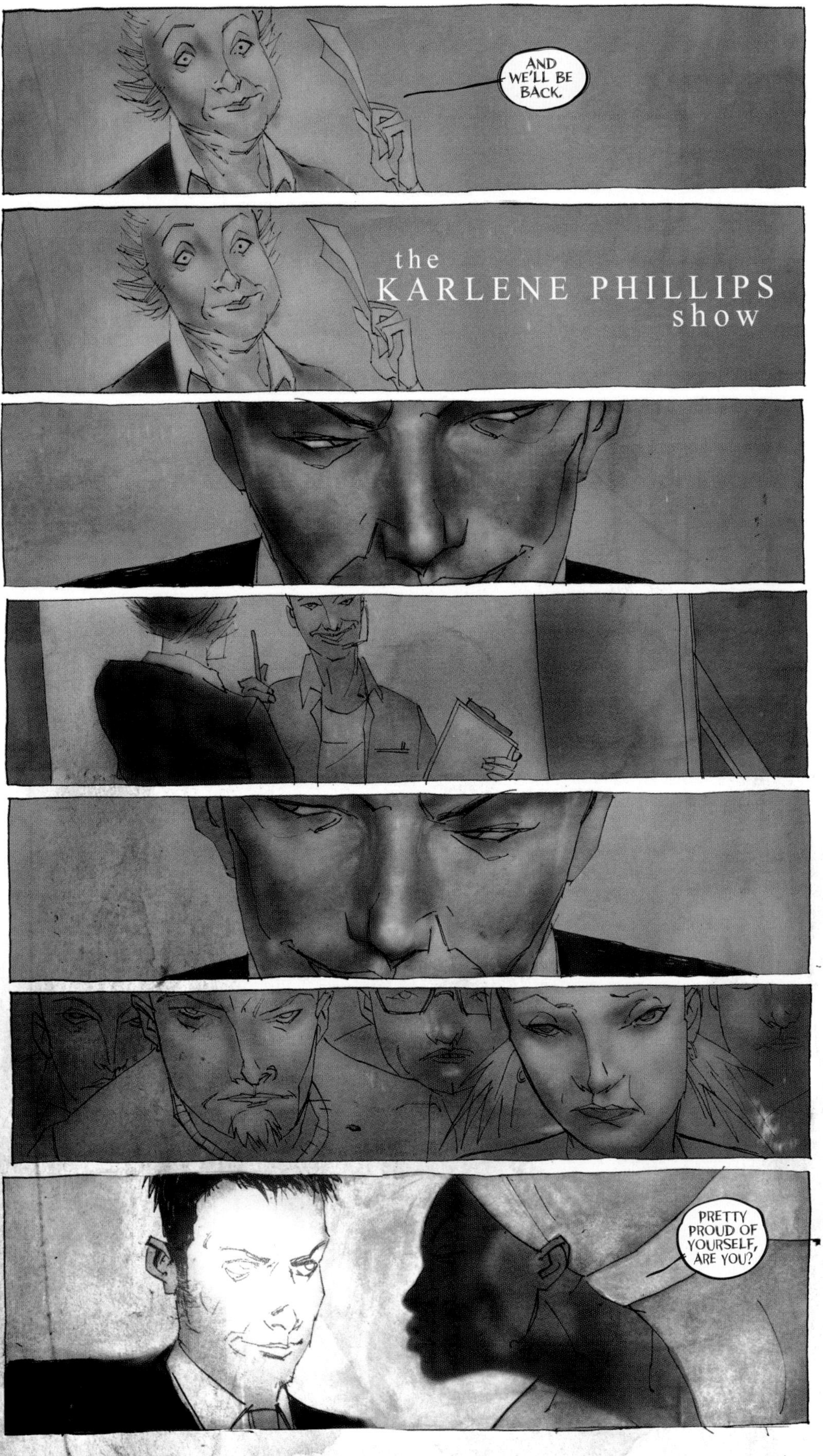
AND WE'LL BE BACK.
the KARLENE PHILLIPS show
PRETTY PROUD OF YOURSELF, ARE YOU?

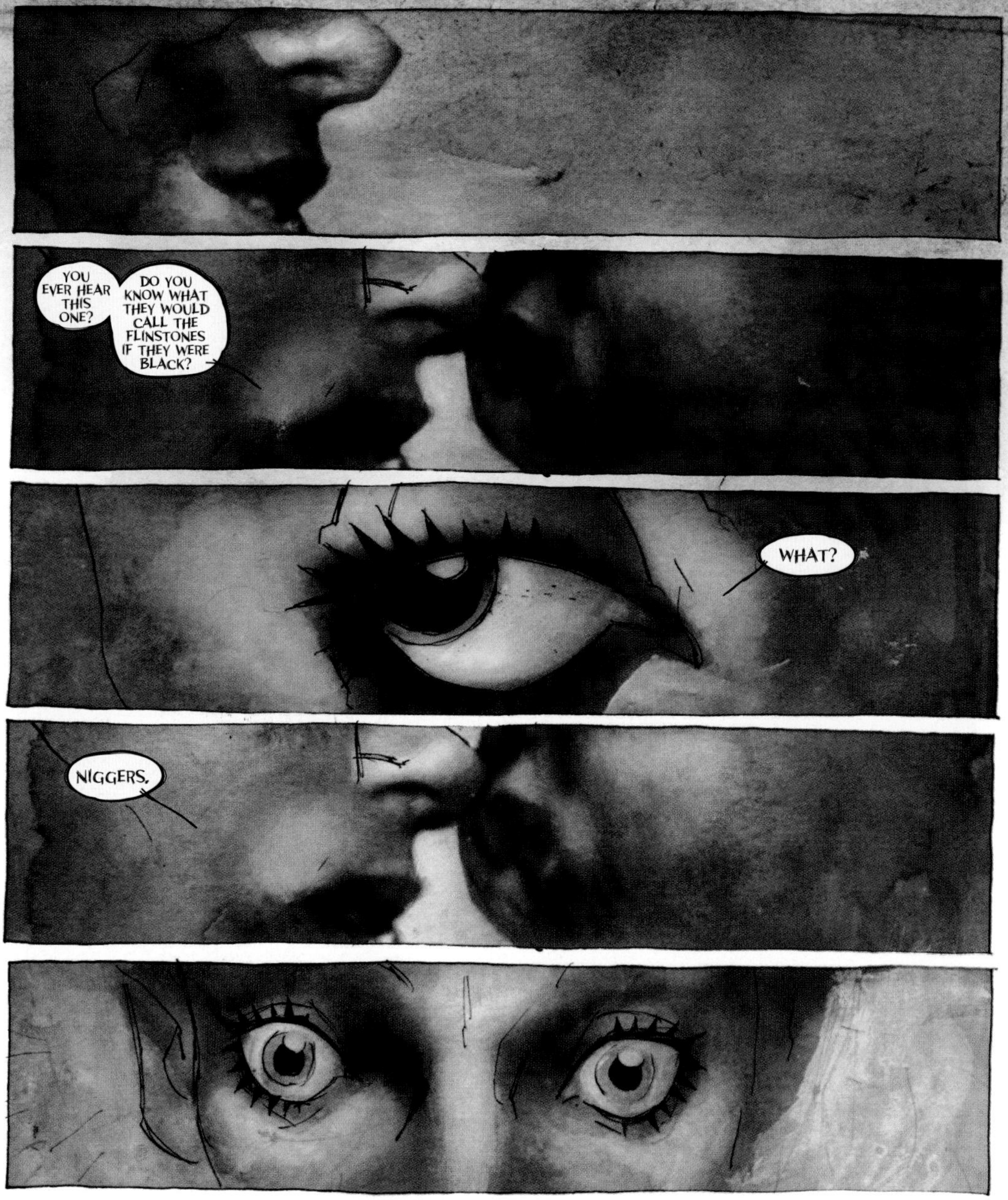
YOU EVER HEAR THIS ONE?
DO YOU KNOW WHAT THEY WOULD CALL THE FLINSTONES IF THEY WERE BLACK?
WHAT?
NIGGERS.

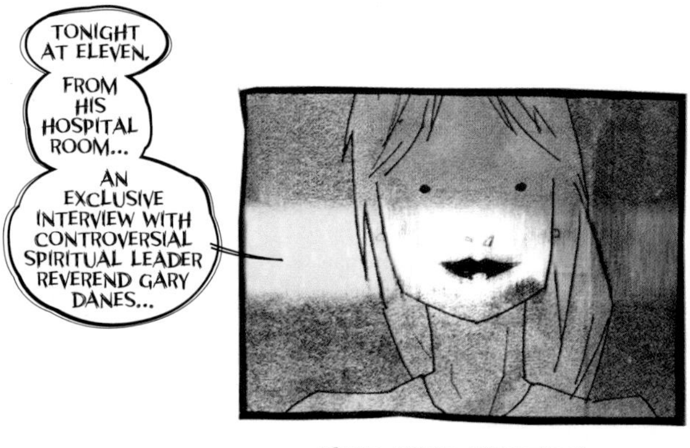
TONIGHT AT ELEVEN.
FROM HIS HOSPITAL ROOM...
AN EXCLUSIVE INTERVIEW WITH CONTROVERSIAL SPIRITUAL LEADER REVEREND GARY DANES...

NEXT: ISSUE: HATE YOU!

HELL**S**PAWN

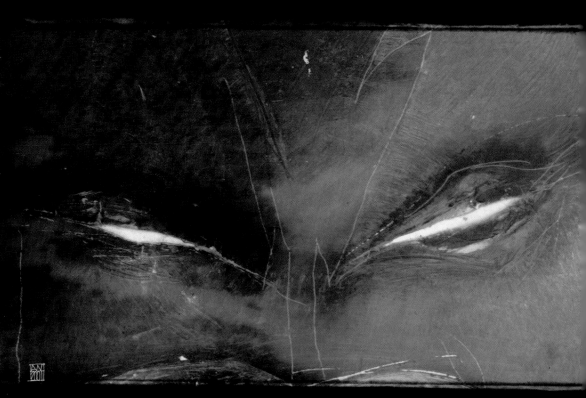

ISSUE FOUR

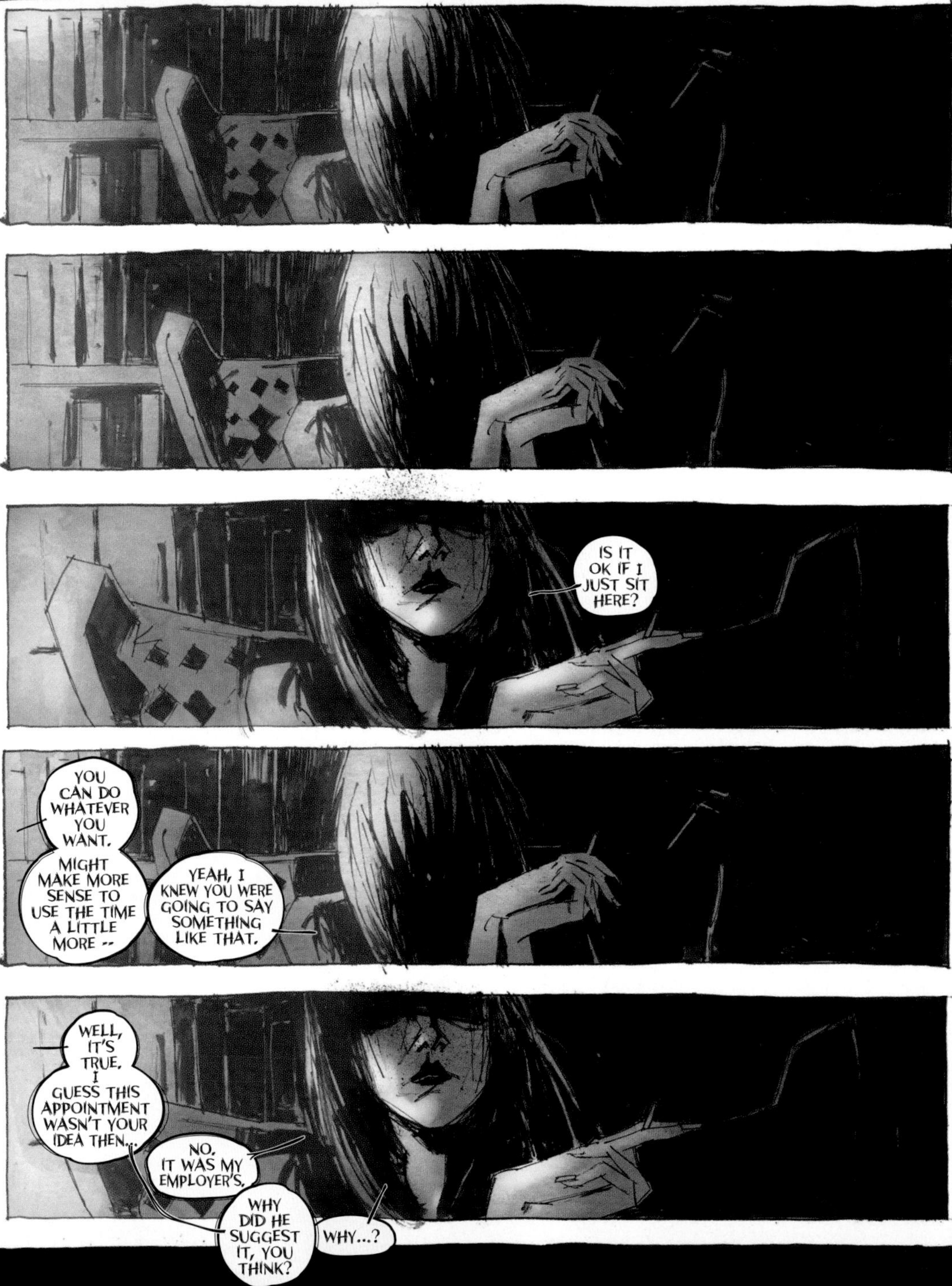
IS IT OK IF I JUST SIT HERE?
YOU CAN DO WHATEVER YOU WANT.
MIGHT MAKE MORE SENSE TO USE THE TIME A LITTLE MORE --
YEAH, I KNEW YOU WERE GOING TO SAY SOMETHING LIKE THAT.
WELL, IT'S TRUE. I GUESS THIS APPOINTMENT WASN'T YOUR IDEA THEN...
NO. IT WAS MY EMPLOYER'S.
WHY DID HE SUGGEST IT, YOU THINK?
WHY...?

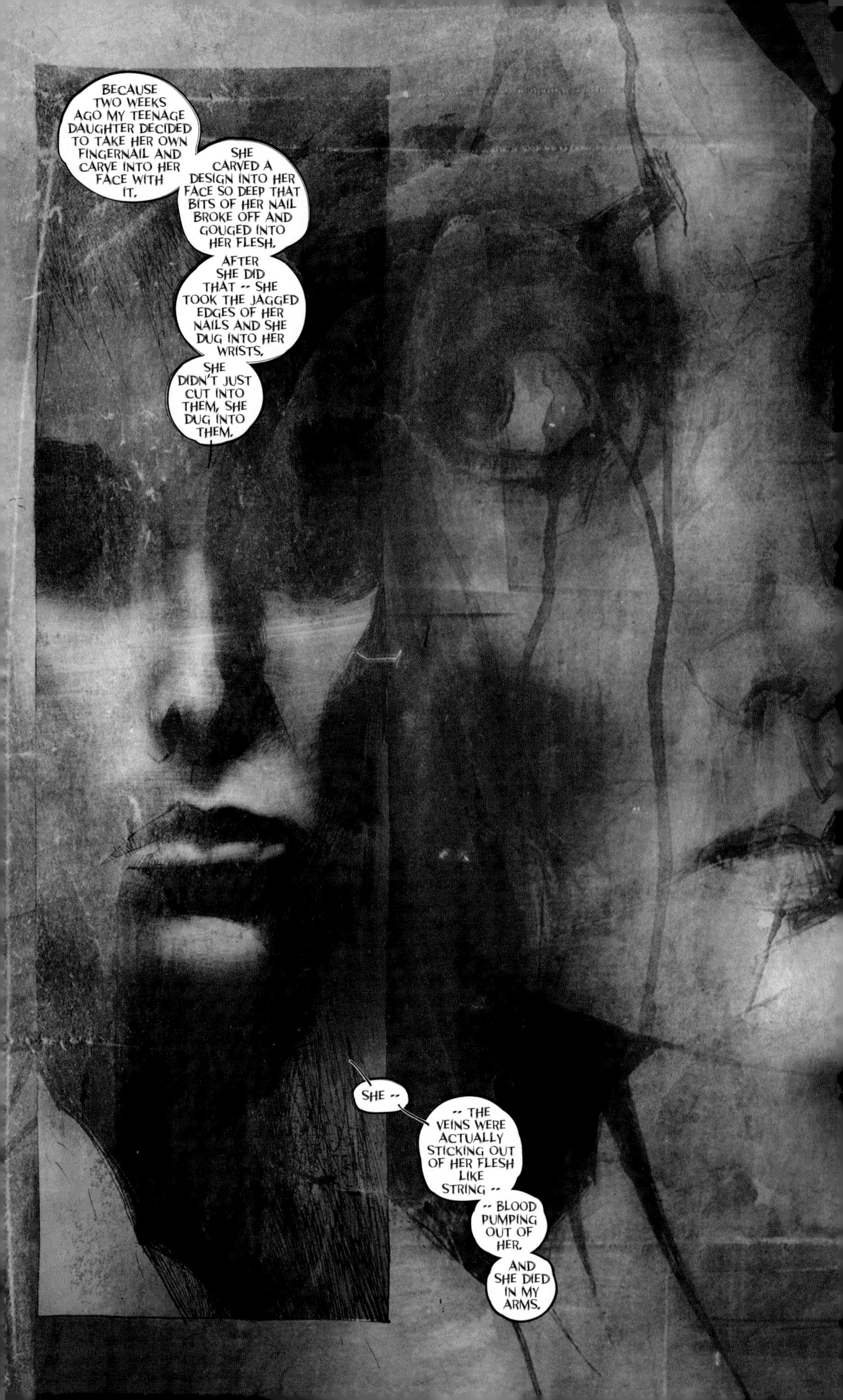
BECAUSE TWO WEEKS AGO MY TEENAGE DAUGHTER DECIDED TO TAKE HER OWN FINGERNAIL AND CARVE INTO HER FACE WITH IT.
SHE CARVED A DESIGN INTO HER FACE SO DEEP THAT BITS OF HER NAIL BROKE OFF AND GOUGED INTO HER FLESH.
AFTER SHE DID THAT -- SHE TOOK THE JAGGED EDGES OF HER NAILS AND SHE DUG INTO HER WRISTS.
SHE DIDN'T JUST CUT INTO THEM, SHE DUG INTO THEM.
SHE --
-- THE VEINS WERE ACTUALLY STICKING OUT OF HER FLESH LIKE STRING --
-- BLOOD PUMPING OUT OF HER.
AND SHE DIED IN MY ARMS.

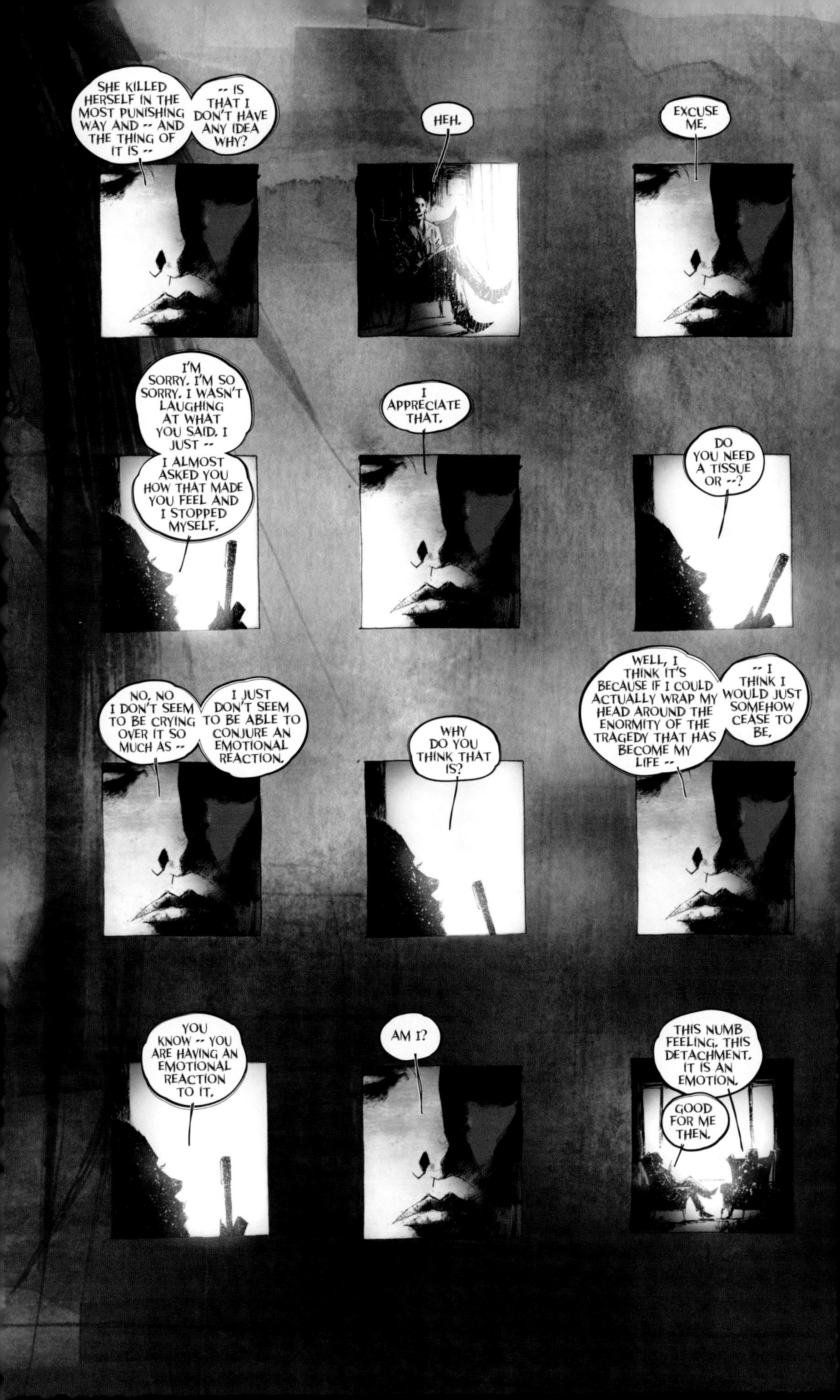
SHE KILLED HERSELF IN THE MOST PUNISHING WAY AND -- AND THE THING OF IT IS --
-- IS THAT I DON'T HAVE ANY IDEA WHY?
HEH.
EXCUSE ME.
I'M SORRY. I'M SO SORRY. I WASN'T LAUGHING AT WHAT YOU SAID. I JUST --
I ALMOST ASKED YOU HOW THAT MADE YOU FEEL AND I STOPPED MYSELF.
I APPRECIATE THAT.
DO YOU NEED A TISSUE OR --?
NO. NO I DON'T SEEM TO BE CRYING OVER IT SO MUCH AS --
I JUST DON'T SEEM TO BE ABLE TO CONJURE AN EMOTIONAL REACTION.
WHY DO YOU THINK THAT IS?
WELL, I THINK IT'S BECAUSE IF I COULD ACTUALLY WRAP MY HEAD AROUND THE ENORMITY OF THE TRAGEDY THAT HAS BECOME MY LIFE --
-- I THINK I WOULD JUST SOMEHOW CEASE TO BE.
YOU KNOW -- YOU ARE HAVING AN EMOTIONAL REACTION TO IT.
AM I?
THIS NUMB FEELING. THIS DETACHMENT. IT IS AN EMOTION.
GOOD FOR ME THEN.

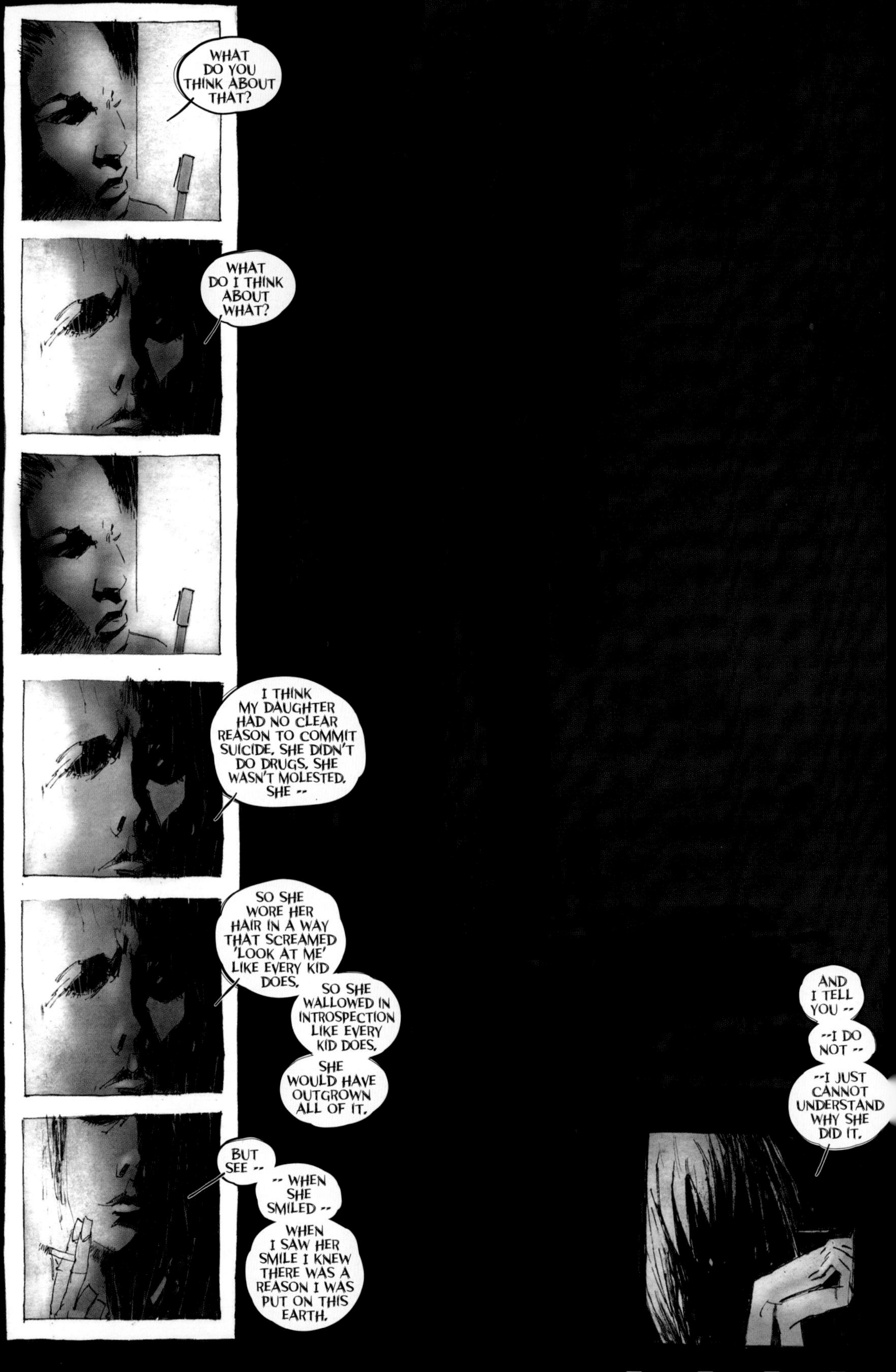
WHAT DO YOU THINK ABOUT THAT?
WHAT DO I THINK ABOUT WHAT?
I THINK MY DAUGHTER HAD NO CLEAR REASON TO COMMIT SUICIDE. SHE DIDN'T DO DRUGS. SHE WASN'T MOLESTED. SHE --
SO SHE WORE HER HAIR IN A WAY THAT SCREAMED 'LOOK AT ME' LIKE EVERY KID DOES.
SO SHE WALLOWED IN INTROSPECTION LIKE EVERY KID DOES.
SHE WOULD HAVE OUTGROWN ALL OF IT.
BUT SEE --
-- WHEN SHE SMILED --
WHEN I SAW HER SMILE I KNEW THERE WAS A REASON I WAS PUT ON THIS EARTH.
AND I TELL YOU --
--I DO NOT --
--I JUST CANNOT UNDERSTAND WHY SHE DID IT.
BEEP BEEP BEEP BEEP

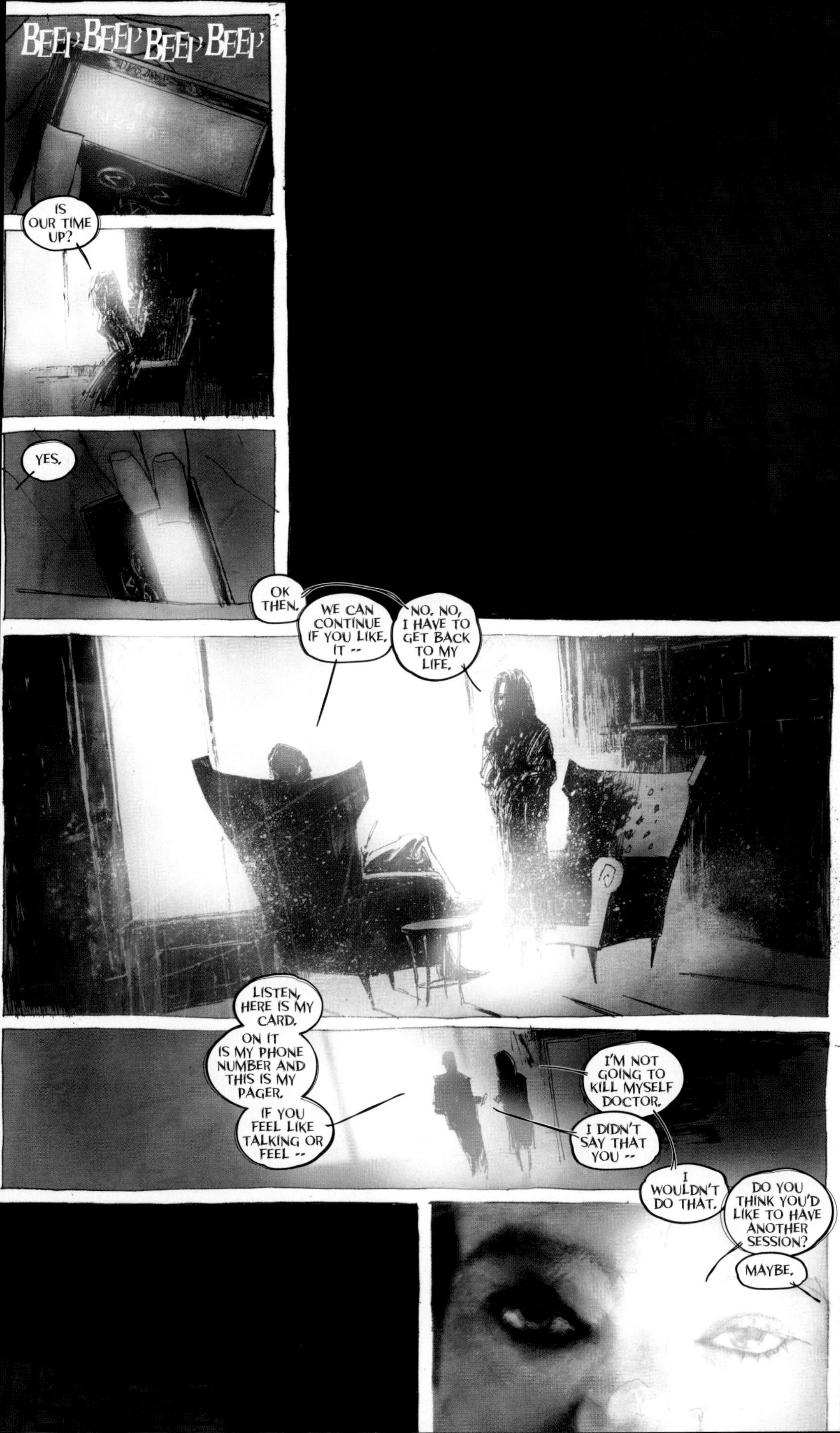
BEEP BEEP BEEP BEEP
IS OUR TIME UP?
YES.
OK THEN.
WE CAN CONTINUE IF YOU LIKE. IT --
NO. NO, I HAVE TO GET BACK TO MY LIFE.
LISTEN, HERE IS MY CARD.
ON IT IS MY PHONE NUMBER AND THIS IS MY PAGER.
IF YOU FEEL LIKE TALKING OR FEEL --
I'M NOT GOING TO KILL MYSELF DOCTOR.
I DIDN'T SAY THAT YOU --
I WOULDN'T DO THAT.
DO YOU THINK YOU'D LIKE TO HAVE ANOTHER SESSION?
MAYBE.

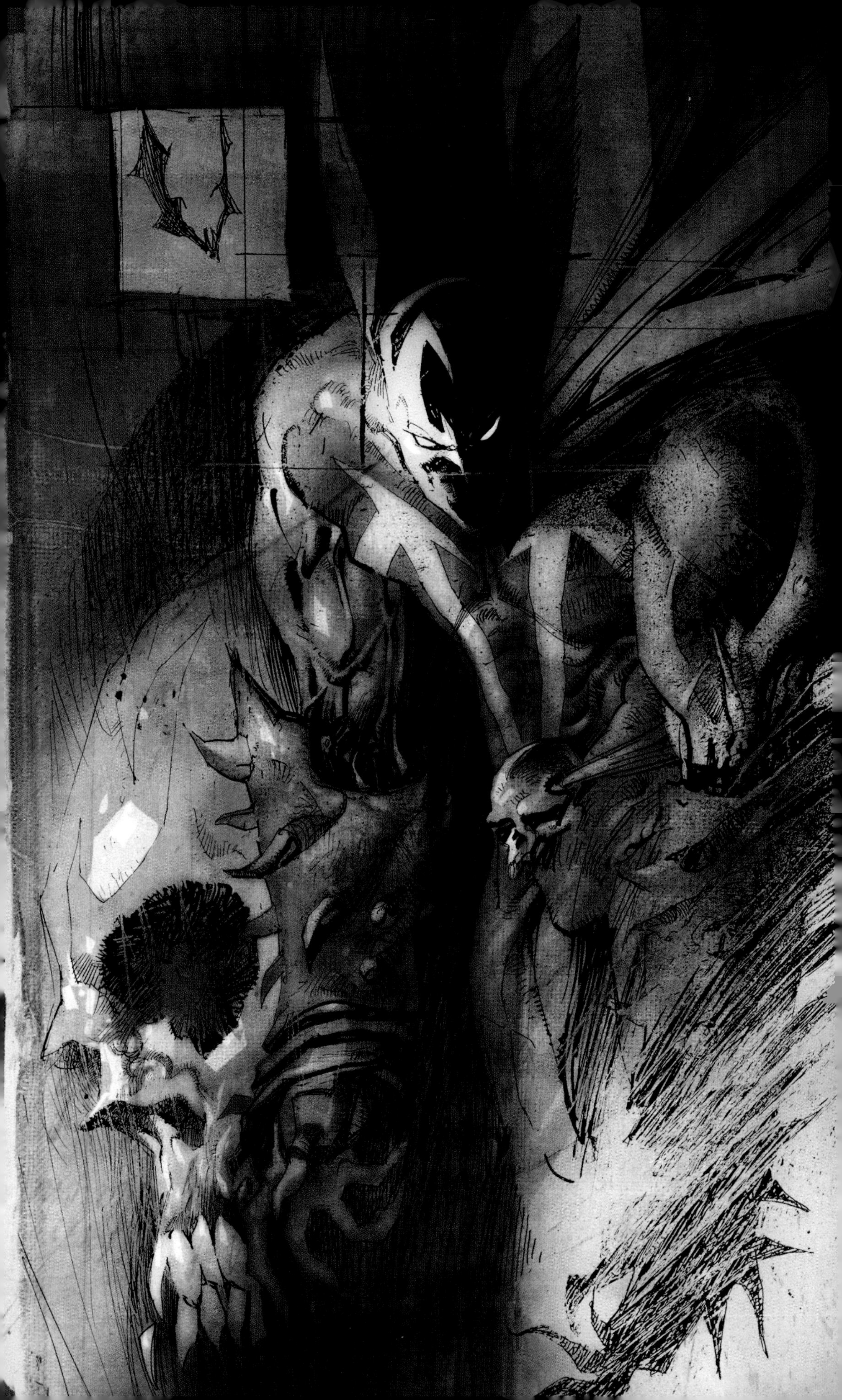

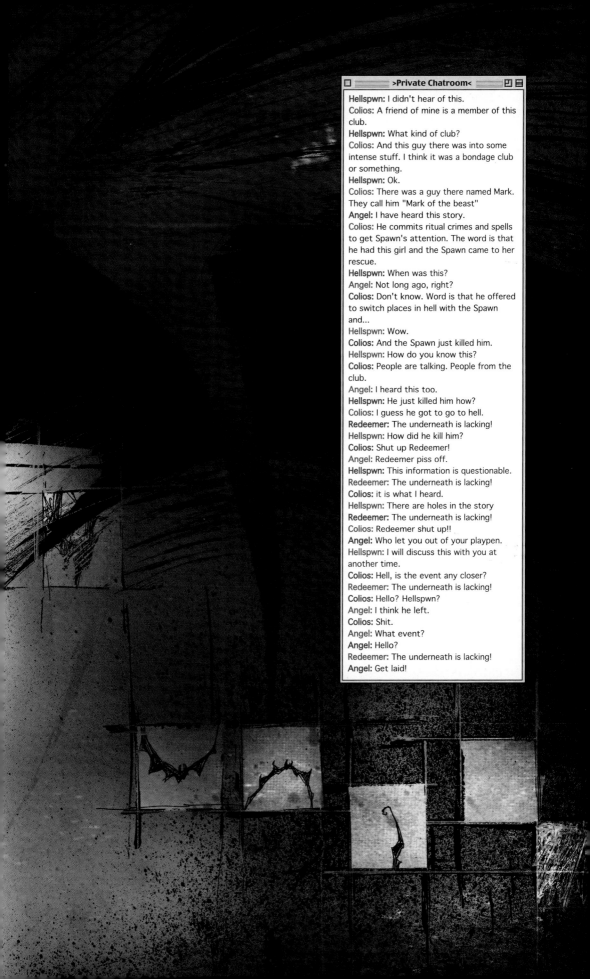

>Private Chatroom<

Hellspwn: I didn't hear of this.
Colios: A friend of mine is a member of this club.
Hellspwn: What kind of club?
Colios: And this guy there was into some intense stuff. I think it was a bondage club or something.
Hellspwn: Ok.
Colios: There was a guy there named Mark. They call him "Mark of the beast"
Angel: I have heard this story.
Colios: He commits ritual crimes and spells to get Spawn's attention. The word is that he had this girl and the Spawn came to her rescue.
Hellspwn: When was this?
Angel: Not long ago, right?
Colios: Don't know. Word is that he offered to switch places in hell with the Spawn and...
Hellspwn: Wow.
Colios: And the Spawn just killed him.
Hellspwn: How do you know this?
Colios: People are talking. People from the club.
Angel: I heard this too.
Hellspwn: He just killed him how?
Colios: I guess he got to go to hell.
Redeemer: The underneath is lacking!
Hellspwn: How did he kill him?
Colios: Shut up Redeemer!
Angel: Redeemer piss off.
Hellspwn: This information is questionable.
Redeemer: The underneath is lacking!
Colios: it is what I heard.
Hellspwn: There are holes in the story
Redeemer: The underneath is lacking!
Colios: Redeemer shut up!!
Angel: Who let you out of your playpen.
Hellspwn: I will discuss this with you at another time.
Colios: Hell, is the event any closer?
Redeemer: The underneath is lacking!
Colios: Hello? Hellspwn?
Angel: I think he left.
Colios: Shit.
Angel: What event?
Angel: Hello?
Redeemer: The underneath is lacking!
Angel: Get laid!

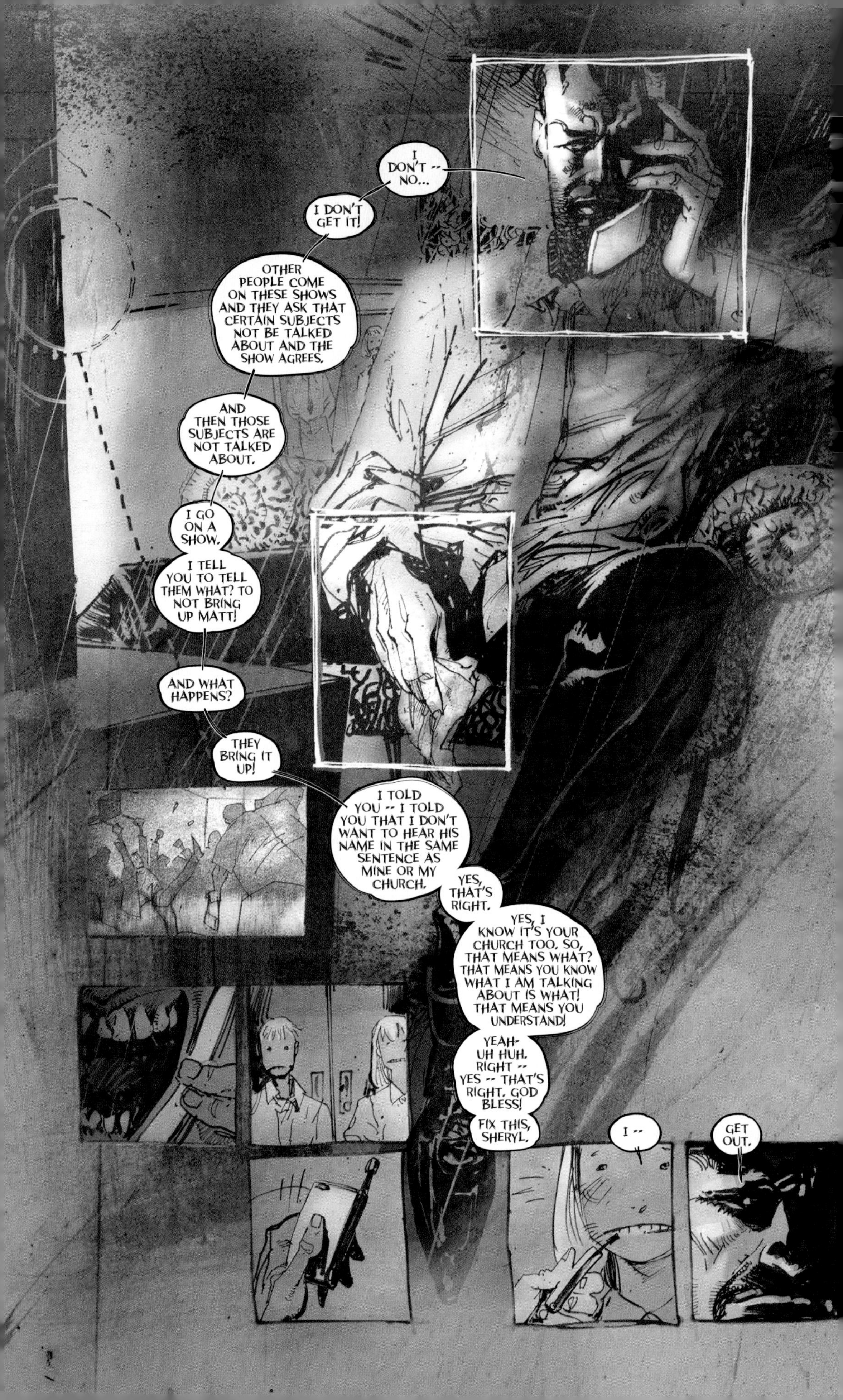

I DON'T -- NO...
I DON'T GET IT!
OTHER PEOPLE COME ON THESE SHOWS AND THEY ASK THAT CERTAIN SUBJECTS NOT BE TALKED ABOUT AND THE SHOW AGREES.
AND THEN THOSE SUBJECTS ARE NOT TALKED ABOUT.
I GO ON A SHOW.
I TELL YOU TO TELL THEM WHAT? TO NOT BRING UP MATT!
AND WHAT HAPPENS?
THEY BRING IT UP!
I TOLD YOU -- I TOLD YOU THAT I DON'T WANT TO HEAR HIS NAME IN THE SAME SENTENCE AS MINE OR MY CHURCH.
YES, THAT'S RIGHT.
YES, I KNOW IT'S YOUR CHURCH TOO. SO, THAT MEANS WHAT? THAT MEANS YOU KNOW WHAT I AM TALKING ABOUT IS WHAT! THAT MEANS YOU UNDERSTAND!
YEAH-UH HUH. RIGHT -- YES -- THAT'S RIGHT. GOD BLESS!
FIX THIS, SHERYL.
I --
GET OUT.

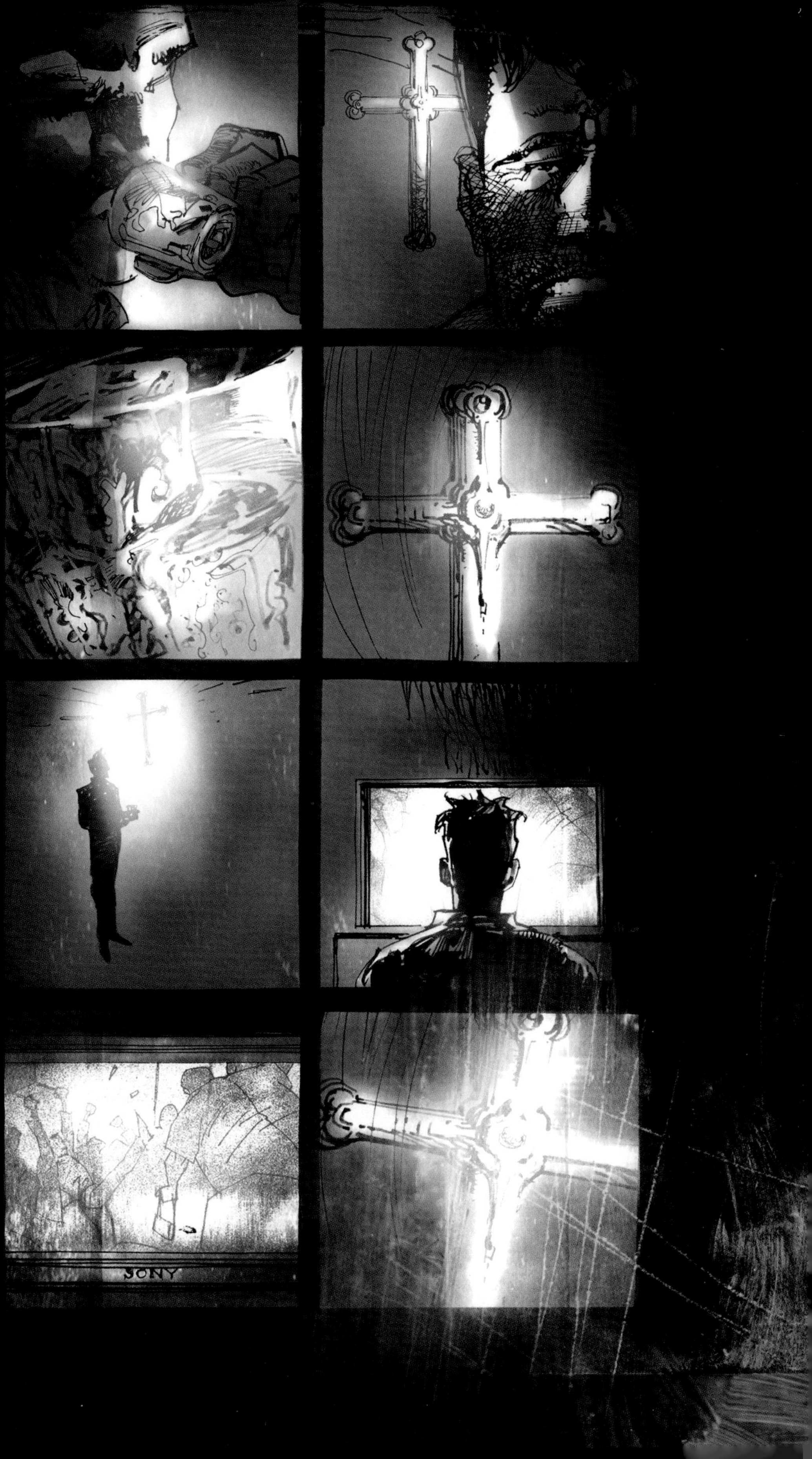
SONY

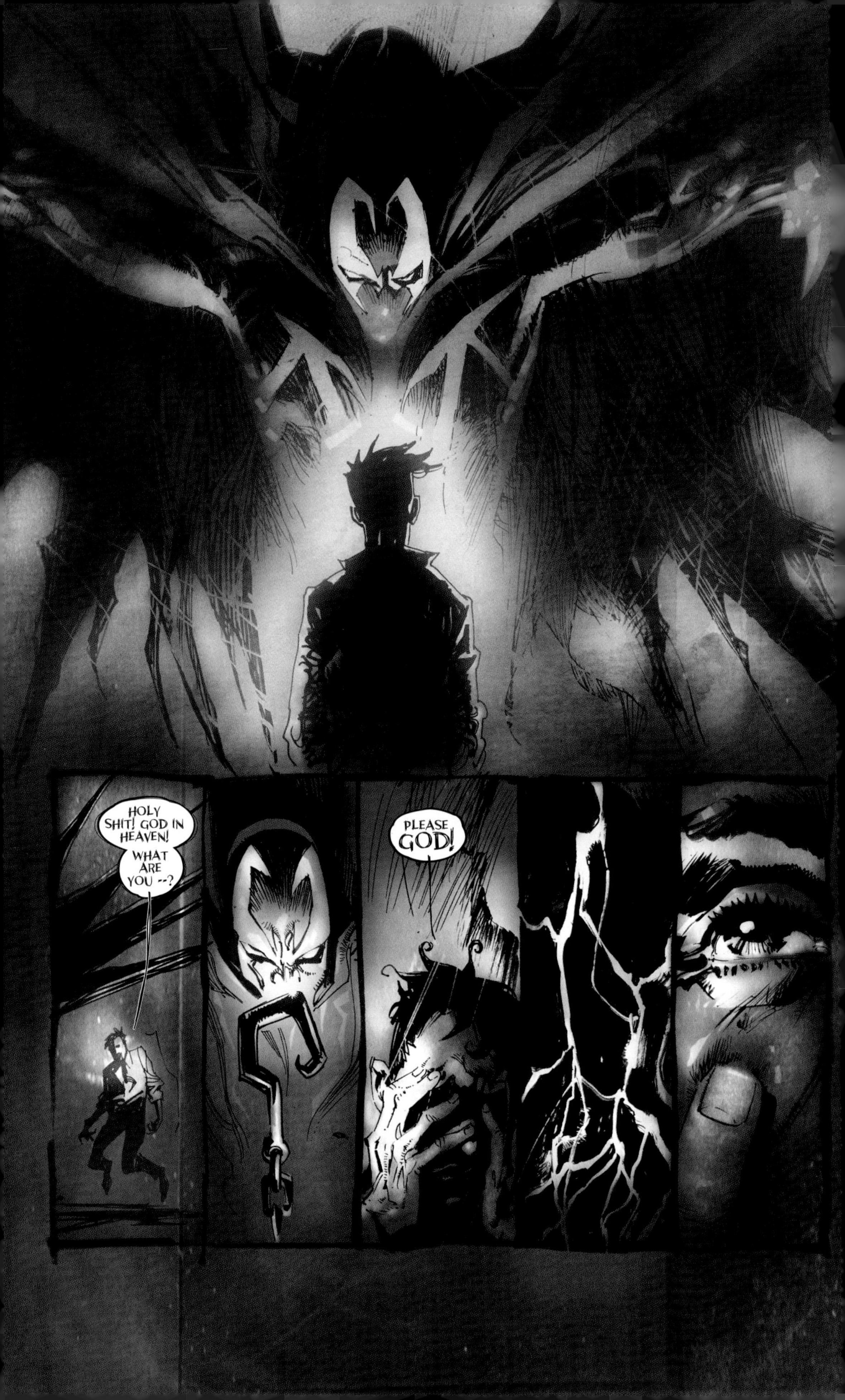
HOLY SHIT! GOD IN HEAVEN!
WHAT ARE YOU --?
PLEASE GOD!

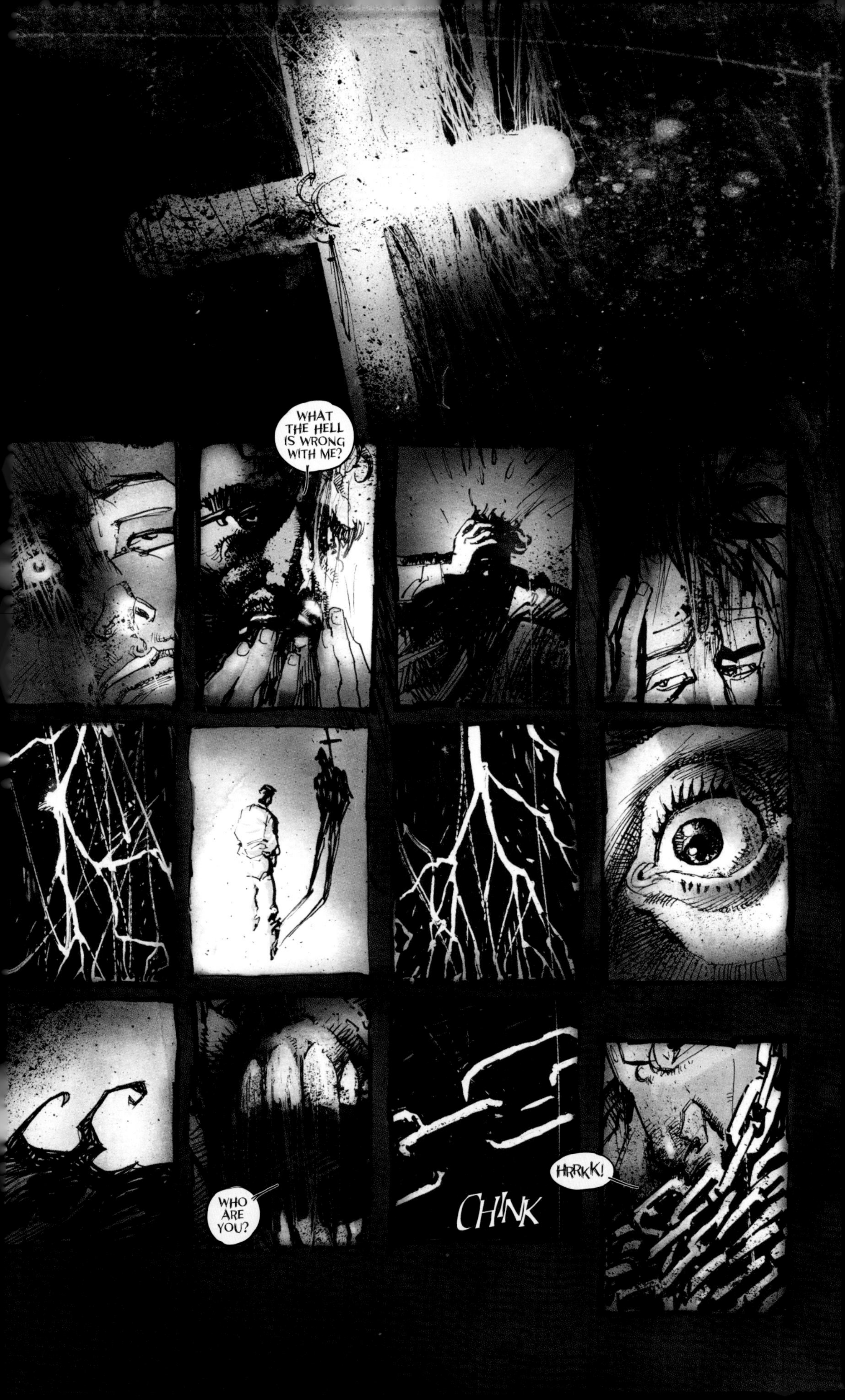

WHAT THE HELL IS WRONG WITH ME?
WHO ARE YOU?
CHINK
HRRKK!

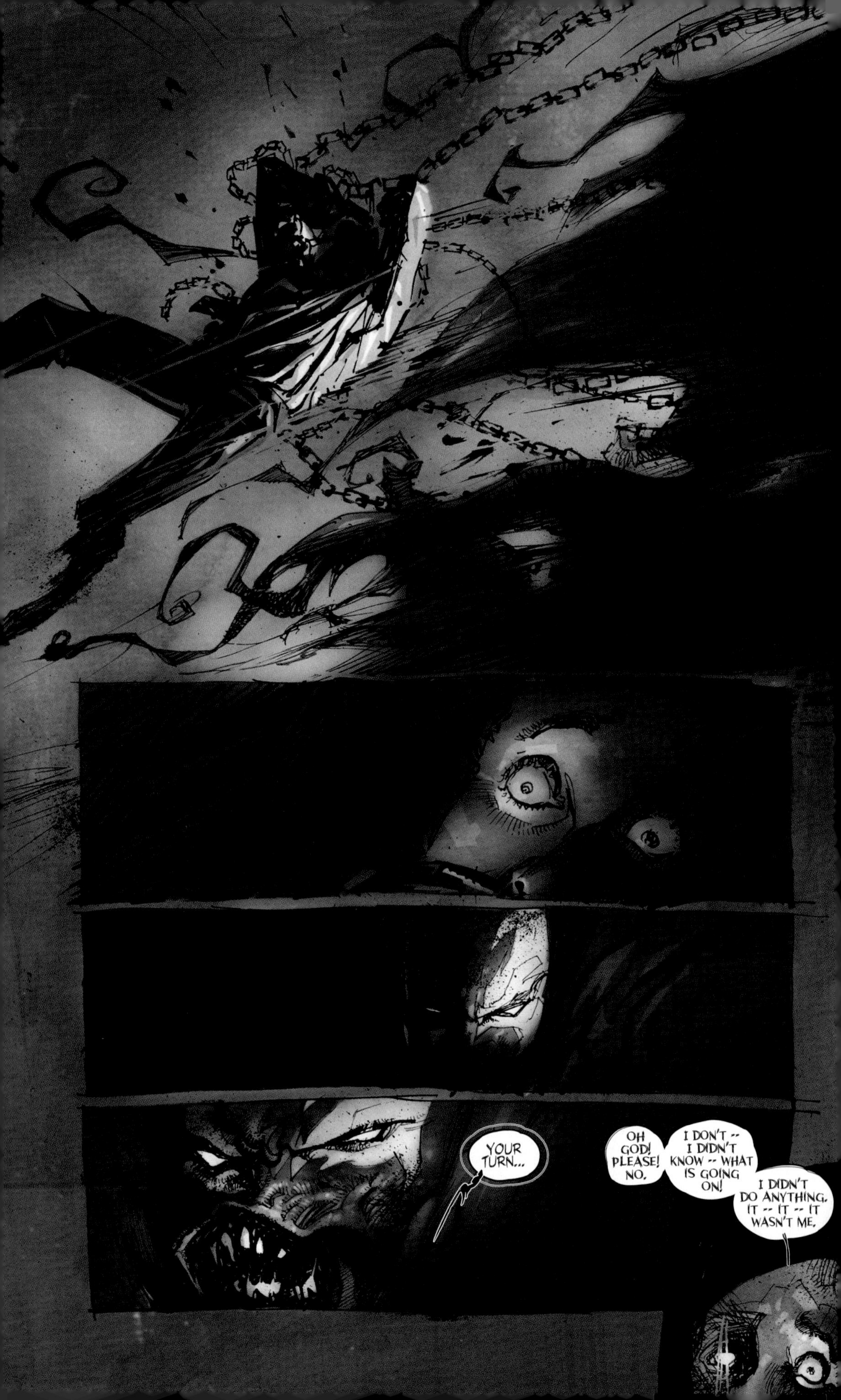
YOUR TURN...
OH GOD! PLEASE! NO.
I DON'T -- I DIDN'T KNOW -- WHAT IS GOING ON!
I DIDN'T DO ANYTHING. IT -- IT -- IT WASN'T ME.

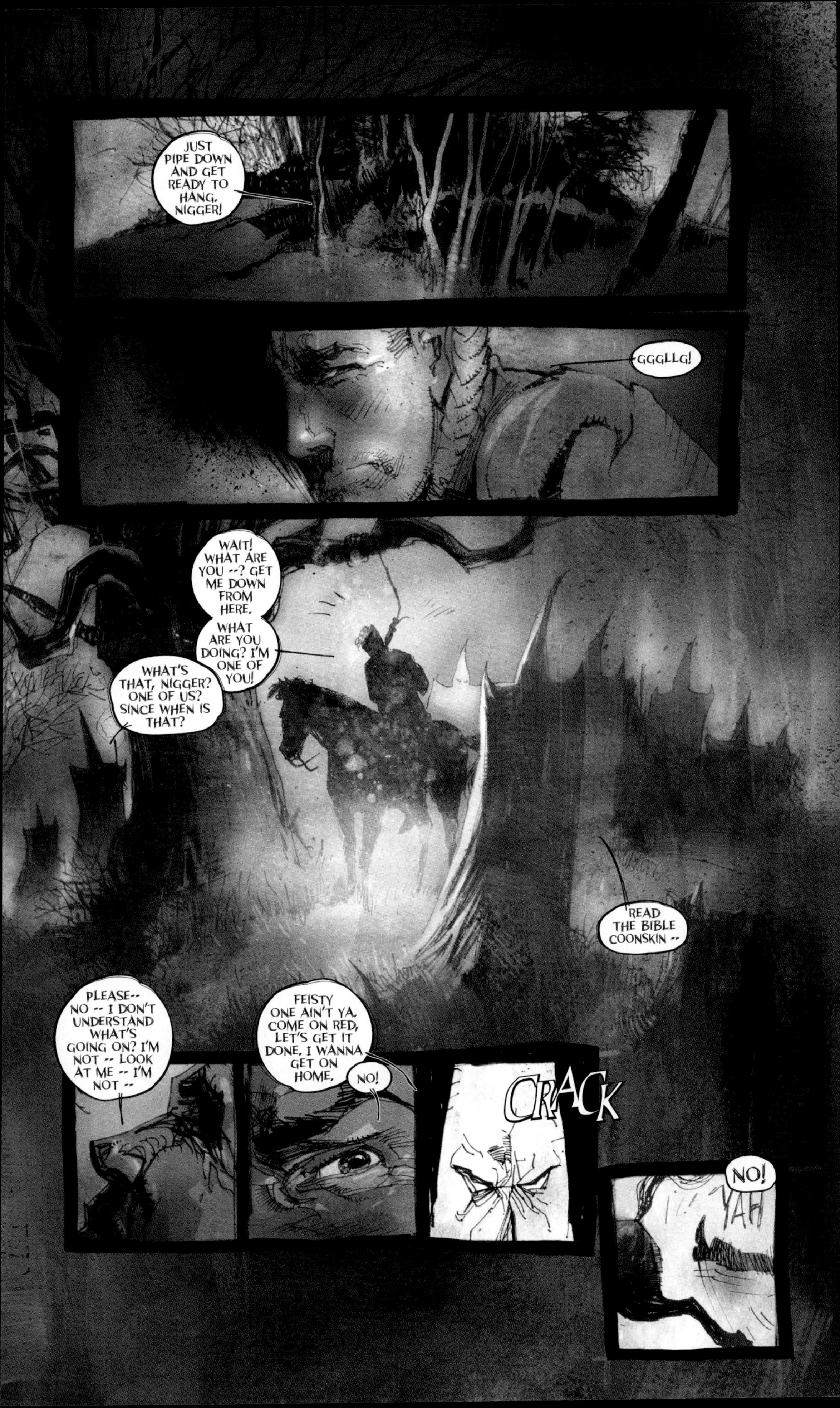
JUST PIPE DOWN AND GET READY TO HANG, NIGGER!
GGGLLG!
WAIT! WHAT ARE YOU --? GET ME DOWN FROM HERE.
WHAT ARE YOU DOING? I'M ONE OF YOU!
WHAT'S THAT, NIGGER? ONE OF US? SINCE WHEN IS THAT?
READ THE BIBLE COONSKIN --
PLEASE-- NO -- I DON'T UNDERSTAND WHAT'S GOING ON? I'M NOT -- LOOK AT ME -- I'M NOT --
FEISTY ONE AIN'T YA, COME ON RED, LET'S GET IT DONE, I WANNA GET ON HOME.
NO!
CRACK
NO!
YAH

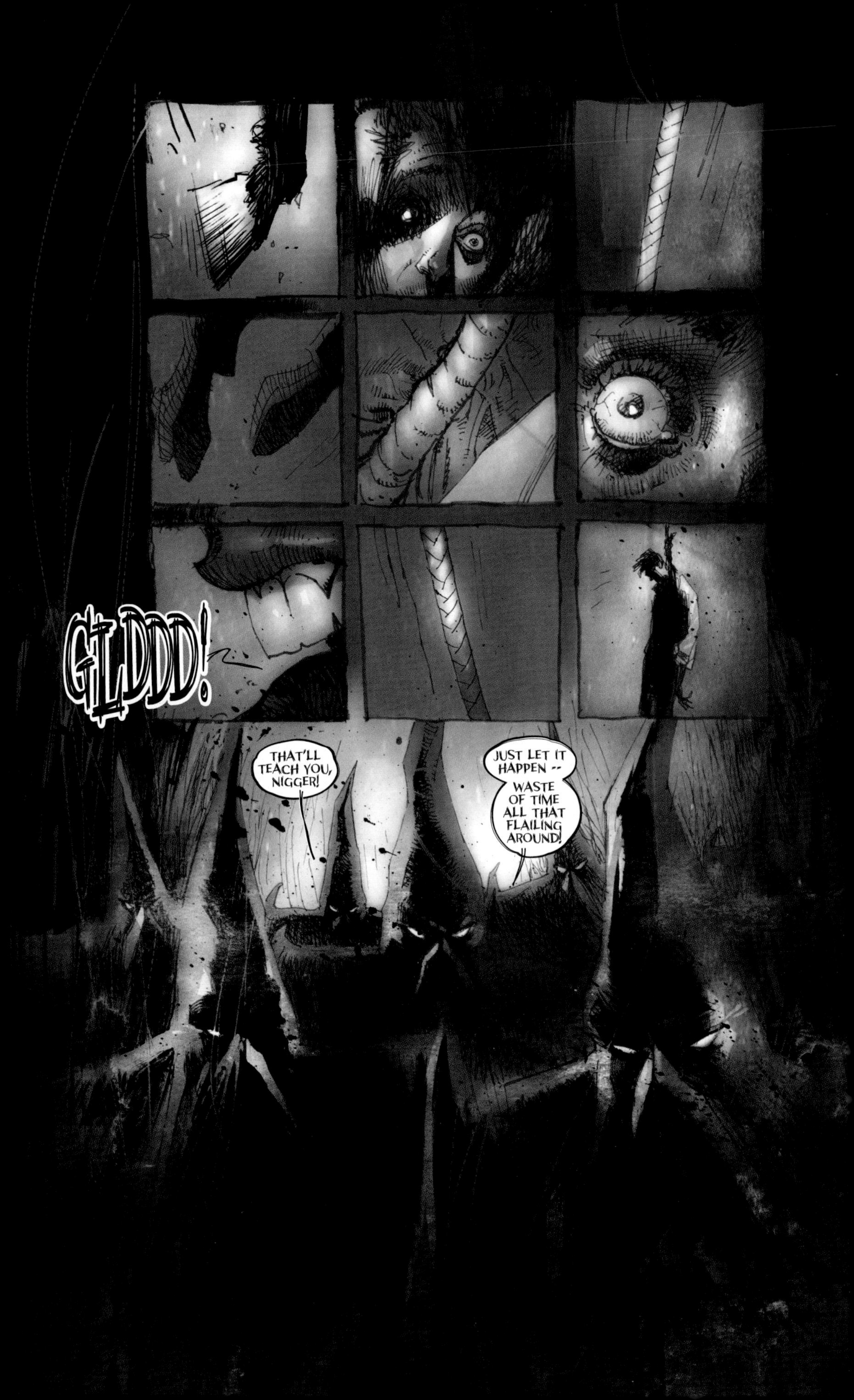
GLDDD!
THAT'LL TEACH YOU, NIGGER!
JUST LET IT HAPPEN -- WASTE OF TIME ALL THAT FLAILING AROUND!

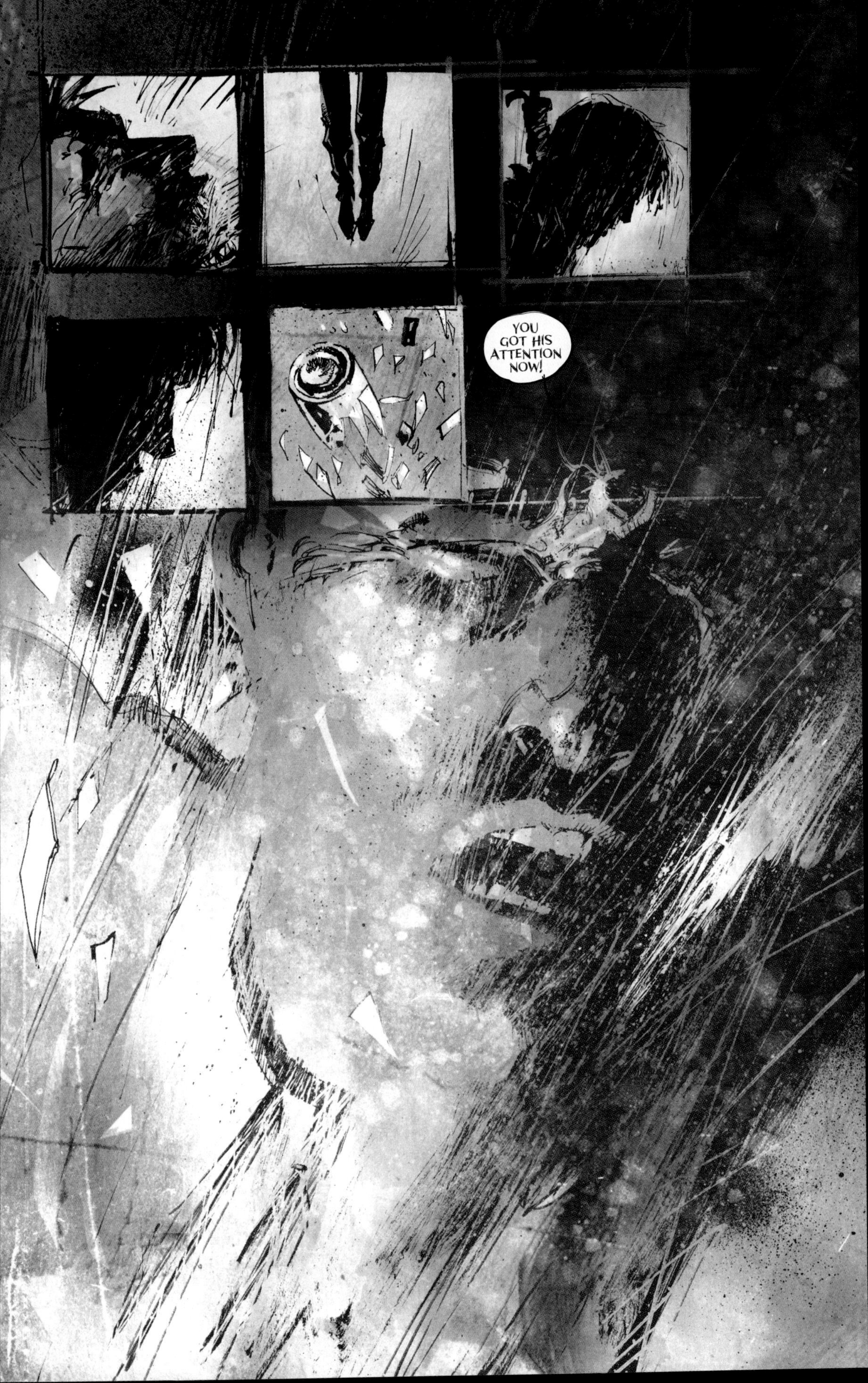
YOU GOT HIS ATTENTION NOW!

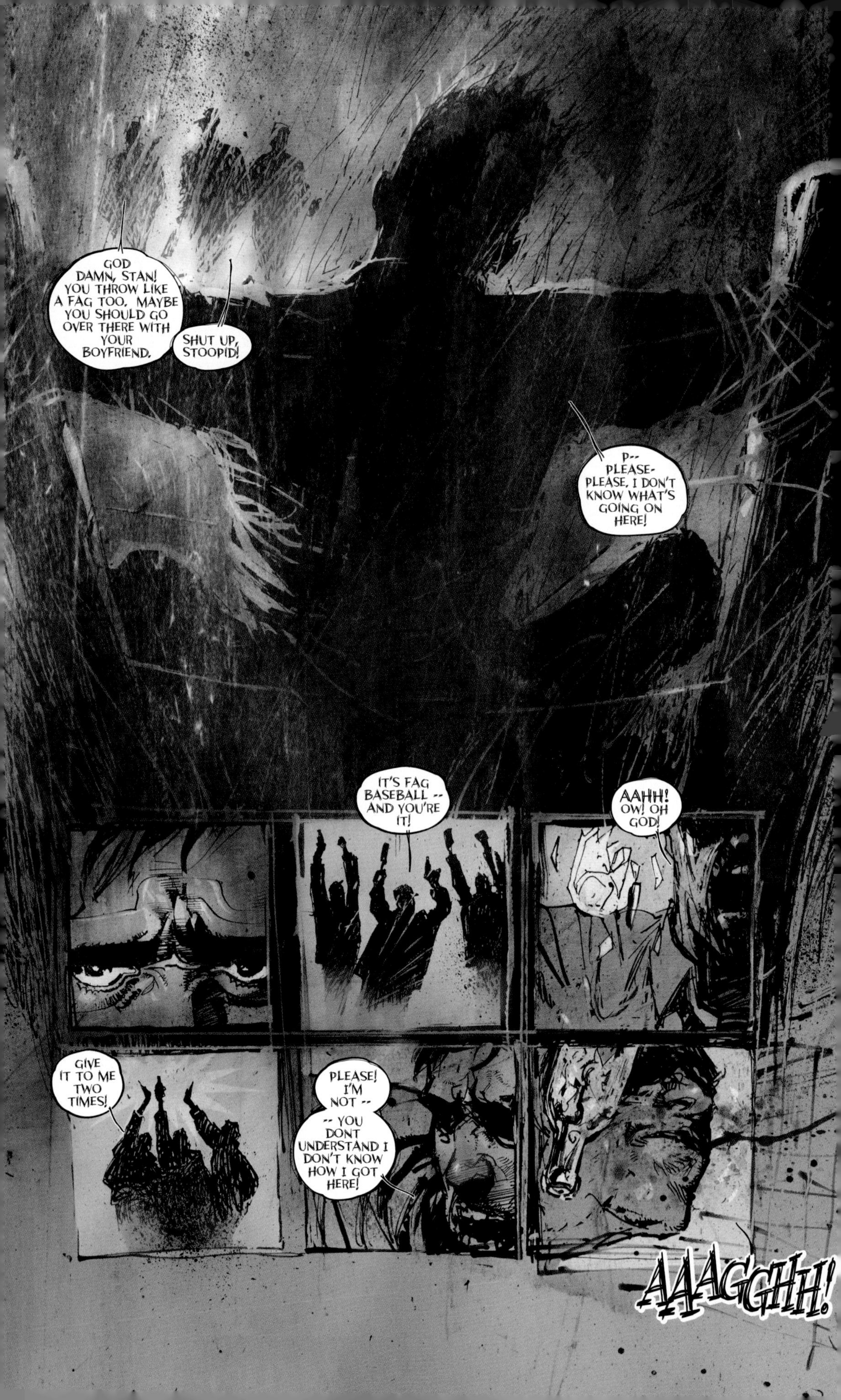
GOD DAMN, STAN! YOU THROW LIKE A FAG TOO. MAYBE YOU SHOULD GO OVER THERE WITH YOUR BOYFRIEND.
SHUT UP, STOOPID!
P-- PLEASE- PLEASE, I DON'T KNOW WHAT'S GOING ON HERE!
IT'S FAG BASEBALL -- AND YOU'RE IT!
AAHH! OW! OH GOD!
GIVE IT TO ME TWO TIMES!
PLEASE! I'M NOT --
-- YOU DONT UNDERSTAND I DON'T KNOW HOW I GOT HERE!
AAAGGHH!

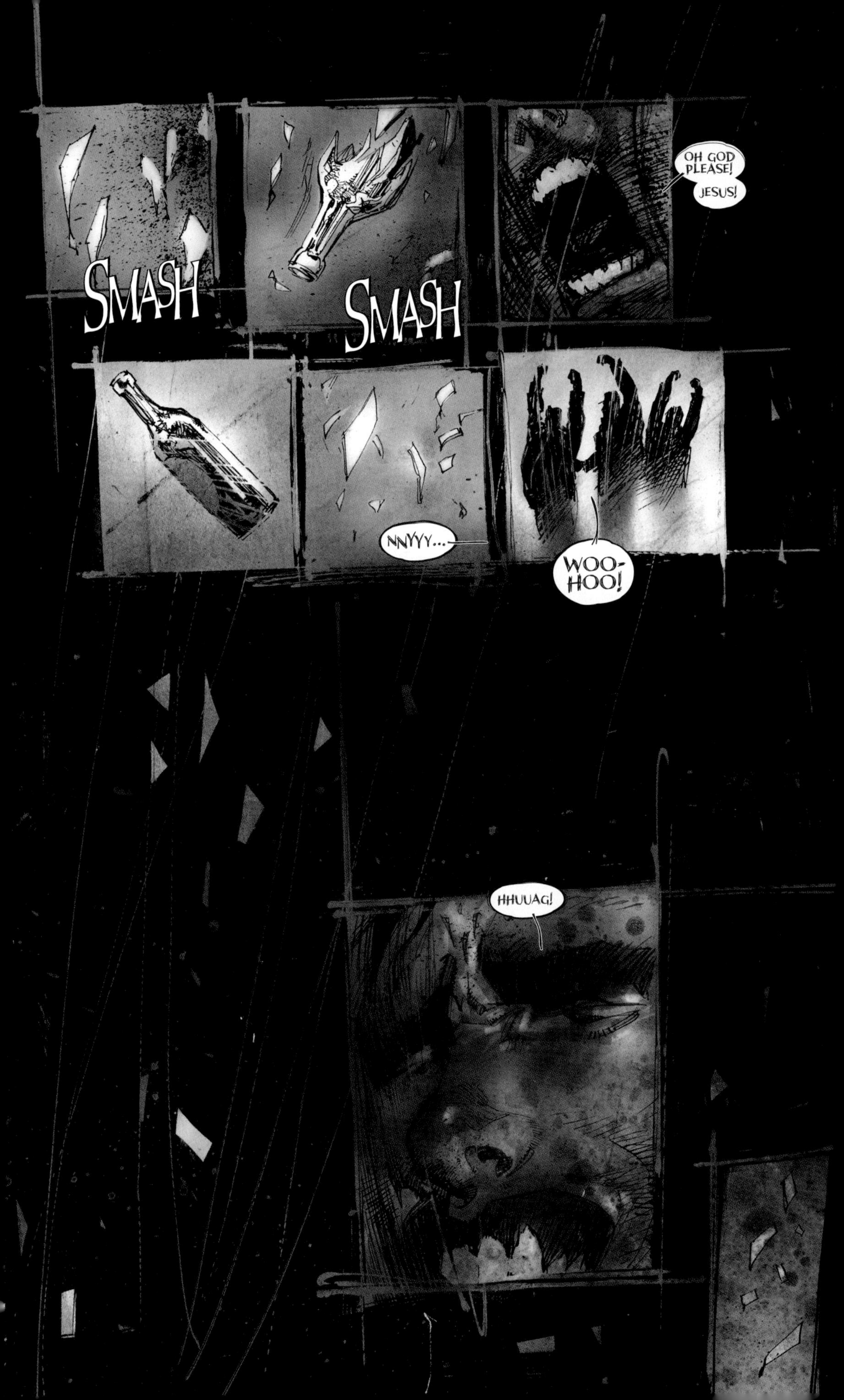
SMASH
SMASH
OH GOD PLEASE!
JESUS!
NNYYY...
WOO-HOO!
HHUUAG!

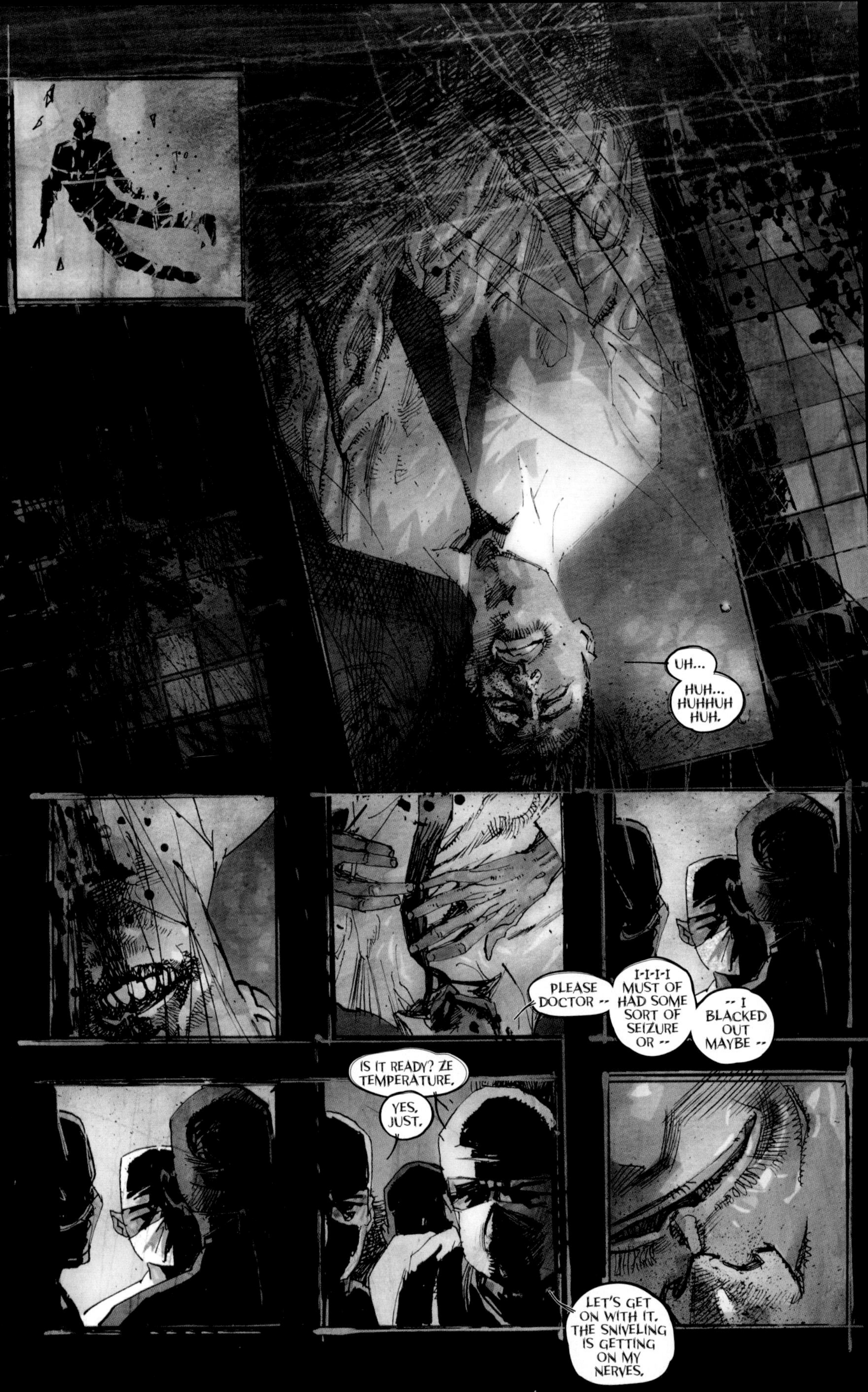
UH...
HUH... HUHHUH HUH.
PLEASE DOCTOR --
I-I-I-I MUST OF HAD SOME SORT OF SEIZURE OR --
-- I BLACKED OUT MAYBE --
IS IT READY? ZE TEMPERATURE.
YES, JUST.
LET'S GET ON WITH IT. THE SNIVELING IS GETTING ON MY NERVES.

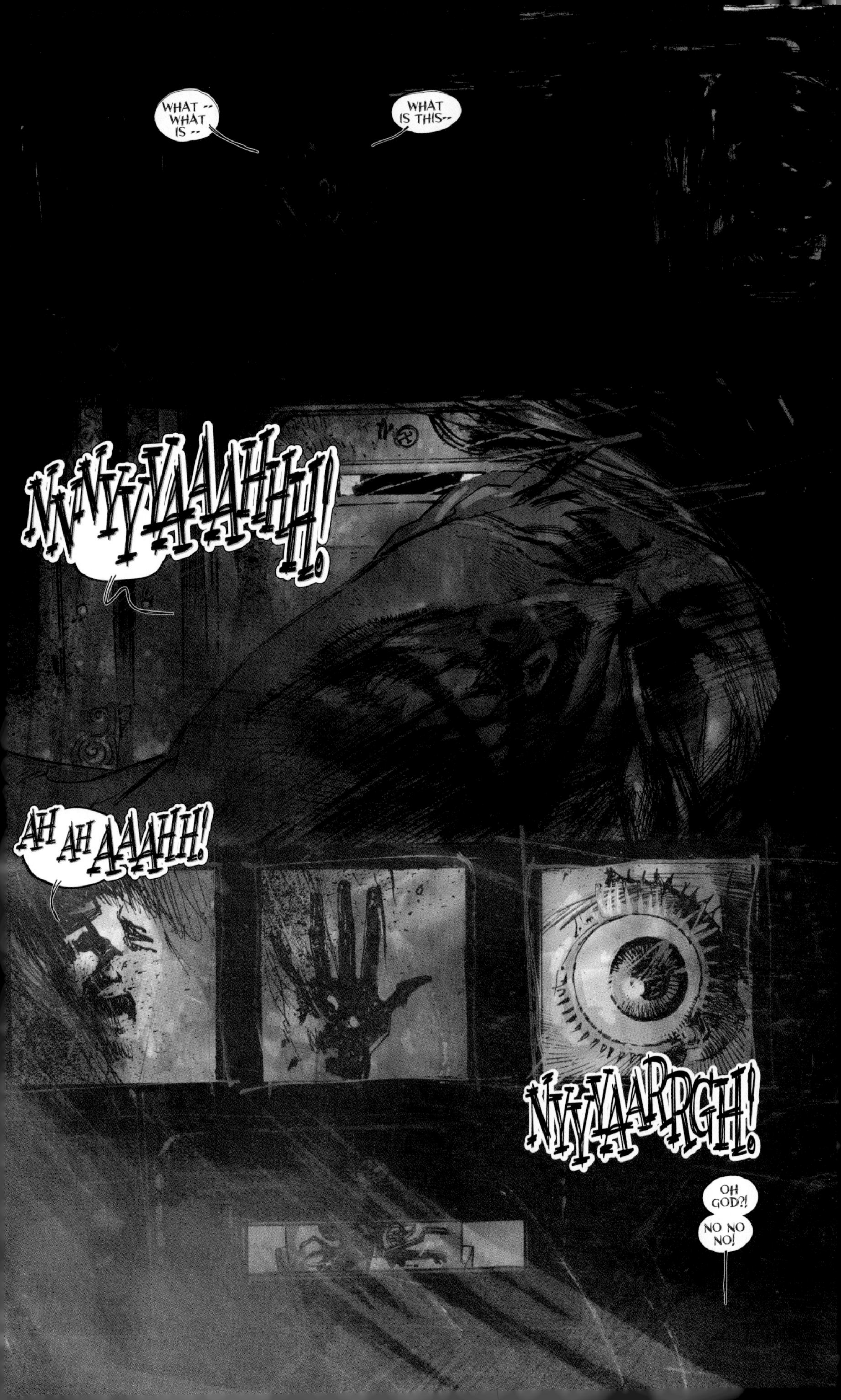
WHAT -- WHAT IS --
WHAT IS THIS--
NNNYYAAAHHH!
AH AH AAAHH!
NYYAARRGH!
OH GOD?!
NO NO NO!

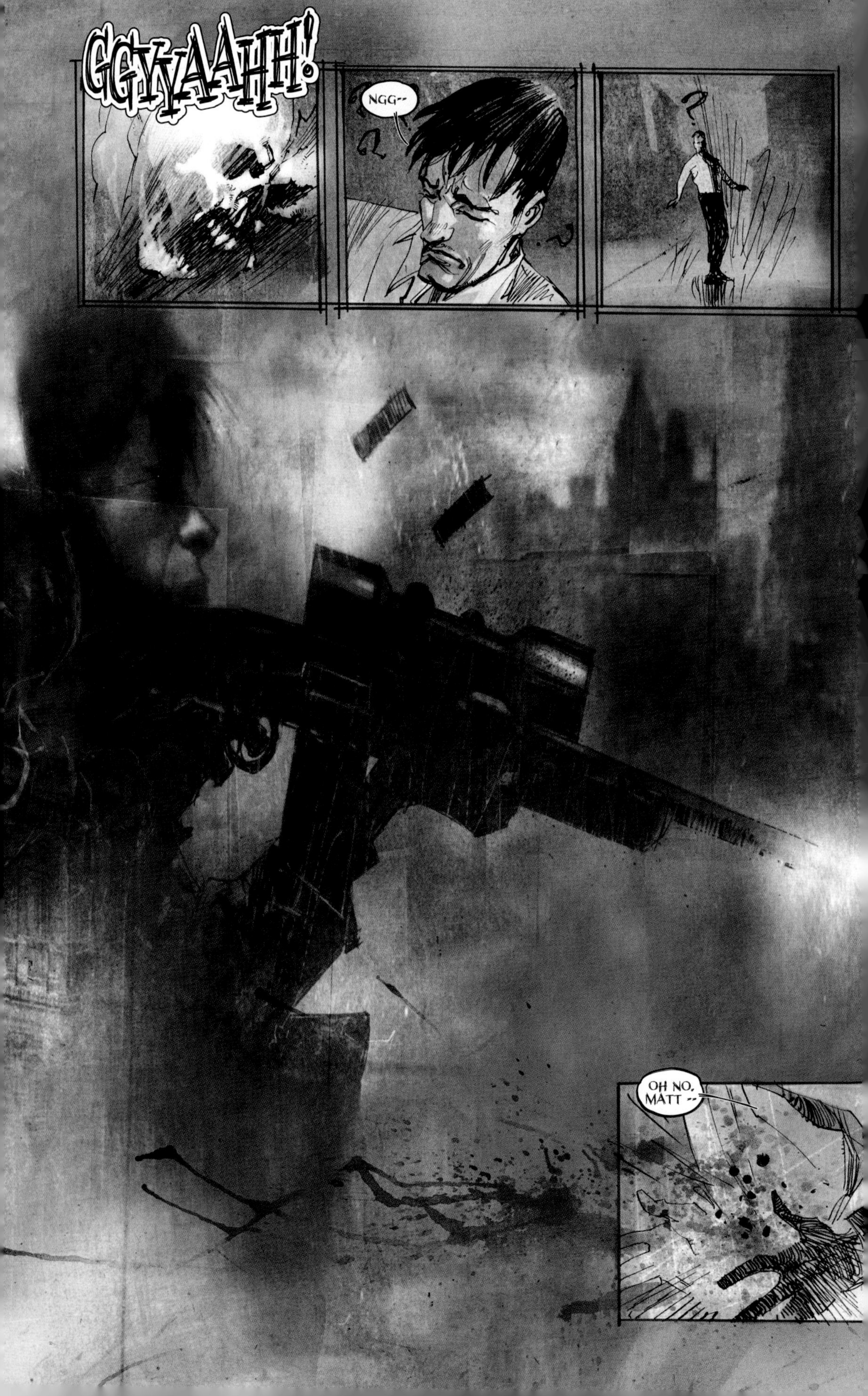
GGYAAHH!
NGG--
OH NO, MATT --

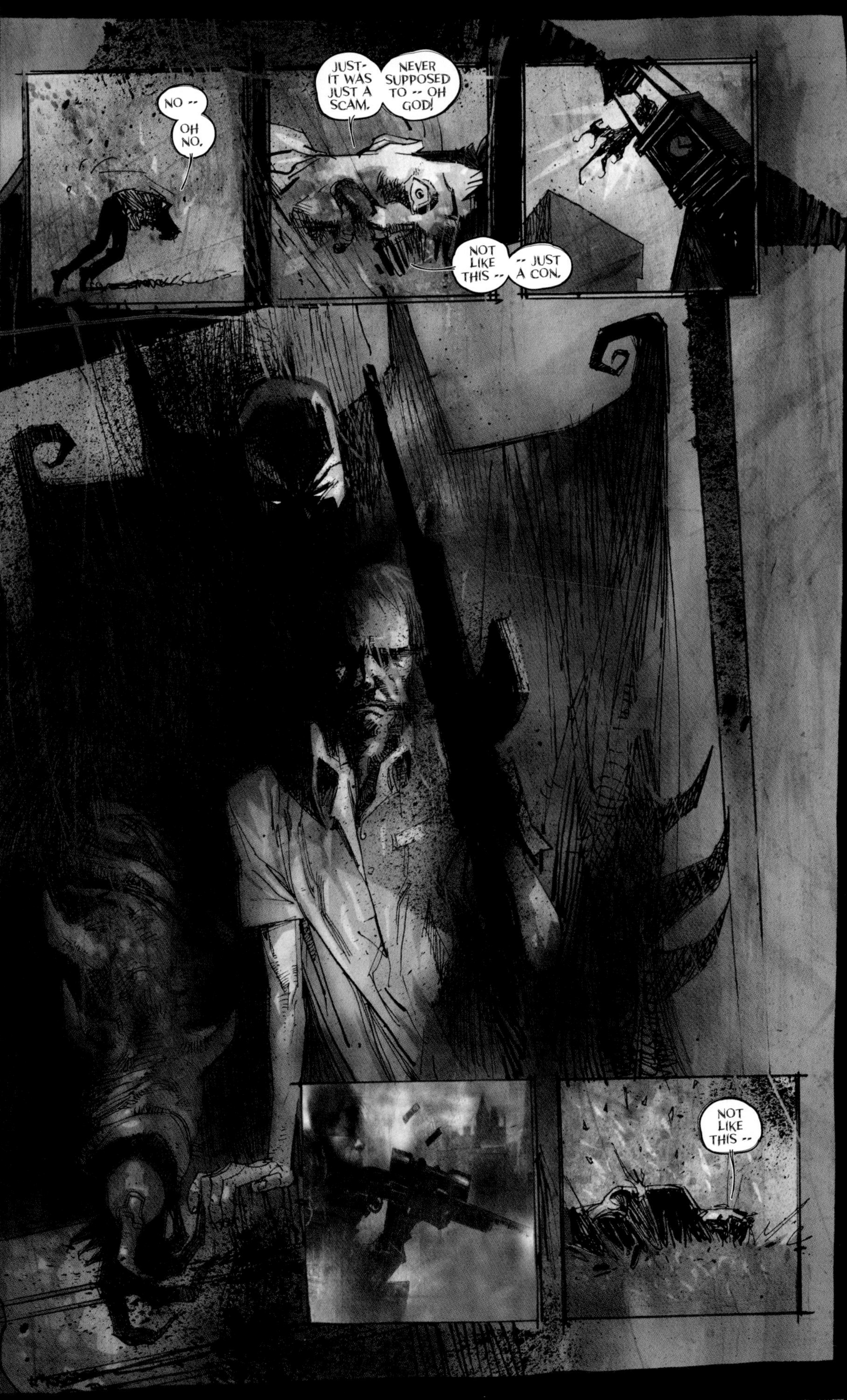
NO --
OH NO.
JUST- IT WAS JUST A SCAM.
NEVER SUPPOSED TO -- OH GOD!
NOT LIKE THIS --
-- JUST A CON.
NOT LIKE THIS --

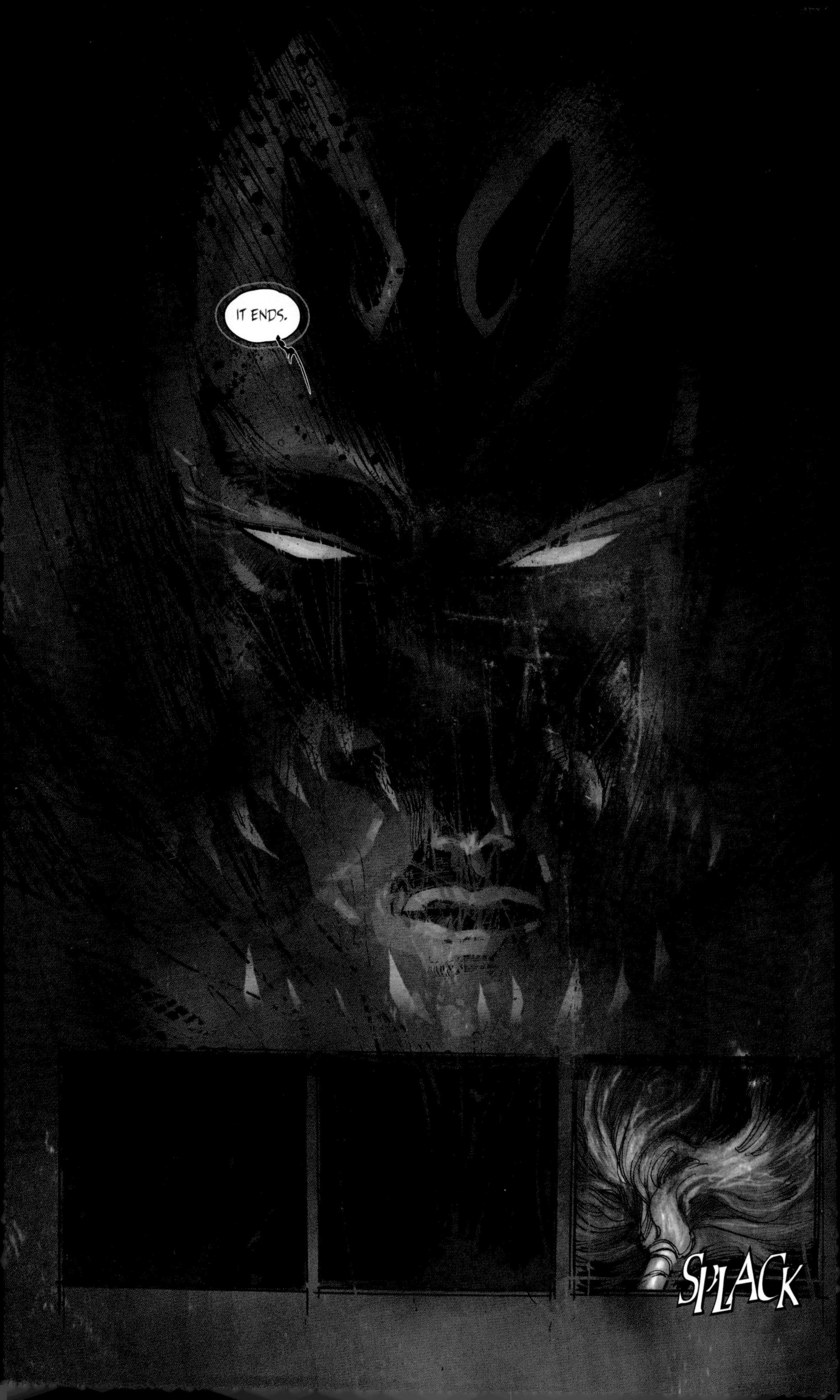
IT ENDS.
SPLACK

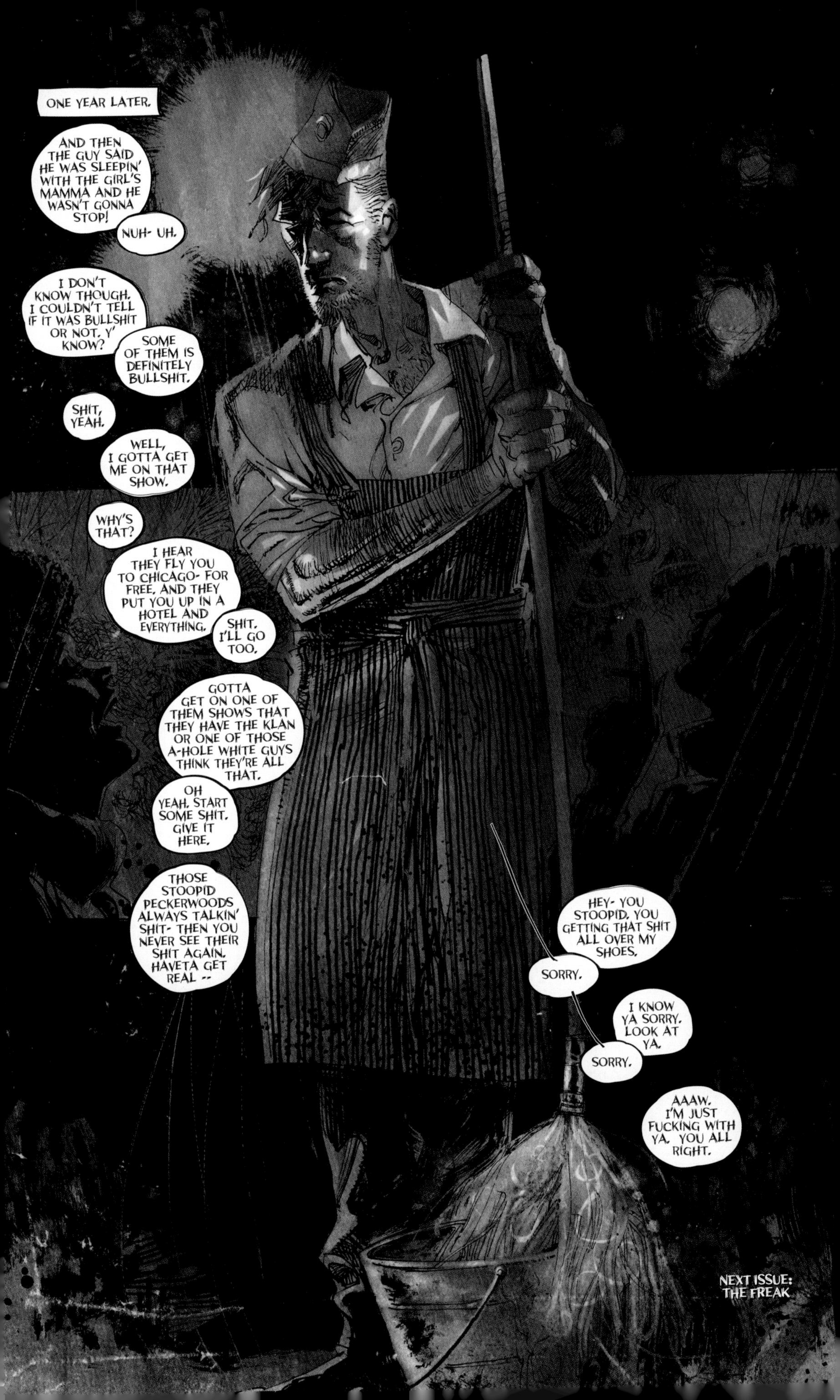
ONE YEAR LATER.
AND THEN THE GUY SAID HE WAS SLEEPIN' WITH THE GIRL'S MAMMA AND HE WASN'T GONNA STOP!
NUH- UH.
I DON'T KNOW THOUGH. I COULDN'T TELL IF IT WAS BULLSHIT OR NOT. Y' KNOW?
SOME OF THEM IS DEFINITELY BULLSHIT.
SHIT, YEAH.
WELL, I GOTTA GET ME ON THAT SHOW.
WHY'S THAT?
I HEAR THEY FLY YOU TO CHICAGO- FOR FREE, AND THEY PUT YOU UP IN A HOTEL AND EVERYTHING.
SHIT. I'LL GO TOO.
GOTTA GET ON ONE OF THEM SHOWS THAT THEY HAVE THE KLAN OR ONE OF THOSE A-HOLE WHITE GUYS THINK THEY'RE ALL THAT.
OH YEAH. START SOME SHIT. GIVE IT HERE.
THOSE STOOPID PECKERWOODS ALWAYS TALKIN' SHIT- THEN YOU NEVER SEE THEIR SHIT AGAIN. HAVETA GET REAL --
HEY- YOU STOOPID. YOU GETTING THAT SHIT ALL OVER MY SHOES.
SORRY.
I KNOW YA SORRY. LOOK AT YA.
SORRY.
AAAW. I'M JUST FUCKING WITH YA. YOU ALL RIGHT.
NEXT ISSUE: THE FREAK

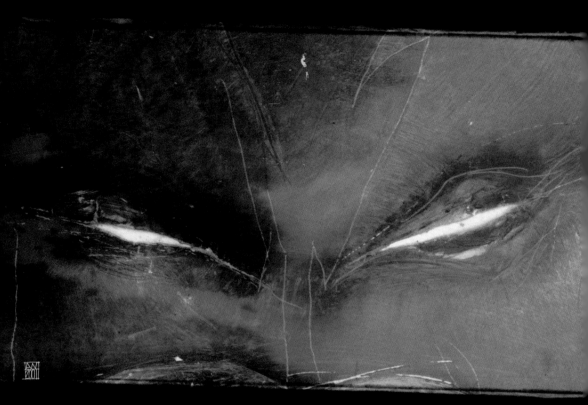

ISSUE FIVE

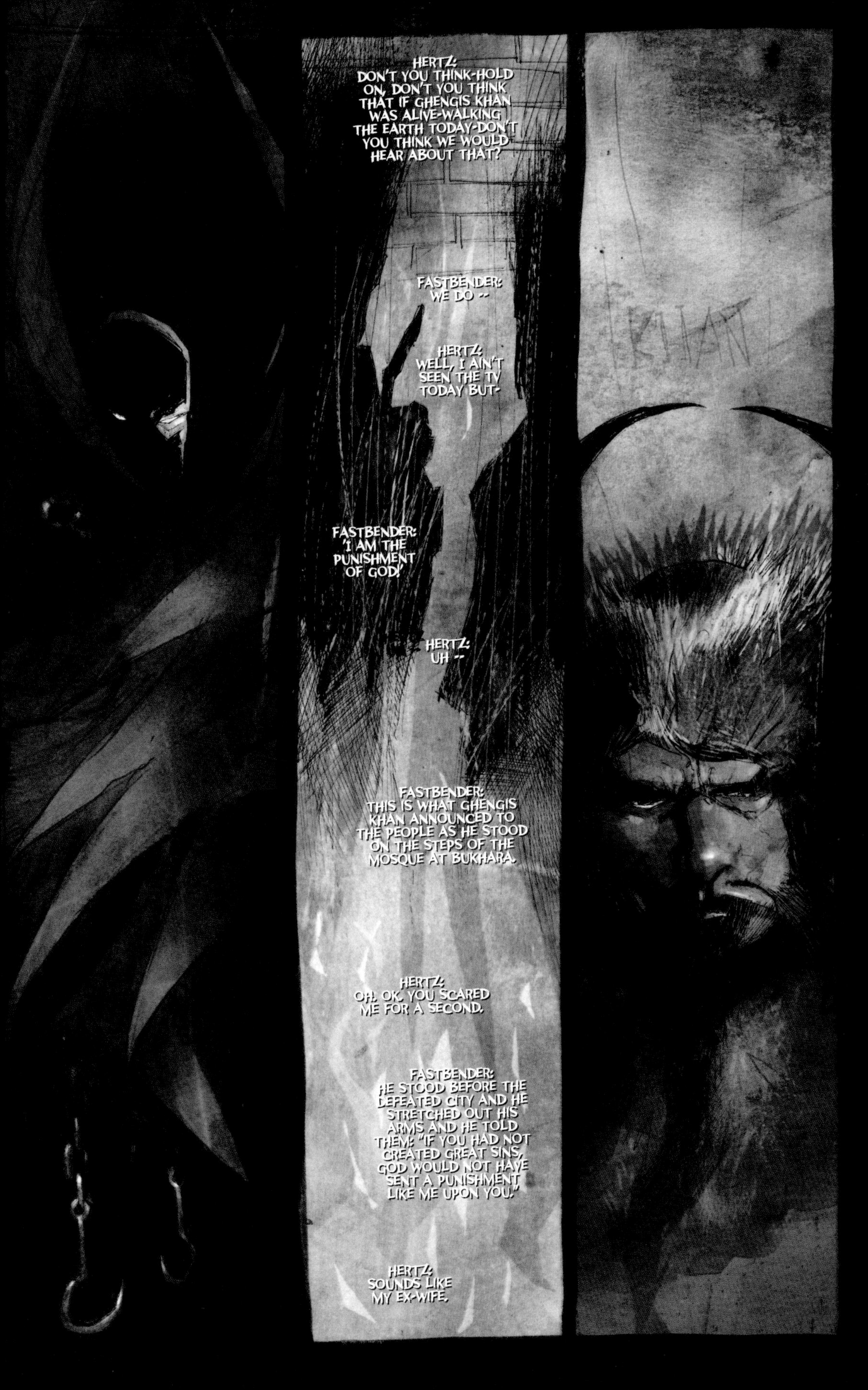
HERTZ:
DON'T YOU THINK-HOLD ON, DON'T YOU THINK THAT IF GHENGIS KHAN WAS ALIVE-WALKING THE EARTH TODAY-DON'T YOU THINK WE WOULD HEAR ABOUT THAT?
FASTBENDER:
WE DO --
HERTZ:
WELL, I AIN'T SEEN THE TV TODAY BUT-
FASTBENDER:
'I AM THE PUNISHMENT OF GOD!'
HERTZ:
UH --
FASTBENDER:
THIS IS WHAT GHENGIS KHAN ANNOUNCED TO THE PEOPLE AS HE STOOD ON THE STEPS OF THE MOSQUE AT BUKHARA.
HERTZ:
OH. OK. YOU SCARED ME FOR A SECOND.
FASTBENDER:
HE STOOD BEFORE THE DEFEATED CITY AND HE STRETCHED OUT HIS ARMS AND HE TOLD THEM: "IF YOU HAD NOT CREATED GREAT SINS, GOD WOULD NOT HAVE SENT A PUNISHMENT LIKE ME UPON YOU."
HERTZ:
SOUNDS LIKE MY EX-WIFE.
KHAN

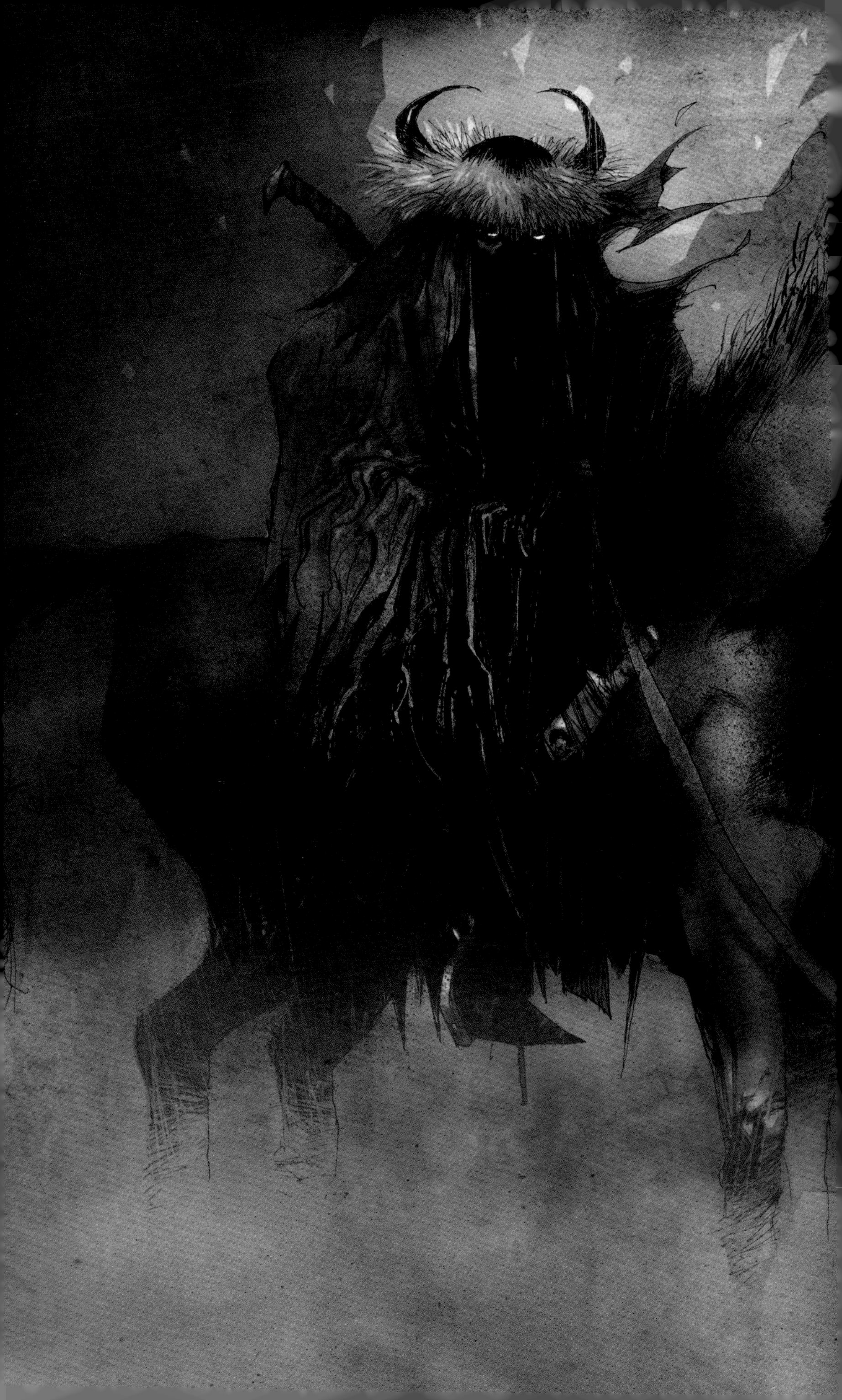

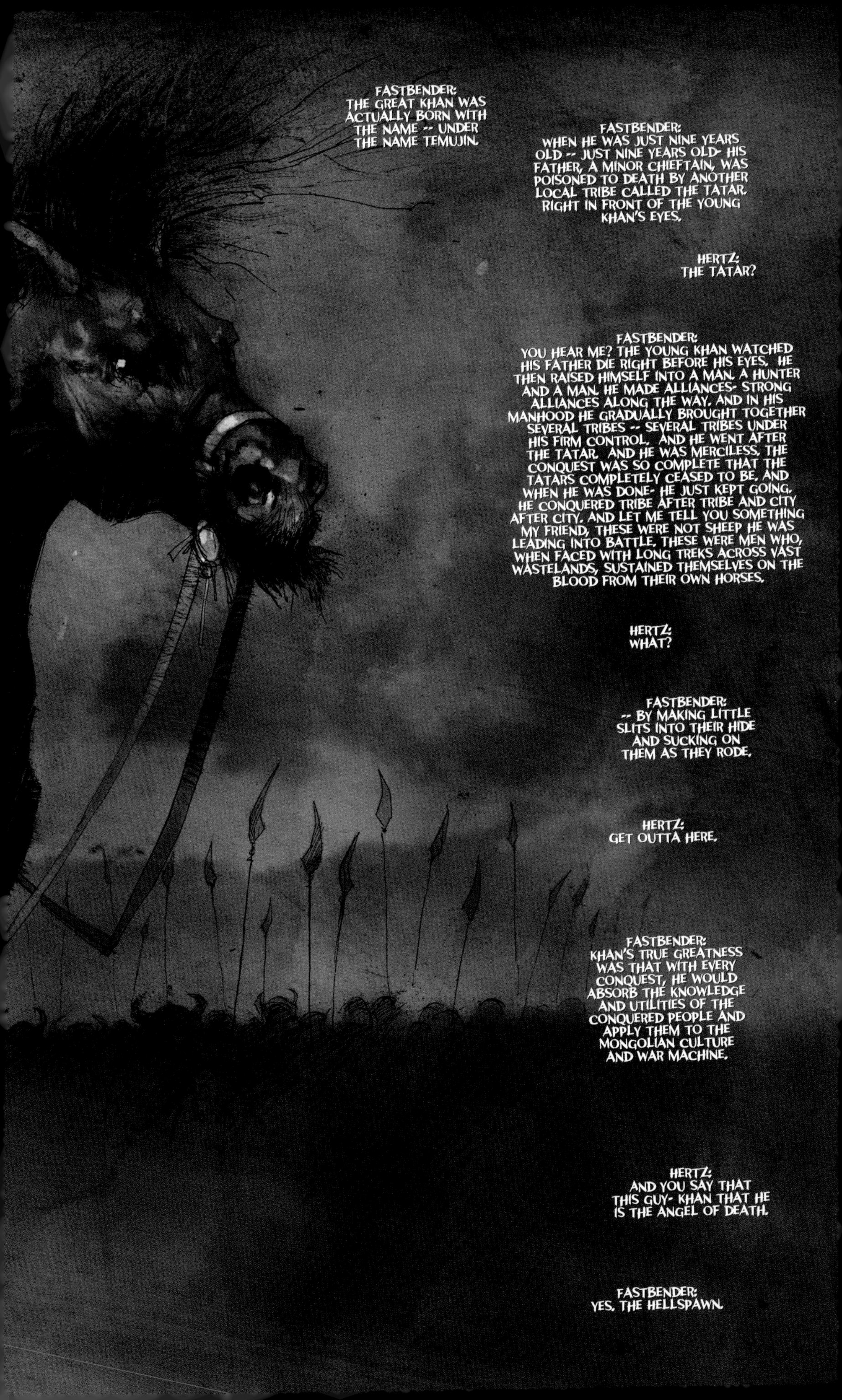
FASTBENDER: THE GREAT KHAN WAS ACTUALLY BORN WITH THE NAME -- UNDER THE NAME TEMUJIN.
FASTBENDER: WHEN HE WAS JUST NINE YEARS OLD -- JUST NINE YEARS OLD- HIS FATHER, A MINOR CHIEFTAIN, WAS POISONED TO DEATH BY ANOTHER LOCAL TRIBE CALLED THE TATAR. RIGHT IN FRONT OF THE YOUNG KHAN'S EYES.
HERTZ: THE TATAR?
FASTBENDER: YOU HEAR ME? THE YOUNG KHAN WATCHED HIS FATHER DIE RIGHT BEFORE HIS EYES. HE THEN RAISED HIMSELF INTO A MAN. A HUNTER AND A MAN. HE MADE ALLIANCES- STRONG ALLIANCES ALONG THE WAY. AND IN HIS MANHOOD HE GRADUALLY BROUGHT TOGETHER SEVERAL TRIBES -- SEVERAL TRIBES UNDER HIS FIRM CONTROL. AND HE WENT AFTER THE TATAR. AND HE WAS MERCILESS. THE CONQUEST WAS SO COMPLETE THAT THE TATARS COMPLETELY CEASED TO BE. AND WHEN HE WAS DONE- HE JUST KEPT GOING. HE CONQUERED TRIBE AFTER TRIBE AND CITY AFTER CITY. AND LET ME TELL YOU SOMETHING MY FRIEND, THESE WERE NOT SHEEP HE WAS LEADING INTO BATTLE. THESE WERE MEN WHO, WHEN FACED WITH LONG TREKS ACROSS VAST WASTELANDS, SUSTAINED THEMSELVES ON THE BLOOD FROM THEIR OWN HORSES.
HERTZ: WHAT?
FASTBENDER: -- BY MAKING LITTLE SLITS INTO THEIR HIDE AND SUCKING ON THEM AS THEY RODE.
HERTZ: GET OUTTA HERE.
FASTBENDER: KHAN'S TRUE GREATNESS WAS THAT WITH EVERY CONQUEST, HE WOULD ABSORB THE KNOWLEDGE AND UTILITIES OF THE CONQUERED PEOPLE AND APPLY THEM TO THE MONGOLIAN CULTURE AND WAR MACHINE.
HERTZ: AND YOU SAY THAT THIS GUY- KHAN THAT HE IS THE ANGEL OF DEATH.
FASTBENDER: YES. THE HELLSPAWN.

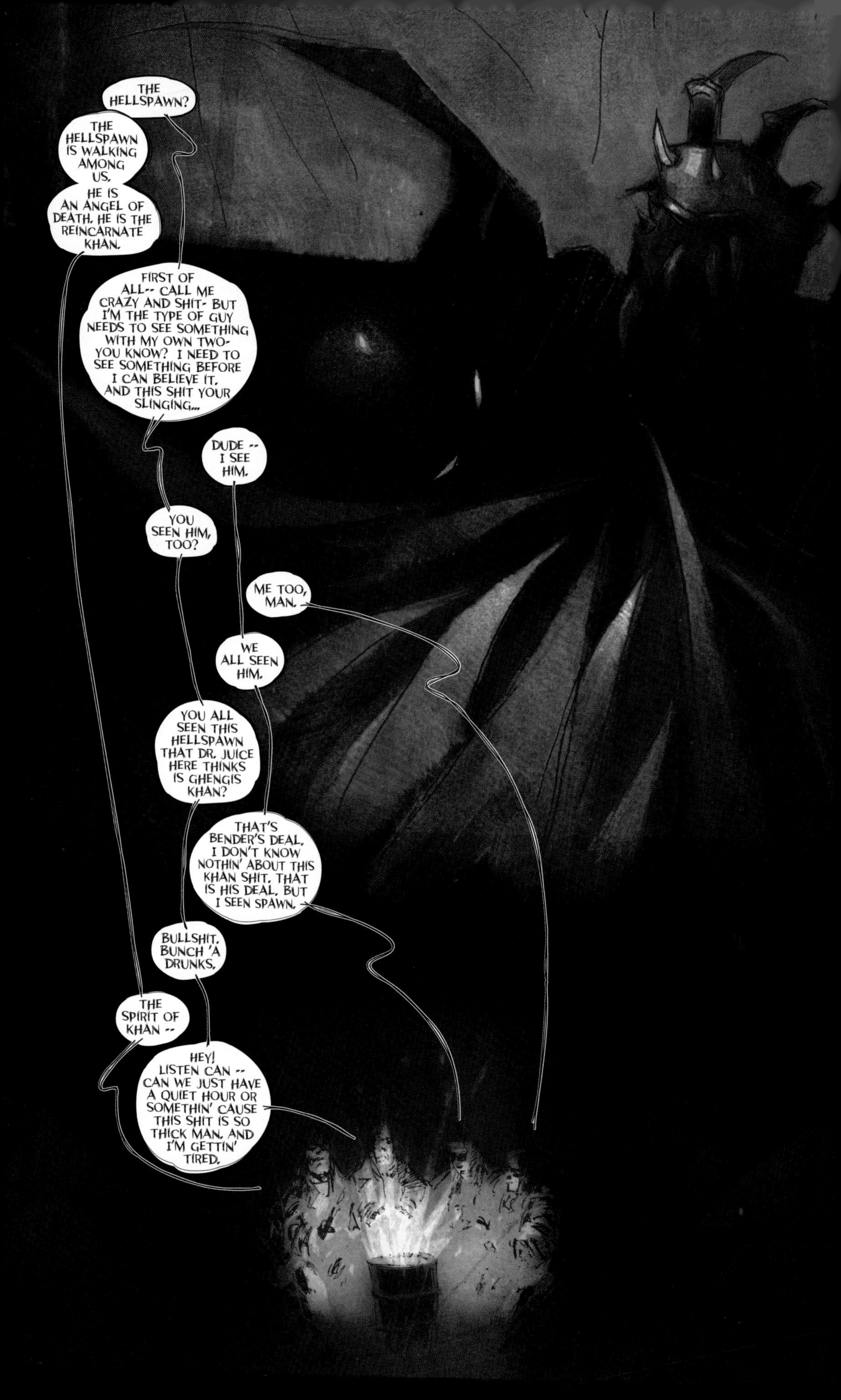
THE HELLSPAWN?
THE HELLSPAWN IS WALKING AMONG US.
HE IS AN ANGEL OF DEATH. HE IS THE REINCARNATE KHAN.
FIRST OF ALL-- CALL ME CRAZY AND SHIT- BUT I'M THE TYPE OF GUY NEEDS TO SEE SOMETHING WITH MY OWN TWO- YOU KNOW? I NEED TO SEE SOMETHING BEFORE I CAN BELIEVE IT. AND THIS SHIT YOUR SLINGING...
DUDE -- I SEE HIM.
YOU SEEN HIM, TOO?
ME TOO, MAN.
WE ALL SEEN HIM.
YOU ALL SEEN THIS HELLSPAWN THAT DR. JUICE HERE THINKS IS GHENGIS KHAN?
THAT'S BENDER'S DEAL. I DON'T KNOW NOTHIN' ABOUT THIS KHAN SHIT. THAT IS HIS DEAL. BUT I SEEN SPAWN.
BULLSHIT. BUNCH 'A DRUNKS.
THE SPIRIT OF KHAN --
HEY! LISTEN CAN -- CAN WE JUST HAVE A QUIET HOUR OR SOMETHIN' CAUSE THIS SHIT IS SO THICK MAN. AND I'M GETTIN' TIRED.

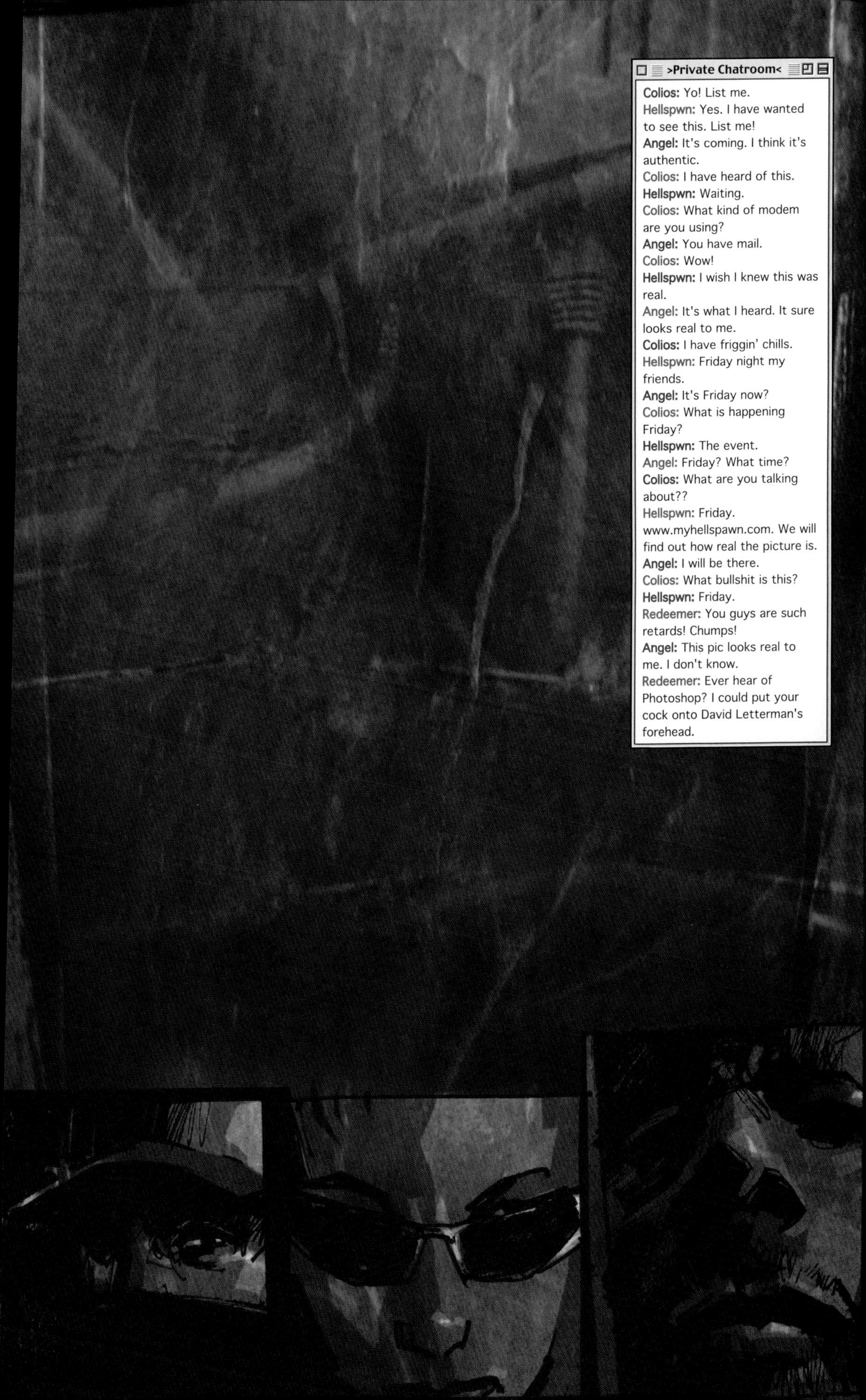
>Private Chatroom<
Colios: Yo! List me.
Hellspwn: Yes. I have wanted to see this. List me!
Angel: It's coming. I think it's authentic.
Colios: I have heard of this.
Hellspwn: Waiting.
Colios: What kind of modem are you using?
Angel: You have mail.
Colios: Wow!
Hellspwn: I wish I knew this was real.
Angel: It's what I heard. It sure looks real to me.
Colios: I have friggin' chills.
Hellspwn: Friday night my friends.
Angel: It's Friday now?
Colios: What is happening Friday?
Hellspwn: The event.
Angel: Friday? What time?
Colios: What are you talking about??
Hellspwn: Friday. www.myhellspawn.com. We will find out how real the picture is.
Angel: I will be there.
Colios: What bullshit is this?
Hellspwn: Friday.
Redeemer: You guys are such retards! Chumps!
Angel: This pic looks real to me. I don't know.
Redeemer: Ever hear of Photoshop? I could put your cock onto David Letterman's forehead.

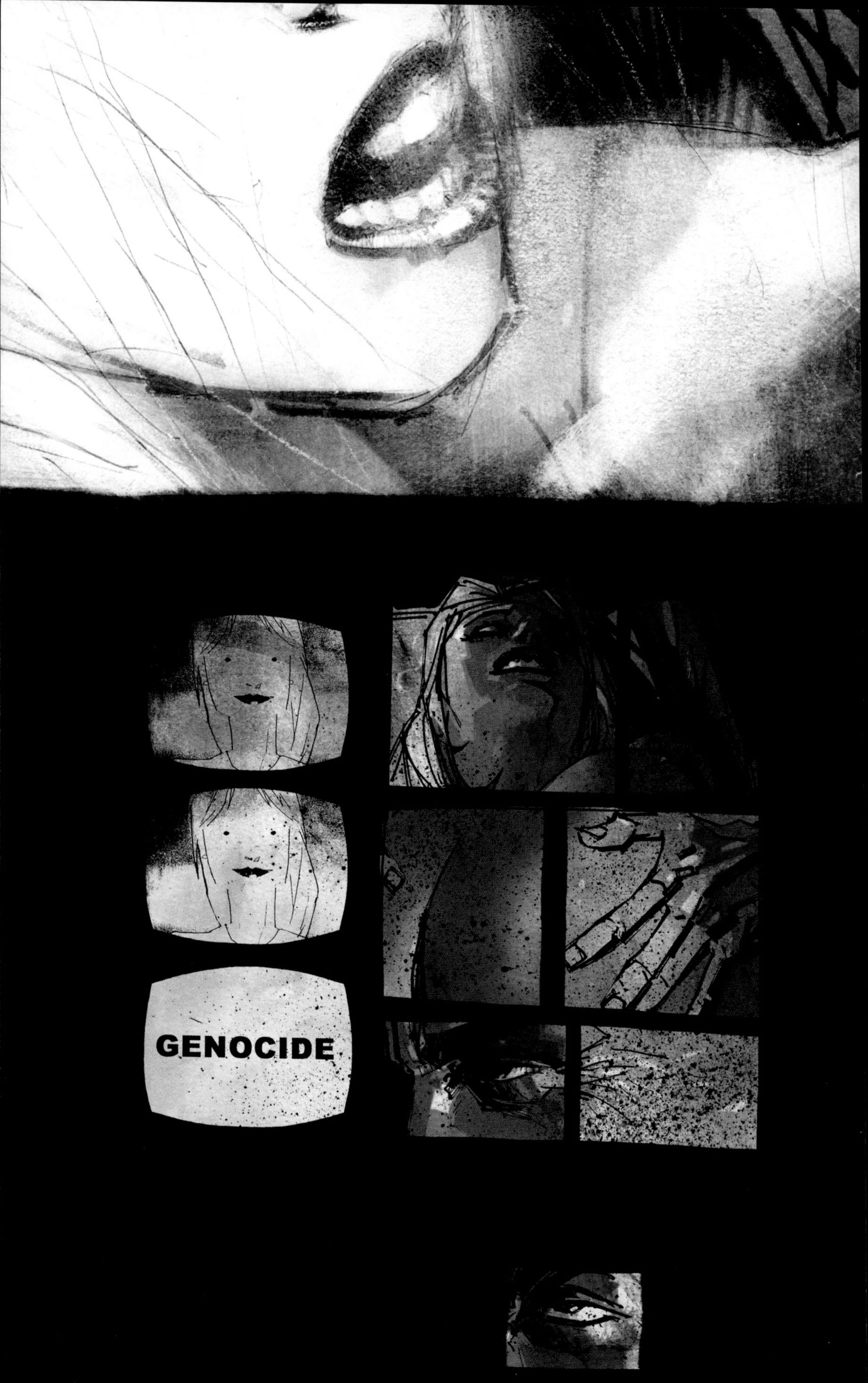
GENOCIDE

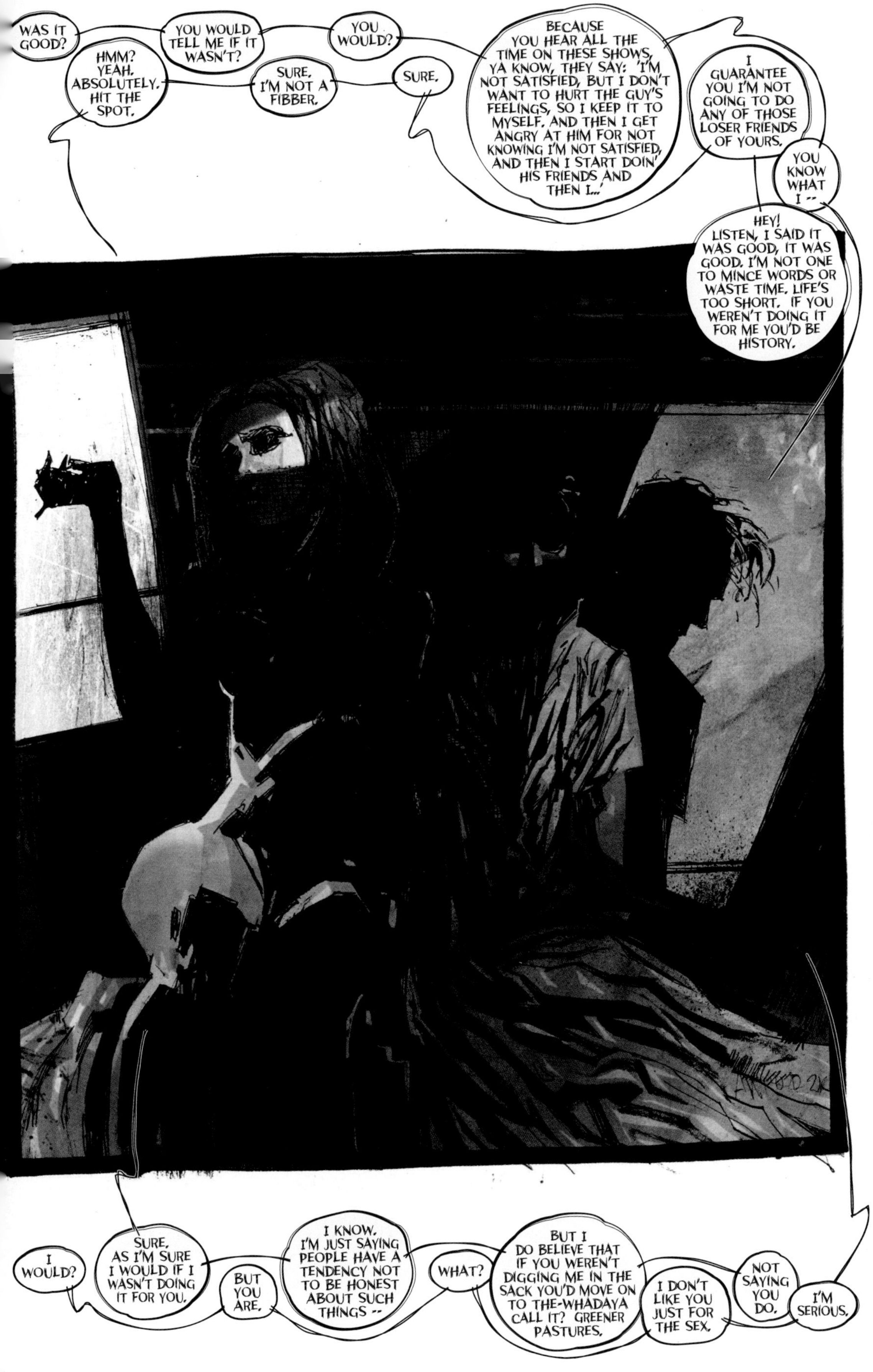

WAS IT GOOD?
HMM? YEAH, ABSOLUTELY. HIT THE SPOT.
YOU WOULD TELL ME IF IT WASN'T?
SURE, I'M NOT A FIBBER.
YOU WOULD?
SURE.
BECAUSE YOU HEAR ALL THE TIME ON THESE SHOWS, YA KNOW, THEY SAY: 'I'M NOT SATISFIED, BUT I DON'T WANT TO HURT THE GUY'S FEELINGS, SO I KEEP IT TO MYSELF. AND THEN I GET ANGRY AT HIM FOR NOT KNOWING I'M NOT SATISFIED, AND THEN I START DOIN' HIS FRIENDS AND THEN I...'
I GUARANTEE YOU I'M NOT GOING TO DO ANY OF THOSE LOSER FRIENDS OF YOURS.
YOU KNOW WHAT I --
HEY! LISTEN, I SAID IT WAS GOOD, IT WAS GOOD. I'M NOT ONE TO MINCE WORDS OR WASTE TIME. LIFE'S TOO SHORT. IF YOU WEREN'T DOING IT FOR ME YOU'D BE HISTORY.
I WOULD?
SURE, AS I'M SURE I WOULD IF I WASN'T DOING IT FOR YOU.
BUT YOU ARE.
I KNOW. I'M JUST SAYING PEOPLE HAVE A TENDENCY NOT TO BE HONEST ABOUT SUCH THINGS --
WHAT?
BUT I DO BELIEVE THAT IF YOU WEREN'T DIGGING ME IN THE SACK YOU'D MOVE ON TO THE-WHADAYA CALL IT? GREENER PASTURES.
I DON'T LIKE YOU JUST FOR THE SEX.
NOT SAYING YOU DO.
I'M SERIOUS.

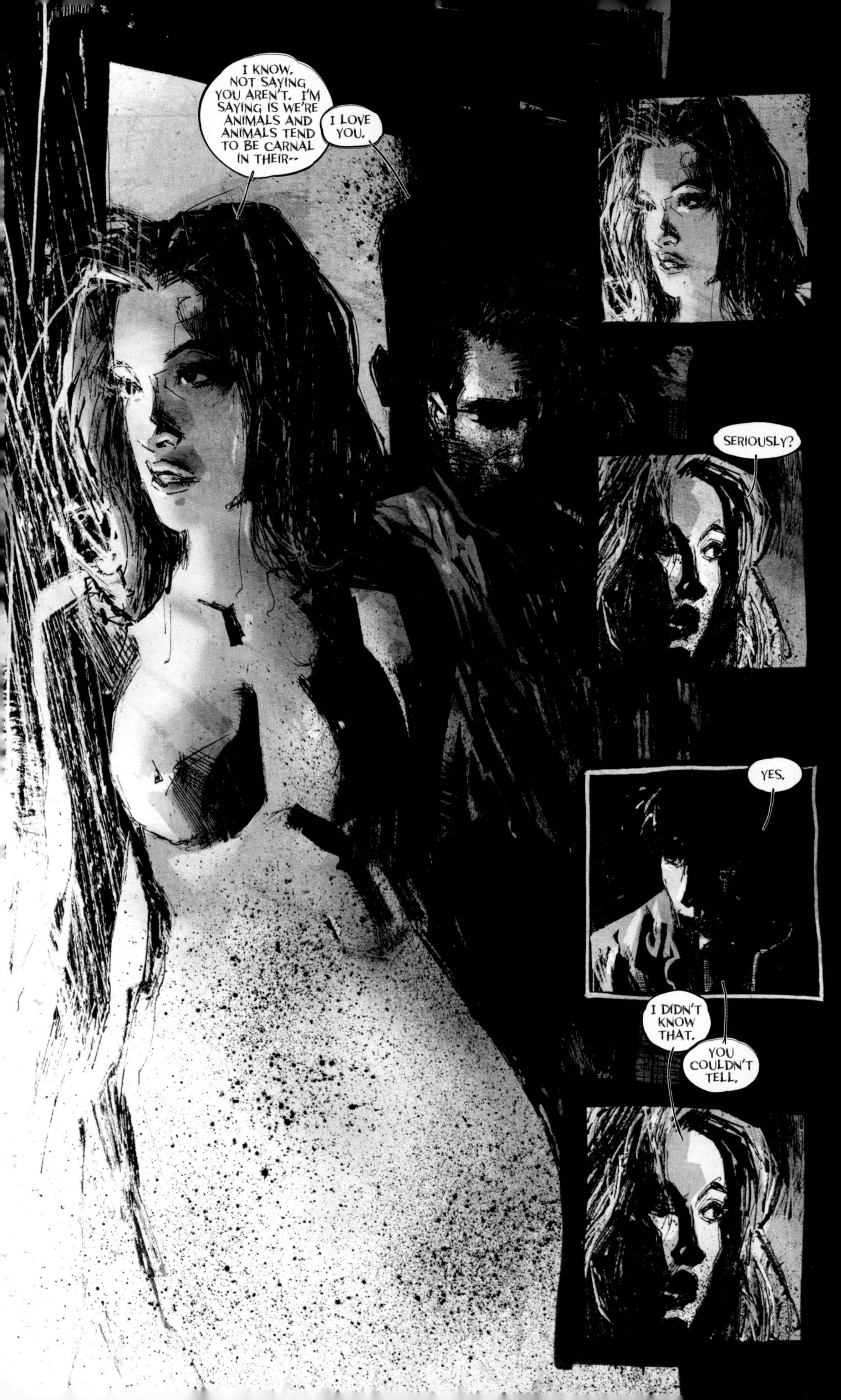
I KNOW. NOT SAYING YOU AREN'T. I'M SAYING IS WE'RE ANIMALS AND ANIMALS TEND TO BE CARNAL IN THEIR--
I LOVE YOU.
SERIOUSLY?
YES.
I DIDN'T KNOW THAT.
YOU COULDN'T TELL.

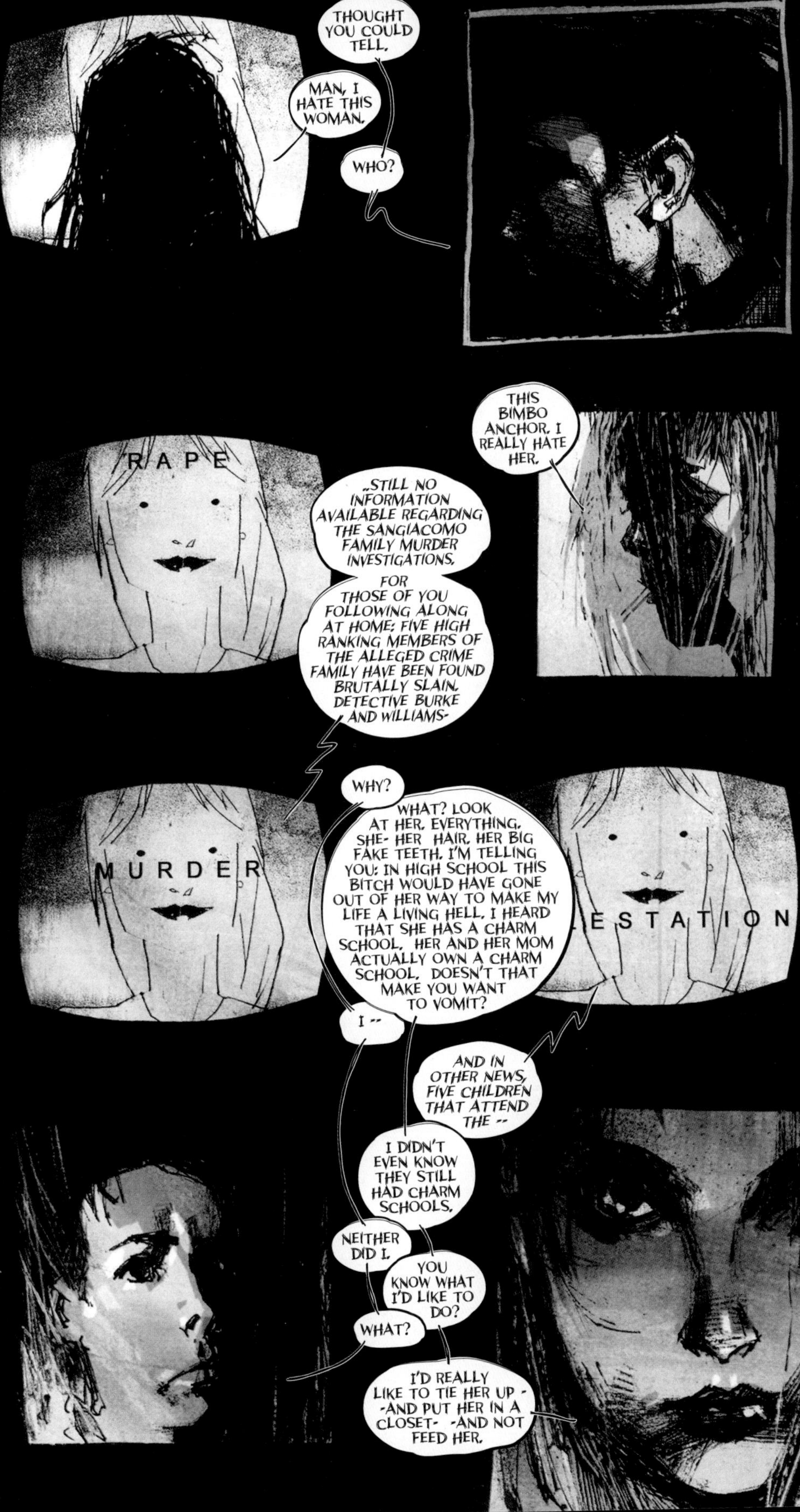
THOUGHT YOU COULD TELL.
MAN, I HATE THIS WOMAN.
WHO?
THIS BIMBO ANCHOR. I REALLY HATE HER.
RAPE
..STILL NO INFORMATION AVAILABLE REGARDING THE SANGIACOMO FAMILY MURDER INVESTIGATIONS.
FOR THOSE OF YOU FOLLOWING ALONG AT HOME: FIVE HIGH RANKING MEMBERS OF THE ALLEGED CRIME FAMILY HAVE BEEN FOUND BRUTALLY SLAIN. DETECTIVE BURKE AND WILLIAMS-
MURDER
WHY?
WHAT? LOOK AT HER. EVERYTHING. SHE- HER HAIR. HER BIG FAKE TEETH. I'M TELLING YOU: IN HIGH SCHOOL THIS BITCH WOULD HAVE GONE OUT OF HER WAY TO MAKE MY LIFE A LIVING HELL. I HEARD THAT SHE HAS A CHARM SCHOOL. HER AND HER MOM ACTUALLY OWN A CHARM SCHOOL. DOESN'T THAT MAKE YOU WANT TO VOMIT?
LESTATION
I --
AND IN OTHER NEWS, FIVE CHILDREN THAT ATTEND THE --
I DIDN'T EVEN KNOW THEY STILL HAD CHARM SCHOOLS.
NEITHER DID I.
YOU KNOW WHAT I'D LIKE TO DO?
WHAT?
I'D REALLY LIKE TO TIE HER UP - -AND PUT HER IN A CLOSET- -AND NOT FEED HER.

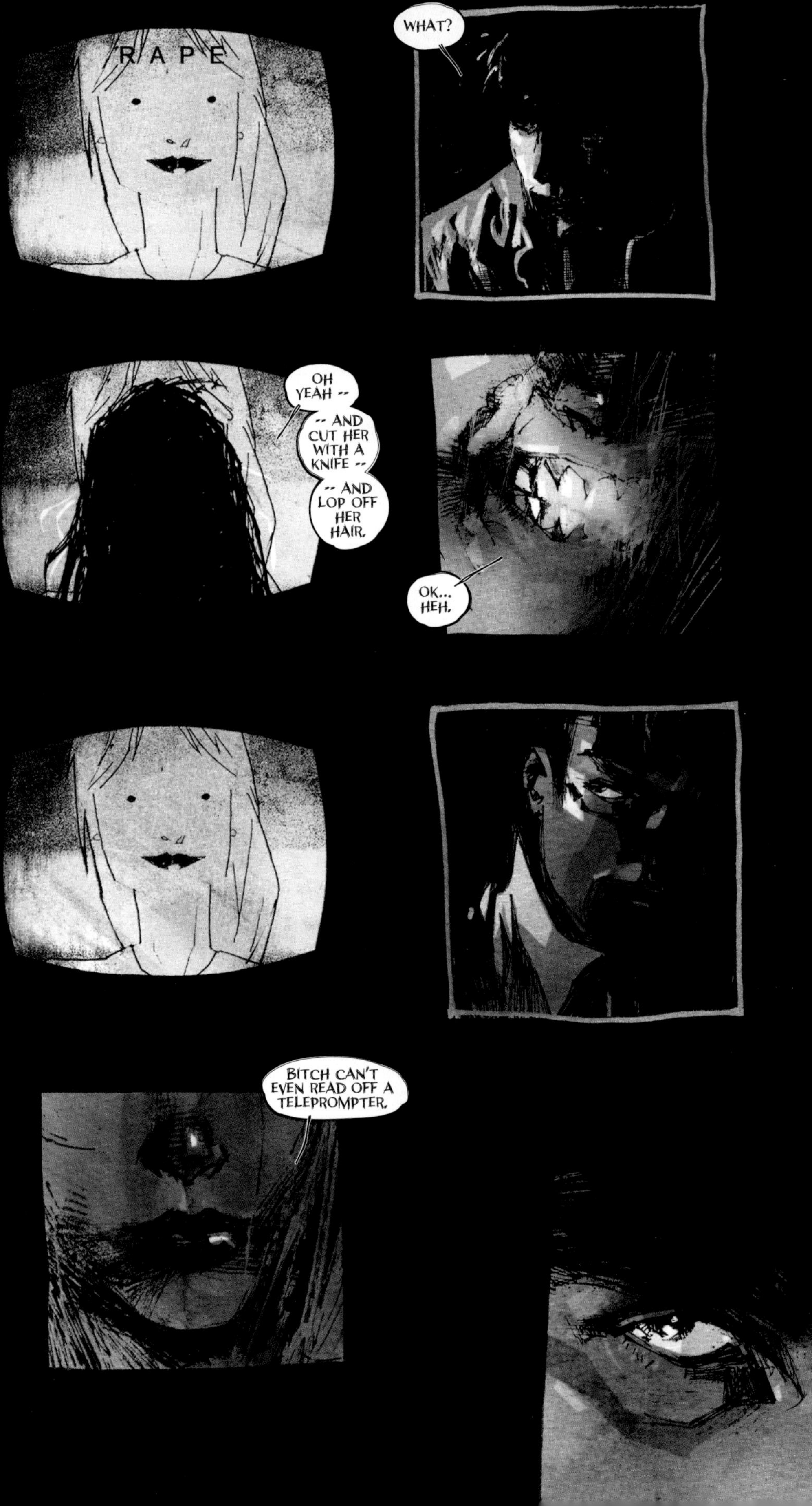
RAPE
WHAT?
OH YEAH --
-- AND CUT HER WITH A KNIFE --
-- AND LOP OFF HER HAIR.
OK... HEH.
BITCH CAN'T EVEN READ OFF A TELEPROMPTER.

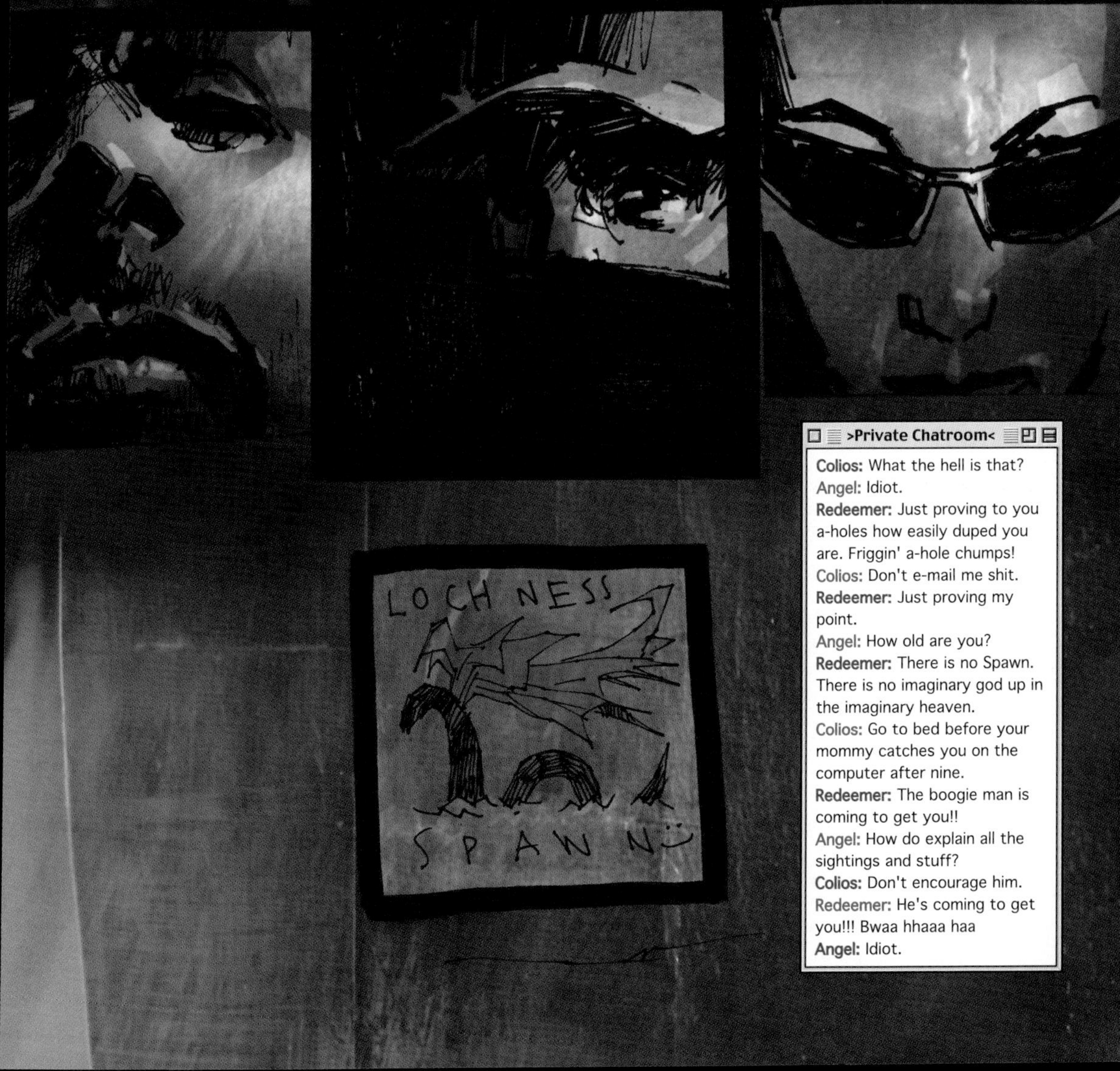

>Private Chatroom<
Colios: What the hell is that?
Angel: Idiot.
Redeemer: Just proving to you a-holes how easily duped you are. Friggin' a-hole chumps!
Colios: Don't e-mail me shit.
Redeemer: Just proving my point.
Angel: How old are you?
Redeemer: There is no Spawn. There is no imaginary god up in the imaginary heaven.
Colios: Go to bed before your mommy catches you on the computer after nine.
Redeemer: The boogie man is coming to get you!!
Angel: How do explain all the sightings and stuff?
Colios: Don't encourage him.
Redeemer: He's coming to get you!!! Bwaa hhaaa haa
Angel: Idiot.
LOCH NESS
SPAWN

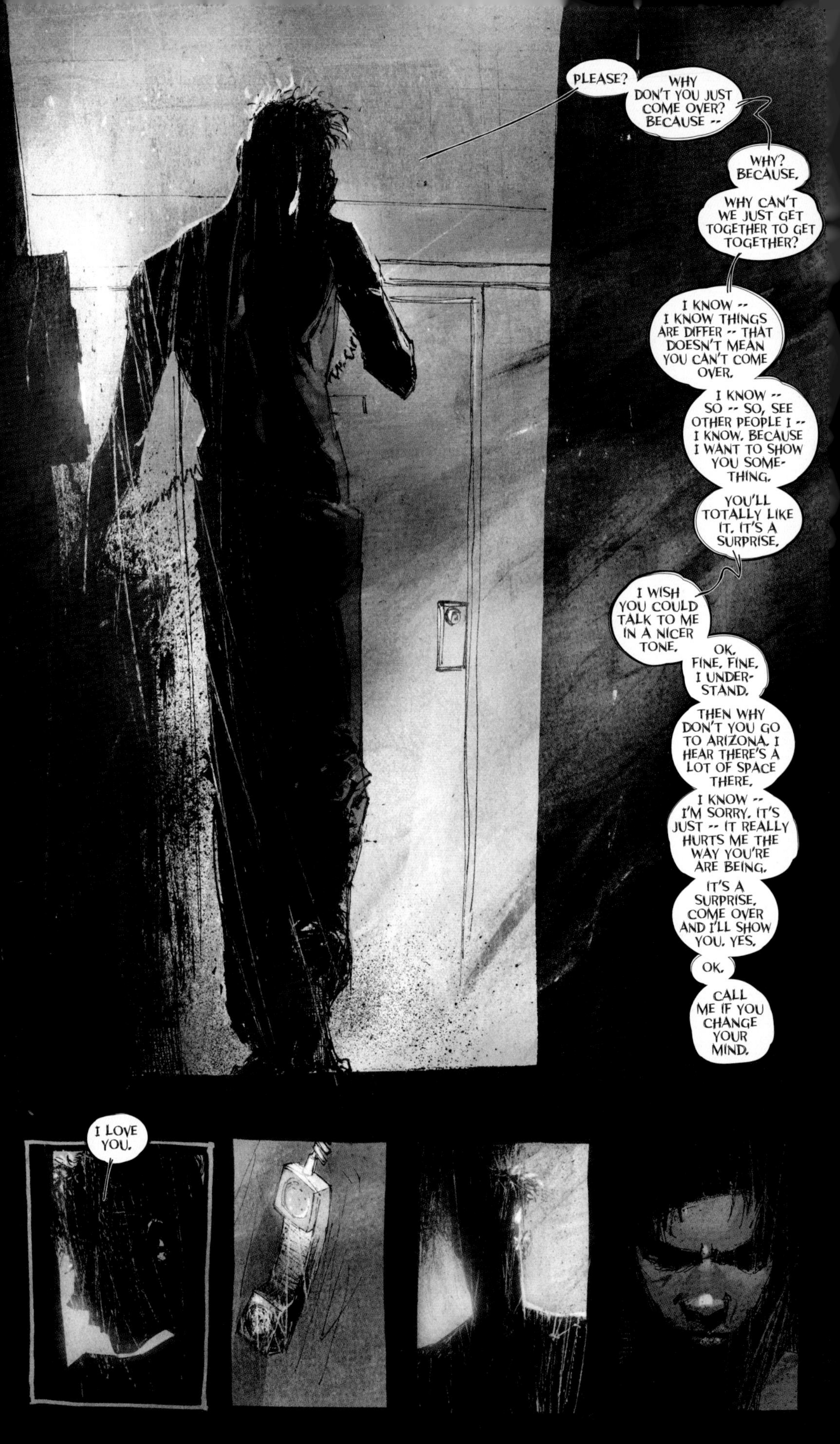
PLEASE?
WHY DON'T YOU JUST COME OVER? BECAUSE --
WHY? BECAUSE.
WHY CAN'T WE JUST GET TOGETHER TO GET TOGETHER?
I KNOW -- I KNOW THINGS ARE DIFFER -- THAT DOESN'T MEAN YOU CAN'T COME OVER.
I KNOW -- SO -- SO, SEE OTHER PEOPLE I -- I KNOW. BECAUSE I WANT TO SHOW YOU SOME-THING.
YOU'LL TOTALLY LIKE IT. IT'S A SURPRISE.
I WISH YOU COULD TALK TO ME IN A NICER TONE.
OK. FINE. FINE. I UNDER-STAND.
THEN WHY DON'T YOU GO TO ARIZONA. I HEAR THERE'S A LOT OF SPACE THERE.
I KNOW -- I'M SORRY. IT'S JUST -- IT REALLY HURTS ME THE WAY YOU'RE ARE BEING.
IT'S A SURPRISE. COME OVER AND I'LL SHOW YOU. YES.
OK.
CALL ME IF YOU CHANGE YOUR MIND.
I LOVE YOU.

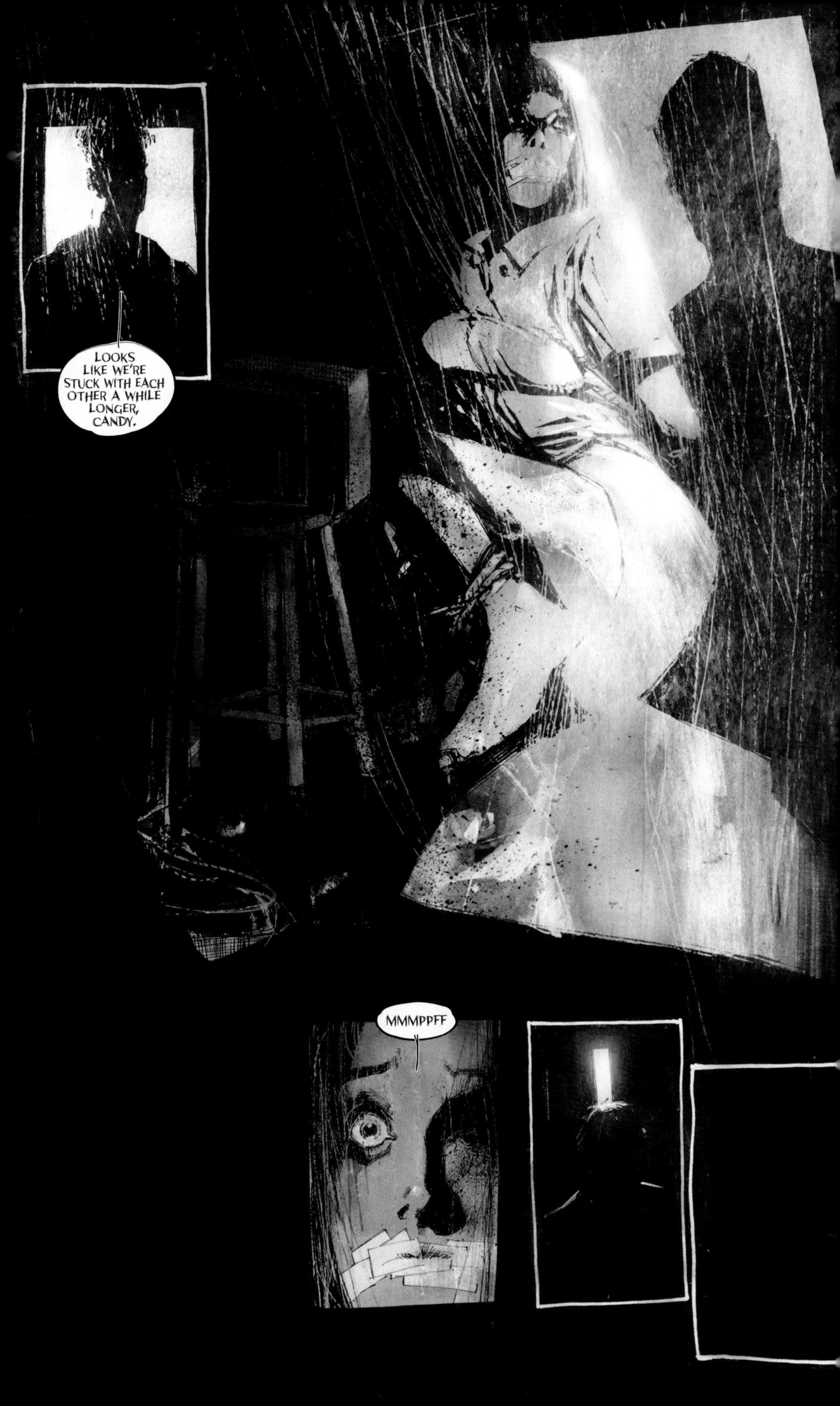
LOOKS LIKE WE'RE STUCK WITH EACH OTHER A WHILE LONGER, CANDY.
MMMPPFF

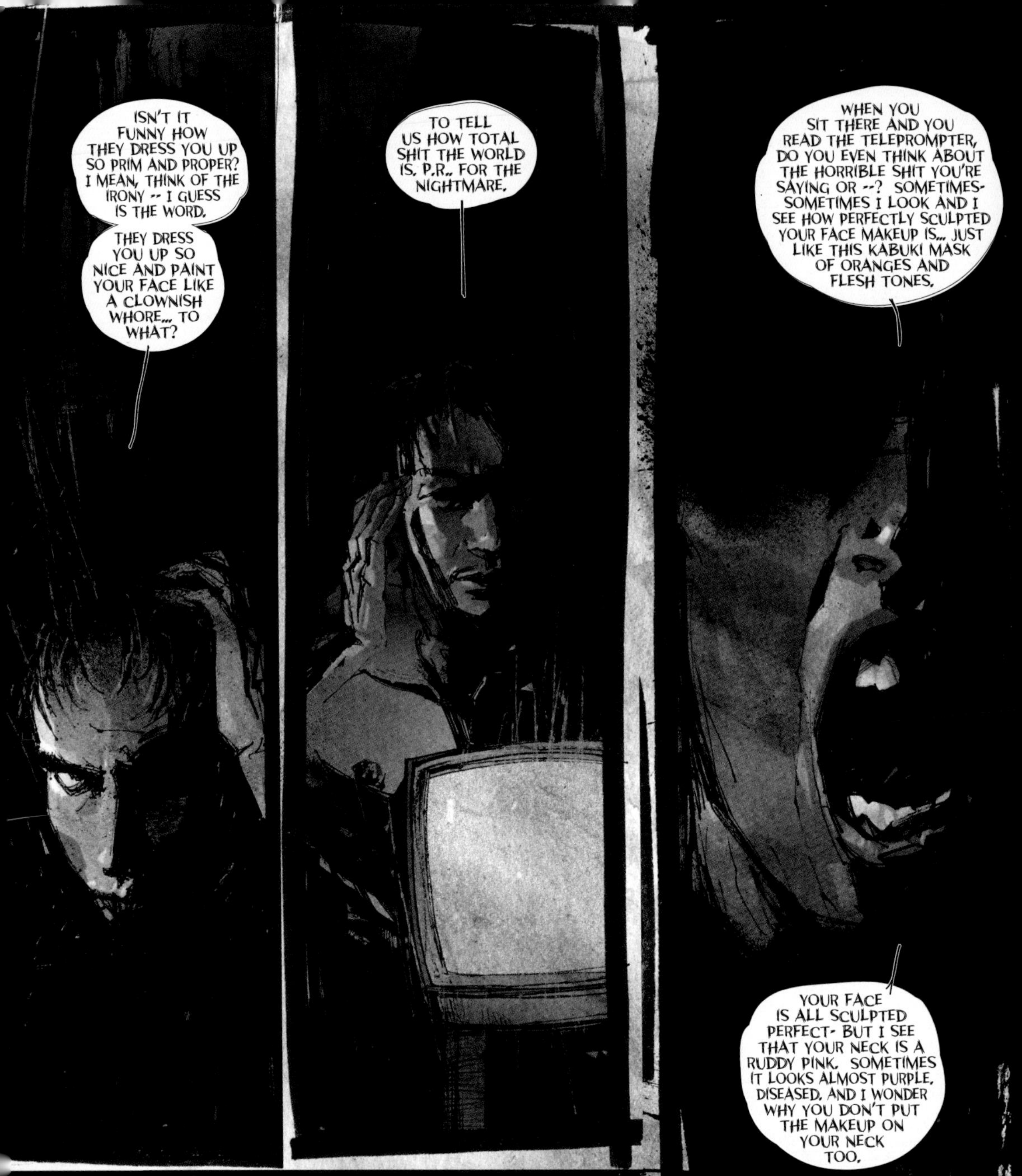
ISN'T IT FUNNY HOW THEY DRESS YOU UP SO PRIM AND PROPER? I MEAN, THINK OF THE IRONY -- I GUESS IS THE WORD.
THEY DRESS YOU UP SO NICE AND PAINT YOUR FACE LIKE A CLOWNISH WHORE... TO WHAT?
TO TELL US HOW TOTAL SHIT THE WORLD IS. P.R.. FOR THE NIGHTMARE.
WHEN YOU SIT THERE AND YOU READ THE TELEPROMPTER, DO YOU EVEN THINK ABOUT THE HORRIBLE SHIT YOU'RE SAYING OR --? SOMETIMES-SOMETIMES I LOOK AND I SEE HOW PERFECTLY SCULPTED YOUR FACE MAKEUP IS... JUST LIKE THIS KABUKI MASK OF ORANGES AND FLESH TONES.
YOUR FACE IS ALL SCULPTED PERFECT- BUT I SEE THAT YOUR NECK IS A RUDDY PINK. SOMETIMES IT LOOKS ALMOST PURPLE, DISEASED. AND I WONDER WHY YOU DON'T PUT THE MAKEUP ON YOUR NECK TOO.

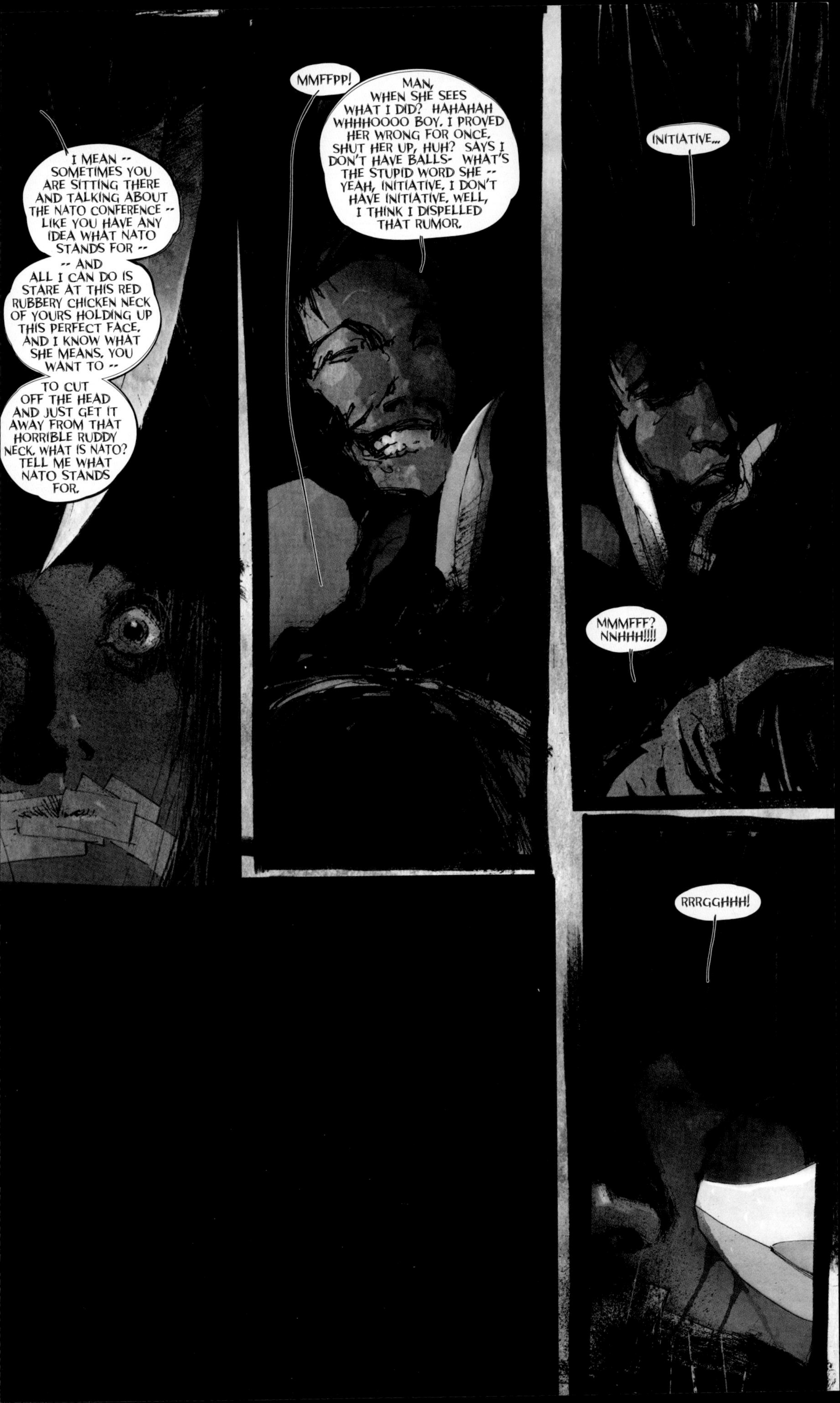
I MEAN -- SOMETIMES YOU ARE SITTING THERE AND TALKING ABOUT THE NATO CONFERENCE -- LIKE YOU HAVE ANY IDEA WHAT NATO STANDS FOR --
-- AND ALL I CAN DO IS STARE AT THIS RED RUBBERY CHICKEN NECK OF YOURS HOLDING UP THIS PERFECT FACE, AND I KNOW WHAT SHE MEANS. YOU WANT TO --
TO CUT OFF THE HEAD AND JUST GET IT AWAY FROM THAT HORRIBLE RUDDY NECK. WHAT IS NATO? TELL ME WHAT NATO STANDS FOR.
MMFFPP!
MAN, WHEN SHE SEES WHAT I DID? HAHAHAH WHHHOOOO BOY. I PROVED HER WRONG FOR ONCE, SHUT HER UP, HUH? SAYS I DON'T HAVE BALLS- WHAT'S THE STUPID WORD SHE -- YEAH, INITIATIVE. I DON'T HAVE INITIATIVE. WELL, I THINK I DISPELLED THAT RUMOR.
INITIATIVE...
MMMFFF? NNHHH!!!!
RRRGGHHH!

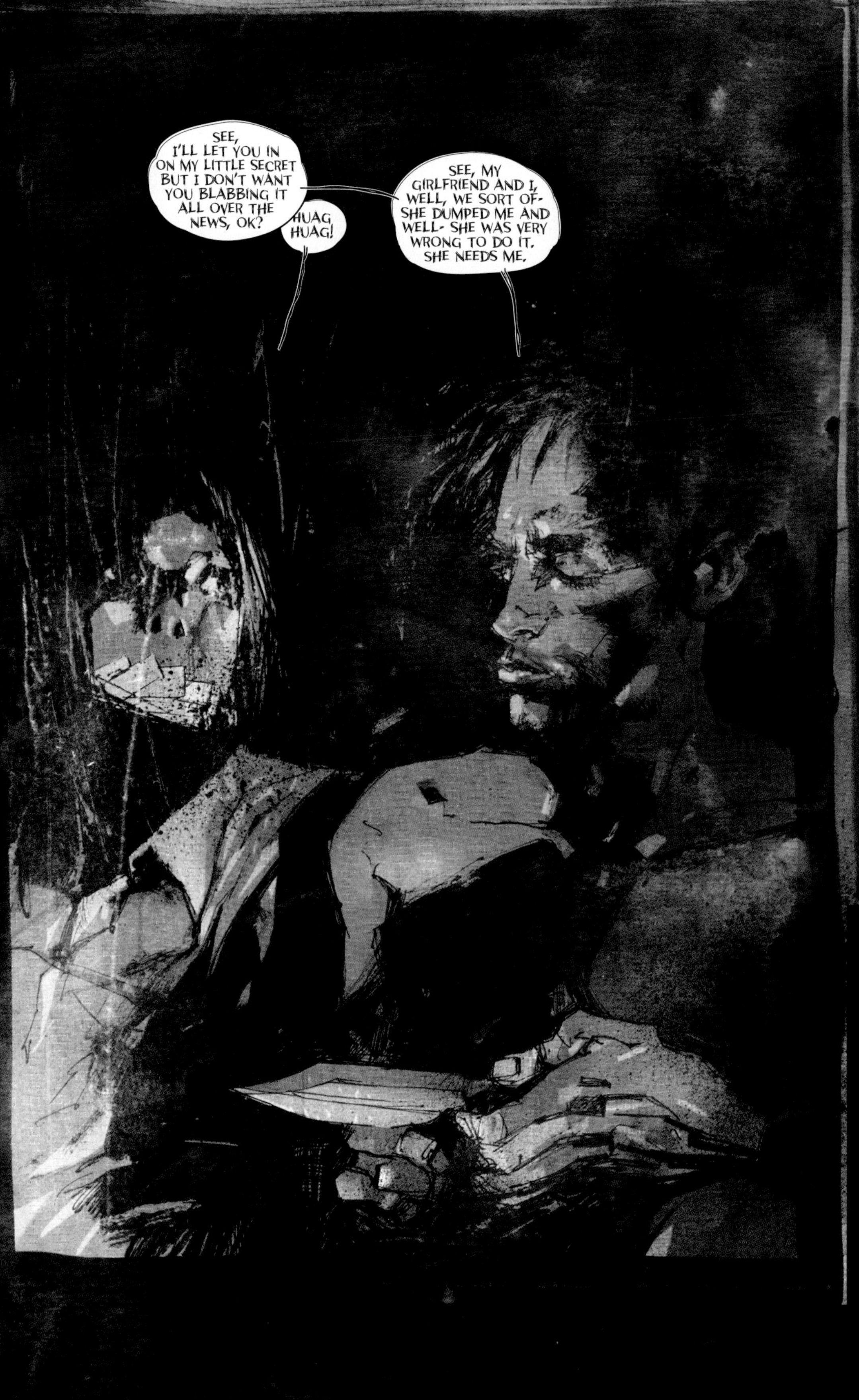
SEE, I'LL LET YOU IN ON MY LITTLE SECRET BUT I DON'T WANT YOU BLABBING IT ALL OVER THE NEWS, OK?
HUAG HUAG!
SEE, MY GIRLFRIEND AND I, WELL, WE SORT OF- SHE DUMPED ME AND WELL- SHE WAS VERY WRONG TO DO IT. SHE NEEDS ME.

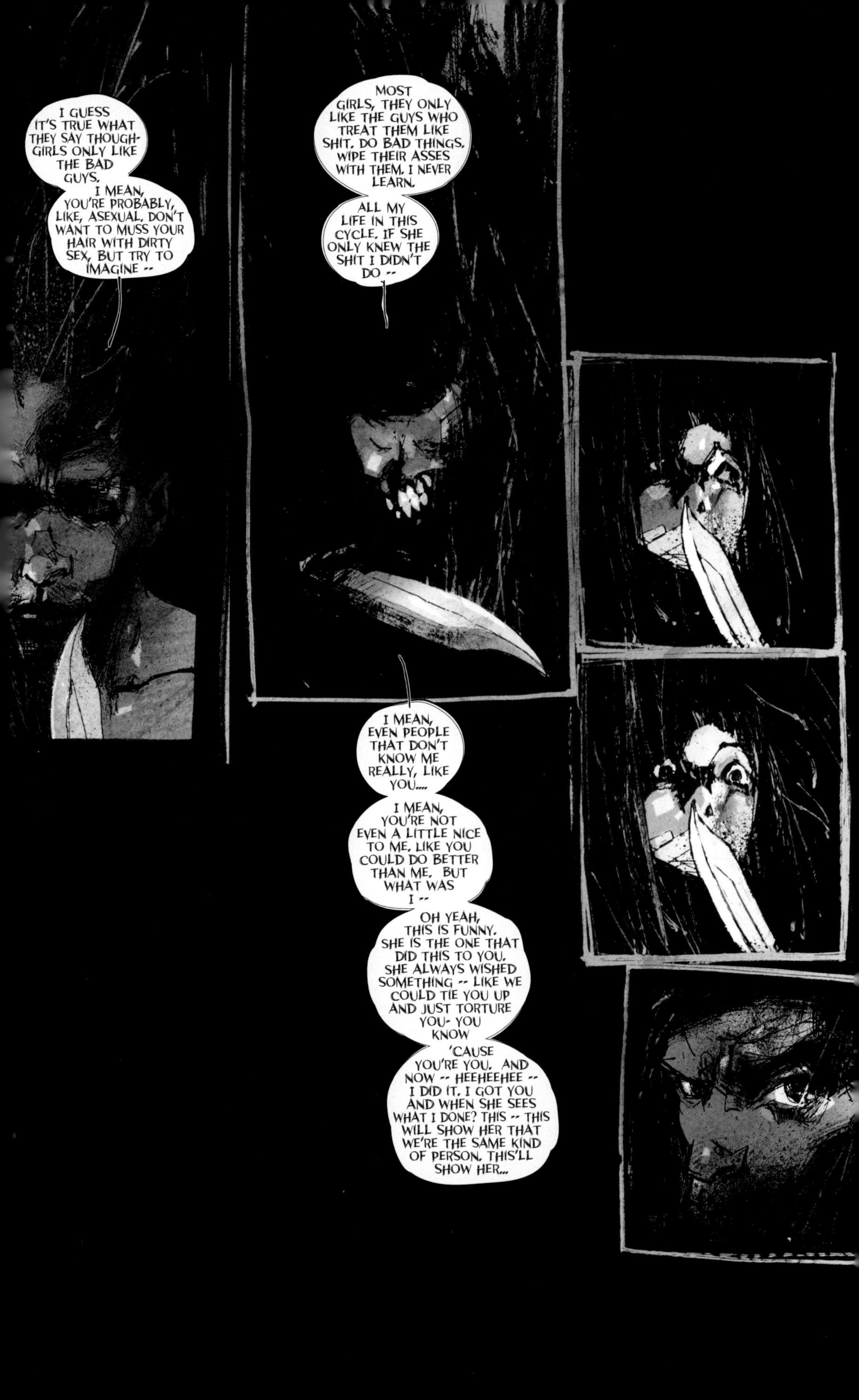
I GUESS IT'S TRUE WHAT THEY SAY THOUGH- GIRLS ONLY LIKE THE BAD GUYS.
I MEAN, YOU'RE PROBABLY, LIKE, ASEXUAL. DON'T WANT TO MUSS YOUR HAIR WITH DIRTY SEX, BUT TRY TO IMAGINE --
MOST GIRLS, THEY ONLY LIKE THE GUYS WHO TREAT THEM LIKE SHIT. DO BAD THINGS. WIPE THEIR ASSES WITH THEM. I NEVER LEARN.
ALL MY LIFE IN THIS CYCLE. IF SHE ONLY KNEW THE SHIT I DIDN'T DO --
I MEAN, EVEN PEOPLE THAT DON'T KNOW ME REALLY, LIKE YOU....
I MEAN, YOU'RE NOT EVEN A LITTLE NICE TO ME. LIKE YOU COULD DO BETTER THAN ME. BUT WHAT WAS I --
OH YEAH, THIS IS FUNNY. SHE IS THE ONE THAT DID THIS TO YOU. SHE ALWAYS WISHED SOMETHING -- LIKE WE COULD TIE YOU UP AND JUST TORTURE YOU- YOU KNOW
'CAUSE YOU'RE YOU. AND NOW -- HEEHEEHEE -- I DID IT. I GOT YOU AND WHEN SHE SEES WHAT I DONE? THIS -- THIS WILL SHOW HER THAT WE'RE THE SAME KIND OF PERSON. THIS'LL SHOW HER...

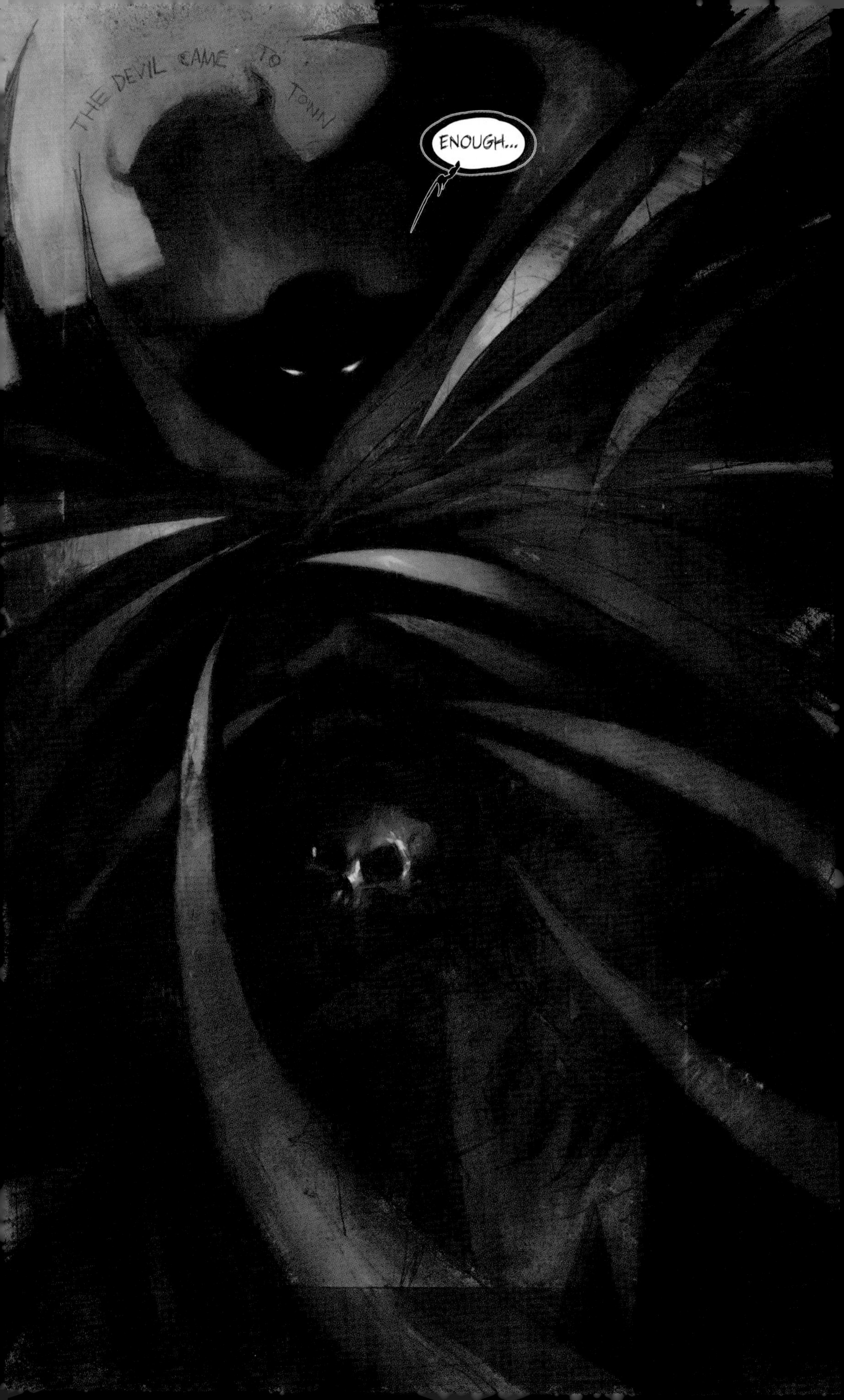
THE DEVIL CAME TO TOWN
ENOUGH...

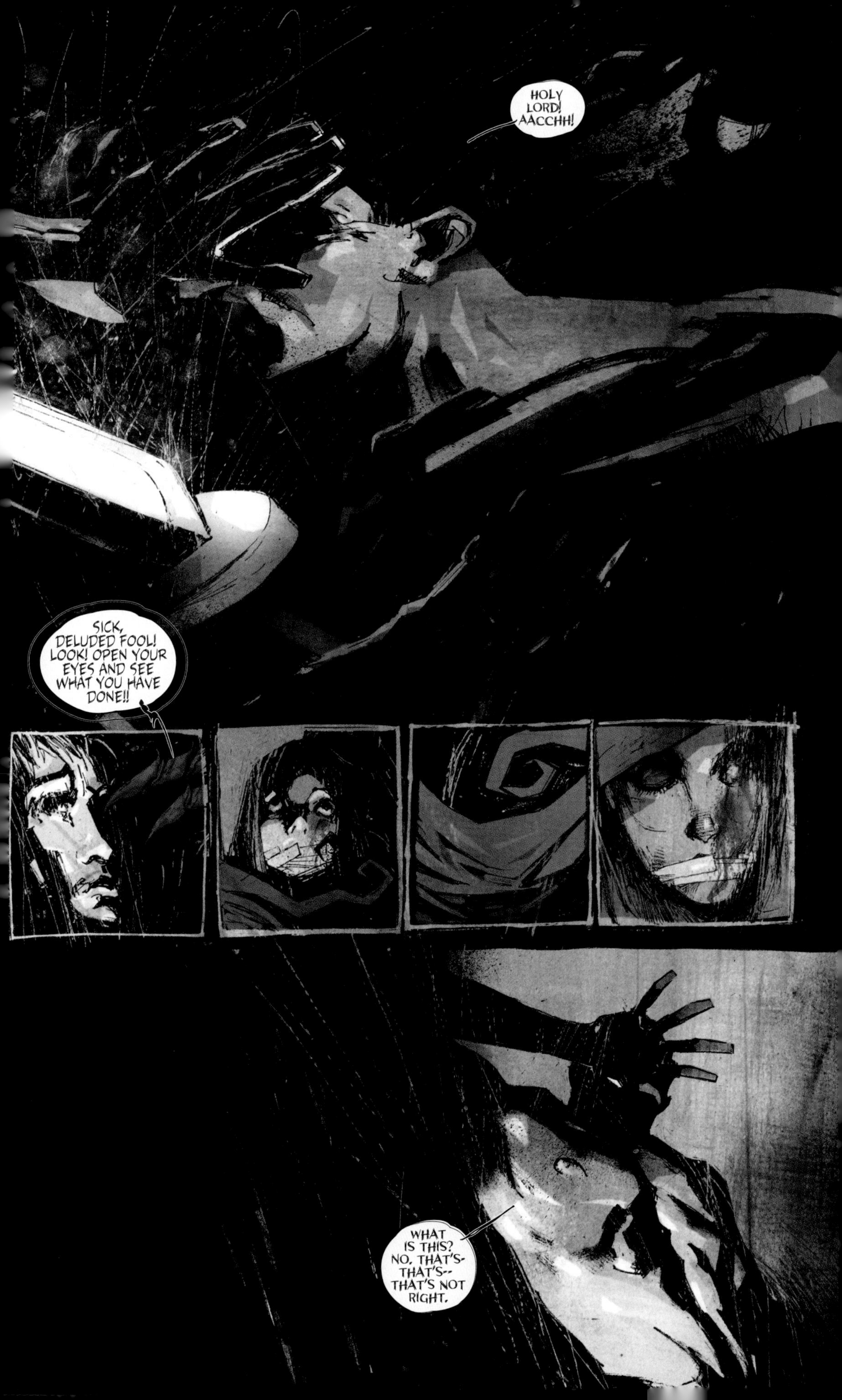
HOLY LORD! AACCHH!
SICK, DELUDED FOOL! LOOK! OPEN YOUR EYES AND SEE WHAT YOU HAVE DONE!!
WHAT IS THIS? NO. THAT'S- THAT'S-- THAT'S NOT RIGHT.

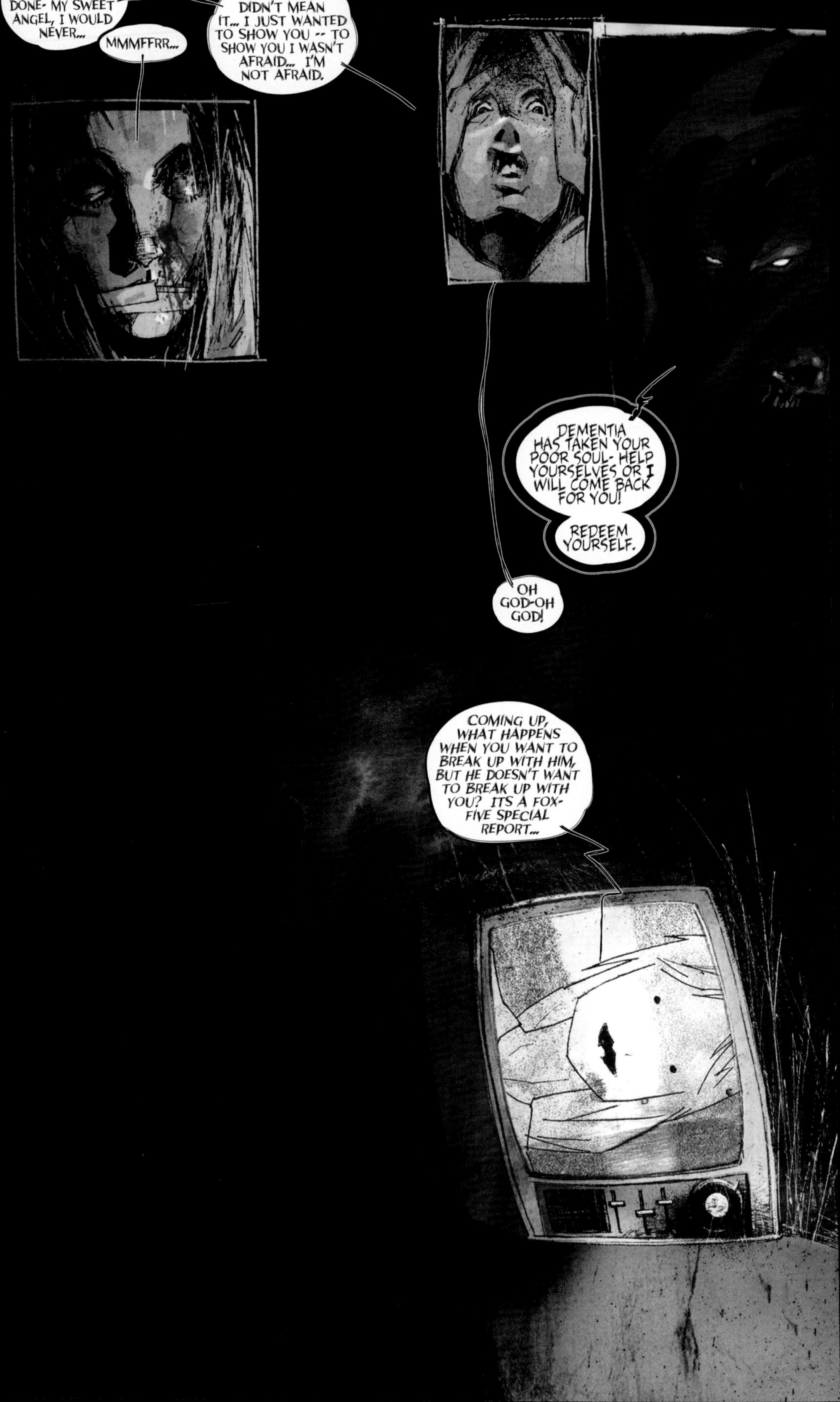

DONE- MY SWEET ANGEL, I WOULD NEVER...
MMMFFRR...
DIDN'T MEAN IT... I JUST WANTED TO SHOW YOU -- TO SHOW YOU I WASN'T AFRAID... I'M NOT AFRAID.
DEMENTIA HAS TAKEN YOUR POOR SOUL- HELP YOURSELVES OR I WILL COME BACK FOR YOU!
REDEEM YOURSELF.
OH GOD-OH GOD!
COMING UP, WHAT HAPPENS WHEN YOU WANT TO BREAK UP WITH HIM, BUT HE DOESN'T WANT TO BREAK UP WITH YOU? ITS A FOX-FIVE SPECIAL REPORT...

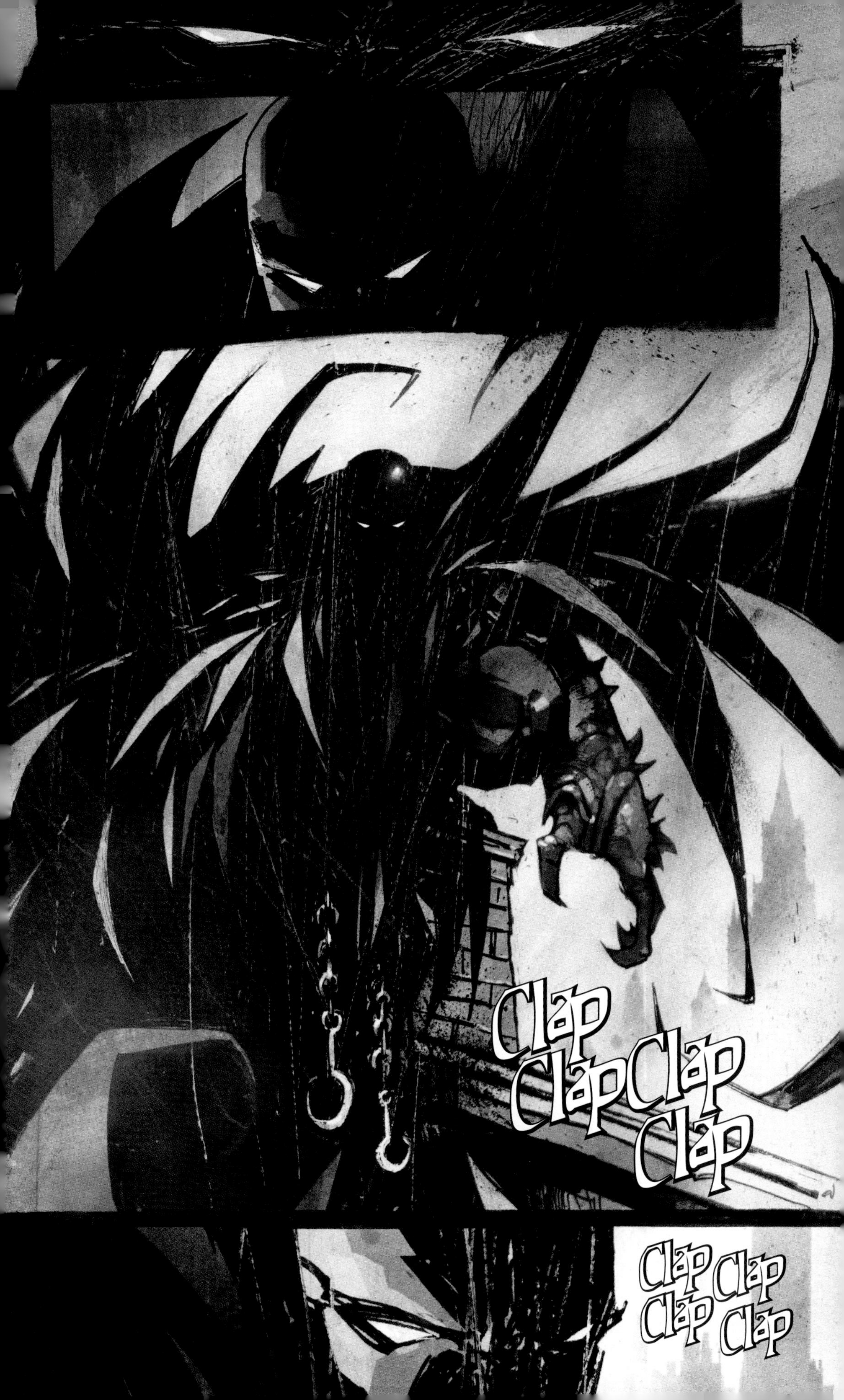
Clap
Clap Clap
Clap
Clap Clap
Clap Clap

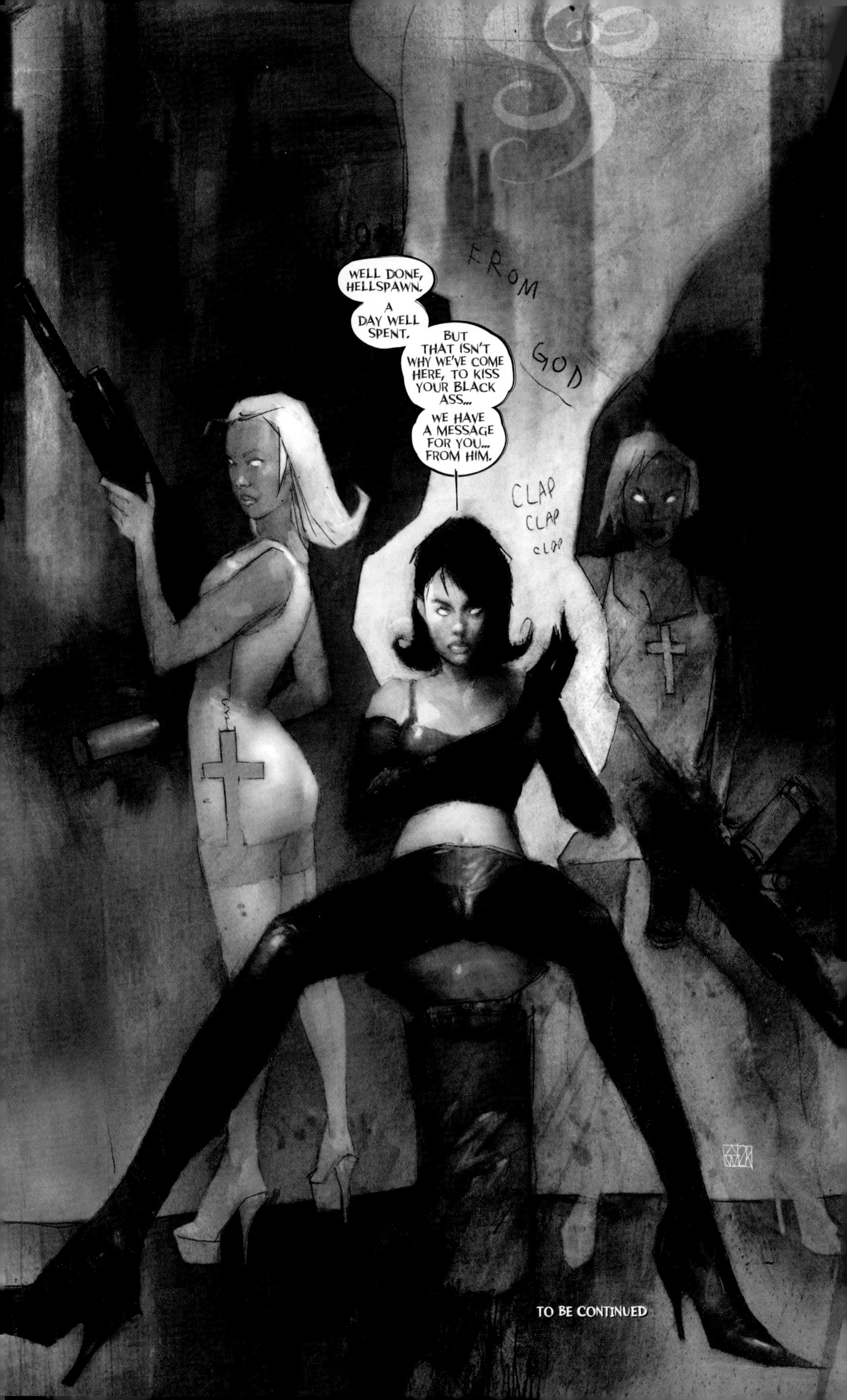
WELL DONE, HELLSPAWN.
A DAY WELL SPENT.
BUT THAT ISN'T WHY WE'VE COME HERE, TO KISS YOUR BLACK ASS...
WE HAVE A MESSAGE FOR YOU... FROM HIM.
FROM GOD
CLAP CLAP CLAP
TO BE CONTINUED

HELLSPAWN

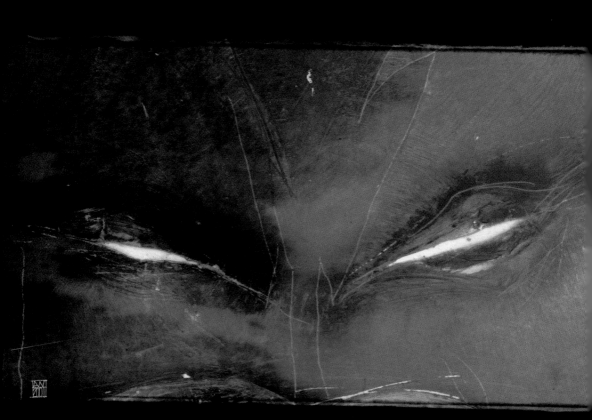

ISSUE SIX

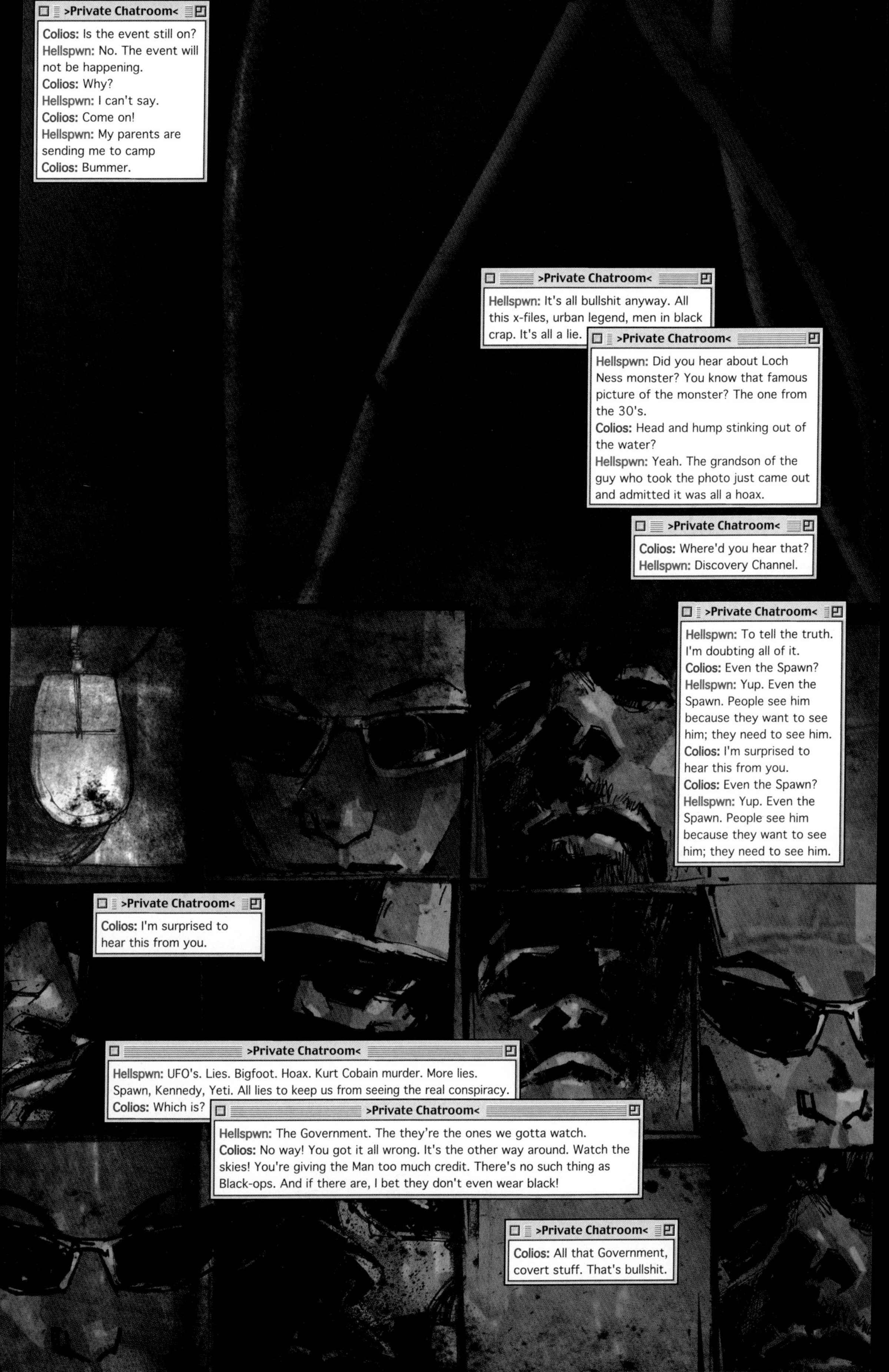
>Private Chatroom<
Colios: Is the event still on?
Hellspwn: No. The event will not be happening.
Colios: Why?
Hellspwn: I can't say.
Colios: Come on!
Hellspwn: My parents are sending me to camp
Colios: Bummer.
>Private Chatroom<
Hellspwn: It's all bullshit anyway. All this x-files, urban legend, men in black crap. It's all a lie.
>Private Chatroom<
Hellspwn: Did you hear about Loch Ness monster? You know that famous picture of the monster? The one from the 30's.
Colios: Head and hump stinking out of the water?
Hellspwn: Yeah. The grandson of the guy who took the photo just came out and admitted it was all a hoax.
>Private Chatroom<
Colios: Where'd you hear that?
Hellspwn: Discovery Channel.
>Private Chatroom<
Hellspwn: To tell the truth. I'm doubting all of it.
Colios: Even the Spawn?
Hellspwn: Yup. Even the Spawn. People see him because they want to see him; they need to see him.
Colios: I'm surprised to hear this from you.
Colios: Even the Spawn?
Hellspwn: Yup. Even the Spawn. People see him because they want to see him; they need to see him.
>Private Chatroom<
Colios: I'm surprised to hear this from you.
>Private Chatroom<
Hellspwn: UFO's. Lies. Bigfoot. Hoax. Kurt Cobain murder. More lies. Spawn, Kennedy, Yeti. All lies to keep us from seeing the real conspiracy.
Colios: Which is?
>Private Chatroom<
Hellspwn: The Government. The they're the ones we gotta watch.
Colios: No way! You got it all wrong. It's the other way around. Watch the skies! You're giving the Man too much credit. There's no such thing as Black-ops. And if there are, I bet they don't even wear black!
>Private Chatroom<
Colios: All that Government, covert stuff. That's bullshit.

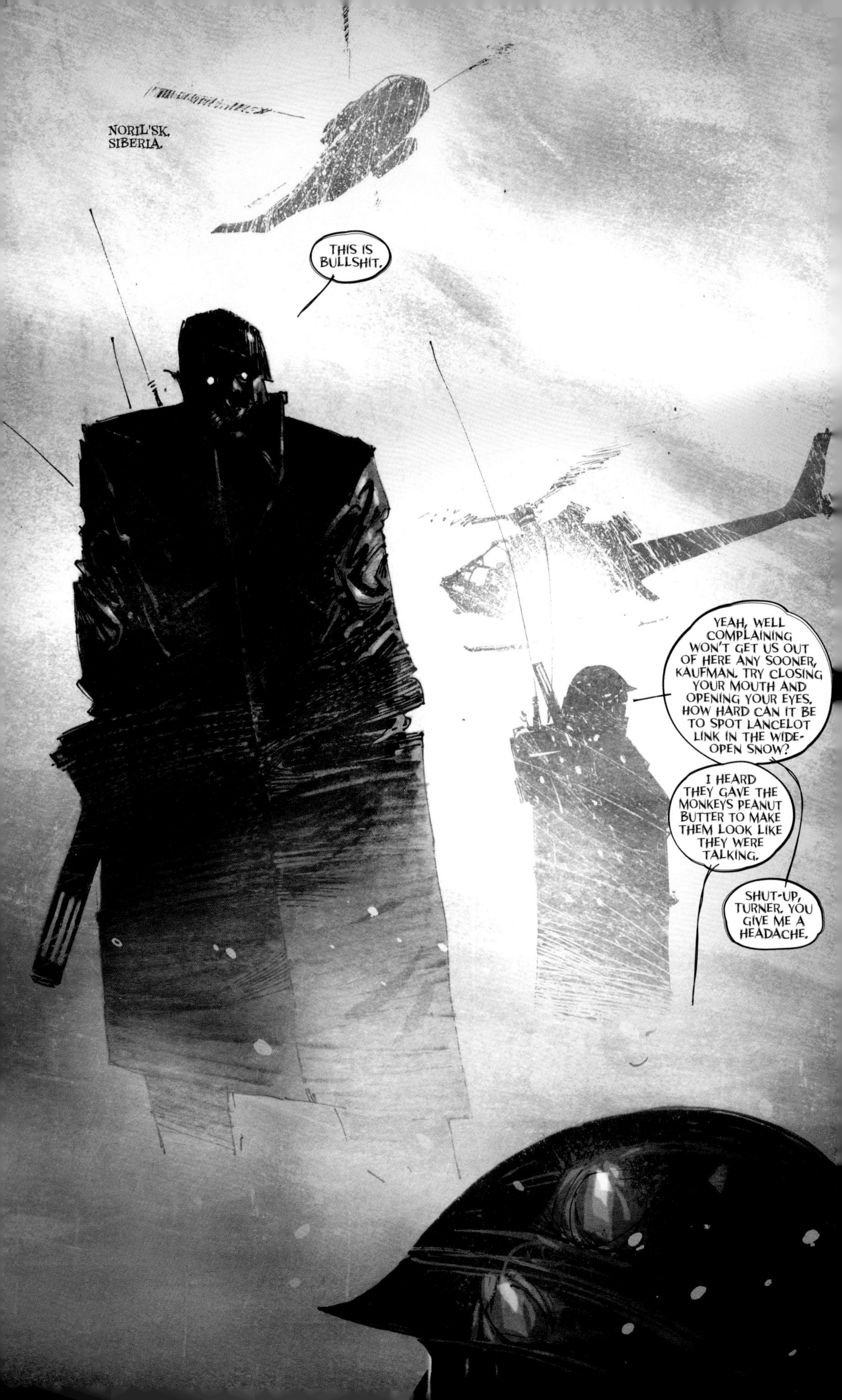
NORIL'SK, SIBERIA.
THIS IS BULLSHIT.
YEAH, WELL COMPLAINING WON'T GET US OUT OF HERE ANY SOONER, KAUFMAN. TRY CLOSING YOUR MOUTH AND OPENING YOUR EYES. HOW HARD CAN IT BE TO SPOT LANCELOT LINK IN THE WIDE-OPEN SNOW?
I HEARD THEY GAVE THE MONKEYS PEANUT BUTTER TO MAKE THEM LOOK LIKE THEY WERE TALKING.
SHUT-UP, TURNER. YOU GIVE ME A HEADACHE.

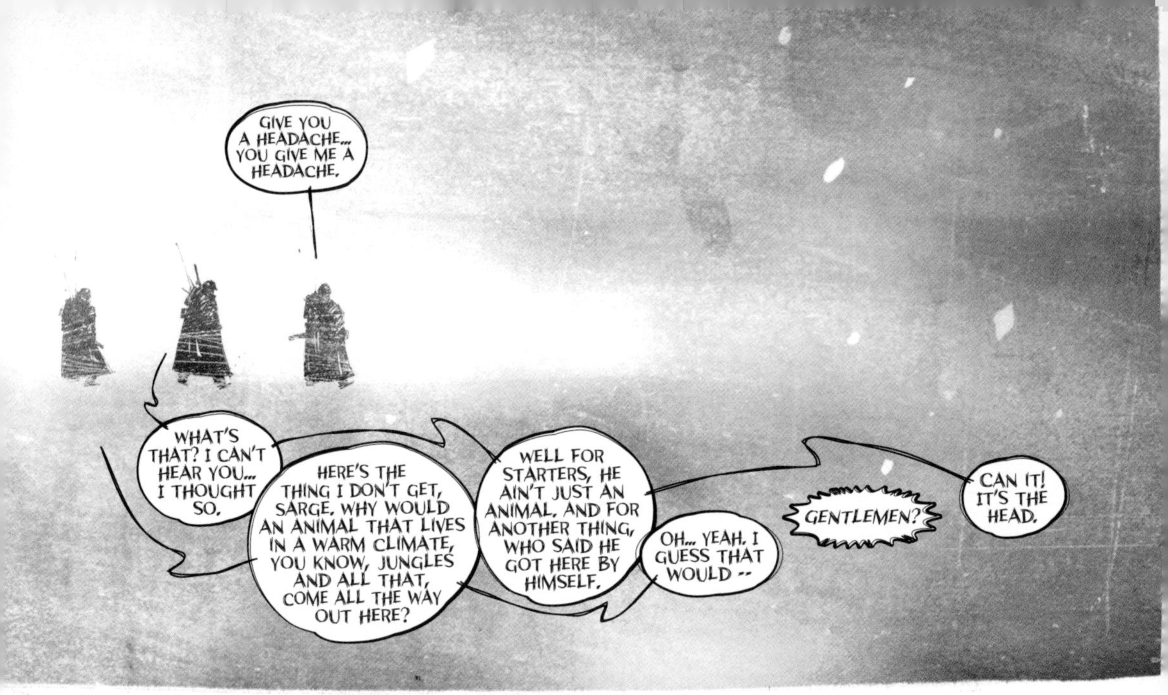
GIVE YOU A HEADACHE... YOU GIVE ME A HEADACHE.
WHAT'S THAT? I CAN'T HEAR YOU... I THOUGHT SO.
HERE'S THE THING I DON'T GET, SARGE. WHY WOULD AN ANIMAL THAT LIVES IN A WARM CLIMATE, YOU KNOW, JUNGLES AND ALL THAT, COME ALL THE WAY OUT HERE?
WELL FOR STARTERS, HE AIN'T JUST AN ANIMAL. AND FOR ANOTHER THING, WHO SAID HE GOT HERE BY HIMSELF.
OH... YEAH. I GUESS THAT WOULD --
GENTLEMEN?
CAN IT! IT'S THE HEAD.

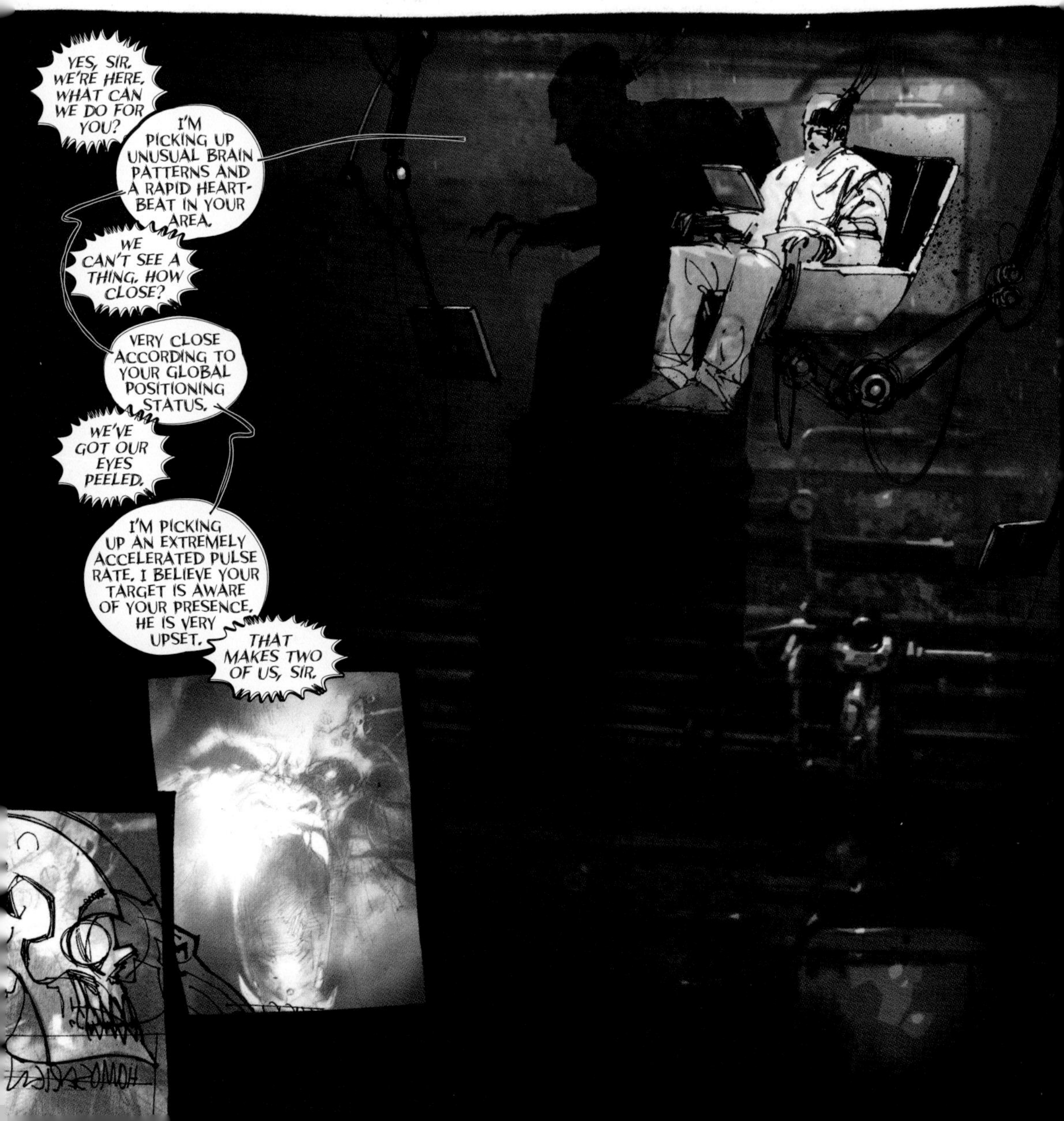
YES, SIR. WE'RE HERE. WHAT CAN WE DO FOR YOU?
I'M PICKING UP UNUSUAL BRAIN PATTERNS AND A RAPID HEART-BEAT IN YOUR AREA.
WE CAN'T SEE A THING. HOW CLOSE?
VERY CLOSE ACCORDING TO YOUR GLOBAL POSITIONING STATUS.
WE'VE GOT OUR EYES PEELED.
I'M PICKING UP AN EXTREMELY ACCELERATED PULSE RATE. I BELIEVE YOUR TARGET IS AWARE OF YOUR PRESENCE. HE IS VERY UPSET.
THAT MAKES TWO OF US, SIR.

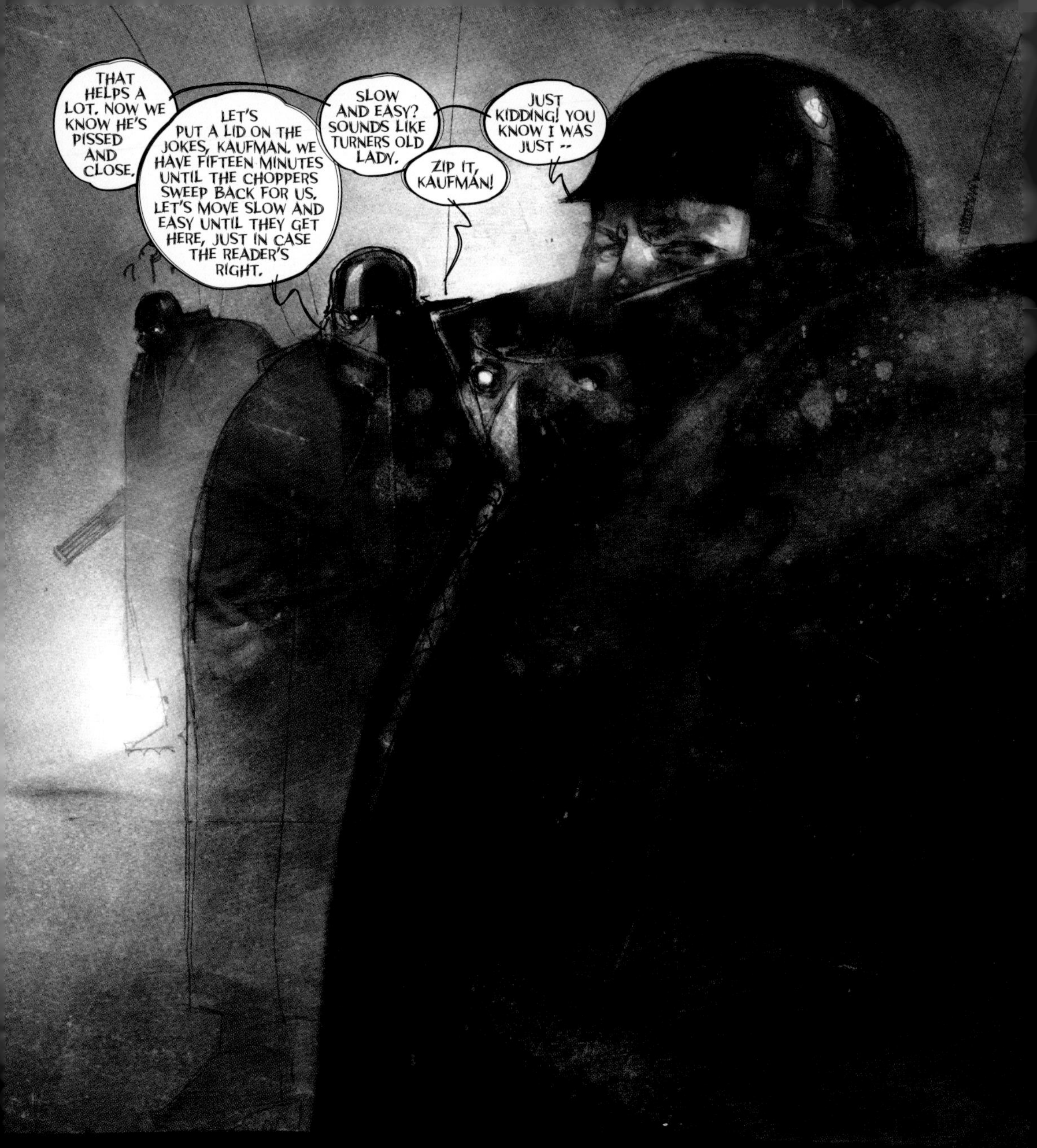
THAT HELPS A LOT. NOW WE KNOW HE'S PISSED AND CLOSE.
LET'S PUT A LID ON THE JOKES, KAUFMAN. WE HAVE FIFTEEN MINUTES UNTIL THE CHOPPERS SWEEP BACK FOR US. LET'S MOVE SLOW AND EASY UNTIL THEY GET HERE, JUST IN CASE THE READER'S RIGHT.
SLOW AND EASY? SOUNDS LIKE TURNERS OLD LADY.
JUST KIDDING! YOU KNOW I WAS JUST --
ZIP IT, KAUFMAN!

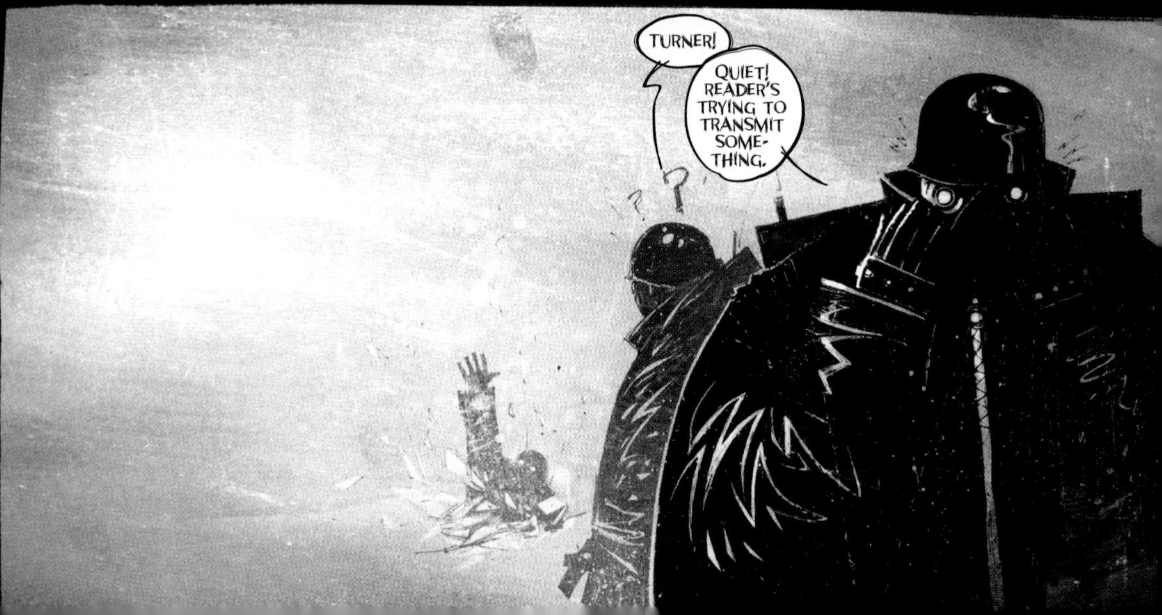
TURNER!
QUIET! READER'S TRYING TO TRANSMIT SOME-THING.

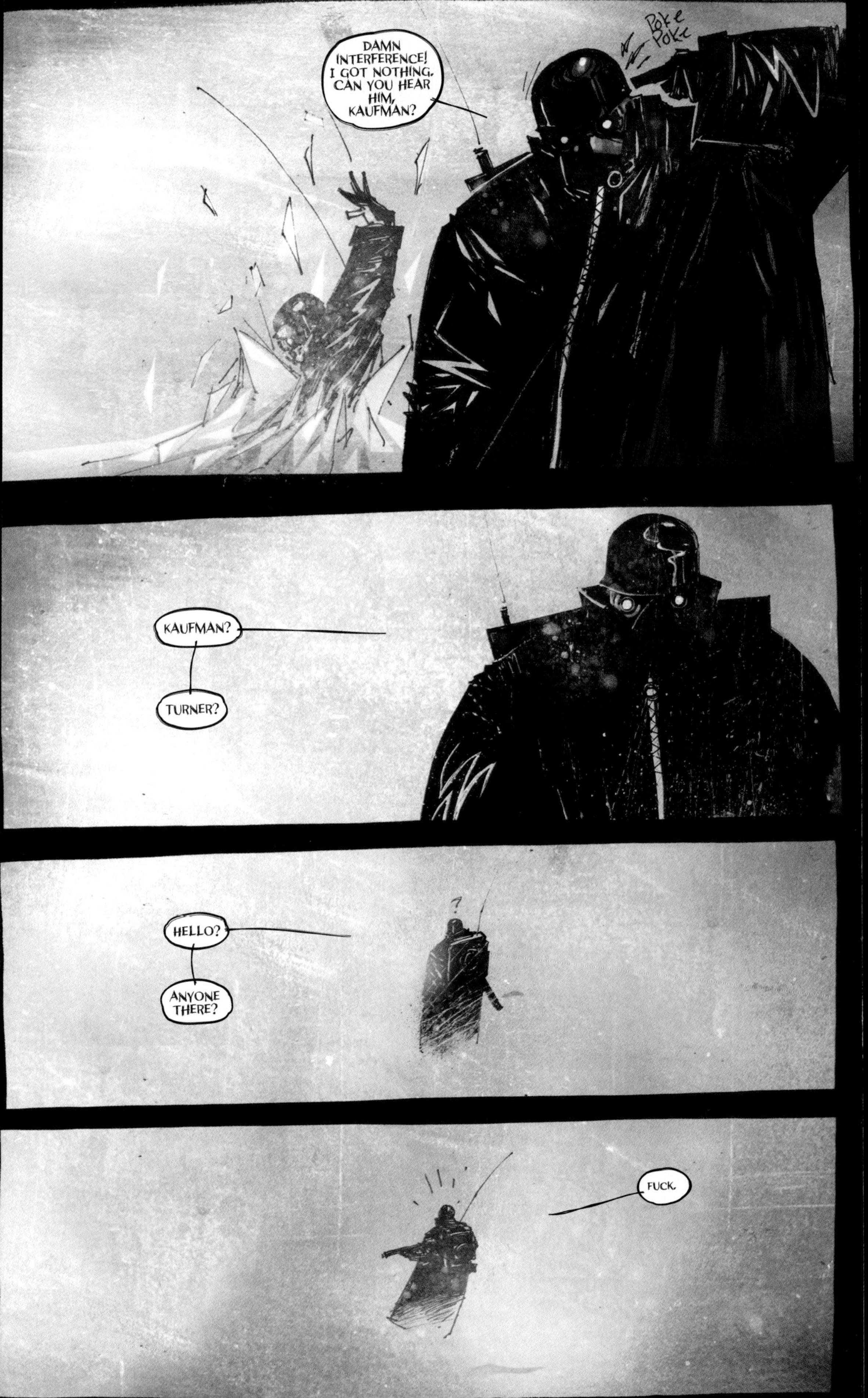
POKE POKE
DAMN INTERFERENCE! I GOT NOTHING. CAN YOU HEAR HIM, KAUFMAN?
KAUFMAN?
TURNER?
HELLO?
ANYONE THERE?
FUCK.

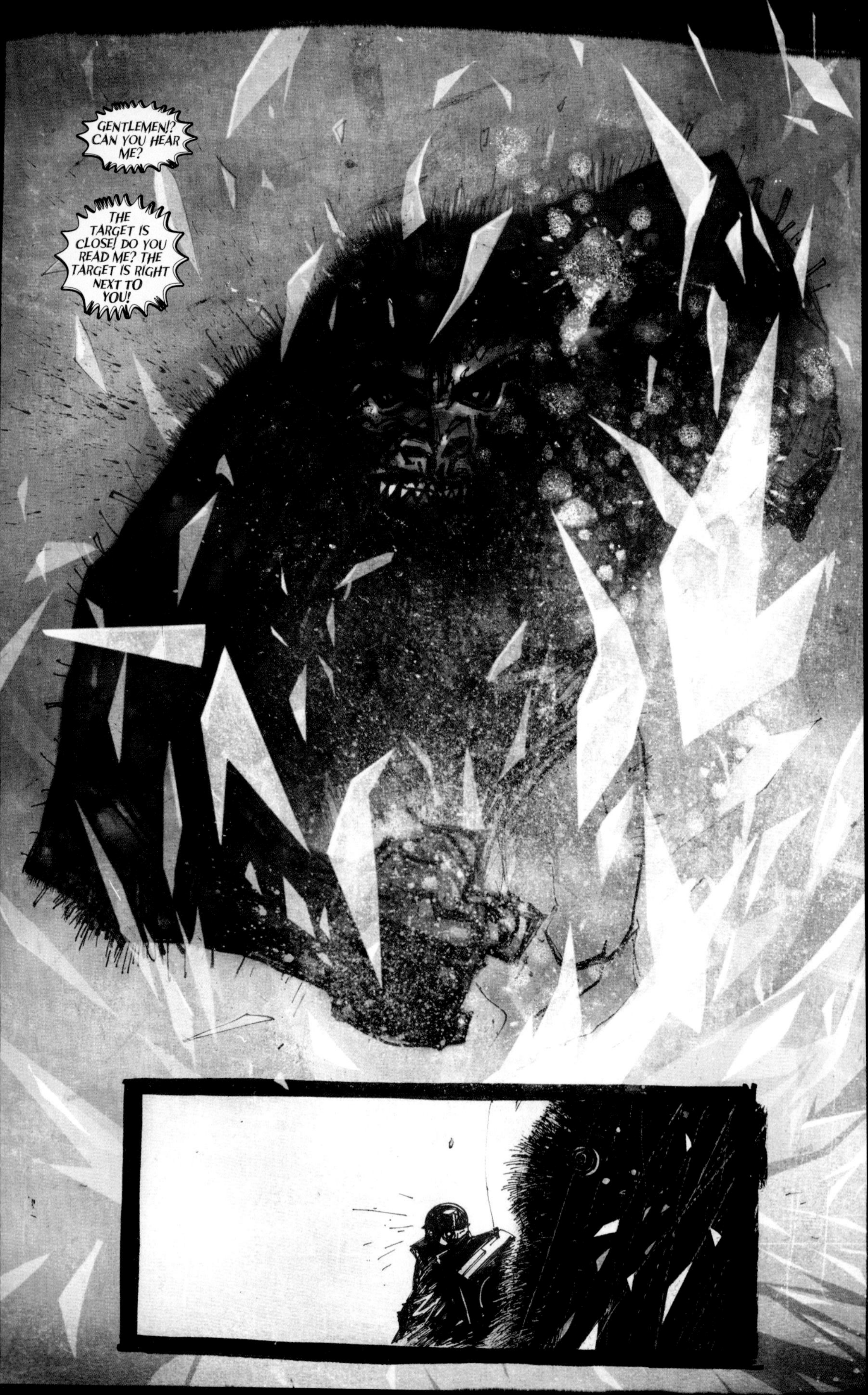
GENTLEMEN!? CAN YOU HEAR ME?
THE TARGET IS CLOSE! DO YOU READ ME? THE TARGET IS RIGHT NEXT TO YOU!

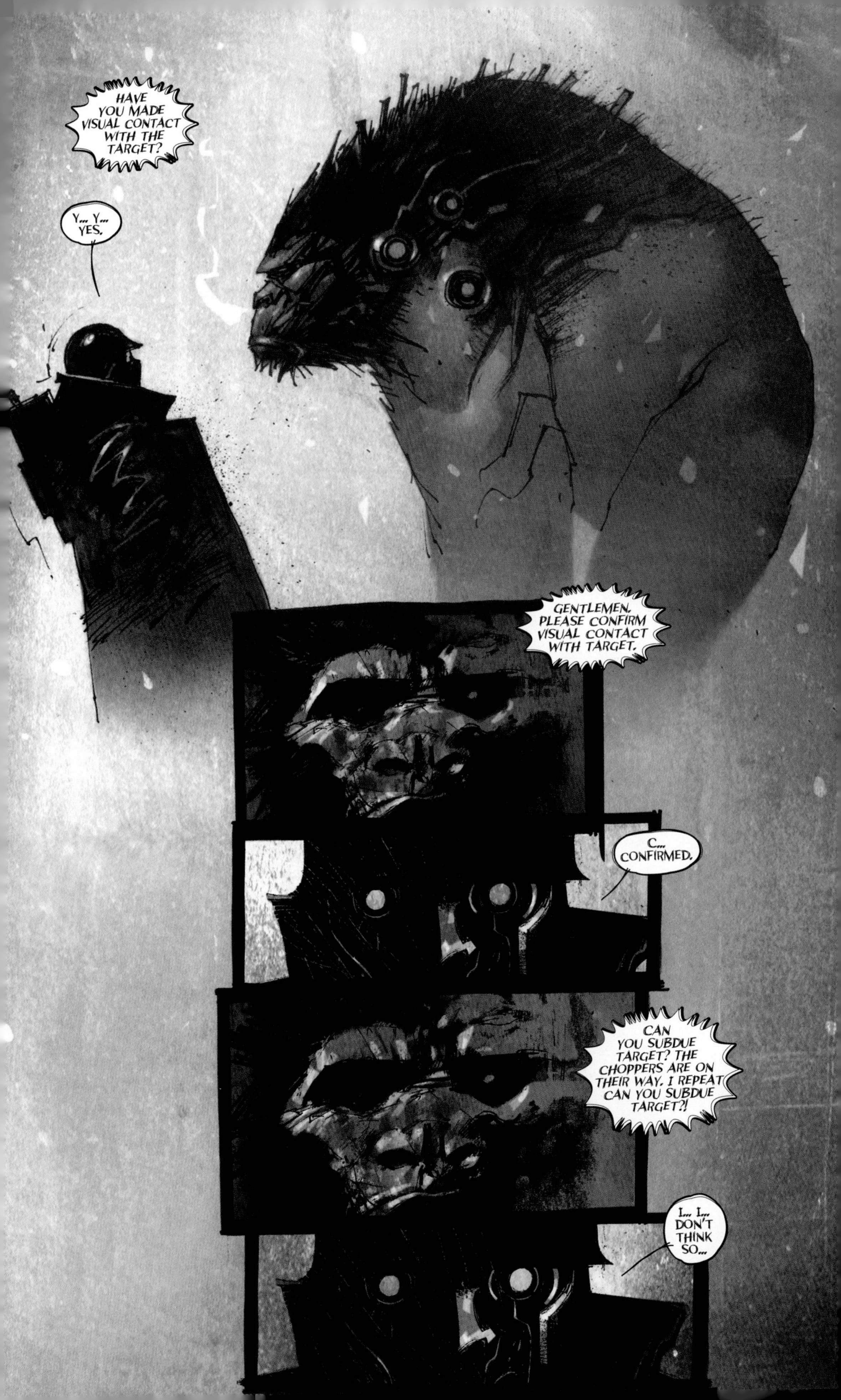
HAVE YOU MADE VISUAL CONTACT WITH THE TARGET?
Y... Y... YES.
GENTLEMEN. PLEASE CONFIRM VISUAL CONTACT WITH TARGET.
C... CONFIRMED.
CAN YOU SUBDUE TARGET? THE CHOPPERS ARE ON THEIR WAY. I REPEAT CAN YOU SUBDUE TARGET?!
I... I... DON'T THINK SO...

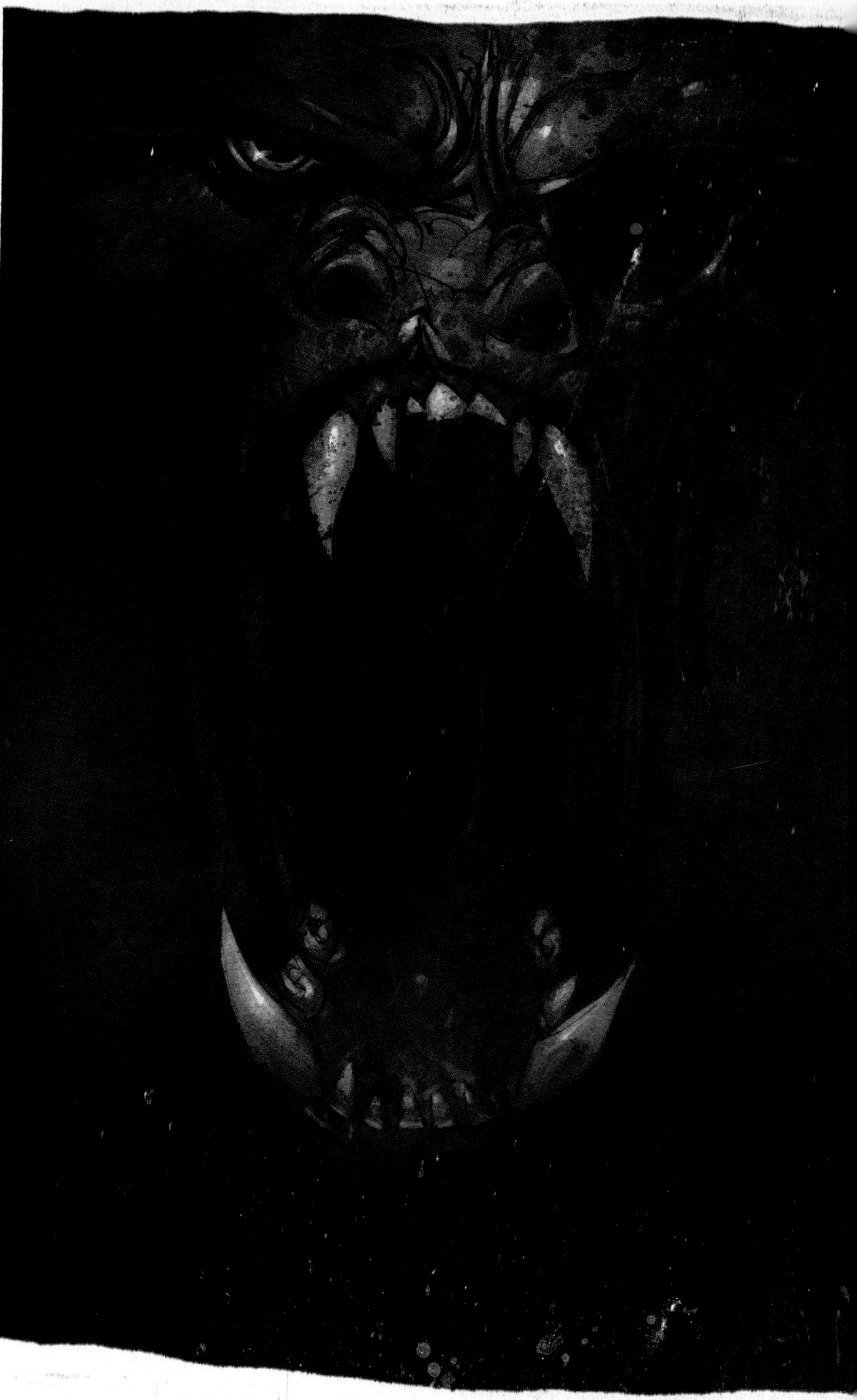

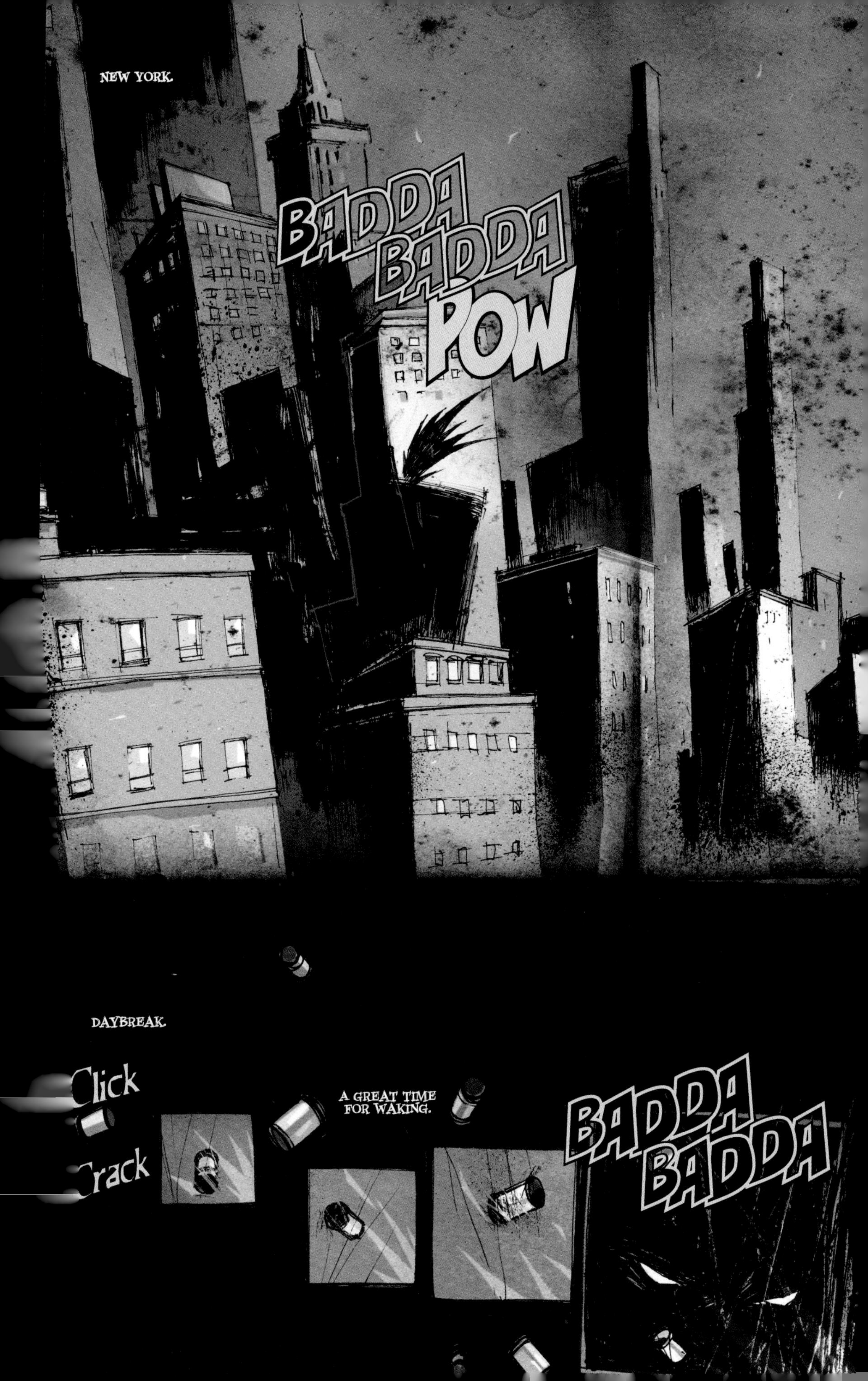

NEW YORK.
BADDA BADDA POW
DAYBREAK.
Click
Crack
A GREAT TIME FOR WAKING.
BADDA BADDA

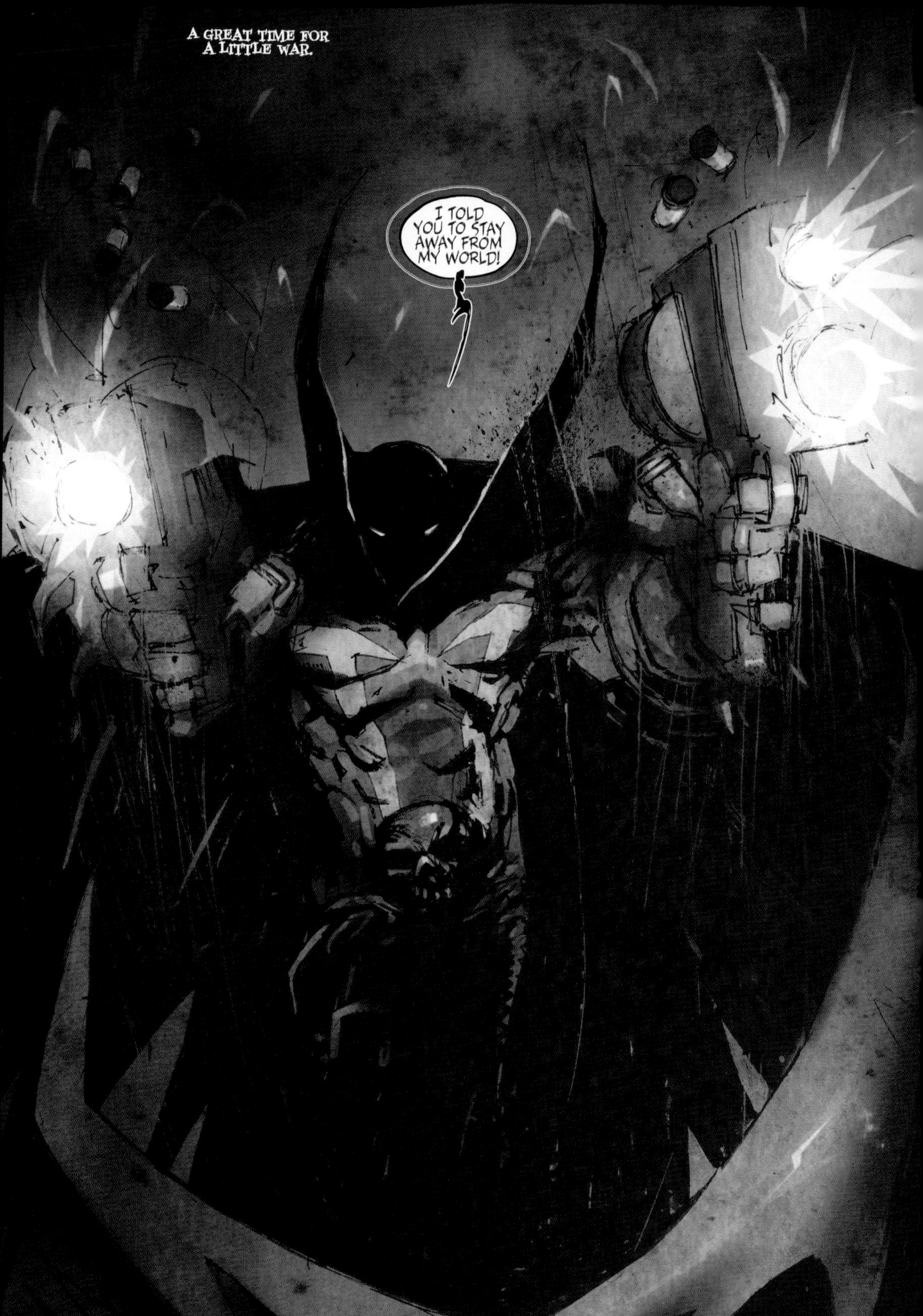
A GREAT TIME FOR
A LITTLE WAR.
I TOLD YOU TO STAY AWAY FROM MY WORLD!

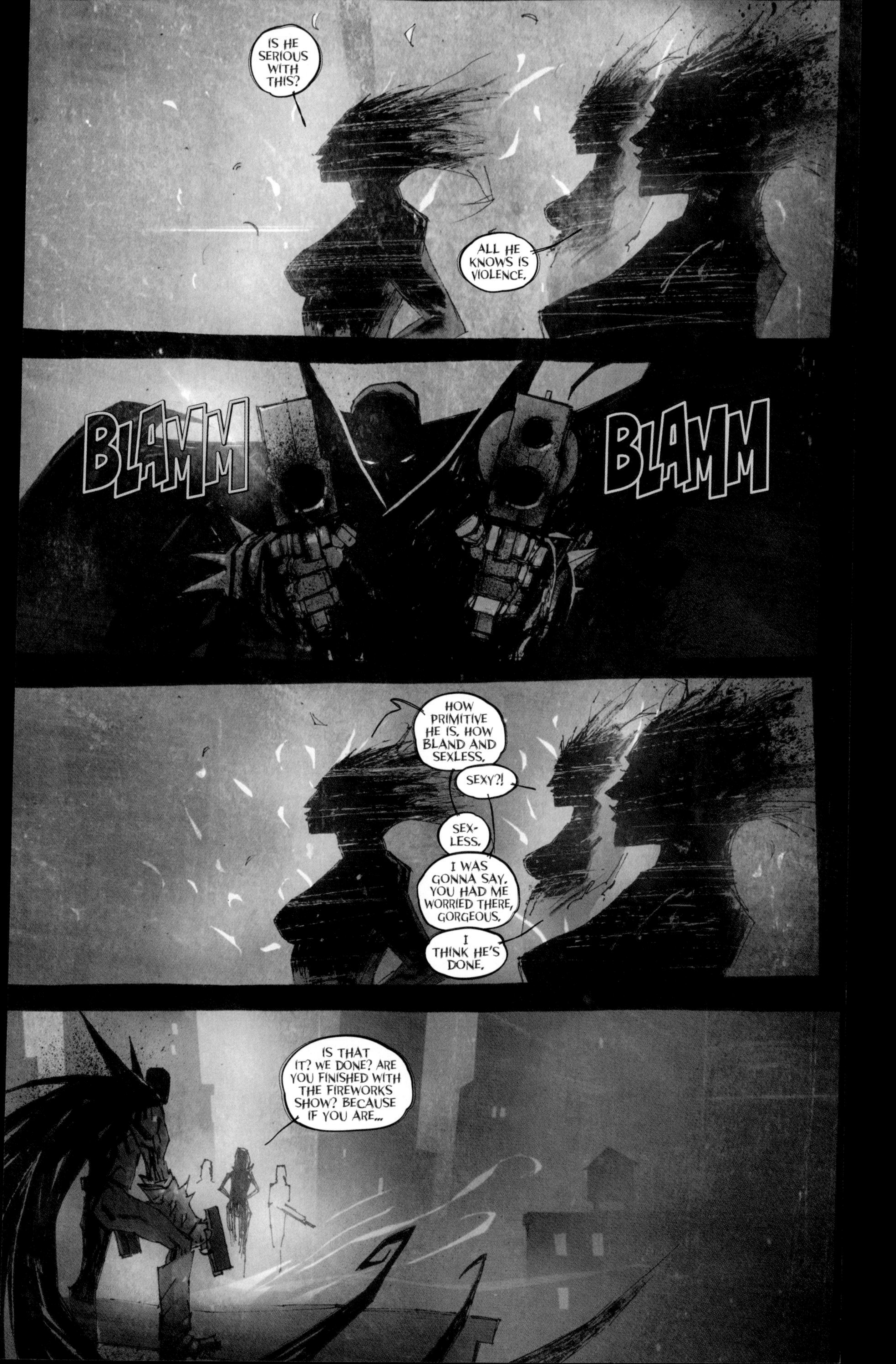
IS HE SERIOUS WITH THIS?
ALL HE KNOWS IS VIOLENCE.
BLAMM
BLAMM
HOW PRIMITIVE HE IS. HOW BLAND AND SEXLESS.
SEXY?!
SEX-LESS.
I WAS GONNA SAY. YOU HAD ME WORRIED THERE, GORGEOUS.
I THINK HE'S DONE.
IS THAT IT? WE DONE? ARE YOU FINISHED WITH THE FIREWORKS SHOW? BECAUSE IF YOU ARE...

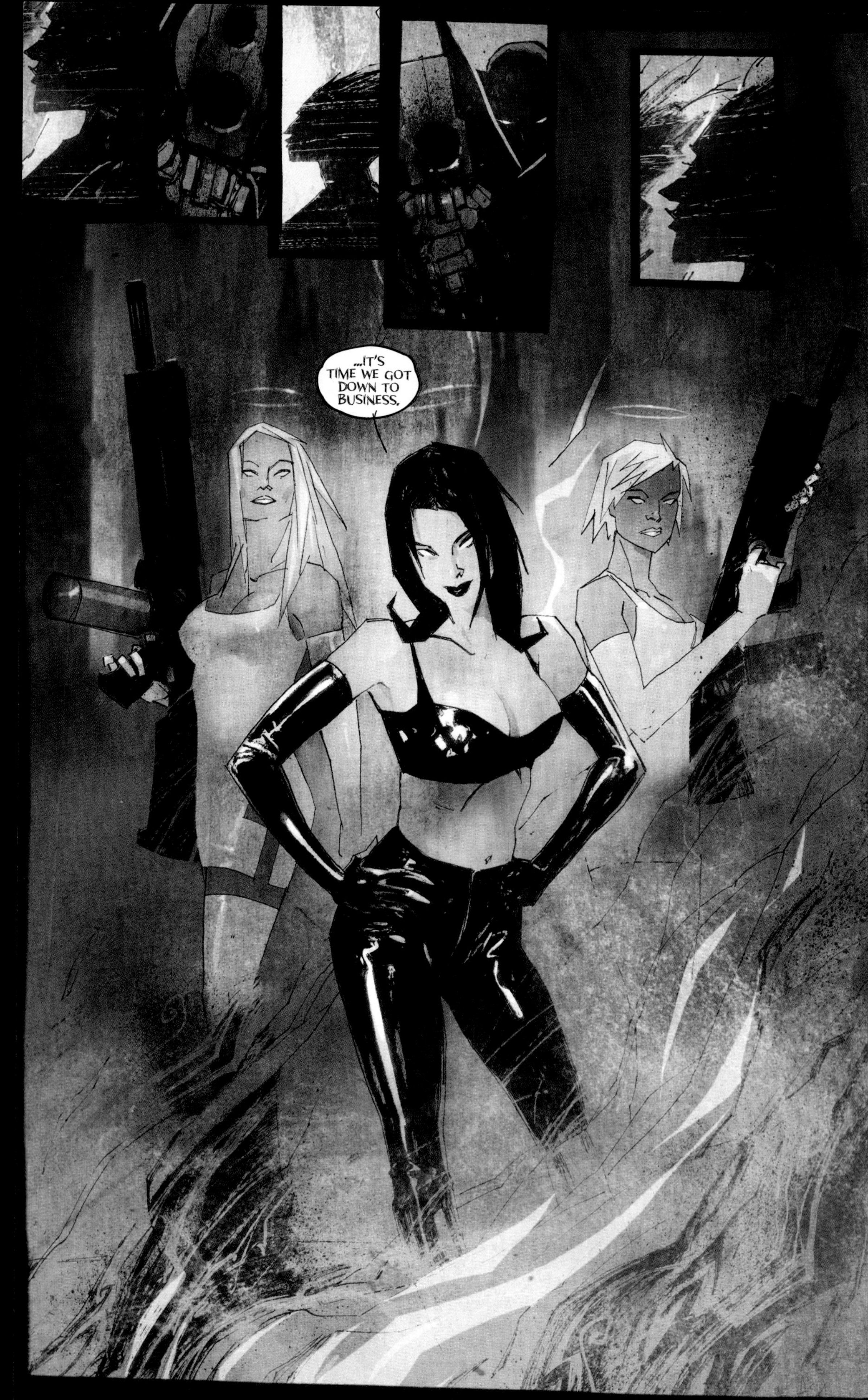
...IT'S TIME WE GOT DOWN TO BUSINESS.

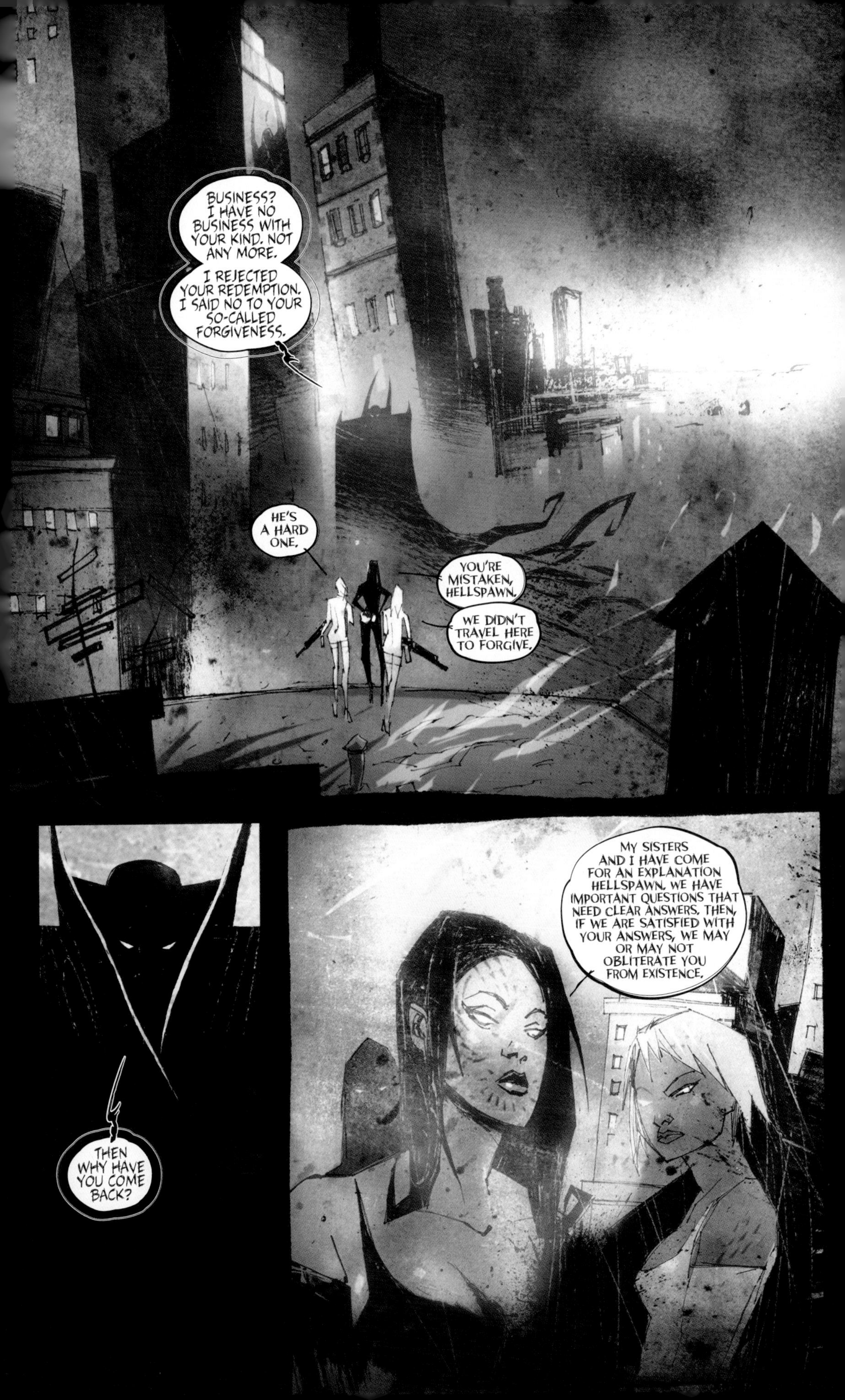
BUSINESS? I HAVE NO BUSINESS WITH YOUR KIND. NOT ANY MORE.
I REJECTED YOUR REDEMPTION. I SAID NO TO YOUR SO-CALLED FORGIVENESS.
HE'S A HARD ONE.
YOU'RE MISTAKEN, HELLSPAWN.
WE DIDN'T TRAVEL HERE TO FORGIVE.
THEN WHY HAVE YOU COME BACK?
MY SISTERS AND I HAVE COME FOR AN EXPLANATION HELLSPAWN. WE HAVE IMPORTANT QUESTIONS THAT NEED CLEAR ANSWERS. THEN, IF WE ARE SATISFIED WITH YOUR ANSWERS, WE MAY OR MAY NOT OBLITERATE YOU FROM EXISTENCE.

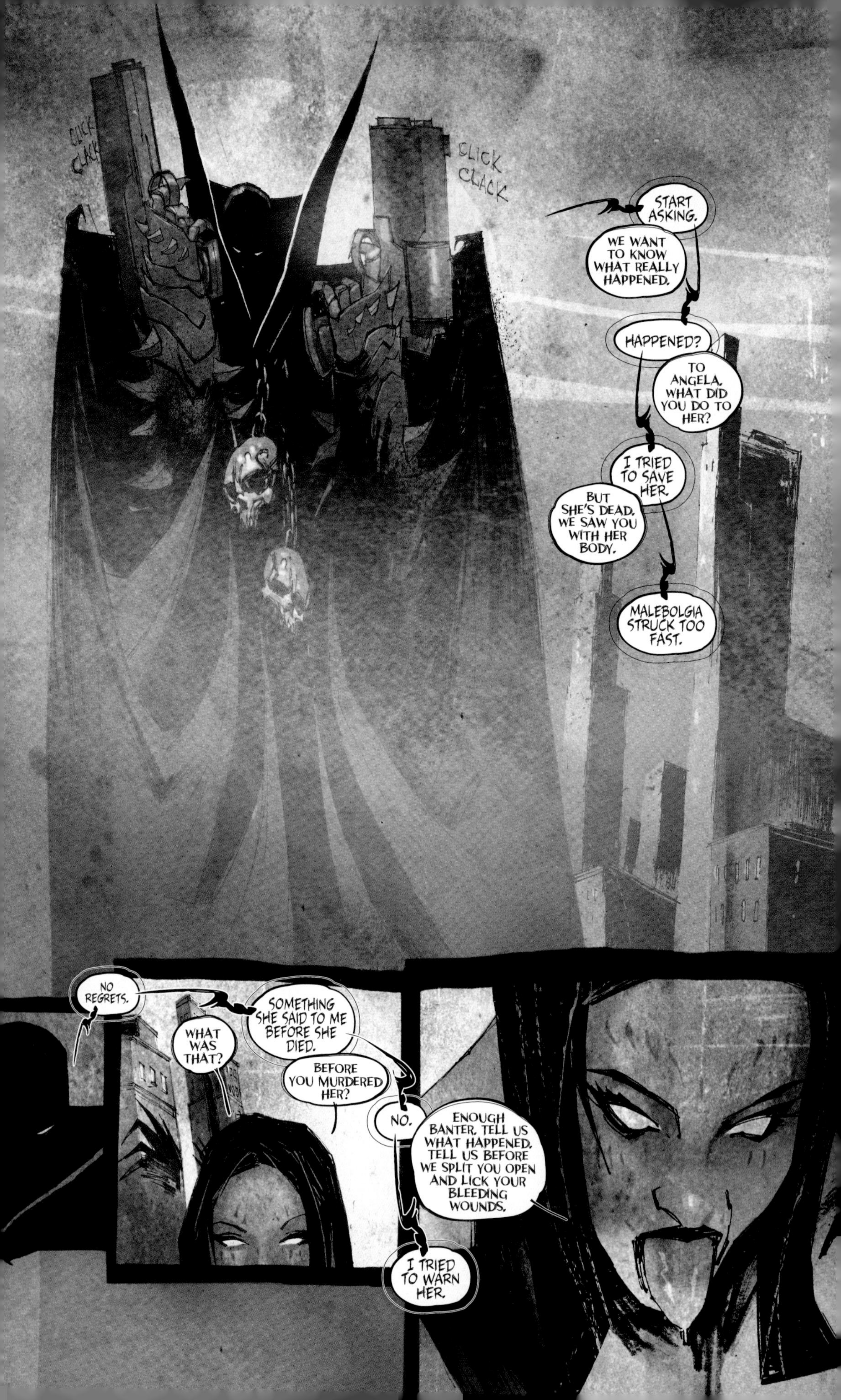
CLICK CLACK
CLICK CLACK
START ASKING.
WE WANT TO KNOW WHAT REALLY HAPPENED.
HAPPENED?
TO ANGELA. WHAT DID YOU DO TO HER?
I TRIED TO SAVE HER.
BUT SHE'S DEAD. WE SAW YOU WITH HER BODY.
MALEBOLGIA STRUCK TOO FAST.
NO REGRETS.
WHAT WAS THAT?
SOMETHING SHE SAID TO ME BEFORE SHE DIED.
BEFORE YOU MURDERED HER?
NO.
ENOUGH BANTER. TELL US WHAT HAPPENED. TELL US BEFORE WE SPLIT YOU OPEN AND LICK YOUR BLEEDING WOUNDS.
I TRIED TO WARN HER.

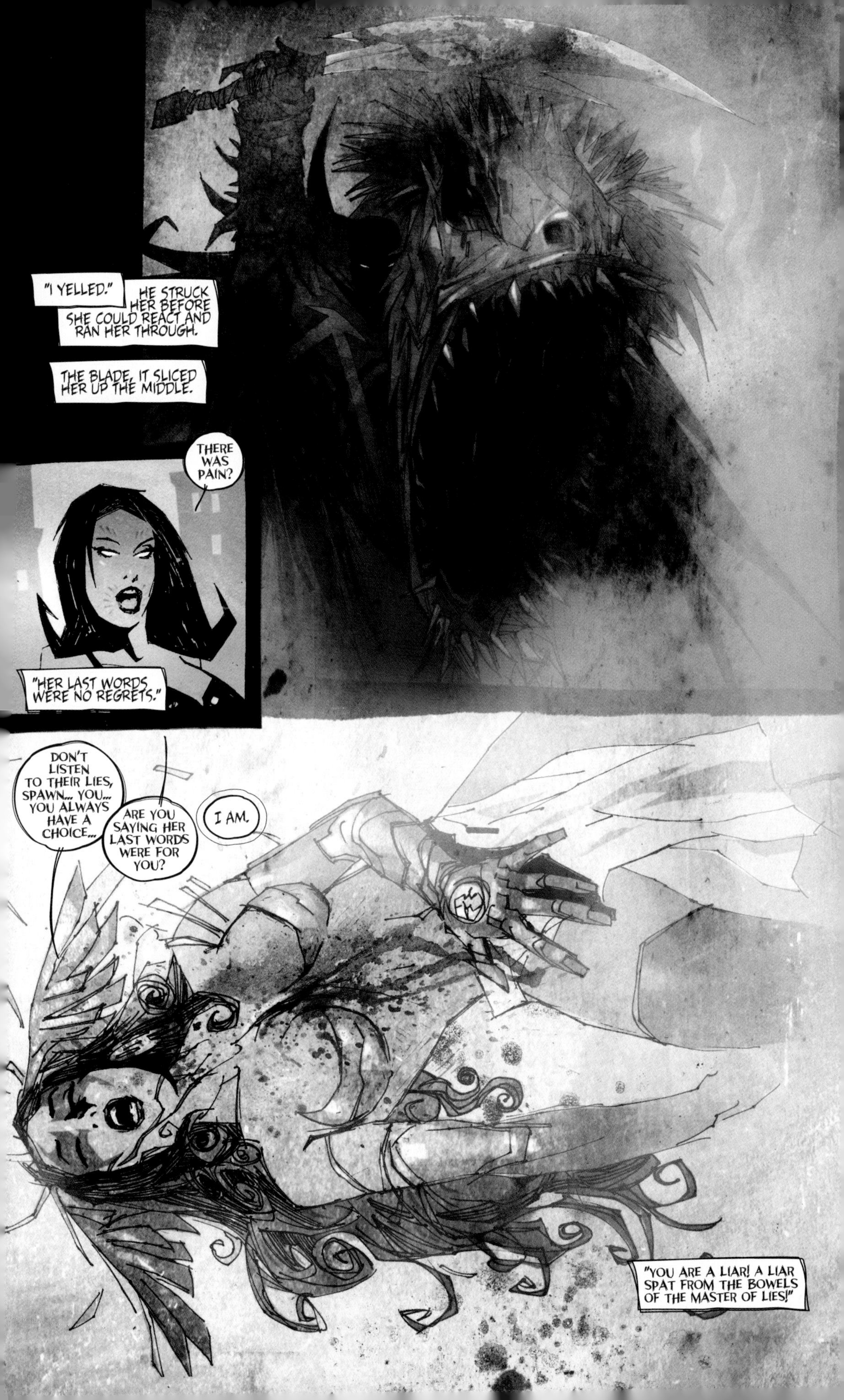
"I YELLED." HE STRUCK HER BEFORE SHE COULD REACT AND RAN HER THROUGH.
THE BLADE, IT SLICED HER UP THE MIDDLE.
THERE WAS PAIN?
"HER LAST WORDS WERE NO REGRETS."
DON'T LISTEN TO THEIR LIES, SPAWN... YOU... YOU ALWAYS HAVE A CHOICE...
ARE YOU SAYING HER LAST WORDS WERE FOR YOU?
I AM.
"YOU ARE A LIAR! A LIAR SPAT FROM THE BOWELS OF THE MASTER OF LIES!"

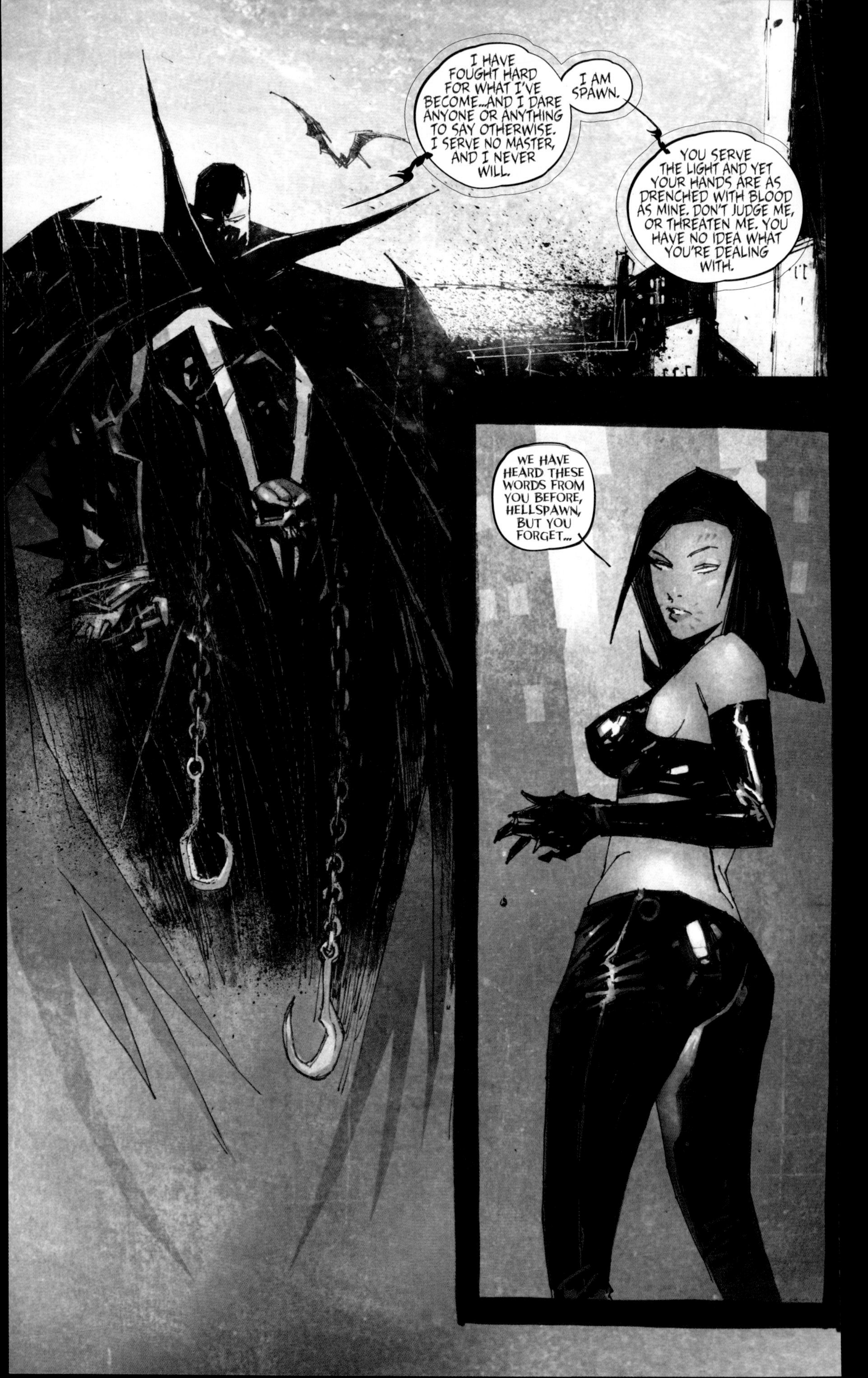
I HAVE FOUGHT HARD FOR WHAT I'VE BECOME...AND I DARE ANYONE OR ANYTHING TO SAY OTHERWISE. I SERVE NO MASTER, AND I NEVER WILL.
I AM SPAWN.
YOU SERVE THE LIGHT AND YET YOUR HANDS ARE AS DRENCHED WITH BLOOD AS MINE. DON'T JUDGE ME, OR THREATEN ME. YOU HAVE NO IDEA WHAT YOU'RE DEALING WITH.
WE HAVE HEARD THESE WORDS FROM YOU BEFORE, HELLSPAWN, BUT YOU FORGET...

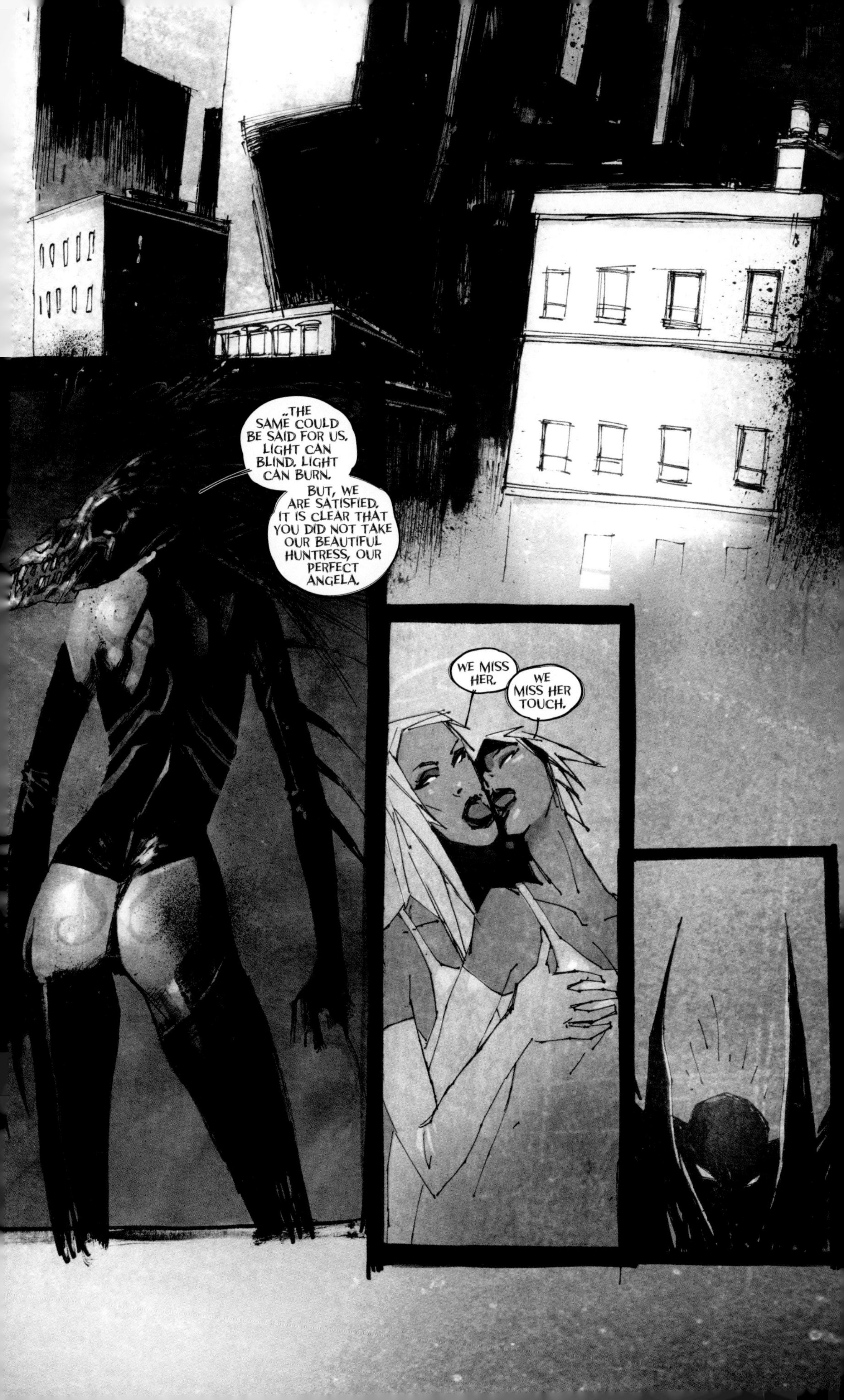
..THE SAME COULD BE SAID FOR US. LIGHT CAN BLIND. LIGHT CAN BURN.
BUT, WE ARE SATISFIED. IT IS CLEAR THAT YOU DID NOT TAKE OUR BEAUTIFUL HUNTRESS, OUR PERFECT ANGELA.
WE MISS HER.
WE MISS HER TOUCH.

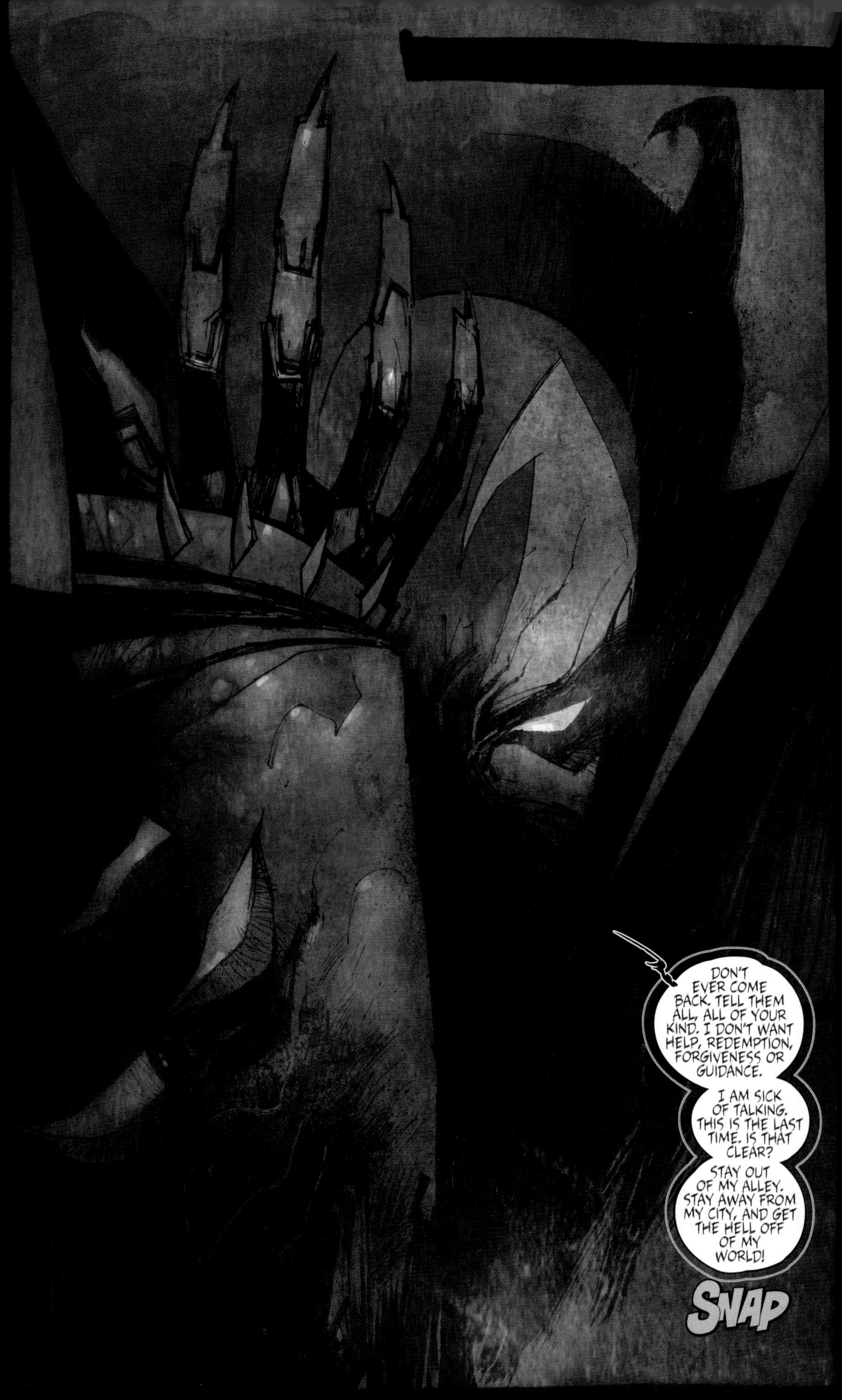
DON'T EVER COME BACK. TELL THEM ALL, ALL OF YOUR KIND. I DON'T WANT HELP, REDEMPTION, FORGIVENESS OR GUIDANCE.
I AM SICK OF TALKING. THIS IS THE LAST TIME. IS THAT CLEAR?
STAY OUT OF MY ALLEY. STAY AWAY FROM MY CITY, AND GET THE HELL OFF OF MY WORLD!
SNAP

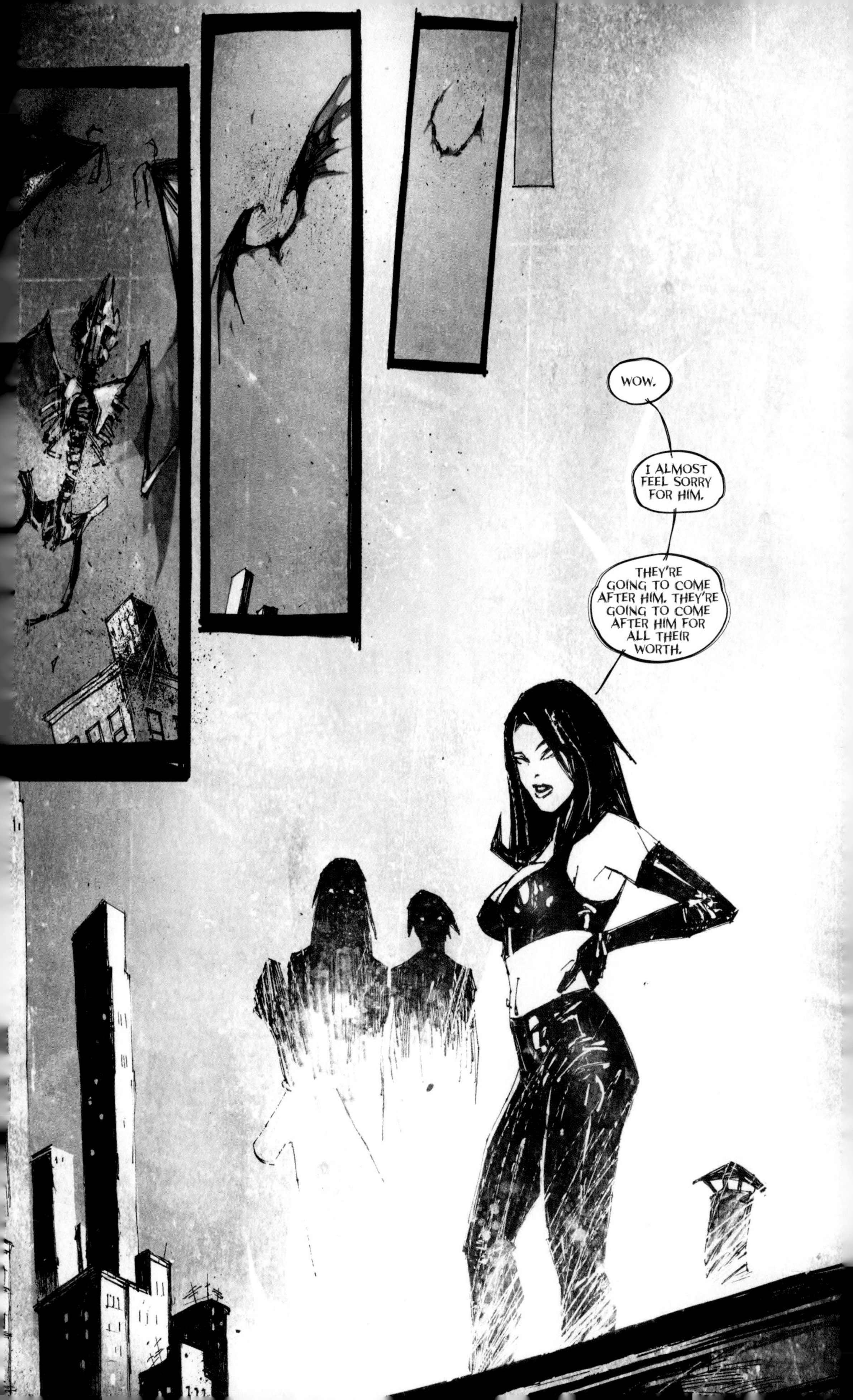
WOW.
I ALMOST FEEL SORRY FOR HIM.
THEY'RE GOING TO COME AFTER HIM. THEY'RE GOING TO COME AFTER HIM FOR ALL THEIR WORTH.

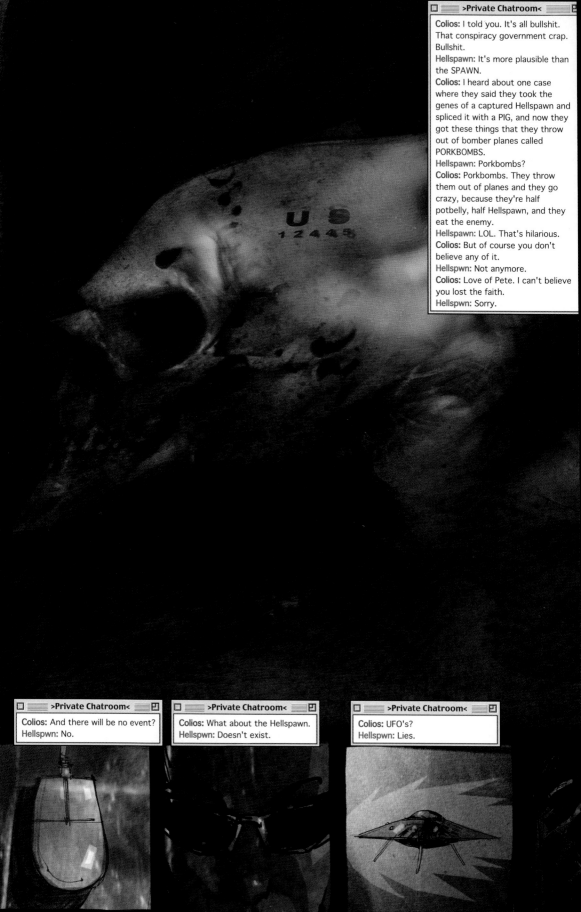

Colios: I told you. It's all bullshit. That conspiracy government crap. Bullshit.

Hellspawn: It's more plausible than the SPAWN.

Colios: I heard about one case where they said they took the genes of a captured Hellspawn and spliced it with a PIG, and now they got these things that they throw out of bomber planes called PORKBOMBS.

Hellspawn: Porkbombs?

Colios: Porkbombs. They throw them out of planes and they go crazy, because they're half potbelly, half Hellspawn, and they eat the enemy.

Hellspawn: LOL. That's hilarious.

Colios: But of course you don't believe any of it.

Hellspwn: Not anymore.

Colios: Love of Pete. I can't believe you lost the faith.

Hellspwn: Sorry.

>Private Chatroom<

Colios: And there will be no event?

Hellspwn: No.

>Private Chatroom<

Colios: What about the Hellspawn.

Hellspwn: Doesn't exist.

>Private Chatroom<

Colios: UFO's?

Hellspwn: Lies.

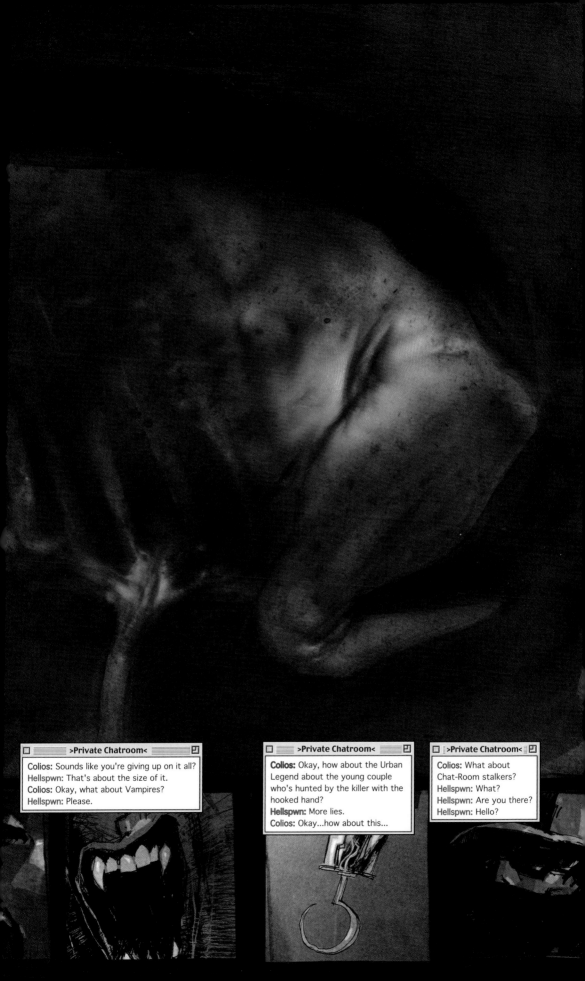

>Private Chatroom<

Colios: Sounds like you're giving up on it all?
Hellspwn: That's about the size of it.
Colios: Okay, what about Vampires?
Hellspwn: Please.

>Private Chatroom<

Colios: Okay, how about the Urban Legend about the young couple who's hunted by the killer with the hooked hand?
Hellspwn: More lies.
Colios: Okay...how about this...

>Private Chatroom<

Colios: What about Chat-Room stalkers?
Hellspwn: What?
Hellspwn: Are you there?
Hellspwn: Hello?

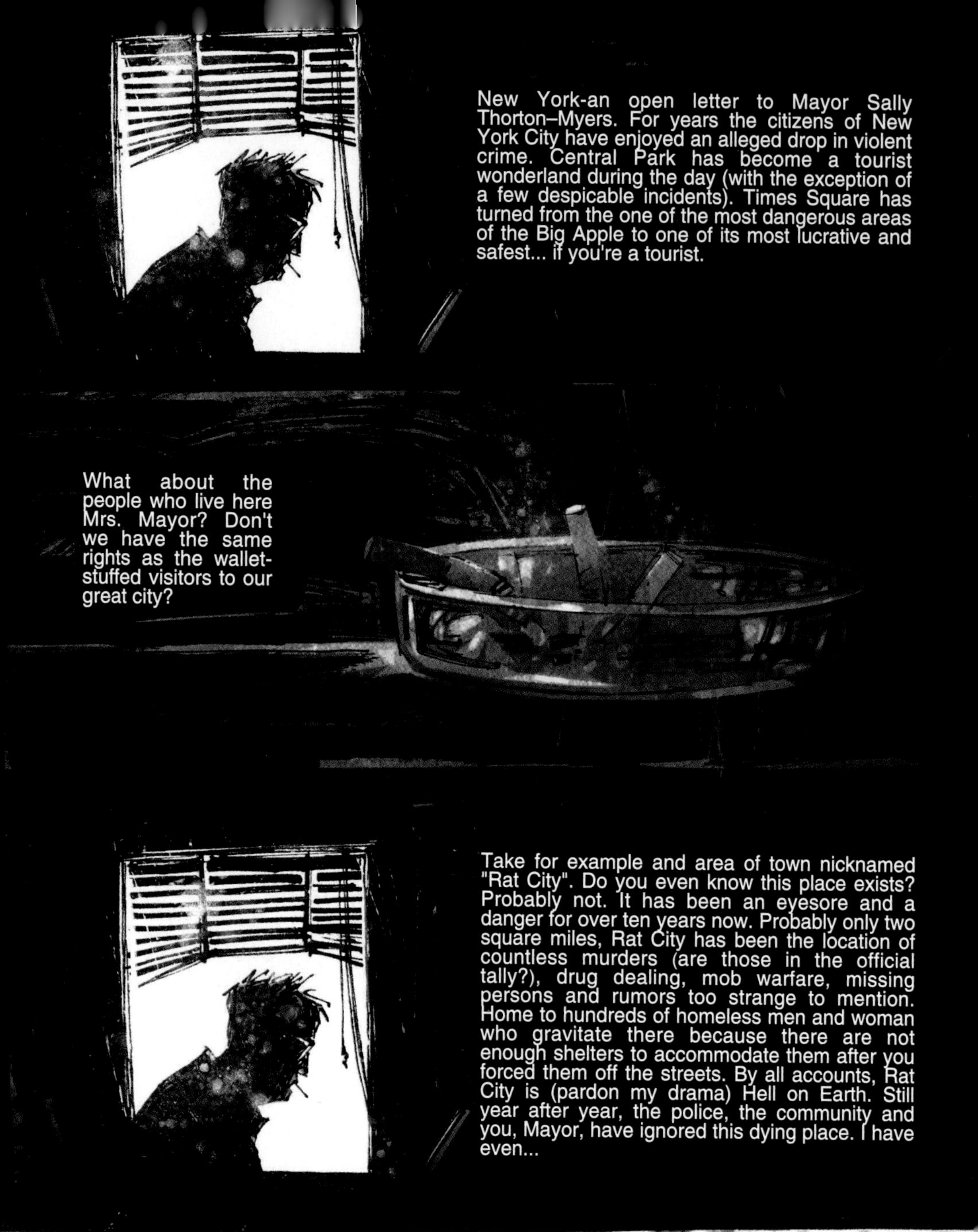
New York-an open letter to Mayor Sally Thorton–Myers. For years the citizens of New York City have enjoyed an alleged drop in violent crime. Central Park has become a tourist wonderland during the day (with the exception of a few despicable incidents). Times Square has turned from the one of the most dangerous areas of the Big Apple to one of its most lucrative and safest... if you're a tourist.
What about the people who live here Mrs. Mayor? Don't we have the same rights as the wallet-stuffed visitors to our great city?
Take for example and area of town nicknamed "Rat City". Do you even know this place exists? Probably not. It has been an eyesore and a danger for over ten years now. Probably only two square miles, Rat City has been the location of countless murders (are those in the official tally?), drug dealing, mob warfare, missing persons and rumors too strange to mention. Home to hundreds of homeless men and woman who gravitate there because there are not enough shelters to accommodate them after you forced them off the streets. By all accounts, Rat City is (pardon my drama) Hell on Earth. Still year after year, the police, the community and you, Mayor, have ignored this dying place. I have even...

Mike Moran

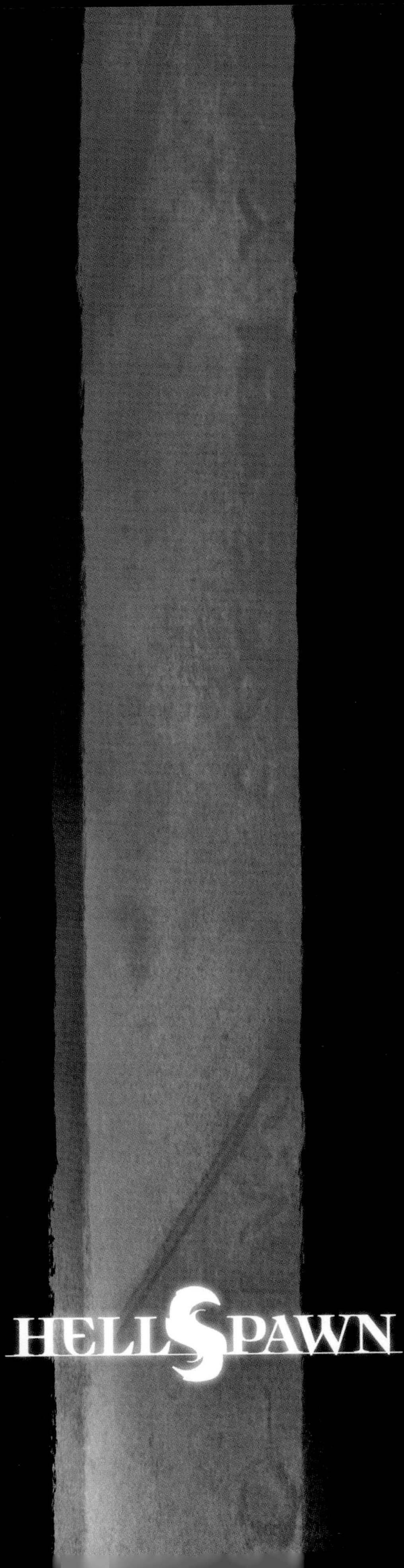
HELLSPAWN

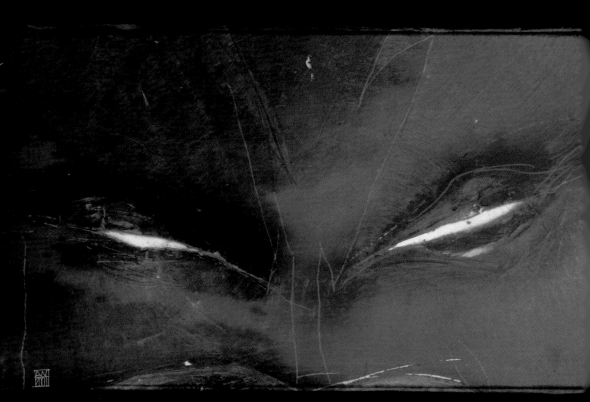

ISSUE SEVEN

meta·mor·pho·sis (mēt'a-mōr' fa-sīs)n. ,pl. noun., plural meta·mor·pho·ses (-sēz') Latin, from Greek metamōrphsis, from metamorphoun to transform, from meta-+morphē form 1 a : change of physical form, structure, or substance especially by supernatural means b : a striking alteration in appearance, character, or circumstances 2 : a marked and more or less abrupt developmental change in the form or structure of an animal (as a fly, frog or maggot) occurring subsequent to birth or hatching.

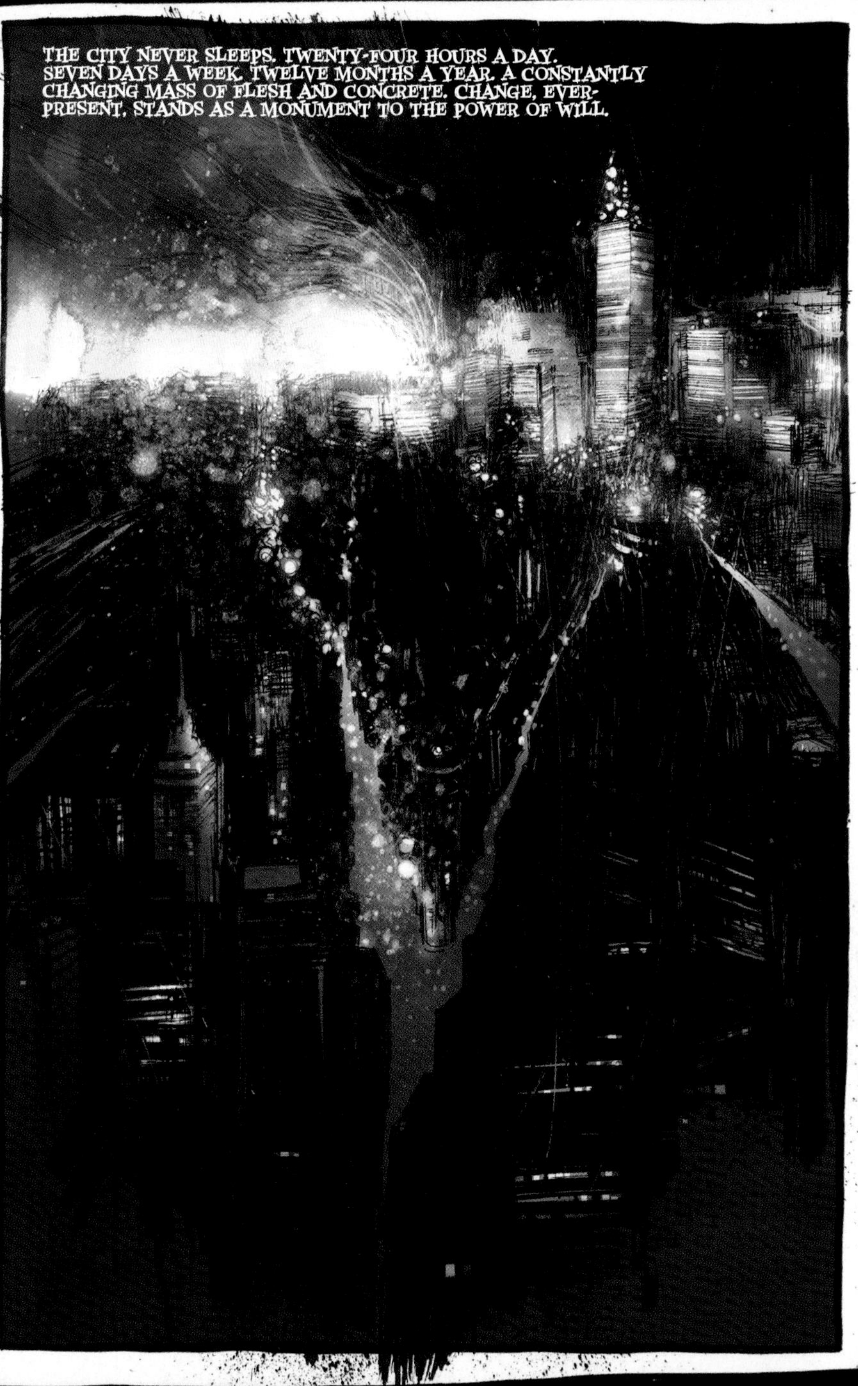
THE CITY NEVER SLEEPS. TWENTY-FOUR HOURS A DAY. SEVEN DAYS A WEEK. TWELVE MONTHS A YEAR. A CONSTANTLY CHANGING MASS OF FLESH AND CONCRETE. CHANGE, EVER-PRESENT, STANDS AS A MONUMENT TO THE POWER OF WILL.

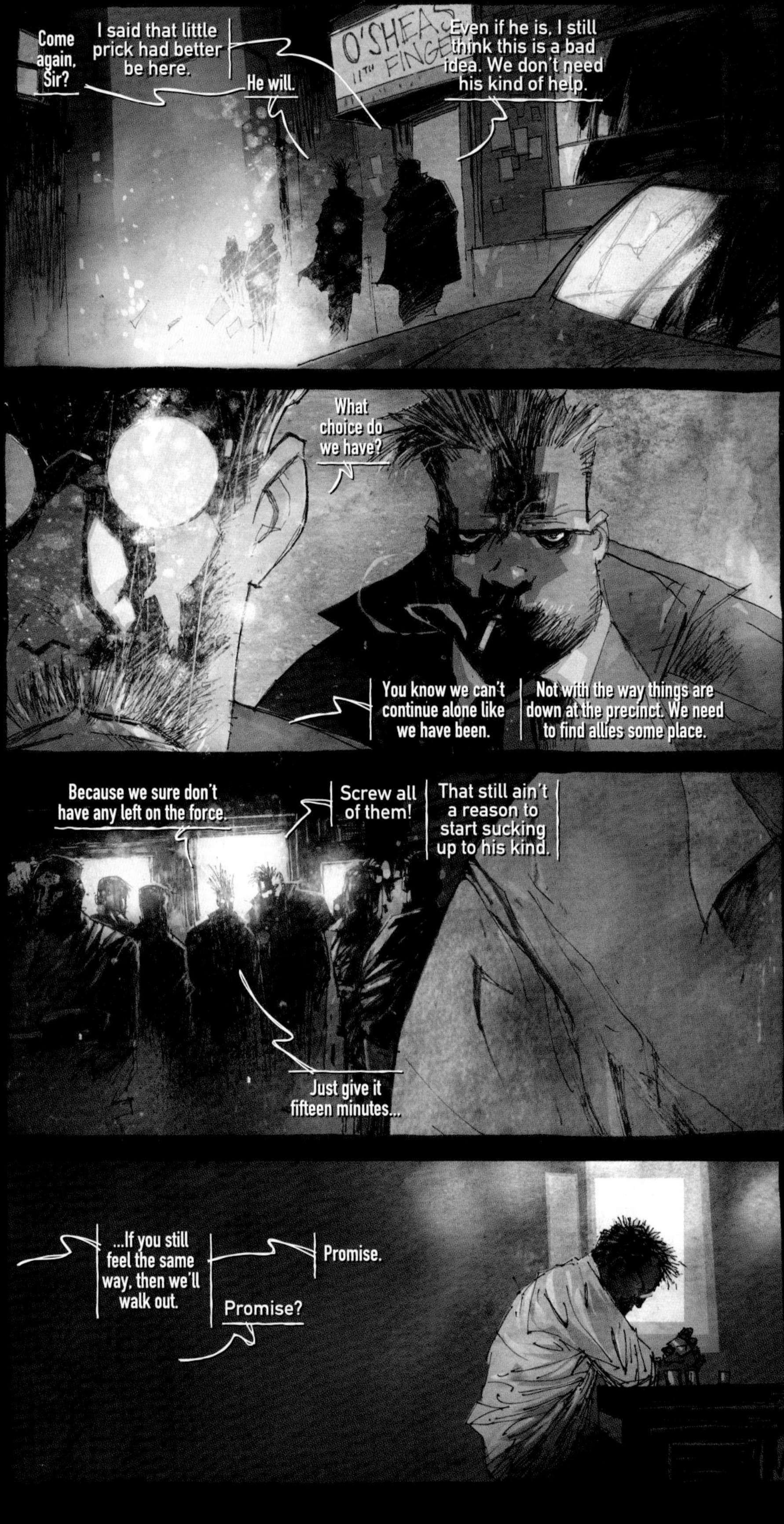
Come again, Sir?
I said that little prick had better be here.
He will.
Even if he is, I still think this is a bad idea. We don't need his kind of help.
What choice do we have?
You know we can't continue alone like we have been.
Not with the way things are down at the precinct. We need to find allies some place.
Because we sure don't have any left on the force.
Screw all of them!
That still ain't a reason to start sucking up to his kind.
Just give it fifteen minutes...
...If you still feel the same way, then we'll walk out.
Promise?
Promise.

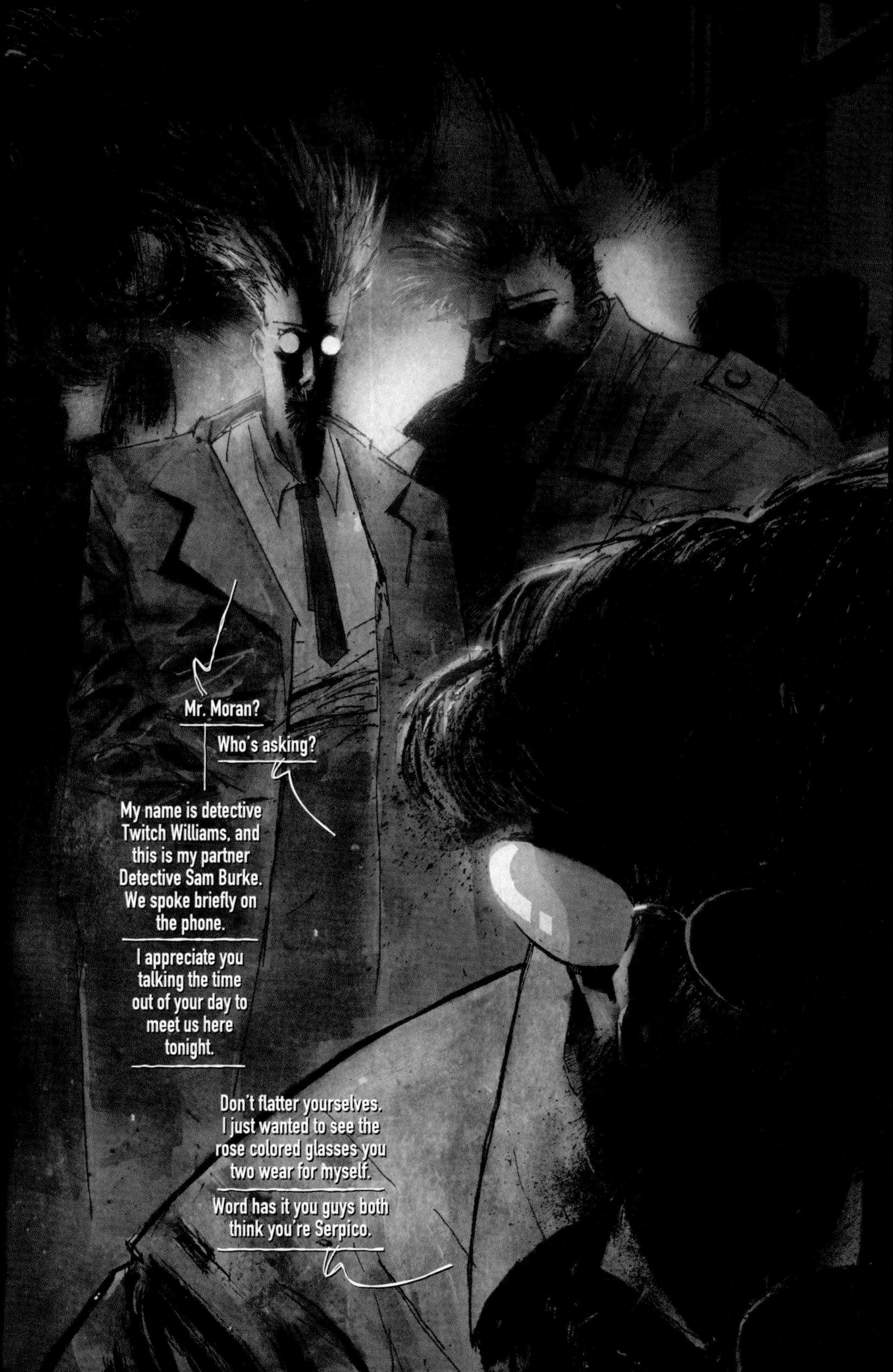
Mr. Moran?
Who's asking?
My name is detective Twitch Williams, and this is my partner Detective Sam Burke. We spoke briefly on the phone.
I appreciate you talking the time out of your day to meet us here tonight.
Don't flatter yourselves. I just wanted to see the rose colored glasses you two wear for myself.
Word has it you guys both think you're Serpico.

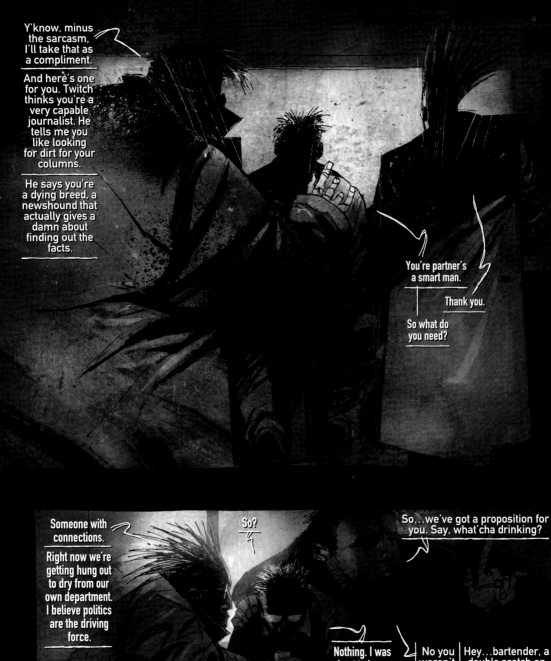

Y'know, minus the sarcasm, I'll take that as a compliment.

And here's one for you. Twitch thinks you're a very capable journalist. He tells me you like looking for dirt for your columns.

He says you're a dying breed, a newshound that actually gives a damn about finding out the facts.

You're partner's a smart man.

Thank you.

So what do you need?

Someone with connections.

Right now we're getting hung out to dry from our own department. I believe politics are the driving force.

So?

So…we've got a proposition for you. Say, what'cha drinking?

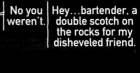

Nothing. I was about to leave.

No you weren't.

Hey…bartender, a double scotch on the rocks for my disheveled friend.

You see, Mr. Moran, much like yourself, we pride ourselves on clean work. Unfortunately, that seems to be a liability for us.

So we were hoping that you might entertain the possibility of us pointing you in the proper direction of some of that "dirt" you report on so much.

And what's in it for you?

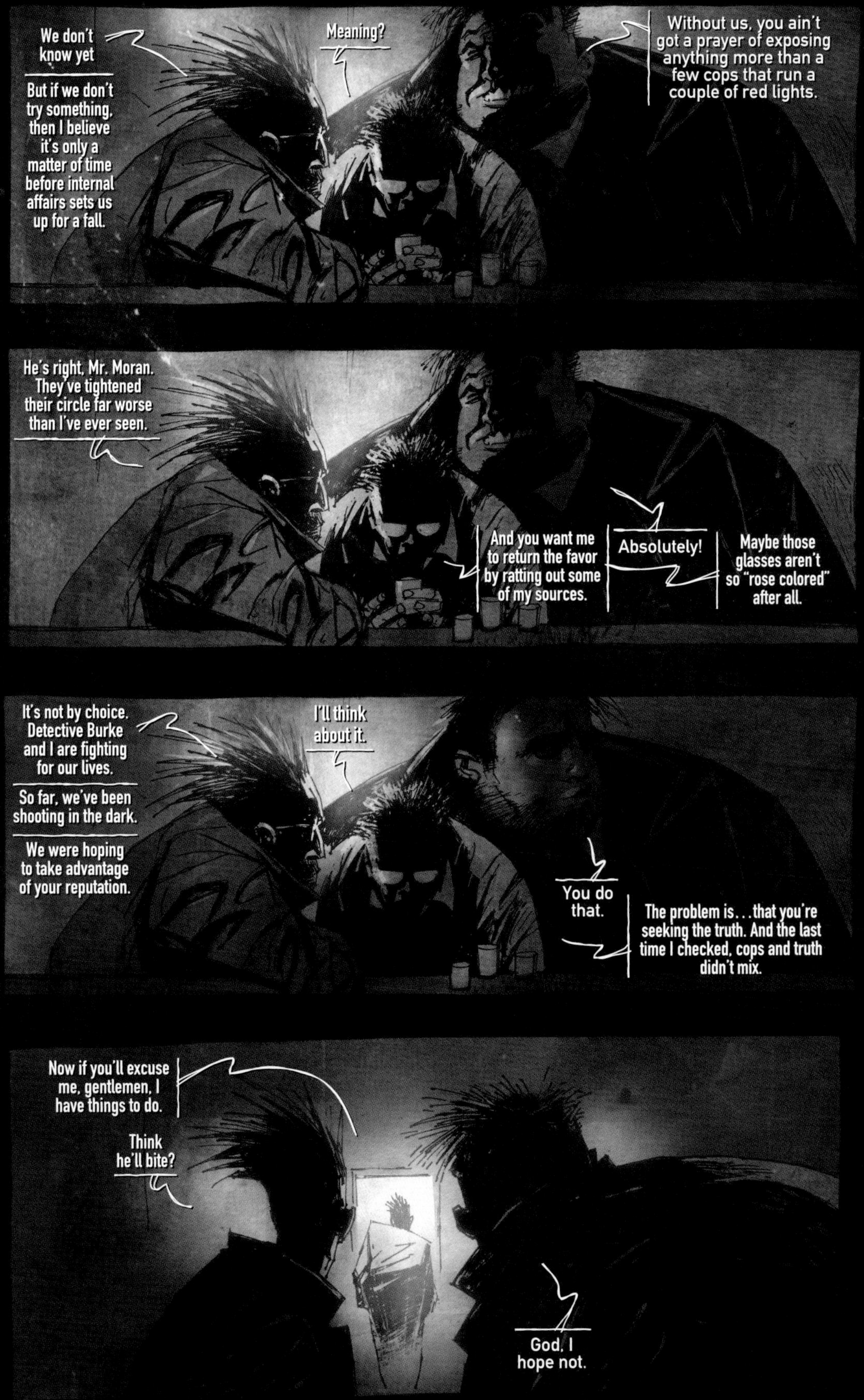
We don't know yet
But if we don't try something, then I believe it's only a matter of time before internal affairs sets us up for a fall.
Meaning?
Without us, you ain't got a prayer of exposing anything more than a few cops that run a couple of red lights.
He's right, Mr. Moran. They've tightened their circle far worse than I've ever seen.
And you want me to return the favor by ratting out some of my sources.
Absolutely!
Maybe those glasses aren't so "rose colored" after all.
It's not by choice. Detective Burke and I are fighting for our lives.
So far, we've been shooting in the dark.
We were hoping to take advantage of your reputation.
I'll think about it.
You do that.
The problem is...that you're seeking the truth. And the last time I checked, cops and truth didn't mix.
Now if you'll excuse me, gentlemen, I have things to do.
Think he'll bite?
God, I hope not.

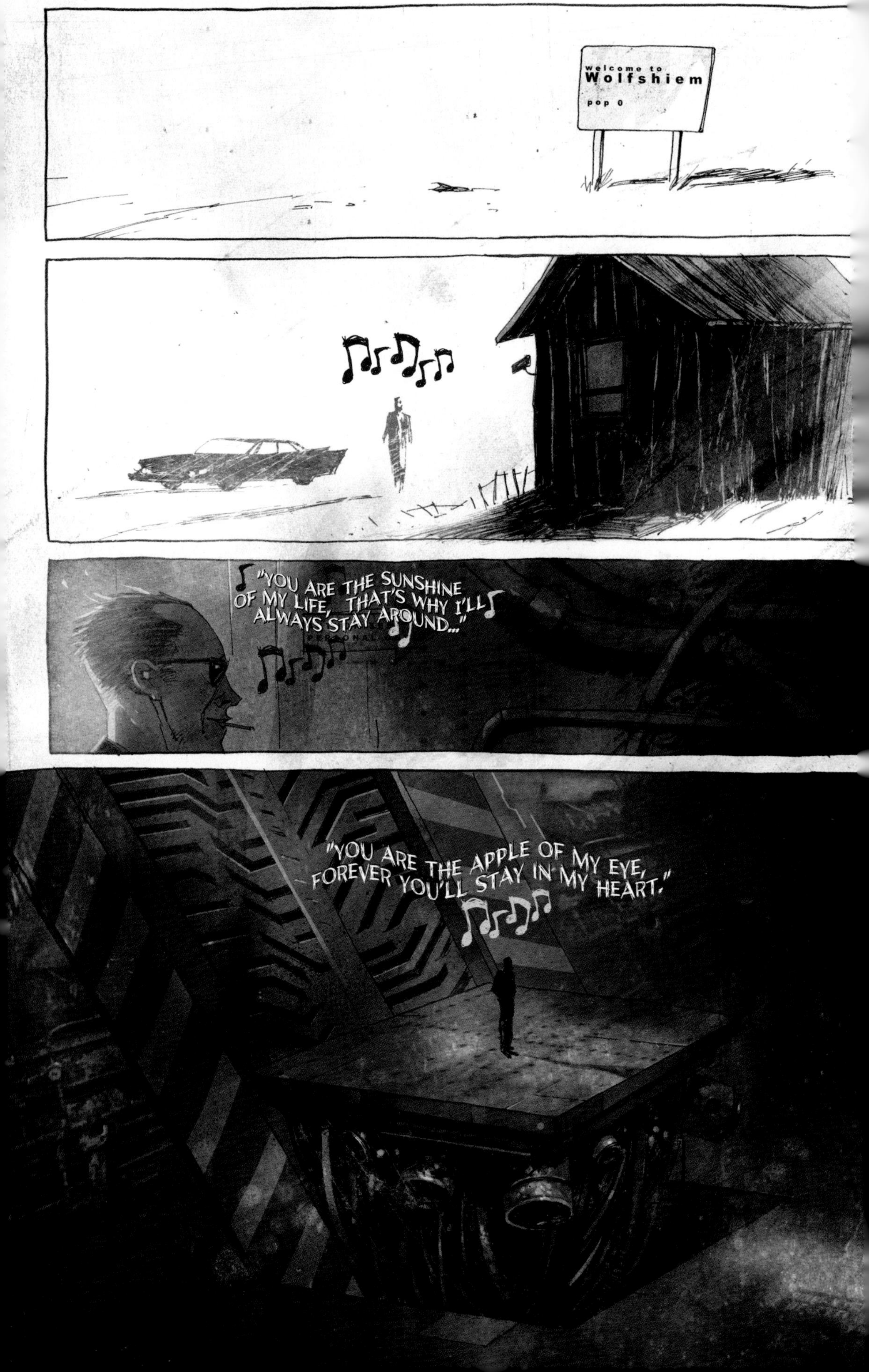
welcome to
Wolfshiem
pop 0
"YOU ARE THE SUNSHINE OF MY LIFE, THAT'S WHY I'LL ALWAYS STAY AROUND..."
"YOU ARE THE APPLE OF MY EYE, FOREVER YOU'LL STAY IN MY HEART."

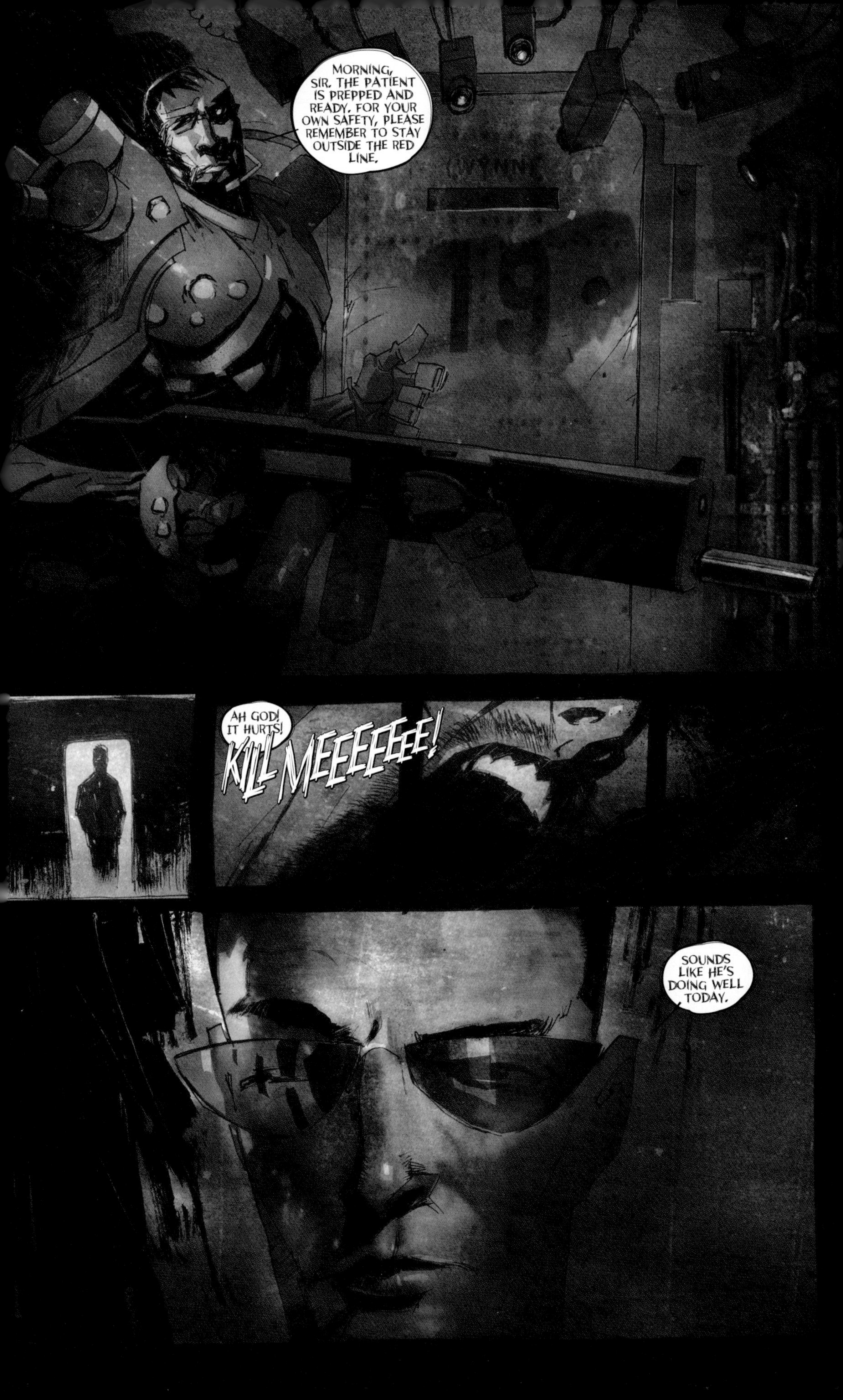
MORNING, SIR. THE PATIENT IS PREPPED AND READY. FOR YOUR OWN SAFETY, PLEASE REMEMBER TO STAY OUTSIDE THE RED LINE.
19
AH GOD! IT HURTS!
KILL MEEEEEEEE!
SOUNDS LIKE HE'S DOING WELL TODAY.

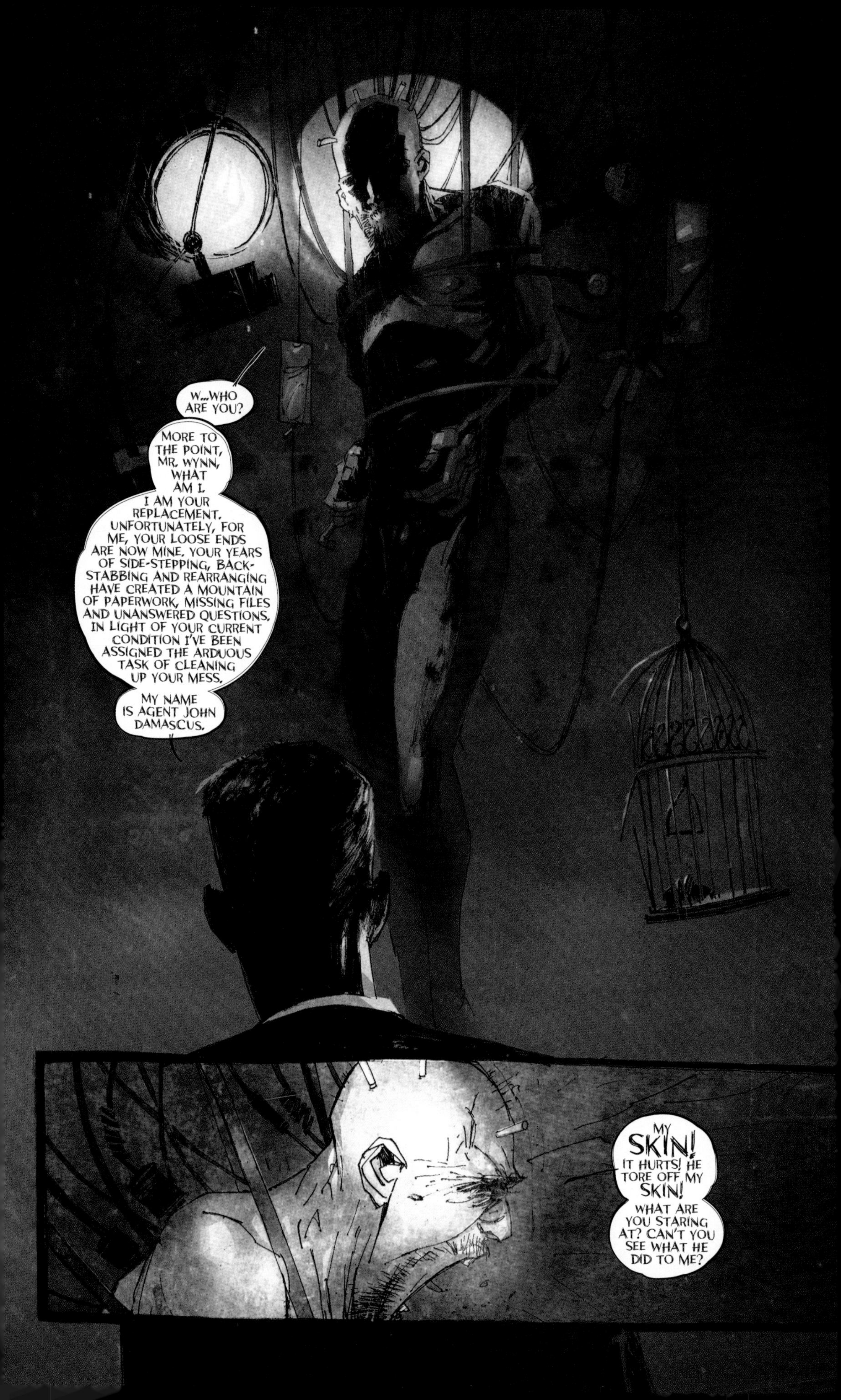

W...WHO ARE YOU?
MORE TO THE POINT, MR. WYNN, WHAT AM I. I AM YOUR REPLACEMENT. UNFORTUNATELY, FOR ME, YOUR LOOSE ENDS ARE NOW MINE. YOUR YEARS OF SIDE-STEPPING, BACK-STABBING AND REARRANGING HAVE CREATED A MOUNTAIN OF PAPERWORK, MISSING FILES AND UNANSWERED QUESTIONS. IN LIGHT OF YOUR CURRENT CONDITION I'VE BEEN ASSIGNED THE ARDUOUS TASK OF CLEANING UP YOUR MESS.
MY NAME IS AGENT JOHN DAMASCUS.
MY SKIN! IT HURTS! HE TORE OFF MY SKIN! WHAT ARE YOU STARING AT? CAN'T YOU SEE WHAT HE DID TO ME?

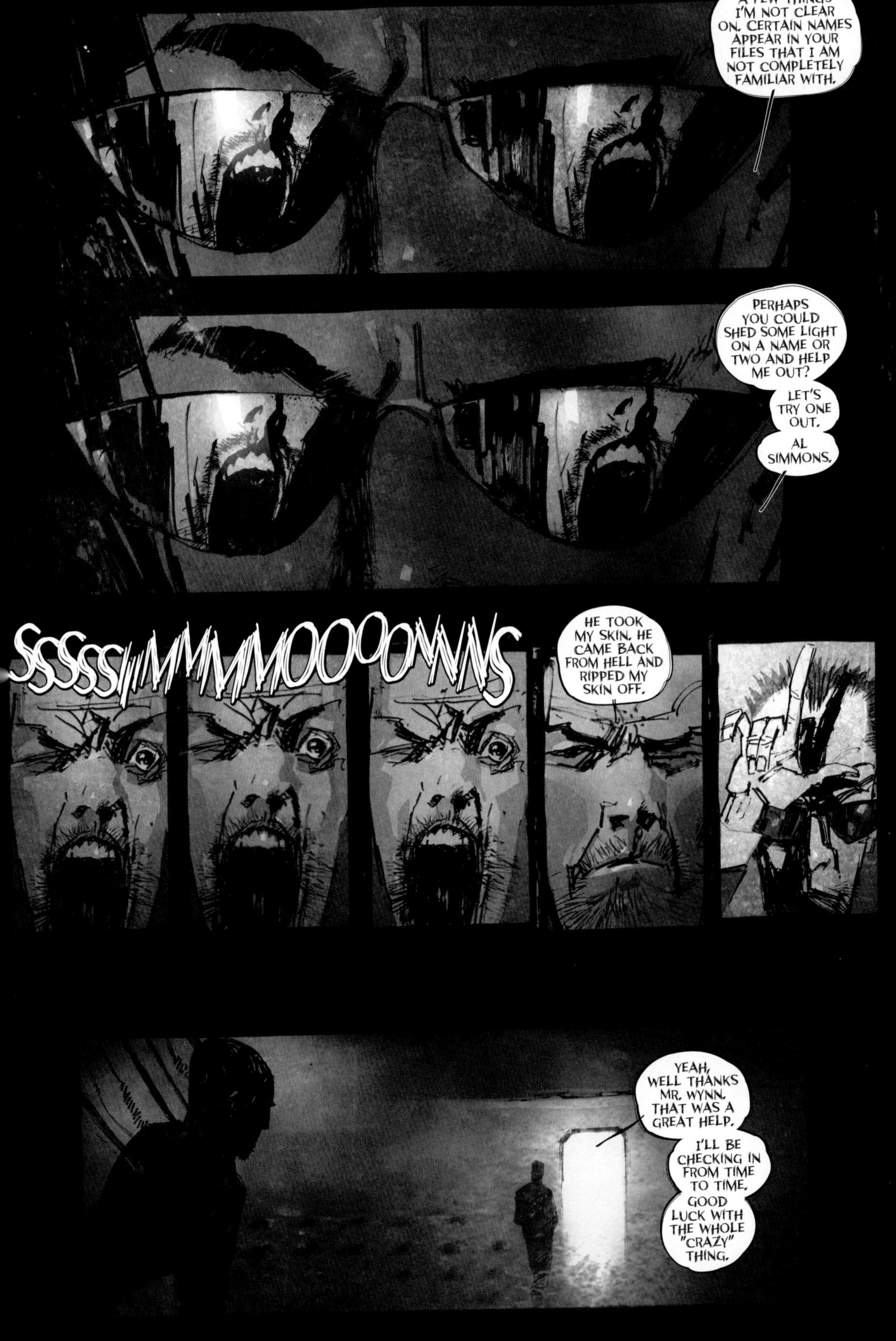

THERE ARE A FEW THINGS I'M NOT CLEAR ON. CERTAIN NAMES APPEAR IN YOUR FILES THAT I AM NOT COMPLETELY FAMILIAR WITH.
PERHAPS YOU COULD SHED SOME LIGHT ON A NAME OR TWO AND HELP ME OUT?
LET'S TRY ONE OUT.
AL SIMMONS.
SSSSSIIMMMMOOOOOWNS
HE TOOK MY SKIN. HE CAME BACK FROM HELL AND RIPPED MY SKIN OFF.
YEAH, WELL THANKS MR. WYNN. THAT WAS A GREAT HELP.
I'LL BE CHECKING IN FROM TIME TO TIME.
GOOD LUCK WITH THE WHOLE "CRAZY" THING.

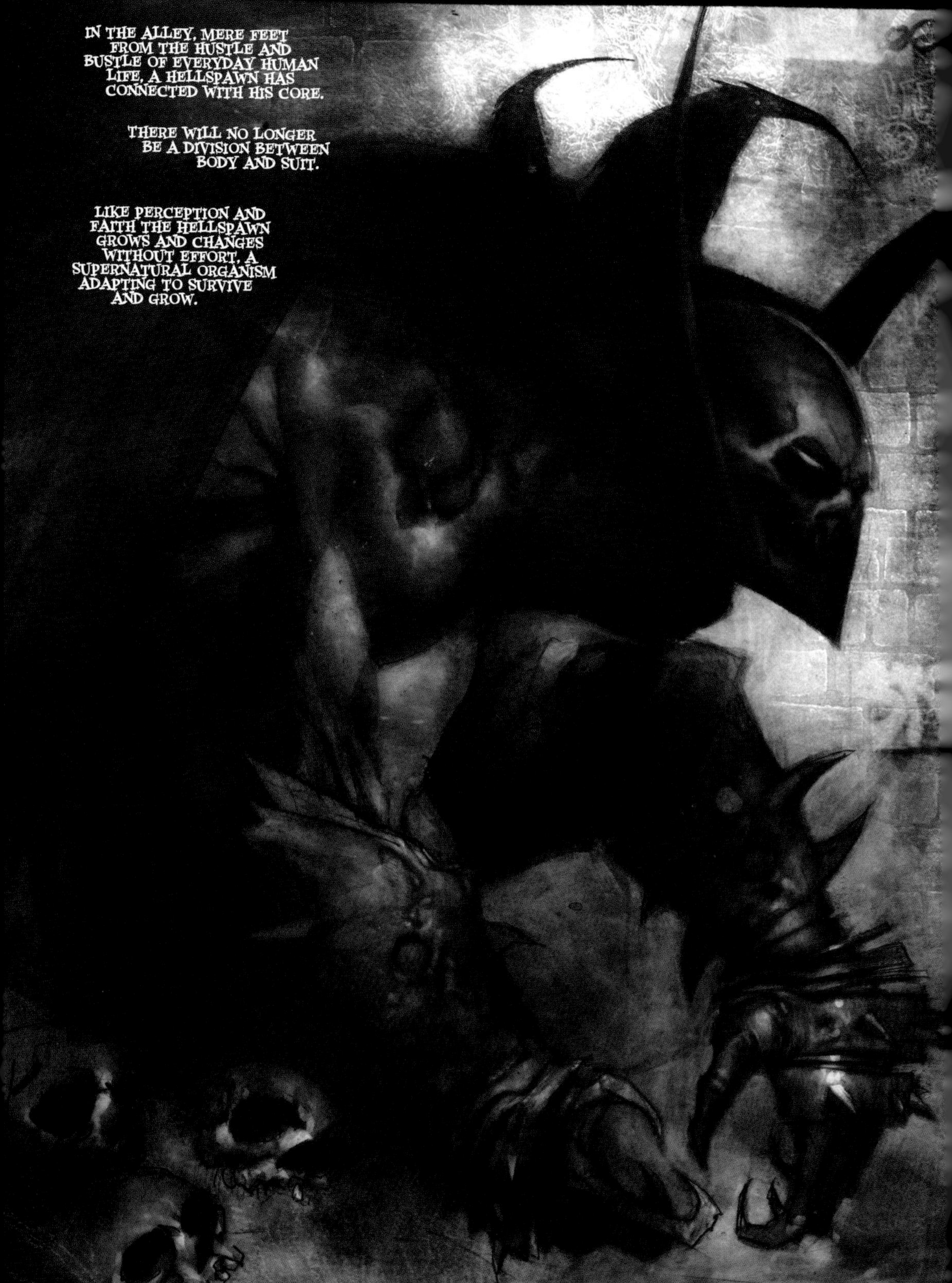
IN THE ALLEY, MERE FEET FROM THE HUSTLE AND BUSTLE OF EVERYDAY HUMAN LIFE, A HELLSPAWN HAS CONNECTED WITH HIS CORE.
THERE WILL NO LONGER BE A DIVISION BETWEEN BODY AND SUIT.
LIKE PERCEPTION AND FAITH THE HELLSPAWN GROWS AND CHANGES WITHOUT EFFORT, A SUPERNATURAL ORGANISM ADAPTING TO SURVIVE AND GROW.

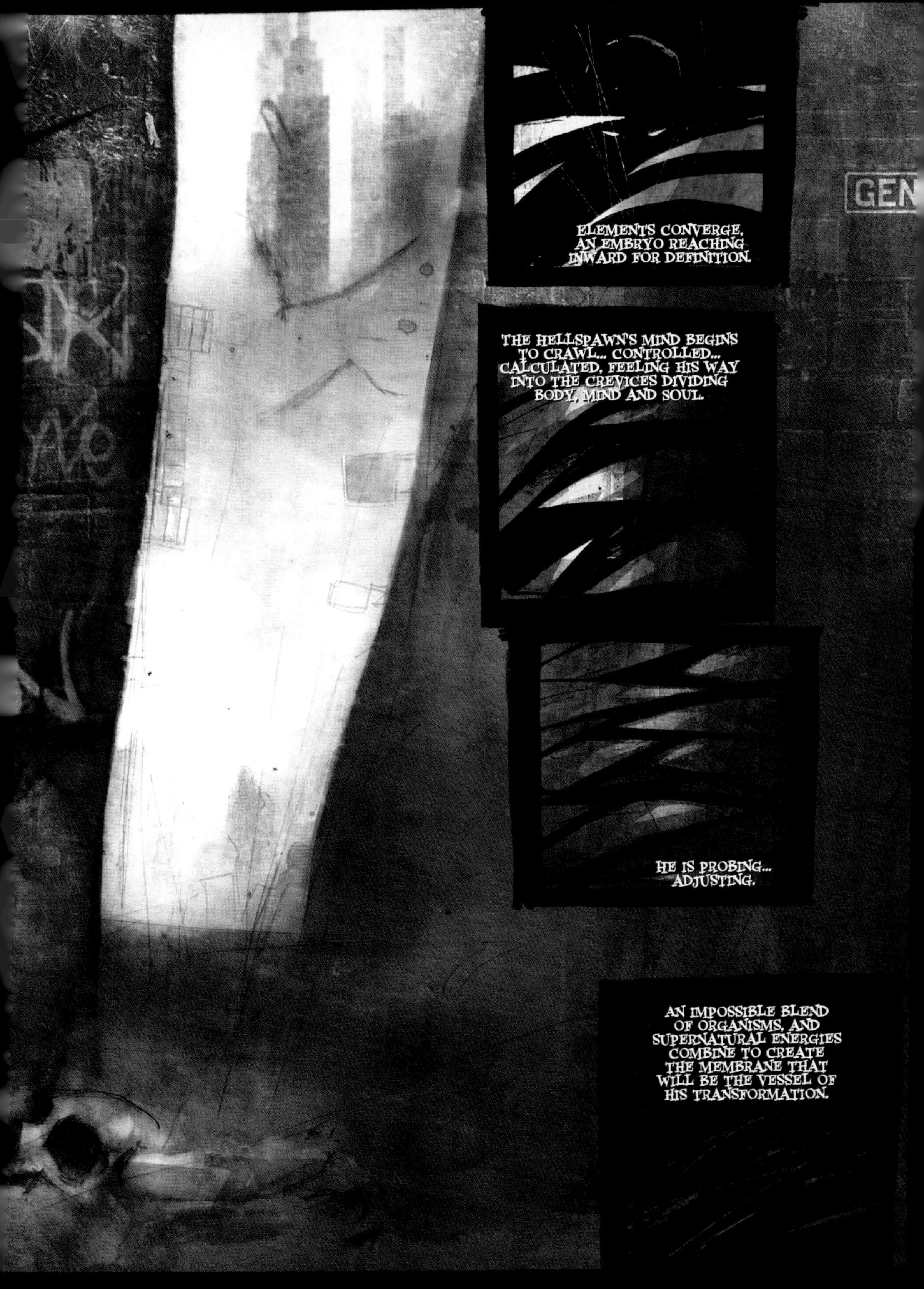
ELEMENT'S CONVERGE, AN EMBRYO REACHING INWARD FOR DEFINITION.
GEN
THE HELLSPAWN'S MIND BEGINS TO CRAWL... CONTROLLED... CALCULATED, FEELING HIS WAY INTO THE CREVICES DIVIDING BODY, MIND AND SOUL.
HE IS PROBING... ADJUSTING.
AN IMPOSSIBLE BLEND OF ORGANISMS, AND SUPERNATURAL ENERGIES COMBINE TO CREATE THE MEMBRANE THAT WILL BE THE VESSEL OF HIS TRANSFORMATION.

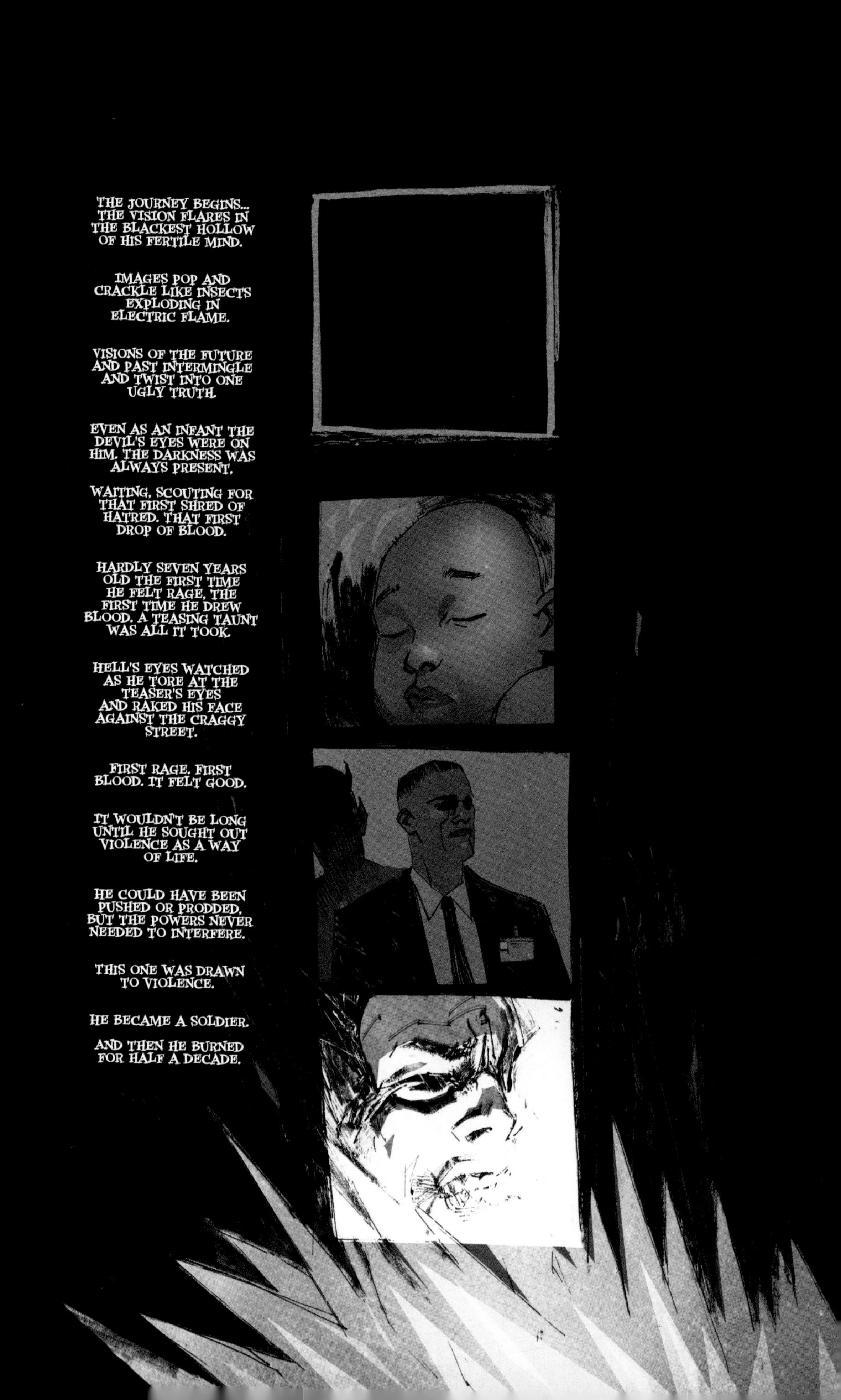
THE JOURNEY BEGINS... THE VISION FLARES IN THE BLACKEST HOLLOW OF HIS FERTILE MIND.
IMAGES POP AND CRACKLE LIKE INSECTS EXPLODING IN ELECTRIC FLAME.
VISIONS OF THE FUTURE AND PAST INTERMINGLE AND TWIST INTO ONE UGLY TRUTH.
EVEN AS AN INFANT THE DEVIL'S EYES WERE ON HIM. THE DARKNESS WAS ALWAYS PRESENT,
WAITING, SCOUTING FOR THAT FIRST SHRED OF HATRED. THAT FIRST DROP OF BLOOD.
HARDLY SEVEN YEARS OLD THE FIRST TIME HE FELT RAGE, THE FIRST TIME HE DREW BLOOD. A TEASING TAUNT WAS ALL IT TOOK.
HELL'S EYES WATCHED AS HE TORE AT THE TEASER'S EYES AND RAKED HIS FACE AGAINST THE CRAGGY STREET.
FIRST RAGE. FIRST BLOOD. IT FELT GOOD.
IT WOULDN'T BE LONG UNTIL HE SOUGHT OUT VIOLENCE AS A WAY OF LIFE.
HE COULD HAVE BEEN PUSHED OR PRODDED, BUT THE POWERS NEVER NEEDED TO INTERFERE.
THIS ONE WAS DRAWN TO VIOLENCE.
HE BECAME A SOLDIER.
AND THEN HE BURNED FOR HALF A DECADE.

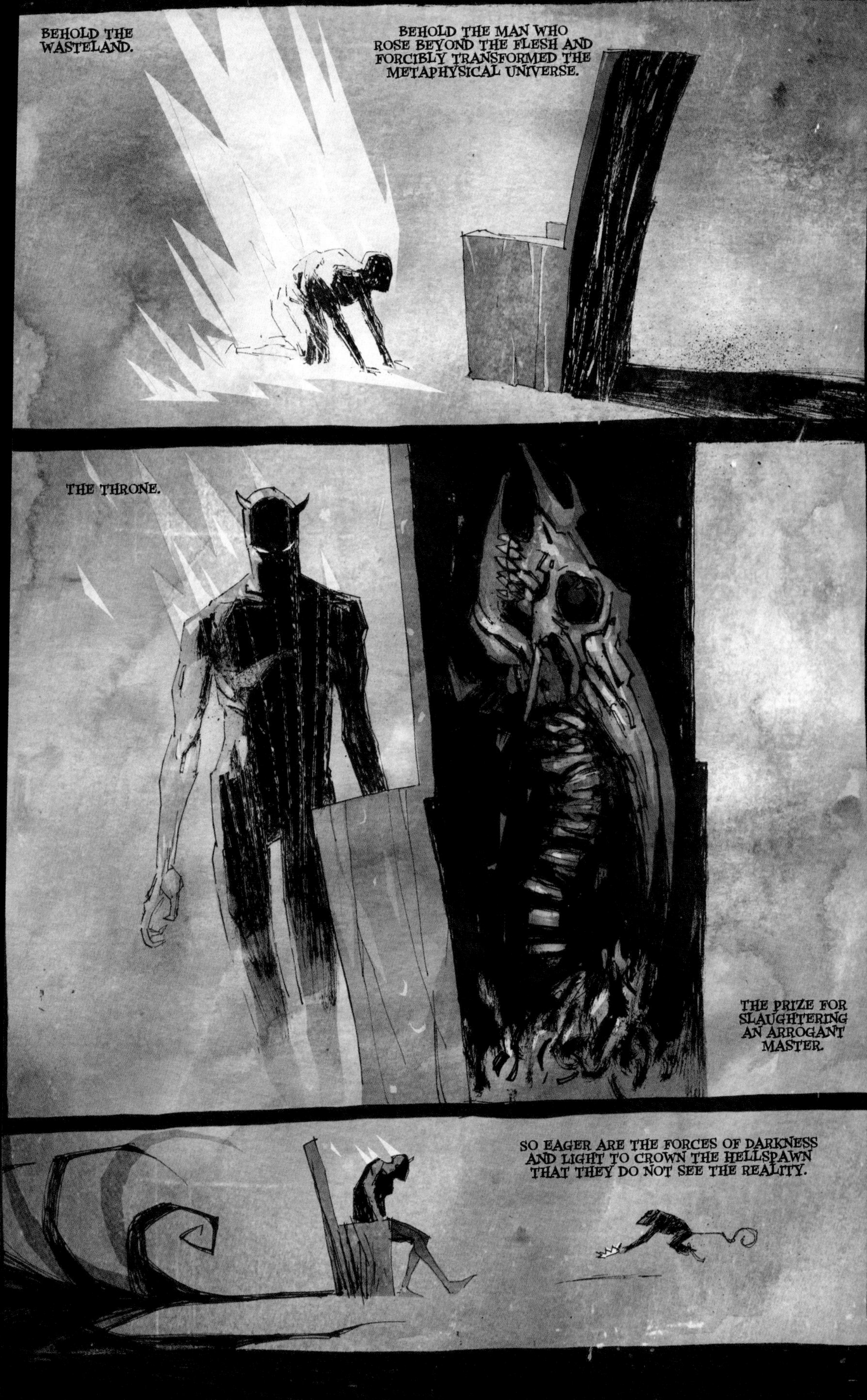
BEHOLD THE WASTELAND.
BEHOLD THE MAN WHO ROSE BEYOND THE FLESH AND FORCIBLY TRANSFORMED THE METAPHYSICAL UNIVERSE.
THE THRONE.
THE PRIZE FOR SLAUGHTERING AN ARROGANT MASTER.
SO EAGER ARE THE FORCES OF DARKNESS AND LIGHT TO CROWN THE HELLSPAWN THAT THEY DO NOT SEE THE REALITY.

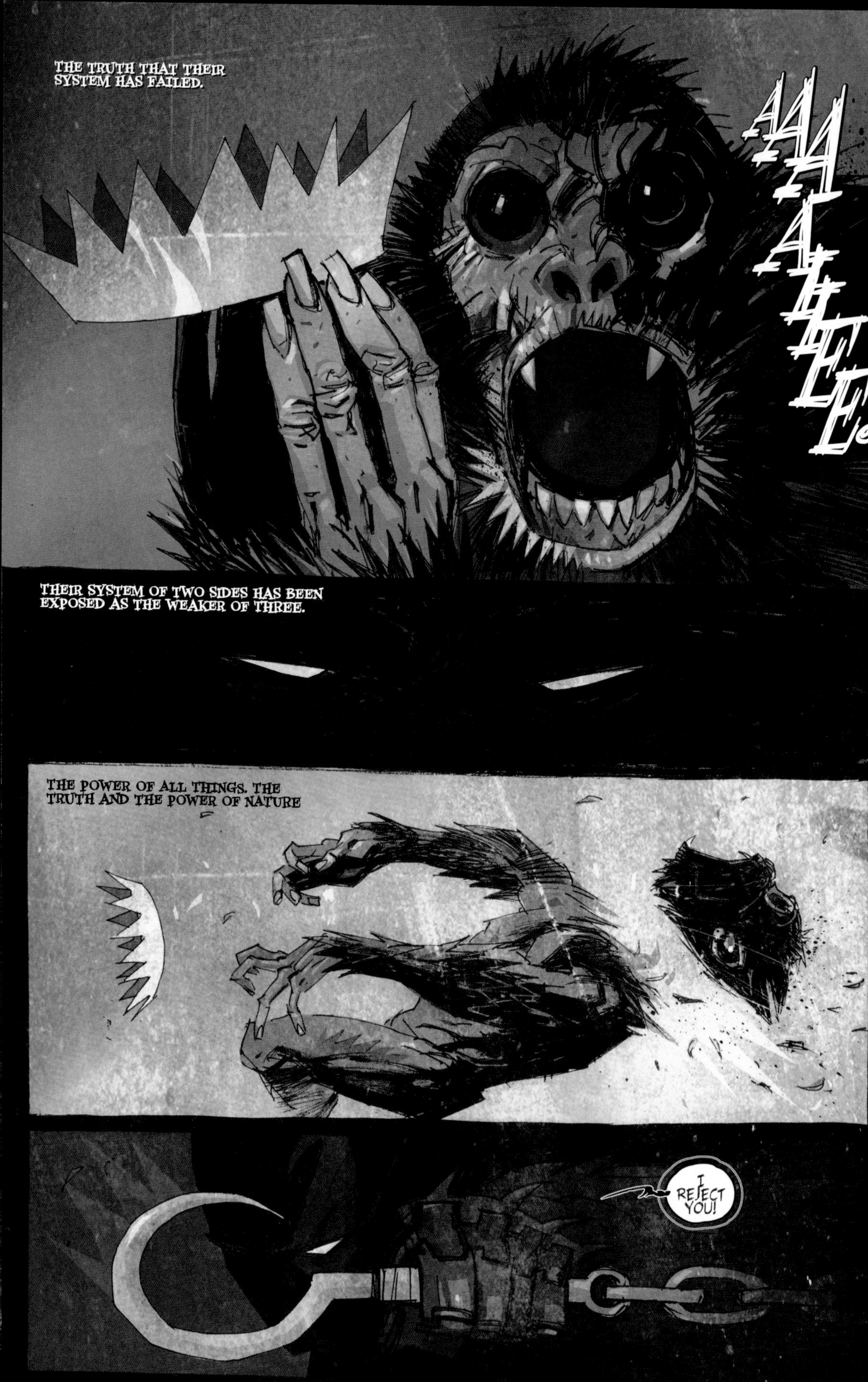
THE TRUTH THAT THEIR SYSTEM HAS FAILED.
AAAAEEE!
THEIR SYSTEM OF TWO SIDES HAS BEEN EXPOSED AS THE WEAKER OF THREE.
THE POWER OF ALL THINGS. THE TRUTH AND THE POWER OF NATURE
I REJECT YOU!

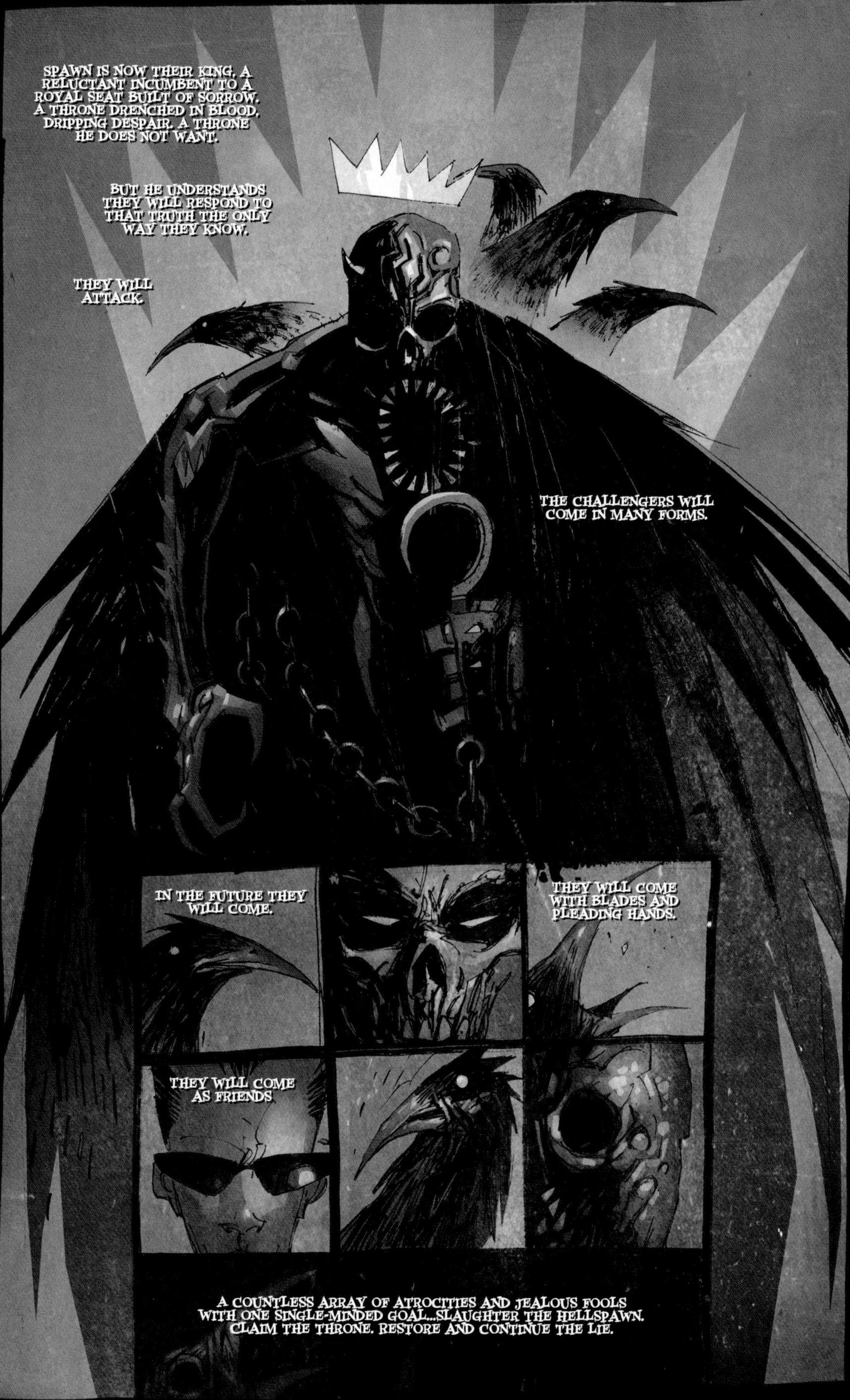
SPAWN IS NOW THEIR KING. A RELUCTANT INCUMBENT TO A ROYAL SEAT BUILT OF SORROW. A THRONE DRENCHED IN BLOOD. DRIPPING DESPAIR. A THRONE HE DOES NOT WANT.
BUT HE UNDERSTANDS THEY WILL RESPOND TO THAT TRUTH THE ONLY WAY THEY KNOW.
THEY WILL ATTACK.
THE CHALLENGERS WILL COME IN MANY FORMS.
IN THE FUTURE THEY WILL COME.
THEY WILL COME WITH BLADES AND PLEADING HANDS.
THEY WILL COME AS FRIENDS
A COUNTLESS ARRAY OF ATROCITIES AND JEALOUS FOOLS WITH ONE SINGLE-MINDED GOAL...SLAUGHTER THE HELLSPAWN. CLAIM THE THRONE. RESTORE AND CONTINUE THE LIE.

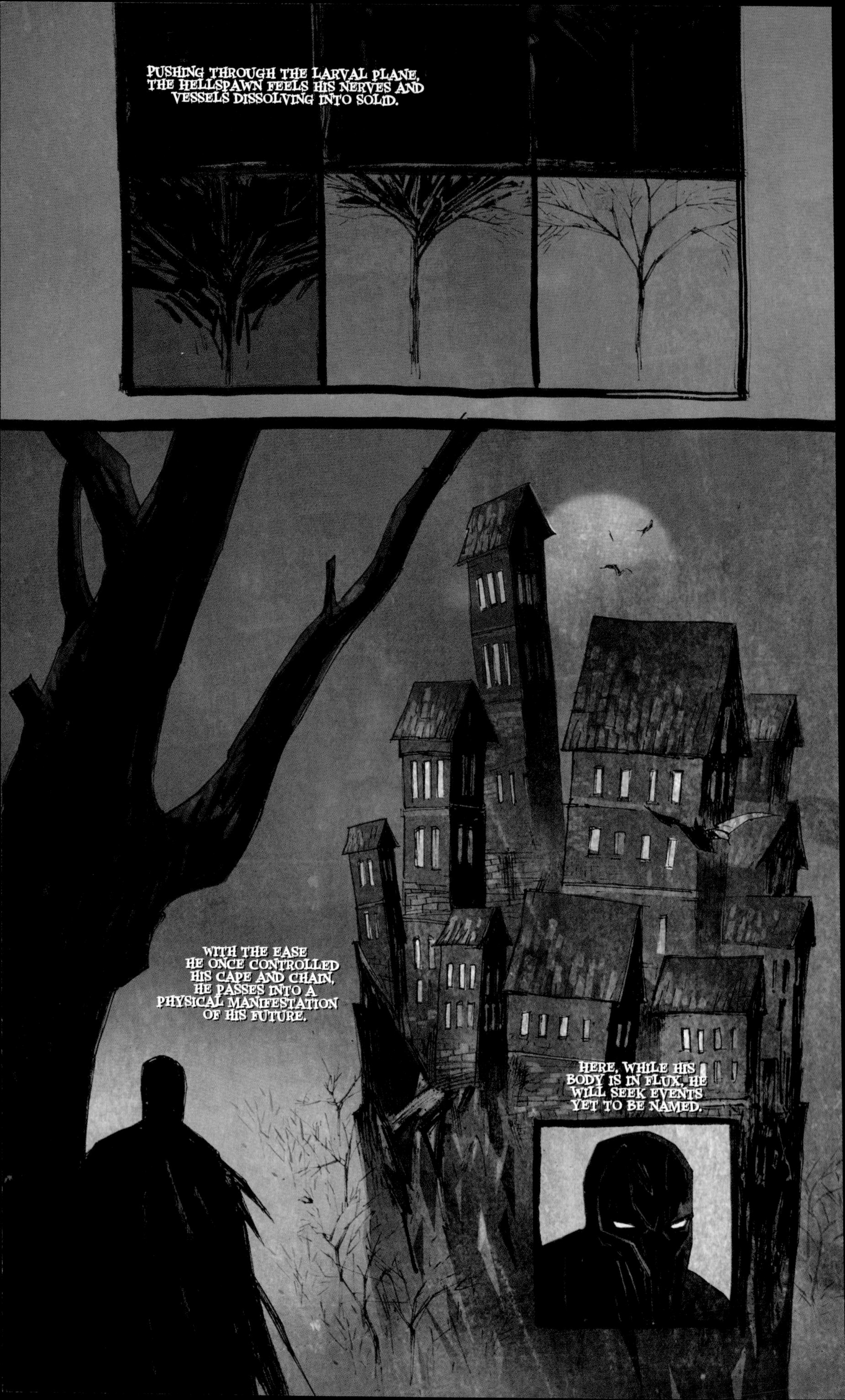
PUSHING THROUGH THE LARVAL PLANE, THE HELLSPAWN FEELS HIS NERVES AND VESSELS DISSOLVING INTO SOLID.
WITH THE EASE HE ONCE CONTROLLED HIS CAPE AND CHAIN, HE PASSES INTO A PHYSICAL MANIFESTATION OF HIS FUTURE.
HERE, WHILE HIS BODY IS IN FLUX, HE WILL SEEK EVENTS YET TO BE NAMED.

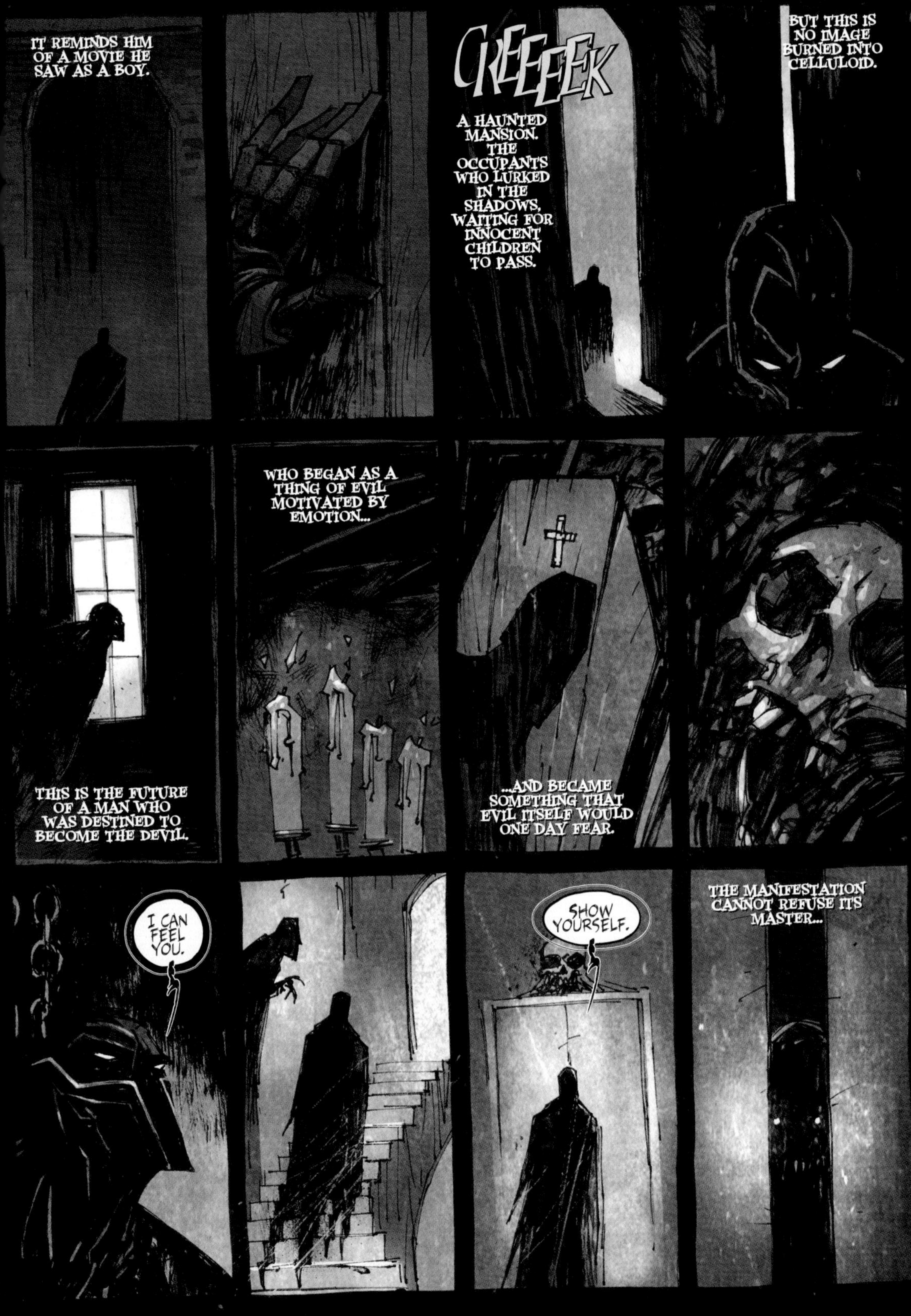
IT REMINDS HIM OF A MOVIE HE SAW AS A BOY.
CREEEEK
A HAUNTED MANSION. THE OCCUPANTS WHO LURKED IN THE SHADOWS, WAITING FOR INNOCENT CHILDREN TO PASS.
BUT THIS IS NO IMAGE BURNED INTO CELLULOID.
THIS IS THE FUTURE OF A MAN WHO WAS DESTINED TO BECOME THE DEVIL.
WHO BEGAN AS A THING OF EVIL MOTIVATED BY EMOTION...
...AND BECAME SOMETHING THAT EVIL ITSELF WOULD ONE DAY FEAR.
I CAN FEEL YOU.
SHOW YOURSELF.
THE MANIFESTATION CANNOT REFUSE ITS MASTER...

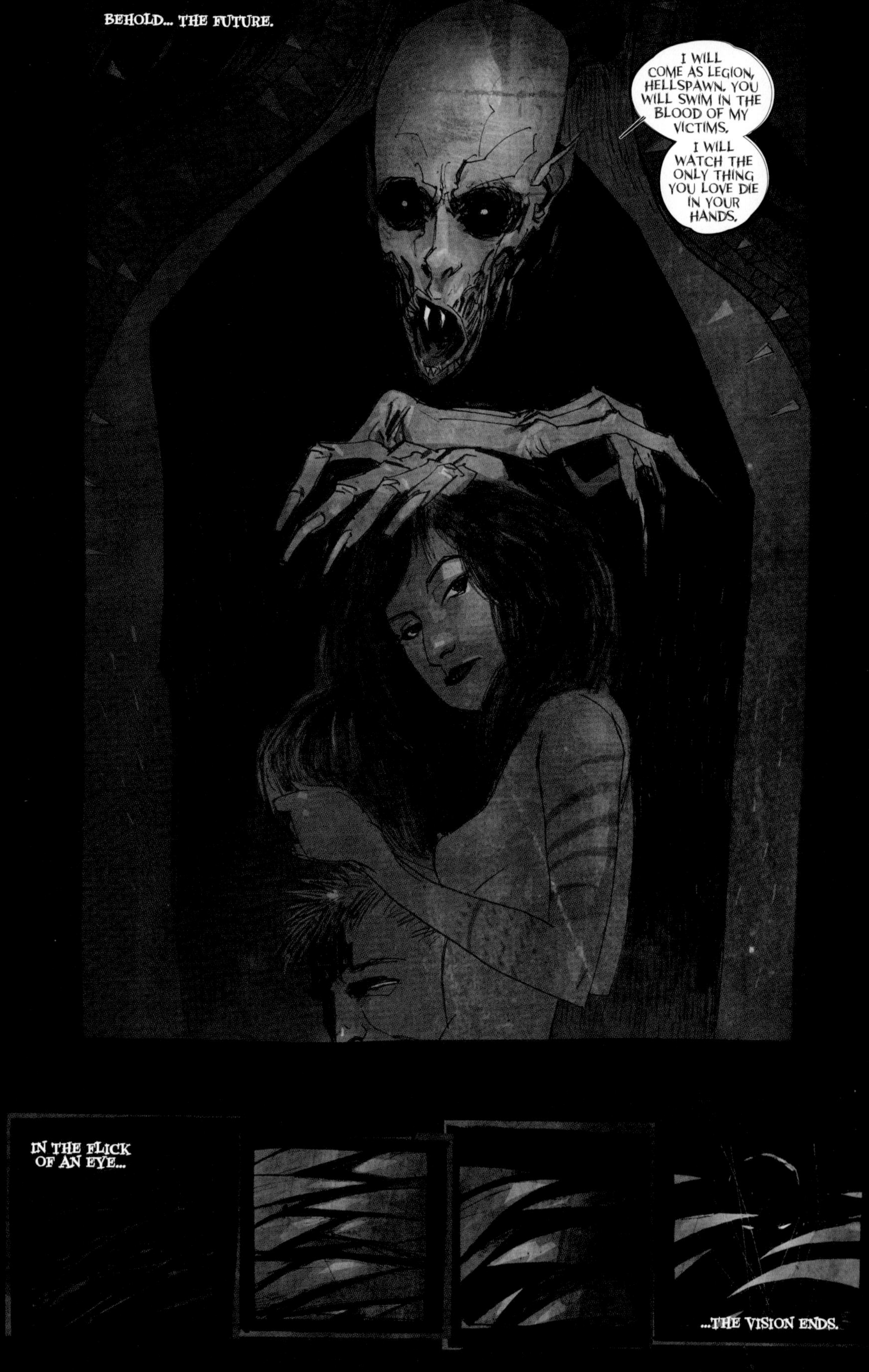

BEHOLD... THE FUTURE.
I WILL COME AS LEGION, HELLSPAWN. YOU WILL SWIM IN THE BLOOD OF MY VICTIMS.
I WILL WATCH THE ONLY THING YOU LOVE DIE IN YOUR HANDS.
IN THE FLICK OF AN EYE...
...THE VISION ENDS.

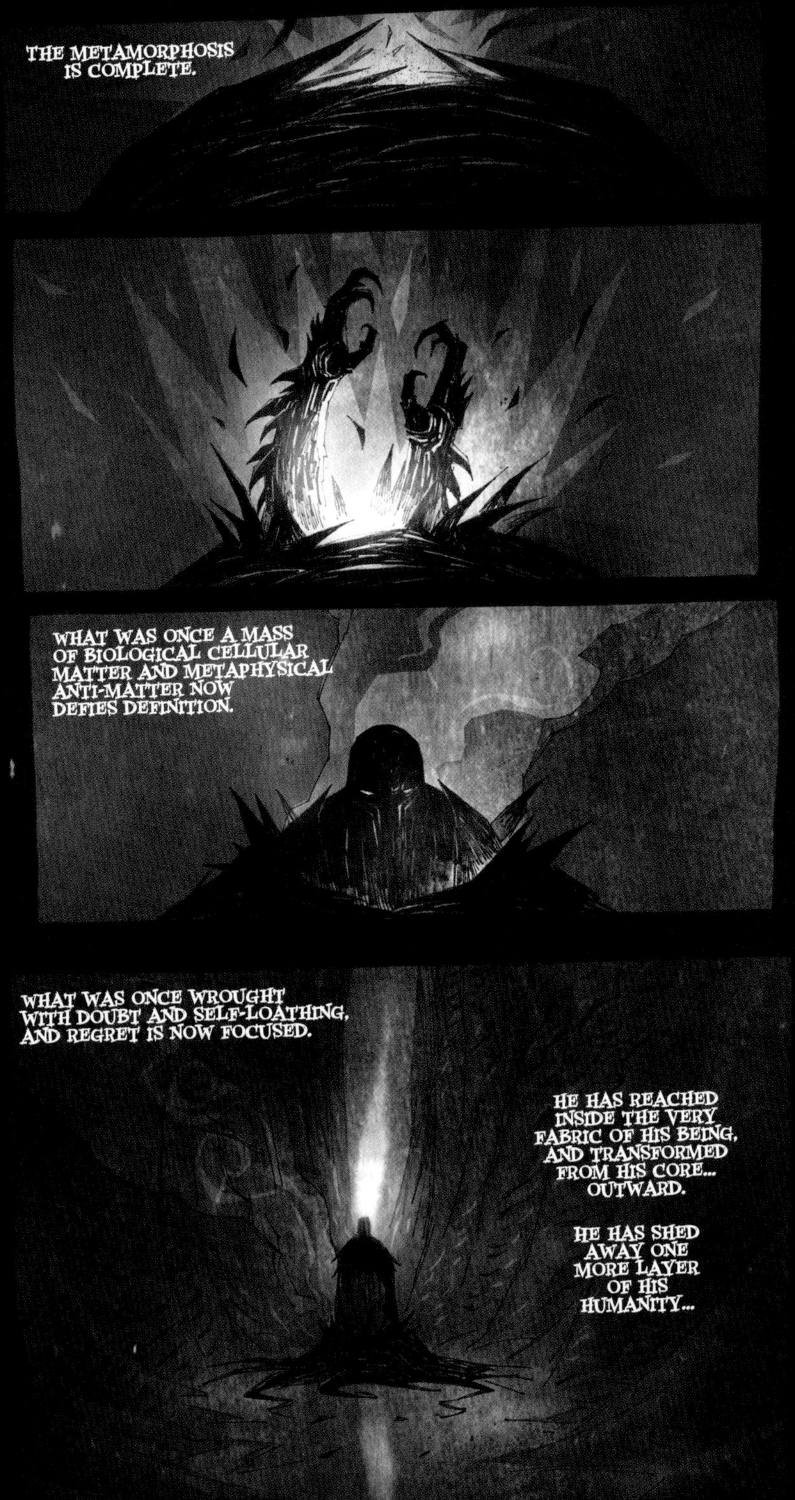
THE METAMORPHOSIS IS COMPLETE.
WHAT WAS ONCE A MASS OF BIOLOGICAL CELLULAR MATTER AND METAPHYSICAL ANTI-MATTER NOW DEFIES DEFINITION.
WHAT WAS ONCE WROUGHT WITH DOUBT AND SELF-LOATHING, AND REGRET IS NOW FOCUSED.
HE HAS REACHED INSIDE THE VERY FABRIC OF HIS BEING, AND TRANSFORMED FROM HIS CORE... OUTWARD.
HE HAS SHED AWAY ONE MORE LAYER OF HIS HUMANITY...

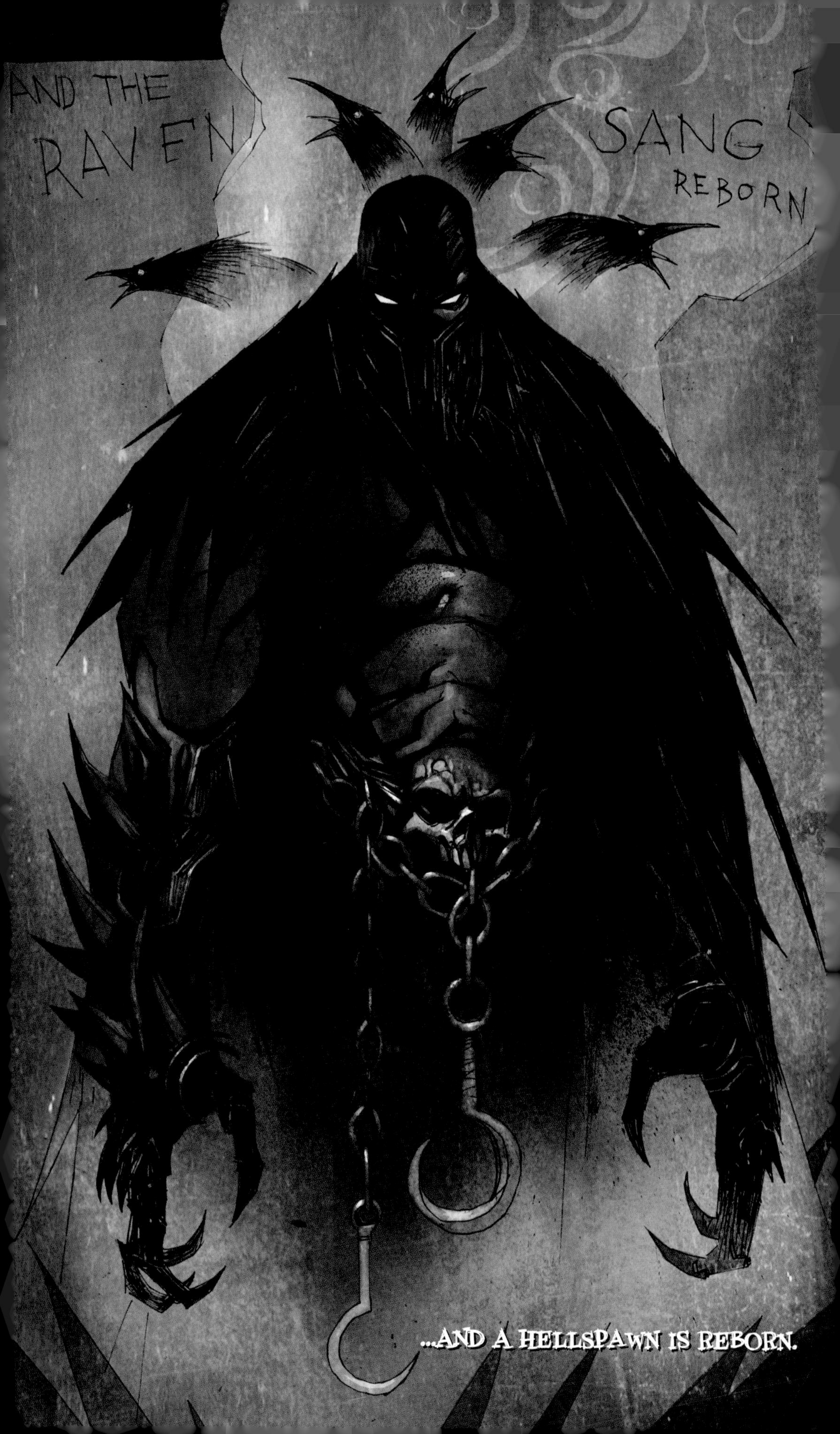
AND THE RAVEN SANG
REBORN
...AND A HELLSPAWN IS REBORN.

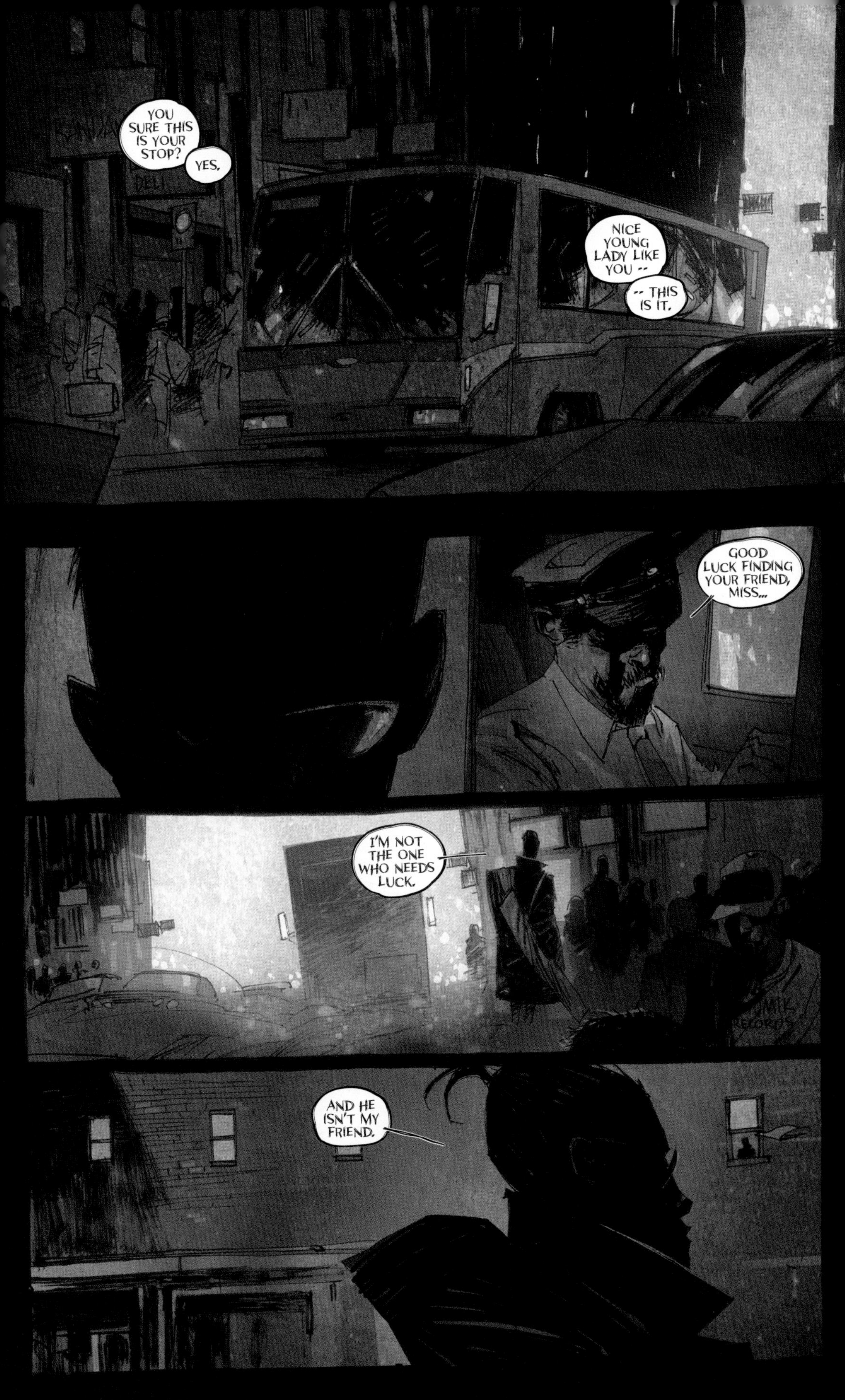
YOU SURE THIS IS YOUR STOP?
YES.
NICE YOUNG LADY LIKE YOU --
-- THIS IS IT.
GOOD LUCK FINDING YOUR FRIEND, MISS...
I'M NOT THE ONE WHO NEEDS LUCK.
AND HE ISN'T MY FRIEND.

YOU MIND THAT I CALLED? WHAT TIME IS IT THERE?
OH, SORRY. I ALWAYS FORGET.
I THINK THIS TIME APART WILL DO US GOOD... WHAT?
KEEPING BUSY. THE PAPERS GIVING ME A COLUMN.
YEAH, YOU KNOW CITY BEAT COVERAGE... YEAH FLUFF.
YOU SHOULD SEE THIS PLACE THEY PUT ME UP... YEAH... BIGGER THAN BUCKINGHAM PALACE.
BIG BED, THREE ROOMS AND A TV WITH CABLE, ROOM SERVICE.
I LIKE IT HERE.
YOU SHOULD COME HERE. I MISS YOU.
OKAY. I KNOW. SORRY.
DON'T START. CHRIST!
NO. DON'T YOU DARE --
-- HANG UP.
CLICK
..DAMN!
ATOMIK
record

HELLSPAWN

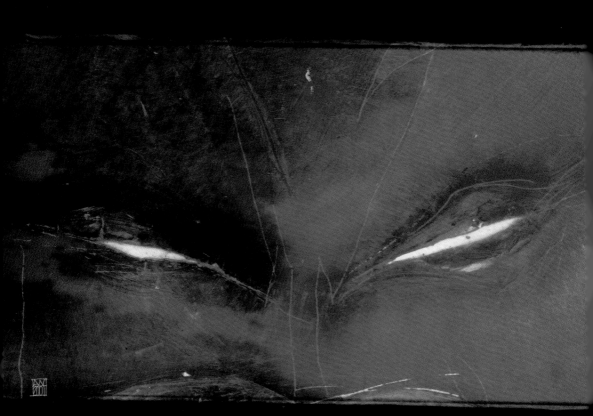

ISSUE EIGHT

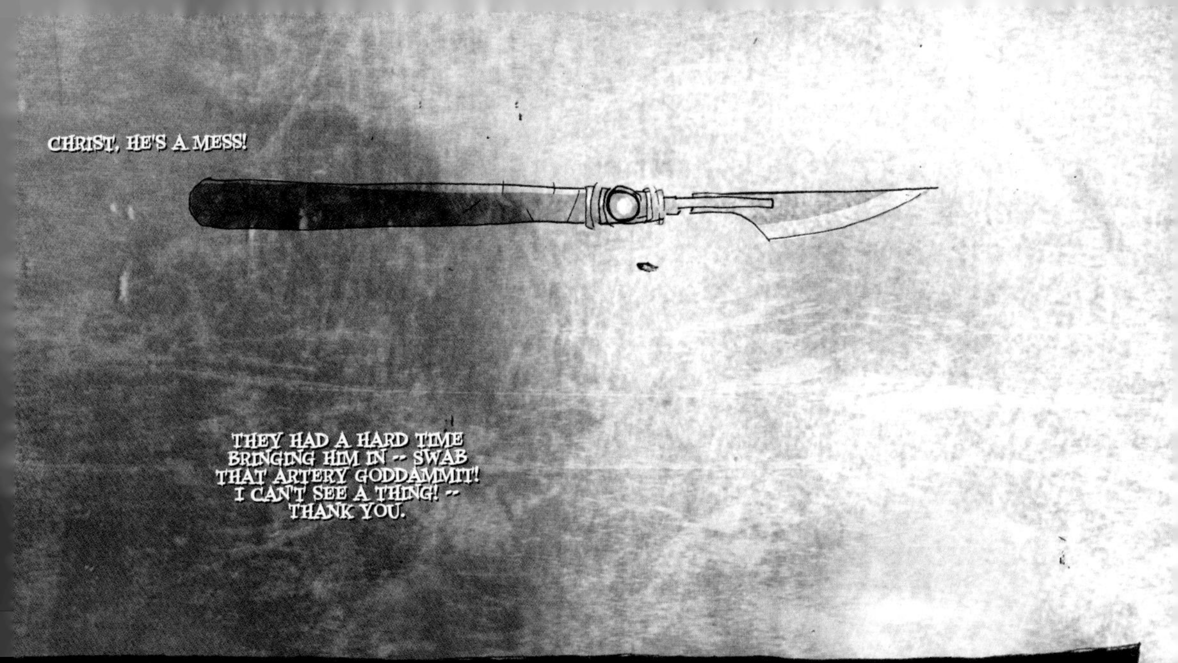
CHRIST, HE'S A MESS!
THEY HAD A HARD TIME BRINGING HIM IN -- SWAB THAT ARTERY GODDAMMIT! I CAN'T SEE A THING! -- THANK YOU.

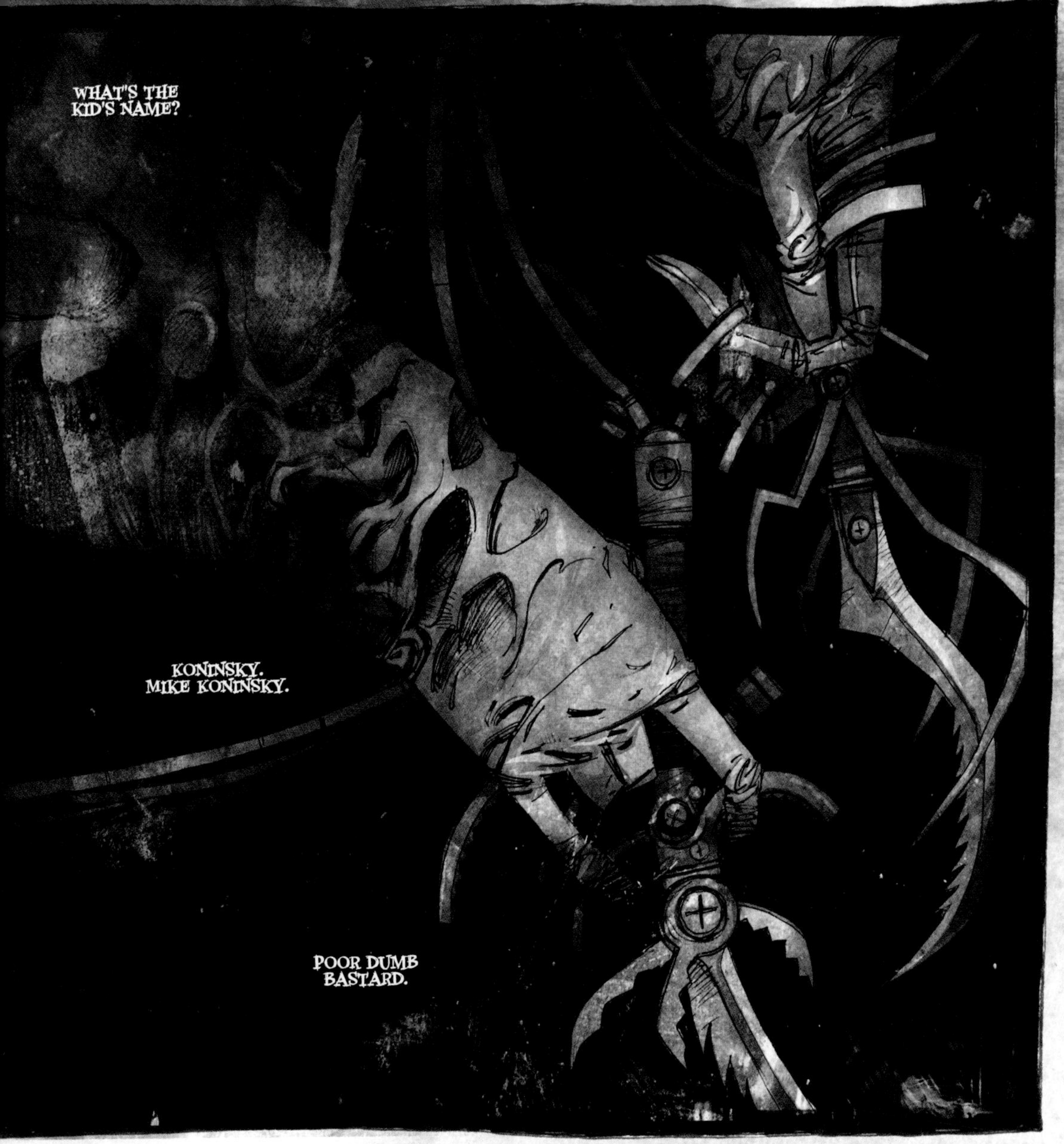
WHAT'S THE KID'S NAME?
KONINSKY. MIKE KONINSKY.
POOR DUMB BASTARD.

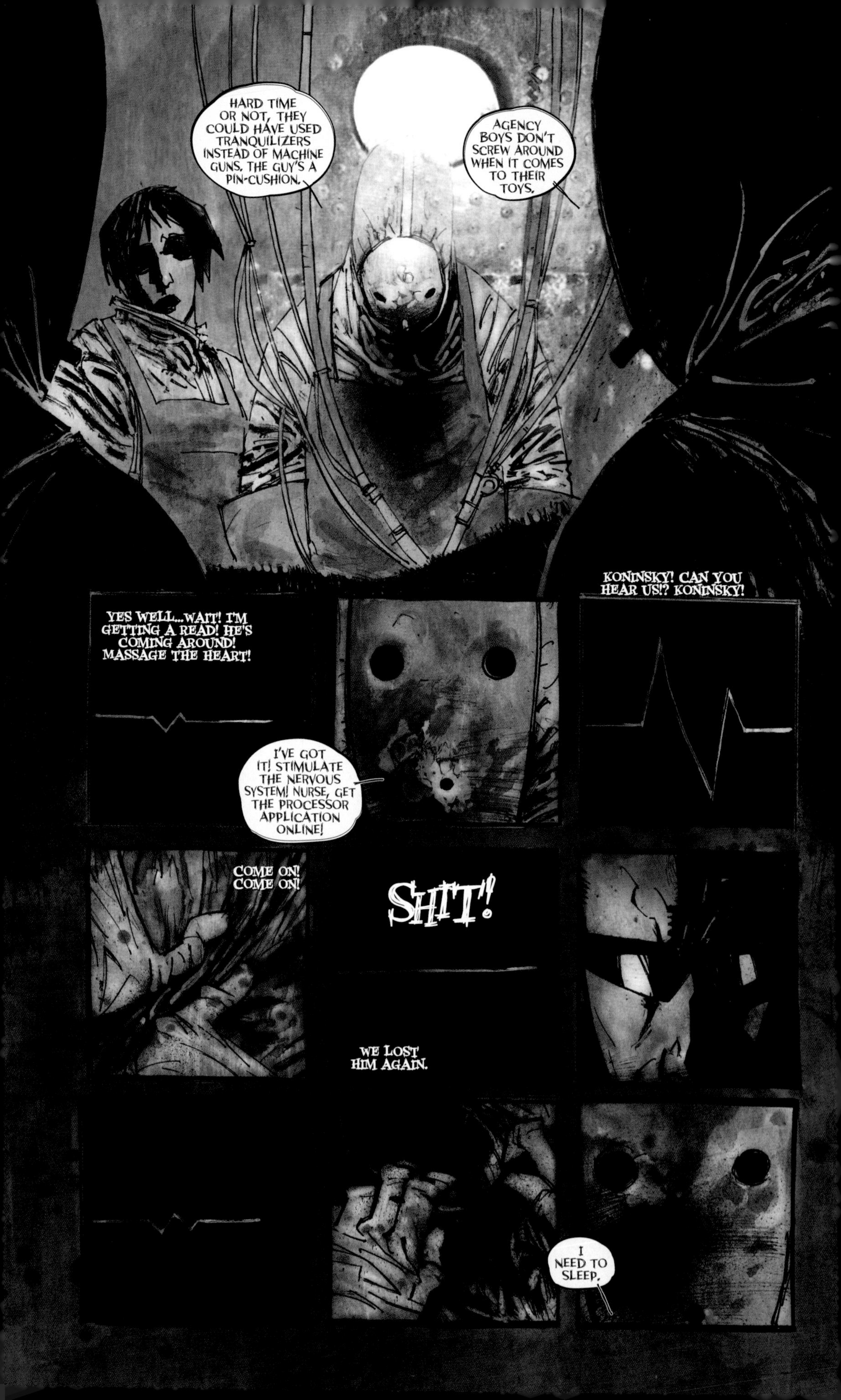
HARD TIME OR NOT, THEY COULD HAVE USED TRANQUILIZERS INSTEAD OF MACHINE GUNS. THE GUY'S A PIN-CUSHION.
AGENCY BOYS DON'T SCREW AROUND WHEN IT COMES TO THEIR TOYS.
YES WELL...WAIT! I'M GETTING A READ! HE'S COMING AROUND! MASSAGE THE HEART!
I'VE GOT IT! STIMULATE THE NERVOUS SYSTEM! NURSE, GET THE PROCESSOR APPLICATION ONLINE!
KONINSKY! CAN YOU HEAR US!? KONINSKY!
COME ON! COME ON!
SHIT!
WE LOST HIM AGAIN.
I NEED TO SLEEP.

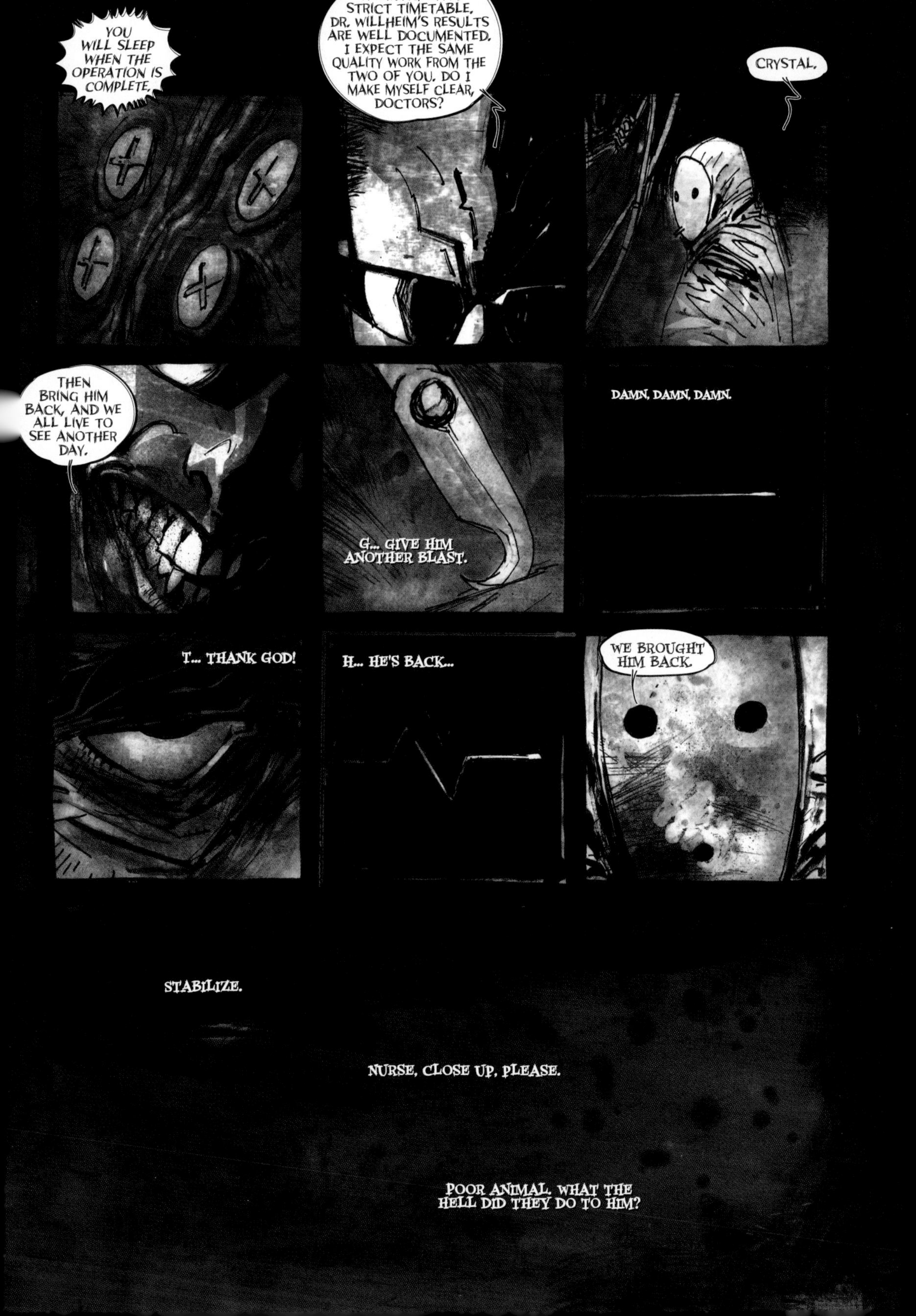
YOU WILL SLEEP WHEN THE OPERATION IS COMPLETE.
WE ARE WORKING ON A STRICT TIMETABLE. DR. WILLHEIM'S RESULTS ARE WELL DOCUMENTED. I EXPECT THE SAME QUALITY WORK FROM THE TWO OF YOU. DO I MAKE MYSELF CLEAR, DOCTORS?
CRYSTAL.
THEN BRING HIM BACK, AND WE ALL LIVE TO SEE ANOTHER DAY.
G... GIVE HIM ANOTHER BLAST.
DAMN. DAMN. DAMN.
T... THANK GOD!
H... HE'S BACK...
WE BROUGHT HIM BACK.
STABILIZE.
NURSE, CLOSE UP, PLEASE.
POOR ANIMAL. WHAT THE HELL DID THEY DO TO HIM?

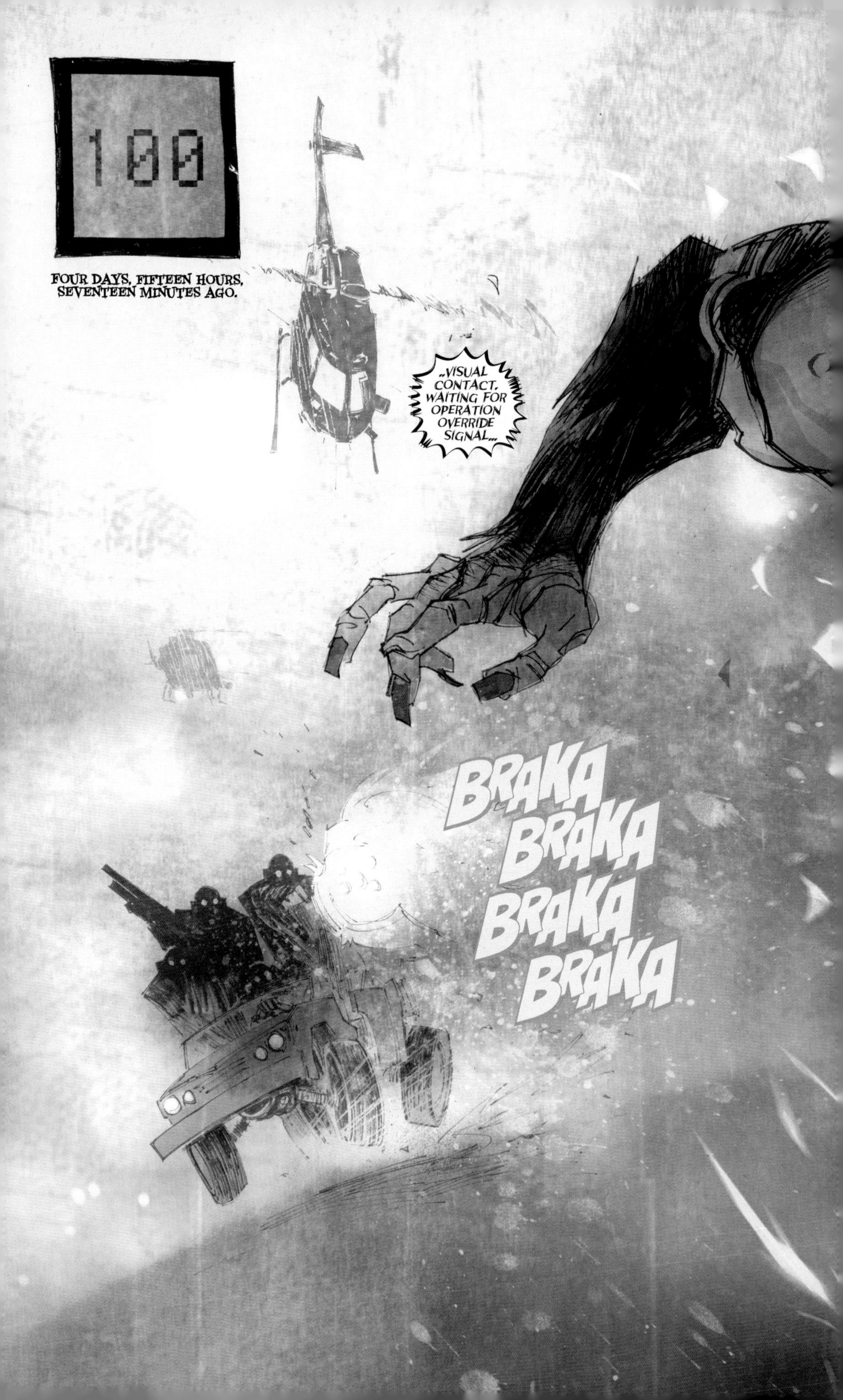
100
FOUR DAYS, FIFTEEN HOURS, SEVENTEEN MINUTES AGO.
...VISUAL CONTACT, WAITING FOR OPERATION OVERRIDE SIGNAL...
BRAKA
BRAKA
BRAKA
BRAKA

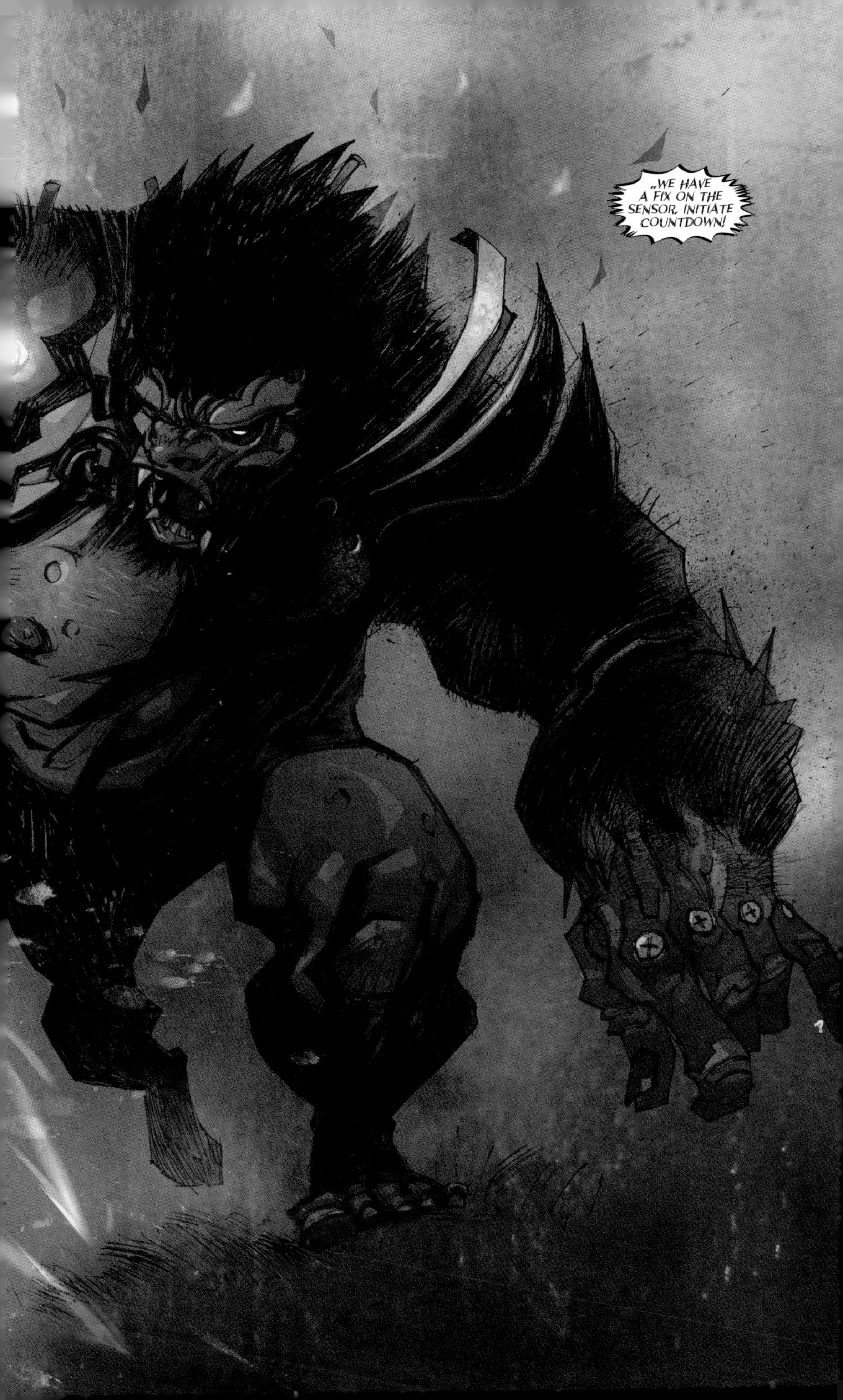
..WE HAVE A FIX ON THE SENSOR, INITIATE COUNTDOWN!

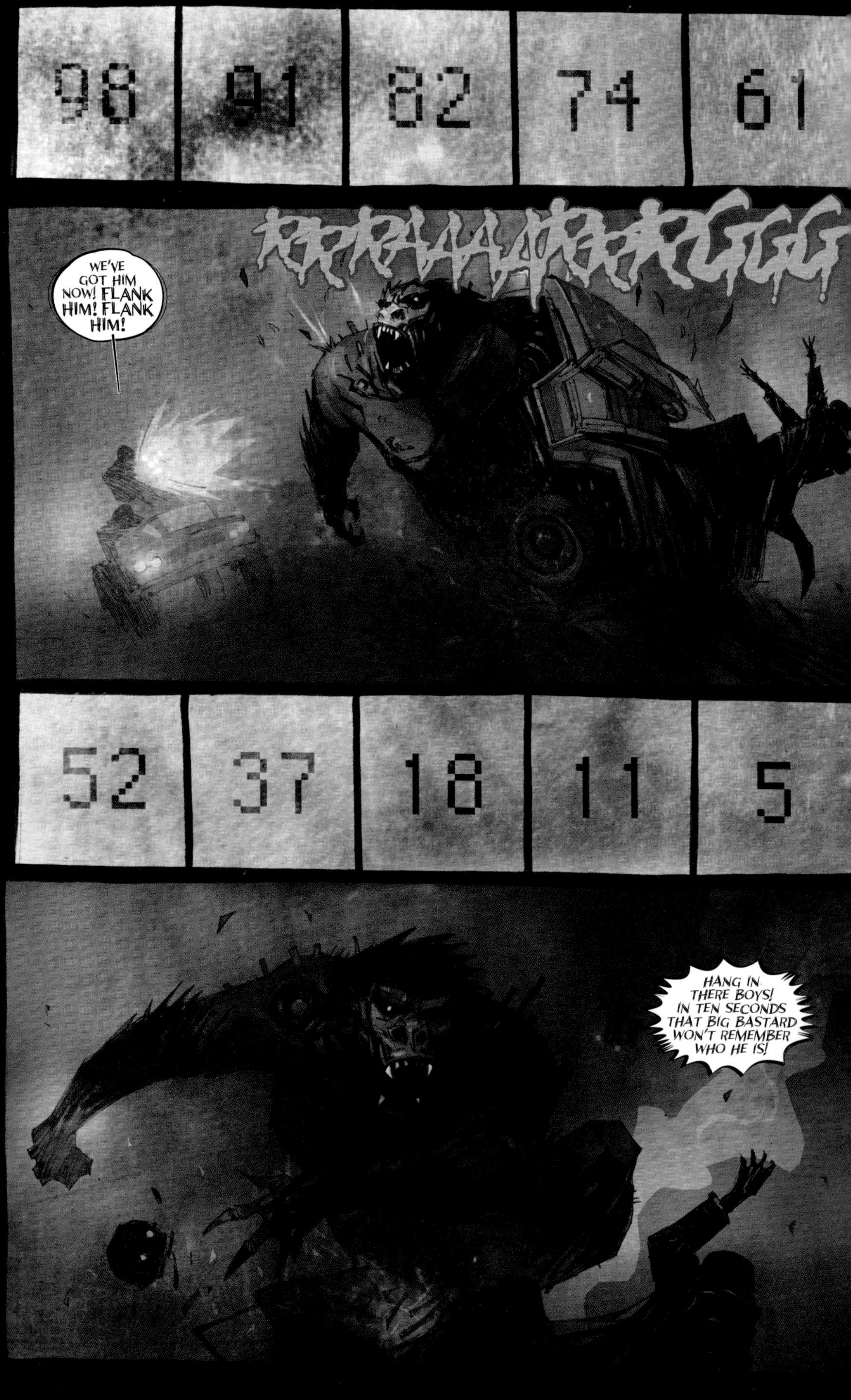

98
91
82
74
61
RRRAAAARRRGGG!
WE'VE GOT HIM NOW! FLANK HIM! FLANK HIM!
52
37
18
11
5
HANG IN THERE BOYS! IN TEN SECONDS THAT BIG BASTARD WON'T REMEMBER WHO HE IS!

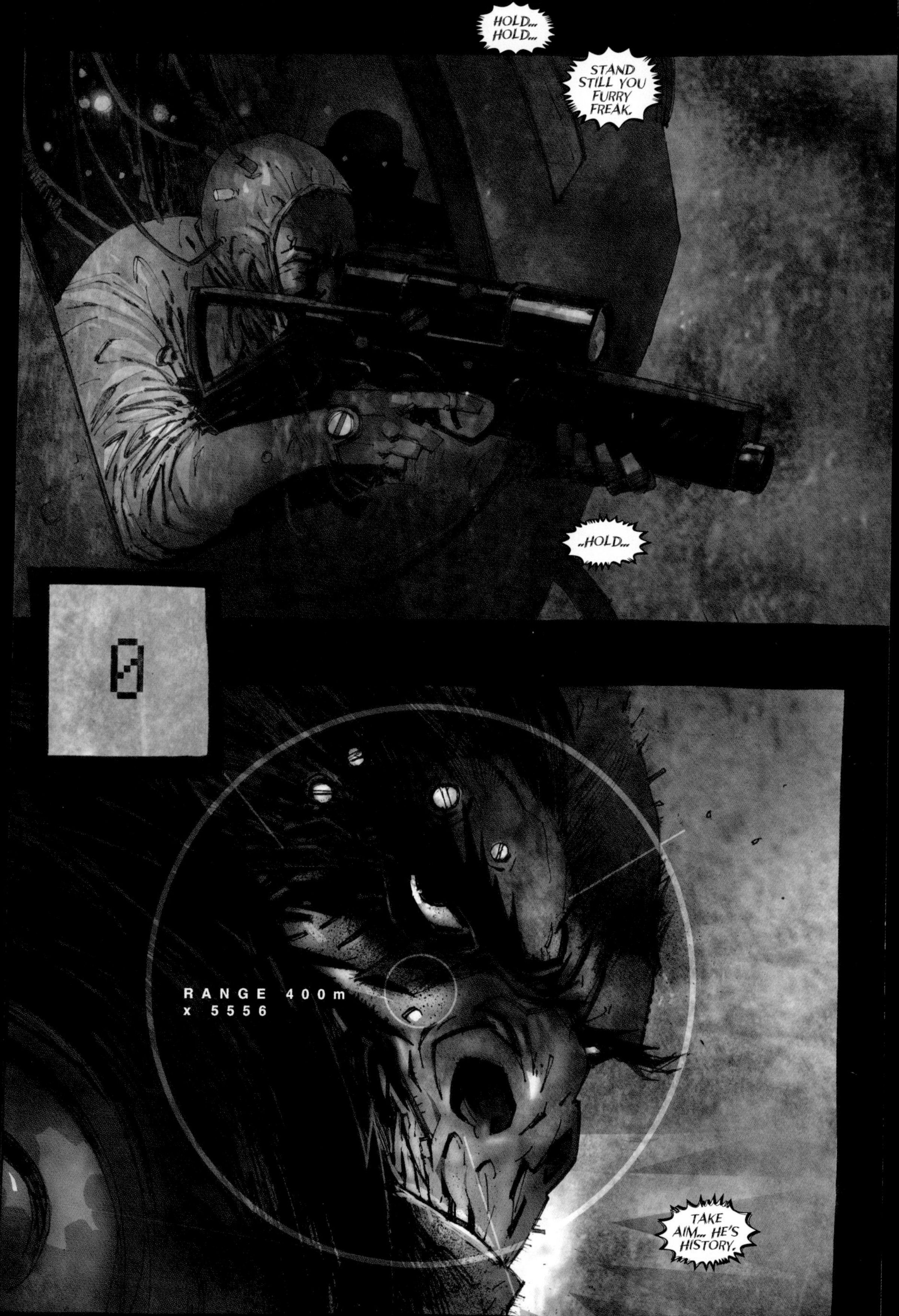
HOLD... HOLD...
STAND STILL YOU FURRY FREAK.
..HOLD...
0
RANGE 400m
x 5556
TAKE AIM... HE'S HISTORY.

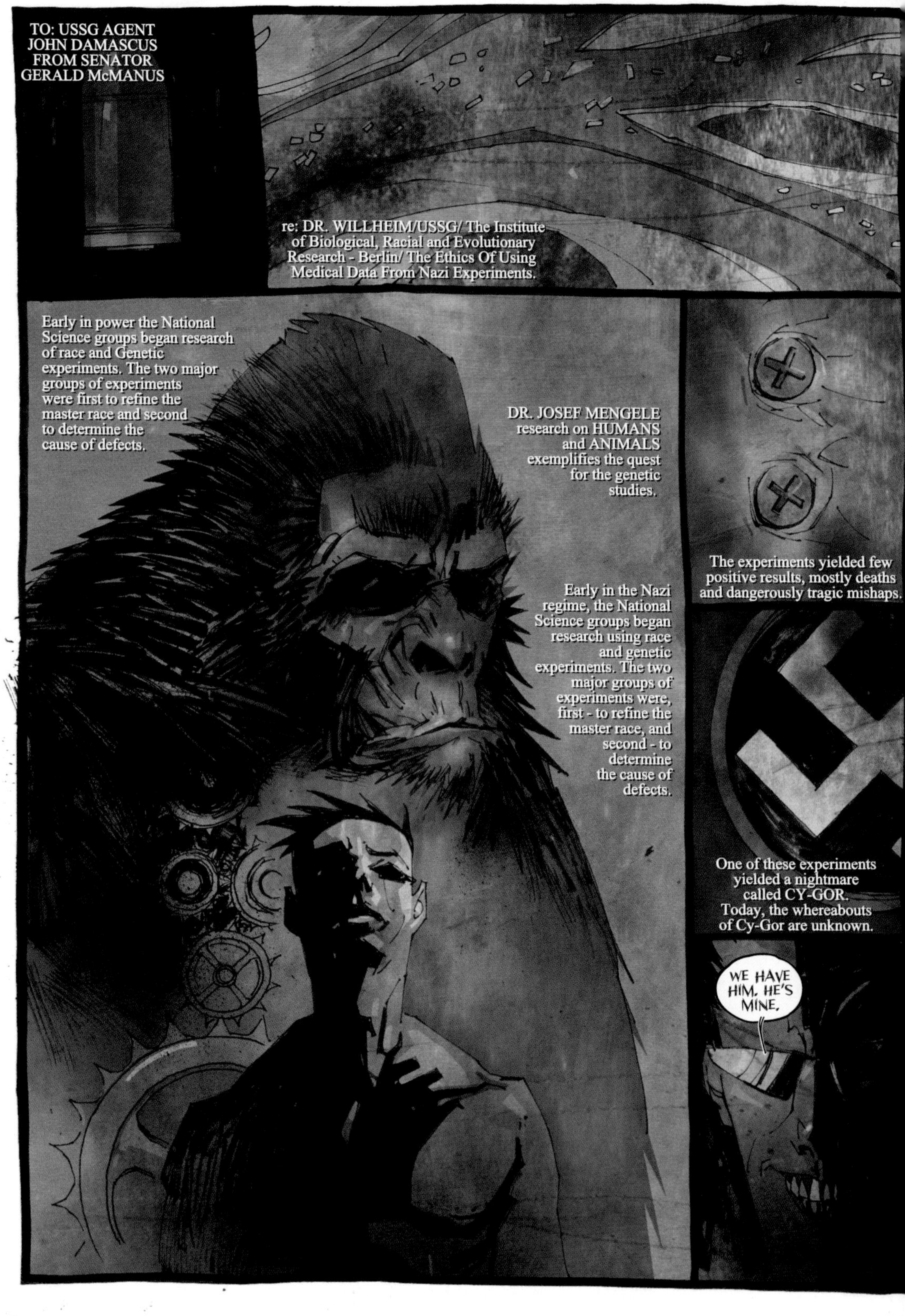

TO: USSG AGENT JOHN DAMASCUS FROM SENATOR GERALD McMANUS
re: DR. WILLHEIM/USSG/ The Institute of Biological, Racial and Evolutionary Research - Berlin/ The Ethics Of Using Medical Data From Nazi Experiments.
Early in power the National Science groups began research of race and Genetic experiments. The two major groups of experiments were first to refine the master race and second to determine the cause of defects.
DR. JOSEF MENGELE research on HUMANS and ANIMALS exemplifies the quest for the genetic studies.
Early in the Nazi regime, the National Science groups began research using race and genetic experiments. The two major groups of experiments were, first - to refine the master race, and second - to determine the cause of defects.
The experiments yielded few positive results, mostly deaths and dangerously tragic mishaps.
One of these experiments yielded a nightmare called CY-GOR. Today, the whereabouts of Cy-Gor are unknown.
WE HAVE HIM. HE'S MINE.

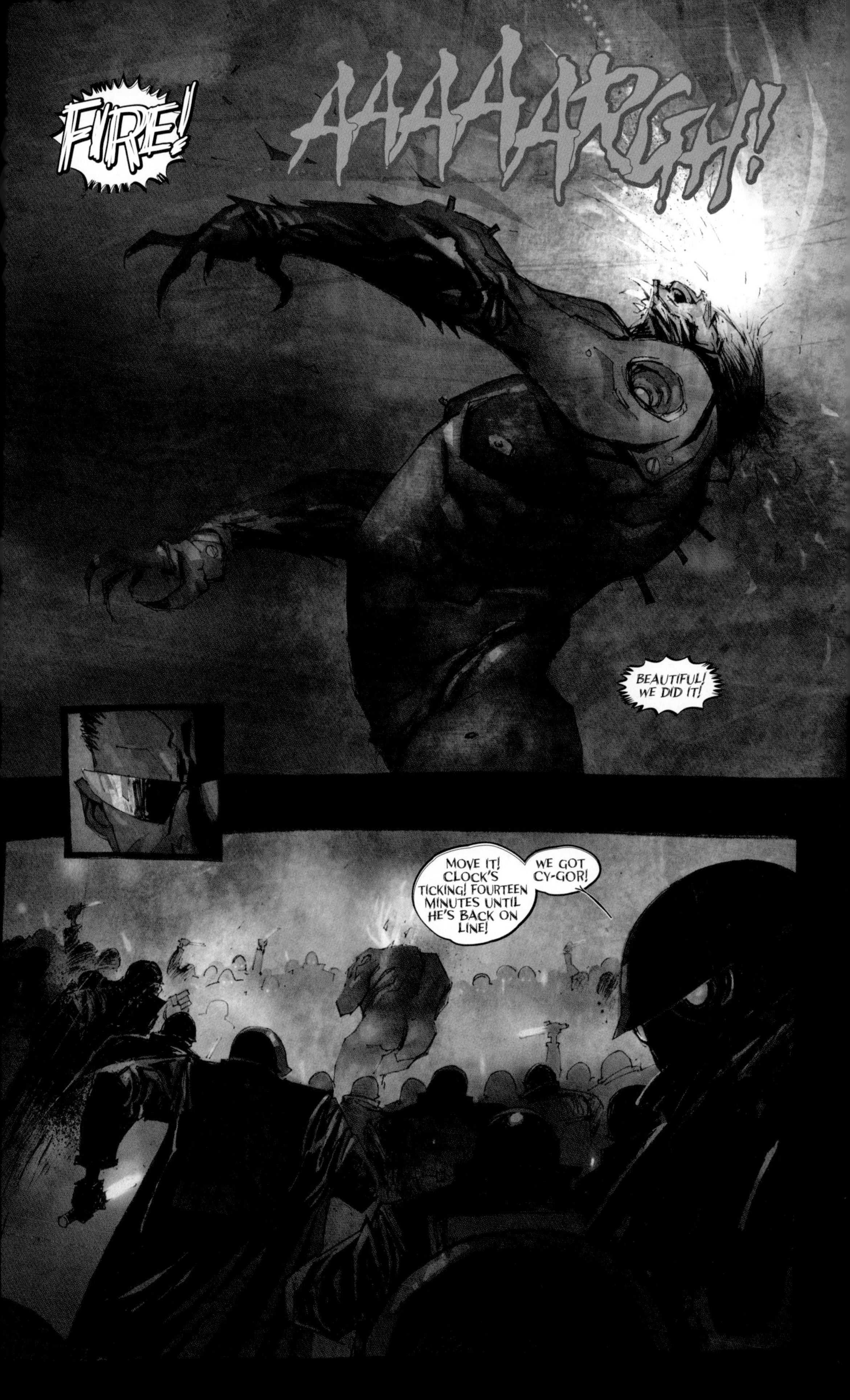
FIRE!
AAAAARGH!
BEAUTIFUL! WE DID IT!
MOVE IT! CLOCK'S TICKING! FOURTEEN MINUTES UNTIL HE'S BACK ON LINE!
WE GOT CY-GOR!

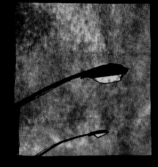

THE ALLEY.

A COLD, LONELY STRETCH OF DESPAIR WHERE ONLY THE DEAD AND THE DAMNED VENTURE.

DARK, FORBIDDING. A BLACK HOLE WITHIN THE SHADOWS.

JUST THROW THE JUNK AWAY, JIMMY! BEFORE THEY CATCH US!

NO WAY, MOVE FASTER YOU STUPID BITCH!

IT IS A DEAD SPOT IN THE CENTER OF A VITAL, LIVING METROPOLIS.

I AIN'T GETTING PITCHED CUZ YOU CAN'T RUN! THEY WON'T FOLLOW US IN HERE.

WHAT'RE YOU DOIN'?

I...UM...NO.

PLACE GIVES ME THE FUCKIN' CREEPS.

SURE AS SHIT AIN'T GOING IN THERE, YOU WANT TO TAKE IT ON FOOT?

THEN LET'S GET THE HELL OUT OF HERE. THE ALLEY CAN HAVE THOSE TWO.

THE WALLS SQUIRM, THE SHADOWS BREATH
THERE IS NO SAFER PLACE ON EARTH FOR A HELLSPAWN TO LIVE.
THEY TURNED AROUND! WHAT A BREAK. PRETTY COOL?
YOU LISTENING TO ME BITCH?
I HAVE A NAME, JIMMY.
REMEMBER? IT'S EDEN.

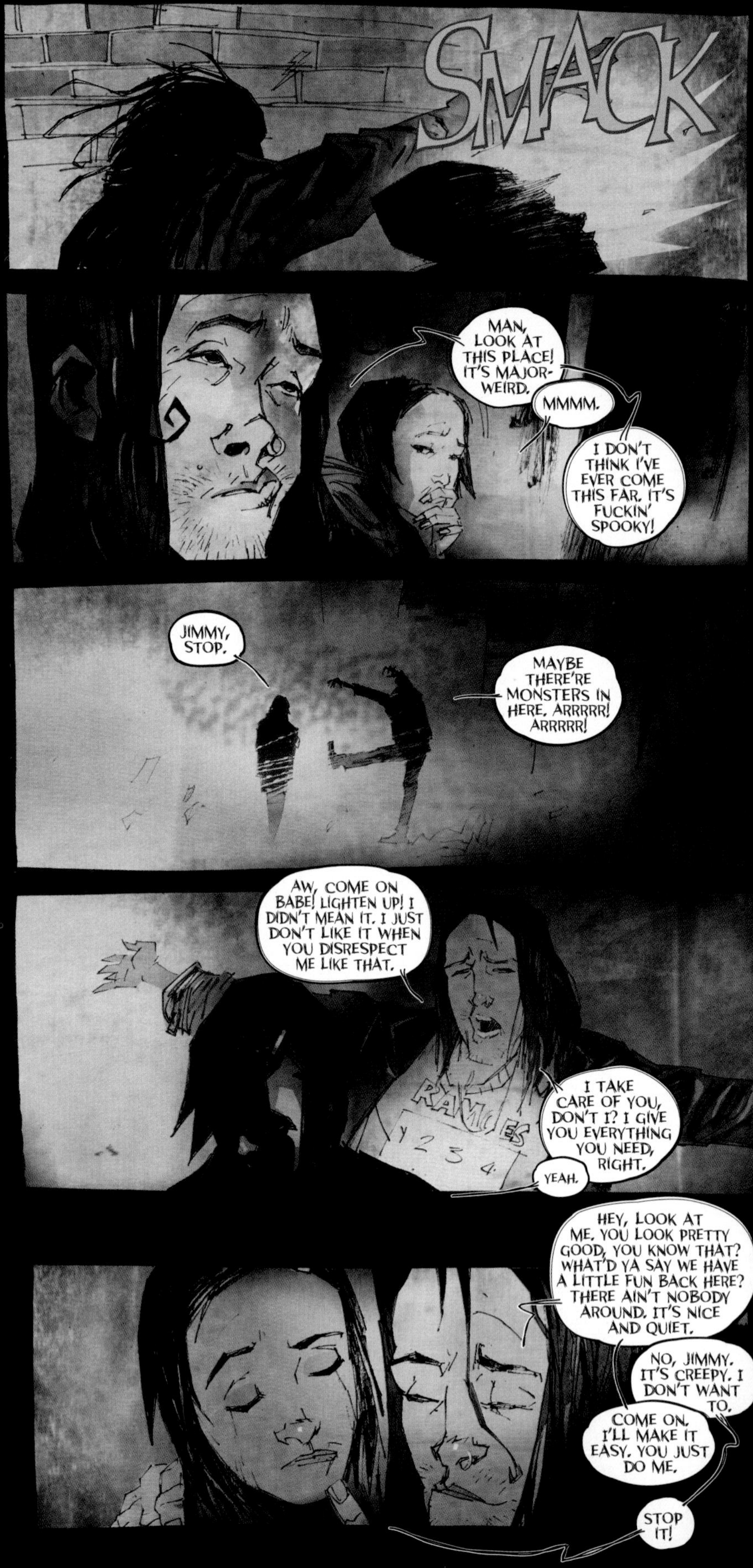

SMACK
MAN, LOOK AT THIS PLACE! IT'S MAJOR-WEIRD.
MMMM.
I DON'T THINK I'VE EVER COME THIS FAR. IT'S FUCKIN' SPOOKY!
JIMMY, STOP.
MAYBE THERE'RE MONSTERS IN HERE. ARRRRR! ARRRRR!
AW, COME ON BABE! LIGHTEN UP! I DIDN'T MEAN IT. I JUST DON'T LIKE IT WHEN YOU DISRESPECT ME LIKE THAT.
I TAKE CARE OF YOU, DON'T I? I GIVE YOU EVERYTHING YOU NEED, RIGHT.
YEAH.
HEY, LOOK AT ME. YOU LOOK PRETTY GOOD, YOU KNOW THAT? WHAT'D YA SAY WE HAVE A LITTLE FUN BACK HERE? THERE AIN'T NOBODY AROUND. IT'S NICE AND QUIET.
NO, JIMMY. IT'S CREEPY. I DON'T WANT TO.
COME ON. I'LL MAKE IT EASY. YOU JUST DO ME.
STOP IT!

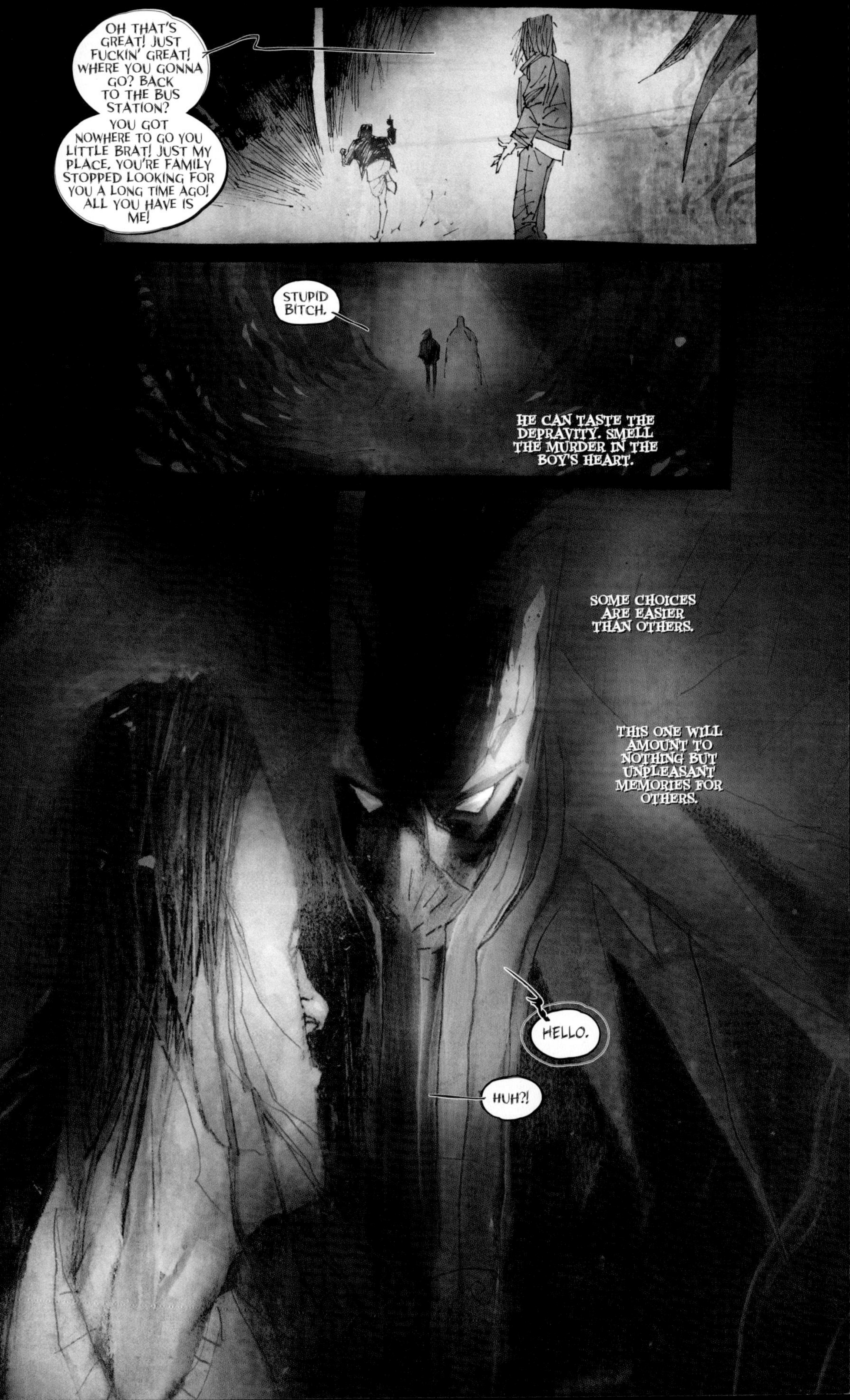
OH THAT'S GREAT! JUST FUCKIN' GREAT! WHERE YOU GONNA GO? BACK TO THE BUS STATION?
YOU GOT NOWHERE TO GO YOU LITTLE BRAT! JUST MY PLACE. YOU'RE FAMILY STOPPED LOOKING FOR YOU A LONG TIME AGO! ALL YOU HAVE IS ME!
STUPID BITCH.
HE CAN TASTE THE DEPRAVITY. SMELL THE MURDER IN THE BOY'S HEART.
SOME CHOICES ARE EASIER THAN OTHERS.
THIS ONE WILL AMOUNT TO NOTHING BUT UNPLEASANT MEMORIES FOR OTHERS.
HELLO.
HUH?!

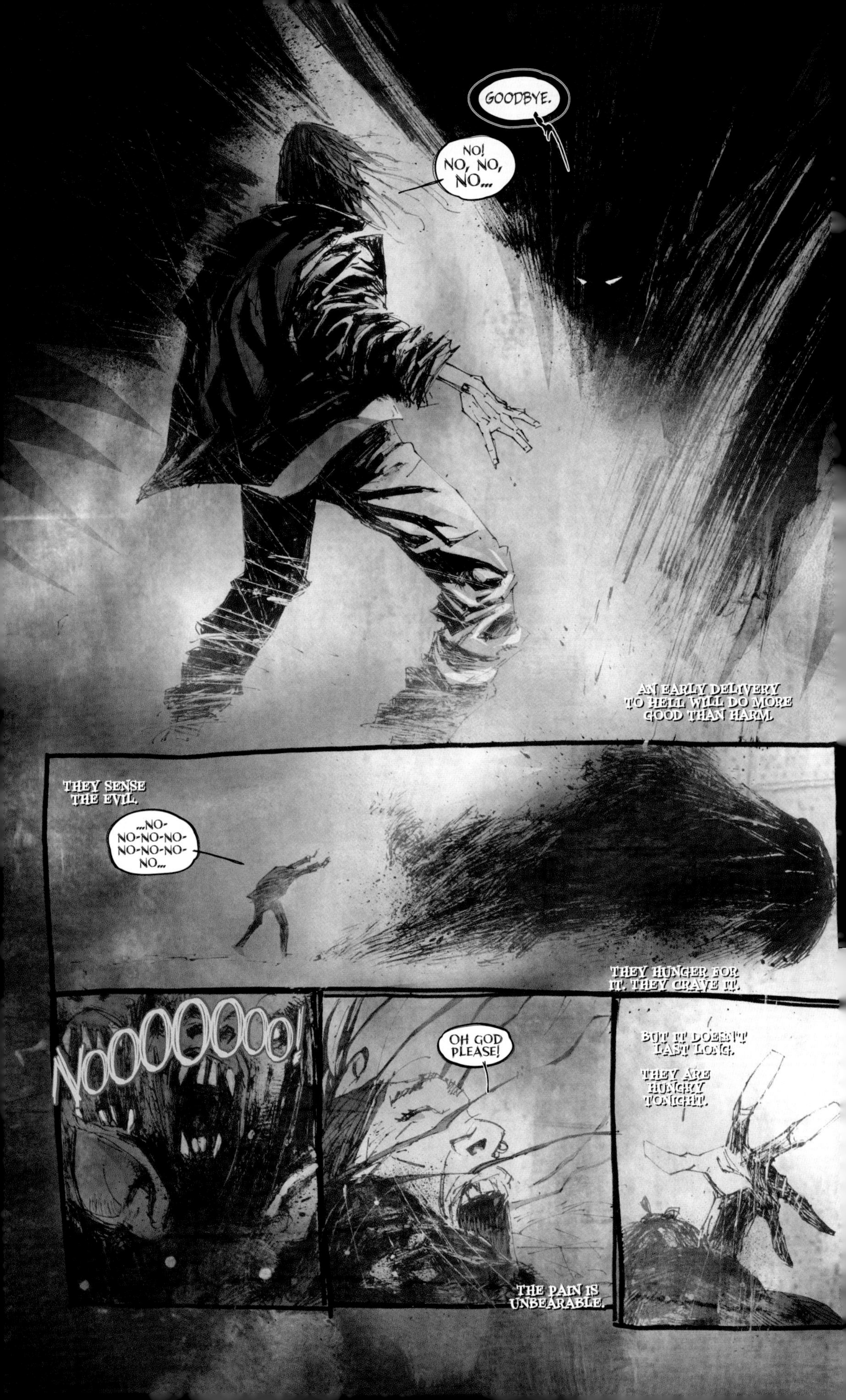

GOODBYE.
NO! NO, NO, NO...
AN EARLY DELIVERY TO HELL WILL DO MORE GOOD THAN HARM.
THEY SENSE THE EVIL.
...NO-NO-NO-NO-NO-NO-NO-NO-NO...
THEY HUNGER FOR IT. THEY CRAVE IT.
NOOOOOOO!
OH GOD PLEASE!
THE PAIN IS UNBEARABLE.
BUT IT DOESN'T LAST LONG.
THEY ARE HUNGRY TONIGHT.

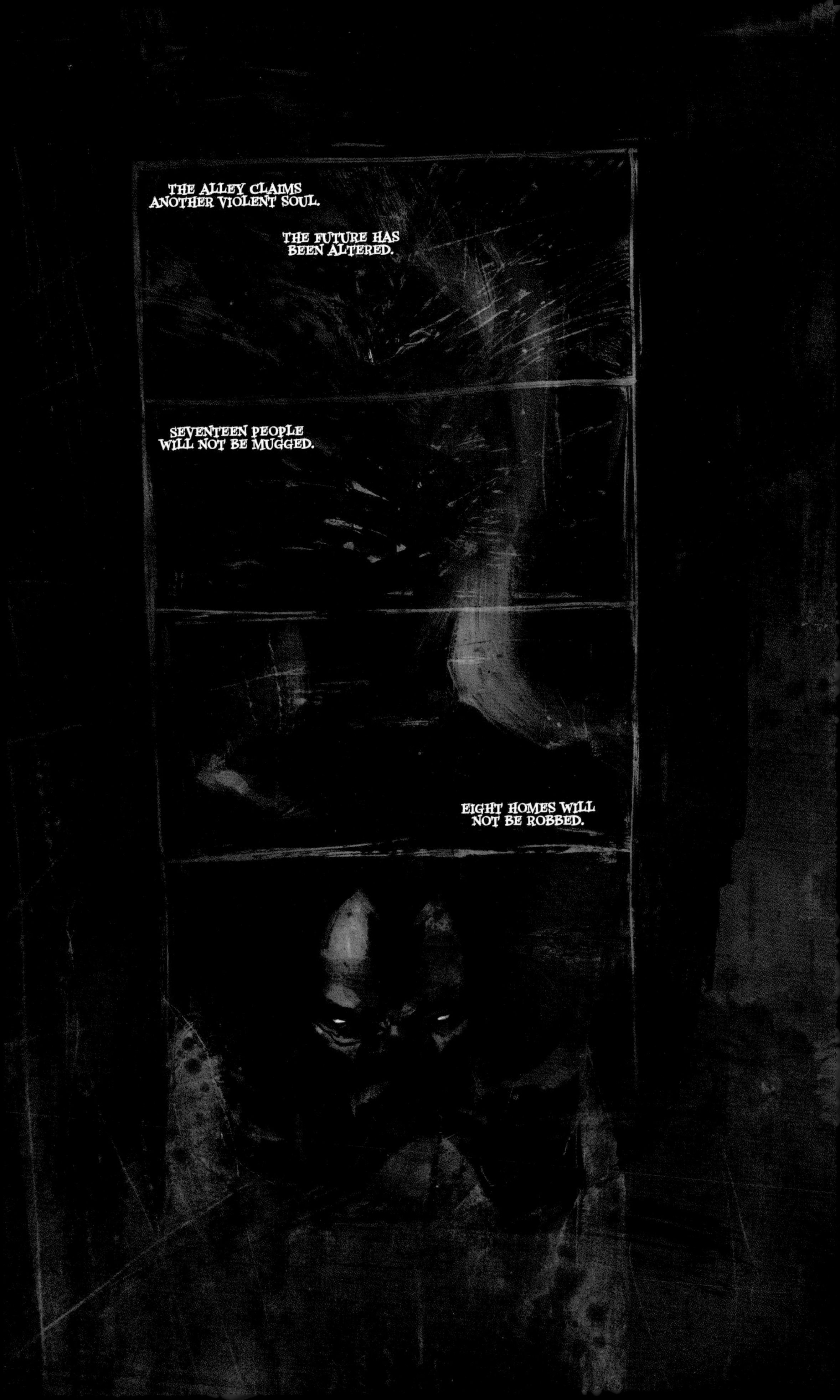
THE ALLEY CLAIMS ANOTHER VIOLENT SOUL.
THE FUTURE HAS BEEN ALTERED.
SEVENTEEN PEOPLE WILL NOT BE MUGGED.
EIGHT HOMES WILL NOT BE ROBBED.

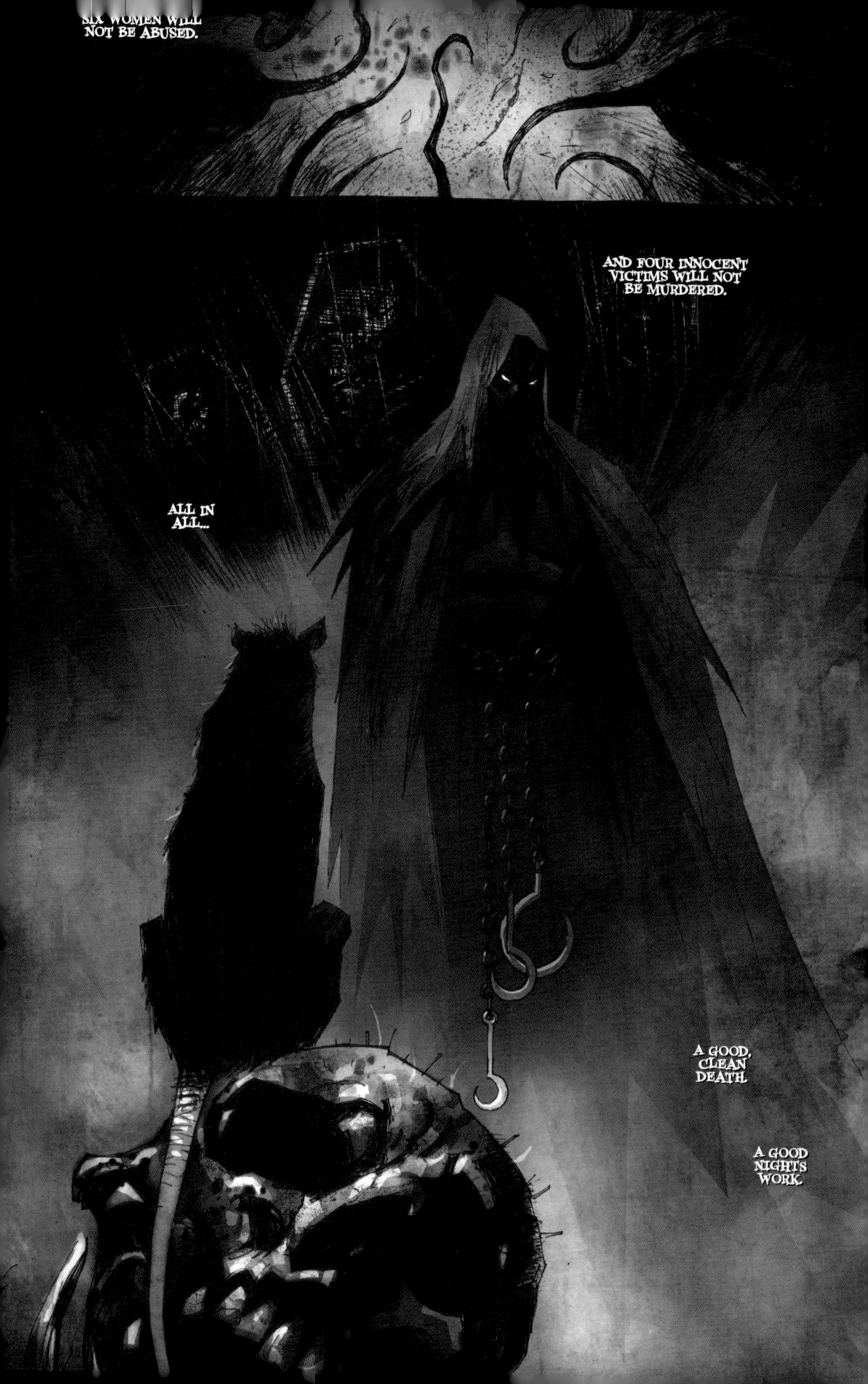
SIX WOMEN WILL NOT BE ABUSED.
AND FOUR INNOCENT VICTIMS WILL NOT BE MURDERED.
ALL IN ALL...
A GOOD, CLEAN DEATH.
A GOOD NIGHTS WORK.

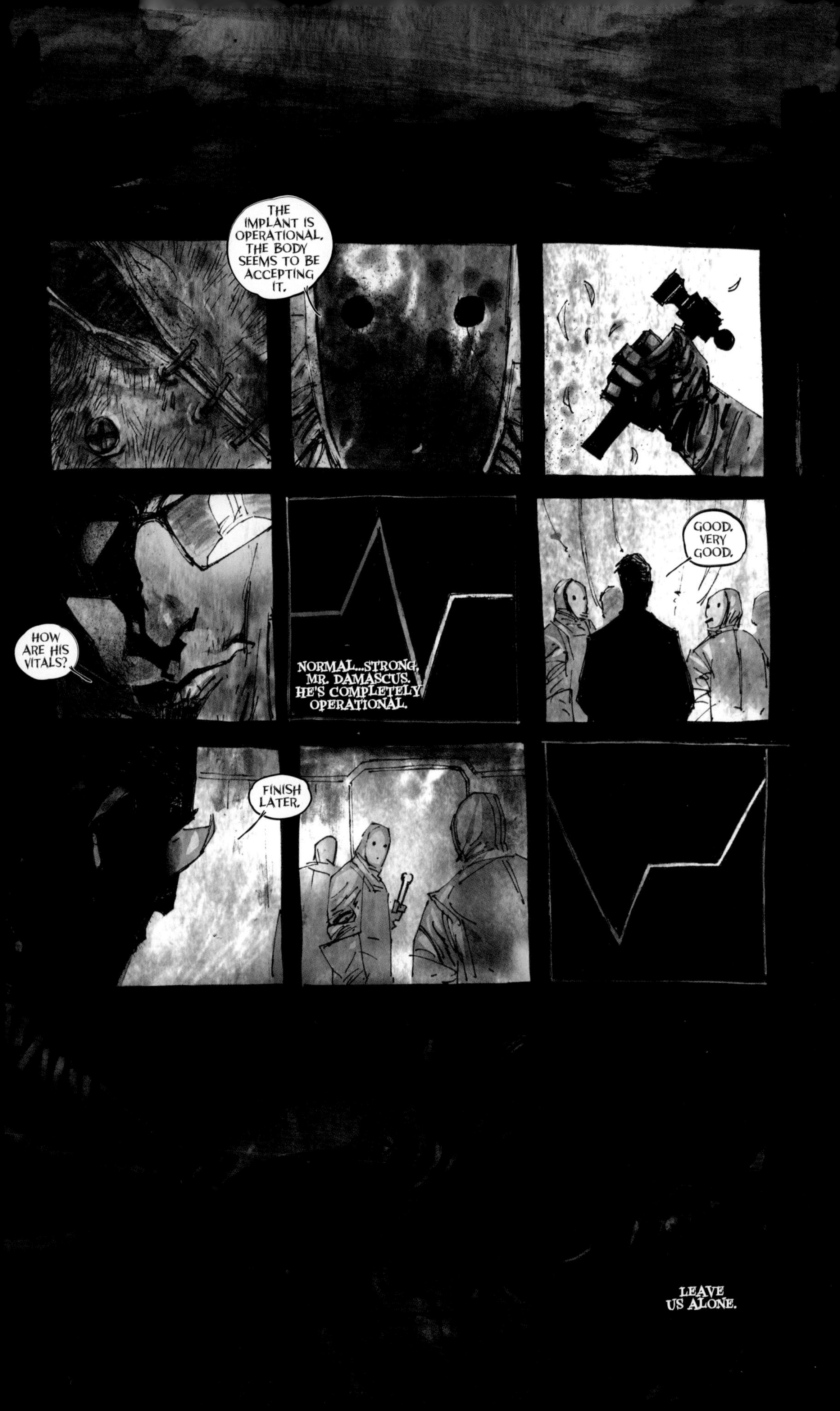
THE IMPLANT IS OPERATIONAL. THE BODY SEEMS TO BE ACCEPTING IT.
HOW ARE HIS VITALS?
NORMAL...STRONG, MR. DAMASCUS. HE'S COMPLETELY OPERATIONAL.
GOOD. VERY GOOD.
FINISH LATER.
LEAVE US ALONE.

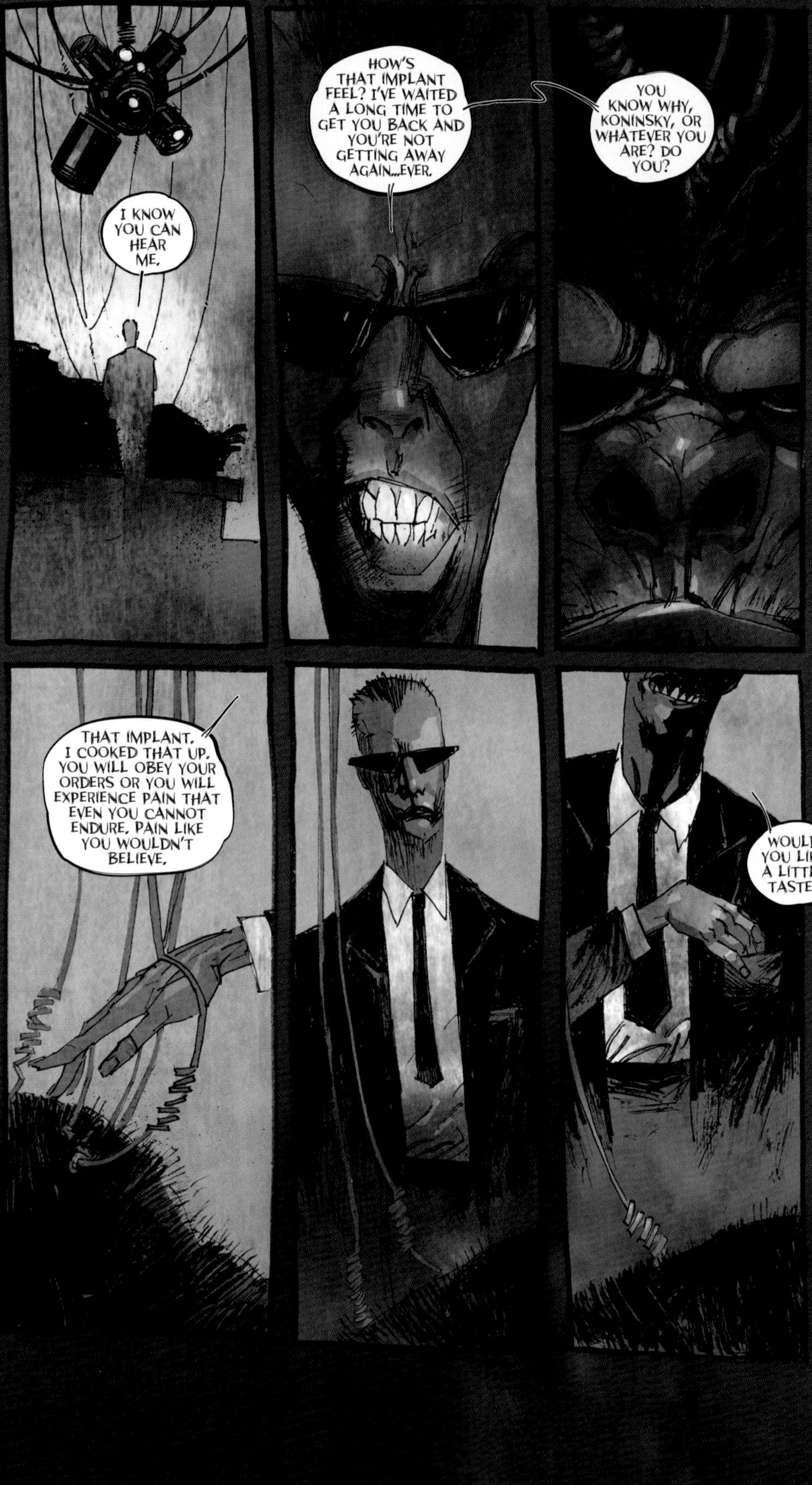
I KNOW YOU CAN HEAR ME.
HOW'S THAT IMPLANT FEEL? I'VE WAITED A LONG TIME TO GET YOU BACK AND YOU'RE NOT GETTING AWAY AGAIN...EVER.
YOU KNOW WHY, KONINSKY, OR WHATEVER YOU ARE? DO YOU?
THAT IMPLANT. I COOKED THAT UP. YOU WILL OBEY YOUR ORDERS OR YOU WILL EXPERIENCE PAIN THAT EVEN YOU CANNOT ENDURE. PAIN LIKE YOU WOULDN'T BELIEVE.
WOULD YOU LIKE A LITTLE TASTE?

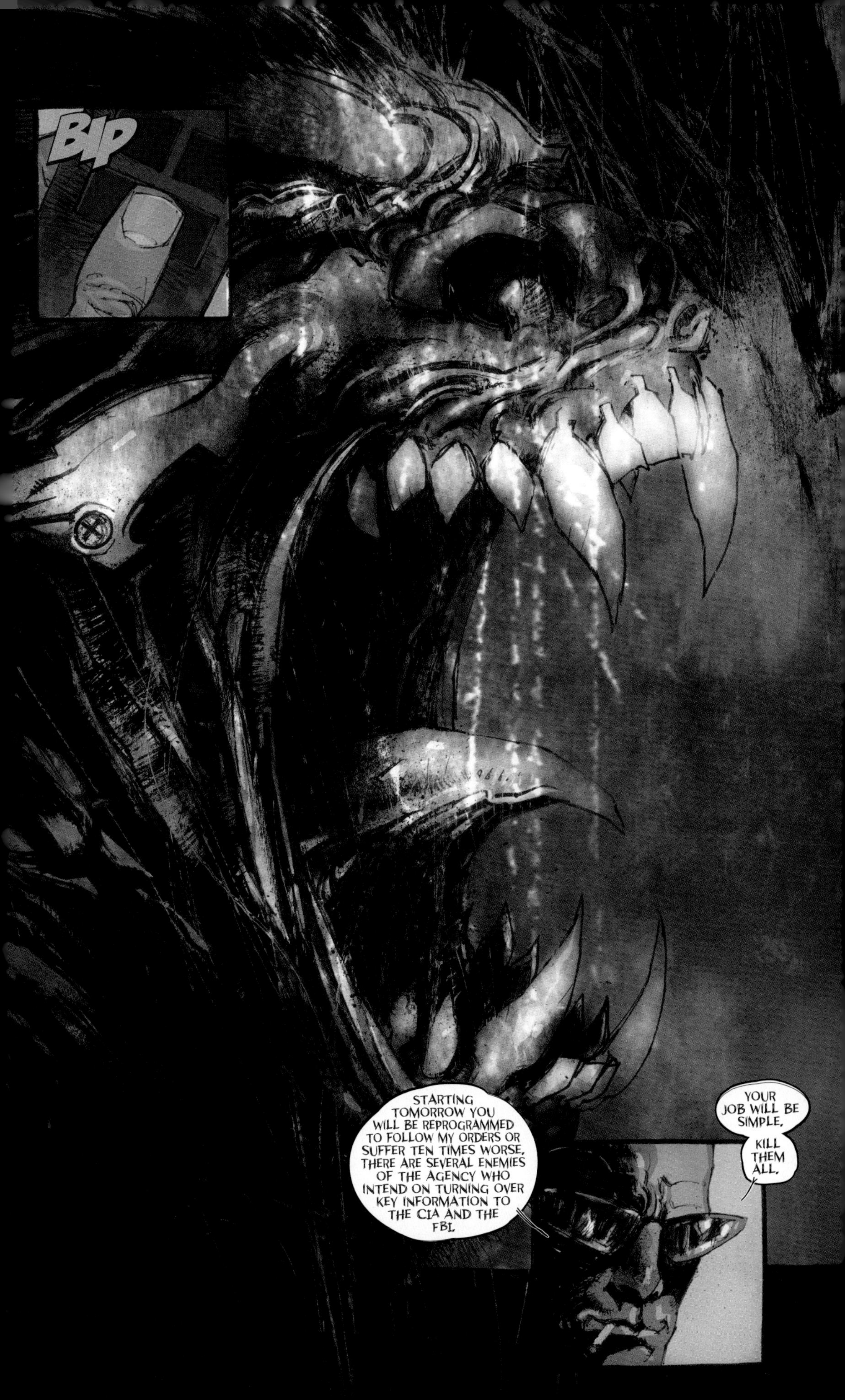
BIP
STARTING TOMORROW YOU WILL BE REPROGRAMMED TO FOLLOW MY ORDERS OR SUFFER TEN TIMES WORSE. THERE ARE SEVERAL ENEMIES OF THE AGENCY WHO INTEND ON TURNING OVER KEY INFORMATION TO THE CIA AND THE FBI.
YOUR JOB WILL BE SIMPLE.
KILL THEM ALL.

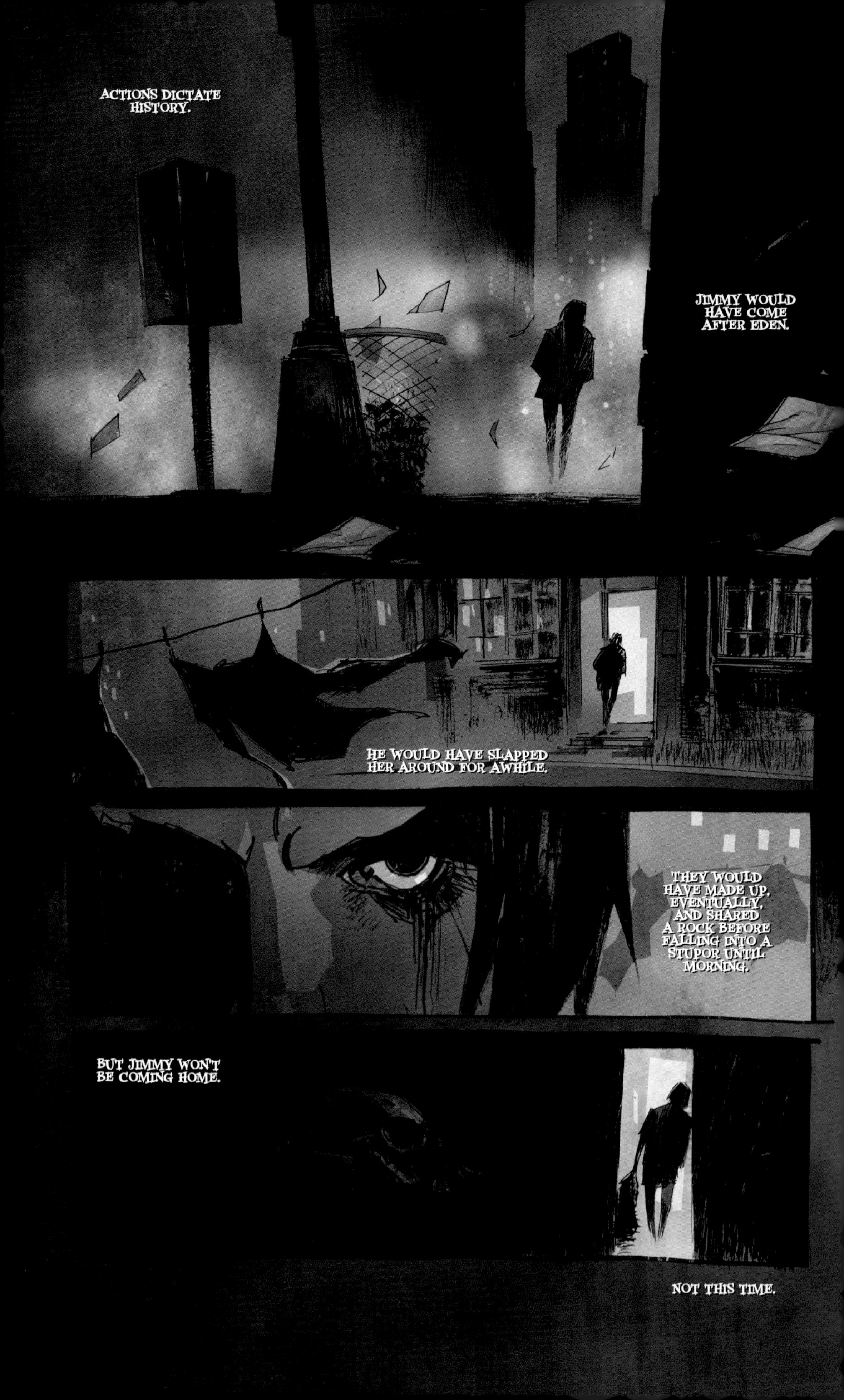

ACTIONS DICTATE HISTORY.
JIMMY WOULD HAVE COME AFTER EDEN.
HE WOULD HAVE SLAPPED HER AROUND FOR AWHILE.
THEY WOULD HAVE MADE UP, EVENTUALLY, AND SHARED A ROCK BEFORE FALLING INTO A STUPOR UNTIL MORNING.
BUT JIMMY WON'T BE COMING HOME.
NOT THIS TIME.

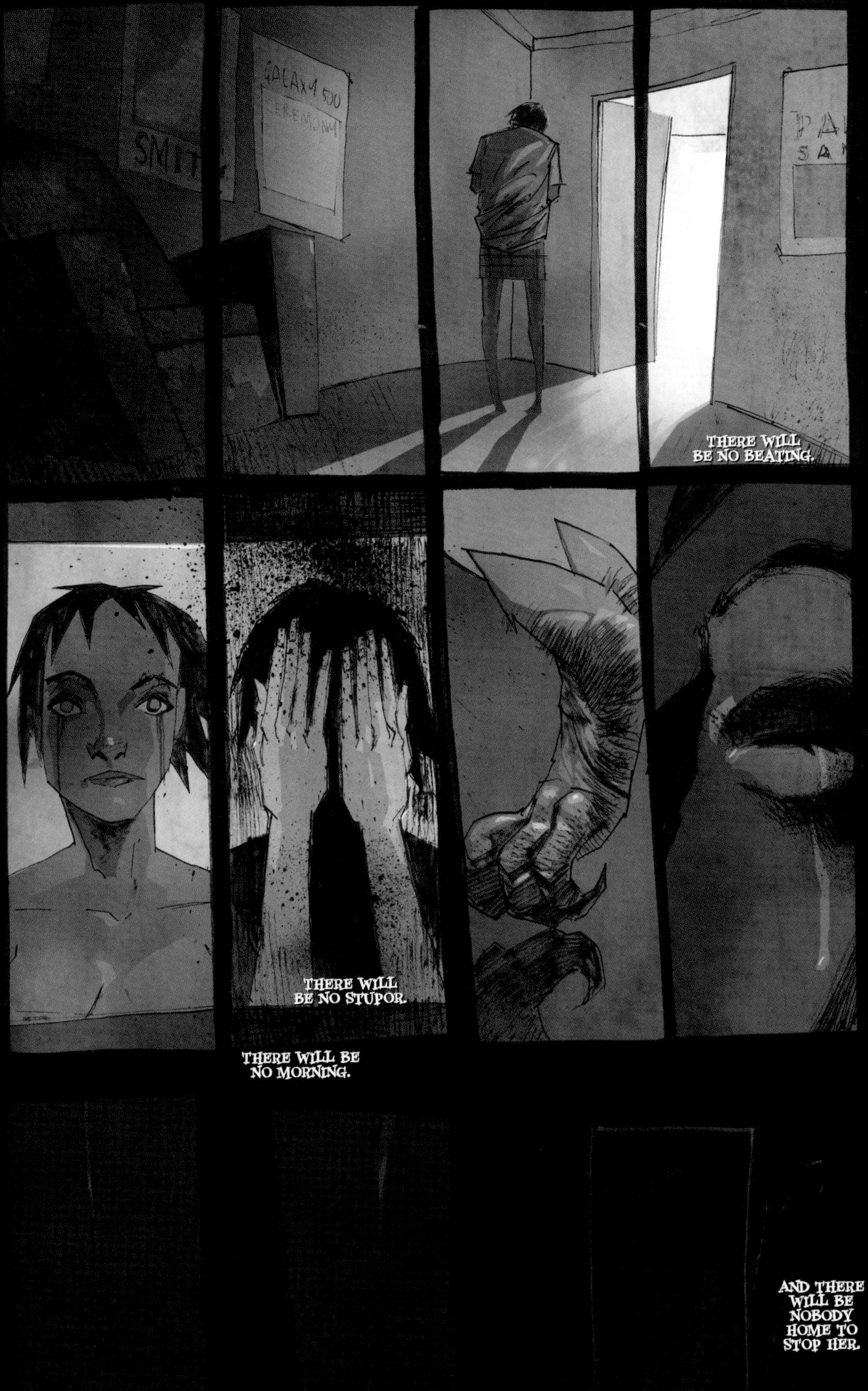
THERE WILL BE NO BEATING.
THERE WILL BE NO STUPOR.
THERE WILL BE NO MORNING.
AND THERE WILL BE NOBODY HOME TO STOP HER.

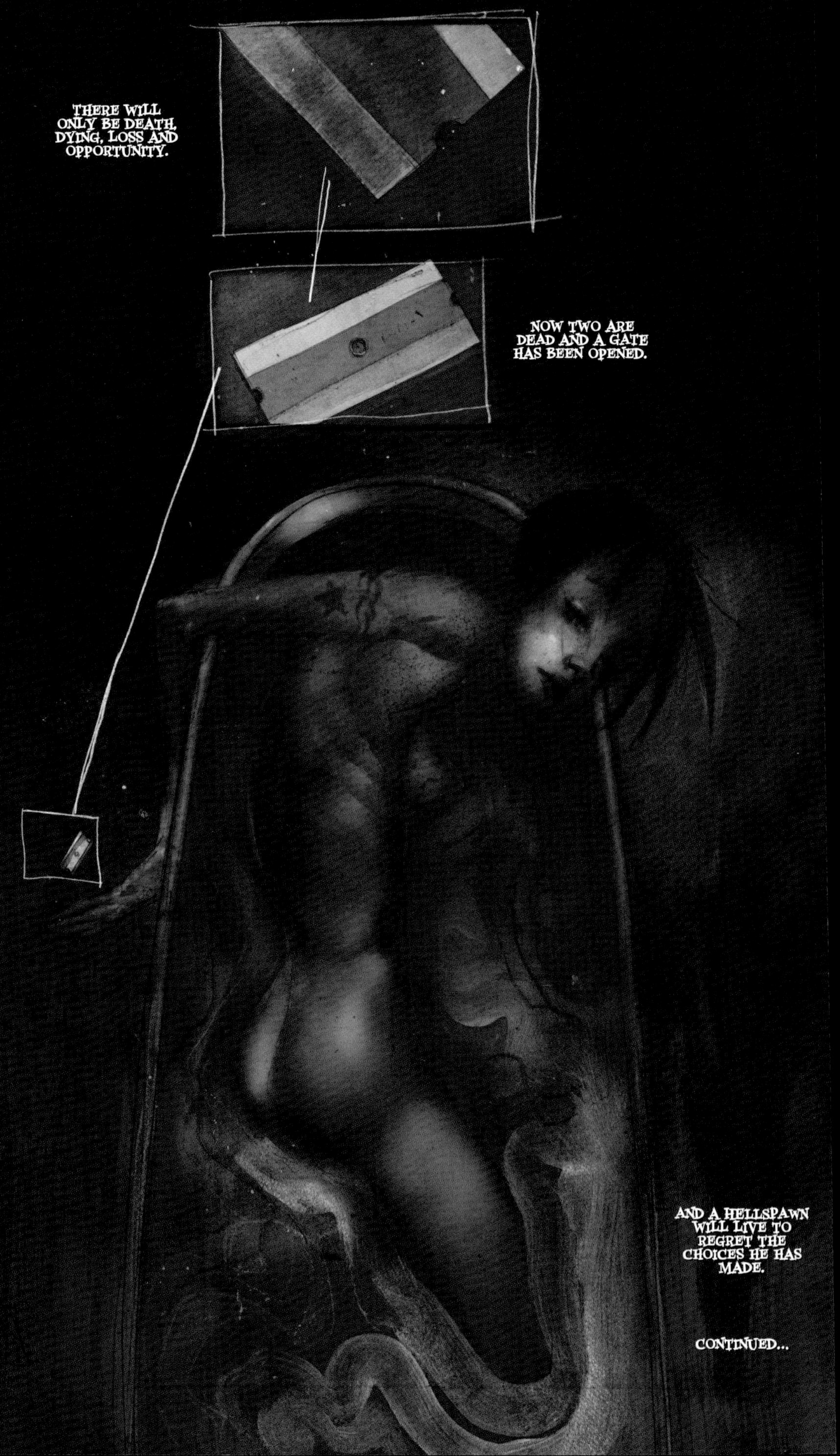
THERE WILL ONLY BE DEATH, DYING, LOSS AND OPPORTUNITY.
NOW TWO ARE DEAD AND A GATE HAS BEEN OPENED.
AND A HELLSPAWN WILL LIVE TO REGRET THE CHOICES HE HAS MADE.
CONTINUED...

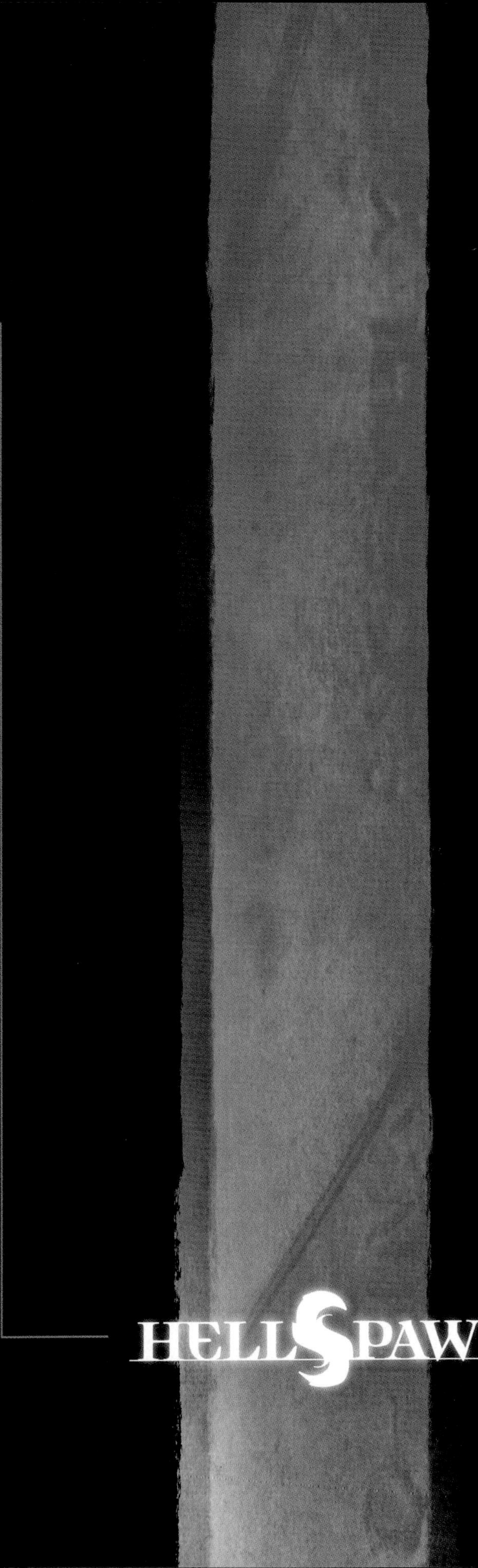
HELLSPAW

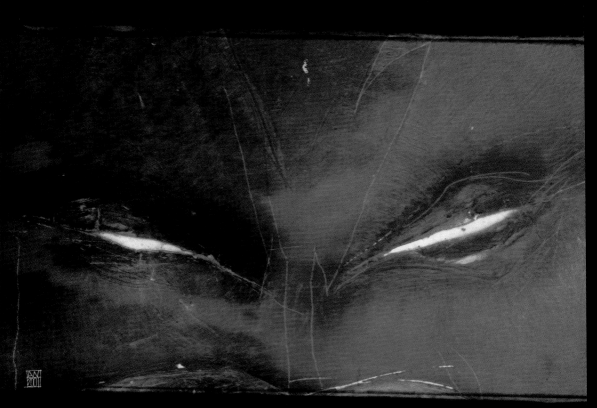

ISSUE NINE

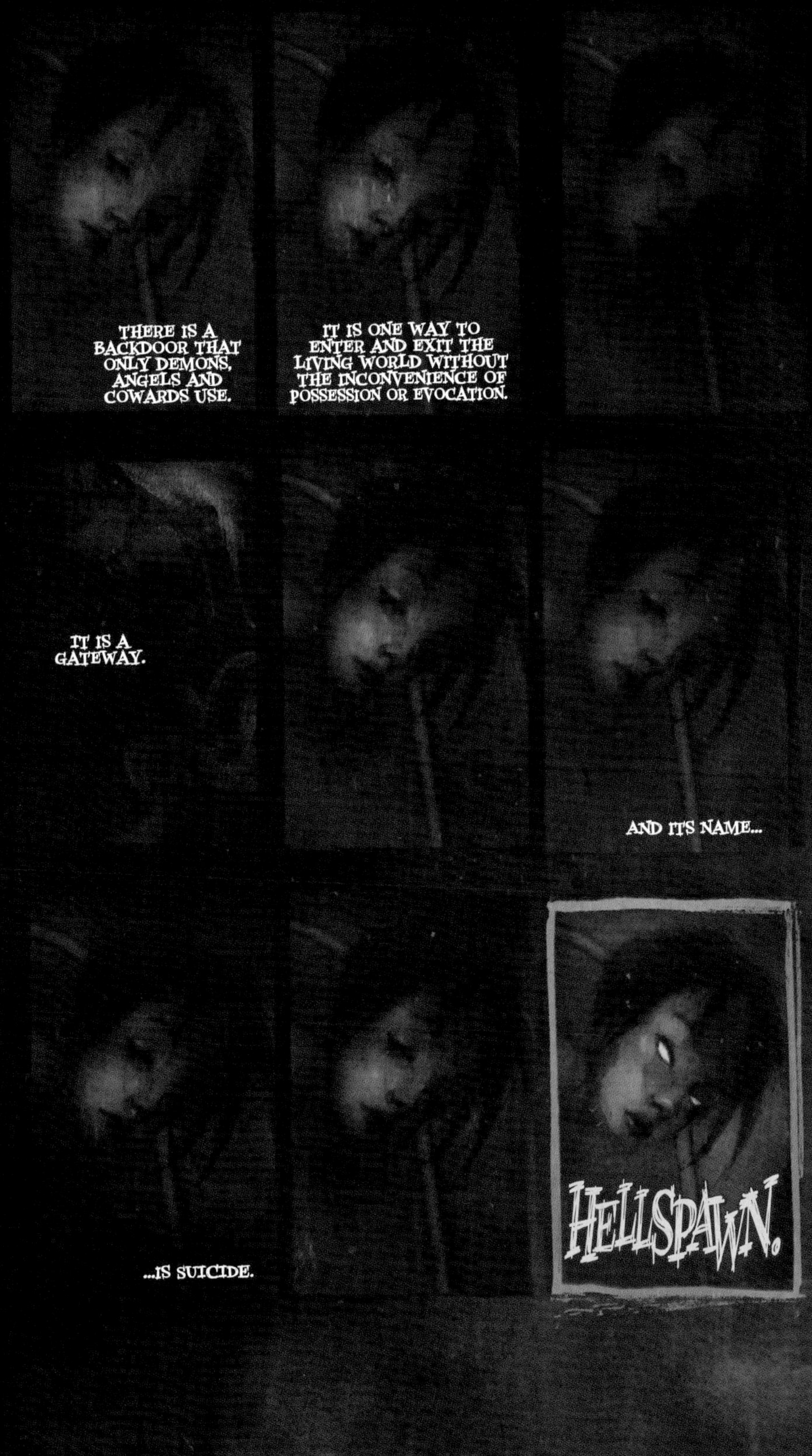

THERE IS A BACKDOOR THAT ONLY DEMONS, ANGELS AND COWARDS USE.
IT IS ONE WAY TO ENTER AND EXIT THE LIVING WORLD WITHOUT THE INCONVENIENCE OF POSSESSION OR EVOCATION.
IT IS A GATEWAY.
AND IT'S NAME...
...IS SUICIDE.
HELLSPAWN.

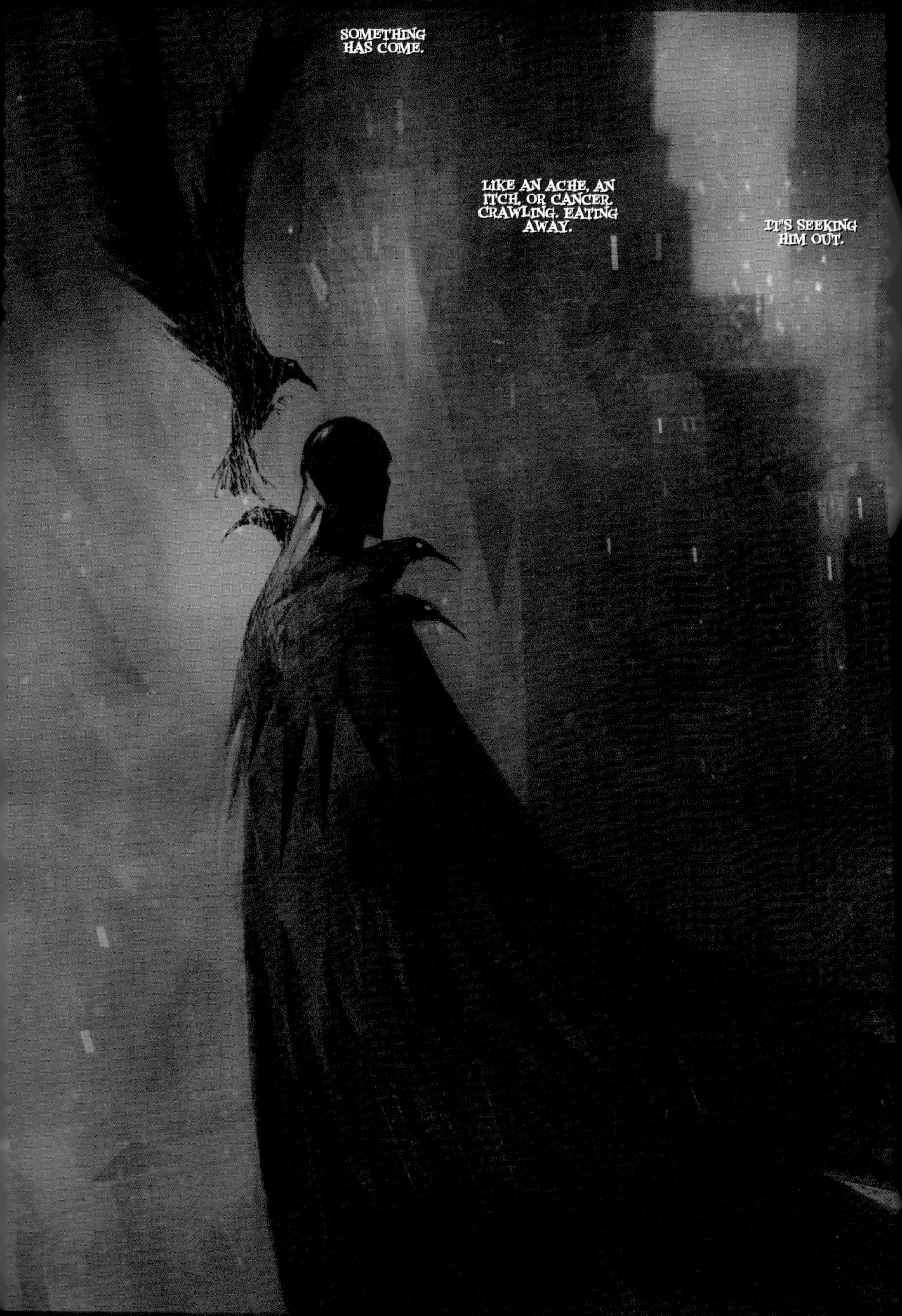
SOMETHING HAS COME.
LIKE AN ACHE, AN ITCH, OR CANCER. CRAWLING. EATING AWAY.
IT'S SEEKING HIM OUT.

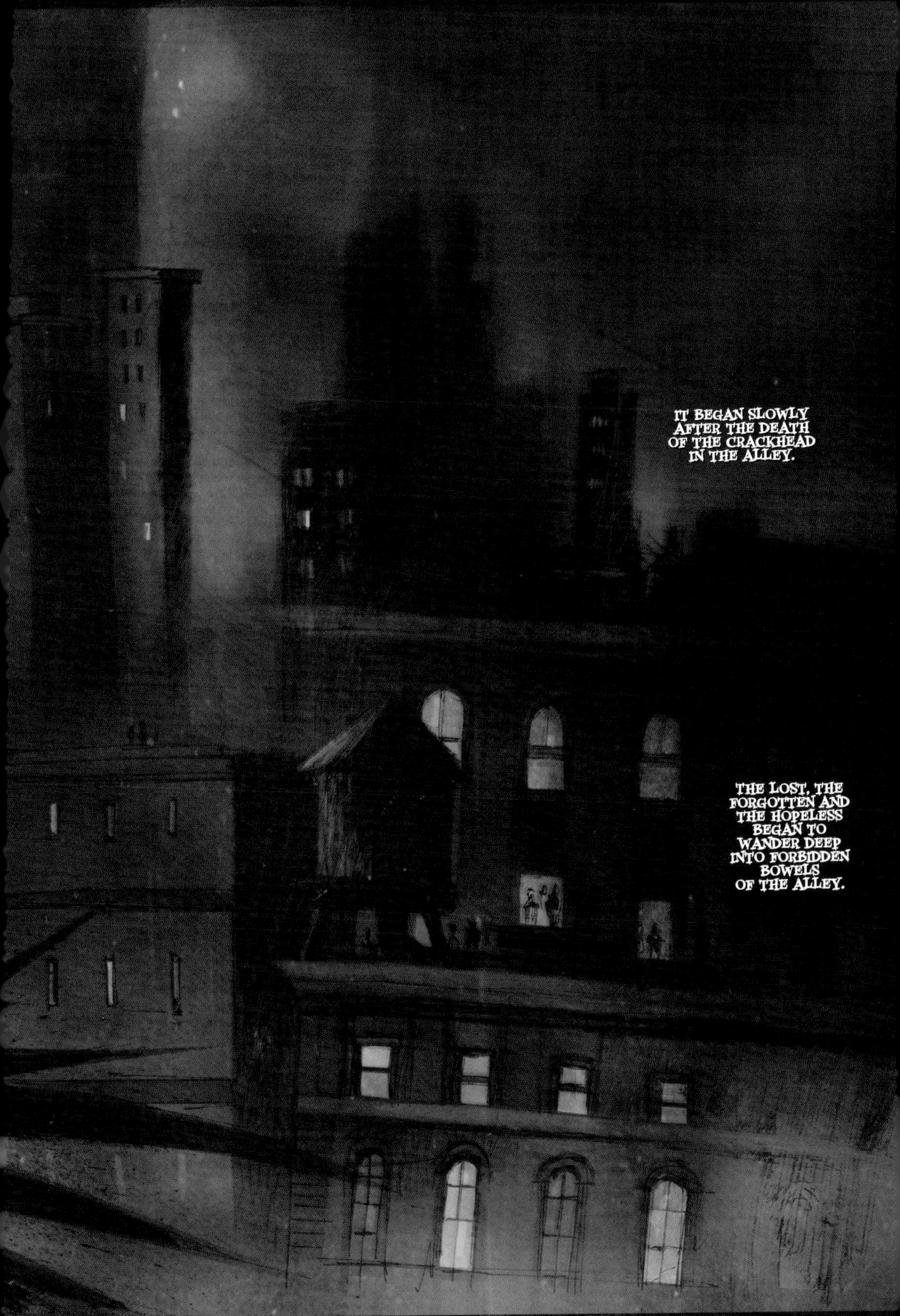
IT BEGAN SLOWLY AFTER THE DEATH OF THE CRACKHEAD IN THE ALLEY.
THE LOST, THE FORGOTTEN AND THE HOPELESS BEGAN TO WANDER DEEP INTO FORBIDDEN BOWELS OF THE ALLEY.

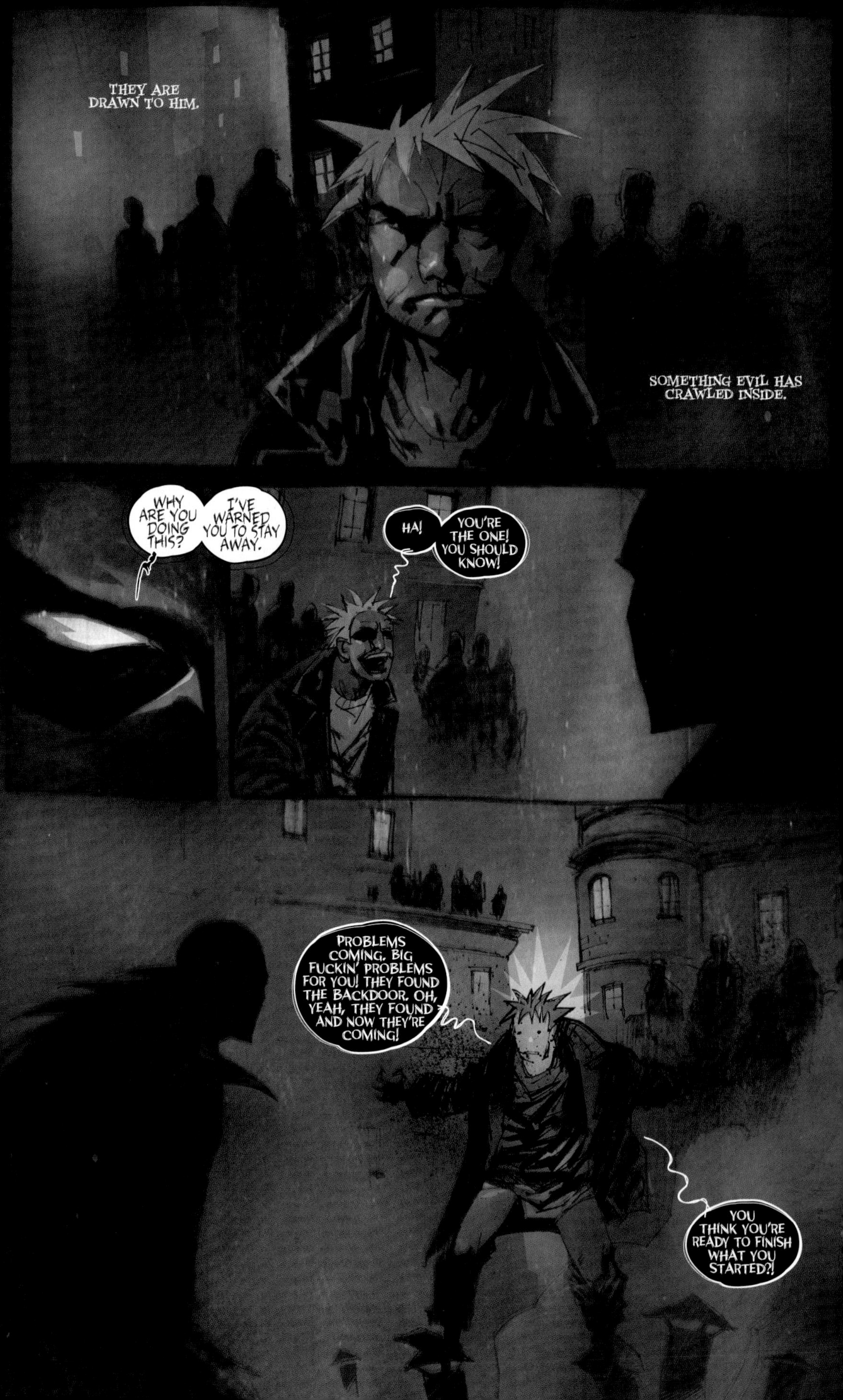
THEY ARE DRAWN TO HIM.
SOMETHING EVIL HAS CRAWLED INSIDE.
WHY ARE YOU DOING THIS?
I'VE WARNED YOU TO STAY AWAY.
HA!
YOU'RE THE ONE! YOU SHOULD KNOW!
PROBLEMS COMING. BIG FUCKIN' PROBLEMS FOR YOU! THEY FOUND THE BACKDOOR. OH, YEAH, THEY FOUND AND NOW THEY'RE COMING!
YOU THINK YOU'RE READY TO FINISH WHAT YOU STARTED?!

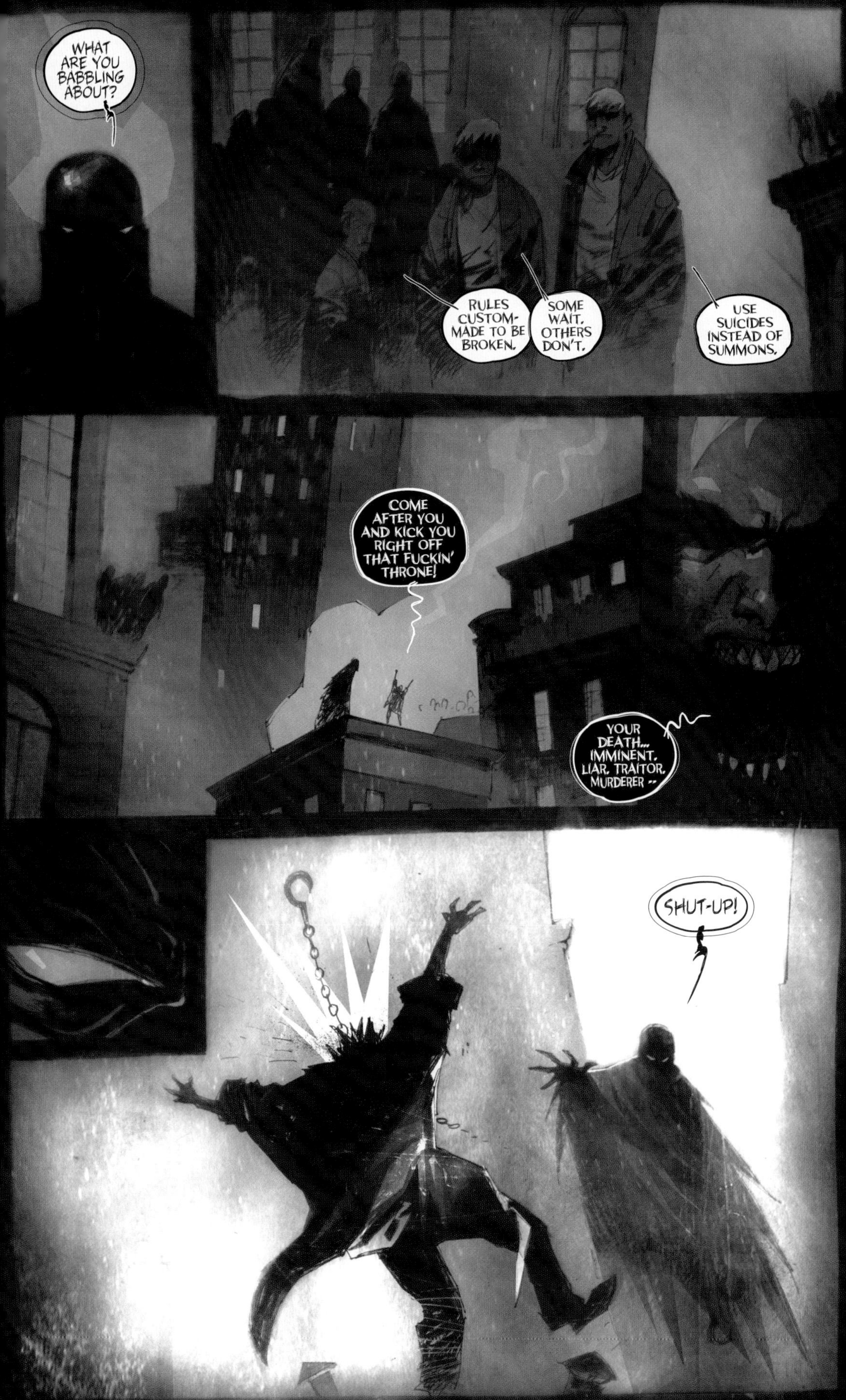
WHAT ARE YOU BABBLING ABOUT?
RULES CUSTOM-MADE TO BE BROKEN.
SOME WAIT. OTHERS DON'T.
USE SUICIDES INSTEAD OF SUMMONS.
COME AFTER YOU AND KICK YOU RIGHT OFF THAT FUCKIN' THRONE!
YOUR DEATH... IMMINENT. LIAR. TRAITOR. MURDERER --
SHUT-UP!

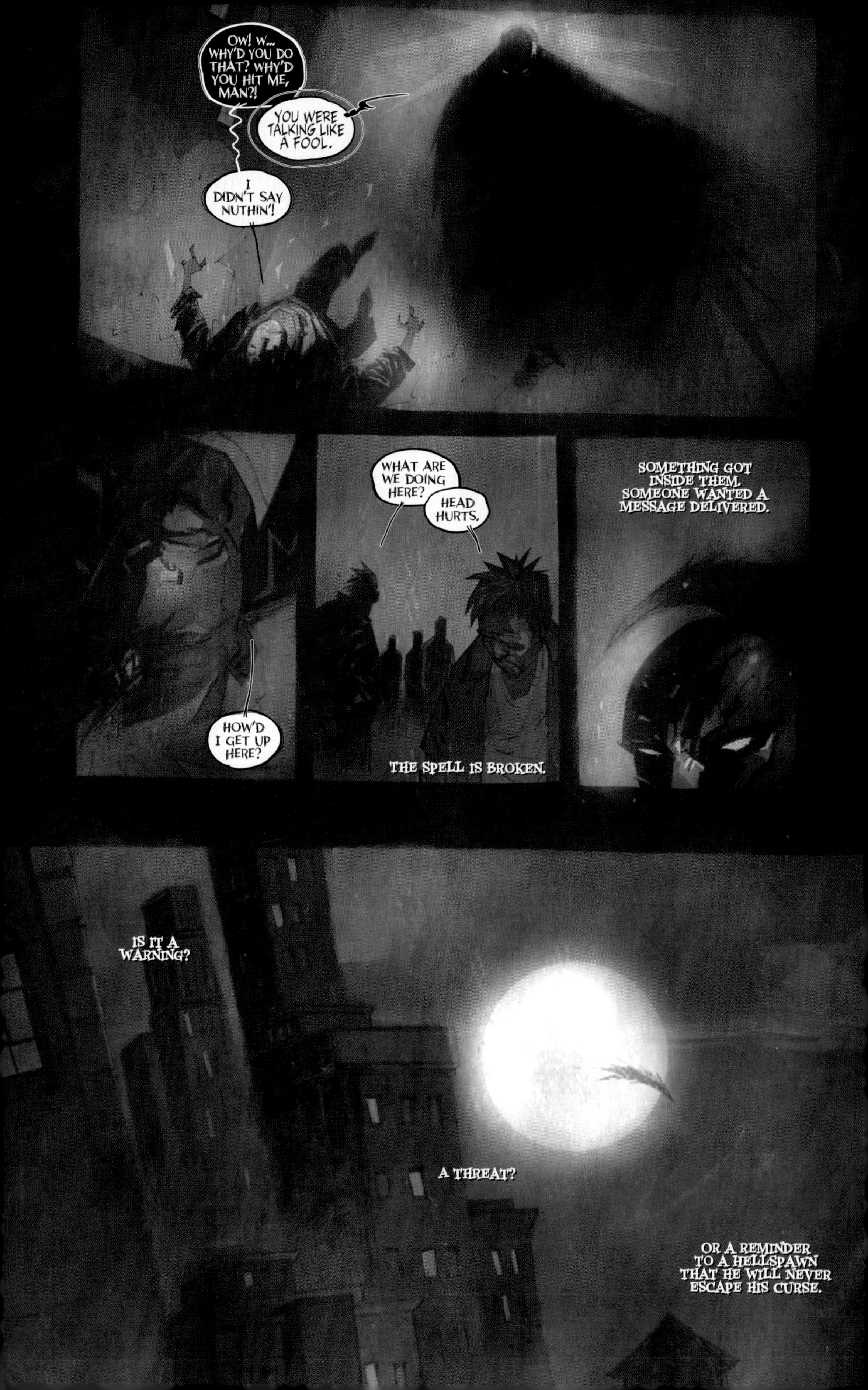
OW! W... WHY'D YOU DO THAT? WHY'D YOU HIT ME, MAN?!
YOU WERE TALKING LIKE A FOOL.
I DIDN'T SAY NUTHIN'!
HOW'D I GET UP HERE?
WHAT ARE WE DOING HERE?
HEAD HURTS.
THE SPELL IS BROKEN.
SOMETHING GOT INSIDE THEM. SOMEONE WANTED A MESSAGE DELIVERED.
IS IT A WARNING?
A THREAT?
OR A REMINDER TO A HELLSPAWN THAT HE WILL NEVER ESCAPE HIS CURSE.

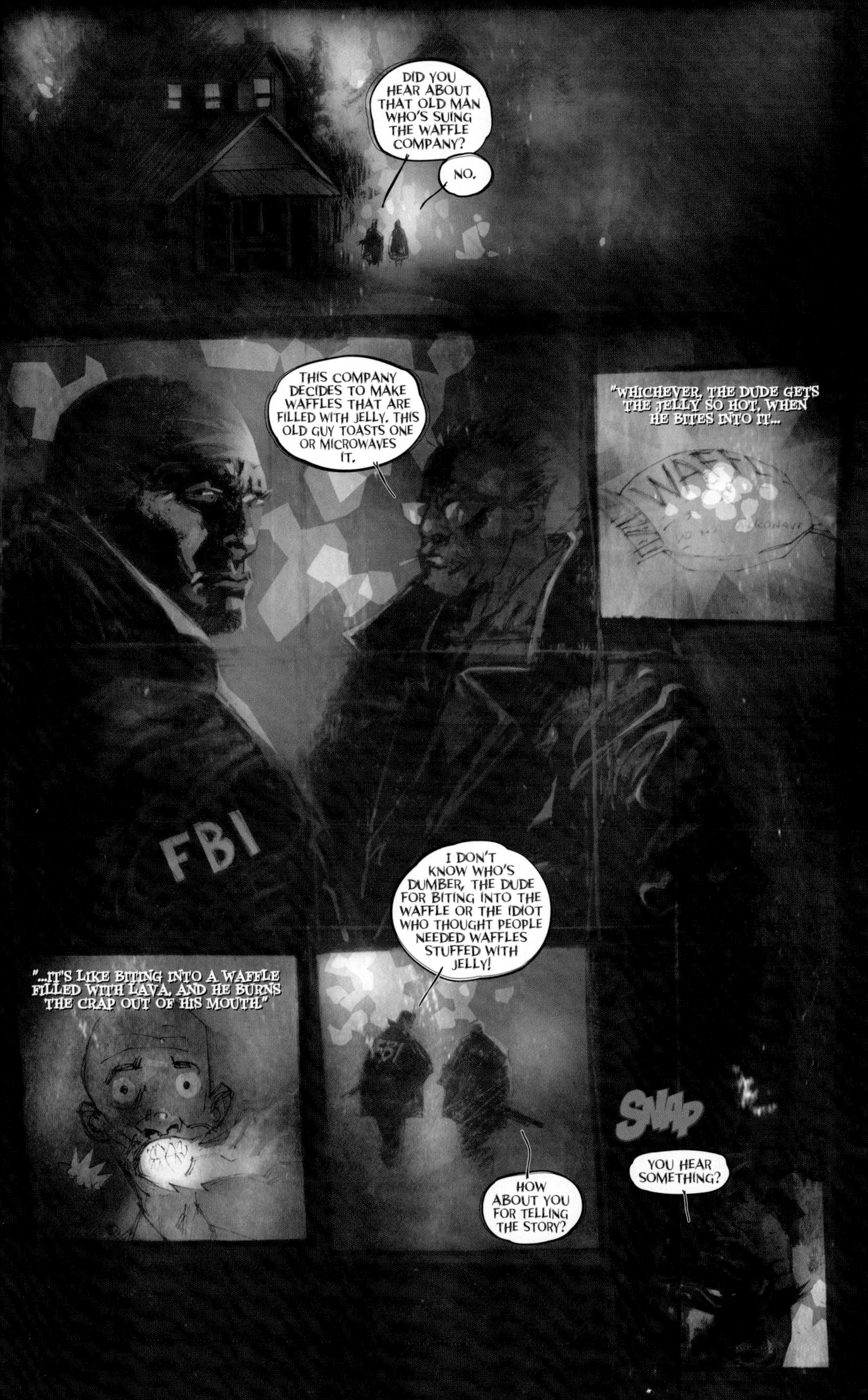

DID YOU HEAR ABOUT THAT OLD MAN WHO'S SUING THE WAFFLE COMPANY?
NO.
THIS COMPANY DECIDES TO MAKE WAFFLES THAT ARE FILLED WITH JELLY. THIS OLD GUY TOASTS ONE OR MICROWAVES IT.
"WHICHEVER, THE DUDE GETS THE JELLY SO HOT, WHEN HE BITES INTO IT...
FBI
I DON'T KNOW WHO'S DUMBER, THE DUDE FOR BITING INTO THE WAFFLE OR THE IDIOT WHO THOUGHT PEOPLE NEEDED WAFFLES STUFFED WITH JELLY!
"...IT'S LIKE BITING INTO A WAFFLE FILLED WITH LAVA, AND HE BURNS THE CRAP OUT OF HIS MOUTH."
HOW ABOUT YOU FOR TELLING THE STORY?
SNAP
YOU HEAR SOMETHING?

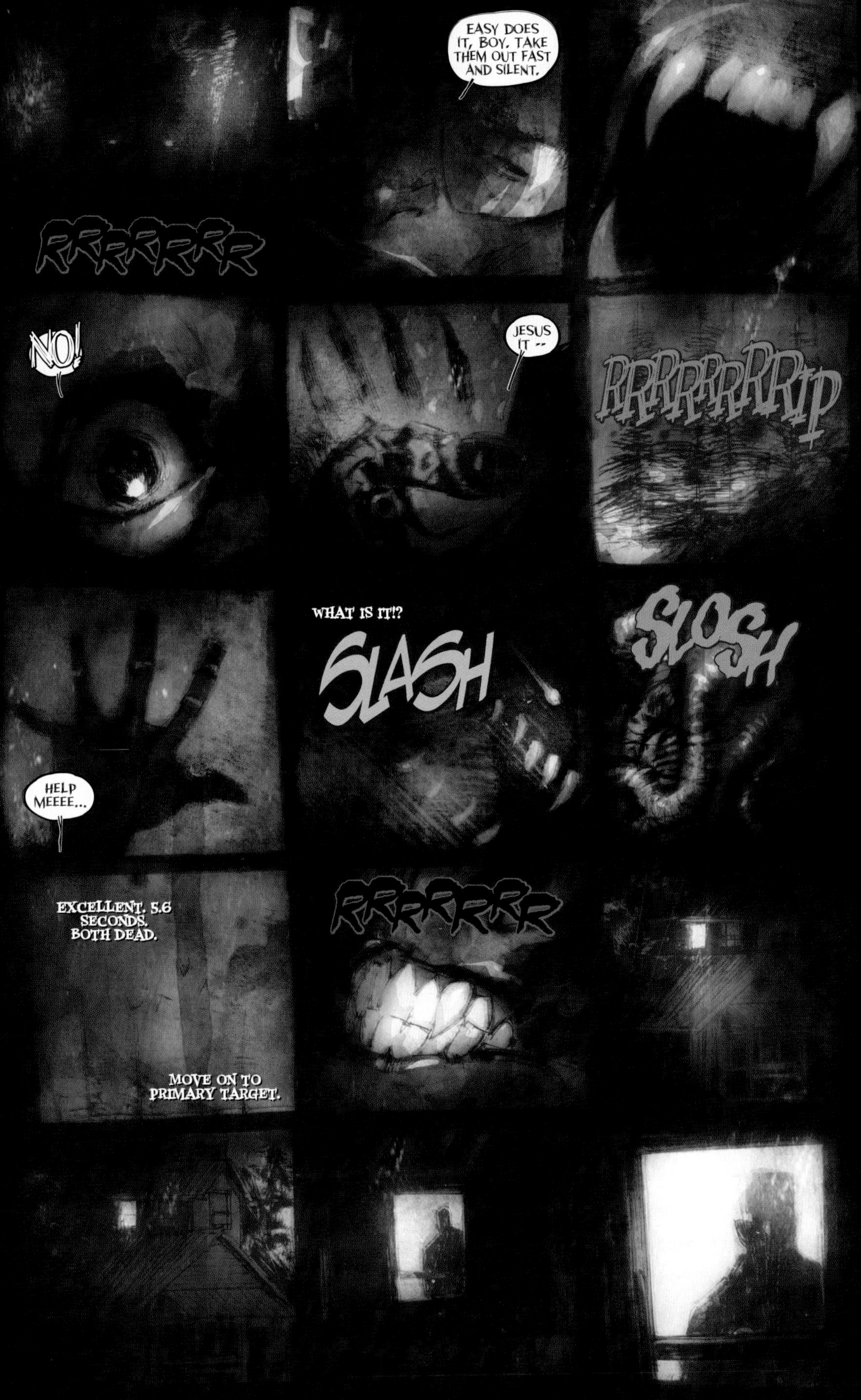
RRRRRRR
EASY DOES IT, BOY. TAKE THEM OUT FAST AND SILENT.
NO!
JESUS IT --
RRRRRRRRRIP
HELP MEEEE...
WHAT IS IT!?
SLASH
SLOSH
EXCELLENT. 5.6 SECONDS. BOTH DEAD.
MOVE ON TO PRIMARY TARGET.
RRRRRRR

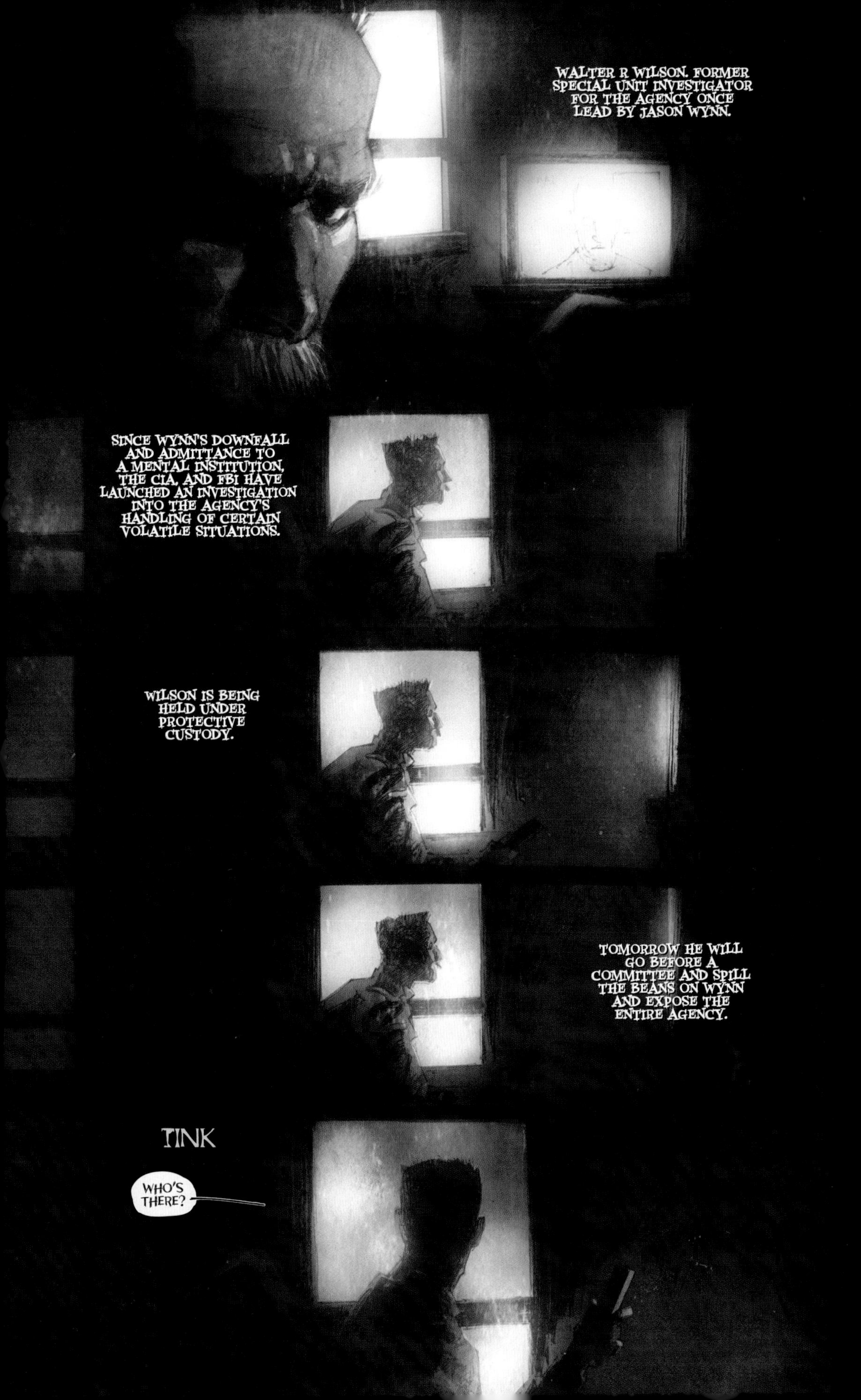
WALTER R WILSON. FORMER SPECIAL UNIT INVESTIGATOR FOR THE AGENCY ONCE LEAD BY JASON WYNN.
SINCE WYNN'S DOWNFALL AND ADMITTANCE TO A MENTAL INSTITUTION, THE CIA, AND FBI HAVE LAUNCHED AN INVESTIGATION INTO THE AGENCY'S HANDLING OF CERTAIN VOLATILE SITUATIONS.
WILSON IS BEING HELD UNDER PROTECTIVE CUSTODY.
TOMORROW HE WILL GO BEFORE A COMMITTEE AND SPILL THE BEANS ON WYNN AND EXPOSE THE ENTIRE AGENCY.
TINK
WHO'S THERE?

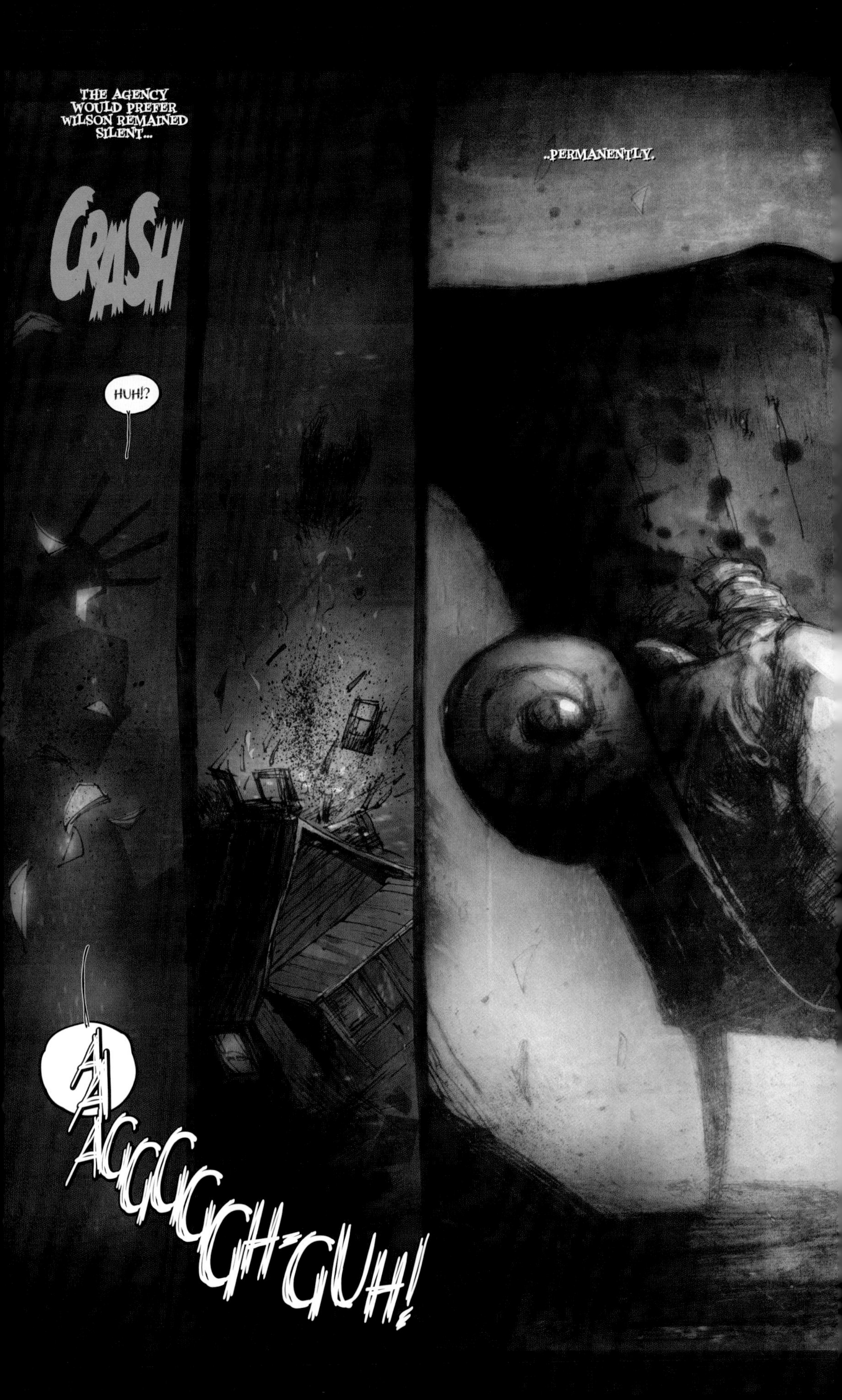

THE AGENCY WOULD PREFER WILSON REMAINED SILENT...
CRASH
HUH!?
AAAGGGGGH-GUH!
..PERMANENTLY.

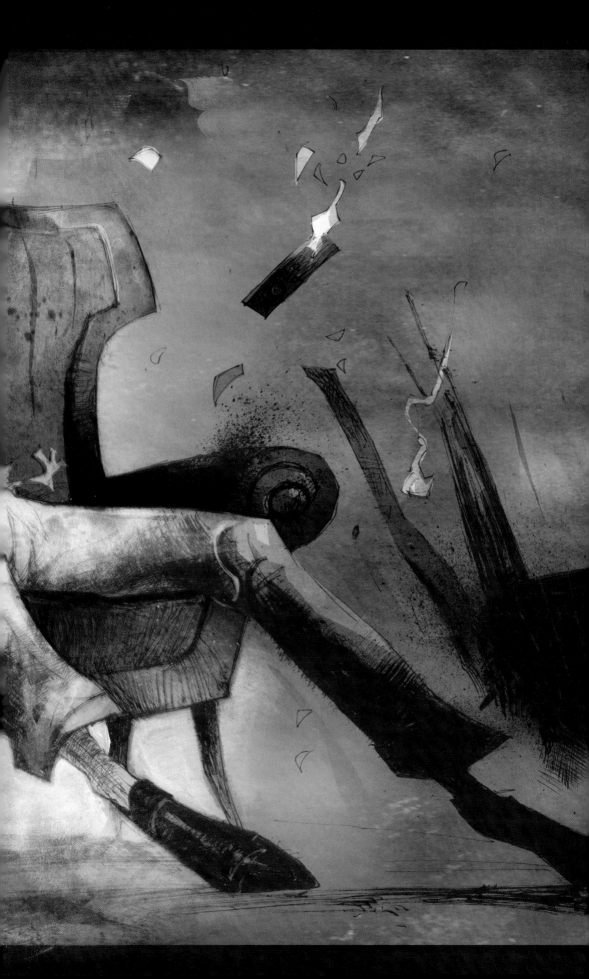

AND THAT IS THE END OF THAT.
THE APE IS RESPONDING PERFECTLY TO COMMANDS. HE'S HEADING BACK THIS WAY.
TWO MORE TRAITORS TO GO AND THEN WE GET BACK TO BUSINESS. THOSE FED BOYS WILL BE SCRATCHING THEIR HEADS FOR YEARS.
UM.. THE MONKEY JUST STOPPED.
WHAT!? MOVE!
EVERYTHING LOOKS NORMAL. PULSE RATE IS STEADY.
WHAT'S THE DAMN THING DOING?!
JUST STANDING THERE.

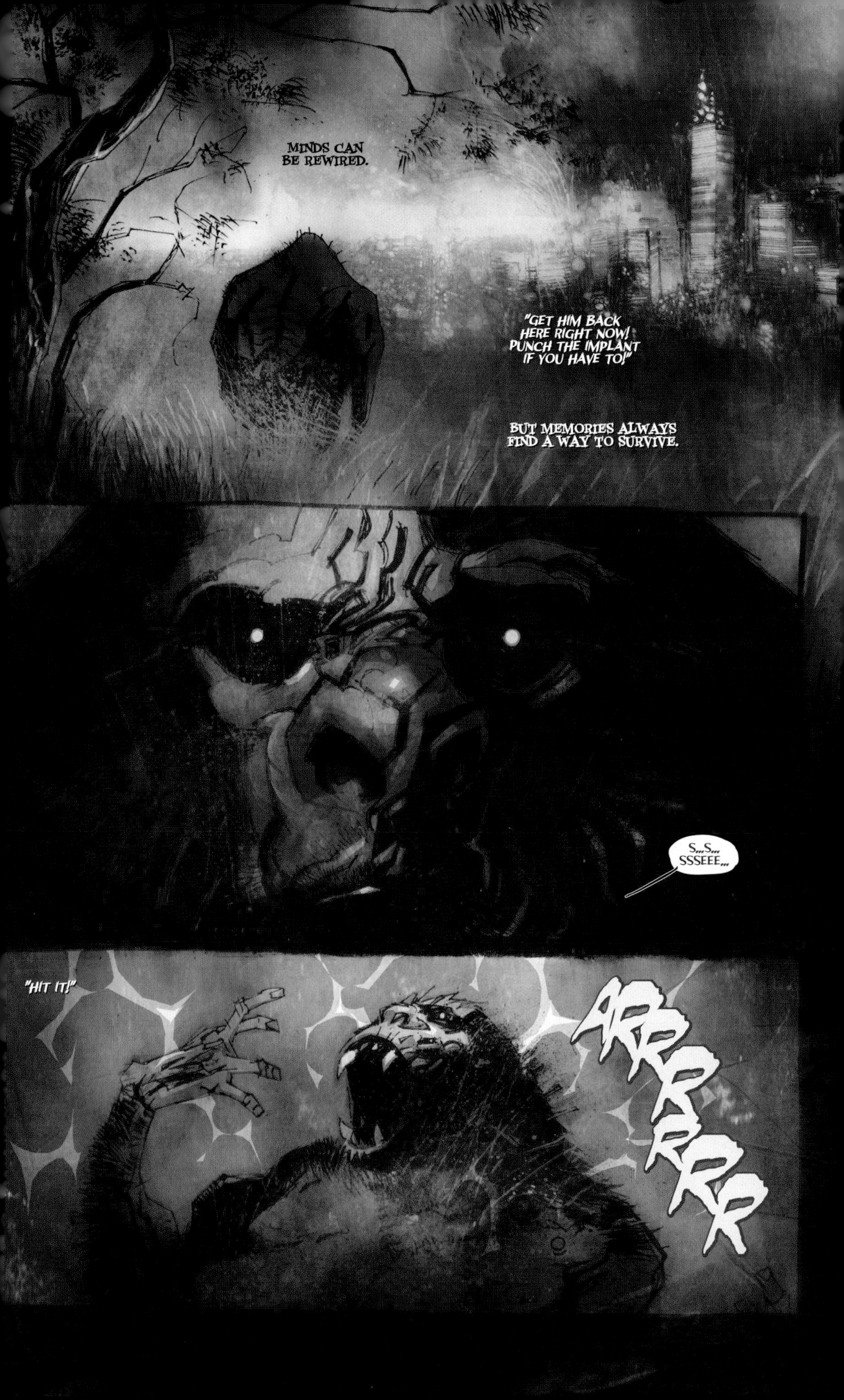

MINDS CAN BE REWIRED.
"GET HIM BACK HERE RIGHT NOW! PUNCH THE IMPLANT IF YOU HAVE TO!"
BUT MEMORIES ALWAYS FIND A WAY TO SURVIVE.
S...S... SSSEEE...
"HIT IT!"
ARRRRRR

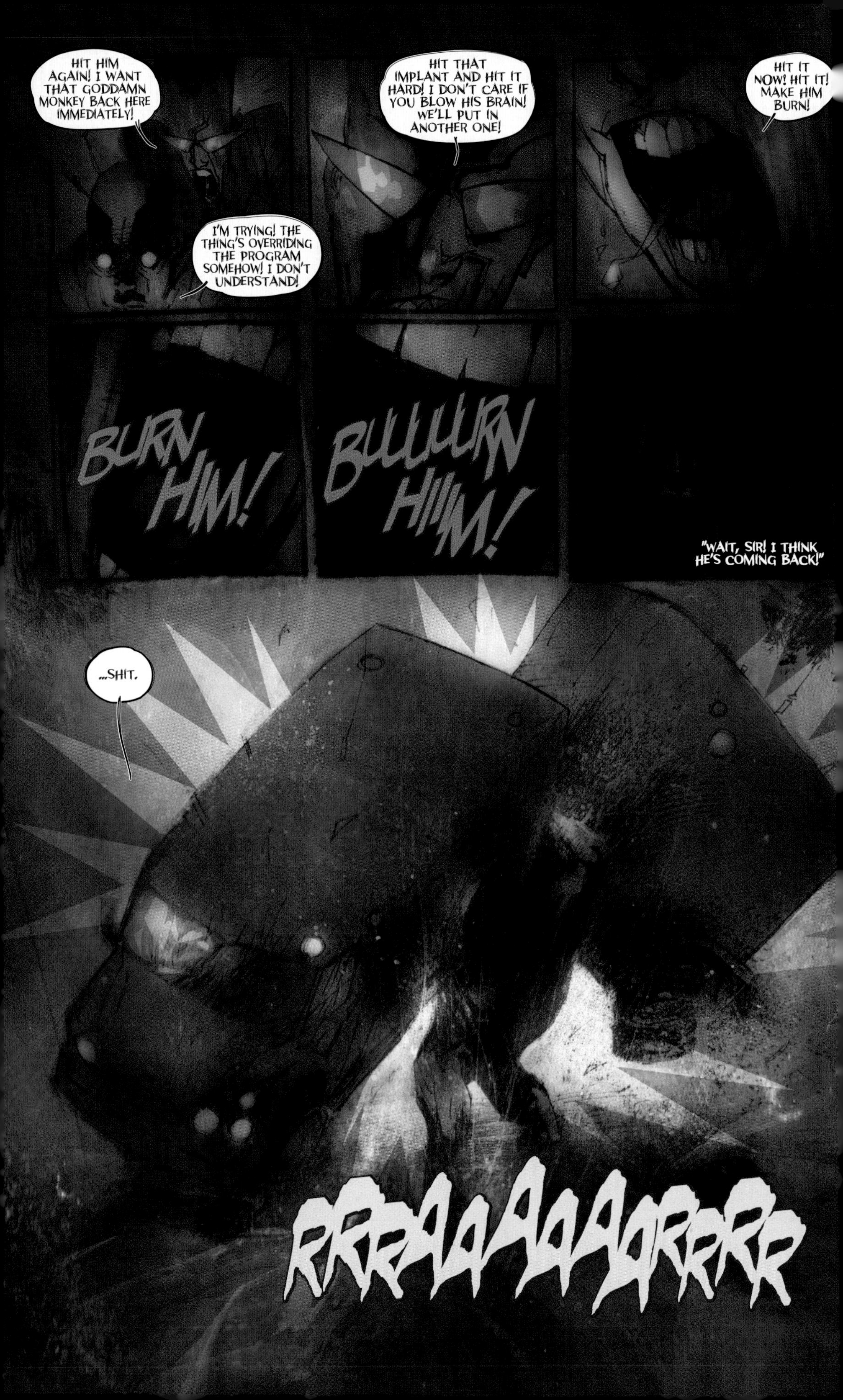
HIT HIM AGAIN! I WANT THAT GODDAMN MONKEY BACK HERE IMMEDIATELY!
I'M TRYING! THE THING'S OVERRIDING THE PROGRAM SOMEHOW! I DON'T UNDERSTAND!
HIT THAT IMPLANT AND HIT IT HARD! I DON'T CARE IF YOU BLOW HIS BRAIN! WE'LL PUT IN ANOTHER ONE!
HIT IT NOW! HIT IT! MAKE HIM BURN!
BURN HIM!
BUUUURN HIIIM!
"WAIT, SIR! I THINK HE'S COMING BACK!"
...SHIT.
RRRAAAAAARRRR

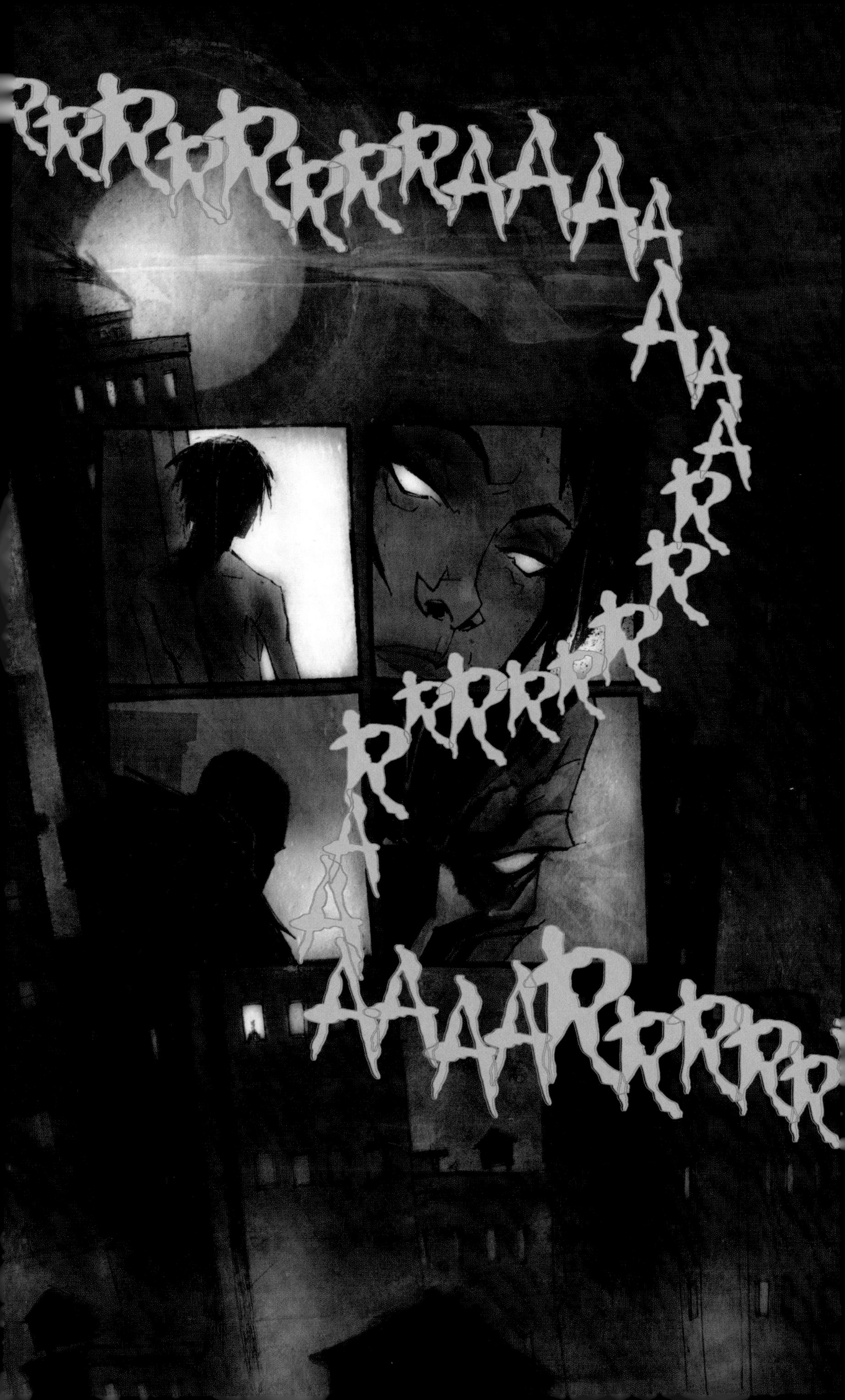
RRRRRRRRRAAAAAAAARRRRRRRRAAAAARRRRRR

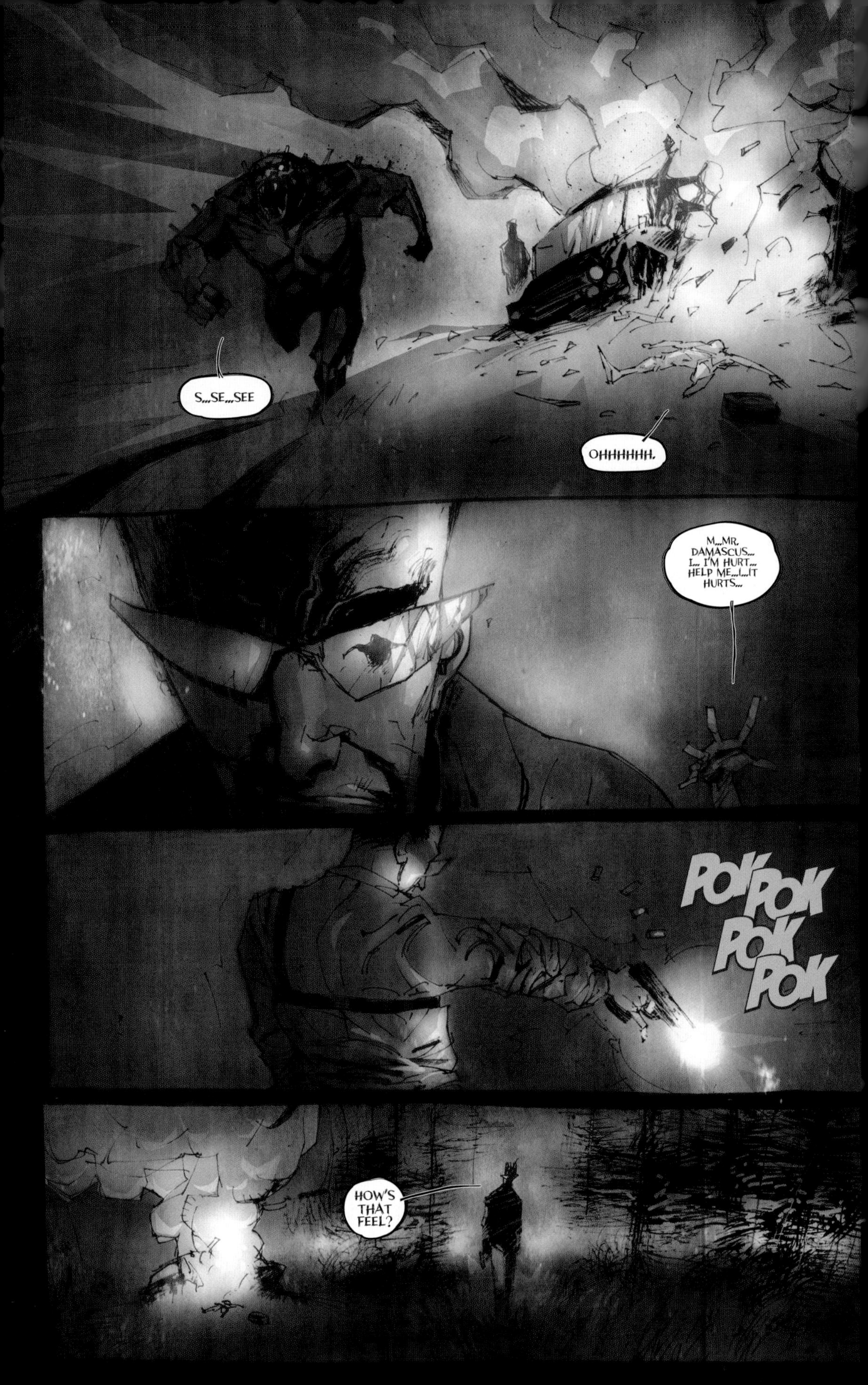
S...SE...SEE
OHHHHHH.
M...MR. DAMASCUS... I... I'M HURT... HELP ME...I...IT HURTS...
POK POK POK POK
HOW'S THAT FEEL?

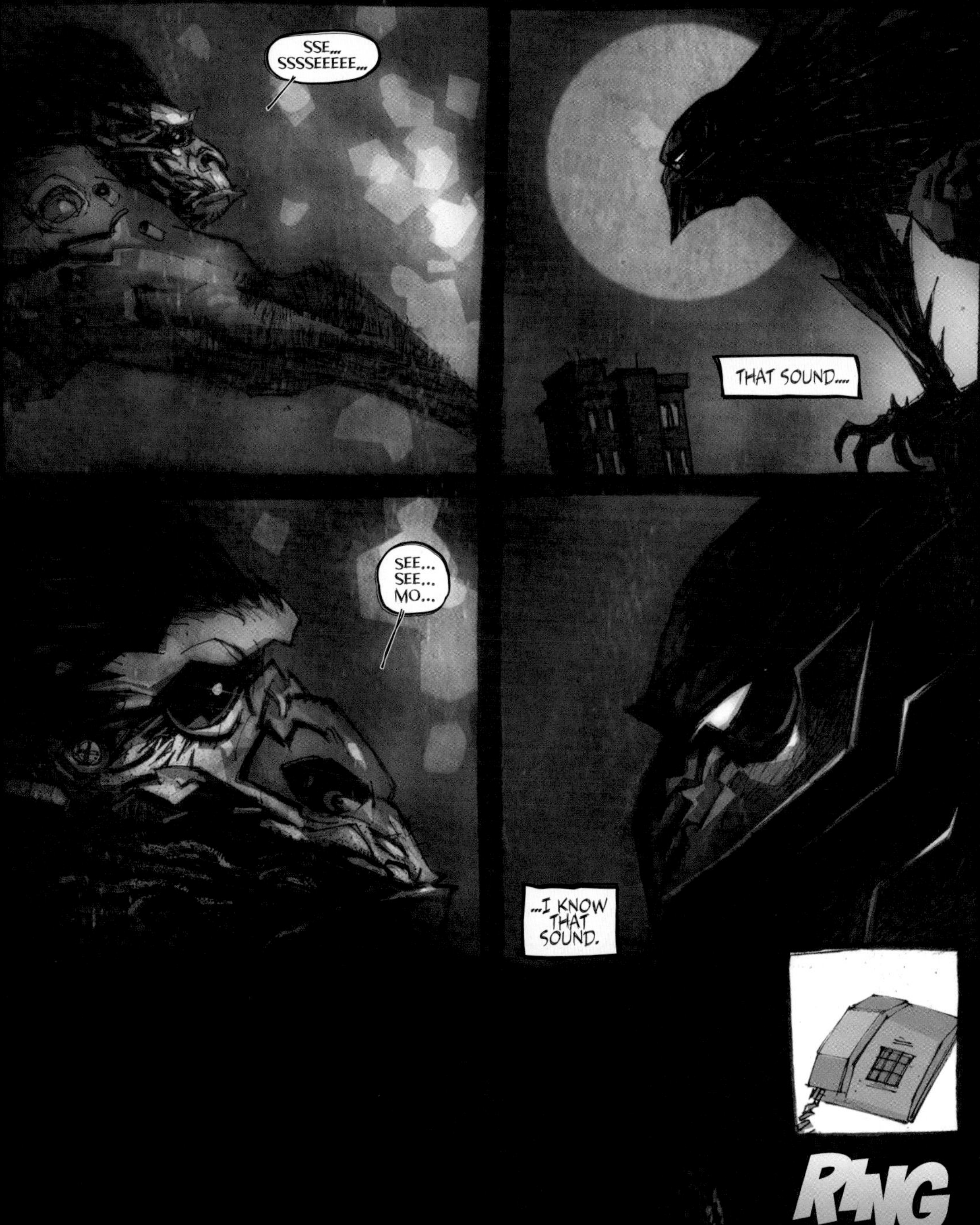
SSE... SSSSEEEEE...
THAT SOUND...
SEE... SEE... MO...
...I KNOW THAT SOUND.
RING

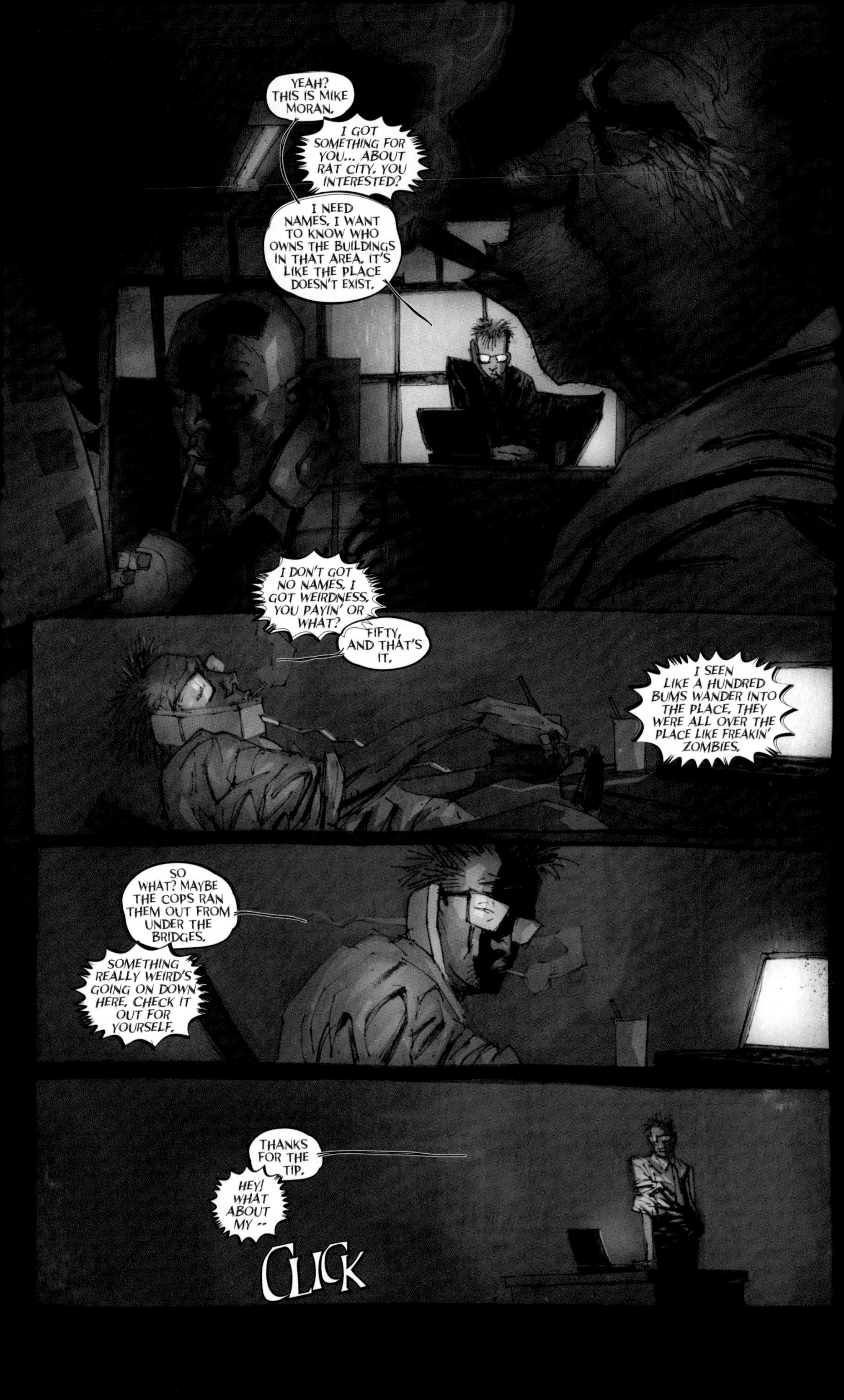
YEAH? THIS IS MIKE MORAN.
I GOT SOMETHING FOR YOU... ABOUT RAT CITY. YOU INTERESTED?
I NEED NAMES. I WANT TO KNOW WHO OWNS THE BUILDINGS IN THAT AREA. IT'S LIKE THE PLACE DOESN'T EXIST.
I DON'T GOT NO NAMES. I GOT WEIRDNESS. YOU PAYIN' OR WHAT?
FIFTY, AND THAT'S IT.
I SEEN LIKE A HUNDRED BUMS WANDER INTO THE PLACE. THEY WERE ALL OVER THE PLACE LIKE FREAKIN' ZOMBIES.
SO WHAT? MAYBE THE COPS RAN THEM OUT FROM UNDER THE BRIDGES.
SOMETHING REALLY WEIRD'S GOING ON DOWN HERE. CHECK IT OUT FOR YOURSELF.
THANKS FOR THE TIP.
HEY! WHAT ABOUT MY --
CLICK

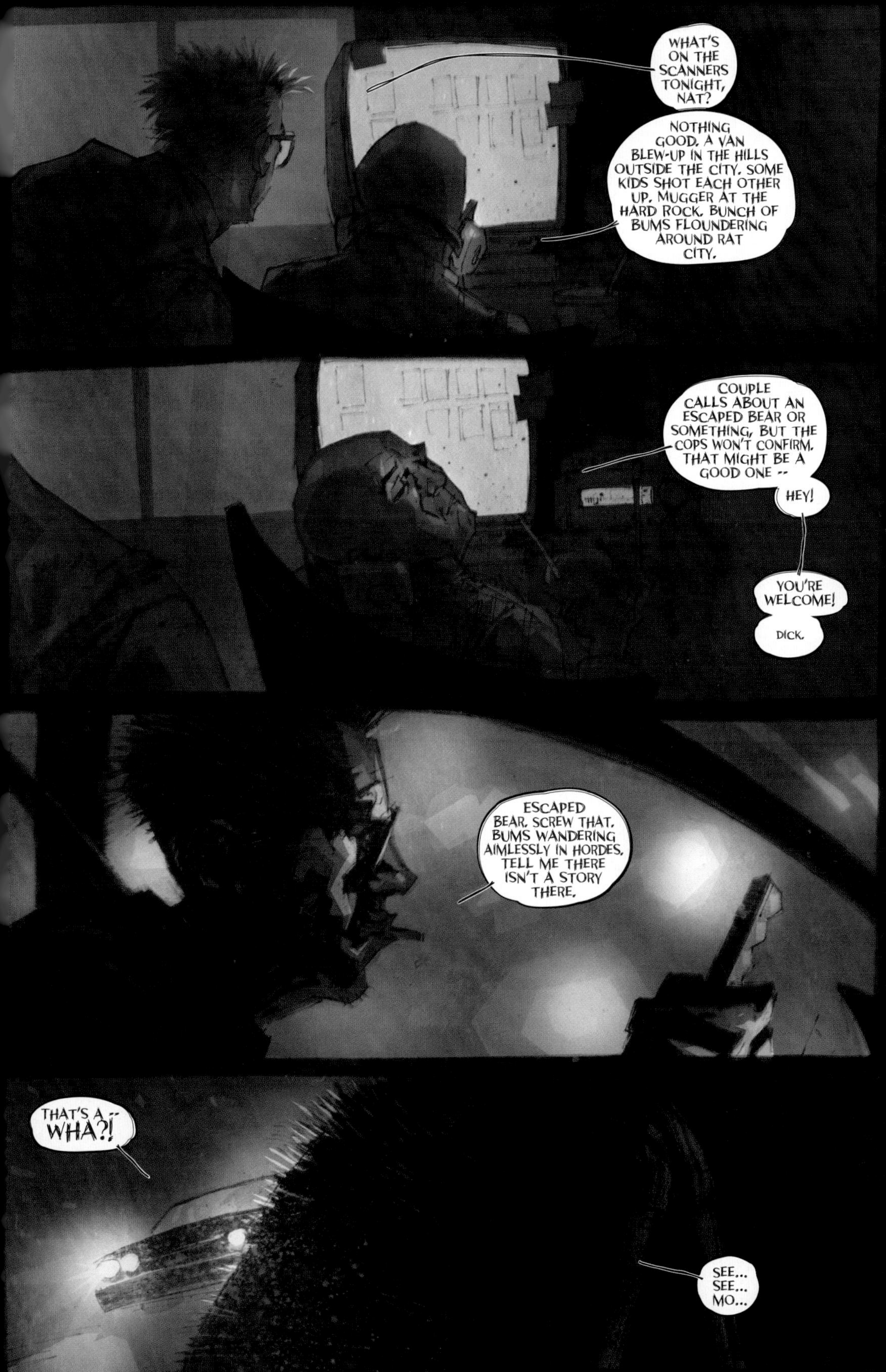
WHAT'S ON THE SCANNERS TONIGHT, NAT?
NOTHING GOOD. A VAN BLEW-UP IN THE HILLS OUTSIDE THE CITY. SOME KIDS SHOT EACH OTHER UP. MUGGER AT THE HARD ROCK. BUNCH OF BUMS FLOUNDERING AROUND RAT CITY.
COUPLE CALLS ABOUT AN ESCAPED BEAR OR SOMETHING, BUT THE COPS WON'T CONFIRM. THAT MIGHT BE A GOOD ONE --
HEY!
YOU'RE WELCOME!
DICK.
ESCAPED BEAR. SCREW THAT. BUMS WANDERING AIMLESSLY IN HORDES. TELL ME THERE ISN'T A STORY THERE.
THAT'S A -- WHA?!
SEE... SEE... MO...

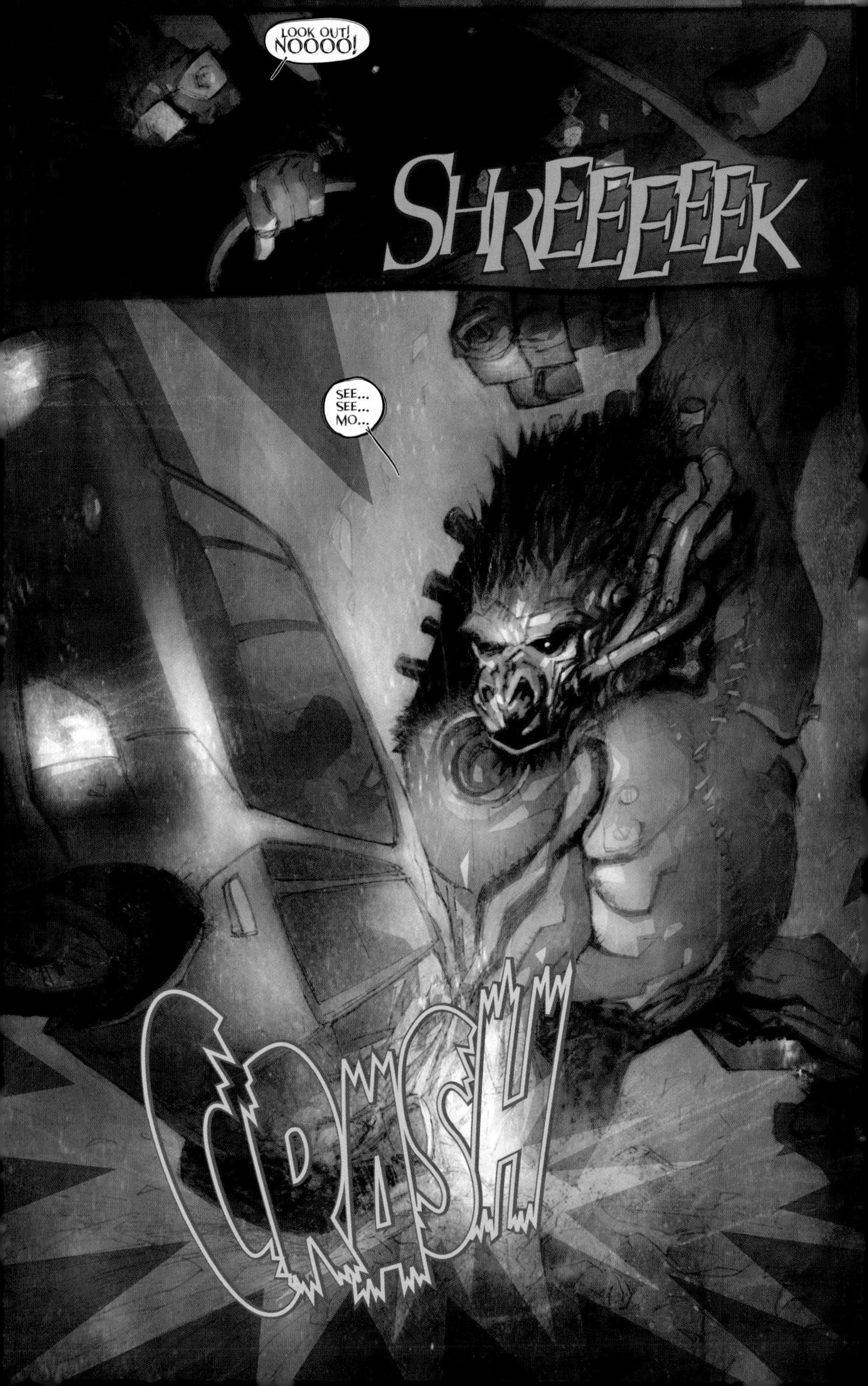
LOOK OUT! NOOOO!
SHREEEEEK
SEE... SEE... MO...
CRASH

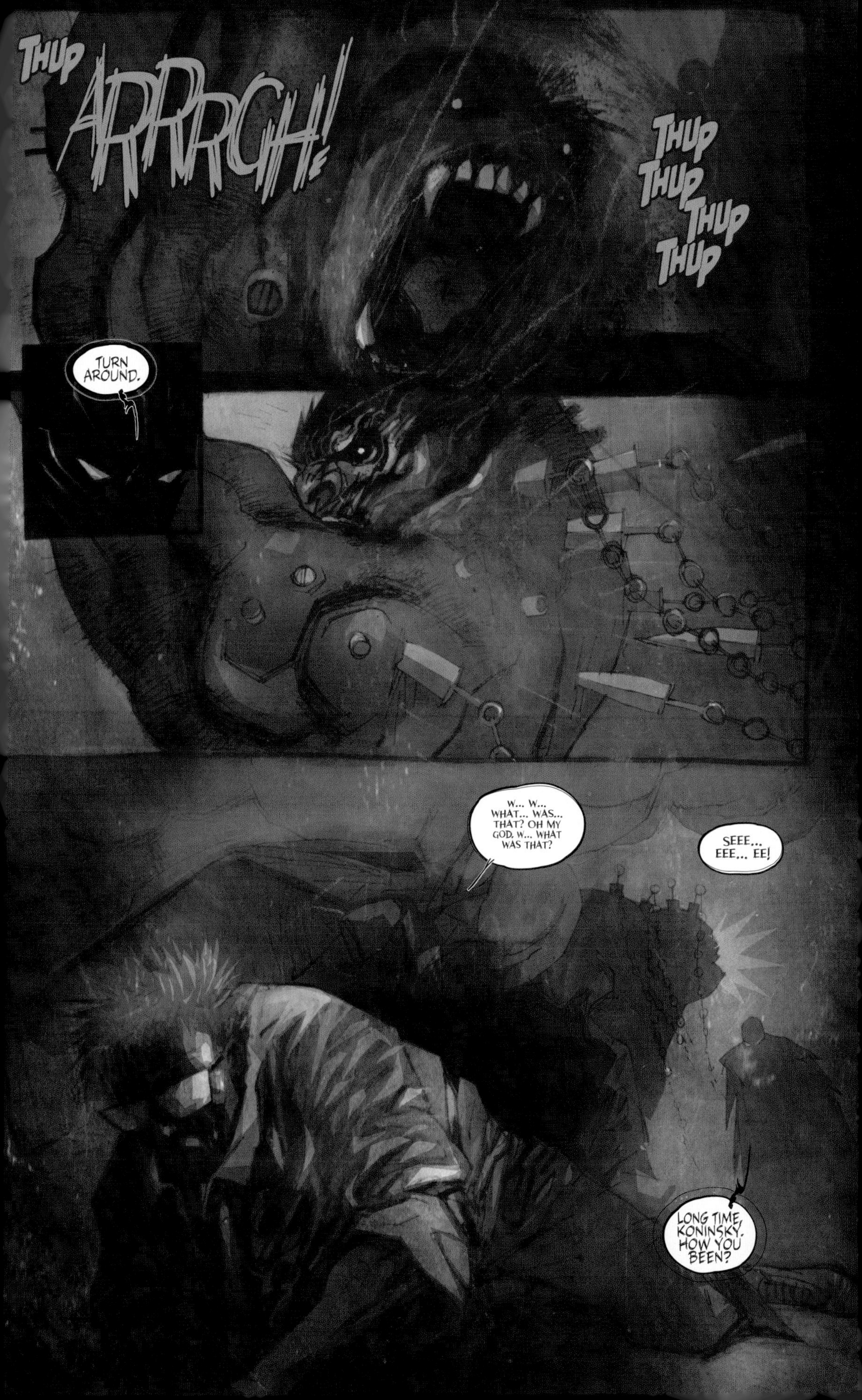
THUP
ARRRRGH!
THUP THUP THUP THUP
TURN AROUND.
W... W... WHAT... WAS... THAT? OH MY GOD. W... WHAT WAS THAT?
SEEE... EEE... EE!
LONG TIME, KONINSKY. HOW YOU BEEN?

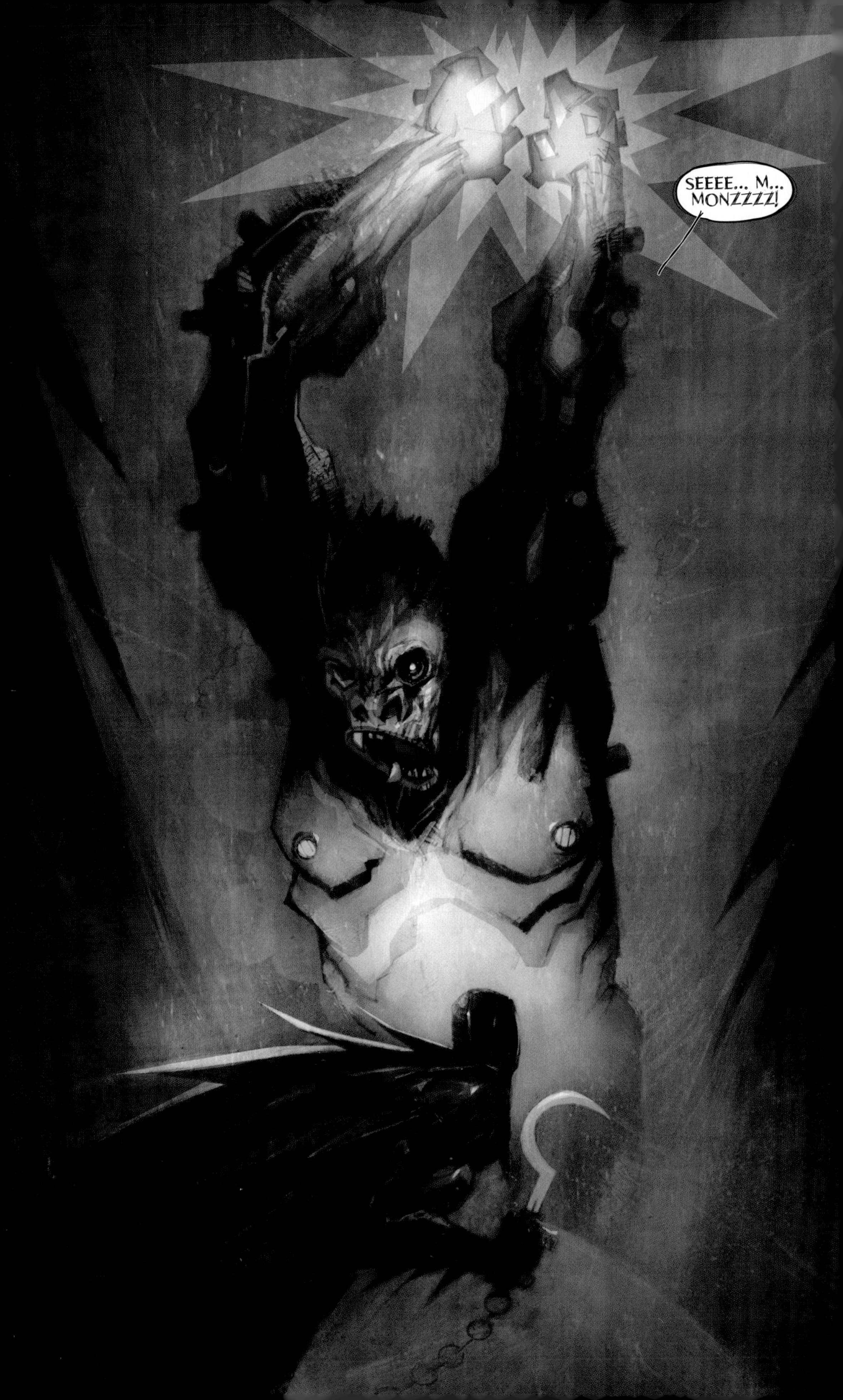
SEEEE... M... MONZZZZZ!

HELL**S**PAWN

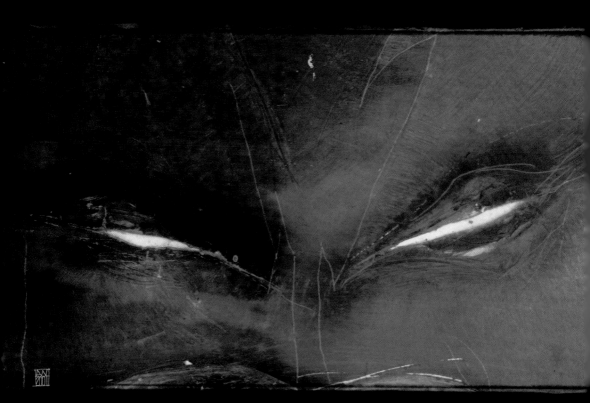

ISSUE TEN

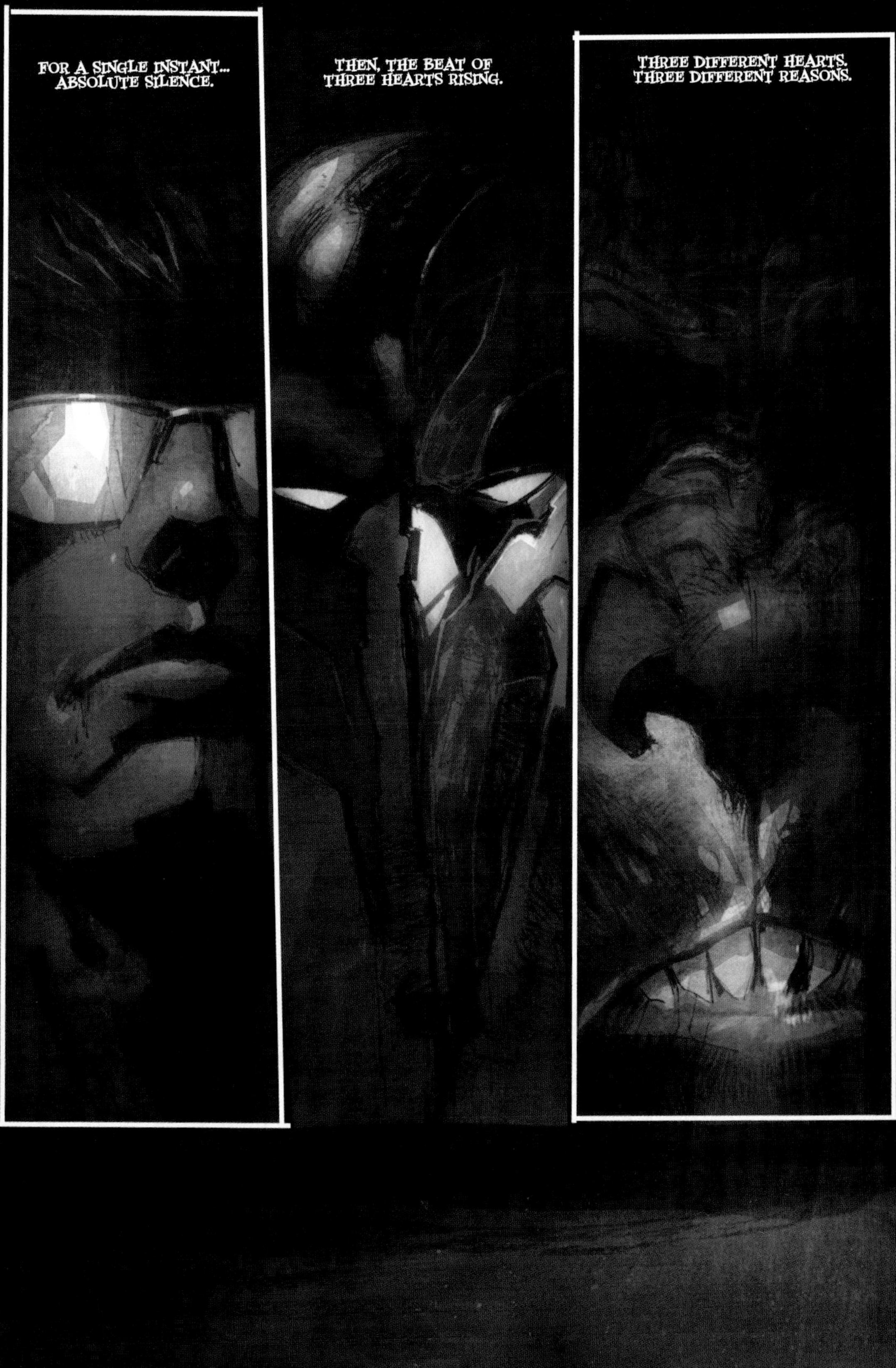
FOR A SINGLE INSTANT... ABSOLUTE SILENCE.
THEN, THE BEAT OF THREE HEARTS RISING.
THREE DIFFERENT HEARTS. THREE DIFFERENT REASONS.

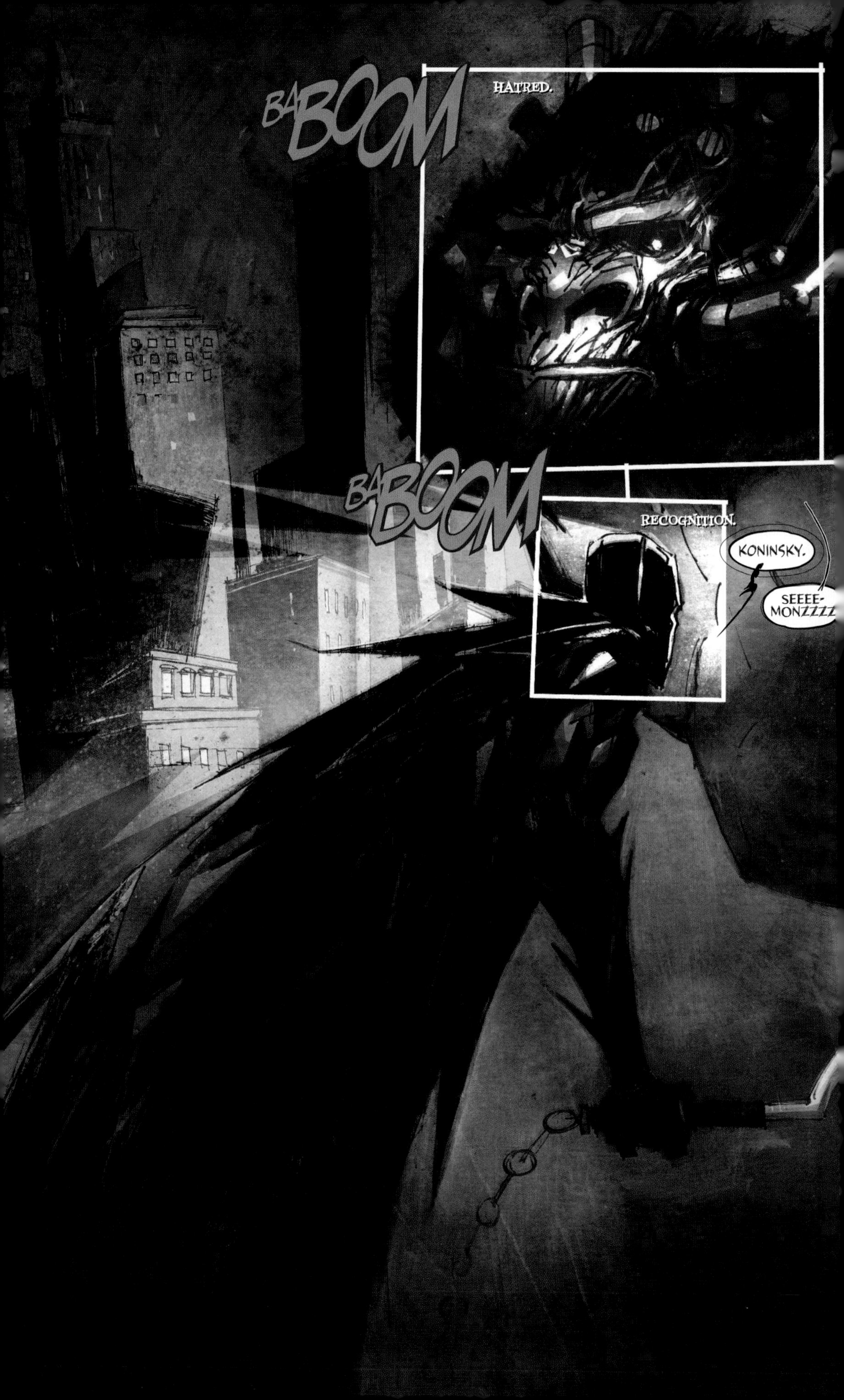
BA-BOOM
HATRED.
BA-BOOM
RECOGNITION.
KONINSKY.
SEEEE-MONZZZZ

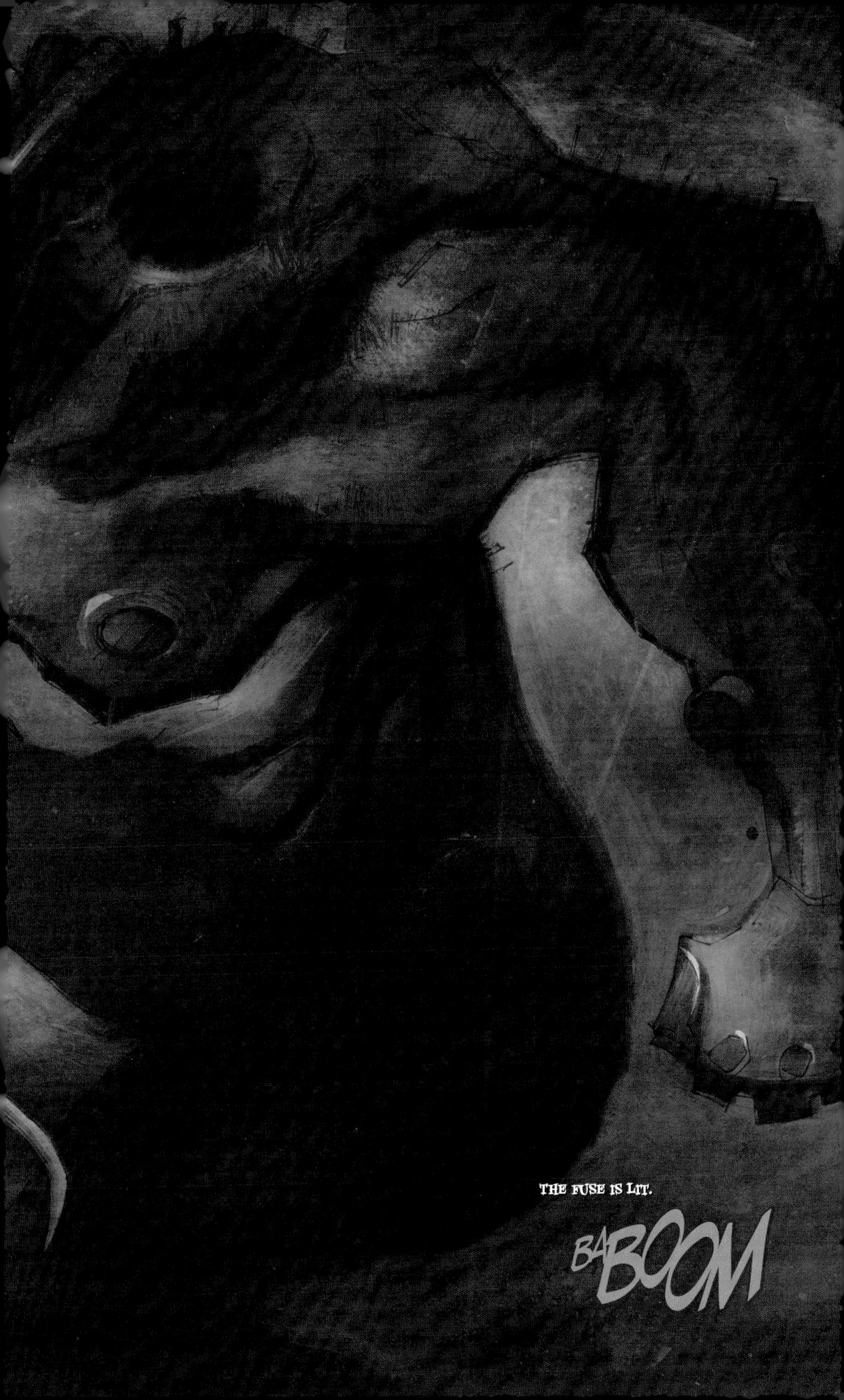
THE FUSE IS LIT.
BA BOOM

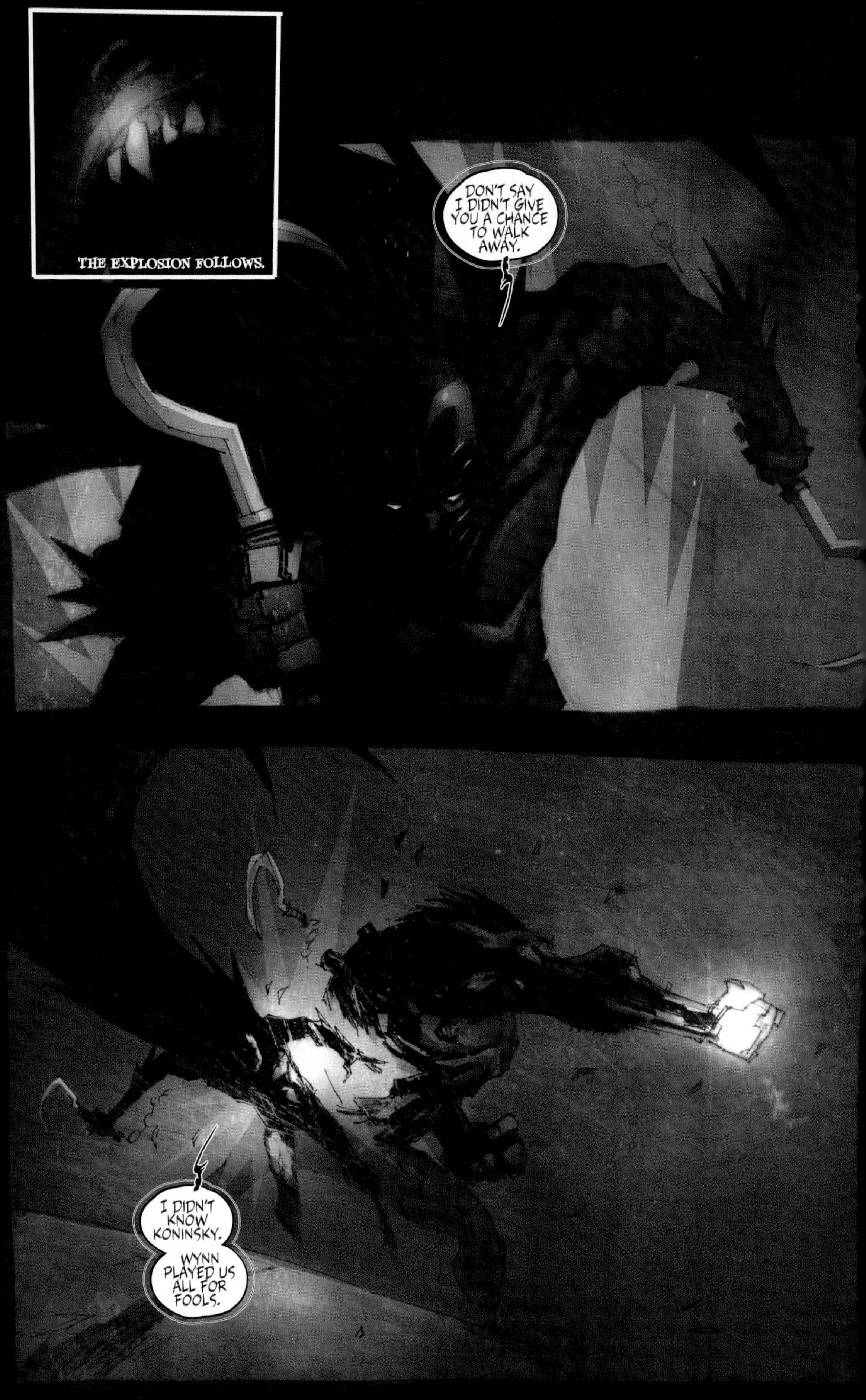
THE EXPLOSION FOLLOWS.
DON'T SAY I DIDN'T GIVE YOU A CHANCE TO WALK AWAY.
I DIDN'T KNOW KONINSKY.
WYNN PLAYED US ALL FOR FOOLS.

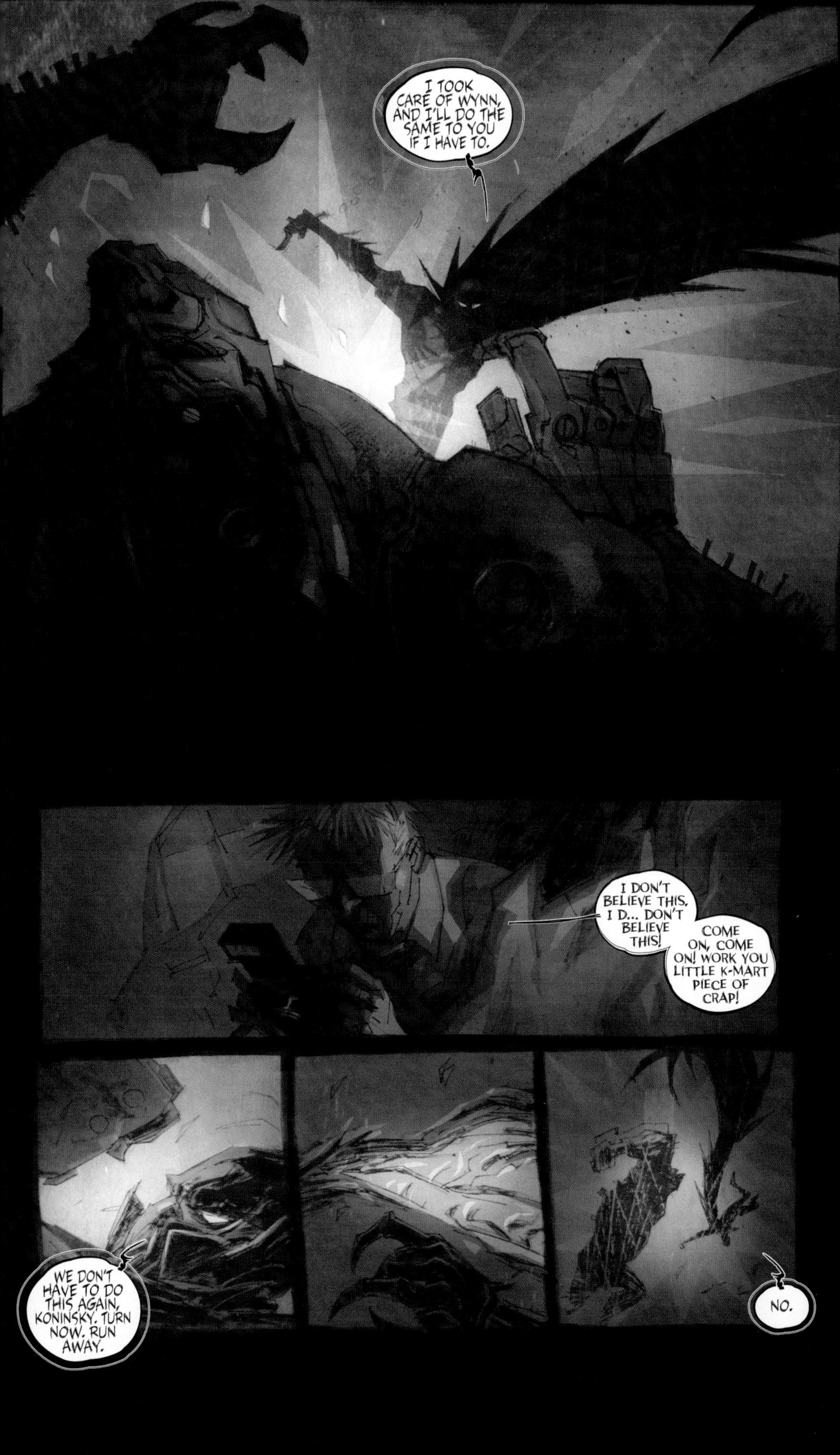
I TOOK CARE OF WYNN, AND I'LL DO THE SAME TO YOU IF I HAVE TO.
I DON'T BELIEVE THIS, I D... DON'T BELIEVE THIS!
COME ON, COME ON! WORK YOU LITTLE K-MART PIECE OF CRAP!
WE DON'T HAVE TO DO THIS AGAIN, KONINSKY. TURN NOW. RUN AWAY.
NO.

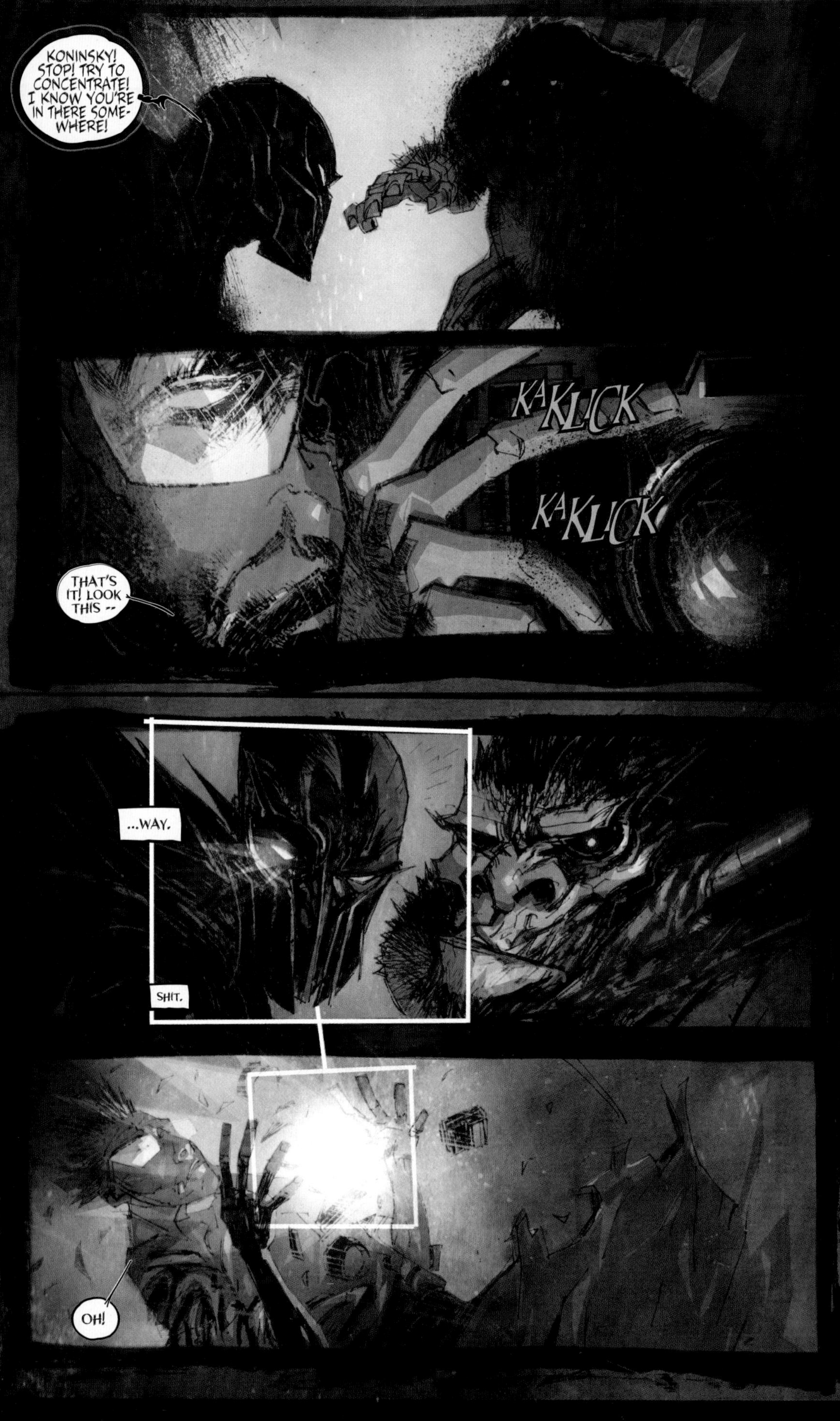
KONINSKY! STOP! TRY TO CONCENTRATE! I KNOW YOU'RE IN THERE SOME-WHERE!
KAKLICK
KAKLICK
THAT'S IT! LOOK THIS --
...WAY.
SHIT.
OH!

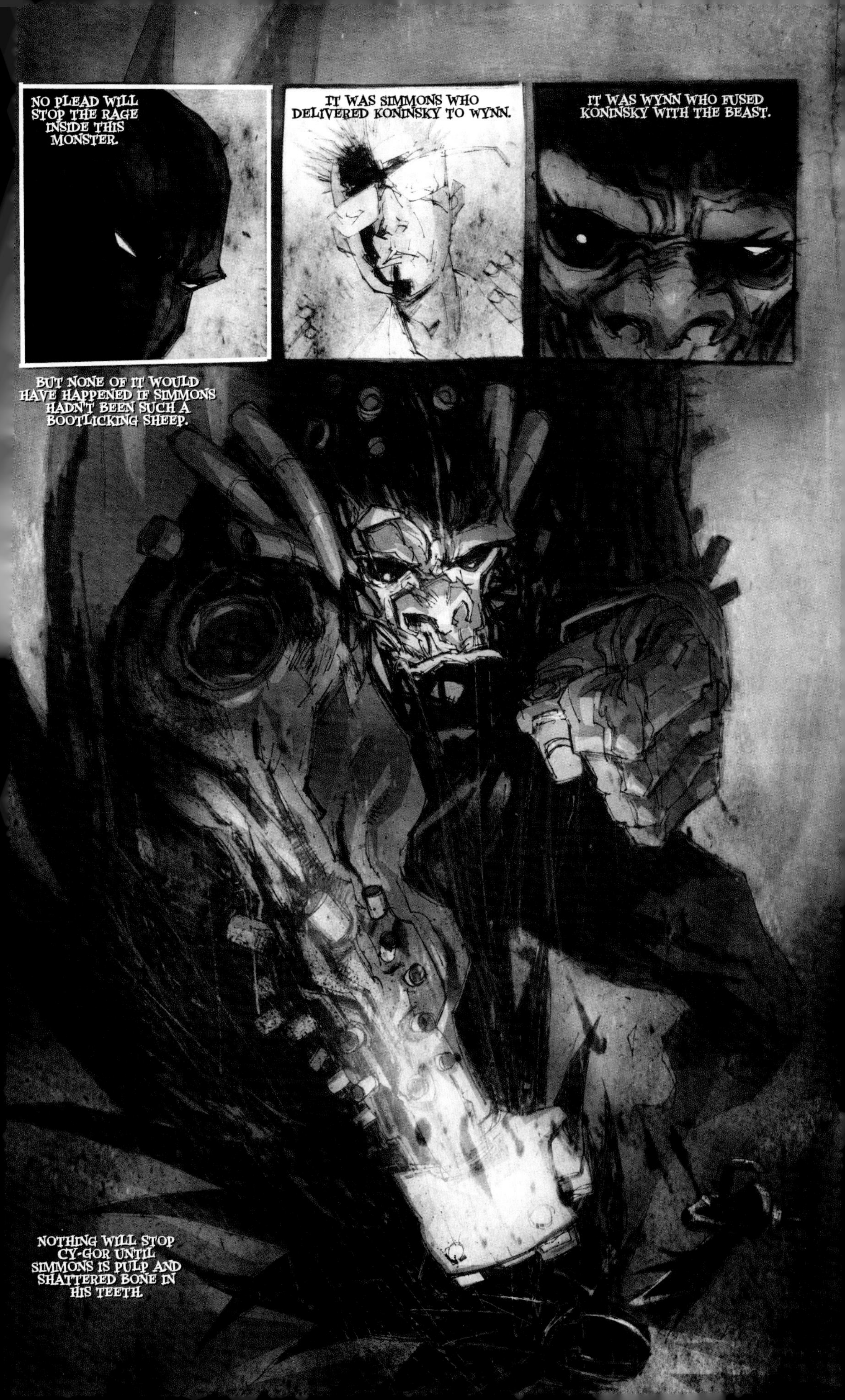
NO PLEAD WILL STOP THE RAGE INSIDE THIS MONSTER.
IT WAS SIMMONS WHO DELIVERED KONINSKY TO WYNN.
IT WAS WYNN WHO FUSED KONINSKY WITH THE BEAST.
BUT NONE OF IT WOULD HAVE HAPPENED IF SIMMONS HADN'T BEEN SUCH A BOOTLICKING SHEEP.
NOTHING WILL STOP CY-GOR UNTIL SIMMONS IS PULP AND SHATTERED BONE IN HIS TEETH.

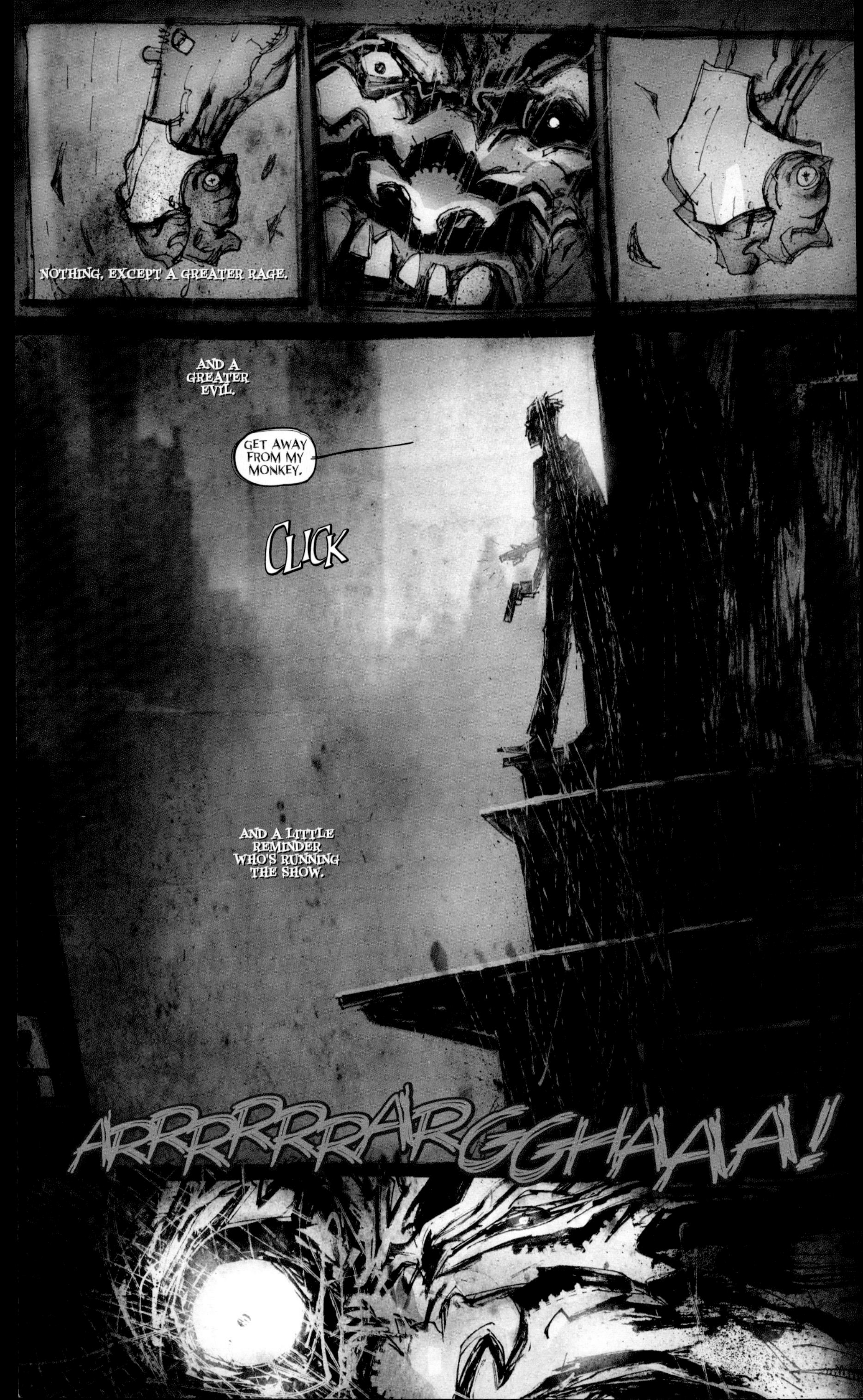
NOTHING, EXCEPT A GREATER RAGE.
AND A GREATER EVIL.
GET AWAY FROM MY MONKEY.
CLICK
AND A LITTLE REMINDER WHO'S RUNNING THE SHOW.
ARRRRRRARGGHAAAA!

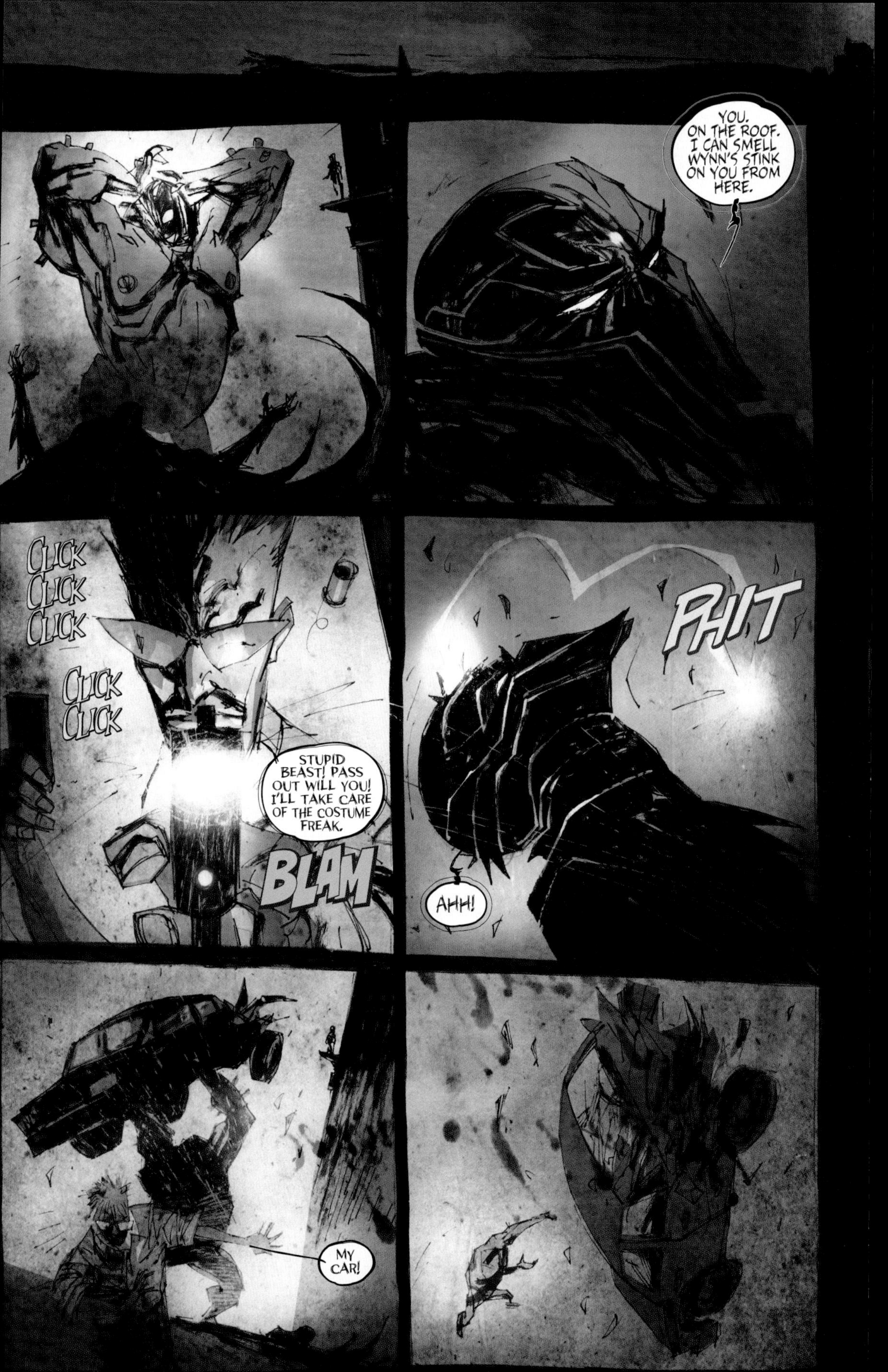
YOU. ON THE ROOF. I CAN SMELL WYNN'S STINK ON YOU FROM HERE.
CLICK CLICK CLICK
CLICK CLICK
STUPID BEAST! PASS OUT WILL YOU! I'LL TAKE CARE OF THE COSTUME FREAK.
BLAM
PHIT
AHH!
MY CAR!

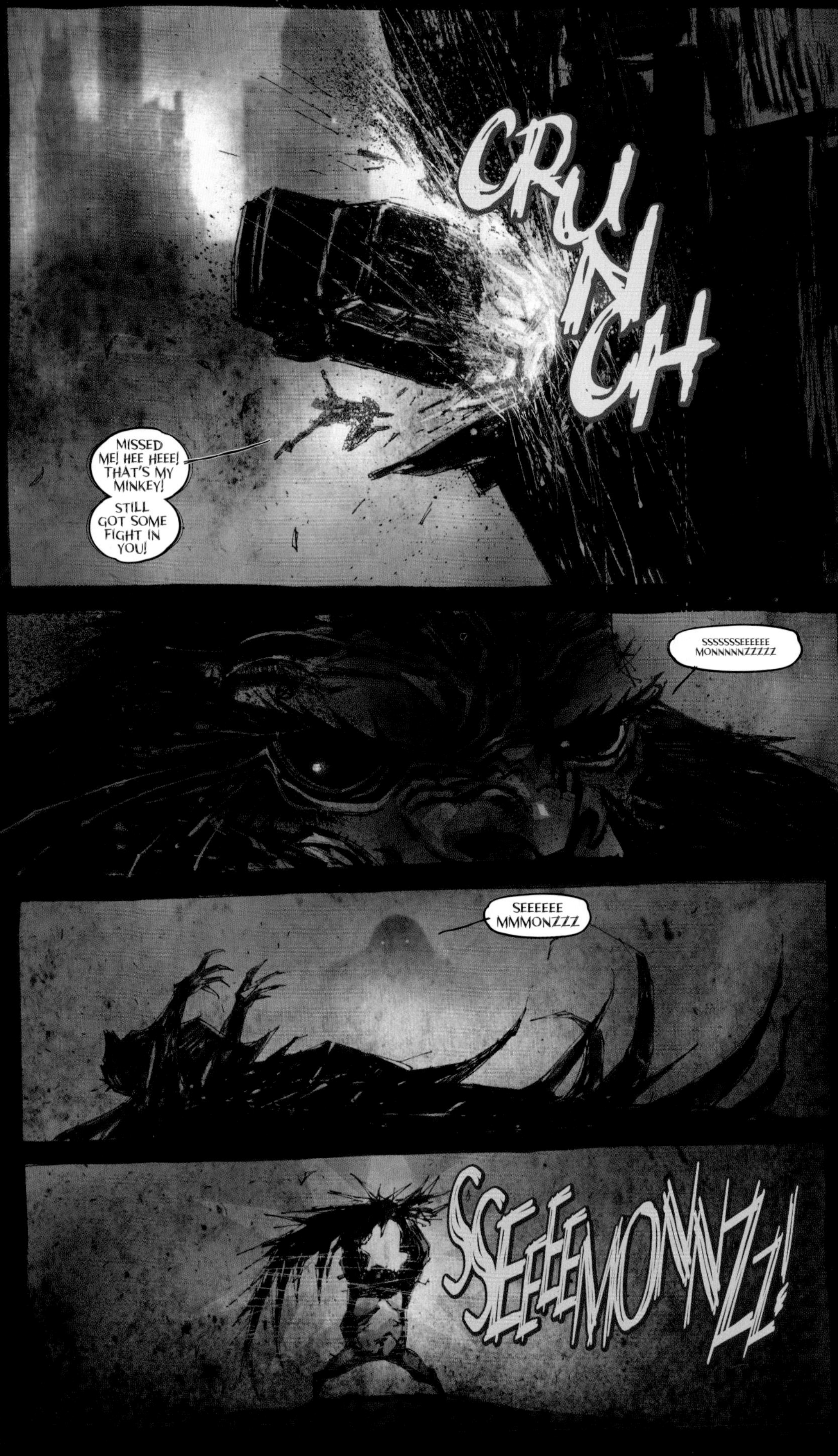
CRUNCH
MISSED ME! HEE HEEE! THAT'S MY MINKEY!
STILL GOT SOME FIGHT IN YOU!
SSSSSSSEEEEEE MONNNNNZZZZZ
SEEEEEE MMMONZZZ
SEEEEMONNZZ!

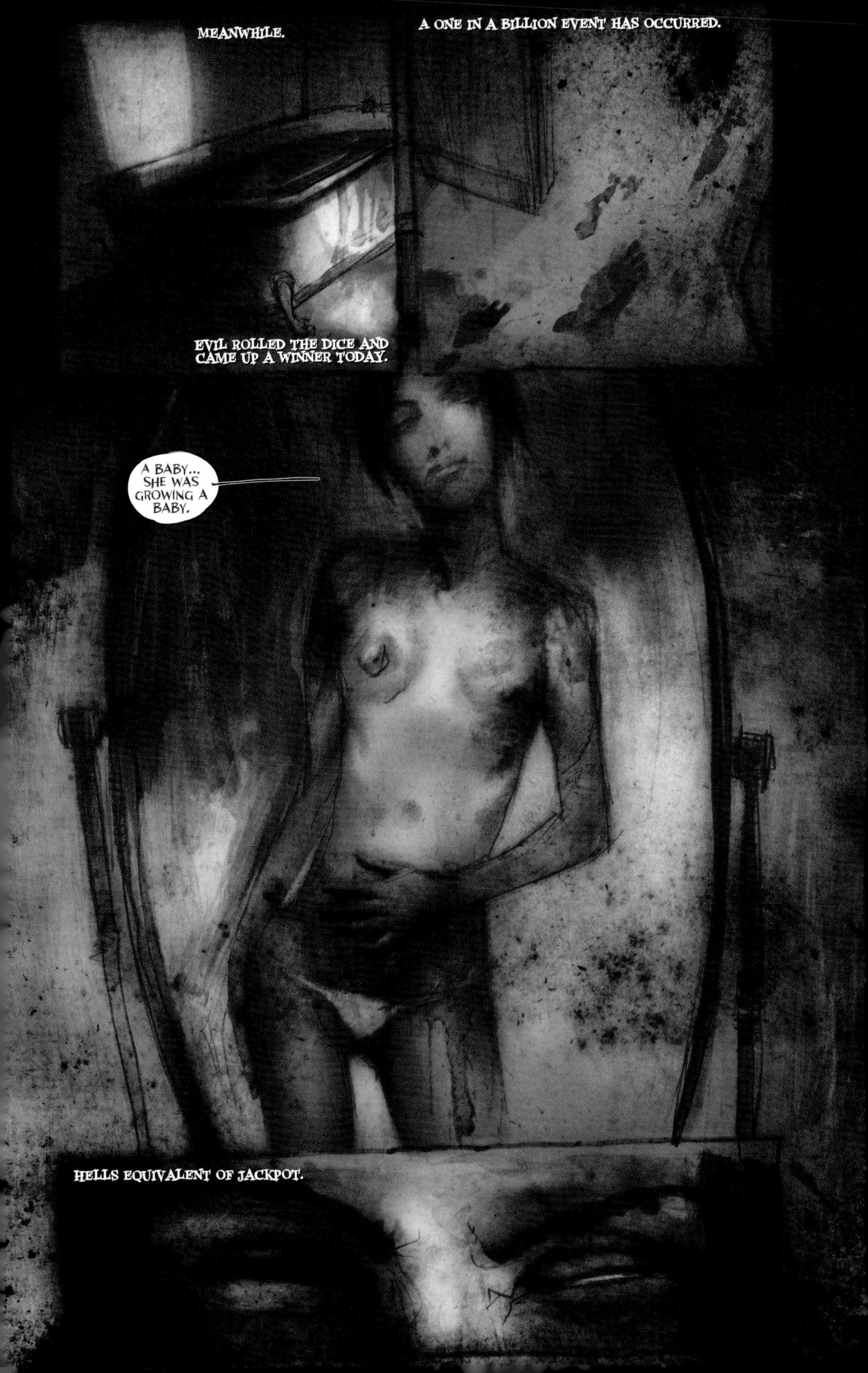

MEANWHILE.
A ONE IN A BILLION EVENT HAS OCCURRED.
EVIL ROLLED THE DICE AND CAME UP A WINNER TODAY.
A BABY... SHE WAS GROWING A BABY.
HELLS EQUIVALENT OF JACKPOT.

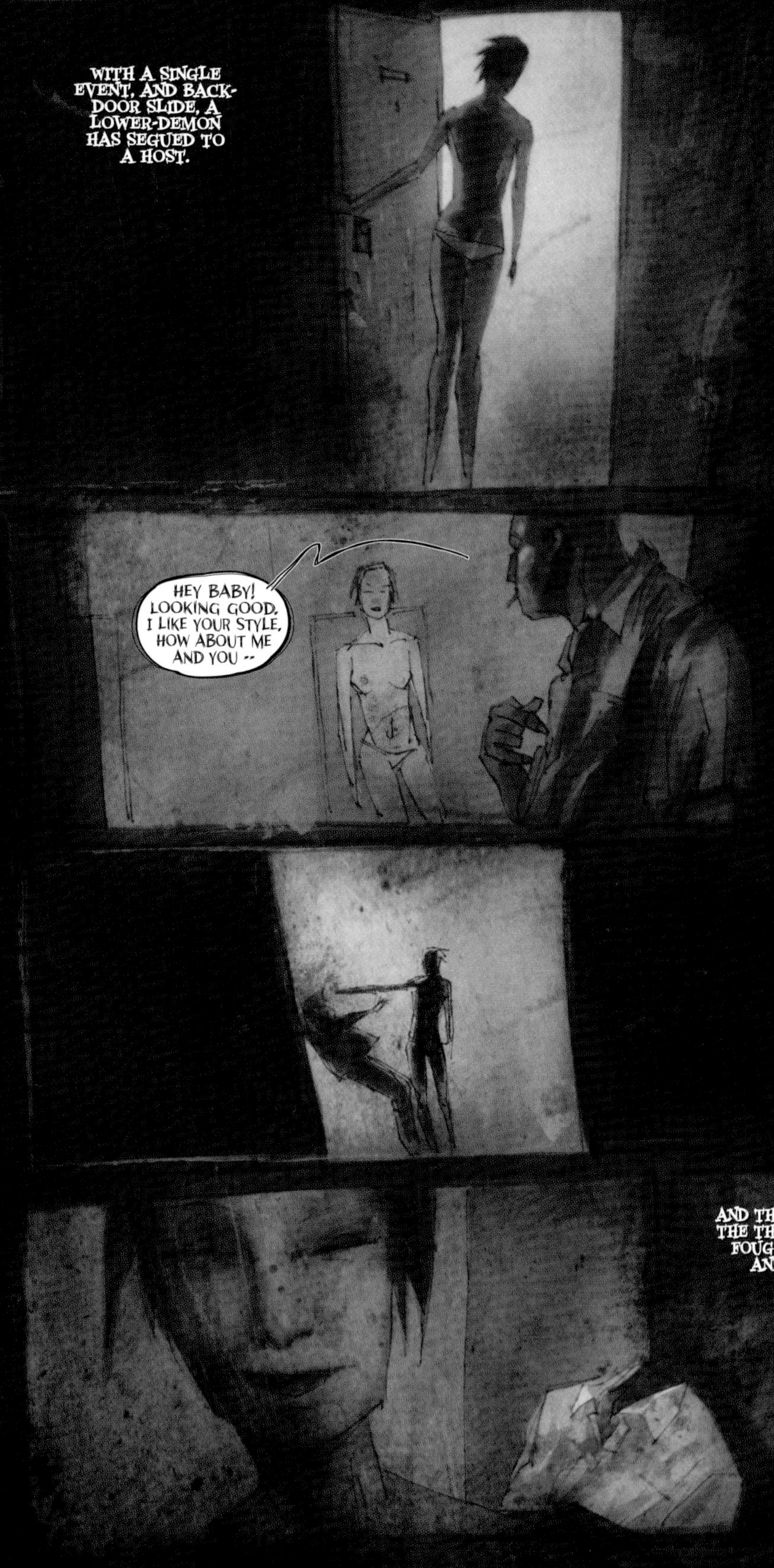
WITH A SINGLE EVENT, AND BACK-DOOR SLIDE, A LOWER-DEMON HAS SEGUED TO A HOST.
HEY BABY! LOOKING GOOD. I LIKE YOUR STYLE, HOW ABOUT ME AND YOU --
AND THE BATTLE FOR THE THRONE WILL BE FOUGHT BY KINGS AND QUEENS.

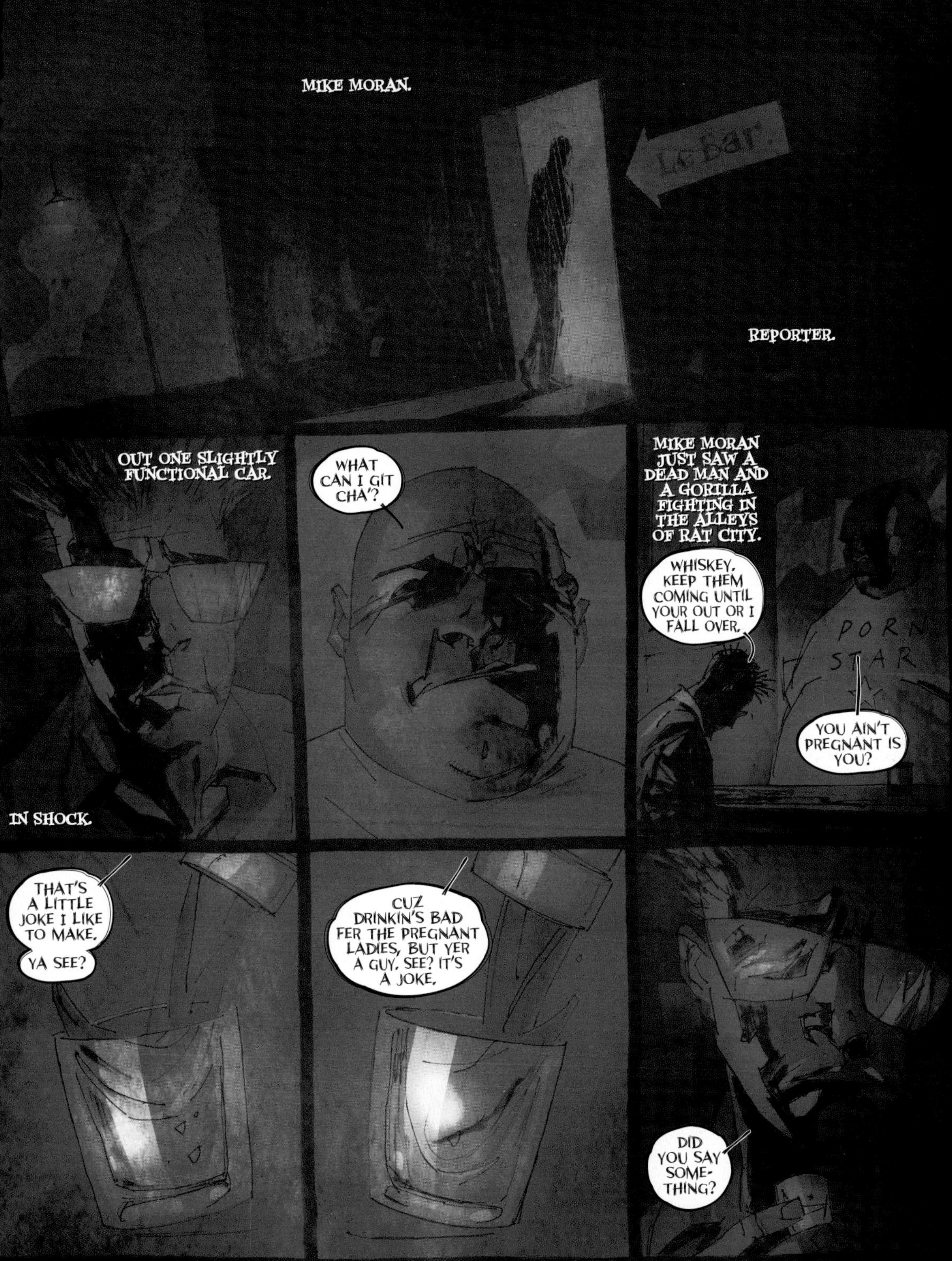
MIKE MORAN.
Le Bar
REPORTER.
OUT ONE SLIGHTLY FUNCTIONAL CAR.
IN SHOCK.
WHAT CAN I GIT CHA'?
MIKE MORAN JUST SAW A DEAD MAN AND A GORILLA FIGHTING IN THE ALLEYS OF RAT CITY.
WHISKEY. KEEP THEM COMING UNTIL YOUR OUT OR I FALL OVER.
PORN STAR
YOU AIN'T PREGNANT IS YOU?
THAT'S A LITTLE JOKE I LIKE TO MAKE.
YA SEE?
CUZ DRINKIN'S BAD FER THE PREGNANT LADIES, BUT YER A GUY. SEE? IT'S A JOKE.
DID YOU SAY SOME-THING?

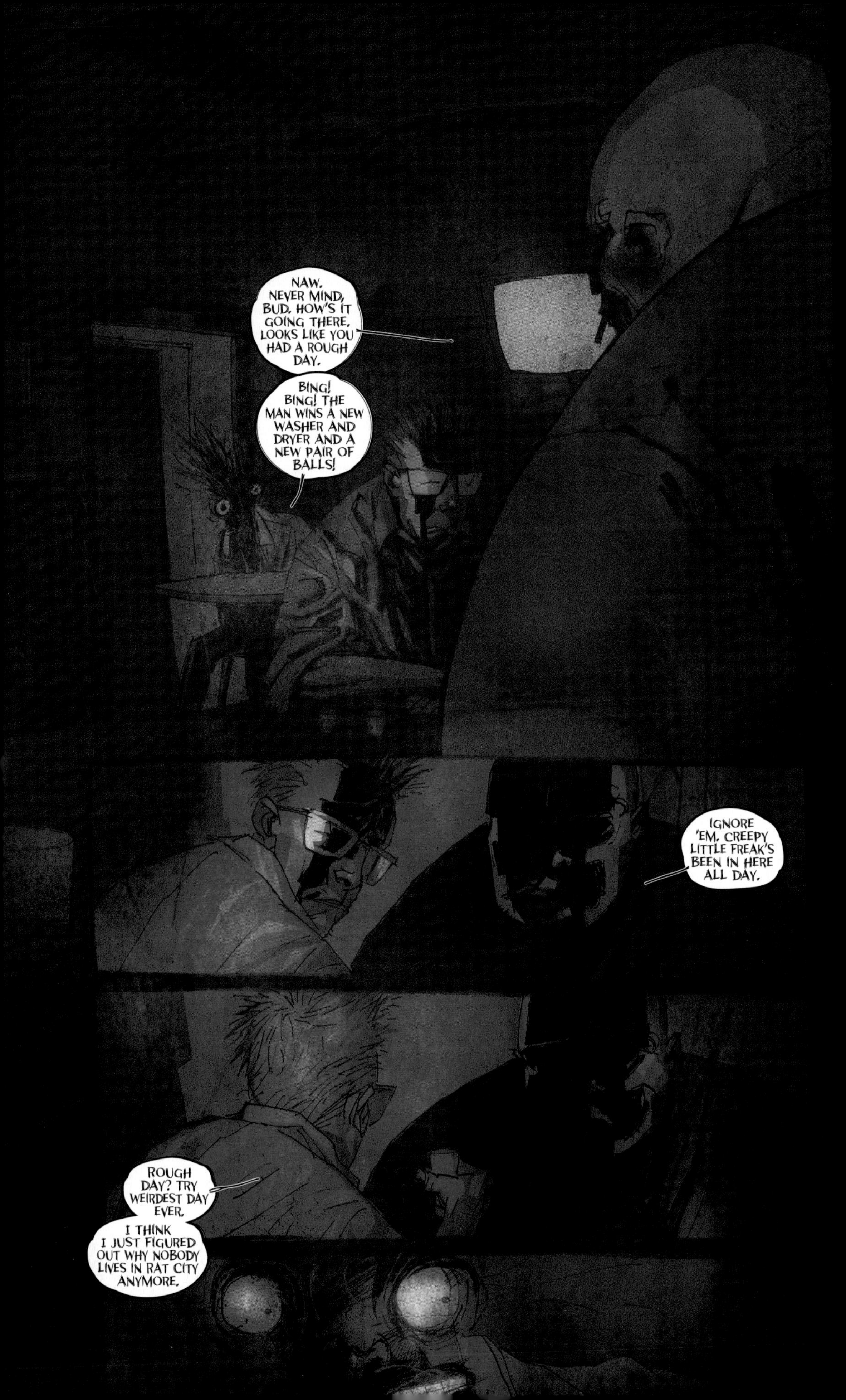
NAW. NEVER MIND, BUD. HOW'S IT GOING THERE. LOOKS LIKE YOU HAD A ROUGH DAY.
BING! BING! THE MAN WINS A NEW WASHER AND DRYER AND A NEW PAIR OF BALLS!
IGNORE 'EM. CREEPY LITTLE FREAK'S BEEN IN HERE ALL DAY.
ROUGH DAY? TRY WEIRDEST DAY EVER.
I THINK I JUST FIGURED OUT WHY NOBODY LIVES IN RAT CITY ANYMORE.

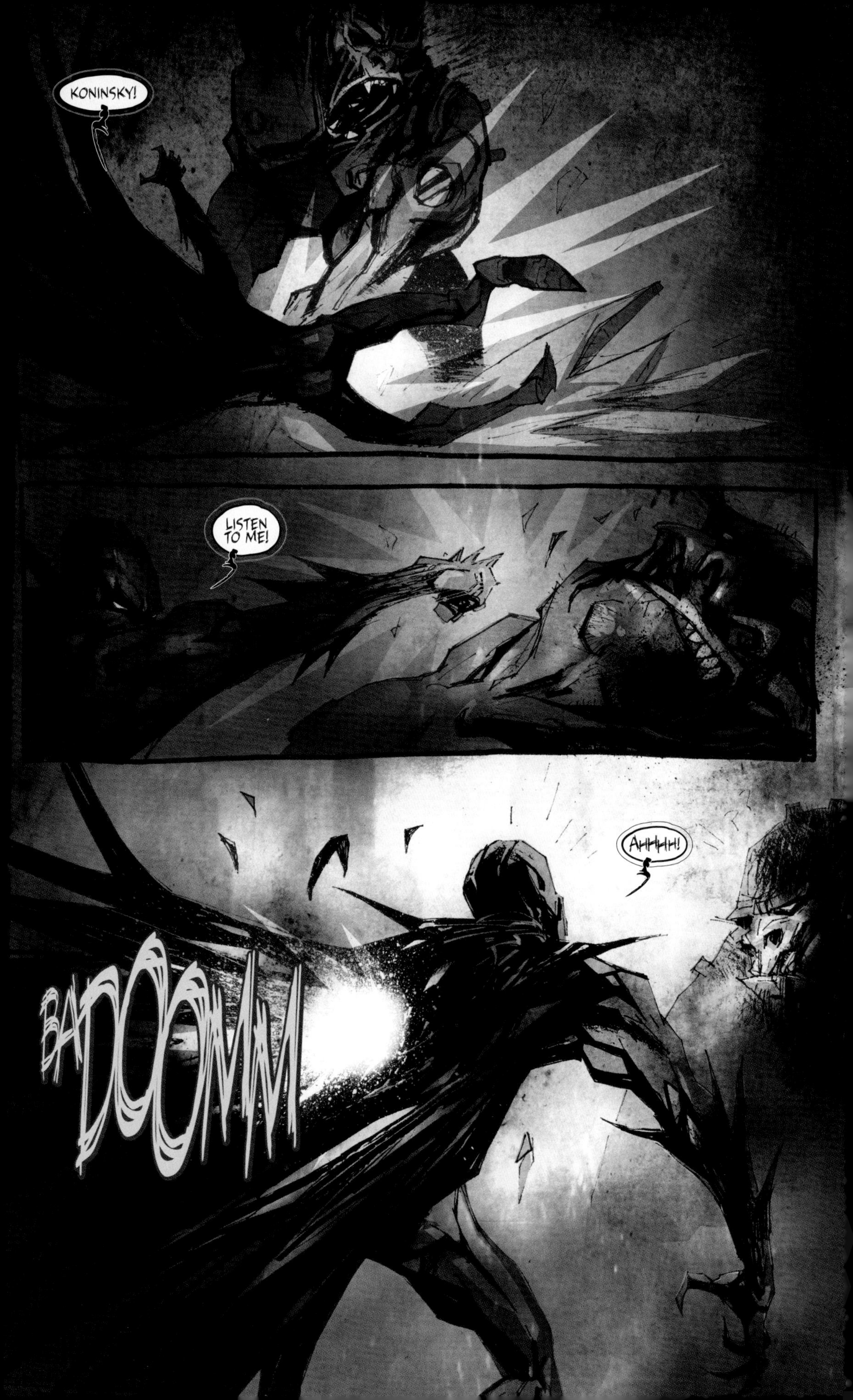
KONINSKY!
LISTEN TO ME!
AHHHH!
BADOOMM

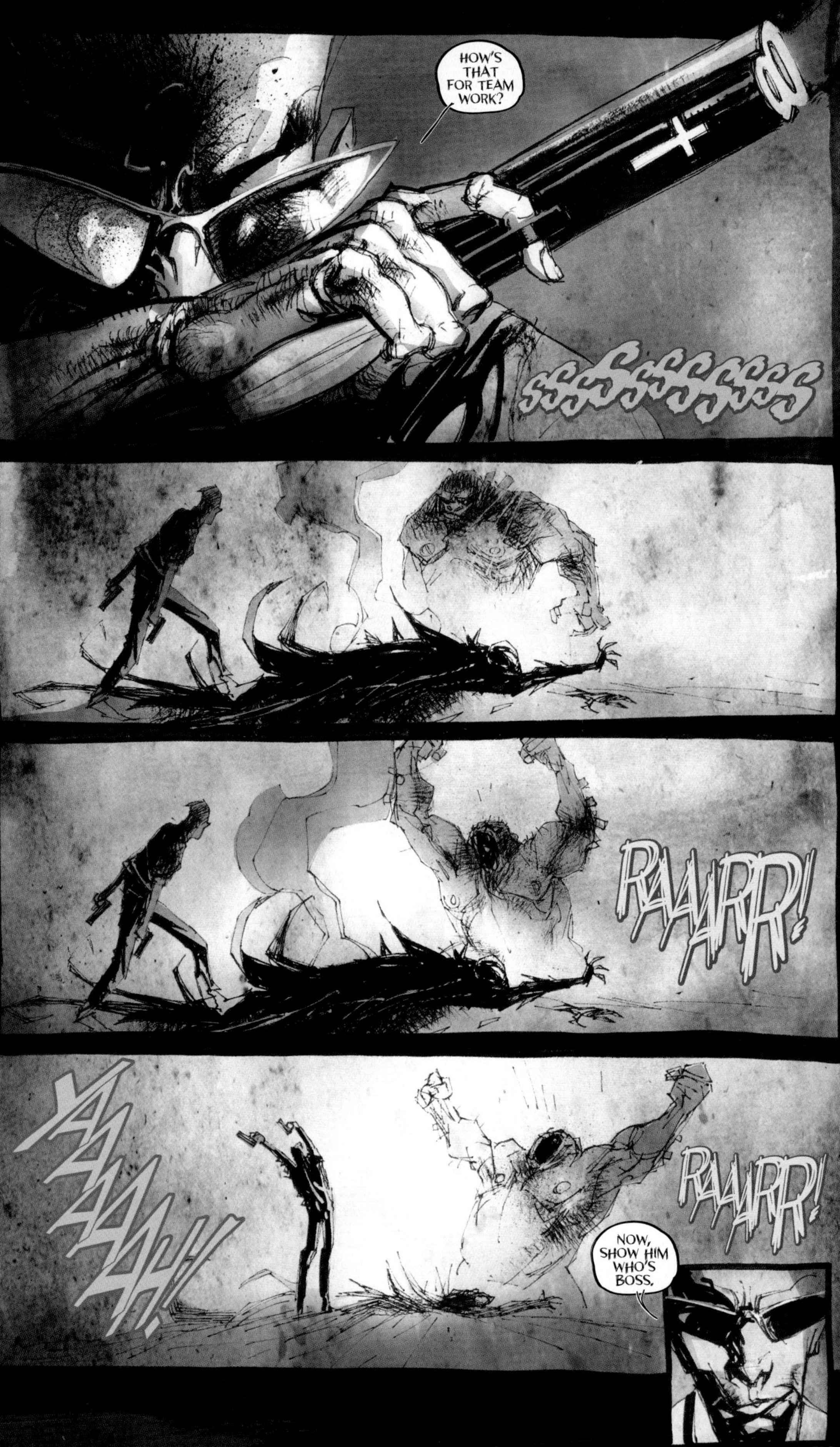
HOW'S THAT FOR TEAM WORK?
SSSSSSSSSSS
RAAARR!
YAAAAAH!
RAAARR!
NOW, SHOW HIM WHO'S BOSS,

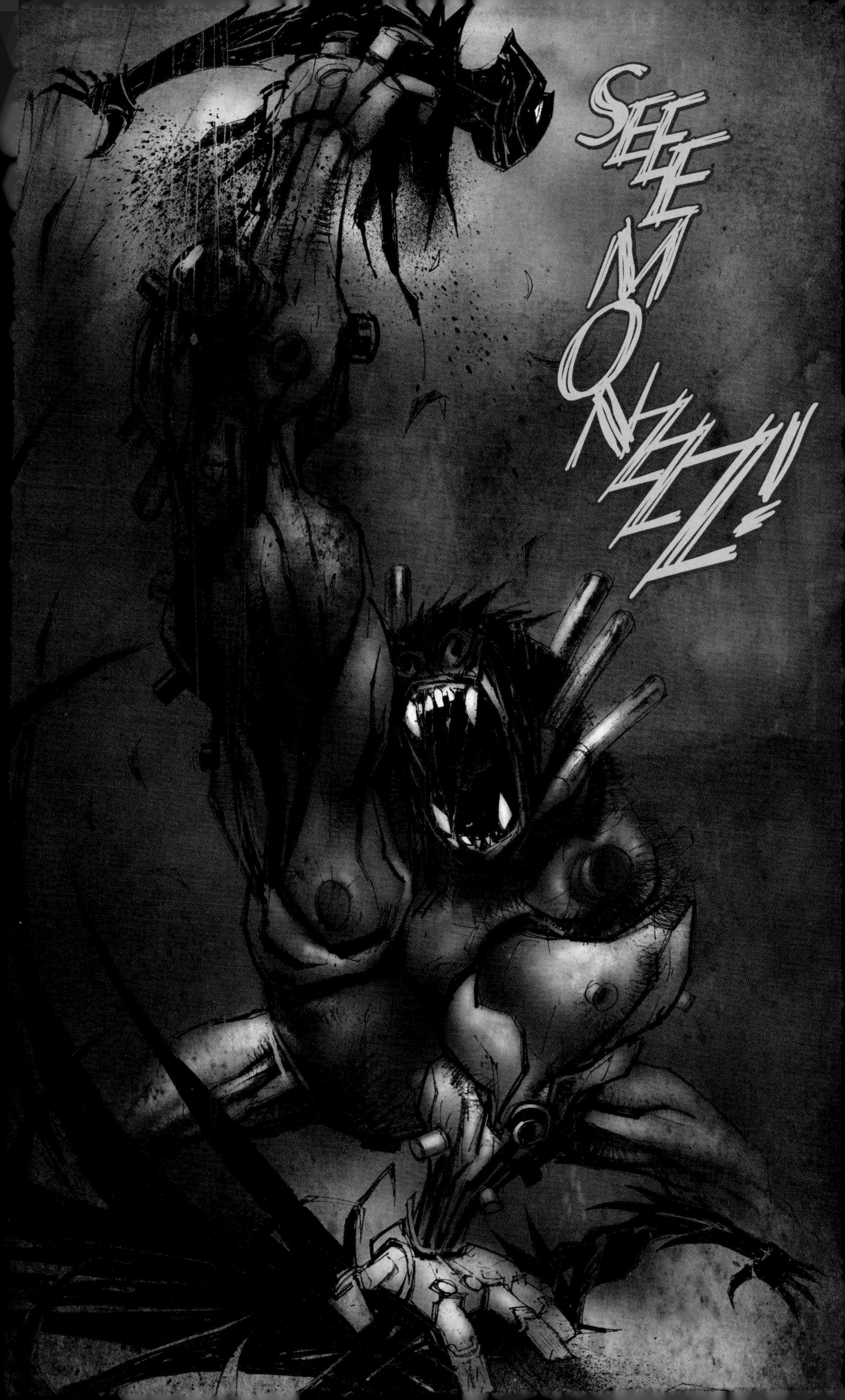
SEEEEMONZZZ!

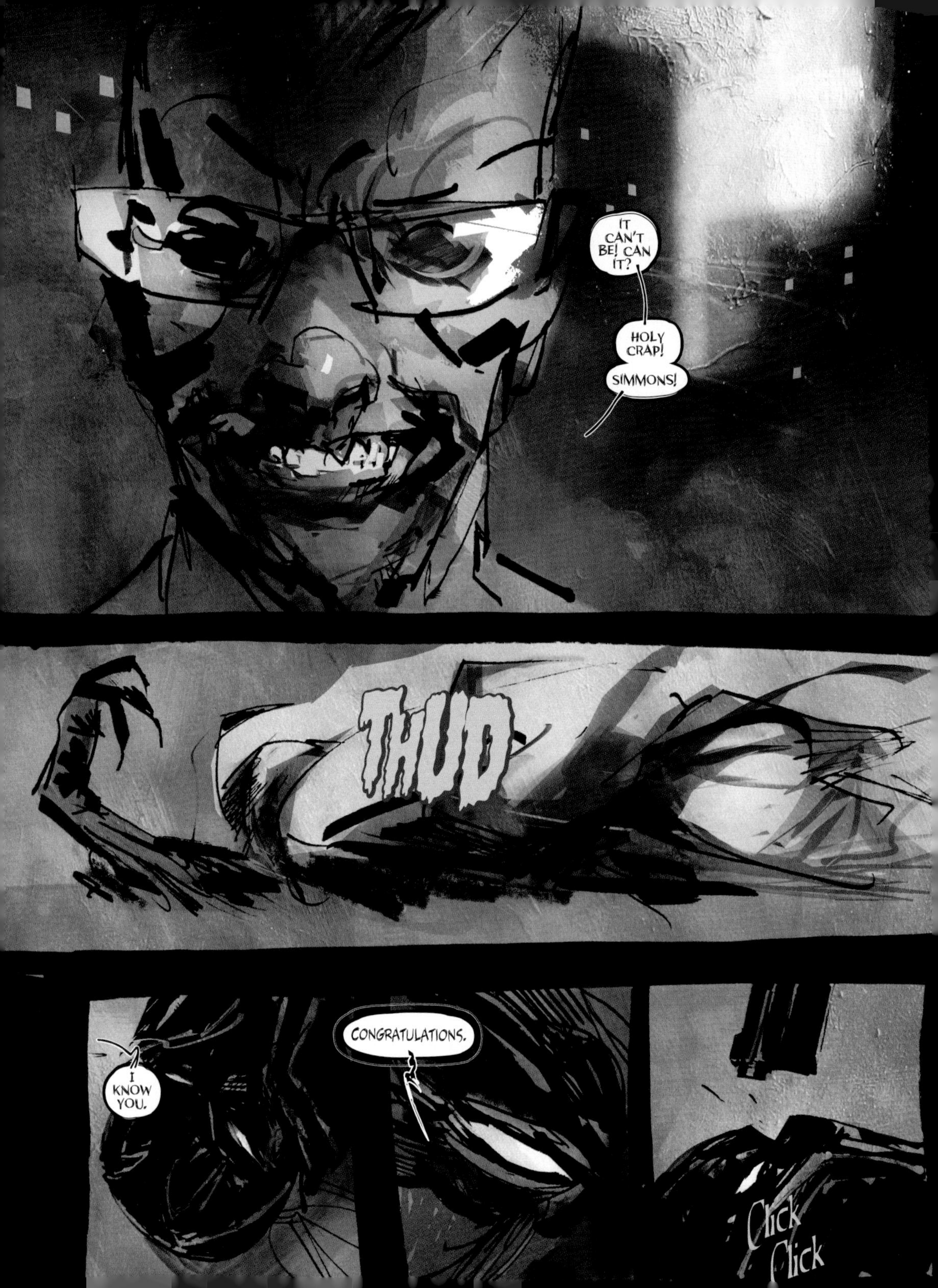

IT CAN'T BE! CAN IT?
HOLY CRAP!
SIMMONS!
THUD
I KNOW YOU.
CONGRATULATIONS.
Click
Click

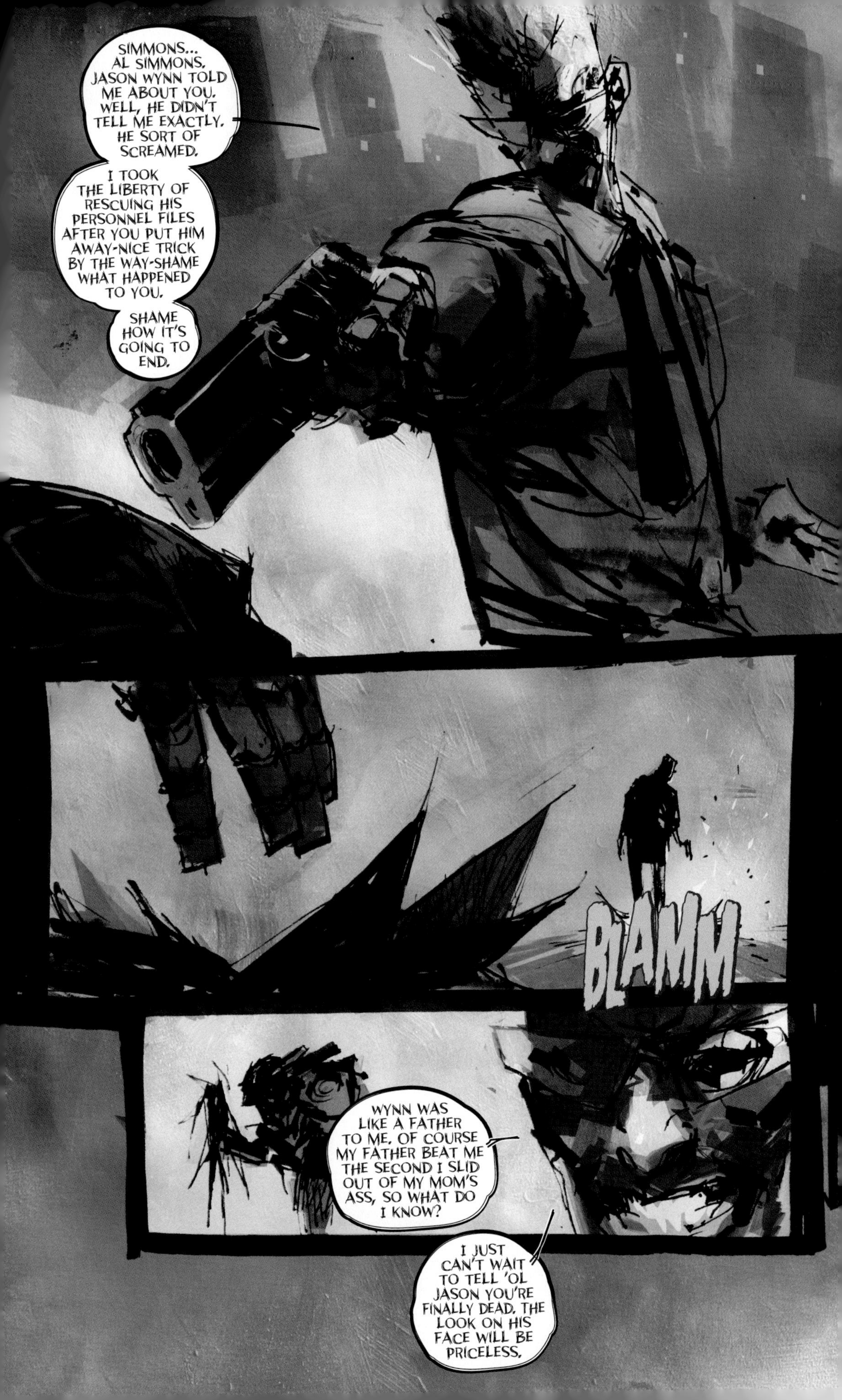

SIMMONS... AL SIMMONS. JASON WYNN TOLD ME ABOUT YOU. WELL, HE DIDN'T TELL ME EXACTLY. HE SORT OF SCREAMED.
I TOOK THE LIBERTY OF RESCUING HIS PERSONNEL FILES AFTER YOU PUT HIM AWAY-NICE TRICK BY THE WAY-SHAME WHAT HAPPENED TO YOU.
SHAME HOW IT'S GOING TO END.
BLAMM
WYNN WAS LIKE A FATHER TO ME, OF COURSE MY FATHER BEAT ME THE SECOND I SLID OUT OF MY MOM'S ASS, SO WHAT DO I KNOW?
I JUST CAN'T WAIT TO TELL 'OL JASON YOU'RE FINALLY DEAD. THE LOOK ON HIS FACE WILL BE PRICELESS.

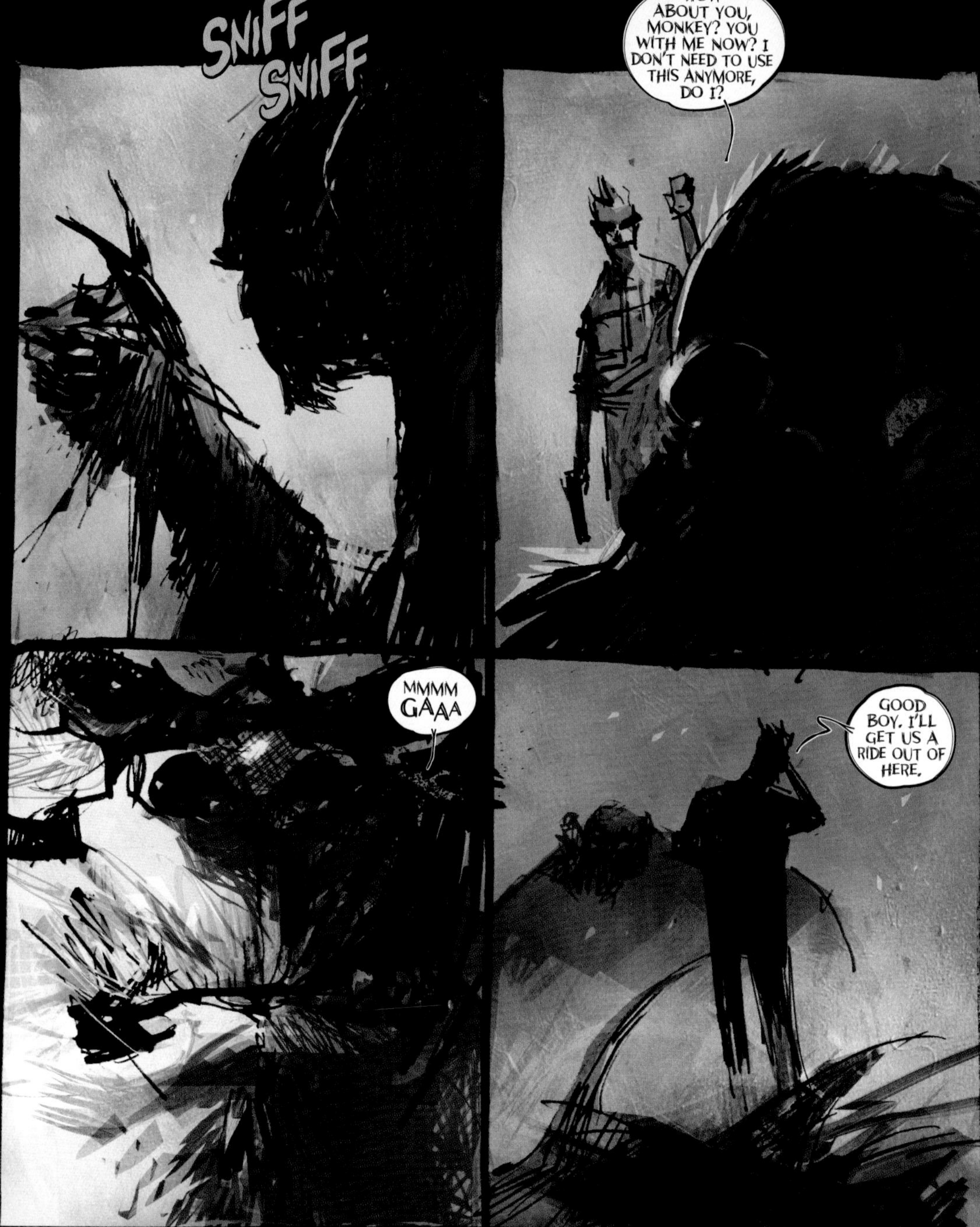
SNIFF
SNIFF
HOW ABOUT YOU, MONKEY? YOU WITH ME NOW? I DON'T NEED TO USE THIS ANYMORE, DO I?
MMMM GAAA
GOOD BOY. I'LL GET US A RIDE OUT OF HERE.

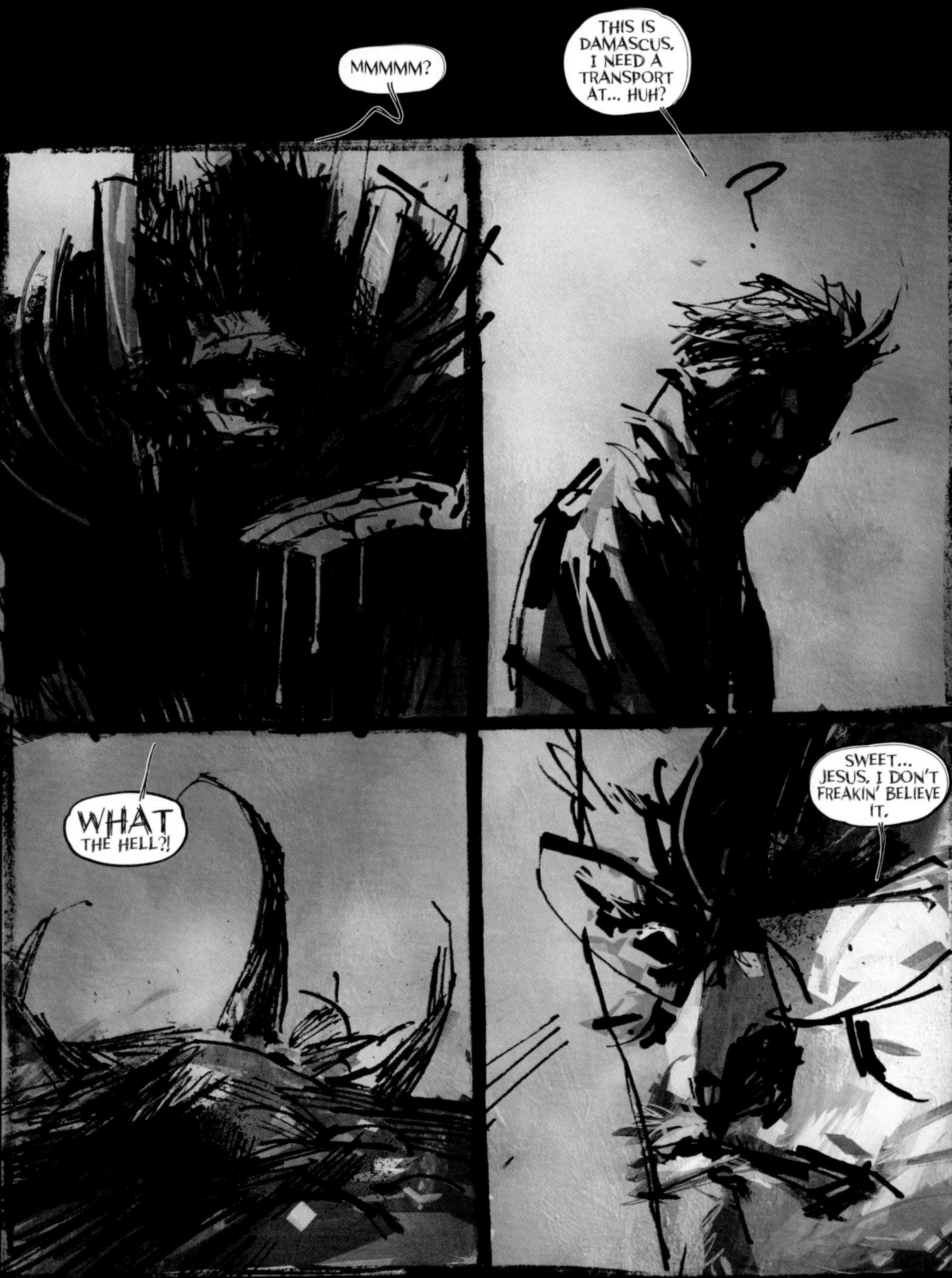
MMMMM?
THIS IS DAMASCUS, I NEED A TRANSPORT AT... HUH?
?
WHAT THE HELL?!
SWEET... JESUS, I DON'T FREAKIN' BELIEVE IT.

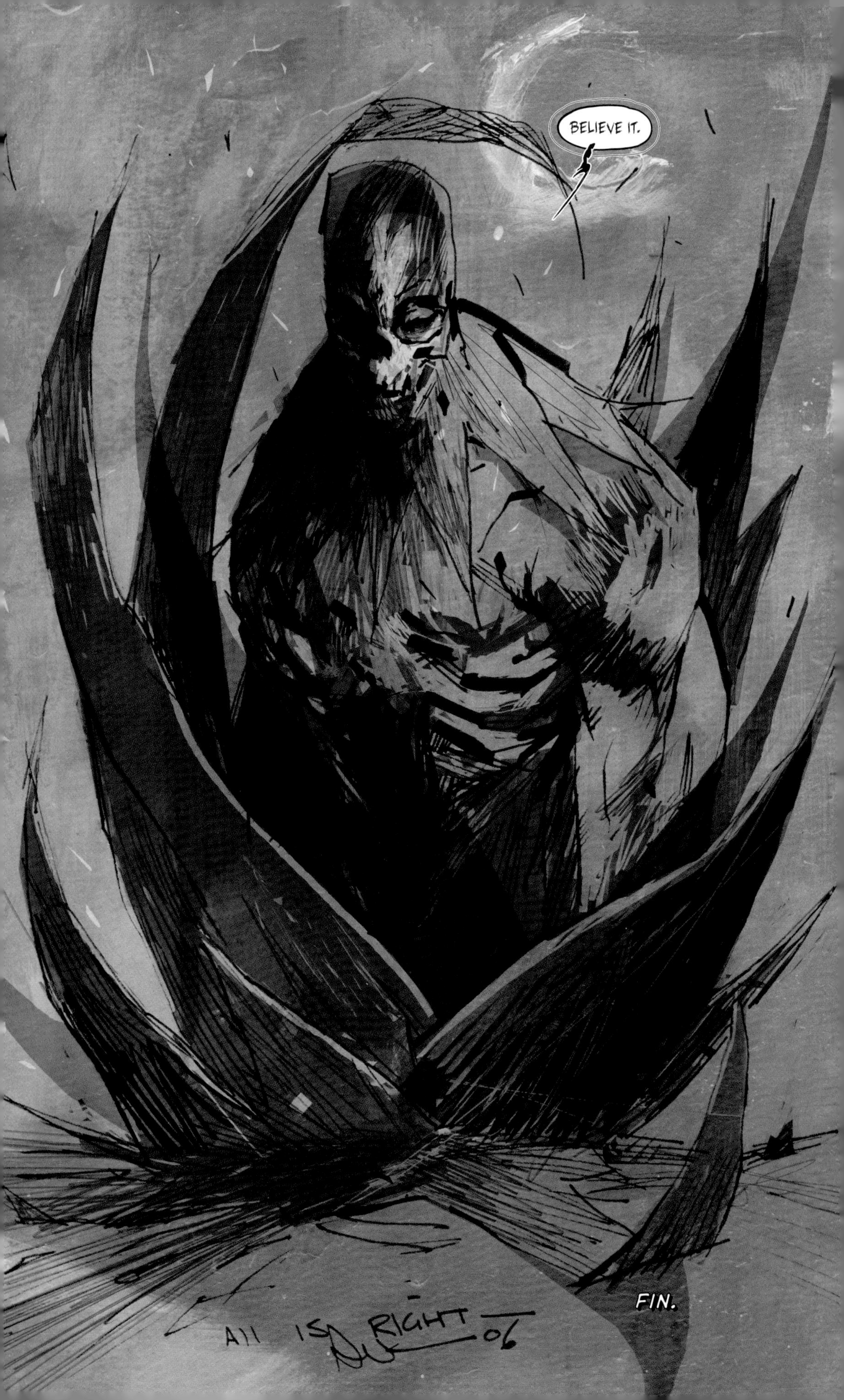
BELIEVE IT.
FIN.
All IS RIGHT 06

Ashley WOOD
sketch & cover gallery

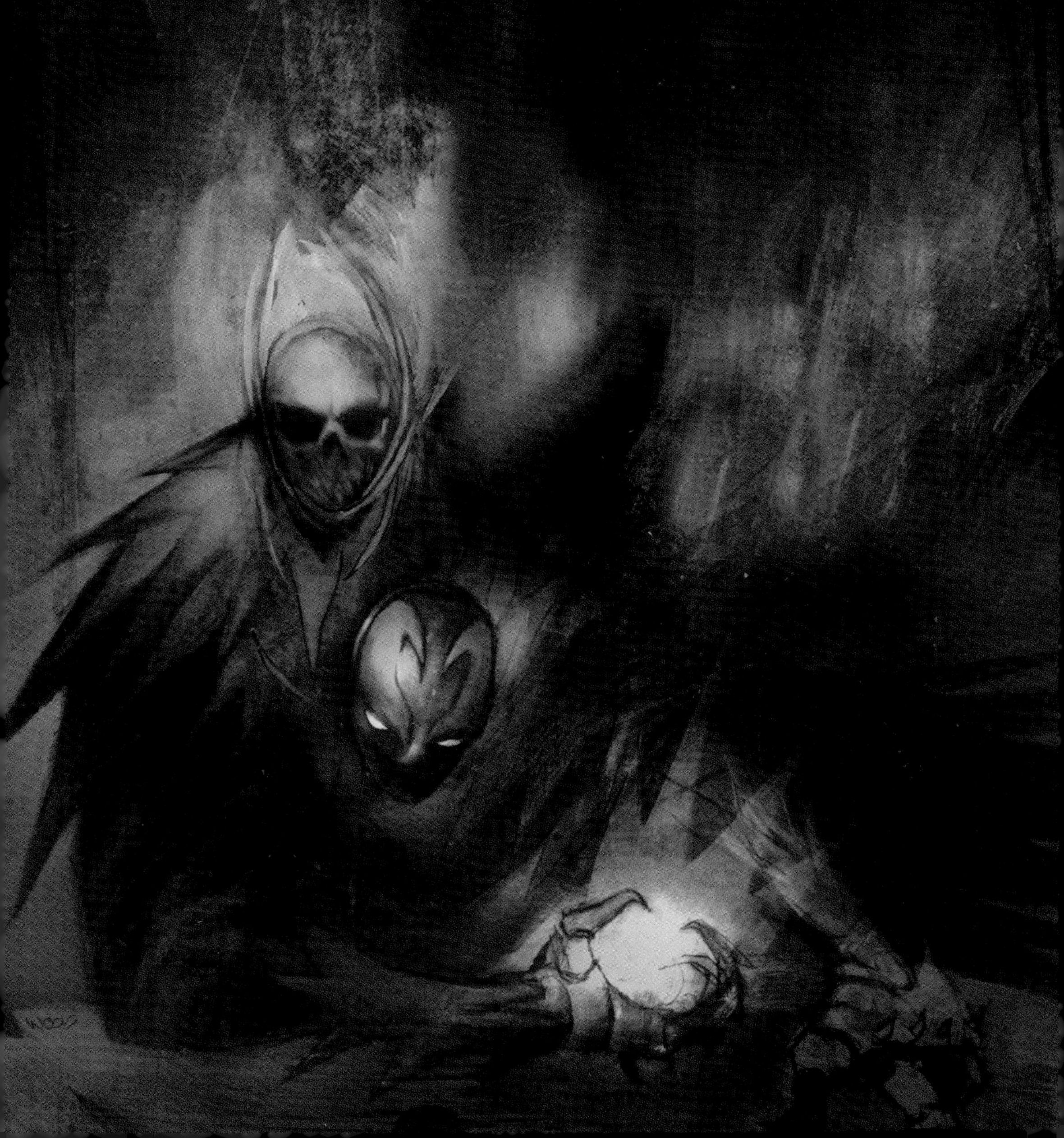

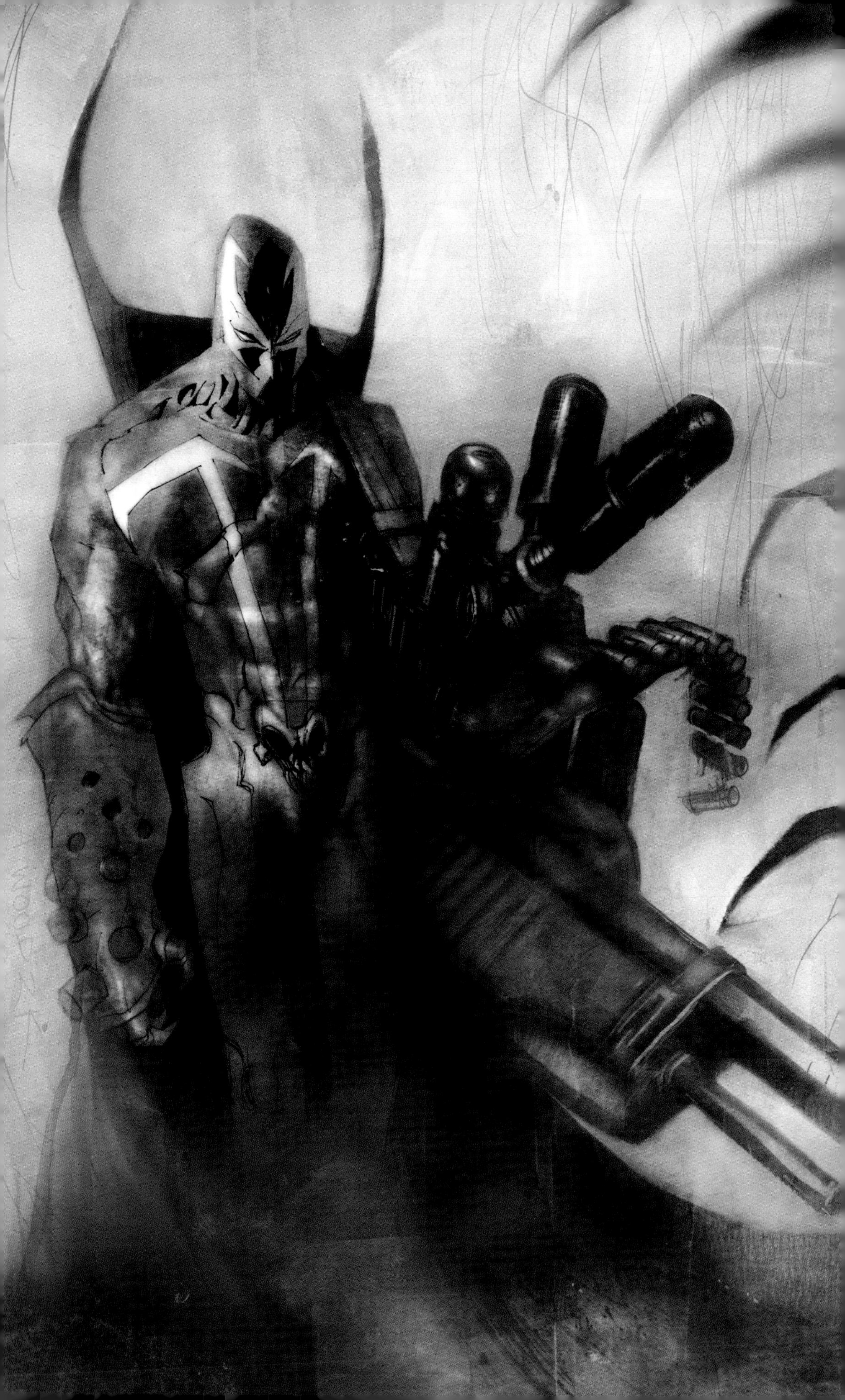

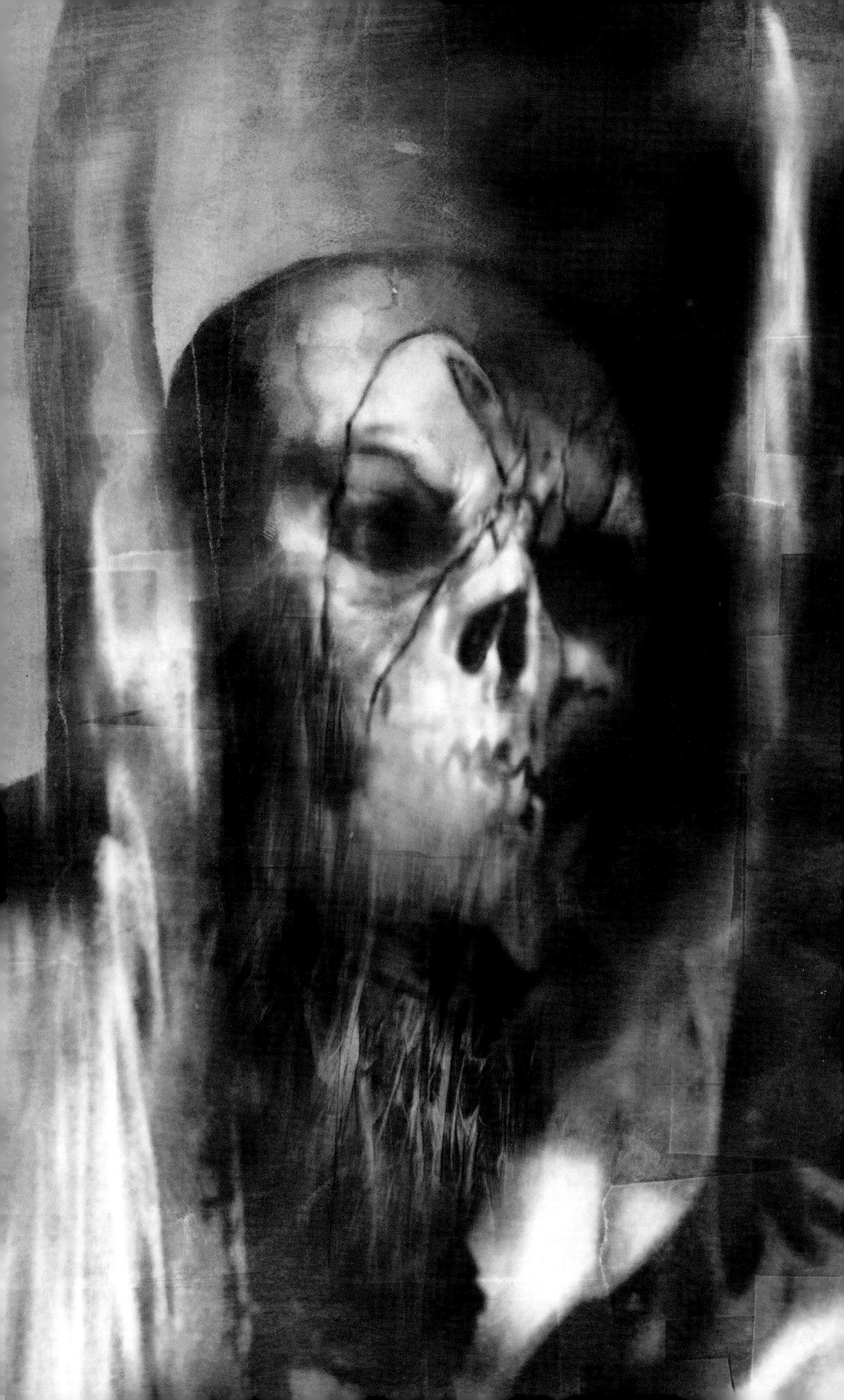

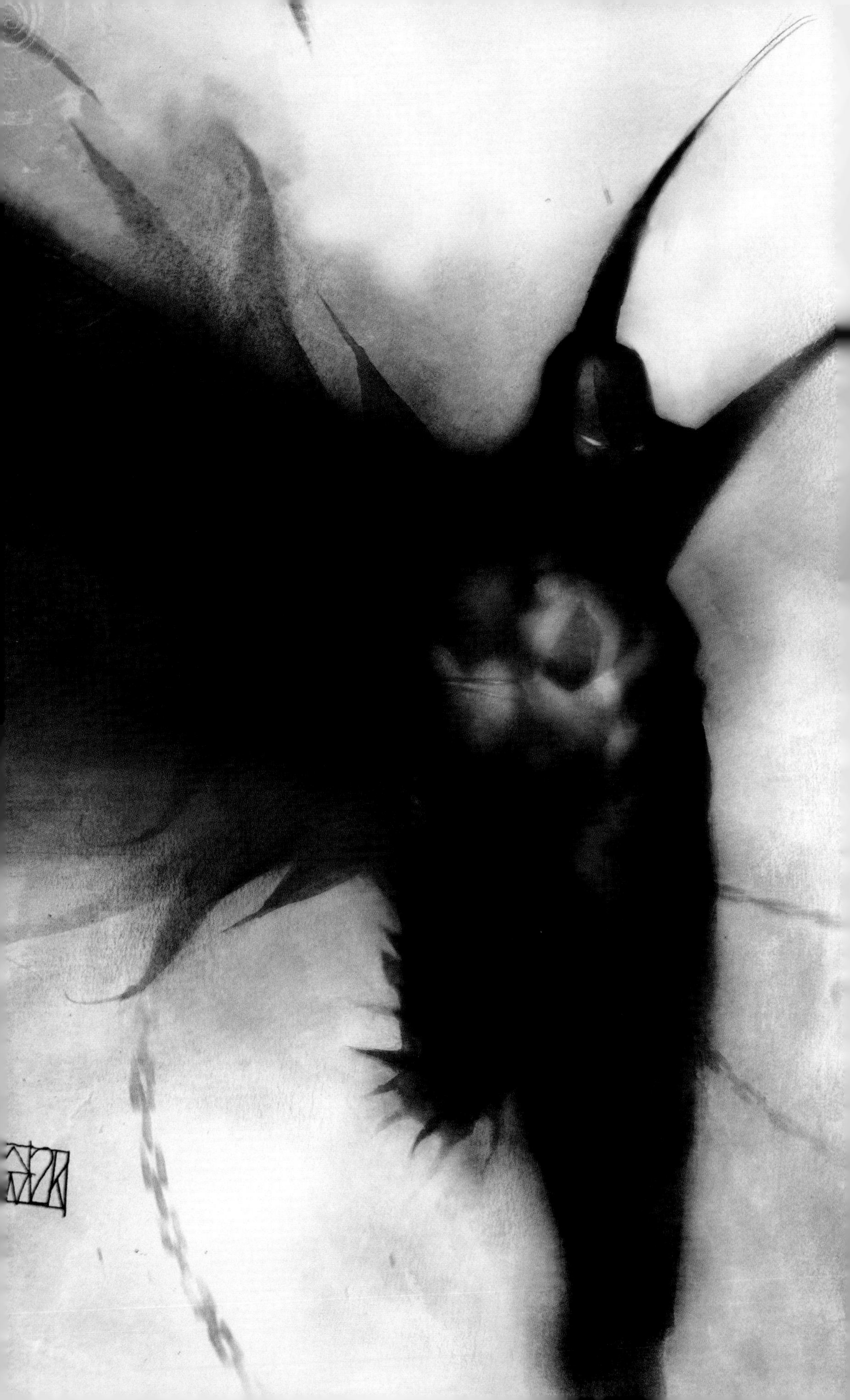

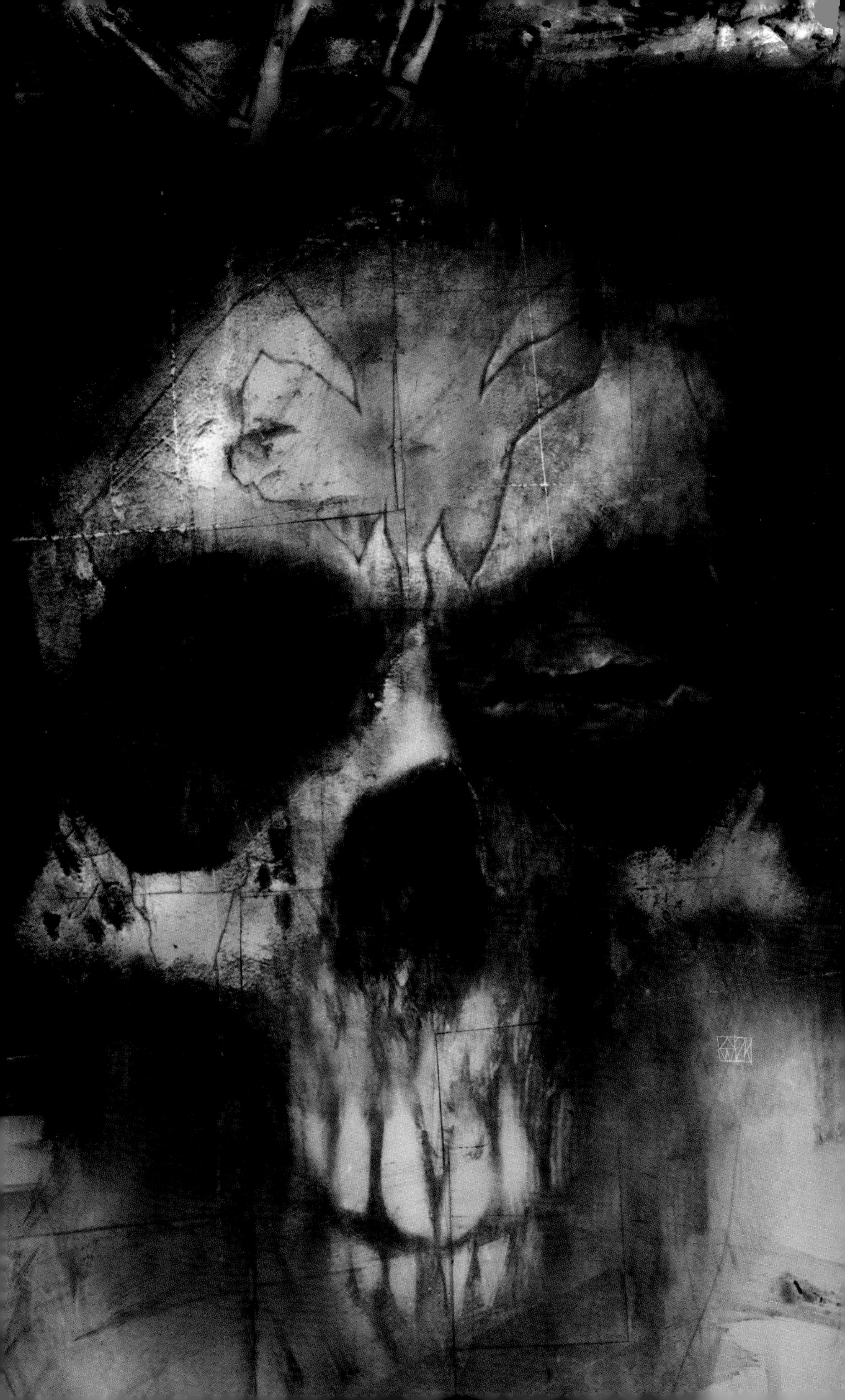

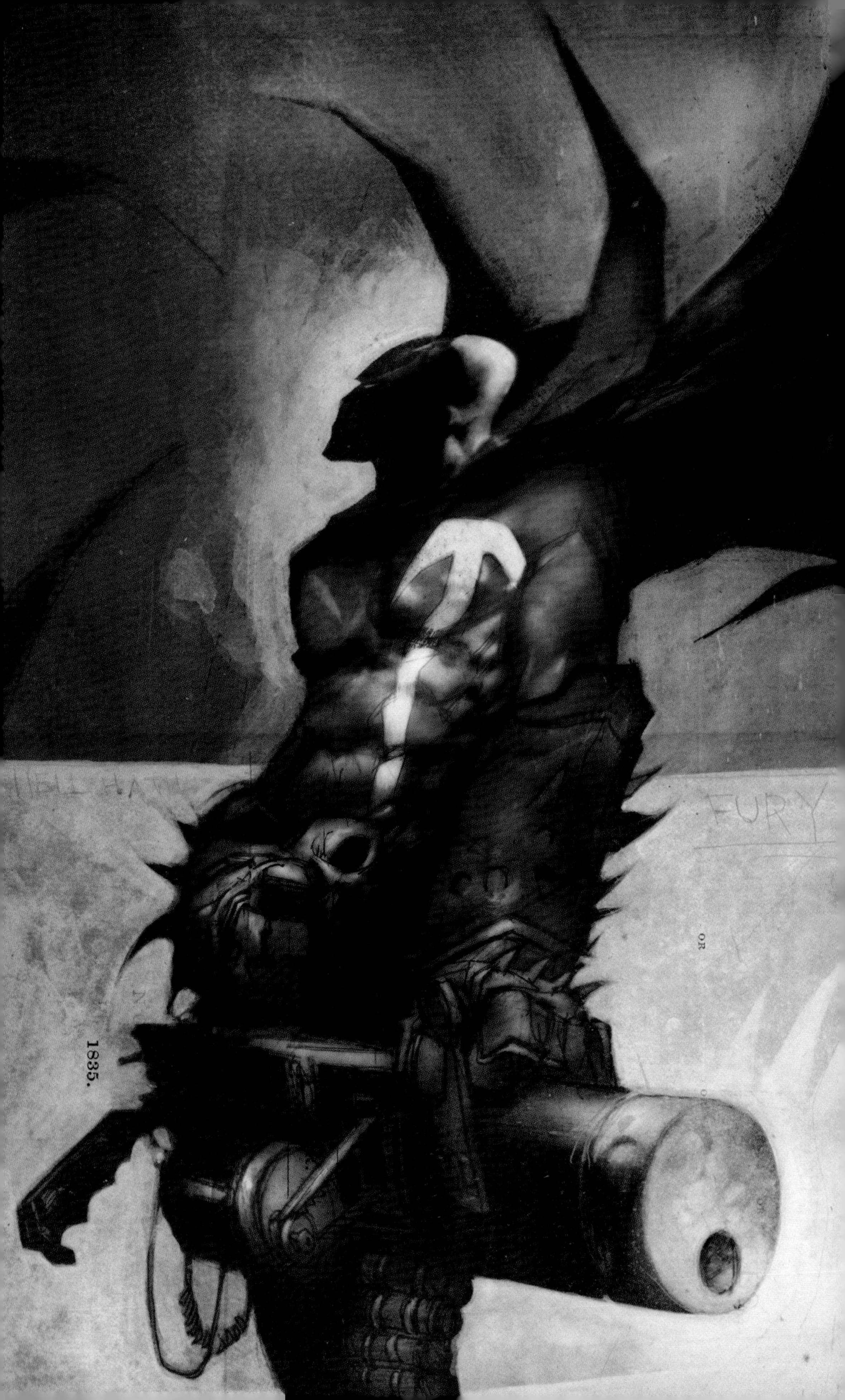
FURY
1835.

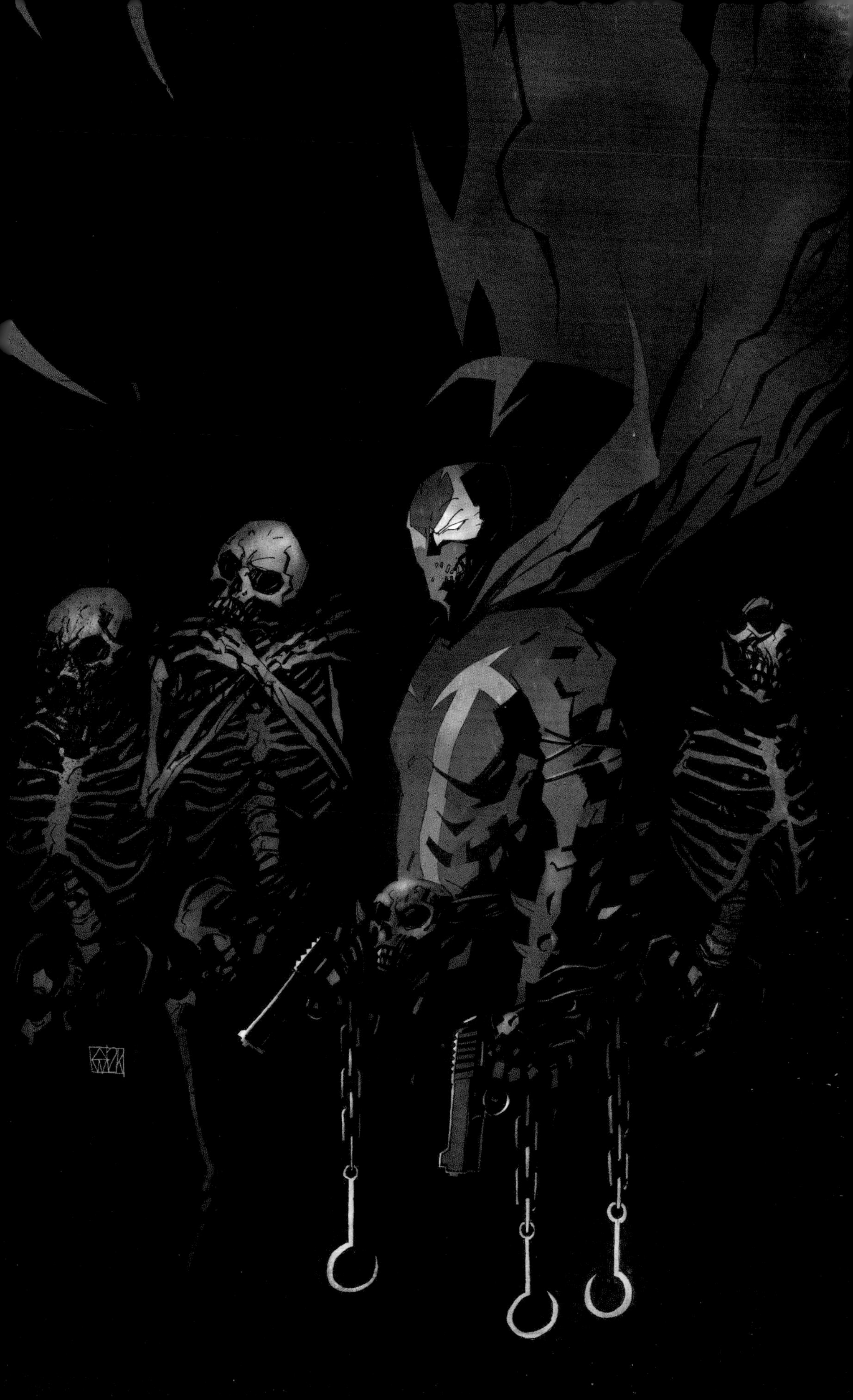

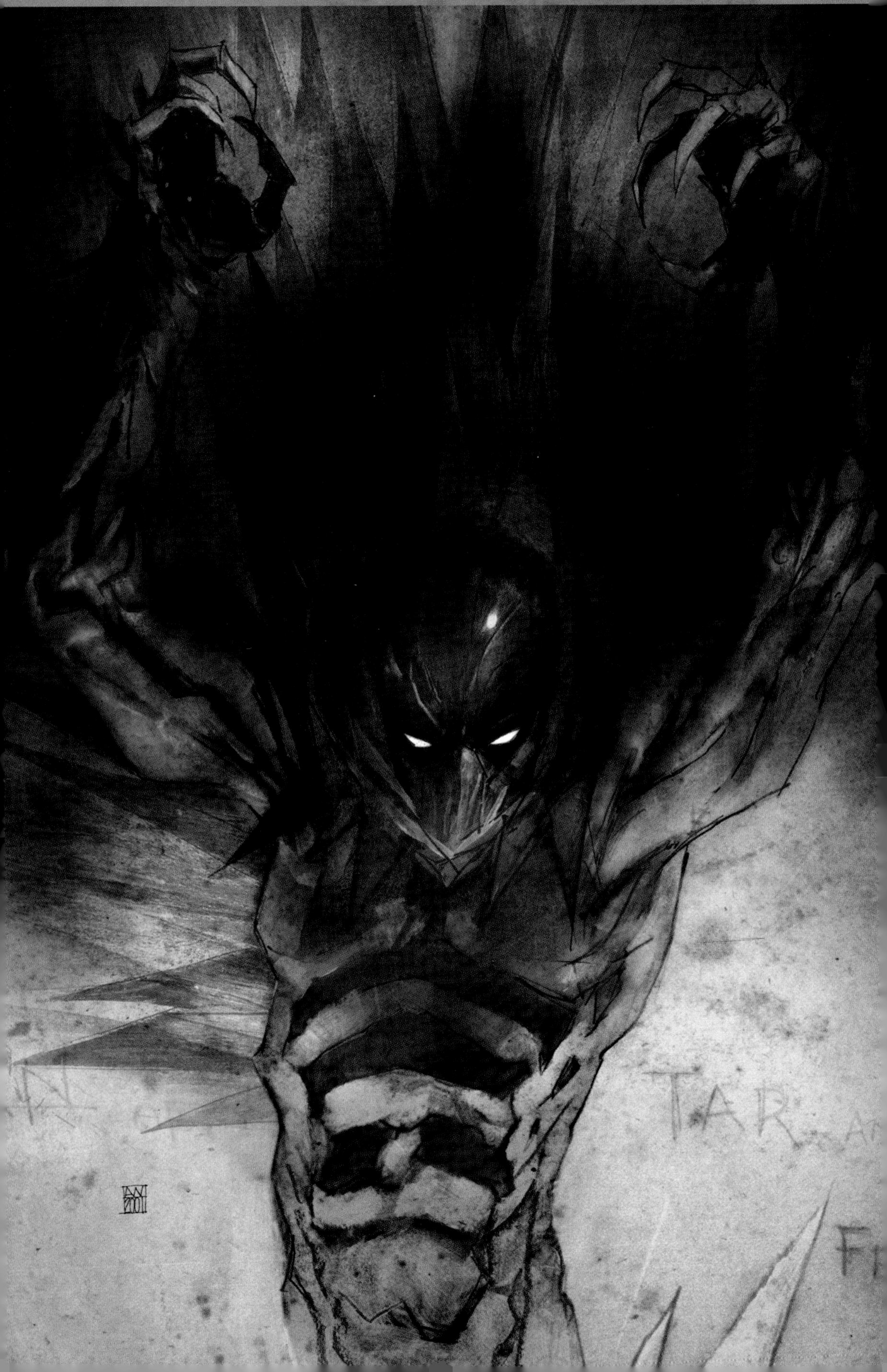

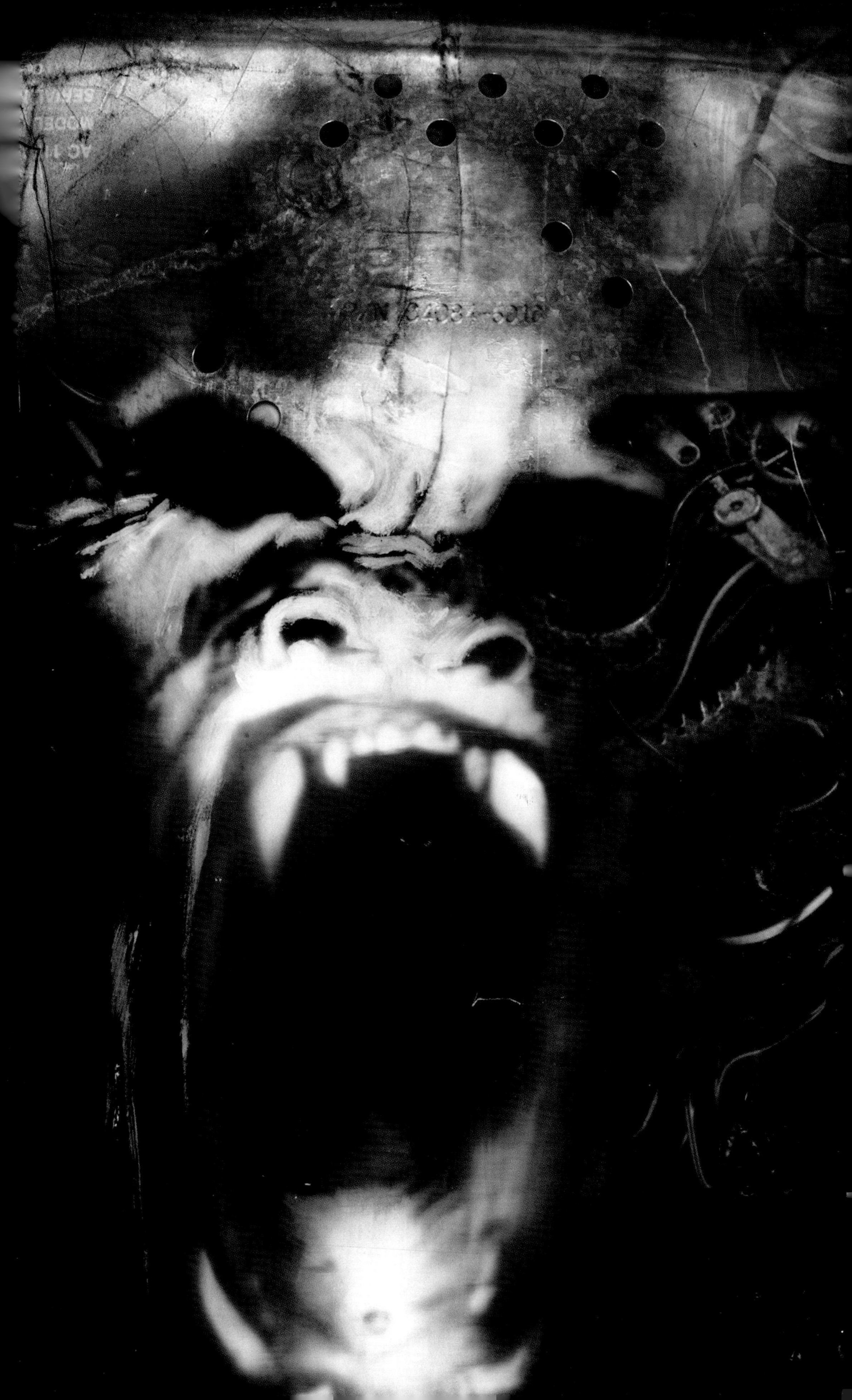

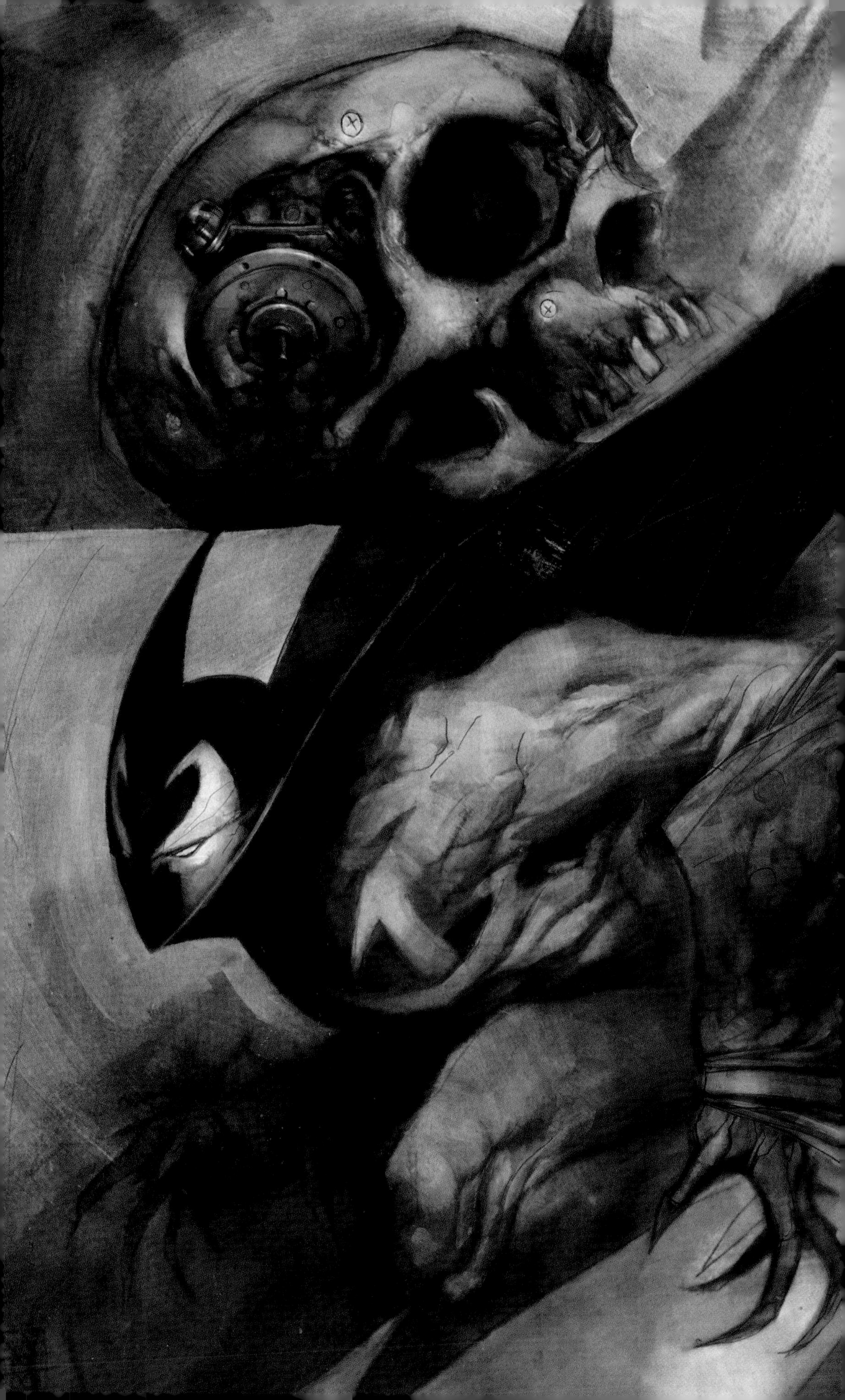

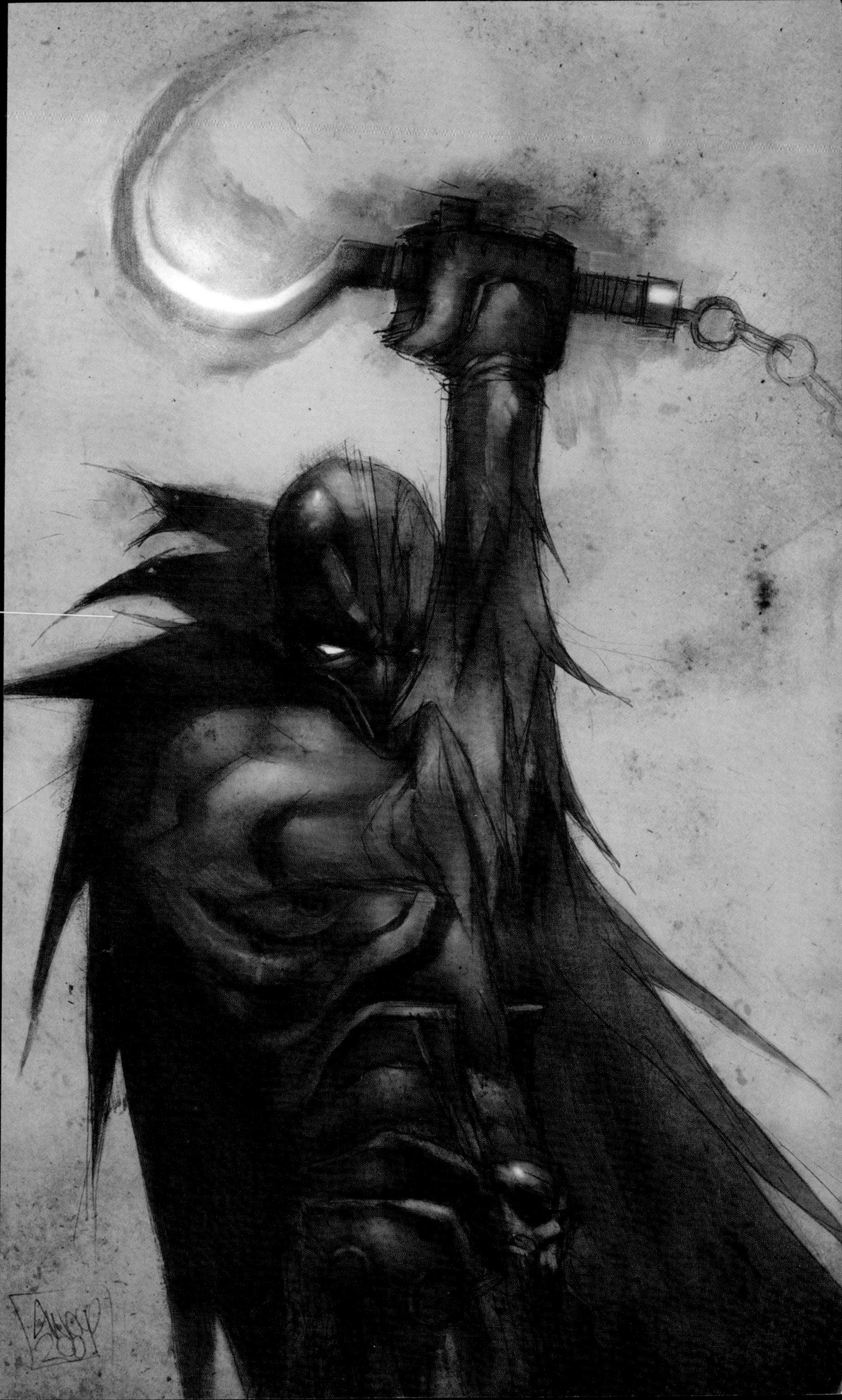

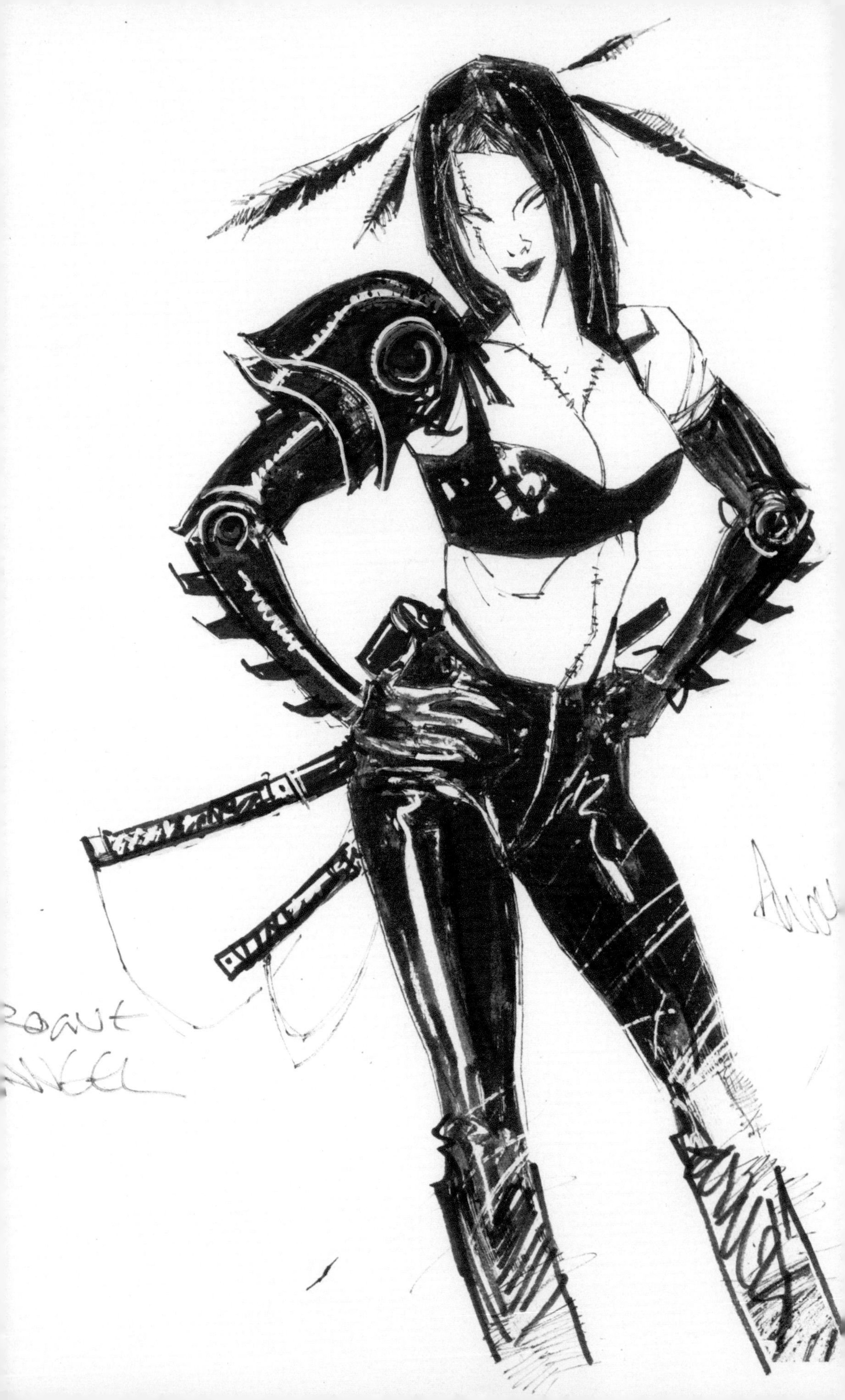

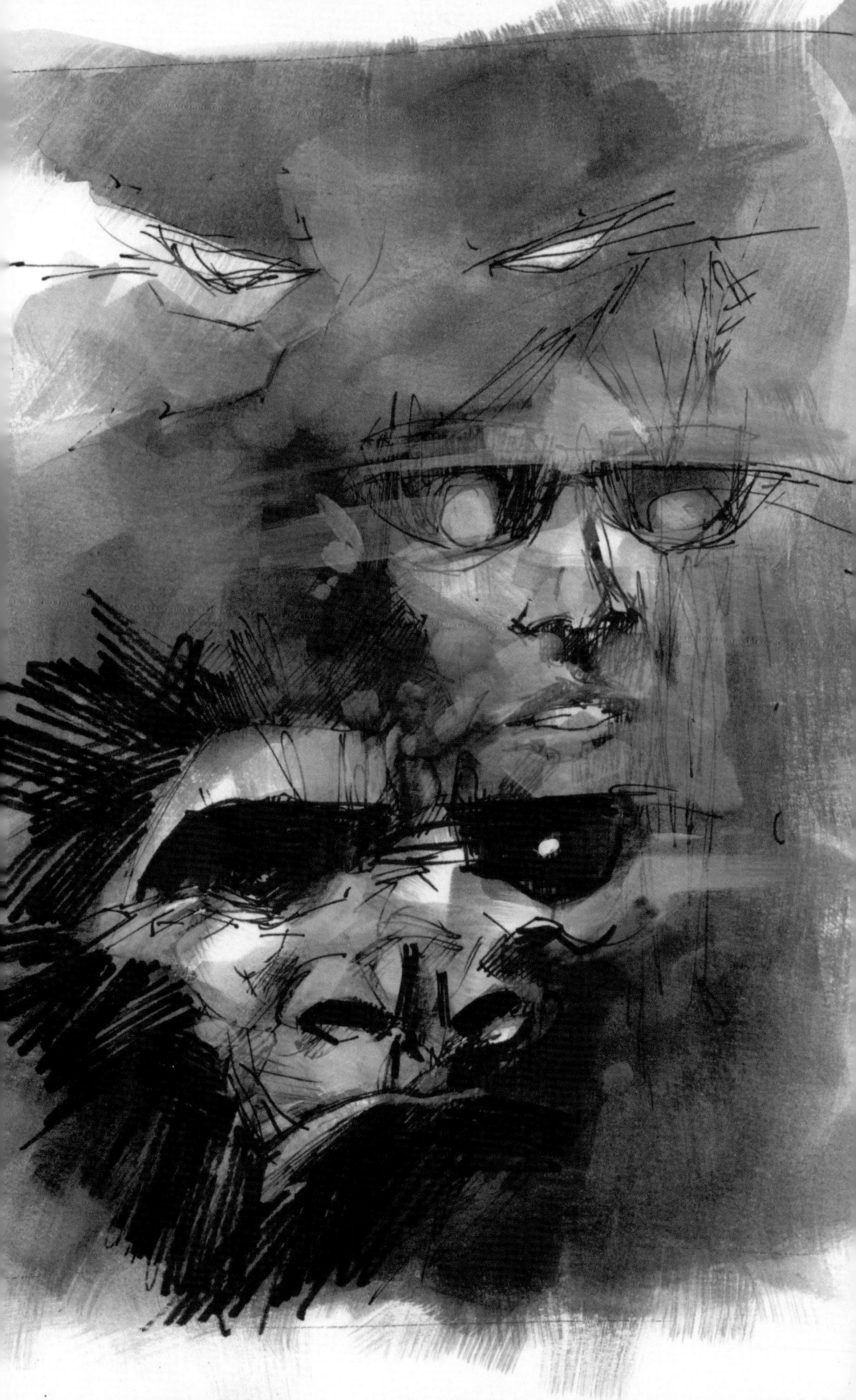

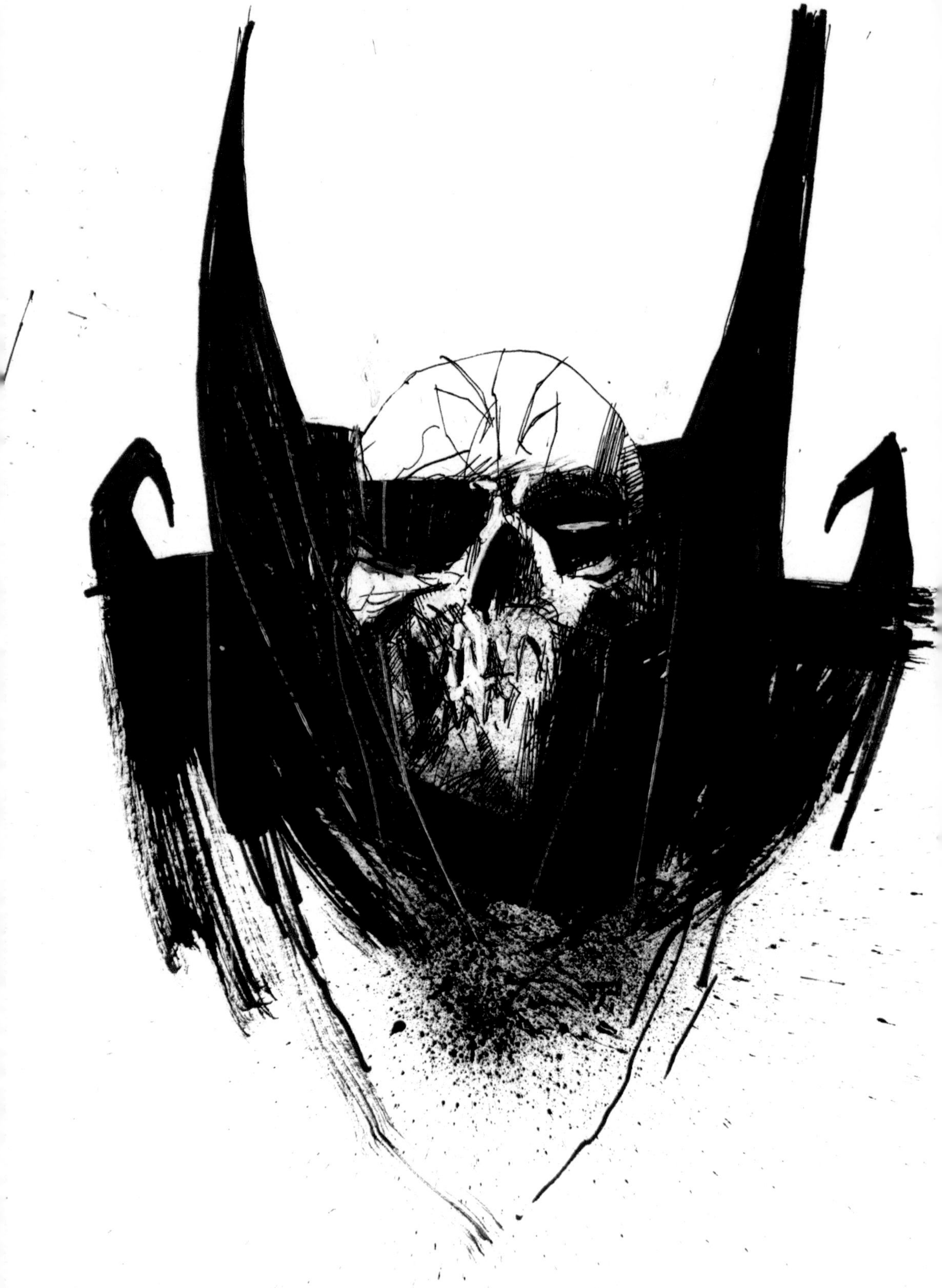

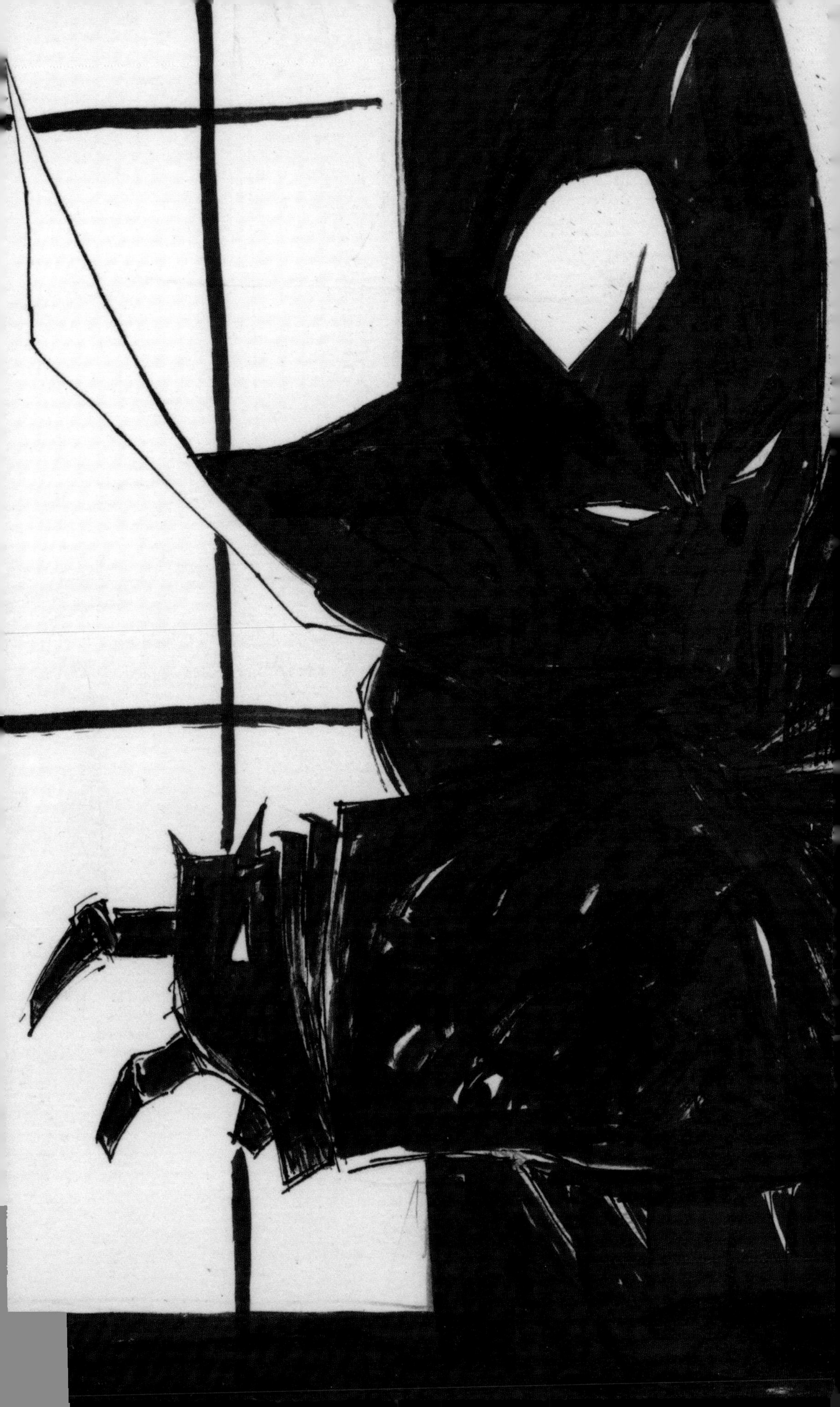

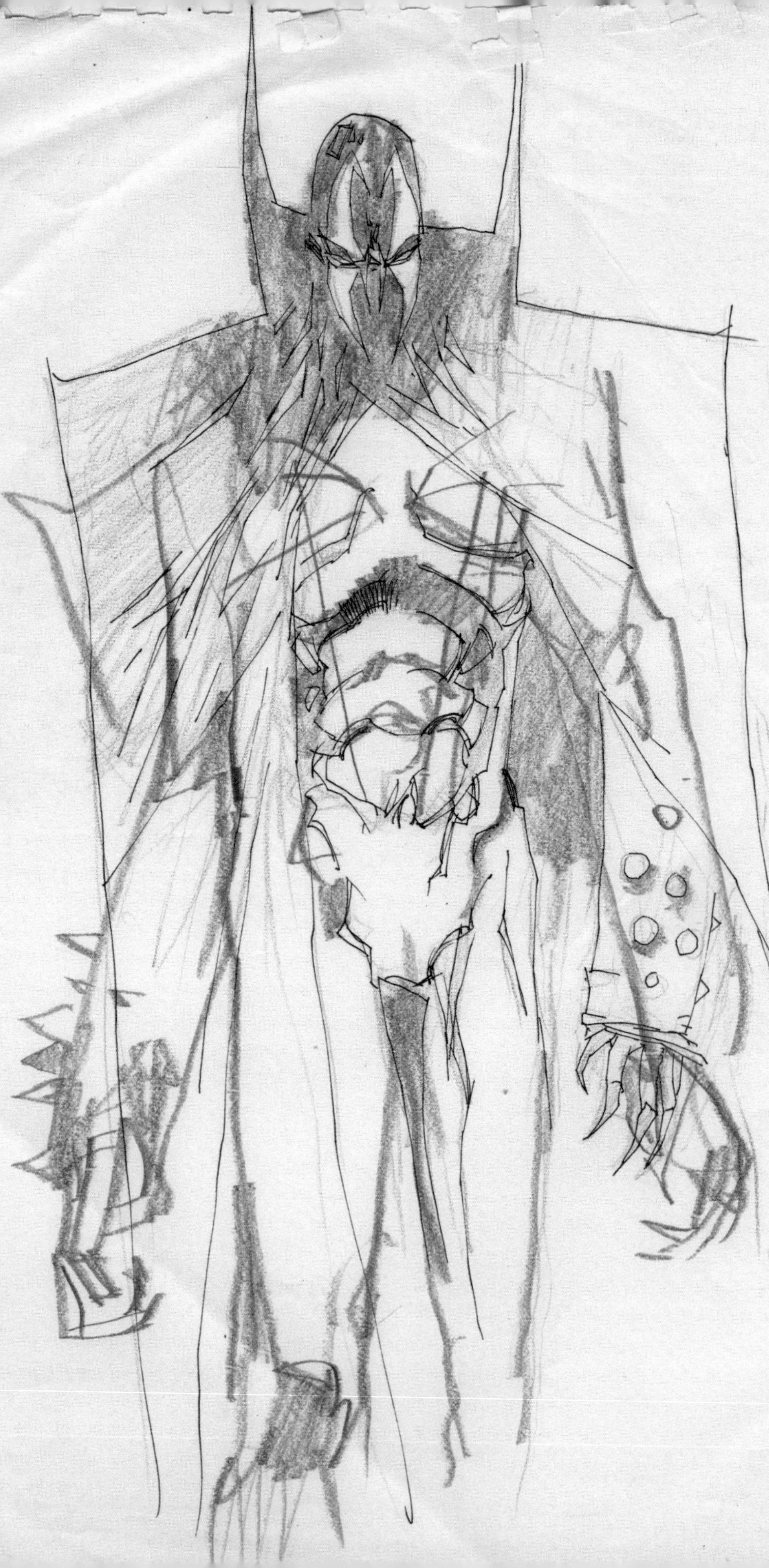